# THE SHIPWRECK OF THEIR HOPES

THE BATTLES FOR CHATTANOOGA

# THE SHIPWRECK OF THEIR HOPES

Peter Cozzens

*Illustrations by Keith Rocco*

UNIVERSITY OF ILLINOIS PRESS
Urbana and Chicago

Library of Congress Cataloging-in-Publication Data

Cozzens, Peter, 1957–
    The shipwreck of their hopes: the battles for Chattanooga / Peter
Cozzens ; illustrations by Keith Rocco.
        p.      cm.
    Includes bibliographical references and index.
    ISBN 0-252-01922-9 (alk. paper)
    1. Chattanooga (Tenn.), Battle of, 1863. I. Title.
E475.97.C779      1994
973.7'359—dc20                                                    94-6269
                                                                         CIP

*For Brittany and Brian*

# Contents

# MAPS

# ILLUSTRATIONS

*In Reserve.* Brigadier General Charles Woods waits with the Thirteenth Illinois Infantry as Federal artillery shells the Confederate position on Lookout Mountain. *Follows page 168.*

*Never Forsake the Colors.* Colonel Holden Putnam urges the Ninety-third Illinois up Tunnel Hill. *Follows page 226.*

*The Rear Guard.* Major General Patrick Cleburne watches the advance of Hooker's Federal infantry against Ringgold Gap. Cleburne sits to the side of the cannon of Lieutenant Richard Goldthwaite. *Follows page 374.*

# ACKNOWLEDGMENTS

*The Shipwreck of Their Hopes* brings to a close my trilogy on the decisive battles in the struggle for the Confederate heartland. I owe my continued gratitude to many people who offered their help in my earlier volumes, as well as to several others whom I have come to know while writing this book.

As always, the kindness of professional librarians and archivists has been of inestimable value in my research. The staffs of all the institutions that appear in my bibliography were most helpful.

Once again, I am deeply indebted to Carley Robison, the archivist of Knox College, Galesburg, Illinois, for her gracious help in providing me with access to the Ray D. Smith Civil War Collection and with a mountain of photocopied pages gleaned from its books.

And again, I am indebted to Dr. Richard Sauers for making available relevant portions of his exhaustive index of the *National Tribune.*

My sincere thanks go to friend and author Jeff Wert, who unselfishly shared his thoughts with me on General Longstreet's role in the Chattanooga campaign.

I also am most grateful to Larry Stevens of Newark, Ohio, for his careful reading of my chapter on Ringgold Gap and for help in clarifying for me many of the troop movements of that confused fight.

Similarly, I am deeply indebted to John Huelskamp of Barrington, Illinois, for sharing both his deep knowledge of and primary source material pertaining to the fighting on Tunnel Hill.

Several individuals offered me the use of materials in their possession pertaining to the campaign. Tom Arliskas of Plainfield, Illinois, made available to me numerous articles from contemporary Illinois newspapers. Steve Calhoun of Richmond, Virginia, provided me with a copy of an important Federal battle report from his private collection.

Karl Hansen, also of Richmond, brought to my attention several letters of Braxton Bragg. Tom Hartzell of Gobles, Michigan, shared with me with the outstanding, unpublished autobiography of his ancestor, John Calvin Hartzell; it is a work that truly merits publication. Charles Van Adder of Forked River, New Jersey, provided me with material from his extensive library. Paul Wagley of Olympia, Washington, graciously sent me passages on the battles from the rich, unpublished memoirs of his grandfather, Ephraim Wagley.

I am grateful to Richard L. Wentworth, director of the University of Illinois Press, for his kind support. To my manuscript editor, Carol Bolton Betts, my deepest gratitude for all her help with *The Shipwreck of Their Hopes* and my earlier books. My sincere thanks to Jim Bier of Champaign, Illinois, for the wonderful maps that have added so much to these works. On the maps and in my text, I have tried where possible to use nineteenth-century place names, not modern ones, to refer to sites on the battlefields.

I would like to close my acknowledgments with special words of thanks to three very dear friends, whose friendship and encouragement alone were of immeasurable value. First, to Keith Rocco, of Edinburg, Virginia, my thanks for another outstanding dust-jacket painting and more great illustrations. To Glenn LaFantasie of Warrenton, Virginia, my thanks for reviewing my chapters on Brown's Ferry and Wauhatchie. And to Adrienne Harmon-Hanrahan, my thanks for digging for difficult source material for me while I was far away in Lima, Peru, and for insightful comments on the manuscript.

CHAPTER ONE

# CHANGES OF VAST MOMENT

MAJOR General Ulysses S. Grant felt miserable. Victory at Vicksburg had made him a public hero, but the laurels fast turned bitter. "In Vicksburg thank God. The backbone of the Rebellion is broken. The Confederacy is divided. . . . The Mississippi River is opened, and General Grant is to be our next President," a captain in Grant's army had written his wife on the day the Mississippi citadel fell. The Northern press shared the young officer's exuberance. Florid headlines trumpeted Grant's success, and the stoop-shouldered, self-effacing Ohioan suddenly found himself the premier general in the Union. Even Lincoln tipped his hat to Grant. Reviewing the campaign, he wrote: "When you first reached the vicinity of Vicksburg, I thought that you should do what you finally did—march the troops across the neck, run the batteries with the transports, and thus go below. When you got below, and took Port Gibson, Grand Gulf, and vicinity, I thought you should go down the river and join General Banks; and when you turned northward west of the Big Black, I feared you had made a mistake. I now wish to make the personal acknowledgment that you were right, and I was wrong," concluded the president graciously.[1]

Gratifying words, but all this adulation proved empty. Within a few short weeks, Grant found himself with neither influence in Washington nor much of an army in the field. The fall of Vicksburg had given General-in-Chief Henry Halleck an idea, from which he conceived a strategy for the West for the remainder of the summer of 1863. With the Mississippi clear of Rebels, he reasoned, the river could be used as "the base of future operations east and west." Union armies along the river could move at will against either half of the severed Confederacy, concentrating their forces with impunity. Only the question of where to strike first remained open.

On this, Halleck solicited Grant's opinion. Grant complied by strongly urging that a seaborne campaign against Mobile, Alabama, be launched from New Orleans. Halleck demurred. He thought it might be "best to clean up a little" in the weaker Trans-Mississippi department before undertaking anything so ambitious in the stronger half of the Confederacy. President Lincoln, in turn, weighed in with his own desire for an expedition into Texas. After rebuffing Grant's suggestion, Halleck proceeded to carve away portions of his army to support his own and Lincoln's proposals. First, four thousand troops were sent to Nathaniel Banks in New Orleans to help that general to carry out the president's Texas operation. Then, five thousand were sent to Arkansas to help roust out a small Confederate army under Sterling Price, one of the mopping-up operations favored by Halleck. Next, the powerful Ninth Corps was returned to Ambrose Burnside in Kentucky, largely to keep him from floundering. Finally, in August, the entire Thirteenth Corps was dispatched to further reinforce Banks.[2]

With nothing better to do, Grant traveled down the Mississippi to New Orleans to celebrate the clearing of the river of Confederate resistance and to review Banks's army—a large part of which until recently had been his. With neither his wife, Julia, nor his punctilious chief of staff, John Rawlins, on hand to steady him, Grant may have taken to the bottle along the way. Certainly there was temptation aplenty once he arrived in New Orleans, where Banks, himself a hard drinker, hosted Grant at a lavish banquet. The next afternoon, while riding back to New Orleans after a grand review of the troops, Grant was thrown from his mount. (Unfriendly wags like Major General William Franklin, a West Point classmate, said that Grant had *tumbled* from his horse, drunk.) The officer behind Grant could not stop his horse, and its hooves cut deep gashes in the general's leg. Grant's own animal may have fallen on top of him as well. In any event, the general was badly hurt. He was patched up at a roadside inn, then hurried off to a hotel in town. From there, he was carried aboard a steamboat bound for Vicksburg. He arrived there a week later, still an invalid. Julia hurried to his side, Rawlins cut short his leave to rejoin his commander, and Grant settled down to recuperate.[3]

His repose was brief. The sudden and startling defeat of the Army of the Cumberland at Chickamauga and its retreat to Chattanooga thrust the ailing Grant back into the limelight. On 23 September, he received orders from the War Department to detail all the forces he could spare to succor Major General William S. Rosecrans. Grant sent his trusted lieutenant William T. Sherman on his way at once with elements of two corps. He put Colonel James H. Wilson, a talented twenty-six-year-old member of his staff, on a steamer for Cairo, Illinois, there better to communicate with Washington.

With an entire army on the brink of destruction, Washington at last admitted its need for more than just Grant's troops. On 29 September, Halleck bade the general travel to Memphis as soon as his health permitted to superintend the movement of troops toward Chattanooga. Low water on the Mississippi and a series of boat breakdowns and navigational mishaps delayed the messenger bearing Halleck's dispatch, so that Grant was not handed it until 5 October. Five days later, Colonel Wilson returned with new, oddly vague orders: Grant was to travel with all haste to Cairo, rather than Memphis. There he would receive further instructions.

Seizing the chance to again play an active role in something, Grant set off at once, steaming into the dirty Illinois river town on 16 October.[4]

There the guessing game continued. The morning after his arrival, a telegram came in telling Grant to continue on to Louisville, Kentucky, where an officer of the War Department would meet him with what presumably were to be his definitive instructions. Grant, Julia, and the general's staff boarded a train an hour later and headed northward into Indiana. The train stopped to take on coal at Indianapolis. As it got up steam and started slowly out of the depot on the last leg of the journey, a messenger ran down the track and waved the locomotive to a halt. He jumped aboard the train and sought out Grant. Breathlessly, he implored the general to wait: Secretary of War Edwin M. Stanton was just then coming into the station by special train from Washington and wanted to see Grant at once. The War Department officer who was to have met Grant in Louisville, then, was no less than the secretary himself. Grant's military fortunes suddenly seemed to be mending faster than his injured leg.[5]

The general and his staff lounged about Grant's private car awaiting their distinguished visitor. Grant and Stanton had never met. In a few moments, the secretary flung open the door and hurried into the car. Breezing past Grant, he rushed up to Doctor Edward Kittoe, the staff surgeon, and, pumping his hand, blurted out: "How do you do, General Grant? I recognize you from your pictures."

"The scene which followed was an embarrassing one," recalled Colonel Wilson wryly. "Kittoe was quite as modest as Grant and all three were momentarily confused. While they were blushing and Rawlins was straightening out the mistake, the rest of the staff could hardly conceal their smiles." A painful interval elapsed before the introductions were completed and the great men of the meeting turned uncomfortably to the business at hand. Although unpretentious by nature, Grant was upset. The egotistical secretary picked up on this and, said Wilson, "became at once less talkative and more reserved than had apparently been his intention."[6]

Stanton recovered sufficiently to thrust two orders into Grant's hand, remarking as he did that Grant might choose between them. The orders were identical in every aspect but one. Both created the Military Division of the Mississippi, a field command of almost unprecedented size that was to be composed of three heretofore independent departments: the Department of the Ohio, then under Burnside; the Department of the Cumberland, under Rosecrans; and Grant's own Department of the Tennessee. In effect, with the exception of Banks's small district, all the territory from the Appalachians to the Mississippi River and including much of the state of Arkansas beyond was to be unified under one commander. Both orders also specified Grant as that commander. Where they differed was with respect to the fate of the departmental commanders: One order left them as they were, the other replaced Rosecrans with his senior corps commander, Major General George Thomas.[7]

There was really no choice to be made, as Stanton, who was eager to cashier Rosecrans, well knew. While he had no special fondness for Thomas, Grant cared even less for Rosecrans. An open secret, their troubles dated back to the fall of 1862, when Rosecrans had held a field command under Grant in northern Mississippi and, to Grant's way of thinking, had botched a chance to destroy an entire Rebel army. Grant chose the second order.[8] As Rawlins explained the matter in a letter home:

> One thing is very certain, General Grant . . . could not in justice to himself or the cause of his country think of again commanding General Rosecrans. . . . Of this the authorities at Washington were fully advised, in General Grant's report of the battles of Iuka and Corinth, in the former of which in consequence of Rosecrans's deviation from the entire plan and order of battle the enemy was enabled to escape and by his tardiness in pursuit in the latter allowed to get off with much less than he should. To this might also be added his general spirit of insubordination toward General Grant, although to his face he professed for him the highest regards both as a man and an officer.[9]

With their immediate business completed, said Wilson, Grant and Stanton lapsed into a long and awkward silence.[10]

They reached the Ohio River that evening, only to find no ferry on hand to take them to the Kentucky side. Together they stood on a windswept wharf under a numbing autumnal rain, Grant balanced on his crutches and the illness-prone Stanton shivering with a chill. At last a boat was rounded up, and the two men, after Lincoln, most responsible for the fate of the Union made their way across the river.

They checked into the comfortable Galt House later that night and then promptly parted company. Stanton went to bed with a terrible cold, from which he told Grant he never expected to recover. To the utter dismay of Rawlins, Grant and most of his staff went off to the theater. Rawlins "did not hesitate to inveigh against it as a thoughtless and undignified proceeding. He was at best rather inclined to be taciturn and moody," remembered Wilson, who by contrast was young, impressionable, and still a bit overawed by service on Grant's staff. Rawlins, continued Wilson, "seemed to think it rather a time for penance and prayer than for enjoyment, however innocent, and was unusually concerned for Grant and the outcome of the new responsibilities which had just been imposed upon him. He realized that his general was now face to face with the greatest task of his life."[11]

It was hardly the first time that Rawlins felt the need to look out for his commander's welfare. By October 1863, the two had forged an intimate friendship, the depth and subtleties of which have eluded historians ever since. They had met in Galena, Illinois, before the war. Grant was then a failed former Regular Army officer who had come home in shame to clerk in his brother's leather store. Rawlins, on the other hand, was an aggressive young attorney on the way up. He won election as city attorney in 1857 and enjoyed the respect of the best elements of the town.

Their characters were as different as their social standing. Grant's modesty and unwillingness to offend are legendary. So gentle were his manners and slow his movements that his true strength of character and quickness when roused to action often surprised his contemporaries. Rawlins, on the other hand, was a man whose emotions were always close to the surface. Passionate and dogmatic, he never compromised his standards for another's sensibilities, not even Grant's.

Despite or perhaps because of their differences, the two men were drawn to one another. "I got to know Grant slowly and respectfully," Rawlins told a newspaperman after the war. The respect was reciprocal. As one of his first acts upon being commissioned a brigadier general in August 1861, Grant had asked Rawlins to leave his law practice and join him as his chief of staff. Rawlins accepted unhesitatingly. The two grew so close that Grant the loner later called Rawlins "the most nearly indispensable" man in his military family.

Rawlins became the quintessential chief of staff. He could digest and present to Grant the conflicting views of staff members and subordinate field commanders with a clarity that enabled Grant to make sound and well-informed decisions. And, by the fall of 1863, the thirty-two-year-old lawyer had learned enough of the military arts to offer his commander good, independent advice from time to time. Indeed, the journalist Sylvanus Cadwallader, a fixture at headquarters who revered Grant and was close to both men, confessed that "no general or broad plan of campaign, or pitched battle, was ever adopted by General Grant without the unqualified assent and approval of Rawlins. The latter was his only military confidant and adviser, and often originated many of the most successful operations." As Rawlins's love for Grant grew, so too did his desire to protect the general, even from Grant himself. "His friendship with Grant was so intense that he would curse him; so valuable that Grant accepted his rage. He wanted so much to be loved by Grant that he could test their friendship by admonishing Grant not to drink," explained Grant's foremost biographer.[12]

So Rawlins fretted around the Galt House. He shared his uneasiness in a letter to Mary Hurlbut: "I feel that [Grant] is equal to the requirements of his present position—as a commander of troops in the field he has no superior. There are those who in the exercise of a quasi-civil as well as military command are far his superiors. His simple, honest, and confiding nature unfits him for contact with the shrewd civilian who would take advantage of unsuspecting honesty [a thinly veiled reference to Stanton]—hence my aversion as you remember to having headquarters in cities." Rawlins was anxious to move on: "His true position is in the field in the immediate command of troops. There he will ever shine without a superior."[13]

Rawlins was about to get his wish. After spending 19 October, his first full day in Louisville, reviewing the military situation in his new command with Stanton, Grant left the Galt House with Julia to visit relatives who lived in the city. Their Sunday evening social calls were cut short, however, by a harried messenger who insisted Grant return with him to the hotel to see Stanton.

As Grant neared the hotel, nearly everyone he met told the general that the secretary was frantically looking for him. "Finding that I was out he became nervous and excited, inquiring of every person he met, including guests of the house, whether they knew where I was, and bidding them find me and send me to him at once," recalled an amused Grant.

The Ohioan obligingly hurried to the secretary's room. There he found Stanton pacing the floor in his nightshirt, waving a dispatch and wailing that a retreat must be prevented. Grant read the message. It was from Assistant Secretary of War Charles Dana, whom Stanton ironically had employed to report on Grant's fitness for command just five months earlier, when the general was blundering about in the swamps around Vicksburg. Grant won him over, and Dana had pronounced the Ohioan fit. Stanton then sent Dana to the Army of the Cumberland, where the assistant secretary, considerably less impressed with his new subjects, took delight in destroying the reputations of Rosecrans and several of his lieutenants. In the dispatch that had shaken Stanton and cut short Grant's and Julia's evening, Dana had warned the secretary that "conditions and prospects grow worse and worse" in Chattanooga. Horses were starving and the soldiers were not far behind. "Amid all this, the practical incapacity of Rosecrans is astonishing, and it often seems difficult to believe him of sound mind," opined Dana. "His imbecility appears to be contagious, and it is difficult for anyone to get anything done."

Grant acted promptly to calm the secretary. A retreat from Chattanooga at that moment would be "a terrible disaster," he assured Stanton. Although then a town of only some 2,500 inhabitants—more "an idea than a place," as one writer has put it—Chattanooga was of vital importance. It enjoyed a national reputation as a transportation hub from which two of the most important of the Confederacy's few railroads penetrated deep into the South's lightly defended interior, thus earning for Chattanooga its popular label as "Gateway to the South." Its occupation was essential both to future Federal operations into the deep South and to continued Union control of Tennessee. No other viable base of operations for Federal armies existed nearer than Nashville.

Grant understood all this. He dictated an order assuming command of the Military Division of the Mississippi and directing the removal of Rosecrans and had it telegraphed to Chattanooga. Just before midnight, he followed it with a terse but firm admonition to Thomas: "Hold Chattanooga at all hazards. I will be there as soon as possible." Thomas replied instantly: "I will hold the town till we starve."[14]

The import of the moment was not lost on the young Colonel Wilson. All present read and applauded Thomas's telegram, said Wilson, who sat down to scratch out his impressions to a friend: "General Grant takes command of . . . the Military Division of the Mississippi, headquarters in the field. Rosecrans is relieved and . . . Thomas takes his place. Sherman commands the Department of the Tennessee. These changes are radical, of vast moment and most intimately concern the Nation's welfare. I think they are in the right direction and if properly backed ought to give us most decisive results. There are many things connected with them I should like to write—but cannot for want of time. We start for the front at daylight."[15]

# CHAPTER TWO

# STARVATION CAMP

NEITHER Grant nor his staff could then appreciate the conviction behind Thomas's manful reply to the Ohioan's demand that he hold Chattanooga. After nearly four weeks of being besieged in the city, the Army of the Cumberland was on the brink of starvation. The same day Thomas wired Grant his promise to hold out, Private John Ely of the Thirty-sixth Illinois reflected in his diary: "If we could only manage to get plenty of rations, we could begin to see out of the woods again." Sergeant Isaac Doan of the Fortieth Ohio expressed the common plaint more pointedly: "This was starvation camp. For a full month we were on less than quarter rations, and the normal condition of the stomach was ravenous."[1]

The degree of suffering varied from unit to unit. Thanks to resourceful quartermasters, a few divisions managed to sustain full rations for a time. Others were put on half rations the day they stumbled into Chattanooga. By mid-October, however, all were reduced to two-thirds or, more commonly, one-half rations, "and we are cheated out of one-half of even these," complained an Ohio private. Some saw even their official allotment dwindle to a mere quarter rations. What all this meant was that the average soldier had to subsist each day on four crackers, each of which was only three inches square and just three times the thickness of a normal soda cracker.[2]

On occasion, the men were issued a bit of salt pork or beef, but the former was usually rancid and the latter indigestible. "Indeed," remembered an Indiana sergeant, "the beef was so poor that the soldiers were in the habit of saying, with a faint facetiousness, that they were living on 'half rations of hard bread and beef dried on the hoof.'" In some commands, the meat ration disappeared altogether. "When rations are reduced to one-third or less on a list of only one-half articles, then starvation commences," lamented Sergeant Frederick Keil of the Thirty-fifth Ohio. "Possibly no set of men were more completely starved, during the war of the rebellion . . . save only the prisoners at Andersonville, and other rebel prison pens," he averred.[3]

A lack of decent clothing and an early onset of autumn, which brought with it cold, drenching rains, compounded the soldiers' misery. Federal troops were accustomed to a new issue of uniforms after a hard campaign, but supply problems precluded this after Chickamauga. Clothing grew threadbare, and shoes gave out altogether. "Many were almost barefoot, and all were more or less ragged," said a Hoosier captain. Private George Kirkpatrick of the Forty-second Indiana was not one to suffer such indignities in silence. "We drew no rations for ten days. We had to go on picket every day, and I stood picket one night, barefooted," he recalled. "I told the captain I would not go on picket without shoes and so I was put into the guard house."[4]

Real though it was, the suffering of the soldiers almost paled beside the agony of the animals. There is no record of a single soldier dying of hunger during the siege, but horses and mules succumbed by the thousands. What little forage existed within the Union lines was fast used up, and hunger-deranged animals chewed to dirt the pastures ringing the town. Some artillery commanders tried to send all or part of their teams back over the mountains to the supply depots at Stevenson or Bridgeport, Alabama, before they became too feeble to walk. Many animals died along the way nevertheless, and those that remained in Chattanooga were no better off for the decreased numbers. Captain Jeremiah Donahower of the Second Minnesota watched the horses of his brigade's battery slowly die:

> Battery I, Fourth United States was drawn by five teams of bay horses, some of these having been sent to Bridgeport, and those retained at Chattanooga soon became too weak to walk to the usual watering place, and as they stood day after day in line along their picket ropes with their noses near the ground, growing leaner and weaker, they drew on our sympathies, but we could do nothing for them. I saw one of the drivers carrying an armful of blackberry brush wood, and I inquired what he intended doing with it, and was told that he intended chopping it fine and then make it into a pulp for feed for his team. A day or two later the same man said his horses could not eat it.[5]

Officers had to post guards over their horses while the animals ate to prevent soldiers from stealing the few ears of corn they had scrounged for them. "When the guard was withdrawn the soldiers would pick up the scattered grains, and wash and parch them for food for themselves," recalled Major John McClenahan of the Fifteenth Ohio sadly.[6]

Hunger indeed drove the men to pathetic extremes. Unloading boxes of crackers, they sifted the dirt beneath supply wagons for crumbs. Canine mascots began to disappear. Soldiers would loiter in groups around the slaughter yards, quarreling with one another for the offal of cattle. A thriving informal market developed. Early in the siege, beef livers topped the list at fifty cents apiece, entrails and heads went for a quarter, and tails sold for fifteen cents, all at a time when a private's salary was thirteen dollars a month.

Unscrupulous army butchers preyed on the famished infantrymen, and as the weeks passed the prices went up. H. H. Hill of the Second Minnesota overcame his revulsion at both the butchers' opportunism and the products they peddled and wandered down to the slaughter yard one afternoon. Some three hundred soldiers had gotten there ahead of him. Pushing his way through the crowd, he implored a butcher to sell him the next fresh liver. "Yes, for three dollars," snarled the butcher, "and if you want to make sure of it, you had better pay for it now, as I am going to make but one more killing today, and all those hungry fellows are after that one liver." Hill paid the man and was quickly swallowed up in the crowd. "Soon afterwards there was a rush made for the butcher, and when I got there I found myself dancing on the extreme outer rim of a large circle, and when the crowd melted away, I found two assistants loading the carcass into a government wagon, the butcher gone, and the liver also." Levi Wagner, an Ohioan who had deftly dodged bullets on the skirmish line at Stones River and Chickamauga, saw his luck continue, in a manner of speaking. His messmate walked proudly into their tent carrying the hide stripped from a beef's head, which he had begged from a butcher. "We heated water and scalded it, scraped off the hair and cooked the hide, and ate it before it had time to get very tender."[7]

Those fortunate enough to be sent out on foraging expeditions along the north bank of the Tennessee River carefully guarded for themselves much of what they found. One member of the Twenty-first Ohio snared a goose and kept it from the sight of his comrades. He brought it back into camp and stuffed the bird into a hole in the company bombproof shelter. Each day he sneaked a nibble or two until some of the men, attracted to the hole by the smell, demanded he bury the putrid remains.[8]

Most soldiers were more clever than gross. In late October a general order went out stating that commissioned officers must obtain their rations in person or send a signed request to the commissaries for them. Shifty enlisted men caught the loophole in the order and would appear at the commissary tent with forged requisitions to claim rations on an officer's behalf. When the victimized officer later applied in person, he was dismissed with the rebuke that he had already gotten his allowance.

The hard-preaching, hard-fighting commander of the Seventy-ninth Illinois, Colonel Allen Buckner, was lucky. His men thought enough of him to cut him in on their take. Remembered Buckner: "One night while quietly sleeping in my tent I heard a racket in front. I came to the door and inquired for the reasons. Someone replied: 'Colonel, go back to bed.' I obeyed orders. I understood that one of our generals had a cow at his headquarters for the purpose of furnishing milk for coffee. She had been locked up but this was bait that starving men must and would have. I had a nice beef steak for my breakfast. I ate that which was set before me and asked no questions for conscience sake."[9]

Years later, Buckner maintained that his troops had borne their hunger and uncertainty with grit and humor. He recalled wandering into the tent of two sick soldiers, who were sitting on their bunks with underwear in hand, busily picking off lice. "Boys, how do you like this?" he asked. "We would rather die than go back across the Tennessee," they purportedly replied. "That was the pluck which put down the rebellion," boasted Buckner. Perhaps. But the feelings of Captain George Lewis of the One Hundred Twenty-fourth Ohio probably came closer to those of the grand majority of the army in the days before Rosecrans's removal. "Never in the history of the Army of the Cumberland had the spirit of its officers and men been more depressed. The battle of Chickamauga had not only been fought and lost, but we also lost what was more than losing a battle. We had lost confidence in our commander."[10]

And their commander seemingly had lost confidence in himself. The army was near collapse, Assistant Secretary Dana had wired Stanton on 16 October, "because our dazed and hazy commander cannot perceive the catastrophe that is close upon us, nor fix his mind upon the means of preventing it. I never saw anything which seemed so lamentable and hopeless."[11]

In the month between the disaster at Chickamauga and his removal, Rosecrans still was able to plan well, but he lacked the strength to sustain a coherent effort to relieve his beleaguered army. His old bursts of energy came less frequently, and the clarity that previously had marked his strategic thinking too often was missing.

Certainly the task before Rosecrans was daunting enough to give any commander pause, particularly one who had just suffered one of the soundest defeats of the war. Few cities or towns on the continent were both so intrinsically vulnerable to siege or offered topographical features so favorable to the defense as Chattanooga. Natural obstacles of imposing grandeur encircled it. If protected, they might keep a besieging army

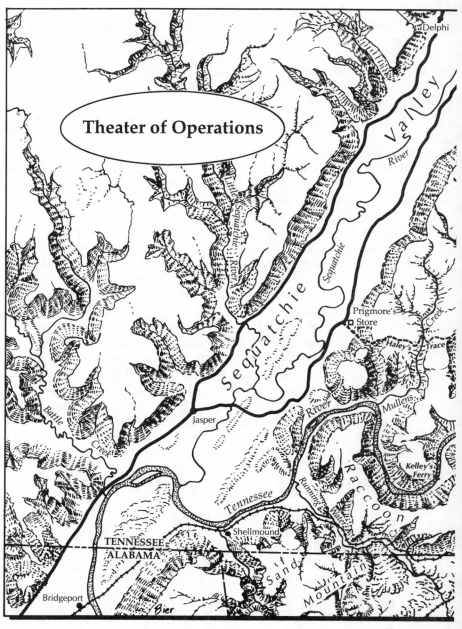

Theater of Operations

Delphi

Valley

River

Little Sequatchie River

Sequatchie

Sequatchie

Prigmore's Store

Haley's Trace

Creek

Mullens

Battle Creek

Jasper

River

Running Water

Raccoon

Kelley's Ferry

Tennessee

Shellmound

TENNESSEE
ALABAMA

Sand Mountain

Bridgeport

Bier

Map Symbols

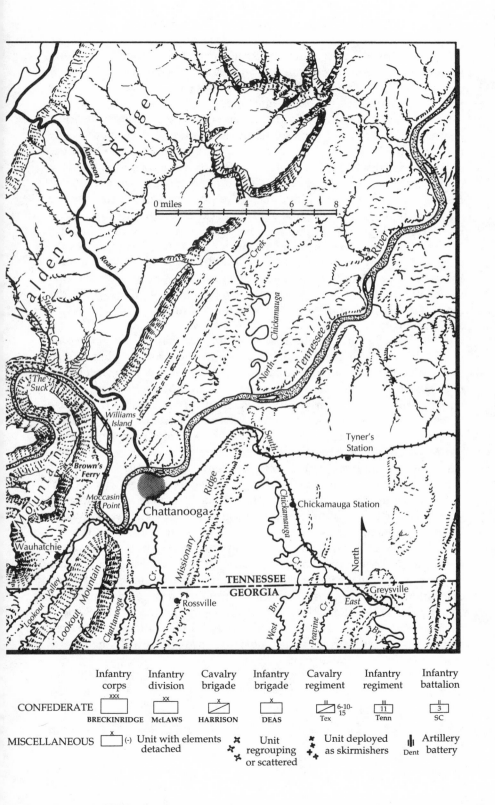

| 0 miles | 2 | 4 | 6 | 8 |

Walden's Ridge

Anderson Road

Stick Cr.

The Suck

Williams Island

Brown's Ferry

Moccasin Point

Chattanooga

Wauhatchie

Lookout Valley

Lookout Mountain

Chattanooga Cr.

Missionary Ridge

Rossville

TENNESSEE
GEORGIA

West Br.

Peavine Cr.

East Br.

Greysville

North Chickamauga Creek

Tennessee River

South Chickamauga

Tyner's Station

Chickamauga Station

Chickamauga Cr.

North

|  | Infantry corps | Infantry division | Cavalry brigade | Infantry brigade | Cavalry regiment | Infantry regiment | Infantry battalion |
|---|---|---|---|---|---|---|---|
| CONFEDERATE | xxx BRECKINRIDGE | xx McLAWS | x HARRISON | x DEAS | ⫽ 6-10-15 Tex | 11 Tenn | 3 SC |

| MISCELLANEOUS | (-) Unit with elements detached | Unit regrouping or scattered | Unit deployed as skirmishers | Artillery Dent battery |

at bay indefinitely; unfortunately, Rosecrans had lost them to General Braxton Bragg's Army of Tennessee without having fired a shot in their defense, and so the Federals found themselves ensnared between a wide river and a series of long ridges and craggy bluffs.

Chattanooga itself lay tucked in a bend of the Tennessee River, on a peninsula that grew out of its southern bank as the river twisted its way through the Cumberland Mountains. The Tennessee flowed from the northeast until within about a mile of Chattanooga, where it changed course and ran nearly due west, with a slight northward curve as it passed the town. Overlooking the northwest corner of the town was a low ridge perhaps four hundred yards long called Cameron Hill. Behind its western slope, the Tennessee River turned abruptly to the south, continuing in that direction for two miles before swinging to the southwest and butting up against Lookout Mountain. As the river rounded the northern extremity of Lookout and again changed course, this time to the northwest, it spilled over the rocky outcrops that formed the mountain bed and created a mild whirlpool that boats had learned to avoid by hugging the northern bank of the river.[12]

A half-mile beyond the base of Lookout Mountain, the river veered nearly due north. It flowed north for two miles before forking at Williams Island. These two major changes of the river's course after Chattanooga—first to the south, then back to the north—created a long, narrow peninsula that early settlers had named Moccasin Point because its shape resembled the footwear of the area's Cherokee inhabitants. A mile wide in most places, Moccasin Point lay directly opposite Lookout Mountain, its southernmost acreage cleared and partly cultivated. The curve in the river at this point was named Moccasin Bend.

From many miles northeast of Chattanooga up to the southern tip of Williams Island, the Tennessee River held fairly steady at an imposing width of three to five hundred yards, its current gentle and waters placid. Where the two branches reunited north of the island, however, the river turned suddenly narrow and rapid. It roared and spat, racing through a long, deep gorge created by the meeting of Raccoon Mountain to the south and Walden's Ridge to the north. Frightened pioneers had given colorful names to the most treacherous stretches of the gorge: Tumbling Shoals, the Frying Pan, the Skillet. The worst spot was the Suck, a chasm beneath the southern cliffs of Walden's Ridge where the river ran so fast that, even at high water, only the most powerful steamboats could hope to best its current.[13]

After thirteen miles of dizzying twists and foaming water, the river calmed and widened near Kelley's Ferry, which lay six miles due west of the northern tip of Lookout Mountain. From Kelley's Ferry, the Tennessee River was easily navigable all the way to the Federal supply depot at Bridgeport, Alabama, some twenty-two miles away.[14]

The ground east of Chattanooga was nearly as formidable a barrier as the river to the north and west. Two miles beyond the town, rising from a broad and partly cleared valley to a height of nearly five hundred feet, loomed the narrow heights of Missionary Ridge.

Missionary Ridge grew out of the southern bank of South Chickamauga Creek, a wide and sluggish tributary that emptied into the Tennessee River about two and a half miles northeast of the city. Cut here and there by wagon roads, broken by ravines, dotted with huge outcroppings, and tangled with fallen timber, Missionary Ridge ran south by slightly southeast for a distance of nearly fifteen miles. Hard to ascend along its entire length, its slopes were particularly precipitous along the eight-mile stretch from South Chickamauga Creek to Rossville, Georgia, where a narrow gap sliced through the ridge.[15]

Missionary Ridge was separated from its more spectacular sister elevation to the west, Lookout Mountain, by the four-mile-wide Chattanooga Valley. Through the center of the valley wound Chattanooga Creek, which flowed north, then curved west to empty into the Tennessee River at the base of Lookout.

Of Lookout Mountain itself, one Northern journalist observed: "As the Tennessee is a geographical inconsistency, so is Lookout Mountain a geological anomaly." Indeed it was, and nearly everyone who saw it came away deeply moved by the majestic and rugged grandeur of the mountain. Forty-five years earlier, Elias Cornelius, a young Congregationalist minister who had ventured into the still unsettled region to convert Indians, climbed its heights and penned his impressions of the view: "The summit of Lookout Mountain overlooks the whole country. And to those who can be delighted with the view of an interminable forest, penetrated by the windings of a bold river, interspersed with hundreds of verdant prairies and broken by many ridges and mountains, furnishes . . . a landscape which yields to few others in extent, variety, or beauty. Even the aborigines had not been insensible to its charms, for the name in the Cherokee language is . . . literally, 'mountains looking at each other.'"[16]

The name Lookout Mountain is a bit of a misnomer. Not a single mountain in the commonly understood sense, it was more of a long, towering ridge that extended southward from the Tennessee River some eighty-five miles. Nearly ten miles wide along its southern reaches, Lookout Mountain narrowed as it neared the river. There it ended, coming to a point—or "nose," as the locals called it—not more than two hundred yards wide and eighteen hundred feet above the Tennessee.

From the riverbank, along a quarter-mile stretch, the mountain rose at a forty-five degree angle to a height of eight hundred feet. Virgin timber blanketed this initial rise. Laurel bushes abounded, and rough, dreary limestone rocks jutted from a thin soil of red clay. About two-thirds of the way between the river and the summit, the slope rose sharply, then abruptly changed grade and became relatively level, giving the appearance, when viewed from the city, of a small hump. This feature terminated in a ledge, or "bench," between 150 and 300 feet wide, which extended for several miles around both sides of the mountain.[17]

From the bench, the grade again became steep. Five hundred or six hundred feet of timber and outcrops brought one abruptly to the "palisades." The war correspondent William Shanks penned one of the best descriptions of the palisades. They were, he wrote, "a ridge of dark, cold, gray rocks, bare even of moss, which rise to the height of fifty or sixty feet, overhanging, arch-like, the beholder who looks up at them from their base; and which, seen from the valley, have the appearance of a crown encircling a human brow."[18]

West of Lookout Mountain loomed Sand Mountain. For nearly seventy miles, the Tennessee River lapped against its western base. On its eastern side, a long valley of varying width and names divided Sand from Lookout Mountain. Although of similar length, Sand Mountain was far wider than Lookout along most of its plateau—up to fifteen miles across in places. Unlike the plateau of Lookout, which was heavily forested, Sand Mountain was oddly barren. Some five miles south of the Tennessee River, Sand Mountain was cut by a mile-wide valley, through which flowed Running Water Creek. North of Running Water Creek Valley, the mountain resumed. This final four-mile stretch to the Tennessee River was called Raccoon Mountain. It lay two miles west of Lookout Mountain. Near the river, the plain separating the two ranges was known as Lookout Valley. A narrow stream called Lookout Creek ran along the western base of Lookout Mountain and emptied into the Tennessee almost due north of the point of the mountain. On either side of the valley, a chain of high foothills rubbed up against the two mountains. The western side of Lookout Mountain was abrupt, the eastern slope of Raccoon Mountain gentle and easily traversed.

The greater range of which Sand and Raccoon mountains were a part resumed on the northern bank of the Tennessee, where it became known as Walden's Ridge. Generally ten miles wide, it ran northeast for forty miles before melting into the plateau of the Cumberland Mountains. Walden's Ridge was bordered on the northwest by the broad Sequatchie Valley and on the southeast by the equally expansive Tennessee River Valley. Barren and wild, Walden's Ridge was as great a barrier to travel north of the river as Sand Mountain was to the south of it.[19]

Of course, this imposing—and confusing—patchwork of natural obstacles rendered lines of supply and communications into Chattanooga from the north and west extremely vulnerable, as Rosecrans learned early. Practically speaking, five routes—four of them short and one quite long—connected Chattanooga with the Federal supply depot at Bridgeport.

The most obvious and rapid route was the Nashville and Chattanooga Railroad, which crossed the Tennessee River at Bridgeport. From there, the track snaked through valleys and mountain passes along the southern bank of the river until it reached the tiny junction of Wauhatchie in Lookout Valley. From Wauhatchie, it ran northward to the point of Lookout Mountain where, turning east, it threaded its way between the base of Lookout and the river into Chattanooga Valley and then continued northeastward on into the city. Unfortunately, the trestle bridges across the Tennessee and at Running Water Creek had been burned, which rendered this first route temporarily useless.[20]

The second route was an improved wagon road that paralleled the railroad between Bridgeport and Chattanooga. The third was the river itself, which was unnavigable after a summer of prolonged drought and problematical beyond Kelley's Ferry in any season. The fourth route was a wagon road of uneven quality along the north bank. From Bridgeport to Jasper, a distance of twelve miles, the road was tolerable. It remained so for another ten miles, from Jasper northeastward across the Sequatchie River to a dusty little crossroads settlement called Prigmore's Store. From there, the most direct route to Chattanooga was a narrow backcountry trail that branched off from the main road, which in turn continued up the Sequatchie Valley. Called Haley's Trace, this short route ran due east from Prigmore's Store, over the southern tip of Walden's Ridge, and down the mountain to the north bank of the Tennessee River opposite the Narrows and the Suck, where the river was less than three hundred yards wide. For the next three miles, the trail hugged the bank. North of Williams Island, Haley's Trace broke out into the open and joined the main roads that approached Chattanooga from the north.[21]

The fifth, and longest, route initially traversed a good country road up the Sequatchie Valley. Two miles short of Delphi, however, it turned onto the Anderson road for the journey over Walden's Ridge. There, atop Walden's Ridge, the going was hard even in the best of weather. In times of drought, the tiny streams along the ridge dried up, leaving animals and men without a source of drinking water. After rains, it became "a greasy, washed-out hell." Also, the ridge long since had been stripped of what little forage it had had to offer. The distance from Bridgeport to Chattanooga over this excruciating course was nearly sixty miles.[22]

Circumstances quickly forced this route on Rosecrans. Three days after falling back to Chattanooga, in an effort to shorten his badly attenuated and as yet unfortified front, Rosecrans pulled his lone brigade off Lookout Mountain and drew in all his forces to the north side of Chattanooga Creek. Bragg promptly occupied the summit at the point of Lookout, gaining control of the railroad and wagon road around the base. Two of five supply routes were thus instantly closed to the Federals.[23]

Rosecrans was concerned but not yet alarmed. "Fighting Joe" Hooker was on his way from the Army of the Potomac with the Eleventh and Twelfth corps, fifteen thousand strong, which Stanton had ordered west with all haste in the first frenetic hours after Chickamauga. The promise of reinforcements temporarily restored Rosecrans's equilibrium and energy, and he quickly fashioned plans for Hooker's column. On 27 September, he telegraphed Hooker: "You will proceed from Louisville direct to Bridgeport without stopping at Nashville." The next day, he ordered all train cars then at Stevenson and Bridgeport to be unloaded at once and sent back to Nashville to forward Hooker's troops.

Rosecrans's plan was simple. Once at Bridgeport, Hooker was to push rapidly across the pontoon bridge laid down by the late Brigadier General William H. Lytle a month earlier and then march over the wagon road to Wauhatchie. From there, Hooker was to force any enemy he might encounter out of Lookout Valley and take control of the mountain passes from the point of Lookout all the way south to Trenton. As soon as Hooker had secured the passes and cut off Bragg from the valley, Rosecrans intended to throw a pontoon bridge across the Tennessee below the mouth of Lookout Creek. Supplies then could be brought upriver from Bridgeport, landed at Kelley's Ferry, and hauled across Lookout Valley to the pontoon bridge near Lookout Creek, thereby avoiding the treacherous waters of the Suck altogether. Rosecrans planned to store those supplies not immediately needed by the army in a depot on Williams Island. With characteristic attention to detail, he directed his engineers to appropriate two old sawmills in the city and begin cutting planks for the pontoons. Rosecrans also ordered the construction of four steamboats at Chattanooga and one at Bridgeport and called for repairs to be hastened on the *Painted Rock*, a Rebel ferryboat that John Wilder's Mounted Infantry had sunk early in the Chickamauga campaign. At the same time, Hooker was to speed repairs on the trestle bridges at Bridgeport and over Running Water Creek. If all went well, both the river and railroad routes would be reopened in short order.[24]

All did not go well. As the tragic month of September drew to a close, heavy rains began to fall. Roads turned to a pasty ooze, and in the mountains, long stretches were washed away altogether. The Confederates seemed to make common cause with nature. At noon on 1 October, a mud-caked courier staggered into the leaky, one-room cottage that served as Rosecrans's headquarters. The news he brought was alarming: Major General Joseph Wheeler had crossed the Tennessee River north of Chattanooga and with his cavalry corps was riding hard toward the Sequatchie Valley.

The report was accurate. Wheeler crossed Walden's Ridge and descended into the valley the next morning. There he found a cavalry commander's dream. Rumbling slowly over Walden's Ridge was a train of eight hundred mule-team wagons, trailed by a large number of sutlers' wagons. The procession stretched for nearly ten miles, from the top of the ridge back down the valley toward Jasper.

As the first whooping and hollering Confederate troopers descended on the train, teamsters panicked. Supply wagons slid off the road and tumbled down the ridge. Ammunition wagons on the summit exploded with a deafening roar that echoed across the valley. The entire train stalled. Rebel horsemen herded the teamsters, soldiers, and their meager guard of infantry into groups, and then went about rummaging. It had all been too easy, and the mood of the Rebels turned festive. They plundered whiskey from sutlers' wagons, cast off their own ragged clothing for new Yankee shoes and trousers, and even held up Union officers for booty. Confederate officers did little to restore discipline, their only order of consequence being to "kill the mules and burn the wagons." Out came the torches. Carbines cracked and mules shrieked. The stench of animal blood mingled with the smoke of nearly four hundred burning wagons. After eight hours of gleeful plundering, Wheeler and his men rode off toward McMinnville, easily outdistancing the Federal cavalry and infantry sent to intercept them.

Bragg and his generals were openly ashamed at the manner in which Wheeler had wrought his destruction. "The facts in regard to Wheeler's circuit of the enemy's rear are becoming developed," Colonel George Brent noted with disgust in his journal at the end of October. "It was a disgraceful raid. Plunder and demoralization were manifested . . . and when the enemy appeared, the race was to keep the booty out of his reach." Brigadier General Arthur Manigault agreed: "There being a large quantity of whiskey and brandy in some of the wagons, the men and officers drank large quantities, and the consequence was a great amount of drunkenness. Hard to control at any time, they now became almost entirely unmanageable."

Although Wheeler's methods had been despicable, the results were highly satisfactory. Three Federal divisions were left without supplies, and the ammunition reserves of the entire army had been rendered dangerously low. Wheeler's raid, bemoaned Rosecrans's biographer, was "the funeral pyre of Rosecrans in top command."[25]

It also brought a swift end to the Ohioan's plans for recovering Lookout Valley. Deeply shaken, Rosecrans afterward told Hooker to distribute the majority of the Twelfth Corps along the railroad from Wartrace to Bridgeport to prevent its destruction by Wheeler, and with the remainder of his command to take up headquarters near Bridgeport, there to await further instructions.[26]

Hooker could have done but little more. In a masterful bit of mismanagement, the War Department had instructed the Eleventh and Twelfth corps to turn in their "choice and efficient" trains—horses, wagons, pontoons, and all—before leaving Washington for the West, telling them to draw new wagons and teams at Nashville. Unfortunately, the Nashville depot had been thoroughly depleted. Only unbroken or worn-out horses and crippled wagons remained. Hooker's infantry pushed on by rail, while his quartermaster corps remained behind to fashion a train out of the dregs of the depot. The Eleventh Corps and those units of the Twelfth not detailed to guard the railroad congregated between Stevenson and Bridgeport on schedule, but without transportation they were of little use. Hooker made his headquarters at Stevenson and waited for his artillery and trains. For the moment, the river route to Chattanooga was eliminated as an option.[27]

Matters grew worse. On 8 October, Bragg sent elements of Lieutenant General James Longstreet's corps into Lookout Valley. Rebel pickets fanned out along the south bank of the Tennessee, stretching their line to within cannon shot of Bridgeport. They dug in opposite the Narrows and awaited the approach of the first Yankee train along Haley's Trace. A sergeant of the Eighty-fourth Illinois, on detached duty with the teamsters, remembered the moment when the wagons of Brigadier General Charles Cruft's division rumbled into range: "The enemy sharpshooters let the whole train come quietly into the pass between the river and mountain, and then commenced shooting down the mules near the front and rear, so that the road was completely blocked at both ends. . . . Probably one fourth of the mules of the entire train were shot down before the drivers could cut them loose from the wagons and bring them out."[28]

The closing of Haley's Trace left open only the long route. Rosecrans fell into a perplexed despondency, issuing no orders of real consequence for the next week, while his wagon trains negotiated the nightmarish Anderson road over Walden's Ridge. John Patton of the Ninety-eighth Ohio accompanied several such trains, and the extreme difficulty of the experience deeply impressed him:

Much of the drive was over mountain crests and ridges. The ascent of these was sometimes steep, and always rugged. Often it was over the outcrop of ledges of rock. Over these rock-ribbed steps the mules would clamber and climb, and strain to their utmost to draw the loaded wagons up after them. Descending these rocky steps, the wagons would dash from side to side, and jolt and toss about in a way that might cause one to think that they would soon be dashed to pieces. But few of the cracker boxes after the arrival of our trains at Chattanooga had whole crackers when opened. And some of them were nothing but a box of crumbs, the intense knocking and jarring of the wagons having broken and pulverized the crackers.[29]

Then, in mid-October, the rains returned. Recalled Patton:

> The rain did not come down in showers and at intervals but it poured down for days and nights in succession till the water rushed in torrents down the mountain and tossed and roared in the gorges.
> Every low place in the road became a pool of water; the water filled the ruts cut by the wheels. And in many places, the wheels worked down in the mud and water axle deep. Teams by the hundreds floundered and stuck in the mud. Soldiers of the train escort worked hard, fishing up mules sunk in the deep mud; prying up and helping forward wagons.[30]

It was not the hard labor that most distressed the men, but rather the pitiable plight of the mules. "The poor, abused mule suffered the most," remembered John Duke of the Fifty-third Ohio. "For instance, one of them got off the road and was hanging over a precipice, endangering the other mules of the team. This one was cut loose, and dropped 200 or 300 feet below." And their hunger was so acute, recalled Duke, that "it was no unusual sight to see trees as high as animals could reach, barked and eaten as food."[31] John Patton was equally disturbed:

> But what pen can portray the suffering and abuse to which the poor, patient, long-suffering army mules were compelled to submit to. . . . Starved, and overworked, when they became utterly exhausted and unable to perform any more labor, they were either shot or turned out to die of starvation, and themselves became food for the buzzards that continually circled and swooped above and about the line of our route.
> Yes, when the mules were turned out it was to starve and die for in a range of miles among those mountain barrens, enough of even wild bunch grass could not be found to make one good feed for a hungry mule.
> Mules would sometimes lie down in the harness completely discouraged, hearts broken perhaps, and no whipping or coaxing or pulling on the bridle and twisting of the tail would induce them to make a single effort to rise. And all that could be done was to remove the harness, pull them out of the way, and abandon or shoot them.
> And thus it was that the number of dead mules along the route in-

creased day by day, till the road sides became literally lined with dead mules.[32]

With each wagon that stalled or broke down out on Walden's Ridge, the hunger of the troops in Chattanooga sharpened. The black market in offal boomed, and a cow's tail was bringing ten dollars. A single cracker could be sold for fifty cents. Soldiers slept with their haversacks under their heads to keep them from being stolen. When they did draw rations, the men often devoured several day's worth in a single sitting. That simply brought on acute diarrhea, which laid low entire companies at a time.

Morale slid further. "I found that an empty stomach caused considerable grumbling and fault-finding," wrote a Minnesota drummer boy in an expression of the obvious. "The rations I drew today were one cracker and a half, one half spoonful of coffee, and a little piece of meat for two days," a disgusted Indianian scribbled in his diary. "That was all I got and I could sit down and eat all of it and not have half enough. Now when it gets down to that small rations, it seems to me the Army is pretty near gone up."[33]

Many of the generals agreed. Confessed one: "No military man, officer, or soldier of any intelligence could fail to see the daily disintegration that was going on, or could look forward to anything but a dreadful termination of the then existing state of affairs."[34]

# CHAPTER THREE

# EVERYONE HERE CURSES BRAGG

B RAXTON Bragg was on the attack. Unfortunately for the Southern cause, the object of his offensive was not the badly weakened Army of the Cumberland but rather his own generals. As he had following Perryville and again after Stones River, President Jefferson Davis came a third time to the defense of his beleaguered friend, whose detractors within the Army of Tennessee had achieved a new level of audacity. Indeed, they were on the brink of mutiny. As bloody September ended and the Army of the Cumberland was allowed to entrench unmolested in Chattanooga, twelve of Bragg's most senior generals, including James Longstreet, D. H. Hill, and Simon Bolivar Buckner, signed and submitted to the president a petition bluntly calling for the general's removal from command. Leonidas Polk and Thomas Hindman, whom Bragg had suspended from command on 29 September, did not sign the petition, which was dated 4 October.

Davis left for the front as soon as word of the petition reached him. He arrived at Bragg's headquarters atop Missionary Ridge on 9 October. For five days he listened to the bitter complaints of the factious subordinates and to the equally vehement rebuttals of their petulant commander. Longstreet, who had come west before Chickamauga partly in the hope of getting command of the Army of Tennessee, and Buckner, who had seen his Department of East Tennessee whittled away to nothing by Bragg, led the movement to oust him. Buckner told Davis that Bragg was "wanting in imagination," a man who when faced with a hard choice would "lean upon the advice of a drummer boy." Longstreet was equally impassioned. Davis granted him a private interview that, as Longstreet told it, became "excited, at times warm." Longstreet opened the meeting by suggesting that Joseph Johnston be put in charge of the army. Davis was tired of such talk and bluntly told Longstreet as much. The two men shook hands at the end of the meeting, but Longstreet saw in Davis's parting smile "a bitter look lurking about its margin, and the ground-swell, admonished me that clouds were gathering about headquarters."[1]

Before he left the army, the president shattered any lingering hope Longstreet and his fellow conspirators may have nurtured. He told Brigadier General St. John Liddell, who had a knack for getting others to reveal themselves, that what the army needed was "zealous, unreserved cooperation with the Commander." And that commander would continue to be Bragg. Liddell then sought out Bragg, ostensibly to urge on him "the propriety of making friends and quieting the dissatisfaction among his general officers" but, given Liddell's sadistic bent, probably simply to irritate him. Predictably, Bragg balked at the suggestion. "His mettle was up and beyond the control of dispassionate reason," recalled Liddell. "General," snarled Bragg, "I want to get rid of all such generals. I have better men now in subordinate stations to fill their places. Let them send in their resignations. I shall accept every one without hesitation."[2]

When the resignations were not forthcoming, Bragg acted. He relieved a second corps commander—D. H. Hill—and smugly informed Buckner that his Department of East Tennessee had been broken up officially upon instructions from the president. Buckner had commanded a corps at Chickamauga; he should, Bragg intimated in his letter to the Kentuckian, be grateful for that. Bragg warned: "You are required by the general commanding to desist from the exercise of any other authority in this military department."[3]

Left with the full benediction of the president, Bragg in early November did what he long had desired but had dared not do: he dug out the roots of the opposition through a complete reshuffling of units. Bragg had gotten the president's permission to reorganize the army before Davis departed, on the grounds that having too many brigades from the same state in a division placed undue hardship upon a single community in the event of heavy losses. Whatever the official pretext, Davis understood Bragg's real intent, and he quietly countenanced the dismantling of the powerful Tennessee and Kentucky blocs, which had long nurtured three of Bragg's most powerful foes: Frank Cheatham, John C. Breckinridge, and Simon Bolivar Buckner.[4]

Cheatham got wind of the impending shakeup and tried to resign. Bragg, who for all his personal enmity toward the Tennessean could not deny even to himself that Cheatham had fought capably at Chickamauga, forwarded the request to Richmond without endorsement on 1 November. While awaiting Richmond's reply, Cheatham went on leave, perhaps to avoid having to watch the carving up of his division. At

Chickamauga, four of his five brigades had been composed exclusively of Tennessee regiments whose loyalty to him was unwavering. No more. George Maney's Tennessee brigade was transferred to the division of William "Hell-Fighting Billie" Walker, a Bragg supporter; Otho Strahl's went to the division of A. P. Stewart, who, if not neutral, was at least circumspect in his opposition to Bragg; and Alfred Vaughan and his men found themselves in Hindman's division, now commanded by Patton Anderson, a Bragg favorite. All that was left of Cheatham's famed Tennessee division were six regiments under Marcus Wright, a relative newcomer to the army whose own regimental commanders distrusted him as an incompetent coward. The division was filled out with Walthall's Mississippi brigade and a ragtag brigade of Alabamians under John Moore gathered from paroled Vicksburg defenders and armed with cast-off weapons.[5]

Buckner fared even worse. The dismantling of his corps had begun even before the formal mid-November reorganization. On 18 October, William Preston's division was transferred first to Polk's old corps and then out of the theater altogether. A Kentuckian whose hatred of Bragg ran deep, Preston himself was reduced to brigade command. Buckner too was dropped one notch, to the status of division commander. He counterattacked, complaining bitterly of his treatment in a strong note to Bragg. Davis failed to intervene decisively. Bragg and Buckner ignored the president's pathetic plea for mutual understanding and for the next two weeks kept up an unseemly exchange of letters that wasted far too much of both men's time and ended only when the Kentuckian took ill.[6]

Breckinridge fared substantially better. Although their mutual antipathy ran deep, Bragg respected Breckinridge's ability as a troop commander. He recognized that Breckinridge had fought well at Chickamauga; indeed, the Kentuckian had been one of the few Confederate generals to have thought clearly on that muddled field. For his part, Breckinridge had had the good sense not to sign the petition calling for Bragg's removal, which in a measure kept him in good graces with the commanding general. When the reshuffling was completed, Breckinridge found himself elevated to corps command.[7]

Between Bragg and Longstreet there could be no reconciliation. Since coming west, Longstreet had evinced a lack of respect for his commanding general that bordered on insubordination. He fomented unrest among his fellow lieutenants at every opportunity and was clearly a moving force behind the petition to Davis. When his effort to unseat Bragg failed, he sulked. Bragg continued to hold him in high regard as a commander and entrusted him with key assignments in the early weeks of the campaign, apparently unaware that Longstreet had lost any inclination to obey.[8]

By mid-November the shakeup was complete and the dissidents dispersed. Of the six wing and corps commanders who had fought at Chickamauga, only Walker and Longstreet remained. Bragg had divided the army into two grand wings before the second day at Chickamauga, hoping to facilitate better command and control. The result had been only deeper confusion and jealousy, and Bragg returned to a traditional corps structure.

The reconfigured army consisted of three corps. Breckinridge was handed Stewart's division, which itself had been reshuffled until just one of its original brigades remained. General William Bate's suicidal attacks at Chickamauga had won him the recognition he had sought so assiduously, and Bragg gave him command of Breckinridge's old division. Hindman's division rounded out Breckinridge's corps.

Longstreet kept his corps, less Preston's division, which was broken up, and Walker's division, which was transferred to Polk's old corps in November. Brigadier General Micah Jenkins replaced the convalescing John Bell Hood as a division commander, and Major General Lafayette McLaws, who had arrived too late for Chickamauga, led Longstreet's other remaining division.[9]

Whom to place in command of Polk's former corps posed a problem that President Davis solved for Bragg. After leaving the Army of Tennessee, Davis traveled on to Mississippi, officially to confer with Joseph Johnston and William J. Hardee, his second-in-command, on the state of affairs there since the loss of Vicksburg and to see if any troops could be spared for service before Chattanooga. Davis, however, had a hidden agenda equally important. While passing through Atlanta on the way to Mississippi, Davis had met with his old friend Polk, who was there biding his time after being cashiered by Bragg. Davis told Polk he would dismiss the charges that Bragg had brought against him and restore his reputation by appointing him to corps command in Johnston's department. To make room for Polk, Davis would send Hardee back to the Army of Tennessee to take over the Polk's old corps.[10]

It was a clever bit of maneuvering acceptable to all concerned. Polk had his dignity restored and a field command in the bargain. Bragg had a general he respected; he had, in fact, appealed for Hardee's services as early as 1 October. Although they too had had their differences, Hardee always had been scrupulously careful to avoid blatant politicking, so that Bragg was quite pleased at the prospect of once again having the talented Georgian under his command.

No one was happier with the change than Hardee. Arguably the most accomplished military scholar in the South, Hardee was also a gifted if sometimes pedantic field commander. Since the fall of Vicksburg he had had little to do. Hardee missed Tennessee, recalled a staff officer, T. B. Roy, who wrote that the general was "not at all pleased with Mississippi and gives a gloomy account of everything." In August, the War Department assigned him the thankless task of bringing order to paroled Confederates then assembling in Demopolis, Alabama, and Enterprise, Mississippi, to await formal parole. At Demopolis, Hardee found about a thousand unarmed and demoralized Alabamians under Major General Carter Stevenson and a skeleton brigade of Missourians.[11]

When Davis met with Hardee in Demopolis on 18 October and offered to transfer him to Chattanooga to replace Polk, the Georgian immediately accepted. He started for Tennessee on 27 October with two partially refitted brigades under Stevenson and a solemn charge from Davis. Accompanying the order returning him to the Army of Tennessee was a personal letter from the president, commissioning Hardee as "peacemaker to the army" and begging him to use his considerable influence to heal the divisions within it. "The information from the army at Chattanooga painfully impresses me with the fact that there is a want there of that harmony, among the highest officers, which is essential to success," Davis wrote. "I rely greatly upon you for the restoration of a proper feeling, and know that you will realize the comparative insignificance of personal considerations when weighed against the duty of imparting to the Army all the efficiency of which it is capable."[12]

It was a pathetic appeal, one that reflected Davis's lack of appreciation of the depth of the army's discontent, but the burden probably did not weigh heavily on Hardee.

The general was at that moment deeply in love. The handsome forty-eight-year-old widower enjoyed a wide reputation as a ladies' man. During the Kentucky campaign, it was said, he availed himself of the "privilege of his rank and years, and insisted upon kissing the wives and daughters of all the Kentucky farmers." While in Demopolis, however, he met a young woman who brought his playful flirtations to an abrupt halt. Slim and sophisticated, Mary Foreman Lewis conquered him completely. With more exuberance than tact, he wrote a young lady who had earlier rebuffed his advances: "You have lost your chances. Since his disappointment, he has determined to concentrate his forces and attack in another quarter. See what you have lost! If a forced reconnaissance which he intends to make on Thursday next near Demopolis shall prove successful he intends to bring on a serious engagement immediately." Hardee apparently had his way, and he left for Chattanooga with a light heart.[13]

The officers and men of the Army of Tennessee greeted the news of Hardee's impending return with universal delight. Yet the prospect of "Old Reliable's" presence was insufficient to quell the general disquiet, which, far from disappearing after Davis left, had simply moved back underground. For a few, the hypocrisy was unbearable. Bragg's own chief of staff, the loyal and talented Brigadier General W. W. Mackall, quit rather than compromise himself further. Bragg's "whole soul is in it," he wrote his wife of the general's dedication to the Southern cause, but "he is as much influenced by his enemies as by friends—and does not know how to control the one or preserve the other." He "is as blind as a bat to the circumstances surrounding him." Mackall's departure was a serious blow. Enjoying good relations with both Bragg and his lieutenants, Mackall had been able to smooth many a misunderstanding and clarify the commanding general's orders. Joseph Johnston always believed Mackall "absolutely necessary" to the stability of the army's command structure, particularly during Bragg's frequent bouts of ill health.[14]

St. John Liddell also wanted out. He went to headquarters to remind Bragg of an earlier promise to transfer him to Johnston's department. Instead, Liddell found himself on the short list of candidates to replace Mackall as chief of staff.

"I declined at once in favor of the others," said Liddell. "The fact was I did not believe we could get along smoothly together, or I would have tried it." Apparently the other candidates felt likewise, for the post remained vacant throughout the coming campaign.[15]

The deleterious effect on the army of this unseemly infighting was not lost on the men in ranks. "Everyone here curses Bragg," wrote a young Tennessee lieutenant who dismissed the commanding general as an imbecile. Only Bragg's immediate removal, the subaltern told a friend, would put the troops in good spirits. Predictably, the dismembering of divisions and brigades had eroded morale further. Unit pride was paramount to battlefield success, as in any war, and when men who had fought together for nearly two years suddenly found themselves thrust into unfamiliar surroundings, they grew confused and anxious.[16]

For many, especially the Tennesseans of Cheatham's division, the reorganization of the army was the last straw. "The position of a private soldier in our army [was] worse than that of a servant in peaceable times," Van Buren Oldham of the Ninth Tennessee noted with disgust in his diary. He for one was tired of "being domineered by every 'chap in stripes.'"[17]

Oldham had plenty of company. Desertions climbed at an alarming rate. Colonel Brent of the army staff placed the number at 2,149 for the months of September and October alone, and he listed as among the deserters an officer from Bragg's headquarters guard. The morale of hungry and weary Federal pickets was in a measure sustained by nightly visitations from deserting Rebels, who crawled the couple of hundred yards that separated the picket lines to give themselves up. Frank Phelps of the Tenth Wisconsin wrote home that in one night alone twenty-seven Southerners waded Chattanooga Creek to surrender. The historian of the Ninety-fourth Ohio said a squad of seventeen turned themselves in at a regimental picket station. A soldier of the Nineteenth Alabama confirmed the Yankee claims. Thirty-two members of a neighboring brigade had crossed the lines the night before, he wrote his wife on 13 November, and four from a company in his own regiment had just sneaked off as well.[18]

It was more than just bad generalship that drove the Rebels to desert. Among the besiegers, rations were nearly as short as among the besieged. Accustomed to food wanting in both quantity and quality, Confederates seldom mentioned shortages except in a sort of manly jest. But now they complained bitterly. "In all the history of the war, I cannot remember of more privations and hardships than we went through at Mission Ridge," the generally good-natured Sam Watkins of the First Tennessee averred in early October. "And when in the very acme of our privations and hunger, when the army was most dissatisfied and unhappy, we were ordered into line of battle to be reviewed by Honorable Jefferson Davis," continued Watkins. "When he passed by us, with his great retinue of staff officers and play-outs at full gallop, cheers greeted them, with the words, 'Send us something to eat, Massa Jeff. Give us something to eat, Massa Jeff. I'm hungry! I'm hungry!'"[19]

The appeals fell on deaf ears. Several weeks later, Watkins was still writing of the same hardships: "Never in all my life do I remember of ever experiencing so much oppression and humiliation. The soldiers were starved and almost naked, and covered all over with lice and camp itch and filth and dirt. The men looked sick, hollow-eyed, and heartbroken, living principally upon parched corn, which had been picked out of the mud and dirt under the feet of officers' horses. We thought of nothing but starvation."[20]

Frank Mixson of the First South Carolina remembered scavenging through barns for rats, which were boiled and mixed with whatever else was on hand into a stew. Johnny Green of the Orphan Brigade said his unit got only small portions of unbolted cornmeal and beef pickled in a foul-smelling brine. Officers substantiated the claims of their men. "We were almost starved during this month," Colonel James Cooper of the Twentieth Tennessee wrote in October. "The rations were very scant at best, and then sometimes, the railroad would not come up on time. Then it was dreadful. One occasion I well remember, when for three days, in place of our meat ration of three quarters of a pound of beef, or one sixth of a pound of bacon, we drew one spoonful of sugar daily."[21]

As in the Federal camps, corrupt butchers lined their pockets from the sale of scraps. Beef heart brought a dollar in greenbacks, tongue up to a dollar and a half, and tail fifty cents. A few local women wandered along the lines selling small unleavened and unsalted biscuits for a dollar apiece.

Confederate horses suffered too. Corn and forage were in dangerously short supply. A lieutenant in Darden's Mississippi Battery lamented that "for the want of forage my horses are rapidly falling off." An Arkansas battery commander complained that "during the past five days I have received twelve sacks of corn for sixty-nine horses." During October, half the army's artillery horses were unavailable for duty, having been led to the rear to feed on grass.[22]

Threadbare clothing and a lack of adequate shelter compounded the solders' misery. Some men scavenged boards and built rough shanties, but many lacked even tents. Exposed to the elements, the hungry, poorly clad Confederates suffered acutely from the heavy rains and unseasonably frigid weather that settled over the area. Thousands fell ill. Nearly half the army lay along the western base of Missionary Ridge. When the rains came, water rushed down the slopes in torrents, flooding the camps. "To put this picture nakedly before you, take one fact well known at the time . . . for I saw it myself," attested a member of the Thirteenth Arkansas. "Just as you drew near to our bivouac (we had no tents or shelter save booths or tree branches and a few little fly tents) in the middle of the main road (which was a lake of mud fifty or sixty feet or more wide) there was a long stake stuck up with a board sign on it. On the board was written: 'Mule underneath here.' A mule had actually sunk out of sight in the mud at that spot. I saw that myself."[23]

Despite Bragg's harsh strictures against foraging, few officers were about to let their men starve. Private Frank Mixson's commanding officer detailed a squad to chop down trees and build a raft. During the dark of night, they stole across the Tennessee River to Moccasin Point and brought back some meal and bacon. Longstreet's corps, camped near the eastern base of Lookout Mountain, literally was cut off from the rest of the army by the torrential rains of mid-October. Chattanooga Creek backed up, spilling over its banks and flooding the valley for several hundred yards in both directions. Longstreet's chief of artillery, Edward Porter Alexander, told how troop commanders turned a blind eye as their men descended on nearby cabins, dismantling them to build rafts in order to venture across the creek and into the valley to forage.[24]

Part of the army's shortages was beyond Bragg's immediate control, although his penchant for irritating those who could be helpful only made matters worse. On 29 September, Bragg wrote Commissary General L. B. Northrop, hardly a likable personality himself, that "the question of subsistence should receive early attention, as our supplies are nearly exhausted at Atlanta." Northrop was offended. He reminded Bragg that "the subsistence of [his] army has been a subject of solicitude since its withdrawal from Kentucky," and then went on to suggest that Bragg should have anticipated the problem himself. Northrop closed with a suggestion that Bragg recapture East Tennessee and supply his army from there.[25]

What is remarkable in all this is that at the very moment his men were grumbling about their empty stomachs, Bragg was stockpiling boxes of commissary and quartermaster supplies—many consisting of goods donated by solicitous homefolk—at Tyner's and Chickamauga stations, the former some seven miles and the latter a mere four miles in his rear. Johnny Green and some of his comrades from the Ninth Kentucky, along with several companies from an Alabama regiment, had the good fortune to draw guard duty over the stores. Of course, their hunger overruled their scruples, and under cover of darkness Green and his fellow Kentuckians set about plundering the stores. They bribed an Alabama guard to allow them to carry off their booty, and with him stole into the woods to divide the goods. "It proved to be a rich haul indeed, three hams, delicious pickles and preserves, nice warm woolen socks, two coats, a pair of shoes, and various other good things," recalled Green lustfully. His appetite for plunder only whetted, the compliant Alabama guard tried his hand at stealing a box the next night, only to find when he pried it open that it contained the decomposing remains of a soldier on the way home for burial.[26]

The men could more readily have borne these hardships had they felt that Bragg had some strategy in mind beyond simply waiting for the Federals to starve first. But, bemoaned a Virginian in early October, "Bragg is so much afraid of doing something which would look like taking advantage of an enemy that he does nothing. He would not strike Rosecrans another blow until he has recovered his strength and announces himself ready. Our great victory [of Chickamauga] has been turned to ashes."[27]

There can be no denying that Bragg was absorbed so completely in his internecine struggles that he failed to fashion a coherent plan for compelling the Federals to abandon Chattanooga, or at least to bring them into a fight on favorable terms. The October journal entries of Bragg's meticulously observant staff officer, Colonel Brent, reflect nothing of strategy, but are merely a monotonous recounting of the commanding general's quarrels with Buckner and Longstreet and his periodic bouts of depression.[28]

Bragg's actions against the Federal army at Chattanooga throughout the month were little better than a series of poorly thought out, makeshift measures conceived during the odd moments between battles with his generals.

His troop dispositions offered little possibility of anything more. A direct assault was out of the question. Bragg had a mere forty-six thousand infantrymen stretched out along a seven-mile front that ran from the foot of Lookout Mountain to Missionary Ridge and then northward along the base of the ridge to a point a half-mile south of the Chattanooga and Cleveland Railroad (a section of the longer East Tennessee and Georgia Railroad). Bragg lacked even the troops needed to extend the line to the Tennessee River, which was the only way truly to hem in the Federals. Instead, Bragg shook out a thin picket line up the riverbank as far as the mouth of South Chickamauga Creek to guard against crossings beyond his right flank. Longstreet's corps held the line from the base of Lookout Mountain to the west bank of Chattanooga Creek; Breckinridge occupied the center from the east bank to the Bird's Mill road across Missionary Ridge, and Polk's corps—temporarily under the command of Cheatham—completed the line along the foot of the ridge. The Federals, tucked behind a chain of earthen redoubts and rifle pits, were at least a mile beyond the attenuated Rebel main line in most places. Their lines, by contrast, were neatly compact. Extending from bank to bank of the Tennessee, they formed a half-circle around Chattanooga no more than three miles long. Opposing pickets were often less than two hundred yards apart, placed so as to give ample warning of an advance by either side.[29]

Bragg's first plan, if it may be called a plan, was to avail himself of the heights of Lookout Mountain to try and shell the Yankees out of the city. As commander of the left sector, Longstreet was made responsible for its execution. He in turn passed on the mission to the intelligent and resourceful Porter Alexander, recently arrived from Virginia with his artillery battalion of twenty-three guns.

A cursory glance at Lookout Mountain convinced Alexander of the hopelessness of the task. "Long range, random shelling is far less effective than it is popularly supposed to be," explained the twenty-eight-year-old Georgian, already a master of his trade. Also, "our rifled guns and ammunition were both comparatively inferior. . . . When it came to extreme ranges, a considerable percentage of our rifle shell would tumble, or explode prematurely, or not explode at all. This made accurate shooting almost impossible." Then too there was Alexander's general disdain for his new colleagues. "This army is far inferior to the Army of Northern Virginia in organization and spirit, and I regret very much that I ever left the latter," he complained. Their ammunition and guns, he added, were of even poorer quality than his own.[30]

Still, Alexander tried to comply. For three days, mules hauled his guns up the narrow, rock-strewn road to the summit of Lookout, where the weapons joined two Parrott guns of Garrity's Alabama Battery already posted on the point. A Federal battery neatly concealed behind high parapets on Moccasin Point took potshots at the toiling teams, forcing them to work under the cover of night. By this method, twenty long-range guns and a handful of howitzers eventually were brought to the top and carefully placed behind outcroppings to protect the crews from Yankee counter-battery fire.

After scanning the Federal fortifications with his field glasses, Alexander picked his targets and, at 1:00 P.M. on 29 September, ordered his batteries to open fire.[31]

The results were about what Alexander had expected. The boom of the guns was spectacular. The valley shook as the sound bounced from mountain to mountain, but the damage done was inconsequential. Indeed, the bored and hungry Federals actually looked forward to the daily bombardment as a sort of morbid distraction.

"All the execution I ever heard of those guns doing was to kill a mule that would have died of starvation later on," quipped an Ohio captain. Sergeant David Floyd of the Seventy-fifth Indiana shared the Ohioan's contempt for the Rebel gunnery: "Some of their guns were of large caliber and threw big shells. Very few of our soldiers were hurt by them. We would stand upon the parapets of our intrenchments watching the shots, and would speculate upon their probable effect, while the negroes about our camps would continue their games of marbles." Joked Captain Donahower of the Second Minnesota: "The Confederates indulged in the bad habit of practice shooting just when the Union men morning, noon, and evening were engaged in boiling their coffee, and while the men might escape danger from flying metal, they were in danger of the upsetting of their tin cups and the loss of their coffee during their absence."[32]

The Federal commanders paid no more heed to the shelling than did their troops. The stern, bespectacled Colonel Ferdinand Van Derveer was pacing in front of his works, arms folded behind his back, lost in quiet contemplation, when the first shell from Lookout came spiraling down into the valley. It slammed into the ground a few yards away, showering the colonel with dirt, then rolled to a halt directly in front of him without exploding. Van Derveer tapped it with his foot, announcing to all present: "It looks as though that was intended for me, but I serve notice on Longstreet that if that is the best he can do, in spite of his successes on the Potomac, his laurels will soon wither in this climate." The jolly Indiana brigade commander Colonel Benjamin Scribner asked General Thomas his opinion of the shelling. The damage done was trifling, replied Thomas. "He referred to the expense incurred every time one of those guns was fired, and added that 'the Southern Confederacy had no money to throw away,'" said Scribner.[33]

Alexander agreed. After a week of daily shelling, including a general bombardment by all cannon on 5 October that Bragg ordered, the Confederates called it quits. And none too soon, wrote a Rebel artilleryman wryly: "They are too well posted to be shelled and this business is all foolishness." For his efforts, Alexander had lost one of his best twenty-pounder rifled Parrott guns, which burst on the second day, wounding two gunners, and he had exhausted the ammunition of three others.[34]

Bragg's next effort was the previously mentioned strike by Wheeler into Rosecrans's rear. Wheeler's raid was to have been part of a coordinated effort with Johnston's cavalry in Mississippi both to strike at Sherman's approaching columns and to cut Rosecrans's railroad supply lines from Nashville. Johnston agreed to cooperate with Bragg, but on his own terms. He would send Stephen Dill Lee's cavalry corps across the Tennessee River on the condition that Bragg first detail Philip Roddey's independent cavalry brigade for service under Lee. Roddey was to join Lee near Decatur, Alabama, on the southern bank of the Tennessee. From there, the two commands would cross the river and ride far north into Middle Tennessee to destroy the railroad bridges over the Duck and Elk rivers.

Bragg, however, had different ideas. He sent Roddey on an independent raid over the river nearer Chattanooga to strike at the Federal wagon road between Jasper and Anderson's Crossroads. Meanwhile, far from cooperating with Lee to disrupt the Nashville and Chattanooga Railroad, Wheeler and his inebriated troopers were almost swallowed up by pursuing Federal cavalry under Brigadier General George Crook, who was already demonstrating the bloodhound instincts that were to make him a famed Indian fighter. After an abortive effort to tear up the tracks near Murfreesboro, Wheeler met a with sharp defeat at Farmington. Yankee cavalry recaptured eight hundred mules lost on Walden's Ridge, and an entire regiment of Wheeler's freebooting command deserted into the hills. From there to the river it was a rout, recalled a pursuing Federal, "every man for himself, and hats, caps, coats, guns, and broken-down horses were strewn along the whole route." Wheeler barely made it across the Tennessee River into northern Alabama on 9 October, his once-proud command all but wrecked. Commenting on this sorry denouement, General Manigault declared: "I am inclined to think that this raid, like a great many others, did us more harm than the enemy."[35]

Neither Roddey nor Lee accomplished anything of consequence. In fact, no one even knew Roddey's whereabouts until 21 October, when he sheepishly admitted to army headquarters that he had not even crossed the Tennessee until a few days before Wheeler's retreat from Farmington. Word of Wheeler's debacle was enough to send him back to the safety of the southern bank of the river.

Lee got no farther than Decatur. With no sign of Roddey and news of Wheeler's ill-fortune, he gave up the expedition as lost.[36]

When it became clear that neither his artillery nor his cavalry alone were sufficient to starve Rosecrans out of the city, Bragg finally turned his attention to doing what he should have done at the start: closing off the Federal supply route along Haley's Trace. As previously recounted, Bragg correctly surmised that a line of sharpshooters posted along the southern bank of the Tennessee in the vicinity of the Narrows could wreak havoc on passing Yankee trains. Once again, the task of wedging the Federals out of Chattanooga fell to Longstreet. On 8 October, Bragg directed him to close Haley's Trace.[37]

Longstreet assigned the duty to Brigadier General Evander McIvor Law, a twenty-seven-year-old former teacher who had helped found a military high school in Tuskegee, Alabama. Alert and able, Law also could be petty and sulking, especially when he felt his achievements were not adequately recognized.[38]

In keeping with his instructions, Law sent one small regiment, the Fourth Alabama, to fulfill the critical mission. Its commander, Colonel Pinckney Bowles, dutifully deployed his men as pickets, from the shore directly opposite the Suck eastward toward Williams Island as far he could stretch them, and then had the Alabamians dig in. Their success in shooting down Federal mules and closing off Haley's Trace along the river was, as earlier related, instant and complete. Still, Bowles's tiny force was vulnerable, with its nearest support five miles away on the east side of Lookout Mountain. Longstreet recognized the absurdity of this and on 12 October ordered Law to send another regiment into the valley to extend the picket line. Over the nose of Lookout in the dark of night went the Fifteenth Alabama. Its commander was Colonel William C. Oates, a giant of a man at six feet, four inches tall. Despite a penchant for getting lost on the field of battle, as he had on both days at Chickamauga, Oates was a tough character who never shrank from a fight once he found it.[39]

Oates tried to make the best of his seemingly impossible task. He shook out four of his companies along the riverbank to picket from Bowles's right flank southward to a gap in the foothills known as Brown's Ferry. Disturbed by the susceptibility of the five-mile-long picket line to a breach at any point, he held his remaining six companies in reserve, along with a section of Moody's Louisiana Battery, in a field near the ferry.[40]

Law too was uneasy over the security of his two isolated regiments. Riding along the riverbank, he saw that the Yankees could, if they wished, cross the Tennessee easily anywhere between the base of Lookout Mountain and foot of Raccoon Mountain and crack the thin shell of Rebel pickets. It was only a matter of time, he surmised, before the Federals would try to reopen communications with Bridgeport via Lookout Valley in this manner. Law shared his concerns in a letter to Longstreet. Arguing that he would need a division to render the valley safe beyond question, Law added that he would attempt it with his brigade, assuming his three reserve regiments could be sent over at once. Longstreet concurred only with Law's offer to try to hold Lookout Valley with his own brigade; no other troops would be forthcoming. When his remaining three regiments and a section of Barret's Missouri Battery came over the mountain, Law posted them in the valley near the mouth of Lookout Creek. Somewhat assuaged, Law obtained a short leave of absence and rode away to visit the wounded John Bell Hood.[41]

Longstreet had paid scant attention to Law's letter because he had in mind a grander scheme that, if successful, would render the Alabamian's concerns moot. When it became obvious that the closing of Haley's Trace would merely lead Rosecrans to rely on the longer route over Walden's Ridge, Bragg looked for another way to compel a Federal evacuation of Chattanooga. Goaded by Davis, he now seemed receptive to suggestions from his lieutenants. On 11 October, the president called a council of war at Bragg's headquarters to develop a coherent plan.

What transpired during the meeting in the little white frame house atop Missionary Ridge is uncertain. At least two conflicting proposals were put forward. From Charleston, Pierre G. T. Beauregard, the perennial advocate of a strong western concentration, had sent a letter suggesting a massive reinforcement of the Army of Tennessee from Lee and Johnston to crush Rosecrans, presumably by first crossing the Tennessee north of Chattanooga and flanking him out of the city.

Davis liked the plan, despite his antipathy for its Creole author, and Bragg promised to present it to the council. He did, but was vague on specifics. Bragg failed to explain where he intended to cross the river or how he intended to bring the Federals to battle. Sensing the muddle in Bragg's thinking, the president grew lukewarm and called for other suggestions. Longstreet was the only general to speak up. For several days he had been discussing with Porter Alexander and others of his staff the possibility of a change of base to Rome, Georgia, from whence the army might march rapidly on Bridgeport. There, he conjectured, it could cross the railroad bridge (which Longstreet did not know had been burned), seize the supply depot, and disrupt Rosecrans's line of supply at its source. General Hooker—whose command was still scattered between Bridgeport and Stevenson—would be prevented from joining Rosecrans, and the Army of the Cumberland compelled "to precipitate battle or retreat."[42]

So confident was Longstreet of his scheme that he had sent Alexander on a secret reconnaissance to Bridgeport even before presenting the plan to Bragg. Alexander crept to within hailing distance of the Federal blockhouse on the south bank of the Tennessee. Although he found the railroad bridge destroyed, Alexander liked the exposed nature of the pontoon bridge built in its place. Observed Alexander:

> The situation seemed to me to give very fair chances for a surprise. If once the block house on the southern bank could be captured, or silenced, the three or four dozen pontoon boats making the southern bridge would be easily cut loose and floated down the river under cover of the woods on the island, filled with our infantry and then rowing, down past the island, they could land on the northern shore, below the enemy's camps, and make a lodgment. Then the boats could be used as ferry boats to bring over a sufficient additional force to capture all the enemy had at hand.

Alexander made a sketch of the area and rode back to Longstreet's headquarters in a high state of excitement.[43]

Davis also liked Longstreet's proposal, so much so that he rejected Beauregard's plan and, according to Longstreet, ordered the army to withdraw to Rome preparatory to moving against Bridgeport.[44]

Bragg, however, had neither the interest nor, given his low spirits and fragile health, the strength to comply. After Davis's departure, he found one excuse after another for delaying and then finally canceling the movement. First it was the heavy rains, he wrote Davis on 17 October, which "have broken our temporary bridges. Will only result in delay of a forward movement," he assured the president. Then it was the muddy roads. Within a few days he had dropped all pretense of moving, and the army remained in its miasmal camps in the Chattanooga Valley.[45]

Bragg clearly was out of serious ideas. He authorized some resourceful Rebel units on the army's right flank to build rafts and float them downriver in an attempt to break the Federal pontoon bridge near Chattanooga Island. Most of the rafts ran harmlessly aground, but enough got through to rupture the vital lifeline for a couple of days. After that, Yankee guards were posted on the island with long ropes strong across the river to intercept the rafts.[46]

After making his excuses to the president on 17 October, Bragg spent his time sulking about headquarters, scratching out impassioned rebuttals to Buckner's ceaseless letters, and reading, with considerably less interest, ciphered messages warning of the approach of Sherman's corps from Mississippi.[47]

With Bragg sunk in a self-absorbed torpor, the next move would be up to the Federals.

# CHAPTER FOUR

# AUDACITY MIGHT YET BRING US THROUGH

BRIGADIER General William Farrar Smith was a man of many parts. That he was an officer of considerable talent and imagination none disputed. Nicknamed "Baldy" by his colleagues to distinguish him from the numerous other Smiths holding the rank of general, the thirty-nine-year-old Vermonter had graduated fourth in his class from West Point in 1845. In recognition of his abilities, he was soon recalled to the Military Academy to teach. Smith rose rapidly in the early days of the war, from command of the Third Vermont Infantry to that of a division during the Peninsula Campaign. It was then that he first exhibited a penchant for irritating superiors through an almost puerile inability to control his tongue. The commander of the Second Corps, Major General Edwin Sumner, "was not a man to reason with," snarled Smith, who had a greater "feeling of admiration for the old plantation Negro who had shown more knowledge of strategy than the second officer in rank in the Army of the Potomac." Smith's immediate salvation was his close friendship with George B. McClellan, whom he regarded as one of the few great generals of the war. McClellan transferred Smith and his division to the Sixth Corps of William Franklin, another of Smith's seemingly few friends. In the general shakeup of the Army of the Potomac after Antietam, Smith was given command of the Sixth Corps and recommended to the Senate for promotion to major general. After Fredericksburg, however, he fell into ill-favor with Lincoln and the War Department when he and Franklin wrote a scathing, insubordinate letter damning Major General Ambrose E. Burnside's conduct during that campaign. That indiscretion cost Smith both his corps and his promotion.[1]

During Lee's invasion of the North, Smith was shunted off to Harrisburg, Pennsylvania, to bring order to a patchwork force hurriedly assembled there to guard the state capital. After that humiliating duty, he was ordered to New York to await further instructions. While pothering about the city, he gained the sympathy of several prominent New Yorkers, who went to Washington on his behalf to ask Stanton to return him to duty. The secretary acceded, and on the very day news of the defeat at Chickamauga reached New York, Smith received orders to report to the Army of the Cumberland. He departed at once, determined to make a fresh start. "To avoid delay I left my baggage at Stevenson to go by the wagon train while I took a trail over the mountain on horseback."[2]

Perhaps his longtime friend and later biographer, James Harrison Wilson, one of Grant's staff members, best summed up the character of the man so anxious to reach Chattanooga and prove himself. "He was one of those distinguished men of the old army whose sharp tongue and sententious speech had done much to make enemies and mar his immediate career," explained Wilson. "He was popular with his subordinates, for he was a conscientious, painstaking, and industrious officer who spared no effort to keep his soldiers in good condition or to lead them successfully, no matter how great the difficulties which surrounded them."[3]

Rosecrans, himself no stranger to controversy, was pleased to see Smith but had no idea what to do with him. The Vermonter's rank entitled him to a division, but Rosecrans was reluctant to replace any of his division commanders just then. After much discussion, on 3 October Smith was assigned to duty as chief engineer of the Department of the Cumberland.[4]

Smith accepted his assignment philosophically, and he set about to make himself useful. He superintended the work of Captain Perrin Fox and his First Michigan Engineers in sawing lumber for boats and bridges at the two old sawmills outside of town. He saw to it that needed timber and logs were floated to the mills, scrounged nails, and confiscated cotton for caulking pontoons. Smith also hurried along repairs to the steamer *Painted Rock*.[5]

Important though they were, none of these duties challenged Smith's considerable intellect. With ample time on his hands, he pondered ways to improve upon Rosecrans's plan for reopening the short route to Bridgeport. Smith disagreed strongly with Rosecrans's conviction that General Hooker must occupy Lookout Valley and seize the passes of Lookout Mountain *before* a bridge could be thrown across the Tennessee from Moccasin Point.

"Movements from Bridgeport and Chattanooga must be coincident in time," mused Smith. If Hooker crossed the Tennessee at Bridgeport and advanced along the southern bank first, it would be a simple matter for Bragg to shift enough troops into Lookout Valley either to close the passes of Raccoon Mountain or to allow Hooker to enter the valley and then crush him with superior numbers. An attempt to lay the bridge first also would tip the Federal hand, and Bragg reasonably could be expected to seal off the passes through Raccoon Mountain and throw up a line of works covering the western approach to the bridge, thereby rendering it worthless. In short, either plan "was a move only to be made in desperation," he reasoned. Smith understood that Rosecrans also had hoped to carry Lookout Mountain, but doubted Hooker's troops would be up to dislodging Longstreet from the heights. "The throwing of the bridge must be quickly followed by the entrance of troops from Bridgeport into Lookout Valley," he concluded.

Smith also wondered if the lower reaches (that is to say, the northern portion) of Lookout Valley, near the eastern base of Raccoon Mountain, might not offer a more propitious point at which to bridge the Tennessee than the ground near Lookout Creek, which Smith rightly feared was both too close to Longstreet's main body and commanded by the Rebel guns atop Lookout Mountain.[6]

On the evening of 18 October, Smith rode to army headquarters to share his thoughts with Rosecrans and ask permission to ride downriver the next morning to study the country. Perhaps, he told Rosecrans, he could find an alternate bridging site that would hasten the prospects of putting into play Rosecrans's earlier plan to use Williams Island as a supply depot. Rosecrans had all but given up on any sort of movement until the railroad was repaired at Bridgeport and Running Water and Hooker's wagons reached him from Nashville. Nevertheless, he endorsed the proposal. "That is a good idea; I will go with you," Rosecrans replied. "I have a long day before me, and must start early," Smith dictated with typical bullheadedness. Fine, deferred Rosecrans, "fix your own hour for starting."[7]

Monday morning, 19 October, dawned bright with the promise of a brilliant Indian summer day. At 8:00 A.M., Rosecrans, Smith, and the commanding general's retinue cantered out of Chattanooga and over the pontoon bridge to the north bank of the Tennessee. Once across, Rosecrans stopped to visit a nearby hospital where the wounded of Chickamauga lay recuperating. Smith waited outside. As the minutes slipped away, his impatience got the better of him. Turning his horse, Smith set out alone over a narrow dirt road across the spongy fields of Moccasin Point. At the road's end, on the east bank of the river, he chanced upon a small earthwork manned by the Eighteenth Ohio Battery. The commanding officer told Smith they had been stationed there to prevent a Rebel crossing, as the road continued on the opposite bank. The site, he added, was known locally as Brown's Ferry. Smith dismounted to have a closer look. Finding that the pickets on both sides of the river were on friendly terms, Smith stepped through the brush to the water's edge.

There he sat for an hour, carefully studying the far bank where, as the Ohio captain had reported, the road resumed. Its tactical importance was obvious. The only road along that stretch of the river, it cut through a gap in a line of foothills that lined the shore from the mouth of Lookout Creek northward to a point opposite the southern tip of Williams Island. More significant, less than a quarter mile beyond the gap the road turned south and became the primary wagon road through Lookout Valley as far south as Wauhatchie, where it forked, meeting a road that ran west all the way to Kelley's Ferry.

The gap itself struck Smith as an ideal crossing site. Narrow but deep, it split the foothills just slightly above the level of the river. A decrepit little shanty stood on the north edge of the gap. Smoke rose in narrow white threads from behind the hills, betraying the few scattered Rebel picket posts in the area. No other Confederates were in evidence. Through the defile, Smith had a clear view of Raccoon Mountain, which rose temptingly less than a mile away.[8]

Smith was alive with the thrill of discovery:

> If that ridge of hills could be surprised, and held, and a bridge built there, then we could throw troops into Lookout Valley faster than the rebels, and any force disputing its passes leading through the mountains to Bridgeport would have us on their flank if they made a fight there against our force in our direction and Hooker's force coming at right angles. Hooker once in the valley and connected with us by the bridge made one really compact army, the river was opened, the army fed, and no further question of our ability to hold the army there during the winter and collect supplies for a forward movement in the spring.[9]

Still, as he galloped back to headquarters to report his findings, a few doubts troubled him: "The topographical features [of Brown's Ferry] left nothing to be desired. If Bragg had left it carelessly guarded, as I believed, we could recover the short line. If I were mistaken, we might be repulsed. Our desperate situation required us to take any risk on which a hope might be hung, without action, the end was almost at hand; audacity and luck might yet bring us through. All depended upon the nerve of the General Commanding."

Unbeknownst to Smith as he recrossed the pontoon bridge into Chattanooga amid the gathering shades of evening, Rosecrans had that very day been relieved of command.[10]

On the evening of 21 October, the train carrying Grant and his staff creaked into Stevenson, "a dirty little town with some half dozen miserable houses." Rosecrans was there, on his way north, sick and heartbroken. Swallowing the last of his pride, he climbed aboard Grant's private car to brief his old antagonist on the situation at Chattanooga and his tentative steps to reopen the short route. "The meeting was brief and courteous but not effusive," observed Colonel Wilson. "They were far from sympathetic with each other." Still, Grant appreciated the gesture and Rosecrans's "excellent suggestions as to what should be done. My only wonder was that he had not carried them out," he added sarcastically in his memoirs.[11]

Also waiting on the platform to pay his respects to Grant was Major General Oliver Otis Howard, commander of the Eleventh Corps. Howard had never met Grant and probably approached his car with trepidation. The thirty-two-year-old former West Point mathematics instructor had a lot to prove, both to himself and to his new commander. He had come west with the stigma of Chancellorsville, where his corps had been demolished by Stonewall Jackson, still fresh. At Gettysburg his performance most charitably could be termed mediocre. As a final burden, Howard was serving again under Joe Hooker, who held him to blame for the defeat of his army at Chancellorsville. Between the two was a deep and irreconcilable bitterness.[12]

To Howard's immense relief, he and Grant hit it off nicely. Too infirm from his injuries to rise from his chair, Grant smiled warmly and extended his hand as Howard was introduced. Despite Grant's injury, which left him pallid, Howard "liked his appearance better than that of any major general I have seen. He is modest, quiet, and thoughtful. He looks the picture of firmness." And, in an interesting aside, the Bible-thumping, teetotaling Howard later assured his wife that Grant "does not drink liquor and never swears."[13]

Notably absent was Hooker. Like Howard, the cashiered commander of the Army of the Potomac was at a crisis point in his career. After the Lincoln administration, to Hooker's surprise, had accepted his request to be relieved on the eve of Gettysburg, he had lingered about Washington, a broken man lost in his rancor. About all Hooker had had going for him was his longtime friendship with Lincoln, who admired his fighting qualities and appreciated his lack of political ambitions. But even that friendship had seemed to fail him. After Chancellorsville, he had asked the journalist Noah Brooks, a mutual acquaintance, how

Lincoln regarded him. Brooks drew a thoughtless analogy, saying that the president looked on him as a father might look on a son who was incurably handicapped. Tears clouded Hooker's eyes as he stammered: "Well, the President may regard me as a cripple, but if he will give me a chance I will yet show him that I know how to fight."[14]

Chickamauga gave Hooker his chance. As he rode the rails west in the closing days of September, his characteristic arrogance returned. So too, apparently, did his famed robust appearance. An Illinois lieutenant who met him shortly after his arrival sized him up as "an exceedingly fine looking man—one of the finest I ever saw. He must be fully six feet tall, and strangely one might say, heavily built, dressed in military uniform, very florid complexion and light hair, with a little patch of gray whiskers under each ear and extending down an inch on the cheek."[15]

While Grant and Howard were exchanging pleasantries, a staff officer from Hooker's headquarters entered the car. Hooker was not feeling well, the officer told Grant, and wondered if Grant might not like to call on him at his quarters. "They had been brother officers and boon companions years before, but had not met since the outbreak of the war. It was evident that Hooker was 'trying it on' with Grant," deduced Colonel Wilson. Rawlins agreed. In a tone that brooked no reply, he told the staff officer: "General Grant himself is not very well and will not leave his car tonight. He expects General Hooker and all other generals who have business with him to call at once, as he will start overland to Chattanooga early tomorrow morning." That was right, Grant added: "If General Hooker wishes to see me he will find me on this train."[16]

Hooker understood. In a matter of minutes he showed up at the train. Grant politely but firmly declined Hooker's offer of lodging for the night. "Grant took this first occasion to assert himself," recalled Howard with obvious delight. "He never left the necessity for gaining a proper ascendancy over subordinate generals, where it was likely to be questioned, to a second interview." As if to drive home the point, Grant continued on to Bridgeport that same night, where he shared a tent with Howard.[17]

The hard part of the journey began the next morning. After two days of blue, Indian summer skies, the rain returned with a vengeance; a cold, blowing rain that quickly churned the wagon road up the Sequatchie Valley into paste. Amid the downpour, remembered Howard, Rawlins lifted Grant, "lame and suffering, as if he had been a child, into the saddle" for the long ride to Chattanooga.

It was the first time Grant had mounted a horse since his spill at New Orleans, and every jolting step the horse took along the slippery trail pained him. With him were Rawlins, Wilson, Dana—who had traveled to Nashville to meet Grant—and a small escort. The tiny party made it a few miles beyond Jasper before stopping for the night in a nonde-script hamlet that may have been Cheekville. Wilson and Dana, how-ever, pressed on in order to give fair warning to Thomas of Grant's impending arrival.[18]

Dawn of 23 October saw no letup in the downpour. Again Rawlins lifted Grant into the saddle, and they began the tortuous ascent of Walden's Ridge. What they met there stunned Rawlins. Rotting mule carcasses by the thousands and broken wagons by the score littered the road, which he called "the roughest and steepest of ascent and descent ever crossed by army wagons and mules." In places where the rains had washed away the road, Grant had to be lifted off his horse and carried. His escort did not notice one rough spot until it was too late, and Grant's horse slipped and fell heavily with the general, badly jamming his in-jured leg.

Compounding the bleakness was a steady procession of civilians that passed them along the ridge—"Union families, refugees from their homes," wrote Rawlins. "Mothers with little children in their arms covered with only one thin garment exposed to the beatings of the storm, wet and shivering with cold. I have seen much of human mis-ery consequent of this war but never before in so distressing a form as this."[19]

Grant and his party rode over the pontoon bridge and into Chattanoo-ga just before nightfall. They drew rein in front of the tiny, whitewashed, one-story wooden house that served as headquarters for the Army of the Cumberland. Wilson and Dana had reported to General Thomas that morning, but had badly overestimated Grant's time of arrival. "We had been advised that he was on his way, but hardly expected that he would reach Chattanooga that night, considering the state of the weather, the wretched condition of the roads . . . and the severe injury to his leg," recalled Captain Horace Porter of Thomas's staff.[20]

The unexpected hour of Grant's arrival could hardly excuse what followed. When Colonel Wilson walked into headquarters a few min-utes after Grant, he found the Ohioan seated beside a fireplace on one side of the tiny living room, steam rising from a puddle beneath his drenched clothing. Thomas stood on the other side of the room. The silence was disconcerting; both looked "glum and ill at ease," observed Wilson. Rawlins whispered testily to the colonel that neither Thomas nor his staff had yet bothered to attend to Grant's comfort. Knowing that Grant would not condescend to beg a favor, Wilson stepped forward. "General Thomas, General Grant is wet and tired and ought to have some dry clothes, particularly a pair of socks and a pair of slippers. He is hungry besides, and needs something to eat," said Wilson. "Can't you officers attend to these matters for him."[21]

That shook Thomas out of his reverie. He urged Grant to step into a bedroom and change. Grant apparently declined the offer, but did accept the light supper that was quickly proffered. Conversation began to flow. "Baldy" Smith dropped by to pay his respects. The mood lightened. Nevertheless, Thomas's odd aloofness had set the tone for future dealings between the two and their staffs. His coolness was so apparent, said Wilson, that Grant hastened to establish his own headquarters, without waiting for his wagons of personal baggage to come up. Thomas's behavior, said Wilson, "was perceived and imitated by his staff and cordial and friendly relations were never established between their respective headquarters." Rawlins particularly disliked Thomas's assistant adjutant general, Brigadier General William Whipple, a crusty but capable regular officer whose pedantic objections to Rawlins's instructions in the coming weeks were tinged with gratuitous rudeness.

Thomas left behind no personal papers, so the reasons for his rudeness toward Grant can only be conjectured. None of Thomas's biographers has ventured a convincing guess. The explanation of Colonel Wilson, who held both in high esteem, seems the most plausible: "I have always been inclined to think that Thomas, having graduated higher at West Point, entered a more scientific arm of service and served generally with great distinction, regarded himself as a better soldier than Grant, and that he thereby, perhaps unconsciously, resented Grant's assignment to duty over him . . . and was not disposed to change his attitude merely because Grant was now his commanding officer. He doubtless believed to the end that while Grant had put him in Rosecrans's place, it was not because he loved Thomas more, but because he distrusted Rosecrans too much to keep him in command at all." On that point, at least, there can be no dispute.[22]

Grant finished his supper and drew closer to the fire. Thrusting his feet forward to dry out his boots, he bade Thomas proceed with a formal briefing. The Virginian made a few general remarks, then gave the floor over to Smith.[23]

The Vermonter was ready for the moment. When he found that Rosecrans had been removed from command, Smith had sought out Thomas at once with his plan to seize Brown's Ferry. Thomas presented the proposal to his staff. Most ridiculed it as preposterous. Thomas, however, was willing to gamble on Smith, and a full three days before Grant's arrival had told the Vermonter to begin assembling the boats and bridging material he would need to carry out his plan.[24]

Surrounded now by many of the same staff officers who had snickered behind his back, Smith stood before a large map of the region. He spoke passionately of his plan to Grant, who lounged quietly by the fire. With well-rehearsed precision, Smith detailed the army's dilemma and his idea of a way out of it. Grant was deeply impressed: "He explained the situation of the two armies and the topography of the country so plainly that I could see it without an inspection." Grant asked a series of probing questions to demonstrate to all that he was not only still awake but alert and well informed. He asked Captain Porter, as chief of ordnance, if the army had enough ammunition on hand to carry out Smith's plan. "There is barely enough here to fight one day's battle," answered Porter candidly, then added, as if to tantalize Grant into a decision, "but an ample supply has been accumulated at Bridgeport to await the opening of communications." Grant tentatively approved Smith's scheme for "opening up the cracker line," as the hungry Federals came to call the supply route that Smith's plan eventually created, but deferred final approval until he could ride out and look the ground over the next day with Thomas and Smith.[25]

It was 9:30 P.M. before Smith finished—thirteen and a half hours after Rawlins had eased Grant into the saddle for what may have been the most physically grueling day of his wartime service. Still, Grant kept at it a bit longer. With the Cracker Line operation largely settled, his thoughts turned to his friend and confidant, William T. Sherman, whose detachments from the Army of the Tennessee were snaking their way across northern Mississippi toward Chattanooga. Turning from the fire to a nearby table, Grant scrawled a brief telegram to General-in-Chief Halleck. "Have just arrived; I will write tomorrow. Please approve order placing Sherman in command of Department of the Tennessee, with headquarters in the field." Grant, observed Porter, "had scarcely begun to exercise the authority conferred upon him by his new promotion when his mind turned to securing advancement for Sherman." Grant's loyalty was to prove invaluable to the wizened fellow Ohioan in the weeks to come.

At 10:30 P.M., Grant at last arose, said goodnight to Thomas and Smith, and, with a limp that pained all who noticed it, hobbled into an adjoining bedroom to sleep.[26]

# CHAPTER FIVE

# A MEDAL OF HONOR OR TWO EARS OF CORN

N EARLY five weeks of siege had left both the besieged and the besiegers not only hungry and sick but bored and anxious; many found it difficult to decide which was harder to bear, the acute physical suffering or the more subtle emotional strain. "The monotony and dreariness of a siege can be appreciated only by those that have taken part therein," explained Captain George Lewis of the One Hundred Twenty-fourth Ohio. "Language fails me to give you anything like an adequate idea of its listless torments. While on the march the scenery is constantly changing. The exercise of marching keeps one healthy, and keeps one's mind employed and the banishment from home and loved ones does not occupy so much of one's thoughts. But in the siege every day was like all the others."[1]

Indian summer had been fleeting, a handful of bright, balmy days scattered among weeks of gray dampness. On those occasional mornings when it didn't rain, a chill fog greeted the soldiers. As it lifted, opposing pickets flopped down on their stomachs and peered under the fog to be sure their opposites had drawn no closer during the night. They never did, and so began another day of idleness.

The boredom drove a few to incredible acts of stupidity. Recalled Captain Donahower of the Second Minnesota: "On a cold morning while a few men were warming their hands over a small fire, an idle soldier wishing to frighten the men around the fire, not realizing the danger to himself and the others, picked up a very long and heavy unexploded rebel shell and dropped it into the fire, and it exploded instantly, and the heedless man had a leg broken, and one of the bystanders was killed."[2]

Most passed the time with better judgment, if not greater morality.

One of the few things to make it from Bridgeport intact had been the monthly payroll. That was a mixed blessing for soldiers besieged in a town where nothing remained for sale but mediocre food at exorbitant prices. Finding little to buy, the troops hit upon other ways to dispose of their money. Scarcely had his men left the paymaster's table and broken ranks, remembered Lieutenant John Hartzell of the One Hundred Fifth Ohio, when the gamblers set about "their miserable work. In all kinds of out of the way places, you can see groups of soldiers, and if you crowd in, you will find a rubber blanket spread on the ground with soldiers sitting on it, piles of money all about and dice boxes rattling, or maybe cards, and many of the poor fellows are soon fleeced of all they have."[3]

Gambling was against regulations in the Army of the Cumberland, but the patrols that occasionally wandered through the camps to enforce the rules did so only halfheartedly.[4]

Things were about the same across the valley. Echoing the sentiments of George Lewis, Captain Samuel Foster of the Twenty-fourth Texas lamented: "Soldiers, who have been accustomed to marching and fighting, as we, must be kept busy. True soldiers want to march or to drill, every day if possible. Here we have done neither. Instead, we have set aside an area about the size of half a mile, called 'Half Acre.' It is a curious place. . . . The men play all kinds of games there. They also hold an auction in full blast. You can buy a watch, or an old pair of shoes. The place just cannot be described."[5]

Few officers on either side shared the indignation of Captain Foster. They played cards as zestfully as their men—and for higher stakes. Food may have been scarce, but a bottle always seemed to turn up in the officers' messes. Lieutenant Hartzell of the One Hundred Fifth Ohio envied the officers of the largely German Ninth Ohio their ample supply of liquor. He struck up a friendship with some of them and was rewarded with an invitation to one of their nightly gatherings in the quartermaster's tent. Laying open the flap, he found everyone from the colonel to the most junior lieutenant sitting in a half-circle. A big pan of hot water, condensed milk, and spirits circulated among the officers. Each took a gulp, then passed on the pan. "Thus the evening slips away finely for all are good singers and sociable," recalled Hartzell happily.[6]

Not everyone tolerated the decline in discipline. Brigadier General Philip Sheridan, for one, raised hell about it at every opportunity. Early in the siege, General Thomas had sent an aide to Bragg to suggest a halt to the constant but purposeless picket firing. Bragg agreed, and from that moment on, pickets could safely stand in plain sight of one another without fear of being shot.[7] It was not long before they availed themselves of the truce to swap stories and merchandise. They wandered out of their little rifle pits—or "gopher holes" as the men called them—to meet casually between the lines and trade New York and Chicago dailies for Richmond and Atlanta newspapers, Yankee coffee for Rebel tobacco. Some officers tried to stop the fraternization, most ignored it, and not a few profited by it.[8]

Then, one morning, along came Sheridan, making the grand rounds of the picket posts as the army's Officer-of-the-Day. Despite his poor showing at Chickamauga, the little Irishman was still a division commander and as feisty as ever. At the crack of dawn, he descended upon the brigade of Colonel Ferdinand Van Derveer, whose misfortune it was to have drawn picket duty that day.

Lieutenant Hartzell was rousting his detachment of off-duty men from the One Hundred Fifth Ohio out of their shelters for a change of pickets. The sentinel barked, "Grand rounds, fall in," and Hartzell's men, fumbling with their waist belts, walked—cold, wet, and stiff—toward their stacked rifle-muskets. Out of the fog appeared Sheridan. "When [he] saw our fix, he put spurs to his horse and came up with a dash and began using very naughty language, which so upset my little bedraggled squad that as fast as each man got his strap tightened, he grabbed his gun out of the stack; of course, the stack fell over, and so it went. Little Phil saw me standing like a stick and my lads picking their guns off the ground," confessed Hartzell, who gradually recovered from the shock. "I waited as patiently as I could, and when all were ready, presented arms and he acknowledged the salute." Hartzell waited for the inevitable rebuke. "Now here was a pretty kettle of fish; I expected he would take away my old toad sticker, send me to camp, and I'd be tried and used scandalously." But Sheridan had his eye on larger game. He whirled in the saddle and bore down on the Ohioans' grand reserve, which happened to be Colonel Gustave Kammerling's Ninth Ohio. "The Dutchmen were in about the same fix," said Hartzell sadly of his drinking companions. "Old Colonel Kammerling lost his sword for a few days, and had to tag around in undress uniform."[9]

Lieutenant Colonel Judson Bishop, who had handled the Second Minnesota with great skill at Chickamauga while the regiment's rheumatic colonel merely had looked on, was one of those officers who tolerated the fraternizing between the lines. Now formally in command of the Second, he too was visited by Sheridan. Although at least awake and dressed, his men for the most part were lounging along the line of rifle pits or chatting with the Rebels across the way, their rifle-muskets neatly stacked a few yards beyond reach. Sheridan galloped down on the stacked arms. Bishop yelled the command to fall in, and the men tumbled toward their weapons, but it was too late. Sheridan and his escort interposed themselves between the Minnesotans and their arms. "Stand back; don't touch those guns; they are mine! I captured them, and they belong to me. If we had been rebels, how easy it would have been to have captured you all," Sheridan scolded. Bishop was luckier than Kammerling. Sheridan vented his spleen, wheeled his horse, and was gone, and that was the last the regiment heard of the matter. "We knew he was Officer of the Day by his sash, which nearly covered him," said Corporal H. H. Hill of Company I, "but who the little crabbed, crusty cuss was nobody knew."[10]

The very informality along the picket lines that threw Sheridan into such a frenzy actually served his new commanding general quite nicely. As agreed upon, Grant was up and in the saddle by 8:00 A.M. on 24 October, his first morning in Chattanooga, for the ride out to Brown's Ferry with Thomas and Smith. The rain had stopped during the night, yielding to a cold and misty dawn. The Ohioan and his procession rode over the pontoon bridge north of town, then turned west to cross the neck of Moccasin Point. As Smith had done four days earlier, Grant took advantage of the good relations between the opposing pickets. Dismounting in the woods just shy of the bank, he, Thomas, and Smith walked to the river's edge. "There was a picket station of the enemy on the opposite side, of about twenty men, in full view, and we were within easy range," remembered Grant. "They did not fire upon us nor seem disturbed by our presence. They must have seen that we were all commissioned officers. But, I suppose, they looked upon the garrison of Chattanooga as prisoners of war, feeding or starving themselves, and thought it would be inhuman to kill any of them except in self-defense."[11]

Grant was duly impressed with Smith's choice of a bridging site. Returning to Chattanooga shortly after noon, he formally approved the operation, leaving the manner of its execution to Thomas and Smith.[12]

The two worked quickly. At 2:30 P.M. Thomas wired Hooker detailed marching orders. He was to detach Major General Henry Slocum, who despised Hooker as thoroughly as did Howard, with one division of the Twelfth Corps to guard the precarious rail line from Murfreesboro to Bridgeport. With the remaining division of the corps, under Brigadier General John Geary, and Howard's Eleventh Corps, Hooker was to cross the Tennessee River at Bridgeport as soon as possible and move rapidly to Rankin's Ferry, a point two miles short of Running Water Creek, being careful to watch his right flank for any Rebel counterthrust from the direction of Lookout Valley. Simultaneous with Hooker's crossing at Bridgeport, two brigades under Major General John Palmer, who had taken over the Fourteenth Corps upon Thomas's elevation to army command, would move along the north side of the river from Chattanooga to Rankin's Ferry to cover Hooker's rear. Once Palmer was in place, Hooker was to push on into Lookout Valley to link up with the bridgehead at Brown's Ferry.

Thomas shared none of Rosecrans's earlier anxiety over Hooker's transportation. With or without his wagons, Hooker was to move. In fact, Thomas doubted the wisdom of bringing wagons over the river until the linkup with Brown's Ferry was made, and he told Hooker as much. To make sure his wishes were understood, he sent Colonel Wilson to Bridgeport to accompany Hooker into Lookout Valley.[13]

Thomas spelled things out in such excruciating detail for Hooker in large part because Dana had poisoned the waters between the men. After Grant reached Chattanooga, the assistant secretary had returned to Bridgeport to check up on Hooker. Unacquainted with the particulars of the Brown's Ferry operation or the part Thomas expected Hooker to play in it, Dana on 23 October sent Stanton and Thomas a telegram scathingly critical of the general. He condemned Hooker for having failed to concentrate his forces at Bridgeport and for a lack of "zeal in the enterprise."[14]

In one sense, Dana's emotional blast was unfair. Neither Rosecrans nor Thomas had issued Hooker orders to concentrate at Bridgeport; moreover, the last one hundred wagons of his dilapidated train did not even creak into Bridgeport until 24 October, less nearly half the animals, which had died along the way. On the other hand, Hooker made no secret of his doubts about the Brown's Ferry plan when he did receive his orders. Fearful that the enemy would sweep down on his flank from Lookout Mountain while he marched up the valley, Hooker told Howard: "It is a very hazardous operation, and almost certain to procure us a defeat." Still, he did his best to comply. He issued orders that evening for Geary to hurry his division forward from Dechard, a distance of thirty miles, and for Howard to call in his forces, which were scattered between Stevenson and Battle Creek. More than that, he could not do: the roads were still miserable quagmires from the rains, and the railroad was out between Dechard and Bridgeport. It would be at least a day, perhaps two, before he would be ready to move, Hooker hinted to Thomas.

Grant was annoyed but not alarmed. He no longer shared Smith's conviction that Hooker's thrust into Lookout Valley and the seizure of Brown's Ferry must occur simultaneously. As he now saw things, the immediate capture of Brown's Ferry and the hills flanking it would permit him to forestall the sort of Rebel concentration in Lookout Valley designed to drive back Hooker that Smith so feared. A lodgment at Brown's Ferry would enable Grant to throw a force against the right flank of any Rebel units that ventured into the valley.[15]

As Thomas kept an eye on Hooker's progress, Smith set about organizing the assault on Brown's Ferry. Although Hooker's reply and Grant's own evolving views overruled Smith's desire for concurrent movements into Lookout Valley, the Vermonter nevertheless approached his mission with relish. He calculated that two brigades of infantry and three batteries of artillery would suffice to take the ferry. Every available flatboat and pontoon was to be assembled to carry one brigade downriver under the cover of darkness from Chattanooga to Brown's Ferry; there the troops were to disembark and capture the gorge and hills on the west bank. The hazards were clear: the men would be floating targets for nine miles, seven of which were within easy range of enemy pickets. Rebel batteries atop Lookout might reduce the flotilla to splinters. Nevertheless, reasoned Smith, "it was deemed better to take this risk than to attempt to launch the boats near the ferry, because they would move more rapidly than intelligence could be taken by infantry pickets, and, although the enemy might be alarmed, he would not know where the landing was to be attempted, and therefore could not concentrate with certainty against us."[16]

While the first brigade risked drowning and decimation on the river, the second brigade and the artillery were to march across the neck of Moccasin Point to the ferry, taking care to encamp in the woods near the east bank of the river, out of sight of Rebel pickets. Leaving Chattanooga so as to be in place ahead of the flotilla, this brigade would cross the river in support of the assaulting force after the boats had unloaded their first passengers.[17]

Smith chose his brigades wisely. For the river-borne force he selected the command of fellow Vermonter Brigadier General William Hazen, a proven fighter whose daring was exceeded only by his ambition. At Stones River, Hazen's brigade had held a critical piece of ground called the Round Forest against repeated Rebel attacks, buying Rosecrans the time needed to forge a new line of battle for the army. At Chickamauga, Hazen had thrown his brigade into a breach nearly as critical at the Brotherton farm, once again trading lives for time. There was no doubt that he was the man for the mission at hand.

To lead the supporting brigade, Smith called on the "Mad Russian," Brigadier General John Turchin, a former colonel of the Czar's Imperial Guard. Although many disliked the overbearing Ukrainian emigré, after Chickamauga none questioned his ability. There he had fought as well as Hazen, perhaps better. Command of the three artillery batter-

The "Suck"

Confederate Picket Line

Williams Island

Tennessee River

Raccoon Mountain

Brown's Ferry

Moccasin Point

Kelley's Ferry

Cravens House

Wauhatchie

Lookout Creek

Summertown

Lookout Mountain

0 miles   1   2

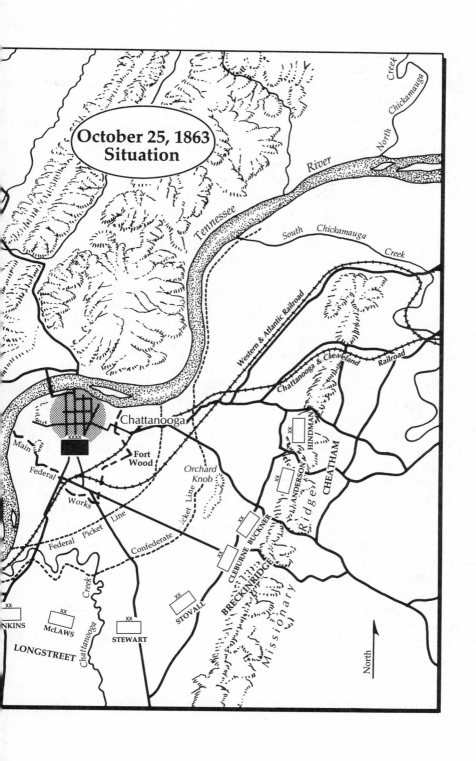

October 25, 1863
Situation

Creek

North Chickamauga

River

Tennessee

South Chickamauga

Creek

Western & Atlantic Railroad

Chattanooga & Cleveland Railroad

Chattanooga

HINDMAN

CHEATHAM

Ridge

ANDERSON

Fort
Wood

Main

Orchard
Knob

Federal

Picket Line

BUCKNER

Works

CLEBURNE

BRECKINRIDGE

Federal        Picket          Line

Confederate

Missionary

Creek

Chattanooga

STOVALL

KINS

McLAWS

STEWART

North

LONGSTREET

ies went to Major John Mendenhall, one of the most reliable artillery officers in the Army of the Cumberland. Colonel Timothy Stanley of the Eighteenth Ohio, a talented young officer who had lost his badly decimated brigade in the consolidation of units after Chickamauga, was placed in charge of the pontoons.

Obviously, the success of the mission depended largely on surprise. With opposing pickets on intimate terms, absolute secrecy was imperative. Only Grant, Thomas, Smith, key staff officers, and the commanders of the units directly involved were briefed on the operation.[18]

Not until the morning of 25 October, when he was summoned to army headquarters, did Hazen learn of the lead role he was to play. There Smith "told me his plan for opening the river, and informed me of the 'delicate duty' of carrying my brigade in boats at night down the river past the enemy's pickets to Brown's Ferry," said Hazen. Colonel Stanley had found only fifty serviceable pontoons, each of which was capable of carrying four crewmen and twenty-five passengers. He had scrounged two flatboats, one that could hold forty troops, the other, seventy-five, but that was all. The lack of boats forced Smith to cut back the size of the river-borne expedition to slightly under fourteen hundred men; the remaining seven hundred soldiers of Hazen's brigade would have to follow Turchin across Moccasin Point by foot. Smith told Hazen to spend 25 October organizing his command, then dismissed him with orders to return at dawn the following day to visit the landing site.[19]

If Hazen had any doubts he hid them well. Joined by Lieutenant Colonel Robert Kimberly of the Forty-first Ohio, who was to act as guide for the flotilla, Hazen rode out with Smith to the ferry early on Monday morning, 26 October. There, recalled Hazen, Smith "pointed out the precise spot he had already chosen for the landing, made plain at night by a gap in the hills which lined the [west] bank of the river; and we selected a point some five hundred yards above, on the opposite side, where, from a line of signal fires which I should make, I would know when to begin pulling for the other shore."[20]

Smith and Hazen fell into an animated discussion of the particulars of the expedition. Considering that neither had any experience at river-borne operations, their planning was admirably thorough. Hazen was to seize the two hills—each of them three hundred feet high—immediately to the left of the gorge. Smith and Hazen agreed that the first contingent of troops—composed of seventy-five men crammed into the larger flatboat—should disembark at the gorge and push out rapidly along the road to clear and hold it. They decided to divide the remainder of the water-borne force into two commands of equal size that would subsequently land to carry the hills. These two commands were further broken down into landing parties of twenty-five men each. Two men from each party were to carry axes with which to begin felling trees to fortify the hills as soon as they were secured. The seven hundred men of Hazen's brigade left with Turchin would be poised on the east bank, ready to cross in support as soon as the boats were free. Turchin's brigade would come over last and carry the line of hills to the right of the gorge. Hazen was to begin embarking his troops at midnight and shove off no later than 3:00 A.M. on the twenty-seventh.[21]

Hazen exuded enthusiasm. He could see only two tiny Rebel picket posts in the way of his objective—one beside a log cabin at the gorge, the other in a small depression between the two hills. Lieutenant Colonel Kimberly was more pensive. No one could be sure what force lay in the valley beyond the hills, and, as he reminded the generals, the riverbank was picketed all the way down from Lookout Mountain. "It was not an inviting prospect, especially the pontoon part of it" he reflected. "These rough boats were heavy and as clumsy in the water as a square box."[22]

Kimberly worried needlessly. No one at Bragg's headquarters atop Missionary Ridge yet had an inkling of what was about to unfold over in Lookout Valley. And they were not going to find out, if matters were left to General Longstreet. Bragg had accurate information on Sherman's progress across northern Mississippi, thanks to Stephen Dill Lee's cavalry. Closer to home, he learned from scouts on 25 October that Hooker was preparing to cross the river at Bridgeport. That same day, Major James Austin's Ninth Kentucky Cavalry came upon Yankee engineers rebuilding the railroad trestles in the gorge of Running Water Creek.[23]

Austin's report in particular worried Bragg. He ordered Longstreet to make a close reconnaissance in the direction of Bridgeport and to protect his left flank, presumably by moving additional units into Lookout Valley.

Nothing happened. Longstreet did not bother to acknowledge the order until the next day, 26 October. Although he promised to send a brigade from Jenkins's division all the way to Bridgeport, Longstreet took no action whatsoever; he simply laid aside Bragg's instructions. Longstreet had lost interest in anything Bragg had to say. Still smarting over President Davis's decision to retain Bragg, which he certainly took as a personal rebuke, Longstreet probably reasoned that, if he could not command the army, he might at least run his corps the way he saw fit.[24]

In truth, Longstreet was doing a poor job at even that. After committing the defense of Lookout Valley to Law's brigade in early October, he seems to have given no further thought to that all important avenue of approach. Longstreet neglected even to ride over Lookout Mountain to check on Law's dispositions.

Law, it will be recalled, had gone on a short leave of absence to visit the wounded General Hood, which left Colonel Oates of the Fifteenth Alabama as the ranking officer in the valley. Oates, in turn, not only was unaware of Law's departure, but was not even told where he had posted his three reserve regiments. "I suppose that General Law encamped the other three regiments of his brigade near the western base of Lookout on the creek," surmised the Alabamian. "I was not informed, nor was I given any instructions—only to picket the river, keep the enemy from using it, and to gather all the supplies for the men I could."[25]

Sadly, Oates was wrong in his only assumption. For reasons known only to himself, on 25 October Micah Jenkins had taken advantage of Law's absence to recall his three reserve regiments to the east side of Lookout Mountain. Oates was on his own.

Unaware of his predicament, Oates passed the twenty-sixth anxiously watching the subtle but unmistakable signs of a Federal buildup across the river. From the hills above Brown's Ferry he caught a glimpse of Mendenhall's batteries rumbling across Moccasin Point. Federal pickets along the east bank suddenly doubled in strength. Cavalry scouts brought in additional reports of increased Yankee activity at Bridgeport, where a crossing appeared imminent. Oates penned a note to Longstreet relating all this and requesting reinforcements without delay; at the very least, he needed one regiment that night. "The courier returned before midnight and stated that he had delivered my communication to General Longstreet, as I had directed, and had a receipt for it," recalled Oates. "No other response came, and I lay down and tried to sleep."[26]

Law reported to division headquarters off leave that night, about the same time Hazen was preparing to wake his men and begin embarking for Brown's Ferry. Law was stunned to find his reserve regiments quietly encamped nearby. "The withdrawal of these troops, without rhyme or reason for there was no earthly necessity for them on the east side of Lookout, opened an easy way for the enemy to throw a force across the river into Lookout Valley with a fair prospect of cutting off entirely the two regiments remaining there and reopening the blockaded roads," Law later rambled angrily. "Why this order was issued has always been a mystery to me."

The fiery Alabamian returned to his own camp after midnight. He was about to scribble an angry note of protest to division headquarters when someone told him that Jenkins had just left on a leave of absence of his own, meaning that Law was now in temporary command of the division. Thoroughly confounded, Law told his assistant adjutant general, Captain L. R. Terrell, to go to the valley at once and check on the picket line, while he readied the reserve regiments for the return trip. As Terrell galloped off into the misty darkness, the eerie echoes of scattered firing rolled over Lookout Mountain from the direction of Brown's Ferry.[27]

Sunday, 25 October, had been a day of wild rumors and strange activity in the camp of Hazen's brigade. Early that afternoon, regimental commanders were startled to receive orders enjoining them to form several twenty-five–man squads from among their best men, each to be led by an officer or noncommissioned officer "selected especially for efficiency and courage." Those troops not picked for the squads were to report for duty to Lieutenant Colonel E. B. Langdon of the First Ohio, whom Hazen had chosen to lead the remainder of the brigade.

The special squads were to be mustered and drilled at once, though for what, no one seemed to know. "We were ordered to report for duty on the parade ground at dusk and informed that we were about to undertake a dangerous task. What this was we were not told," attested a private of the Twenty-third Kentucky who was among the chosen. Officers were no better informed. A few, sensing that they had been called on to lead a suicide mission, offered their men an out. "As each man was chosen he was also informed that his work was of the most dangerous character—in fact a forlorn hope—and if any wished to remain in camp, they could do so," remembered a member of the Forty-first Ohio. Levi Wagner of the First Ohio said that his company commander could not bring himself to choose his squad: the captain "declared his men were all good and he would hurt no man's feelings by picking, so he just counted them off by files, beginning at the head, and of course I was among them."[28]

Monday opened a bit more calmly. Hazen waited until that morning to select the leaders for his river-borne force. To Lieutenant Colonel James Foy of the Twenty-third Kentucky, who had shown unusual coolness under fire at Chickamauga, went the dubious distinction of commanding the seventy-five–man party that was to land first and secure the road through the gorge. Twenty-eight-year-old Colonel Aquila Wiley of the Forty-first Ohio and Major William Birch of the Ninety-third Ohio were chosen to lead the storming parties against the hills. Late in the morning, Hazen and his lieutenants rode furtively out of camp to have a look at Brown's Ferry.[29]

The day passed quietly enough, and the men began to forget the rumors of a secret expedition. Then, precisely at midnight, those selected the day before were shaken awake and told to assemble into their squads. Two men per squad were handed axes. All were ordered to shed their knapsacks and blankets, and the squads marched through the deserted streets of Chattanooga toward their rendezvous point on the south bank of the river.

As the men gathered before the gently bobbing pontoons, the moon sank below the horizon. A heavy mist rolled into the valley, blanketing the river. Only then did company officers learn of their destination.

A few last-minute irritants arose. Colonel Foy found his flatboat nearly awash and loaded down by a dozen heavy pieces of iron. His party broke ranks to bail out the boat and toss the iron overboard. Then Foy began to usher the men aboard, only to discover that there was room for just fifty of the seventy-five men in his assault party. Reluctantly, the Kentuckian left the rest behind to find places in other boats. As the remaining parties stepped into their pontoons, they found that someone likewise had overestimated the capacity of their boats. "The pontoons were so crowded that the men must stand, steadying themselves with their guns," complained Colonel Kimberly. "A detail from Stanley's Michigan engineer regiment had been provided to man the oars, but they could do little in the crowded pontoons; the movement must rely mainly on the current of the river, which chanced to be running high."[30]

A mile and a half to the west, Lieutenant Colonel Langdon was growing angry. He had marched the remaining 750 men of Hazen's brigade across Moccasin Point shortly before midnight as ordered, only to find the road choked with ambulances, cannons, caissons, and sleeping soldiers from Turchin's command. In the fog-laced darkness, Langdon tried to move his column around the obstacles. As he neared the edge of the forest, a few hundred feet short of the river, Langdon was stopped by the commander of Battery A, First Middle Tennessee, who warned him not to move out onto the open bank, where enemy pickets would surely spot his party. Langdon halted the column, then rode about looking for Smith and Turchin. Finding neither of them, he told his men to break ranks and try to get some sleep amid the timber. It was 1:00 A.M.[31]

Back at the embarkation point, all was ready by 3:00 A.M. Squad leaders enjoined their men to keep silent, and the Michigan engineers pushed the boats free of the shore. Foy and his party led the way in the large flatboat; Hazen rode in the fourth boat, and Colonel Wiley brought up the rear.[32]

Three hundred yards downriver, the flotilla slowed to pass through a gap in the pontoon bridge that the engineers had opened for them. As his boat waited its turn to shove through, an awestruck Kentucky private blurted out: "This reminds me of a picture I once saw of Washington crossing the Alps." "His mixed history caused a general laugh," recalled a comrade, "which was quickly suppressed by a voice from the boat ahead, in a kind of stage whisper: 'Shut up, you damned fools! Do you think this is a regatta?'"[33]

Slowly and silently, the boats glided toward the looming point of Lookout Mountain. As they turned the bend in the river, the campfires of enemy picket posts flickered into view. "The Rebel pickets could be plainly seen, taking their ease before blazing fires, talking together, or, perchance, humming over some old familiar air with happy unconcern. Holding their breath, as it were, the men passed under the frowning brow of Lookout, rising darkly above them on the left," remembered an Ohio corporal.[34]

A scream and a splash split the night air. A low-hanging branch had knocked a man out of Foy's flatboat. Foy growled an angry reprimand as the soldier sank out of sight. But the Rebel pickets took no notice, and the man was picked up by a trailing pontoon, wet but alive.

At 4:30 A.M., Foy's boat neared a huge signal fire on the east bank just above the ferry. The blaze was his cue to make for the opposite side and disembark. To Hazen's horror, Foy drifted past the fire. "Pull in, Colonel Foy, Pull in! Pull in!" he shouted repeatedly.

That did it. From the west bank, Rebel pickets in the gorge fired a wild volley into the darkness; from the east bank, a dozen of Turchin's men, not knowing who was out in the river, fired back. One of Foy's crew dropped his oar and slumped forward with a bullet through his arm. Cries of "Fall in! The Yanks are coming" echoed in the gorge. Another volley followed. Foy's men ducked low as their boat thudded against the bank, then sprinted up the road, scattering the startled Rebels. One by one, the boats of the flotilla pulled ashore and unloaded their squads. Staring up at the dark hill directly in front of him, a frightened private moaned, "What does that mean?" "That means fight and be damned to you," snapped another.[35]

In fact, there was little fighting to be done. Within five, perhaps ten, minutes after the last pontoon had landed, Brown's Ferry was in Federal hands. Foy and his little band of fifty had sprinted past the log cabin, through the gorge, and five hundred yards beyond, where they were busily throwing up breastworks. Colonel Wiley and Major Birch had their commands atop the two hills. The climb had been hard. Men stumbled and slipped in the gathering morning twilight, but not a single Rebel bullet challenged their ascent. Out came the axes. Trees were felled and dead wood gathered, and the Yankees settled in on the hill crests. Behind them, the empty pontoons were making for the far shore, where Lieutenant

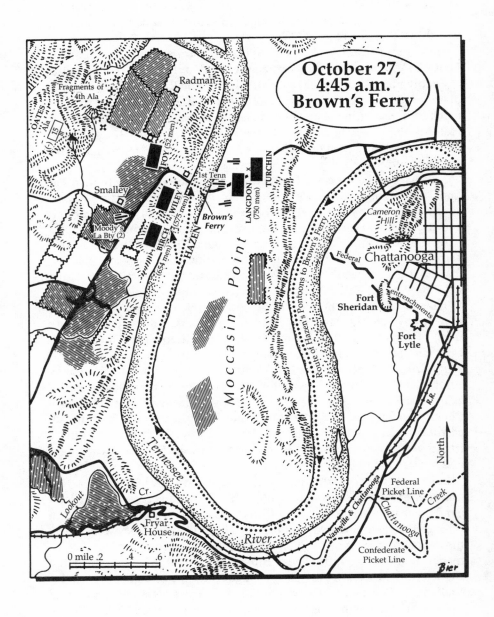

October 27,
4:45 a.m.
Brown's Ferry

Radman

Fragments of
4th Ala

OATES
15 Ala
(-)

FOY (52 men)

1st Tenn

LANGDON
(750 men)

TURCHIN

Smalley

Brown's
Ferry

BIRCH (664 men)

WILEY (575 men)

HAZEN

Moody's
La Bty (2)

Moccasin Point

Cameron
Hill

Federal

Chattanooga

Fort
Sheridan

entrenchments

Fort
Lytle

Route of Hazen's Pontoons to Brown's Ferry

Tennessee

North

River

Cr.

Lookout

Fryar
House

Nashville & Chattanooga

R.R.

Federal
Picket Line

Chattanooga Creek

Confederate
Picket Line

0 mile .2    .4    .6

Bier

Colonel Langdon, who had found Baldy Smith just a few minutes before, was hurriedly gathering the remainder of the brigade.[36]

Out in the valley beyond Brown's Ferry, Colonel Oates was shaken awake just as the first light of dawn touched the hilltops. A frightened private from the scattered picket force, who had grabbed a horse and galloped bareback to find the Alabamian, told Oates of the Yankee crossing. How many were there, asked Oates. "Some seventy-five or one hundred," he replied, obviously having seen only Foy's detachment. The odds sounded about right to Oates. He had the long roll beaten, and the six reserve companies of his Fifteenth Alabama—about 150 men in all—crawled from their tents and formed line of battle. Leaving a couple of sick soldiers behind to guard the camp, Oates swung into the saddle and led his command toward the gorge. Captain Terrell, Law's assistant adjutant general, rode with him. As they came up on Brown's Ferry in the misty twilight, Oates's band was joined by pickets from their regiment falling back from the ferry and by the soldiers of the Fourth Alabama reporting in from farther north.

The cracking of axes against trees told Oates where to find the Federals. Estimating that the Yankees were no more than twenty yards away, Oates whispered to his company commanders to about face. He countermarched one hundred yards, reformed, and then sent forward two companies as skirmishers, telling their captains to "walk right up to the foe, and for every man to place the muzzle of his rifle against the body of a Yankee when he fired."

The Yankees, who happened to be Foy's exposed party, spoiled Oates's bold plan by running. As the Alabamians emerged from the fog, most of Foy's Kentuckians broke for the gorge. Some threw down their rifles, and cries of "We surrender, we surrender" mingled with the vain shouts of Foy and his officers, "Halt! Halt! Where are you going, you damned cowards?" Getting no response, Foy sprinted back toward the landing after his men. Oates pursued.

At the log cabin in the gorge, Foy stumbled upon Lieutenant Colonel Langdon, who had just come across with the First Ohio Infantry and Sixth Indiana Infantry. In reply to Foy's breathless plea for help, Langdon quickly shook out the two regiments into line of battle, but not before Oates had managed to get his three left companies up onto the crest of the hill north of the gorge. From there, at a range of less than a hundred yards, they poured a sharp fire down into the Yankees mingled on the riverbank. For a moment, it looked as though Foy and Langdon's troops might be forced to surrender or swim.[37]

But Oates's right companies had overextended themselves. Dawn broke as they clambered up the steep hill south of the gorge. There was just enough light in the woods to make the Alabamians easy targets for the Federals on the summit, whose line ran far beyond the Rebels' right flank. The Confederates froze on the hillside. Company officers dove behind trees. Bullets cut into the leaderless horde. Oates galloped across the gorge and rode into the mob, trying to urge the men forward. He spurred his horse to within twenty paces of the Yankee breastworks— "I could see their heads as they fired from behind some logs," he recalled. Oates's histrionics were wasted. No one followed him, and while near the summit a minié ball ripped through his right hip and thigh, fracturing the bone an inch below the hip joint. "It struck a blow as though a brick had been hurled against me, and hurt so badly that I started to curse as I fell, and said 'God d——,' when thinking that possibly I was killed, and that it would not seem well for a man to die with an oath in his mouth, I cut it off at that d—— and did not finish the sentence. All this flashed through my mind as I fell," said Oates. Two men came to Oates's assistance, one of them shot through the arm himself, and together the three hobbled down the hill toward the Thompson cabin, two hundred yards west of the gorge. They laid the big Alabamian down in the yard.[38]

Oates's repose was brief. After he fell, what little spirit remained in his confused and badly outnumbered Alabamians had vanished. They held on for about fifteen minutes, then gradually fell back off the hills. Foy led a tentative pursuit back down the road.[39]

Oates knew he was in trouble:

Soon the balls from the enemy were striking the fence, or in the yard, ricocheting, and then hitting the house. The only inmates were two ladies. I was bleeding copiously and became very thirsty. I begged the ladies for a drink of water. One of them came to the door with a dipper of water, when a shot struck the house or fence and she jumped back and shrieked with fright. Seeing that there was no other chance to get the water, and my thirst now being almost unendurable, I crawled and dragged my wounded limb through the dirt of the yard to the doorsteps, when the ladies took me by the arms, helped me into the house, and gave me water—God bless them.

A moment later, Oates's orderly appeared with his other horse. With the help of two nearby troops, the orderly lifted the Alabamian into the saddle, and together they started off along the road up the valley toward Lookout Mountain, passing among survivors of the Fourth and Fifteenth Alabama, who were withdrawing slowly to the safety of the mountain.

Oates made it to the Morris house near the mouth of Lookout Creek at about 7:30 A.M. There, faint from loss of blood, he was lifted off his horse and taken inside. While his surgeon bound the wound, the Alabamian helped himself to a bottle. As Oates was about to lie back and let the warmth of the whiskey sweep through him, General Law stepped into the room, begging to know what had happened. Outside on the road were the three reserve regiments of his brigade, waiting to advance down the valley. "I told him that he was too late, in my opinion, to accomplish anything; that a heavy force had already crossed the river," recalled Oates.

Law rode up the first tall hill north of the mouth of Lookout Creek to have a look. From there, he had an unobstructed view as far as Williams Island. Through the light drizzle that had begun to fall in the valley, he could make out Hazen's brigade entrenched on the hills south of the ferry. Turchin was across and digging in on the hills to the north, and the first pontoons for the bridge were being laid across the river. Law returned to the Morris house. He was quite right, Law told Oates, the Yankees were across in force and getting stronger. Thoroughly disgusted, Law placed his brigade in line of battle to guard the road over Lookout Mountain and reported back to Longstreet on the disaster he and Oates had tried their best to forestall.[40]

Down at the ferry, Hazen was in high spirits. He rode along the line, complimenting the men and declaring that "we had knocked the cover off the cracker box and plenty to eat was in sight if we would hold the ground we had gained." And all this at a loss of only thirty-five men. Later in the day, Hazen showed his gratitude tangibly. He dipped into the meager division stores and on his personal requisition ordered two ears of corn issued to each soldier. The men appreciated the gesture. "Two ears of corn as a reward of bravery may seem like a joke to you companions, as you sit around this well-filled table tonight," a veteran of the Twenty-third Kentucky reminded his comrades at a postwar banquet, "but I assure you that on the occasion referred to, had the option of a medal of honor or two ears of corn been given the troops, very few would have accepted the medal."[41]

# CHAPTER SIX

# OUR LAGGING EFFORTS

B ROWN'S Ferry was a scant three miles from Longstreet's headquarters. It may as well have been in another country, however, for all the attention Longstreet paid it. Moccasin Point and Lookout Mountain not only blocked the general's view of the ferry but also blinded him to its tactical significance. He greeted Law's frenetic dispatch announcing the fall of Brown's Ferry with an indifference that amounted to dereliction of duty. Confident that the Federal crossing was merely a feint, Longstreet tucked away Law's message and gave the matter no further thought; nor did he bother to inform Bragg of what had happened.

Longstreet, it seems, had come up with his own theory regarding Federal intentions in Lookout Valley, one that had no foundation in scouting reports or other intelligence. On 26 October, he had argued in a note to Bragg that any force moving from Bridgeport would not take the short route toward the mouth of Lookout Valley. Rather, Longstreet asserted, it would cross Sand Mountain and enter the valley opposite Johnson's Crook, over twenty miles south of the point of Lookout Mountain. At Johnson's Crook, the Yankees would follow a wagon road up the mountain and, once atop, try to outflank him. This odd notion was the product of Longstreet's imagination. He had neglected to make the reconnaissance toward Bridgeport as ordered by Bragg on the twenty-fifth, nor did he have scouts out in the direction of Johnson's Crook to test his assumption. And he refused to acknowledge contrary indications. When Law, whose disaffection was deepening by the hour, related that his own scouts had reported both a large enemy force—Hooker's command—on the move from Shellmound toward Chattanooga by way of the short route and a body of enemy cavalry probing in the neighborhood of Kelley's Ferry, Longstreet dismissed the warnings. The only other tangible signs of anything amiss were the two Federal brigades now over the river at Brown's Ferry, and these Longstreet simply chose to ignore.[1]

Up on Missionary Ridge, Bragg was restive. He had heard the firing from Brown's Ferry, but was at a loss to understand why Longstreet had sent in no report on it. Lying awake in his tent farther north atop the ridge, Brigadier General St. John Liddell had heard the volleys as well. "Listening attentively, I knew a contest for some object was going on, and my apprehensions led to the quick conclusion that it was injurious to our lagging efforts." With no duties to keep him in camp, Liddell arose at daybreak to ride over to the valley to have a look for himself.

As he passed army headquarters, Liddell noticed Bragg standing at the front gate, obviously distraught. Liddell slowed up, and Bragg asked him where he was going. To learn the nature of the predawn fight, he replied. "When I told him, he expressed great surprise," Liddell recalled. "He said that he had heard nothing from General Longstreet . . . and requested me to report the facts, should anything wrong be going on."

Liddell found plenty wrong, not the least of which was Longstreet's placid indifference. He made his way to the summit of Lookout Mountain, dismounted, and walked out to the rocky edge. Recounted the Louisianian:

> I had to wait some time for the heavy clouds floating over the plains below, like a sea when seen from this high place, to clear off before I could distinguish any object beneath. When this occurred, I could see that the enemy had seized and now occupied a position on our side of the river, having driven away Longstreet's men. The enemy was now busily engaged in throwing a pontoon bridge from the Moccasin Bend across to the lower part of [the] valley. All this quietly progressing, undisturbed by any firing from Longstreet's pickets. I could not understand the indifference on our part at this unmistakable lodgment of the enemy.[2]

Nor could Bragg, when Liddell reported what he had seen. Exploding with rage, Bragg told Liddell he would send for Longstreet and order him to retake the lost ground immediately. He rued ever having given Longstreet so much responsibility. "He complained that Longstreet had boasted to the President that 'he could whip the whole Yankee Army with his Corps alone,'" remembered Liddell. "Mr. Davis, commenting on this absurdity, had instructed Bragg 'to put him at the work.'" He had, and look what it had got him, Bragg snarled.

Liddell went on his way, and Bragg sent Longstreet peremptory orders to reconnoiter the Federal bridgehead and "make all necessary dispositions to dislodge him."[3]

Longstreet did neither. He let the day slip away and permitted Smith's Federals, who expected at any moment to be hit by a fierce counterattack, to strengthen their bridgehead unmolested. Not until dusk did he deign to acknowledge Bragg's order. "Your note of to-day is received," he began laconically. "The enemy's designs seem to be to occupy this bank of the river for the purpose of shortening his line of communication and possibly for the purpose of creating a diversion near the point of Lookout Mountain, while he moves a heavier force to occupy the mountain, via Johnson's Crook. The latter move and object seems to me to be more important, essential indeed, than any such partial move as his present one."[4]

Longstreet's twisted logic caught Bragg off guard, and he not only backed down, but acquiesced to Longstreet's demands. He no longer pressed Longstreet to retake Brown's Ferry, but rather directed him to deploy atop Lookout Mountain so as to prevent the enemy from flanking it from Johnson's Crook.

When Longstreet began to sketch out his plan for stopping the imaginary Federal advance, Bragg had second thoughts, and then the two dickered deep into the night of 27 October. Longstreet warned Bragg that the enemy was moving on Trenton in force. He announced his intention to send Jenkins's division—roughly one-third of his effective force—all the way down to Johnson's Crook at daybreak and implored Bragg to send him another division to replace it. He added, by way of postscript, that the report of a Federal advance upon Trenton had not come from Colonel Warren Grigsby's Kentucky Cavalry Brigade, the only troops then operating in that area, but rather from the signal corps (which, everyone but Longstreet seemed to recall, had proven its ineptness in interpreting enemy troop movements during the Chickamauga campaign).[5]

This strange missive finally convinced Bragg that Longstreet might not have a firm grip on the situation beyond his left flank. Johnson's Crook was too far to send a brigade, much less a division, especially on such meager information. A brigade posted judiciously a few miles south of the point of Lookout Mountain would be enough to hold off an attack from Johnson's Crook until reinforced, countered Bragg. He also suggested that Longstreet move his corps to the west side of Chattanooga Creek before dawn, so as to be in a better position to reinforce the mountain. Breckinridge would shift his corps to the left to close the gap thus created. Bragg then reopened the subject of Brown's Ferry: "Should you ascertain in the morning that the enemy is not advancing on Trenton, the general commanding deems it highly important that you should dislodge the enemy from his position taken today at or near Brown's

Ferry." To prevent further misunderstanding, Bragg told Longstreet he would call on him in the morning to confer in person.[6]

Pleased though they were by the success of Smith's assault, Grant and Thomas recognized the tenuousness of the bridgehead. Although Smith was reporting confidently by midday on 27 October that "this place cannot be carried now," they knew that, absent the arrival of Hooker or strong reinforcements from Thomas's own thinly stretched line, his two brigades were in danger of being swept back into the river. Moreover, the Cracker Line could not be opened until Hooker secured the lower reaches of Lookout Valley and linked up with Smith. Both Grant and Thomas assumed that the Confederates would act rationally and use whatever force was needed to recapture Brown's Ferry, and so they turned their full attention to urging Hooker on.[7]

As Hooker himself had feared, he had run into delays. Early on 25 October, he had, in good faith, ordered Howard to be ready to march out of Bridgeport without wagons the next morning. Howard, however, replied that he had horses and limbers enough to pull just one of his five batteries of artillery. No matter, Hooker told Howard, he was to march on the morrow even if it meant moving without any cannons. Not until early evening, when it became evident that Geary's small division would not arrive on schedule, did Hooker conclude to postpone the movement for at least one more day.[8]

Assistant Secretary Dana, who was still hovering around Hooker's headquarters, disregarded these efforts and instead called attention to Hooker's indiscreet grumbling. Dana again complained to Stanton that the general was stalling. "Troops are now just moving out for Shellmound and Raccoon Mountain," he wrote from Bridgeport on the morning of 27 October. "Hooker . . . is in an unfortunate state of mind for one who has to co-operate, fault finding, criticizing, dissatisfied. No doubt the chaos of Rosecrans's administration is as bad as he describes, but he is quite as truculent toward the plan he is now to execute as toward the impotence and confusion of the old regime." Of course a copy of Dana's telegram found its way to Grant, who already harbored doubts about his ability to work with the petulant Hooker.[9]

Considering the miserable state of the roads, Hooker made good time on the first day's march. Howard, who broke camp at sunrise on 27 October, reached Whiteside's by 8:00 P.M. The decrepit little railroad station on the north bank of Running Water Creek was five miles *beyond* the tentative day's objective of Rankin's Ferry and only ten miles short of Brown's Ferry. Along the way, Howard had detached several regiments to watch the line of communications back to Bridgeport and to guard the trains whenever they finally did move out, leaving him with only two sadly under-strength divisions, or slightly more than five thousand men, with which to complete his mission.

Geary, who followed Howard, made it as far as Shellmound, a railroad station on the bank of the Tennessee that derived its name from the bed of sand and shells upon which it sat. Shellmound was five miles southwest of Rankin's Ferry. "The going was slow because we had a long pontoon train and the roads were very bad," complained an aide to one of Geary's brigade commanders. "In addition to the mud, there were many rocks in the roads, and the going was continually up and down steep hills. We worked nearly all night laying the pontoons." Like Howard, Geary was stripped of troops to repair railroads or build earthwork defenses along the route of march, which reduced his division to a mere six regiments, or about eighteen hundred men in all.[10]

Badgered by Thomas, Hooker issued orders for the march to resume at 5:00 A.M. on 28 October. For Geary's men, it meant three hours' sleep and a quick cup of coffee before they trudged back out onto the muddy road to hike the last twenty miles to Brown's Ferry.[11]

Wednesday, 28 October, dawned cold and cloudy. A gray mist dampened the air. Up from the valley and over the top of Lookout Mountain a chill wind whistled. All in all, it was a most appropriate backdrop for what was sure to be a frosty meeting between Bragg and Longstreet.

The morning began inauspiciously. Bragg stopped at Longstreet's headquarters near the eastern base of Lookout shortly after dawn, expecting to be met by him. Instead, only a few junior staff officers were on hand; their chief had gone up the mountain rather than wait for Bragg.

Bragg and his staff wound their way up the slippery road to the summit of Lookout. They turned north at the tiny resort community of Summertown and were guided toward the point by the boom of Porter Alexander's artillery in its daily conversation with the Yankee cannon on Moccasin Point. Bragg dismounted at the point and walked past the gunners to the very edge of the rocky escarpment. There was no sign of Longstreet, but Baldy Smith's brigades and his neatly laid pontoon bridge were in plain sight, two miles to the north.

The ubiquitous St. John Liddell showed up a few minutes later to gawk again at the Yankees. Once more, his sense of timing was uncanny: "I was observing the effect and accuracy of this artillery duel, when Longstreet came hastily up on foot. Just then a shell exploded above us, causing Longstreet to duck his head considerably. After witnessing a shot from his battery, he went on to see Bragg, who was reconnoitering a little farther on, among the rocks at the point. Apprehensive that Bragg would have an outbreak of words with Longstreet and unwilling to be a witness, I went away to the left side of the mountain," said Liddell of his uncharacteristically decorous exit.[12]

Whatever Bragg had intended to tell Longstreet was cut short by a messenger from a signal station on the west side of the mountain with startling news: a long and powerful Federal column had emerged from the gorge of Running Water Creek and was marching down Lookout Valley. Already its advance guard was a mere six miles away. Bragg rebuked the soldier for repeating what surely was a false report: the Yankees couldn't possibly have come up that soon. The courier held his ground: "General, if you will ride to a point on the west side of the mountain I will show them to you." Bragg and Longstreet followed him across the mountaintop to a large overhanging ledge, called Sunset Rock because of the spectacular view it afforded of sunsets in the valley. Liddell was there ahead of them. As the two walked up, he caught a bit of Bragg's altercation with Longstreet. "Bragg was very restless and complained with bitterness of Longstreet's inactivity and lack of ability, asserting him to be greatly overrated," attested Liddell. Bragg's anger gave way to astonishment. Fourteen hundred feet below and less than a mile due west from where he stood was the head of Hooker's column, closing in on the hamlet of Wauhatchie.[13]

Longstreet was even more astounded: the Yankees had chosen to march through the valley instead of along the mountaintop; the threat from Johnson's Crook was exposed as a chimera.

While Bragg and Longstreet stood and stared, Liddell sent word of the Federal appearance to Colonel Alexander, who galloped up with several rifled guns at 2:00 P.M. A quick survey told him the enemy was too far away to range accurately. He ordered his artillery to open fire all the same; it would be good fun and would give his gunners "an excellent chance and excuse for an afternoon of target practice."[14]

The occasional shells bursting overhead only added to the sense of awe Hooker's Easterners felt as they gazed up at the heights of Lookout Mountain. Accustomed to the gently rolling farmlands of northern Virginia, they had a hard time imagining combat in country so "wild and picturesque"; it was land, said a New York lieutenant, with a beauty "beyond any description that I can give." But the cannon were real enough, as their weirdly cacophonous roar, echoing off Raccoon Mountain and melting back into Lookout Mountain, reminded the men. "The situation was exciting and inspiriting to the last degree," thrilled the lieutenant. "Our color sergeants unfurled their flags, our drummers unslung their drums, and the rattle of some loyal tune sounded our answer back at this gate of the rebel stronghold. There was no use in any attempt at concealment, and none was made. They knew we had come, and we told them then with the flag and drum . . . that we had come to stay."[15]

Fighting Joe Hooker certainly conveyed that impression to the marching men of his corps. "He was the coolest man I ever saw," recalled a private of the One Hundred Thirty-sixth New York who caught a glimpse of him riding by. "He sat jogging along on a white horse, occasionally casting an eye up from under his slouch hat to see how matters looked up on the mountain. I saw one solid shot pass under his horse and go bouncing away for rods beyond, but he appeared in no hurry."[16]

Nor need he be. Apart from the ineffectual shelling from the mountain, which killed just one man in Howard's entire corps, the only resistance Hooker's column met in coming down the valley was a few weak volleys from the Sixth South Carolina of Law's brigade, hidden in heavy timber on a tall hill between Wauhatchie and the mountain. The commander of Howard's lead division, Brigadier General Adolph von Steinwehr, a forty-three-year-old German emigré whose grandfather had been a lieutenant general in the Prussian army and who himself had served the Duke of Brunswick, sent his lead regiments off the road toward the knoll to clear away the Rebels. In this, the first clash of the campaign between troops from the two Eastern armies, the Seventy-third Pennsylvania and Seventy-third Ohio, supported on their flanks by two New York regiments, attacked and, without losing a man, sent the badly isolated South Carolinians scampering down the east slope of the hill and over Lookout Creek in disorder.[17]

The column resumed the march. At 2:30 P.M., Steinwehr cleared Wauhatchie. An hour later, Howard's entire corps was well beyond the range of the Rebel artillery. At 3:45 P.M., the Easterners came within sight of the long hills bordering Brown's Ferry. There, in a marshy field a half mile southwest of the ferry, Howard and Steinwehr suddenly called a halt. The long line of breastworks on the hillsides gave the generals pause: in the gray mist, they were unsure whether the dark forms crouched behind them were friend or foe. Skirmishers inched forward, and Howard strained for a better look through his field glasses. Gazing west from the ferry, General Hazen sensed the Easterners' uncertainty. He ordered his flags unfurled. That erased all doubts. The thrill of mutual recognition, said Howard, "was an unexpected and joyous event to us; and not less so to those so lately besieged. They called out a welcome with the usual loud cheers and shouts, as we came near, and they cried, 'Hurrah! hurrah! you have opened our bread line.'" A few days later, after their rations had been restored and their stomachs filled, the casual Westerners would grow to disdain the smartly uniformed soldiers of the Army of the Potomac—"Eastern pimps," as one Illinoisan labeled them, who in turn came to delight in taunting Thomas's veterans with reminders that they had saved them from starvation. For the moment, however, all were pleased. "When we came in sight of these troops, the scene was most thrilling," a private from Steinwehr's division remembered. "This was the first we had seen of the Army of the Cumberland, and their welcome was most hearty. As our column advanced along the valley, greeted and greeting, the shout was passed from hill-top to hill-top—the bands played, the flags waved, and the very heavens rang with shouts such as are only heard in the army; and their shouts were answered back by our men, with real soldierly enthusiasm." Yes, agreed an officer in Hazen's brigade, the joy of the Westerners was real; "it was beyond description. The depression which had lasted from the days at Chickamauga was gone. The troops felt as if they had been in prison, and were now free."[18]

With the wagon road to Bridgeport now open and the river clear to Kelley's Ferry, Thomas and his staff worked late into the night to see to it that rations would begin to flow over the Cracker Line into Chattanooga. Repairs went on around the clock to the converted Rebel steamer *Painted Rock*, docked on the edge of town; only a few engine parts expected momentarily from Nashville prevented her departure for Bridgeport. A second steamboat was put in trim and made ready to go downriver at dawn, while at Bridgeport, the little flat-bottomed steamboat *Chattanooga* was set to depart simultaneously for Chattanooga. Laden with an initial cargo of thirty-four thousand rations, she had been built from scratch, and her boiler deck was still being laid in place when the first rations were brought aboard. Difficulties remained, but Thomas felt confident enough to wire Halleck that night that he hoped "in a few days to be pretty well supplied."[19]

That, of course, was contingent upon Hooker's and Smith's holding open the wagon road across the northern stretch of Lookout Valley that joined Brown's Ferry with Kelley's Ferry. For the master of Brown's Ferry, that should have been a comparatively easy task, but the normally sanguine Smith was deeply troubled. The source of his anxiety was Hooker. Perhaps the ease of his march down the valley or the rousing reception that greeted his troops had clouded Hooker's judgment; in any case, the manner in which he disposed his troops upon reaching Brown's Ferry was careless in the extreme. Hooker's arrogant chief of staff, Major General Daniel Butterfield, had confessed as much to Thomas when he reported the column's arrival that afternoon. Hooker, he said offhandedly, had "not taken up any military position, but directed the commanders to find good cover for the troops" and encamp for the night.[20]

Smith and Hazen were aghast. Hazen personally implored Hooker to form a compact line across the valley from the hills along the river to the eastern slope of Raccoon Mountain and to consolidate his forces, but Hooker waved him off. Seeing the futility of further conversation with the imperious Easterner, Smith galloped over the pontoon bridge at Brown's Ferry amid the gathering twilight and made for Chattanooga. "I at once went to General Joseph J. Reynolds, the Chief of Staff of General Thomas, and urged him to have General Thomas direct that the troops should take up strong positions for I felt sure the enemy would not give up without a struggle, and as they could see from Lookout Mountain where every regiment was encamped, I did not doubt but that an attack would be made on Hooker that night and that if he was beaten we would lose all we had gained." Smith left headquarters after unburdening himself, only to learn later that Reynolds had neglected to pass on his concerns to Thomas.[21]

Smith's and Hazen's fears were well founded. Hooker's dispositions were deplorable. Although they were at least facing south, toward the enemy, the divisions of Schurz and Steinwehr had bivouacked haphazardly in the cultivated fields and meadows on either side of the road, a half-mile above Brown's Ferry.

Hooker's most egregious error was his placement of Geary's tiny division, down to a mere fifteen hundred men after the Sixtieth New York had been detached to hold the pass near Whiteside's. There were two viable approaches across the valley to Kelley's Ferry, one the wagon road over the northern base of Lookout Mountain near the river, the other a country lane that left the valley road at Wauhatchie and wound its way northwest toward a long, narrow gorge in Raccoon Mountain that ended at the ferry. Hooker felt confident that Howard could intercept any force attempting to move against Kelley's Ferry by way of the northern approach, but worried that the Rebels might use the road from Wauhatchie if it were left undefended. Consequently, he ordered Geary, whose division reached the junction at 4:30 P.M., to halt there for the night. Hooker's report, written to justify this risky decision, revealed more of its foolhardiness than he probably intended:

Geary's division, being in the rear, and being anxious to hold both roads leading to Kelley's Ferry, he was directed to encamp near Wauhatchie, three miles from the position held by Howard's corps. Pickets were thrown out from both camps on all of the approaches, though no attempt was made to establish and preserve a communication between them.

The commands were too small to keep up a substantial communication that distance, and I deemed it more prudent to hold the men well in hand than to have a feeble one. In my judgment, it was essential to retain possession of both approaches to Kelley's Ferry, if practicable, as it would cause us inconvenience to dispossess the enemy if he established himself on either.[22]

Smith and Hazen, of course, disagreed, maintaining (correctly as developments were to prove) that Hooker's command, if judiciously disposed near Brown's Ferry, could so threaten the flank of any Confederate force trying to move across the valley toward Kelley's Ferry, whether by the northern or southern road, as to force it to fall back.

Geary obeyed the order with grave misgivings. The forty-three-old Pennsylvanian was a volunteer officer who had dabbled in a number of trades before the war: teaching school, clerking in a store, studying civil engineering and law, and surveying in Kentucky. A lieutenant in the Pennsylvania militia at the age of sixteen, he had entered Federal service in the Mexican War as lieutenant colonel of the Second Pennsylvania Infantry and fought with Winfield Scott's army from Veracruz to Mexico City. After the war, he moved to California and was elected mayor of San Francisco. It was as territorial governor of strife-torn Kansas in the mid-1850s, however, that Geary gained national attention. Although his administration was by all accounts a failure, he won the respect of radical members of the young Republican party for his staunch antislavery sentiments. At the outbreak of the Civil War, he was elected colonel of the Twenty-eighth Pennsylvania. Geary's rise to division command was rapid.[23]

Geary was a huge man for his day, standing six feet four inches and weighing nearly 250 pounds, with an ego to match his size. Blowhard, glory-seeker, and consummate self-promoter, Geary nevertheless was no fool. He saw the danger of his exposed position under the heights of Lookout, from which the Confederates could watch his every move. As night fell and a brilliant, nearly full moon, hidden now and then by drifting clouds, rose over the valley, Geary ordered the commanders of his two brigades, Major General George Sears Greene and Colonel George A. Cobham, Jr., to bivouac their five regiments upon their arms, with cartridge boxes on. With the infantry were four guns of Knap's Pennsylvania battery, one section of which was led by Geary's young son, Lieutenant Edward Geary. Fires were forbidden, and the men had to make do with a supper of hardtack and cold coffee.

General Greene was even more apprehensive than Geary. He told his staff to keep their horses saddled and bridled and sent his aide to inquire whether the men should not only sleep with their arms but leave their shoes on as well. Geary thought that a bit excessive, but Greene issued the order nonetheless.[24]

The men of the division camped along the northern fringe of a forest about three hundred yards north of the spot where the Trenton Railroad joined the Nashville and Chattanooga line. A broad, roughly cultivated corn field of perhaps one thousand square feet lay beyond the forest. On the southern edge of the field stood a tiny log cabin belonging to a family named Rowden. They had already brought in the harvest, leaving behind the rain-sodden cornstalks. It had been a bad year for crops, and the stunted stalks caused the Federals of Geary's division to label the ground the "stubble field." Northeast of the Rowden cabin was a low knoll. The railroad tracks, which ran upon a steep, three-foot-high embankment, skirted the base of the knoll. Some fifty yards south of the cabin there rose another knoll; atop it Geary planted Knap's battery. The country lane to Kelley's Ferry marked the northern limit of the Rowden field, and a shallow swamp bordered it on the west.[25]

At dusk, Geary summoned Colonel William Rickards, Jr., commander of the Twenty-ninth Pennsylvania, to division headquarters. Rickards had drawn duty as officer-of-the-day, his regiment duty as grand guard.

The two Pennsylvanians discussed the potential threat and the manner to best protect the division against it. Geary assumed that Howard's easy advance down the valley road to Brown's Ferry meant that no enemy lay in that direction. Consequently, he expected any attack would come from the south. Geary told Rickards to post his pickets accordingly, paying special attention to the railroad junction at Wauhatchie.[26]

Rickards personally parceled out his companies to encircle the division bivouac. He placed three companies at the junction, two companies three-quarters of a mile out on the Kelley's Ferry road, two companies a half mile out on the valley road to Brown's Ferry, two companies to cover the ground between the camp and Lookout Creek, and the remaining company in the forest between Wauhatchie and the picket post on the Kelley's Ferry road. From each company, sentinels were pushed still farther out.

Restless and worried, Rickards stopped at every farmhouse in the neighborhood for information on the enemy. Without exception, the occupants assured him there were no Rebels between Wauhatchie and Lookout Mountain. Returning to camp, he stopped at the Rowden place, where the voluble woman of the house told him the truth: troops from Longstreet's corps had been there yesterday and were then lying on the east bank of Lookout Creek at the base of the mountain. Rickards grabbed her husband and dragged him to Geary's headquarters. After a few rough threats, Rickards convinced him to reveal the existence of a footbridge over the creek and the presence of enemy troops just beyond it, a mere mile and a half from Geary's camp.

Rickards galloped out to his companies on the Brown's Ferry road. Riding on in the dark, he found the trail leading to the footbridge and posted a squad to cover it. A bit calmer now, Rickards rode back toward Wauhatchie for a final inspection of his picket stations. In the chill, moonlit darkness, all was quiet. Rickards spoke a few words of encouragement to the shivering soldiers at the junction, then started for camp at 10:30 P.M. to snatch a few minutes' rest. Drowsing in the saddle, he was snapped awake by the crack of rifle shots from the direction of his picket post near the bridge over Lookout Creek.[27]

# CHAPTER SEVEN

# THE CHANCE OF SUCCESS MAY BE CALCULATED AT ZERO

THERE WAS no meeting of the minds between Bragg and Longstreet during their frigid morning encounter of 27 October atop Lookout Mountain. Watching Hooker move inexorably down the valley, Bragg renewed his demand that Longstreet launch an attack against Brown's Ferry, even though it now would mean taking on two additional divisions. Longstreet muttered his assent, begging leave to make the attack by moonlight that night. Bragg agreed—"anything to accomplish the purpose," recalled Liddell—and rode off.

Sadly, as the historian Thomas Connelly incisively observed, "so strong was the resentment between the two officers that they could not even carry through a plan to retrieve the lost situation. . . . There was total confusion as to the objective of the attack and the number of troops Longstreet was to use."[1]

No sooner had Bragg left than Longstreet lost whatever interest, feigned or real, he may have had in making the attack. So complete was his distaste for the plan that he failed during the course of the day to notify Law, whose brigade, being nearest the enemy, would play a key role in any assault, that he should prepare for action at dark. Longstreet probably would have ignored Bragg's order altogether, as he had disregarded his earlier commands, had it not been for Hooker's cavalier deployment of Geary's division. Loitering about Sunset Rock in the waning light of the late autumn afternoon, Longstreet was startled to see what he assessed to be the Yankee rear guard, burdened with a large wagon train, stop and bivouac "immediately in front of the point upon which we stood."[2]

At that moment, Longstreet conceived a plan of his own. He would indeed attack: not the Federal main body at Brown's Ferry, as Bragg had demanded, but the temptingly isolated little force and its wagons at Wauhatchie. Alive with newfound vigor, he sent a courier to tell Micah Jenkins, just back from his short leave, to concentrate his remaining brigades at the eastern base of Lookout Mountain and to bring them over to join Law as soon as it was dark enough to hide their movements from the Yankee batteries on Moccasin Point.

Longstreet alleged that Jenkins joined him on Sunset Rock before dusk and that he explained in detail what he expected of the South Carolinian. With three of his four brigades, Jenkins was to occupy a tall, rough hill on the west bank of the Tennessee River between Lookout Creek and the Brown's Ferry road, in order to prevent Hooker from coming to the rescue of Geary, whom Jenkins was to attack with his remaining brigade. What, if any, other units Longstreet proposed to commit to the operation remains a mystery. Longstreet later insisted that Bragg was still with him on the mountain when he decided to attack Geary and that Bragg had promised to send McLaws's division over the mountain to support Jenkins. However, there is no contemporaneous evidence to substantiate either of Longstreet's claims. Also, it would have been contrary to military etiquette for Bragg to have assumed responsibility for McLaws's division, which belonged to Longstreet's corps.

Indeed, Longstreet's own messages to army headquarters belie his claims. They were addressed to Bragg, a good indication that Bragg was not with him. "There is another column and train just in sight. I hope to be able to attack it in flank soon after dark," he wrote Bragg after seeing Geary halt at Wauhatchie. Then, a little before 6:00 P.M., he sketched out his plan more fully, adding a plea for reinforcements: "I shall try and put Jenkins's brigade [then commanded by Colonel John Bratton] in upon the enemy's rear as soon as it is dark. If we do, we shall probably require more troops on the left of my line or in easy supporting distance of the left. I have given the order for the movement and in case there is no miscarriage of orders, Jenkins will make an attack about nine or ten to-night."

Pleased at the prospect of offensive action of any sort, Bragg consented to Longstreet's plan. Obviously troubled that Longstreet intended to attack with only Jenkins's command, Bragg reminded him that his entire corps—Jenkins's, McLaws's, and Walker's divisions—could be used in the operation. By way of encouragement, he also promised to place the nearest division of Breckinridge's corps at Longstreet's disposal. Regrettably, Bragg stopped short of issuing Longstreet explicit orders to attack with a larger force. Deeply disturbed by the tone of the incoming messages, Colonel Brent took a moment from his official duties to scribble in his journal: "Longstreet writes that he will put a brigade in rear of the enemy at dark and attack him. Should this effort to dislodge him fail I think we shall have to abandon this position."[3]

Brent's instincts were sound. Under the darkening shadows of Lookout Mountain, events were moving toward a tragic denouement. Not even Micah Jenkins fully understood what was expected of him—or what he truly was up against. Captain J. L. Coker, a staff officer who had been with the Sixth South Carolina when it was scattered by the Federal advance guard earlier that afternoon, arrived at division headquarters at sunset to report the encounter. There he found Jenkins issuing orders for the division to fall in. "He told me that his purpose was to cross with the division over Lookout Creek, and with one brigade pass behind a hill up the valley to capture a large wagon train said to be there." Coker remonstrated in vain: "My report indicated that one brigade would be insufficient; that a heavy body of infantry with artillery was with the wagon train mentioned." The South Carolinian was unconvinced, and he carried on with his preparations. If Jenkins indeed had viewed the enemy from atop Lookout Mountain, as Longstreet maintained he did, he had been woefully unobservant.[4]

Longstreet's planning was as erratic as his choice of units to carry out the operation was foolish. Between Jenkins and Law there existed a nasty rivalry that fast was deteriorating into mutual hatred. And, by now, Law was simmering with anger at Longstreet. Law's disgust at having had his repeated warnings of Federal intentions in Lookout Valley ignored was merely the final source of estrangement from his corps commander. The Alabamian had commanded Hood's old division after that general was wounded at Gettysburg and again after Hood lost his leg at Chickamauga. As the ranking brigadier general among the brigades that had fought in all its recent battles, Law naturally assumed permanent command of the division would devolve to him. However, Jenkins's brigade of South Carolinians, which had done garrison duty at Petersburg for nine months and had seen no real fighting since Antietam, was brought west and attached to the division after Chickamauga. Jenkins had date of rank on Law. Longstreet said he recommended to Davis during the president's visit to the army that Law be promoted to major general, but that Davis demurred. Longstreet, for his part, was unwilling to place Law over Jenkins; instead, he turned a blind eye to the tension that inevitably arose between the two. "Law, naturally, thought that he had deserved promotion, and considered himself unjustly kept out of it," explained Porter Alexander. "He would doubtless have made an excellent major general, and no brigadier in the army had fought more bravely. He considered General Longstreet responsible for the injustice being done him."[5]

Such was Law's state of mind when an aide handed him a terse note from Jenkins at sunset. "Let me know where to meet you after dark," was all it said. Meet him for what? "This was the first intimation I had that any offensive movement was contemplated on our part," Law later averred.

The two brigadier generals met shortly after nightfall. Both were young—Jenkins, twenty-seven, Law, only eight months older—and in the fire of their youth easily ruffled. Jenkins briefed Law on what was expected of him. With his own brigade, commanded by Colonel James Sheffield, and that of General Jerome Robertson, Law was to hold the high ground east of the Brown's Ferry road to slash at the flank of any Yankee column that might venture south to succor the force at Wauhatchie, which Jenkins would attack with his brigade under Colonel Bratton. Brigadier General Henry Benning's Georgia Brigade was to be held on Law's left, to reinforce Bratton as needed.[6]

Jenkins then made the mistake of asking Law what he thought of the plan. "I told him plainly that . . . as matters now stood, the Brown's Ferry force and that of Hooker having united, their numbers amounted to at least three times his own, which rendered the success of the attack more than doubtful," said Law. "And even if he gained a temporary success during the night, the light of the next morning would reveal his weakness, with a force of the enemy on both sides of him, each of which would be superior in numbers to his whole force. The chance of success may be calculated by anyone at all conversant with military affairs—and he would be quite safe in estimating them at zero."[7]

Law overestimated Geary's strength, but his points were cogent. He was wasting his breath nonetheless. The orders to proceed were positive, bristled Jenkins, who demanded that Law furnish him with two guides who knew the country to lead his troops across the creek. Law complied and watched Jenkins ride back to fetch Bratton's brigade. A few minutes later, Law led his own brigade over the creek and up the tangled, heavily wooded slope of the hill he was to hold. A drunken Yankee stumbled into his skirmish line, happy to submit to Law's interrogation. He was from Howard's corps, which was encamped just a half mile north of the point the Alabamian was to block, and a division and a half of Slocum's corps was following.[8]

Law's heart sank. Reluctantly he formed his line of battle on the designated hill and began to fortify it, shaking his skirmish line out onto the Brown's Ferry road. At about 10:00 P.M., "Polly" Robertson reported with his brigade. Law told him to hold his command in the open field behind the hill, both to act as a reserve and to watch the gap between Law's right and the river.

Law recrossed Lookout Creek to see Jenkins, perhaps hoping that the whole thing might yet be called off. On the contrary, said Jenkins, Bratton was just then crossing the creek, after which he would push forward along the line of the railroad until he made contact with the enemy. Benning was right behind him, ready to move into position on Law's left as soon as the way was clear. Jenkins again briefed Law: "If [Bratton] encountered only a small force, he was to pick it up. If the enemy proved too strong for him, he was to retire across the creek under cover of the line held by Benning. I was instructed to communicate with Benning and to control the road, so as to prevent reinforcements from moving up it toward the railroad, and in case Bratton's command had to retire to hold my position until he could withdraw his troops."[9]

Surprise obviously was crucial to the success of the enterprise. That was nearly lost at 10:30 P.M., when a 150-man patrol from the One Hundred Forty-first New York, sent forward from Brown's Ferry to reconnoiter Lookout Creek, stumbled upon Law's skirmishers. A few wild shots were exchanged in the darkness before the Confederates melted back into the timber.

This was the racket that had sent Colonel Rickards galloping to his outpost on the bridge trail, in the mistaken belief that his men were under attack. By the time Rickards reached the advance squad, his horse frothing and fagged, the forest to the north had fallen silent. Satisfied that nothing was amiss, the Pennsylvanian began a leisurely ride to camp.[10]

Geary had heard the scattered firing and assembled the division in a matter of minutes. Unsure from which direction the shooting emanated, he ordered the One Hundred Eleventh Pennsylvania out onto the Brown's Ferry road. There it formed, fronting east toward the shadowy base of Lookout Mountain. The next hour passed quietly, and Geary recalled the regiment, allowing the men to drift back into the woods to sleep.[11]

It was now nearly midnight. Long, dark clouds rolled over the valley, blanketing the moon and cutting visibility to less than one hundred yards. Thin moonbeams knifed their way now and then through the gloom, casting weird shadows across the fields around Wauhatchie. In the meadow behind Law's hill, Jenkins and his brigade commanders huddled in empty conversation, awaiting the arrival of McLaws's division.

Up on Sunset Rock, Longstreet had been waiting for the attack to begin. Growing impatient, he came down off the mountain to learn the reason for the delay. Here the story grows murky. In his memoirs, Longstreet said he met his assembled lieutenants, who told him that McLaws had not yet crossed the mountain. Then, said Longstreet, "under the impression that the other division commander [Jenkins] understood that the move had miscarried, I rode back to my head-quarters, failing to give countermanding orders. The gallant Jenkins . . . went to work in its execution by his single division." To excuse his own culpability, Longstreet of course insisted that Bragg had failed to send up McLaws as promised. Even if that claim were true, the crippled Colonel William Oates later wrote, it did not excuse Longstreet's failure to inform Jenkins, with whom he personally conversed, of his decision to call off the attack. "No greater remissness in a general was ever exhibited than Longstreet exhibited in allowing Jenkins to go with one division and attack two corps of the enemy. By his negligence the lives of brave men were sacrificed."[12]

Bratton's South Carolinians had no idea of the fate that awaited them. They stepped off gaily, believing that they were going out to capture a lightly guarded wagon train. The prospect of easy plunder gave the first moments of their advance an almost festive air.[13]

A few minutes after midnight, Bratton's skirmishers collided with Rickards's pickets along the bridge trail. They overran the outpost and drove in Companies C and G of the Twenty-ninth Pennsylvania, which Rickards had deployed across the Brown's Ferry road.

Bratton followed his skirmishers with only a portion of the brigade. Because Benning was still crossing the mountain, Bratton felt compelled to detach the Hampton Legion and the Sixth South Carolina—one-third of his effective force—to guard the ground on Law's left until Benning came up. With his remaining four regiments—the Second South Carolina Rifles, First South Carolina, Fifth South Carolina, and the Palmetto Sharpshooters—he drove up the road toward Wauhatchie, picking up winded stragglers from Rickards's shattered picket force along the way.[14]

In Geary's camp, bedlam reigned. Neither the earlier false alarm nor the careful precautions of Geary and Greene had prepared the Federals for the suddenness or ferocity of Bratton's attack. "The night was still and chilly and the men, roused suddenly from coveted sleep, were dazed and trembled from chilliness and the nervous strain induced by the unexpected situation," remembered the historian of the One Hundred Forty-ninth New York. "They were thoroughly surprised and unprepared for an enemy whose presence they could not divine."

Still, by and large the men moved quickly. The One Hundred Eleventh Pennsylvania of Cobham's brigade sprinted across the field and once again fell in along the Brown's Ferry road, facing east. But as the rifle fire from Bratton's rapidly nearing Rebels rolled down the valley, Geary realized that the Pennsylvanians were facing the wrong way. He hastily issued orders for them to change front to the north, which they did nicely. The right flank of the regiment now touched the railroad embankment and its front extended through the yard of the tiny Rowden cabin, in the cellar of which huddled fourteen frightened mountain folk. The One Hundred Ninth Pennsylvania hurried into place on the left of the One Hundred Eleventh, and the soldiers of both regiments fell to the ground to load their weapons. That done, they frantically tore apart the rail fence that bordered the field and stacked the rails into crude breastworks. On the knoll, Captain Charles Atwell had the four guns of Knap's battery loaded and primed. Beside him was Colonel Rickards, busy rallying the survivors of Companies C and G of his Twenty-ninth Pennsylvania in support of the battery.[15]

Thanks to the negligence of Colonel David Ireland, Geary's front as yet was too short to cover the Kelley's Ferry road. Flouting Greene's explicit order to bivouac the brigade fully dressed, he had allowed the men of his One Hundred Thirty-seventh New York to take off their shoes and loosen their belts. While Cobham's Pennsylvanians were ramming home their first rounds, Ireland's New Yorkers were still back in the woods tying their shoes. As the Pennsylvanians waited for their tardy comrades, they "could distinctly hear the tramp of men at the double quick across the open field in front of us," recalled General Greene's angry aide-de-camp and son, Lieutenant Albert Greene. "It was so dark that they could not be seen, but they seemed to know our position perfectly. We distinctly heard the command to those men, 'By the left flank. . . .'"[16]

The sudden roar of Knap's battery drowned out the rest of the command. "The flash of the four guns lighted up our whole front, showing for an instant the line coming toward us," said Lieutenant Greene. "Then in the darkness the flash of rebel muskets marked their line, and the bullets began to come."[17]

One of the first struck General Greene. It smashed into the left side of his face, shattering his upper jawbone and tearing out a chunk of his right cheek as it plowed through his mouth. Blood bubbled up in his throat. He slumped in the saddle and was led to his tent, dazed and unable to speak. Ironically, brigade command passed to the dilatory Ireland, the senior colonel present. At least Ireland now had his regiment in place across the Kelley's Ford road, which gave Geary's line the appearance of an obtuse angle.[18]

Both sides fought with brutal tenacity, the blackness of the night feeding their fear. With a persistence that eventually degenerated into tragic desperation, Colonel Bratton tried to maneuver his four regiments so as to somehow outflank his numerically equal foe. He spread his command out into a wide "V" that opened toward the Federals. "A hasty observation showed that there was considerable commotion in their camp," said Bratton. "Whether it was of preparation to receive or leave us I could not tell, but the hurrying hither and thither could be seen by the light of their camp fires, which they were then extinguishing." Despite the apparent confusion in the enemy's camp, the ferocity of their fire led Bratton wrongly to assume that he was outnumbered. Nevertheless, he chose to press the attack. Bratton hurled the Second South Carolina Rifles, First South Carolina, and Fifth South Carolina toward the long, bright sheets of flame that marked Geary's front and then sent the Palmetto Sharpshooters to swing around to the left and close in on the railroad at a point he correctly deduced lay beyond the Federal right flank. At the same time, he called up the Hampton Legion and ordered it into the swamp northwest of the Kelley's Ferry road to feel for the enemy's left flank.[19]

The three regiments committed to the frontal assault came within a stone's throw of Geary's line—"so close at hand it was difficult in the darkness to distinguish friend from foe," remembered a terrified New Yorker—before grinding to a halt on the north side of the stubble field. Both sides settled in for a deadly and rapid exchange of volleys that reduced the Rowden cabin to a pile of splinters. Frustrated in their advance, the South Carolinians took aim at the gunners and horses of Knap's battery, atop the knoll only two hundred yards away. As if to help the Rebels, the clouds parted and moonlight spilled over the knoll. The artillerymen were further betrayed by the flash of their own cannon. Cries of "Shoot the gunners! Pick off the artillerists!" passed along the Rebel line.

Their aim was good. Lieutenant Geary bent down to sight a cannon. He stood up again, yelled "Fire," then fell dead with a bullet between the eyes. Captain Atwell crumpled with a bullet in the spine and another in the hip. Twenty-two of forty-eight artillerymen were shot down, along with thirty-seven of their forty-eight horses. The surviving artillerymen shot off every round of canister on hand. Two guns were abandoned for want of ammunition, their crews consolidated to help serve the remaining two pieces. Major John Reynolds, the division chief of artillery, took command of the section still in service. As their casualties mounted, the gunners lost their composure. They aimed badly, throwing several shells into the midst of the One Hundred Eleventh Pennsylvania. "One of these took off the head of the intrepid Lieutenant Pettit, of Company B, and another tore the muscles from both legs of Lieutenant Albert Black, of Company K, which maimed him for life," lamented the regimental historian.[20]

Although he wrought destruction aplenty, Bratton made no real head-

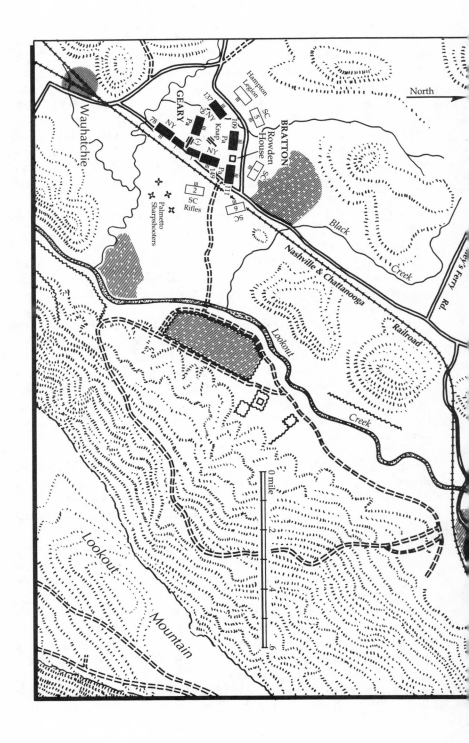

North

Wauhatchie

Hampton
Legion

GEARY

137 NY
29 NY          109
78        Pa Knap    Pa
NY          (-)

Pa
149 NY

2
SC
Rifles

Palmetto
Sharpshooters

SC
5

SC
1

BRATTON

Rowden
House

SC
7

111 Pa

9 SC

Black

Creek

Nashville & Chattanooga

Railroad

Lookout

Creek

Lookout

Mountain

0 mile

2

4

6

ey's Ferry Rd.

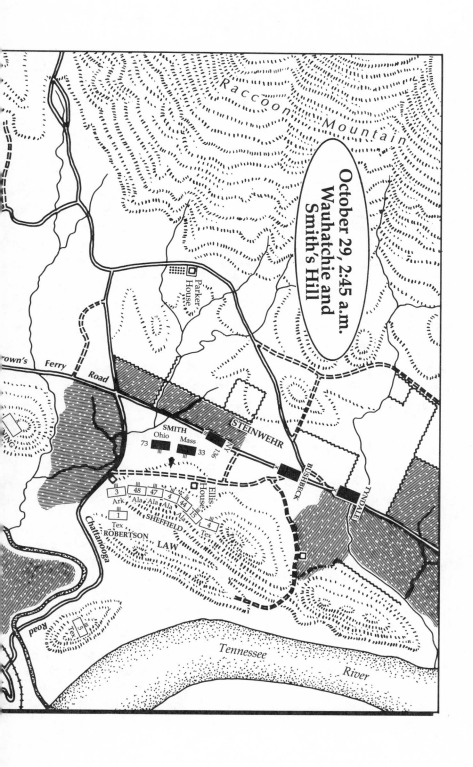

October 29, 2:45 a.m.
Wauhatchie and
Smith's Hill

Raccoon Mountain

Parker House

Brown's Ferry Road

STEINWEHR

SMITH
Ohio        Mass
73                    33
                    136

BUSHBECK

TYNDALE

Ellis House

3        48   47    4
Ark  Ala  Ala  Ala  44  75    4
     1                        Ala  Tex
    Tex              SHEFFIELD
ROBERTSON    LAW

Chattanooga

Tex

Road

Tennessee River

way against Geary's flanks. The Hampton Legion waded through the swamp beyond the Federal left, stepped across the Kelley's Ferry road, and descended into a deep gully. There, despite curses from their commander, Colonel Martin Gary, the South Carolinians preferred to stay. "Everyone was afraid so each one told the other to move forward," recalled Private E. T. Tollison. "I became disgusted at the cowardice shown by our men, so two other men and myself were the first to leave the gully."

Tollison and his comrades were amply rewarded for their daring. Directly ahead lay the Yankee wagon train. A few shots sufficed to scatter the train guards, some of whom hid beneath their blankets as the South Carolinians marched past. Likewise availing themselves of the darkness, scores of Confederates slipped from the ranks to loot the wagons. Mules broke loose from their teams and began braying and stomping about, causing what remained of Gary's line to unravel. A myth arose among the Federals that the bolting mules broke the Confederate attack, but the South Carolinians in fact recovered quickly from their surprise. Nevertheless, the mules had done a bit of good service: by the time Gary got his men reassembled and clear of the animals and the wagons, the One Hundred Thirty-seventh New York had arrived to challenge his further advance.

The dilatory New Yorkers redeemed themselves. As the South Carolinians passed their left flank, the adjutant of the One Hundred Thirty-seventh deftly pulled back the two left companies so as to enfilade the South Carolinians. Stunned by the unexpected fire on their flank, the Hampton Legion withdraw into the swamp.[21]

The mules actually had been rather indiscriminate in their charge. The teams of several ammunition wagons had turned away from Gary's South Carolinians and stampeded directly into the path of the One Hundred Forty-ninth New York, which had been following the One Hundred Thirty-seventh across the Rowden field. The startled New Yorkers parted ranks. A cavalcade of frightened mounted orderlies and three headquarters ambulances, bouncing out of control, completed the work. "The regiment was thus broken to pieces and disorganized, with no company formation, and all exposed to a terrific fire," confessed its commander, Lieutenant Colonel C. B. Randall, who spent the next hour rounding up his men.

By the time Randall rallied the regiment, Geary had discovered the threat the Palmetto Sharpshooters posed to his unguarded right, and he hurried the One Hundred Forty-ninth across the Rowden field with orders to form line of battle behind the railroad embankment. Troubled by a lingering fear for his rear, Geary sent the Seventy-eighth New York across the field as well, with instructions to form on the right of the One Hundred Forty-ninth, fronting toward the southeast.

That the New Yorkers would arrive in time was gravely in doubt. The Palmetto Sharpshooters had settled in on a gentle rise east of the rail-road embankment and were raking the exposed right flank of the One Hundred Eleventh Pennsylvania. The senior company commander drew in his and the two companies nearest him and tucked them behind the embankment to escape the fire, thus refusing the regiment's flank, but their numbers were too few to stop the South Carolinians, should they advance.[22]

Up on the knoll with Knap's battery, Colonel Rickards recognized the danger. He had restored order to Companies C and G of his Twenty-ninth Pennsylvania and was at Lieutenant Geary's side when he fell. Seeing the line of Rebels poised to attack, he yelled at Major Reynolds to take a cannon off the knoll and out across the railroad to enfilade the enemy's left flank. Reynolds protested: the Palmetto Sharpshooters surely would go after the gun; besides, he had no horses to pull it. Rickards brushed him aside. He called on his own two companies to drag the gun over the railroad tracks. They did, and two or three cannon blasts sufficed to sweep the confused South Carolinians from the hill-ock. For good measure, Rickards's little band chased the Rebels back into the forest east of the railroad. As they did, the One Hundred Forty-ninth New York fell in behind the embankment and fired three or four volleys to hurry along the South Carolinians.[23]

It was now nearly 3:00 A.M. Although frustrated in his attempts to turn the Federal flanks, Bratton gave no thought to breaking off the attack. When the Sixth South Carolina reported for duty, he committed it to the fight along the railroad. He reassembled the Palmetto Sharp-shooters, then prepared to launch a final, go-for-broke assault. "The position of things at this time was entirely favorable to a grand charge," he reported. "The enemy line of fire at this time was not more than three hundred to four hundred yards in length . . . the sparkling fire making a splendid pyrotechnic display."

And, as Bratton could not fail to note, that fire was weakening. "With the infantry the officers stripped the dead and wounded of their cap and cartridge boxes and carried them to the line, for the brigade[s] went into that wood with only sixty rounds, and there was no reserve supply," wrote Lieutenant Greene. Fumbling for their last cartridges, the men on the line prepared for the worst. "It looked as if the engagement would end in a hand-to-hand struggle," speculated the adjutant of the One Hundred Eleventh Pennsylvania as he watched his men crawl about in the dark rummaging the cartridge boxes of the dead.

The Pennsylvanian was wrong. At the very instant his confidence surged recklessly to an apex, Bratton was handed a note from Jenkins ordering him to withdraw. A strong Yankee column was pushing up the valley two miles in his rear, the message warned; it had engaged Law and, if successful, would cut off Bratton from the bridge over Lookout Creek. Bratton stuffed the note in his pocket and recalled his troops.[24]

The echoes of the first scattered volleys from Bratton's advance against Geary rang sharp and clear through the cold, crisp October night down Lookout Valley to the camp of Hooker's tired Easterners. Brigade and regimental commanders instinctively roused their troops and called them under arms, then waited expectantly for the command to move out.[25]

It came shortly. Startled by the firing, Hooker was in mortal terror that his earlier disregard of Geary's exposed position might now cost him the division. General Howard hardly had stepped out of his tent when an aide from Hooker galloped up bearing the frenetic message: "Hurry, or you cannot save Geary. He has been attacked." Howard sent orders to his division commanders, Schurz and Steinwehr, to move out at once in the direction of Wauhatchie. Too panicked to trust the chain of command, Hooker dispatched two aides directly to General Schurz, whose division was nearest the fighting, imploring him to hasten forward his lead brigade. He then summoned Schurz to his headquarters to repeat the order in person and enjoin him to "double-quick" his command the entire three miles to Wauhatchie.[26]

Carl Schurz had had little military experience before the war and an unfortunate service record to date, but he was quite capable of carrying out an order without having to hear it three times. Another of the many European emigrés holding high commands in the Union Army, the thirty-four-year-old Prussian hailed from a small village near Cologne. Bespectacled, possessing a long, sharp nose, small, piercing eyes, and wildly wavy hair, Schurz looked every bit the didactic radical Republican that he was. Educated at the University of Bonn, he had fled to France after a brief stint as a lieutenant in the Prussian army. France expelled him as an undesirable, and he lived briefly in England before making his way to the United States in 1852. Blessed with a gift for foreign languages and oratory, Schurz soon became an eloquent spokesman for the German-American community and an outspoken early advocate of abolition. His army commission was an acknowledgment of his political influence. Although his division had been routed both at Chancellorsville and Gettysburg, Schurz had considerable poise on the field of battle.[27]

It was nearly 1:30 A.M. before Schurz returned to his division. While Schurz's brigade commanders were waiting for their final marching orders, Steinwehr had gotten his small, two-brigade division on the road ahead of Schurz and already was on the move. Colonel Orland Smith's brigade took the lead, breaking into double-quick time as soon as it cleared Schurz's camp. Adolphus Bushbeck's brigade followed.

Schurz hurried to catch up. Galloping to the head of Brigadier General Hector Tyndale's brigade, he led it down the road, leaving his chief of staff to bring along the remaining two brigades of Colonels Wladimir Krzyzanowski and Frederick Hecker. Howard and his tiny cavalry escort fell in with Schurz, and together the two generals encouraged Tyndale's brigade forward.[28]

Hooker, meanwhile, had lost his grasp of a situation that his own meddling had muddled. He had, of course, intended that Schurz be the first to move to Geary's relief. Riding with Steinwehr, Hooker had no idea of the order of march and assumed Schurz to be in the lead. Thick woods closed in on the marching columns. Clouds rolled over the moon. Troops were invisible beyond sixty yards. The stage was set for a stumbling comedy.[29]

Colonel Orland Smith was a solid brigade commander whose troops had not endured the trouncing meted out to their German comrades at Chancellorsville. Nevertheless, Smith and the commanders of his three small regiments—which totaled no more than seven hundred riflemen— had ample cause to worry as they neared a darkly timbered hill a mile out of camp that stood to the left of the valley road, nearly astride their line of march. Trying to double-quick his column past its western base, Smith was fired on by Law's Alabama pickets lurking unseen in the woodline just beyond the road. He immediately halted and deployed his lead regiment, the Seventy-third Ohio, in line of battle from the road to the base of the hill, fronting south. Throwing forward skirmishers, Smith pushed on until, coming opposite the base of a hill that was to bear his name after the fight, the Seventy-third Ohio was hit in the left flank by a sharp volley from Law's strong skirmish line posted partway up the rugged hillside. The Ohioans scattered into the plowed field west of the road.[30]

There Smith reformed them. He wheeled the Seventy-third Ohio to the right, leading it across the road and into the tangled underbrush at the base of Smith's Hill, which rose sharply to a height of some two hundred feet in front of the Ohioans. He urged the Thirty-third Massachusetts out of route column and into line on the left of the Seventy-third; held his third regiment, the One Hundred Thirty-sixth New York, in reserve on the road; and then paused to await instructions. The time was nearly 2:30 A.M. Geary already had been fighting for two hours.[31]

Smith's orders came apace. General Howard, who was still a good quarter of a mile down the road with Schurz and Tyndale, had sent his aide-de-camp and brother, Major Charles Howard, off at a gallop to find out the reason for the shooting. After consulting with Smith, the major urged him to attack. Confirmatory orders came from Hooker, who had halted with his staff in a spongy field near the Ellis house.[32]

The unexpected opposition from Smith's Hill shook Hooker profoundly. Already convinced that Geary's division was on the brink of annihilation, Hooker now confronted the strong likelihood that the Rebels also were trying to wedge their way between his relieving column and Brown's Ferry. Hooker grew indecisive. Perhaps the attack on Geary was merely a diversion to lure the Eleventh Corps away from the ferry. The force on Smith's Hill suggested this might be the case. The hill stood just north of the main road to Chattanooga, commanding a quarter-mile gap through which an attacking Confederate force could be expected to penetrate the valley on the way north. Believing it imperative that Smith's Hill be secured, Hooker quite understandably abandoned his resolve to assist Geary with his entire command. Under the mistaken impression that Schurz was leading the march and thus well on his way to Geary, Hooker halted Steinwehr. He ordered Colonel Smith to charge the hill and told Steinwehr to file Bushbeck's brigade off the road in support.[33]

The Seventy-third Ohio and Thirty-third Massachusetts, numbering about 450 nervous rank and file, edged their way up the steep, snarled slope. "Of course we had no means of knowing how large a body of the enemy held the hill, neither did we know how near their lines would be to us when we should arrive at the top," recalled a member of the Thirty-third.[34]

It was better, perhaps, that they were ignorant of what lay ahead. Despite misgivings over his mission, Law had his brigade dug in and ready to receive the Federals. When Jenkins gave him Jerome Robertson's brigade to compensate for his exposed position, Law had turned over the command of his own brigade to Colonel James Sheffield. Sheffield had fed each regiment into line as it trudged up the reverse slope of Smith's Hill. He placed his own Forty-eighth Alabama on the military crest of the western side, its left flank about forty yards from the Brown's Ferry road. Each successive regiment filed off toward the right: the Forty-seventh Alabama fell in on the right of the Forty-eighth, next came the Fourth, then the Forty-fourth, and finally the Fifteenth Alabama. The hill crest bent away from the road toward the northeast, so that the right flank of the Fifteenth Alabama rested nearly two hundred yards from the road. After the last of his regiments came into line at about 1:15 A.M., Sheffield set the men to work throwing up breastworks of rails and logs. A snarl of vines and briars in their front served as a sort of natural abatis. To buttress Sheffield's left, Law asked Robertson to send forward two regiments. The forty-eight-year-old adopted Texan dispatched the Third Arkansas and First Texas, which extended Law's line to the Chattanooga road. At the same time, Robertson threw out pickets to watch the gap between Sheffield's right and the Tennessee River. He also moved the Fifth Texas back a few yards to a rise in the field, from which they could cover the bridge across Lookout Creek behind Law, just in case.[35]

Struggling through the dark, gasping for breath with every step because no one had given the standard order to ground knapsacks, Smith's bluecoats quickly became disordered amid the trees and underbrush. Instinctively they followed the contours of the hill in their ascent, so that the Thirty-third Massachusetts (which had only seven companies present) neared Sheffield's three right regiments first. The forest's black canopy frightened the Massachusetts skirmishers, and they squeezed off a few blind rounds into the darkness. "Don't fire on your own men," came a cry from in front. The skirmishers ceased firing, and the line pressed on. A few dozen men from the main line stumbled into a ravine running parallel to the crest, "the sides of which were almost perpendicular, slippery with leaves and clay, and covered with brush, and its appearance rendered still more formidable by the deceptive moonlight." Regimental alignment disappeared. Struggling out of the ravine individually or by squads, the New Englanders treaded on wearily. "Is that the Seventy-third," a winded officer called out into the gloom. "Yes," came a faceless reply, "what regiment is that?" "Thirty-third Massachusetts," answered the officer.

It was the old Rebel game of baiting the Yankees, lamented a survivor of Thirty-third, for in the next instant the woods to their front lit up with the flash of a thousand muskets. At a distance of just twenty yards, the first Rebel volley savaged the Thirty-third. The adjutant toppled from his horse dead. Colonel Adin Underwood fell, desperately wounded and beyond the reach of his men. Of the 250 who had started up the hill only minutes before, 60 were hit. The consequence of the sudden slaughter was predictable. "The terrible volley . . . so staggered the regiment and no officer taking command and rallying the men they all fell back to the foot of the hill," confessed a sergeant from Company I.[36]

The Seventy-third Ohio fared only slightly better. Forewarned of the

danger by the shattering volley that greeted the Thirty-third Massachusetts, the Ohioans dropped to the ground halfway up the summit to take
stock of the situation. The first Rebel volley passed harmlessly overhead. Regrettably, their commander ordered the men to push on. "We
rose up and went forward; nearer and nearer we came to the summit,
and the rebel fire grew heavier and more effective," recounted the regimental historian. "Finally, about forty paces from the hill-top, we came
out into more open ground, and by the clear moonlight they could see
our line advancing . . . and their whole line now opened on us a most
murderous fire."[37]

Confusion swept through the ranks of the Seventy-third. Since losing
contact with the Thirty-third Massachusetts during the ascent, no one
in the Seventy-third Ohio knew where that regiment had gone. When
from their left front came shouts of "Don't fire into your own men! Cease
firing! You are killing your own friends," which may or may not have
been the case, the Ohioans obliged. They backed off a few dozen yards
and took cover amid the underbrush while their commander, Major Samuel Hurst, sent an officer to look for the Thirty-third.[38]

The unexpected repulse of Smith threw Hooker, his staff, and his chief
lieutenants into a frenzy. Troop commanders pushed on or hesitated,
according to their natures. Bewildered staff officers, separated from their
superiors, issued orders recklessly. The valley road and soggy fields to
the west thronged with troops moving about without a clear purpose.

Carl Schurz chanced to pass Smith's Hill at the head of Tyndale's
brigade just as Smith's regiments took their first volleys on the summit. A few stray shots landed amid Schurz and his staff, toppling an aide
who was riding beside the Prussian. The lead regiment, the Forty-fifth
New York, stopped instinctively and fronted to the left to return the
fire. First Lieutenant Paul Oliver, an aide-de-camp to Hooker, galloped
up and ordered the men to cease firing and move off the road: they were
shooting into the backs of their own men. The New Yorkers trudged
obligingly into a thicket. Schurz extricated them quickly, filed his command back onto the road, and, having no orders to the contrary, resumed
the march toward Wauhatchie.[39]

Unbeknownst to Schurz, the commander of his second brigade did not
share his commitment to relieve Geary. While Schurz pushed south
with Tyndale, Colonel Krzyzanowski called a halt on the valley road,
near a crossroad a quarter mile northwest of Smith's Hill. Trailing Krzyzanowski, Colonel Hecker was forced to stop as well. When a staff officer reported that Krzyzanowski had paused of his own volition, Hecker
announced: "We have no orders to halt, and we will push ahead." He
led his brigade off the road and marched it through the fields to the right
of and past the second brigade, intent on rejoining Schurz.[40]

Just north of the crossroad, Hecker ran into Major Howard, who peremptorily ordered him to edge forward to the crossroad and there deploy fronting toward Smith's Hill, in order to reinforce the attack in that sector as necessary. Whether Major Howard was acting on his own or under instructions from his brother is unclear. Reluctantly, Hecker brought his command into line of battle.

Hooker himself rode up a few minutes later, at about 3:30 A.M. "What troops are these?" he snapped at Hecker. "Third brigade, third division, Eleventh Corps, sir," answered Hecker. Why had he stopped, Hooker demanded. At Major Howard's behest, replied Hecker. Increasingly preoccupied by the prospect of a Confederate counterthrust toward Brown's Ferry, Hooker approved Hecker's dispositions and told him to watch out for a possible attack down the valley as well. Noticing Krzyzanowski's brigade standing on the road a few hundred yards to the north, he asked Hecker to whom they belonged. Hecker answered. "You stay here, Colonel," Hooker barked, then rode off toward Krzyzanowski, so thoroughly distracted that the identity of the two brigades failed to register with him. In Hooker's troubled mind, Schurz was still marching at the double-quick with his entire division to Geary's relief.[41]

In reality, of course, only one brigade of the original two divisions Hooker had dispatched to Geary was then on the move toward Wauhatchie. Now even that small force was distracted from its purpose. Coming up opposite the first rise south of Smith's Hill, Schurz was flagged down once again by Lieutenant Oliver, who instructed him to deploy Tyndale's brigade and take the eminence, which was separated from Smith's Hill by a spongy field nearly a quarter mile wide, through which ran the Chattanooga road. The field and road were logical avenues of approach for a Confederate thrust toward Brown's Ferry and must be closed off, argued the lieutenant. Schurz, who had in the meantime learned from the ubiquitous Major Howard that his second and third brigades were halted nearly a mile behind him, remonstrated with Oliver. "I informed him expressly of the notice I had received about my other brigades, and that, if I placed the only brigade I had in hand on that hill, I would have no troops to send to Geary." Lieutenant Oliver insisted that Hooker wanted the hill occupied and repeated the order. "While this order struck me as contradictory to orders originally received, it struck, also, that circumstances might have changed," reflected Schurz, who could hear clearly the racket over on Smith's Hill. He stopped Tyndale, fronted his brigade toward what was to become known as Tyndale's Hill, and made ready to assault it.[42]

At this point, General Howard ceased to be a player in the dark comedy. Perhaps feeling his presence superfluous, he searched out Hooker and begged to be allowed to continue on his own. "With your approval, I will take the two companies of cavalry and push through to Wauhatchie," he pleaded. "All right, Howard," Hooker replied absentmindedly, "I shall be here to attend to this part of the field."[43]

The only officer above the rank of regimental commander who kept his head seems to have been Colonel Orland Smith. He was at the foot of the hill to greet the stunned survivors of the Thirty-third Massachusetts when they staggered and slipped down the slope. With an equanimity that did much to restore the shattered nerves of his Massachusetts men, Smith rode along their line and calmly announced: "We must take the hill at any cost. Now, when you reach the top again don't stop to fire but rush for them with the bayonet and yell for all you are worth at the same time. It will make them think you have had a reinforcement." The company commanders hesitated to obey the seemingly suicidal order. Finally a young second lieutenant stepped forward, waved his sword over his head, and told the men nearest him to come on. Cries of "Forward, boys, and avenge our colonel" rang along the line, and the Thirty-third started back up the slope.[44]

Smith had no intention of sending the men of the Thirty-third Massachusetts to their deaths. As they moved out, he instructed the One Hundred Thirty-sixth New York, his only remaining regiment, to file off to the road and ascend the hill on the left of the Thirty-third. With luck, the New Yorkers would take the Rebel line in the flank. General Steinwehr lent a hand. Drawing rein in front of the One Hundred Thirty-sixth, he asked in heavily accented English: "What regiment is dat?" Colonel James Wood told him. "That is a good line," he told Wood. Then, addressing the troops, he said: "We want you to take that hill. The rebels are on top of it. You go up. Don't you fire a gun. If you do, that will give them the range to shoot you. Don't say one word until you get right onto them, and then holler like the tuyfel [sic]. They will think the whole corps is behind you."[45]

The cold reality was quite different. Law had availed himself of the lull to strengthen his line, calling up Robertson's last uncommitted regiment, the Fourth Texas, and placing it on Sheffield's right to extend his line at the very point Colonel Wood's New Yorkers hoped to flank. The Alabamian now had perhaps two thousand men in his line to meet an attack by one-third that number.[46]

Numbers, however, meant little in the smoky darkness. The 190 survivors of the Thirty-third Massachusetts threw themselves against the right regiments of Sheffield's brigade a second time. At that moment, Colonel Sheffield made an egregious error. Robertson's pickets had reported the movement of the One Hundred Thirty-sixth New York off the road beyond Sheffield's right. To reinforce that flank, Sheffield drew three companies out of his front line, which opened a thirty-yard gap between the left of the Fifteenth Alabama and the right of the Forty-fourth Alabama. Enough troops from the Thirty-third Massachusetts hopped over this now undefended portion of the breastworks to throw the Forty-fourth Alabama into a confusion from which it never recovered. The commander of the left company of Fifteenth Alabama, however, drew in his line in time to cover his regiment's flank and enable the unit to hold. The Fourth Alabama also held on against the attack from its front, and the majority of the Thirty-third Massachusetts stopped short of the breastworks, compelling those in the gap, now dangerously exposed, to scamper back to their unit under fire.[47]

Matters were equally desperate on Smith's right, where the Seventy-third Ohio had managed to reestablish contact with the left flank of the Thirty-third Massachusetts. The Ohioans rejoined the assault, striking the Third Arkansas and Sheffield's left regiments. The slaughter was terrific. Nearly one-third of the Ohioans were cut down in a tangle of underbrush and fallen trees just short of the breastworks.

Once again, Smith's assault seemed doomed to fail. And it certainly would have, had Law not then given up the contest as lost. Staff officers were bringing in reports that suggested any further sacrifice of lives was pointless. One report, utterly baseless, told of a heavy Federal column moving south along the riverbank toward Law's right rear; another, this one accurate, said that Bratton had been repelled in his attack on Geary and was falling back over Lookout Creek. Since he no longer heard firing from the direction of Wauhatchie, Law concluded that the second report was true. He ordered Sheffield to pull his brigade off Smith's Hill and regroup alongside the Fifth Texas on a bald knob that covered the Chattanooga road at the point where it crossed Lookout Creek.

Law's decision was sound but his timing was terrible. The Alabamians abandoned their line just as the Thirty-third Massachusetts and Seventy-third Ohio launched a third assault. Most of the Alabamians got away safely if in confusion, but some two dozen stragglers were gathered in by the Federals who surged over the empty breastworks.[48]

The Yankees gave no thought to pursuit. "It was a very mixed state of affairs," jibed the absent Colonel William Oates. No one was quite sure what had happened. Troops from both sides groped about to find their commands. Several Rebels were captured through sheer bewilderment. Captain William Richardson, an eccentric but gifted company commander in Oates's Fifteenth Alabama who had never learned to read a compass, got separated from his men in the woods. Hearing voices, he walked right into a squad of Yankees. "Well, boys, that was a devil of a fright we got a while ago," he laughed, convinced he was among his own troops. A Federal laid his hand on Richardson's shoulder and claimed him as his prisoner. "What command is this?" asked the captain. When told he was among Yankees, Richardson protested vigorously: "Look here gentlemen, I am most egregiously mistaken. I thought this was the Fifteenth Alabama. By heavens, this ought not to count!" The Federals laughed and led him to the rear. As governor of Alabama years after the war, Oates visited Richardson, then a babbling inmate of a state insane asylum. "His mind was gone, and he was a pitiable object," said Oates sadly.[49]

Convinced that Bratton was safely over the bridge, Law drew the brigades of Sheffield and Robertson off the knob and recrossed the creek a few minutes before 4:00 A.M.[50]

Unfortunately, neither Law nor Sheffield had bothered to inform the Fourth Texas of the original order to quit Smith's Hill. With Federals combing the forest to their left rear, the Texans stood alone to confront the One Hundred Thirty-sixth New York, then edging its way up the northern slope. It was a fight neither side relished. Going up "was slow work, and we were in no hurry to get to the top," said Sergeant George Metcalf of Company D. Continued Metcalf:

All at once, we found ourselves within a rod of the rebel line, and as we came out of a thick growth of low bushes, I smelt the burnt powder. We gave a most unearthly yell. It was a yell of fright, of terror. We were face to face with death. We fired our guns and yelled, and roared and screamed. If the rebels were not frightened, I was. We ran toward them with our bayonets. They never stopped to ask who we were, or how we got there, or how long we had come to stay, or how many there were of us, or to bid us good-bye. They just ran. They left their guns, their axes, and shovels, and breastworks that they were building.[51]

Metcalf hardly exaggerated the completeness of the Fourth Texas's collapse. Sergeant J. B. Polley, describing from the Confederate perspective the moment when the two lines clashed, told a similar story. On the summit, just before the attack, "the cheerless gloom of an exceedingly great loneliness fell upon us like a pall," he wrote. "It grew intense when, not twenty feet away, we heard the laborious struggling and puffing of the Yankees as they climbed and pulled up the almost precipitous ascent, and became positively unbearable when a dozen or more bullets from the left whistled down the line and the mild beams of the full moon, glinting from what seemed to our agitated minds a hundred thousand bright gun barrels, revealed the near and dangerous presence of the hated foe."

Raked in the flank and hit from behind by volleys from the reformed Thirty-third Massachusetts and absorbing frontal fire from the One Hundred Thirty-sixth New York, the Texans took the only sensible course. "Then and there—deeming it braver to live than die—the officers and privates of the gallant and hitherto invincible Fourth Texas stood not upon the order of their going, but went with a clarity and unanimity truly remarkable, disappeared bodily, stampeded and plunged recklessly into the shadowy depths behind them, flight hastened by the loud huzzaing of the triumphant Yankees and the echoing volleys they poured into the tree tops high above the heads of their retreating antagonists," confessed Polley.[52]

The luckless Texans were the last across Lookout Creek. A few moments before the rout of the Fourth, Tyndale's brigade had crested the hill to the south just as Benning's Georgia brigade was marching down the reverse slope, having successfully covered the withdrawal of Bratton's brigade.

With Tyndale's Hill cleared at the cost of only one man wounded, General Schurz deployed skirmishers and rode back down the valley road to retrieve his errant brigades and resume the march to Wauhatchie. Instead, he ran into Hooker at the crossroads. The carrying of Smith's and Tyndale's hills had done little to settle Hooker's nerves. Shocked to see Schurz, whom he assumed to be at Wauhatchie with his division, Hooker upbraided him mercilessly. Schurz was at a loss to understand why. As he later testified, with commendable understatement: "It was not natural that General Hooker should have expected the same troops which were held at the cross-roads under his instructions, and with his knowledge, should at the same time march to the relief of Geary."

Of course it was not natural. Hooker was behaving irrationally, and the ominous silence from the direction of Wauhatchie only fed his anxiety. Startled and deeply offended, Schurz recalled the brigades of Krzyzanowski and Tyndale and, at 4:30 A.M., set out once again for Geary's camp—on the assumption it still existed.[53]

General Howard and his escort came within sight of Geary's lines shortly before 4:00 A.M. All was silent. Descrying the dim outlines of men moving about the fields to his front, Howard called a halt. "Who goes there," he challenged. "We are Stevens's men," came the reply. Not recognizing the name of the commander, Howard assumed them to be Rebels. He tried a ploy. "All right, have you whipped the Yankees?" The same voice called back: "We were on their flank, but our men in front have gone, and we cannot find our way." Howard's troopers silently encircled them, capturing the lot.

Howard rode on. He entered Geary's lines and dismounted beside the tent of General Greene, who lay on his cot, his face mangled and soaked in blood. Howard stooped down to whisper a few words of sympathy, then moved on to find Geary. It was an emotional meeting. "Geary's hand trembled, and with his tall, strong frame shook with emotion, as he held me by the hand and spoke of the death of his son, during that fearful night."[54]

Young Lieutenant Geary was one of 216 men lost by his father. Bratton had lost 356. It had been a senseless affair. Hooker had left Geary exposed in the valley and invited an attack to no good end. Longstreet had accepted the challenge with a force far too small to offer a reasonable chance of success.

Hooker fumbled for a way to cover up his error in judgment. In his report of the affair, he censured Schurz for not marching as ordered to Geary, but both General Grant and the court of inquiry that exonerated the Prussian understood where the real blame lay.

Colonel Wilson had left Hooker on the evening of the attack to warn Grant of the "disordered and scattered condition of Hooker's camp." The next morning, with a crutch slung over his saddle, Grant rode over the field of battle with Hooker. While Hooker waxed eloquent over the gallant stand of Geary, Grant simmered. Returning to headquarters, he confided to Dana that he would like to relieve Hooker, but preferred to have so serious a move come from the War Department. Still, there was much to be thankful for, as the deeply religious General Howard wrote his wife that morning: "God has been good and sparing and given us the victory and we have opened the river from Bridgeport almost to Chattanooga." Grant too would concede as much. "The Cracker Line" was opened, he later wrote, and "never afterward disturbed."[55]

# CHAPTER EIGHT

# A GOLDEN THREAD THROUGH
# THE TANGLED WEB

BRAGG was less charitable than Grant. Where the Ohioan was forgiving by nature and reluctant to move against an irritating subordinate, Bragg was merciless and quick to act. In the days following the
Wauhatchie fiasco, he looked about for a means to rid himself of the
irksome Longstreet.

Like Hooker, Longstreet tried to explain away his errors. Unlike
Hooker, who censured only Schurz, Longstreet cast a wide net of blame.
He accused Bragg of reneging on a purported promise to send McLaws
to reinforce Jenkins. Playing on the jealousy that existed between Jenkins and Law, he attributed the failure of Bratton's attack not on the
numerical weakness of the assaulting force but rather on Law's inability to hold off Hooker's reinforcing column. As he wrote in his sorry
endorsement of Jenkins's cantankerous report of the affair:

> The reports of Jenkins and Law conflict, each apparently claiming
> that the other was at fault . . . I endeavored to impress upon the minds
> of the officers the fact that one musket at night would make more noise
> than fifty during the day. The only weak point about us was the jeal-
> ousy between the two brigades already mentioned. This I considered,
> and with a momentary doubt about the propriety of executing the plan,
> but concluded after a moment's hesitation that my troops were so
> steady that they would hardly require commanders after they were once
> in position.
> The plan was very simple and very strong. Had we been able to ex-
> ecute promptly, or had Law pressed his advantage after the first or sec-
> ond repulse of the enemy, we should have had a great success at a very
> light cost and trouble.

In his memoirs, Longstreet was more blunt: There was ample evidence, he claimed, that Law had said "that he did not care to win General Jenkins's spurs as a major general."[1]

Of course all this was self-serving fiction, pure and simple. "Longstreet in direct violation of his orders assailed the enemy with only one brigade," countered Colonel Brent. More to the point, as the ever-astute Colonel Oates observed: "If the charges against General Law were true he should have been made to answer for his conduct without delay. Not so much for what he was alleged to have said, as for his alleged withdrawal of his command when most needed at the front. The fact that he never was arrested or tried is persuasive to my mind that the charges were not well founded."[2]

Despite his desire to be free of Longstreet, Bragg sank momentarily into despondency. The morning after the affair, he telegraphed Davis, insinuating "disobedience of orders and slowness of movements" on Longstreet's part and urging the president either to return to Chattanooga and help Bragg in another housecleaning or to relieve him. Davis wired back the next day a response as cloudy as the late autumn skies over Missionary Ridge. He thoroughly sustained Bragg and would not think of relieving him; neither, however, could he see any good to be gained by removing more of his lieutenants. Colonel Brent shared Bragg's depression. "Bragg will regret that he has not insisted on being relieved. It will not be in his power to suppress the jealousies and discontents which exist," Brent recorded in his diary on the dark and blustery afternoon of 30 October.[3]

Lieutenant General William Hardee, upon whom Davis had placed such high—and unrealistic—hopes of restoring harmony to the high command of the Army of Tennessee, reported to headquarters on Halloween morning. Bragg immediately assigned him to the command of Polk's old corps and asked him to ride over to Lookout Mountain to assess the chances for retaking Lookout Valley. Hardee obeyed and, joined by Longstreet and Breckinridge, ventured out to the point. It was bitter cold but clear. The generals had an unimpeded view into the valley, where Hooker now had his entire command entrenched in a long continuous line from a point one mile west of Wauhatchie virtually to the bank of Lookout Creek. Brown's Ferry was guarded now by three brigades, Hazen and Turchin having been reinforced by the brigade of Brigadier General Walter Whitaker. Micah Jenkins's scouts estimated the combined Federal force at twenty thousand. Federal artillery on Moccasin Point dominated the only road around the face of the mountain open to the Confederates.

A cursory look at the blue carpet in the valley convinced Hardee that an attack was impossible, an opinion Longstreet and Breckinridge heartily endorsed.[4]

Bragg's order to Hardee to devise a means to regain the valley was something of a cruel joke, the product of the North Carolinian's tired and tormented mind. While Hardee, Breckinridge, and Longstreet shivered atop Lookout Mountain, groping for a plan to oust Hooker, Bragg was briefing his staff on an entirely different course of action, one that would prove the grandest strategic blunder of the campaign.

Two days earlier, President Davis had reminded Bragg that "the period most favorable for actual operations is rapidly passing away." Rather insouciantly, he suggested that, should the tentative plan to operate against Bridgeport prove impractical (which, with Hooker comfortably settled in Lookout Valley, it already was), Bragg should send Longstreet with his two divisions from the Army of Northern Virginia into East Tennessee to clear out Burnside. This done, Longstreet would be well situated to return to Virginia, where Robert E. Lee was reminding Davis of his urgent need for Longstreet and his fifteen thousand troops. To compensate for the loss of Longstreet's corps, Davis promised Bragg that Hardee would bring with him "two good brigades" from Mississippi.[5]

Davis's suggestion that Bragg detach Longstreet was quixotic, reflecting both his lack of appreciation of the gravity of the Union buildup at Chattanooga and the degree to which he was swayed by Robert E. Lee. Bragg was in a position to know better. Stephen Dill Lee was keeping Bragg closely apprised of the progress of Sherman's powerful columns, which were then in the neighborhood of Tuscumbia, Alabama. Equally important, Bragg already had one division, that of Carter Stevenson, in East Tennessee and was about to send off Cheatham's from the right of the line on Missionary Ridge. That would place eleven thousand men in the long valley between Chattanooga and Knoxville, surely enough to hold the timid Burnside at bay. Stevenson's troops had operated in the region before, knew the country, and had their own transportation. Longstreet, on the other hand, knew little of East Tennessee, had no maps, and had left his wagons in Virginia on coming west. Finally, Longstreet's corps held the far left of Bragg's line; those of Hardee on the right were just a five-mile march from Tyner's Station, the starting point for any transfer into East Tennessee, and thus could make the move with far less disturbance to the Confederate defenses.[6]

But Bragg was beyond the force of logical persuasion. Repossessed of his stubborn energy, he was ready to act. As he confided to St. John Liddell, he wanted to get rid of Longstreet and, somewhat cynically, see what the egotistical Georgian "could do on his own resources."[7]

On 3 November, he called his corps commanders together, ostensibly for a council of war. Longstreet had heard rumors that he was to be sent off, but he was unprepared for the finality of Bragg's decision. Longstreet urged a withdrawal from the Chattanooga front and a movement either across the Tennessee River at Bridgeport, which would effectively bypass Hooker's corps, or thirty miles to the south to Dalton, from which a strong force could be detailed to strike Burnside without risk to the rest of the army. Bragg rebuffed him. Hardee (although he later denied it) meekly supported the Georgian: "I don't think that that is a bad idea of Longstreet's," he began, only to be cut off by Bragg. Longstreet was to move out immediately, his object being "to drive Burnside out of East Tennessee first, or better, to capture or destroy him" and to repair the railroad as far as Loudon. Along the way, he would be joined by Wheeler's cavalry. Bragg would order Stevenson and Cheatham to return to Chattanooga at once, making a net loss to the army of about four thousand infantry and nearly all of its remaining cavalry. The question of when, or if, Longstreet was to return remained undecided.[8]

The council adjourned. Few were sorry to see Longstreet go; "I do not think that the impression he made in the West was a very favorable one," recalled the fair-minded Brigadier General Arthur Manigault. All but Bragg, however, seemed deeply troubled by even a small diminution of the army in the face of the obvious Federal buildup at Chattanooga and by the wild reshuffling of forces along the line that Longstreet's departure from the left would necessitate. Bragg's determination to hold the Chattanooga front at all, now that Lookout Valley had been lost, struck most as foolhardy. When he first learned of Bragg's scheme, even the loyal Colonel Brent had been moved to write in his journal: "Our position, it strikes me, is objectionable. A corps on the west bank of Chattanooga Creek, a swollen stream; our center composed of one corps and two divisions, on an extended single line; and two divisions in East Tennessee. . . . A golden thread through the tangled web would be hailed with joy."[9]

Longstreet certainly did not hold the thread. He left the army for Tyner's Station on 5 November bitter and bereft of hope. Before going, he scratched out his doubts in a letter to Buckner:

> When I heard the report around camp that I was to go into East Tennessee . . . I thought it possible that we might accomplish something by . . . the following plan: to withdraw from our present lines and the forces now in East Tennessee . . . and place our army in a strong concentrated position. The moment the army was together, make a detachment to move rapidly against Burnside and destroy him. Under present arrangements, however, the lines are to be held as they now are and the detachment is to be of say twelve thousand. We thus expose both to failure, and really take no chance to ourselves of great results.[10]

Bragg and Longstreet were not quite finished with their bickering. Arriving at Tyner's Station, Longstreet was startled by the poor quality and small number of ordnance and supply wagons Bragg had detailed for his use. He complained to Bragg, asking also that he be allowed to keep Stevenson's division so that he could meet Burnside on at least equal terms. Bragg dismissed his concerns about transportation, hinting that he move along the badly broken-up railroad line directly toward Knoxville or otherwise fend for himself, and denied his request for Stevenson's division. Over the next week, Longstreet kept badgering Bragg for more wagons to allow him to move cross-country to outflank Burnside, and for more troops. All the while, he moved slowly, encountering one obstacle after another. He had expected to find a commissary depot at Sweetwater to feed his corps, but learned with disgust that it had been ordered back to Chattanooga with Stevenson. Four days were lost in foraging. Not until 13 November, nearly two weeks after the plan for a swift strike against Burnside was laid out, did Longstreet reach Loudon, on the south bank of the Tennessee River. He was still twenty miles short of Knoxville. By then, Bragg and Longstreet, having grown frustrated with their unproductive exchange of letters, had all but lost touch with one another.[11]

Bragg had committed the most egregious error of his checkered career. In all too typical fashion, he had allowed rancor to crowd out rational thought. Without a coherent plan or even the desire for close coordination between the two segments, he had divided his army in the face of a now numerically superior foe who was about to receive even more reinforcements. Colonel Brent was on the verge of despair. "Can we stay here?" he pondered in his journal on 11 November, then answered himself: "I think not." Bragg, interested in the counsel of no one, thought otherwise.[12]

Grant passed the days following the fight at Wauhatchie far more productively than did his harrowed opposite. "Having got the Army of the Cumberland in a comfortable position, I now began to look after the remainder of my new command." Unremitting pressure from Washington "to do something for Burnside's relief" and his own lack of confidence in Burnside led him to turn his immediate attention to East Tennessee. Although many of his problems were creations of his own timid mind, Burnside did indeed face considerable obstacles, as Grant readily conceded. He was "in about as desperate a condition as the Army of the Cumberland had been, only he was not yet besieged. He was a hundred miles from the nearest possible base . . . and much farther from any railroad we had possession of. The roads back were over the mountain, and all supplies along the line had long since been exhausted."[13]

Grant had another, more selfish reason for feeling concern over Burnside's plight. As long as Burnside was relatively helpless, Grant's own left flank was in strategic peril. Should Bragg move between himself and Burnside, "it would greatly trouble us," he said, and "lead to the abandonment of much territory temporarily and to great loss of public property," meaning, of course, the abandonment of Chattanooga and of the loyal mountain country of East Tennessee, so dear to Lincoln. An offensive into Georgia would have to be postponed indefinitely. Although Grant's concerns seem to mitigate Bragg's error in splitting his army, Grant actually was giving Bragg credit for a strategic perspicacity that the weary North Carolinian did not then possess.[14]

Grant knew of the detachment of Stevenson's and Cheatham's divisions from in front of Chattanooga almost as soon as they occurred, as well as their recall and the subsequent departure of Longstreet for East Tennessee. However, he was at a loss how to respond. "We had not at Chattanooga animals to pull a single piece of artillery, much less a supply train. Reinforcements could not help Burnside, because he had neither supplies nor ammunition sufficient for them; hardly, indeed, bread and meat for the men he had," recalled Grant. "There was no relief possible for him except by expelling the enemy from Missionary Ridge and about Chattanooga." And this, as he told Burnside on 1 November, he was then in no position to do: "Thomas' command is not in condition to do more than make a demonstration in their immediate front. This will be done as soon as possible." Four days later, he was only slightly more sanguine. Sherman, he told Burnside, was at least a four days' march from Bridgeport. "Whether Thomas makes any demonstration before his arrival will depend on advice of the enemy's movements."[15]

That advice came the next day, and the ever-resourceful Baldy Smith offered a response. As he explained it:

> On the receipt of the information that Bragg had detached a force to attack Burnside, and also by reason of the fact that we had not in front of us sufficient space to make any manoeuvres, and that the enemy's line was near enough to us for a sudden dash and surprise, I thought it prudent to advance our picket lines, and suggested that, in connection with such a measure, Thomas should draw out his force, but only . . . to threaten the seizure of the northwest extremity of Missionary Ridge. No one knew better than myself that the Army of the Cumberland was at that time incapable of a sustained aggressive effort. . . . There was, however, a possibility that a demonstration might cause Bragg to order the troops, then but just started for East Tennessee, back to his aid. At any rate no harm could follow the outcome of this suggestion.[16]

Or so Smith thought. Grant, however, was under increased pressure from Washington, which "plied me with dispatches faster than ever, urging that something should be done for [Burnside's] relief." Extrapolating more from Smith's counsel than the Vermonter intended, on 7 November Grant ordered Thomas to launch a full-scale attack against the northern end of Missionary Ridge, "with all the force you can bring to bear against it." Should the attack succeed, Thomas was to "threaten, and even attack, if possible, the enemy's line of communications between Dalton and Cleveland." As to how Thomas might move so fast and far having lost nearly ten thousand animals to starvation, Grant offered the facile advice that "where there are not horses to move the artillery, mules must be taken from the teams or horses from ambulances; or, if necessary, officers dismounted and their horses taken." Grant was in no mood for delay or discussion. "Immediate preparations should be made to carry these directions into execution. The movement should not be made one moment later than to-morrow morning," he closed the order.[17]

Smith was mortified. "The whole idea seems to have a crudeness entirely out of place in the mind of a general commanding an army."[18]

Indeed, Grant blithely and egregiously had overestimated the combat readiness of the Army of the Cumberland. On 2 November, he wired Halleck that "steam boats ply regularly between Kelley's Ferry and Bridgeport, thus nearly settling the subsistence and forage problems." Such hopeful reports only fed Washington's expectation of and demand for an early movement.[19]

Quite to the contrary, Thomas's soldiers were still on partial rations; certainly they were too fagged from prolonged hunger to endure the stress of an offensive. The Cracker Line was open, but it would take time to overcome the shortages of the past month, made more acute because the chief commissary officer of the department had neglected to see to it that sufficient fodder for the animals was brought down from Nashville and stored at Stevenson. Two days before Grant issued his unexpected order, a soldier in the Ninety-fourth Ohio recorded in his diary: "Plenty of starvation within the camps—horses and mules dying every day. During the past week the men have received barely enough to keep them alive and on their feet." It was the same in almost every camp. "We drew six small crackers to the man to do one day and a half. The boys are . . . swearing about starving," noted an Indiana sergeant. The clerk of the Eighth Kansas roamed the streets of Chattanooga for something to eat and was happy to find a small pie for twenty-five cents; the regimental historian noted that the command was yet on one-third rations. Even Hooker's recently arrived troops over in Lookout Valley were hungry, as commissary stores intended for them were diverted to the Army of the Cumberland.[20]

Upon hearing of Grant's attack order, Smith sought out Thomas. The normally phlegmatic Virginian was badly shaken. "You must get that order for an advance countermanded; I shall lose my army," Thomas begged. Smith quickly disavowed any role in the order. He shared Thomas's concerns, Smith assured him, but was unable to come up with an excuse that would convince Grant to call off the attack. Perhaps a ride upriver, beyond Thomas's left, would provide a pretense.

Thomas agreed. Together they rode to a steep hill along the west bank of the Tennessee, opposite the mouth of South Chickamauga Creek, to see how far north Bragg's lines ran. "We satisfied ourselves that Bragg extended too far north for Thomas to hope to outflank him without jeopardizing the safety of his own lines," said Smith. While gathering the facts necessary to convince Grant to rescind the order, Smith's fertile mind envisioned a future opportunity. "I studied the ground carefully, for it seemed to offer a method of putting Sherman in to turn Bragg's right flank, which was the one to attack, for the purpose of separating him both from his troops in East Tennessee, and also from his own natural line of retreat."

The two returned to Chattanooga after dark on 7 November and went directly to Grant's headquarters. An immediate attack was out of the question, Smith told Grant. Grant's instincts were right, he went on, only the timing was wrong—everything must wait for Sherman. The ever-present Dana voiced his agreement with Smith. Thomas added, to Grant's evident annoyance, that "he could not move a single piece of artillery." He also expressed unwelcome doubts about the wisdom of the movement at all, stating his own preference for the seizure of Lookout Mountain.[21]

Grant ignored Thomas's latter suggestion but otherwise bowed to the advice of the Virginian and Smith. He countermanded the order, but not without harboring a suspicion that Thomas was stalling. Nearly two weeks later, still simmering, he wired Halleck a thinly veiled criticism of Thomas: "I have never felt such restlessness before as I have at the fixed and immovable condition of the Army of the Cumberland." The mutual distrust between Grant and Thomas deepened.[22]

"Nothing was left to be done but to answer Washington dispatches as best I could; urge Sherman forward, although he was making every effort to get forward, and encourage Burnside to hold on, assuring him that in a short time he would be relieved," Grant wrote in his *Memoirs*.[23]

In truth, Sherman needed little urging during his march across northern Mississippi and Alabama, which went well enough; Stephen Dill

Lee's cavalry harassed but could do nothing to stop the inevitable advance of twenty thousand infantry. "It is not villainous saltpetre that makes one's life so hard, but grub and mules. Still, we make it all right," Sherman wrote his friend, Rear Admiral David Porter, breezily from Iuka, Mississippi, on 27 October. That same day, a courier who had paddled down the Tennessee River from Chattanooga in a canoe handed Sherman new orders from Grant. He was to desist repairing the railroad in his rear, which was his present source of supply; it was a futile endeavor since marauding Rebel cavalry destroyed repairs as quickly as the Federals made them. Instead, Grant told him to detach Brigadier General Grenville Dodge's command of eight thousand men at Athens, Alabama, to set to work to rebuild damaged portions of the track from Nashville, which would have to feed not only the Army of the Cumberland and Hooker's detachment, but now Sherman's as well. Sherman was then to push on with the remainder of his command as quickly as possible across south central Tennessee to Stevenson, Alabama, and from there make his way across the river at Bridgeport and on to Chattanooga over the same route Hooker had taken.[24]

Sherman moved with commendable swiftness; that is, until the head of his column reached Fayetteville, Tennessee, on the morning of 8 November. There, on the bank of the Elk River, he and his command stood before the northern face of the ominously named Plateau of the Barrens, an extension of the Plateau of the Cumberland Mountains even more devoid of forage than the tortuous trails over Walden's Ridge earlier traversed by the trains of the Army of the Cumberland. Seventy miles of such terrain lay between the Army of the Tennessee and Stevenson as the crow flies—nearly one hundred should Sherman choose to follow the line of the railroad, which began at Fayetteville, dipped south in the barrens, turned east to Winchester, and then ran south to Stevenson.[25]

Sherman elected to follow the latter—and only truly practical—route. Once atop the plateau, the men of the Army of the Tennessee confronted the same sort of obstacles that had wrecked countless wagon trains of the Army of the Cumberland along Walden's Ridge. Passages from their diaries sound strikingly similar to those of their counterparts in Thomas's army who had braved the mountains. "There was no forage for beasts and in consequence a large number of mules died from starvation and overwork. It was no unusual sight to see trees as high as the animals could reach, barked and eaten for food," attested a member of the Fifty-third Ohio. Having already tramped over two hundred miles, the soldiers were ill-prepared for the hardships of this final stretch of their march. "We were among the picturesque foothills of the Cumberland range . . . but soldiers with blistering feet are rarely inspired with any sentimental glamour about their pathway, however romantic; and empty stomachs joined with weariness of body are not conducive to enthusiastic scenery," agreed a member of the Fifty-fifth Illinois. "The rations had become woefully deficient, and the incessant toil of the march began to wear upon men and animals."[26]

Five days were lost covering the sixty miles between Fayetteville and Winchester, the tail of Sherman's column not leaving the latter town until 13 November. Once beyond Winchester, the going grew even harder. Instead of a generally level plateau, the route was a series of precipitous ascents and dizzying declines, the slopes covered "with large stones smooth as ice," recalled a Wisconsin artilleryman. "The road was very stony and most of the horses poorly shod, very steep in places. . . . The general and staff were very much scared, it is said, and thought it not safe to ride up so they dismounted, lamenting our fate."[27]

Then, on 14 November, after a week of bright sunshine, the rains returned—hard and cold. Brigadier General Green Raum watched the men and horses of his brigade struggle through the beating rain and whipping wind over roads fast melting into mud: "The animals had to strain every nerve to drag the wagons, over the best part of the road, and when they reached the steepest places the teams were powerless to go forward; at such points groups of twenty or thirty men were assembled; the moment a wagon paused these men seized the wheels and other parts of the wagon and with shouts of encouragement to the team the impediment was overcome."[28]

As steadily as the rain came telegrams from Washington, exhorting Grant to action. Grant shared his deep concern with his friend Sherman: "The enemy have moved a great part of their force from this point toward Burnside. I am anxious to see your old corps here at the earliest moment," he had wired him on 7 November. Six days later, as the last of Sherman's troops left Winchester and his advance elements edged to within a mile of Stevenson, Grant ordered him to have his army assemble at Bridgeport—getting it "ready for moving as soon as possible"— and told the general himself to hurry ahead to Chattanooga to go over plans for offensive operations.[29]

Sherman acknowledged the order at 10:30 P.M. that night. Already at Bridgeport with his staff, Sherman was eager to accommodate his military benefactor. He climbed aboard a steamboat bound for Kelley's Ferry with supplies the next morning, 14 November. Disembarking at the ferry, he found a small group of orderlies and one of Grant's personal horses waiting for him. He mounted the prized animal and set off down the road for Chattanooga.[30]

# CHAPTER NINE

# THE CHAIR OF HONOR?

G RANT had plenty of time on his hands during the two weeks between the Wauhatchie fight and Sherman's arrival at Bridgeport. He had moved from Thomas's cramped—and inhospitable—headquarters into his own in the stately, two-story brick home of one of Chattanooga's leading citizens (and secessionists), James Whiteside. Now, in the evenings, he threw open the Whiteside house to his lieutenants. As Colonel Wilson recalled:

> While waiting for the completion of the road and the arrival of Sherman's army from Memphis, we had a period of rest at Chattanooga, and during the evenings it was customary for the generals to gather at our headquarters. Upon one of these occasions Thomas, Granger, Wood, Brannan, Smith, and several older regulars were gathered about the fire in Grant's sitting room, all official cares thrown aside and all formality discarded. While cracking jokes and telling stories of cadet and army life, it was pleasant to hear them calling each other by their nicknames. Even Thomas unbent and told his reminiscences with wit and good feeling. Both Grant and he, though noted for their capacity "to keep silent in seven languages," were interesting if not brilliant conversationalists upon such occasions.[1]

Neither did Grant have much of consequence to do during the days, apart from answering the War Department's ceaseless exhortations to action and encouraging Burnside to hold on a bit longer. After agreeing to postpone offensive operations until Sherman came up, Grant turned over to Smith and Thomas responsibility for developing the details of the plan that would place Sherman's army in a position to attack Bragg's right flank on the north end of Missionary Ridge. In so doing, he made it clear that no plan would be adopted until Sherman had had a chance to examine and approve it.[2]

Skeptical of the scheme, Thomas conceded the initiative to Smith, who seized it with his usual vigor. Beginning on the morning of 8 November, he made daily rides through the country north of Chattanooga, sometimes in the company of Thomas, systematically reconnoitering the ground from Brown's Ferry to the knoll opposite the mouth of South Chickamauga Creek.

Smith's careful analysis of the terrain revealed two facts of critical importance. First, although the enemy on Lookout Mountain would have a clear view of Sherman's army when it crossed the bridge at Brown's Ferry, the column would disappear from sight after it passed Moccasin Point and entered the range of foothills along the north bank of the river opposite Chattanooga. As Grant put it, the Rebels "would necessarily be at a loss to know whether they were moving to Knoxville or held on the north side of the river for future operations at Chattanooga." Second, Smith's study showed that the northern end of Missionary Ridge was lightly defended. Only a handful of cavalry pickets patrolled the Confederate side of the river from the mouth of South Chickamauga Creek to the right flank of Bragg's army.[3]

By the morning of 14 November, as Sherman was hopping aboard the steamboat at Bridgeport, the general plan of battle had taken shape. Subject to Sherman's blessing, it stood as follows: Roads were to be improved among the foothills north of Chattanooga to allow Sherman's troops to march rapidly to their crossing sites opposite South Chickamauga Creek. Smith, meanwhile, would assemble every available pontoon to ferry the soldiers across the river. Once over, Sherman was to launch the main attack against Bragg's right flank, pushing on along the railroad toward Cleveland to cut the Rebel line of communications. Simultaneously, Thomas would advance directly against Missionary Ridge to pin down the bulk of the Confederate forces. Reliable intelligence suggested that Bragg expected that any attack would come against his left flank. To encourage this misconception, when Sherman reached Whiteside's he was to divert his lead division in the direction of Trenton; with the rest of his army he would continue on toward Chattanooga over concealed roads. On the day of the attack—perhaps in deference to Thomas's desires—Hooker was to assault Lookout Mountain and, if possible, carry it and drive on to Rossville, to be poised to cut off a Confederate retreat southward.[4]

Sherman dismounted in front of the Whiteside house after sunset on the fourteenth. Grant's enthusiasm at seeing the general was in marked contrast to the cool reception Thomas had accorded Grant. Their easy banter and obvious intimacy must have made the Virginian uneasy. As the lanky Ohioan strode into the parlor, Grant hastily proffered him his own seat: "Take the chair of honor, Sherman." "The chair of honor? Oh, no! That belongs to you, general," demurred Sherman. "I don't forget, Sherman, to give proper respect to age," parried Grant. "Well, then, if you put it on that ground, I accept," laughed Sherman.[5]

General Howard was on hand. He watched with interest as the trio settled down to business:

> I had the opportunity of hearing the proposed campaign discussed as never before. Sherman spoke quickly, but evinced much previous knowledge and thought. Grant said that Sherman was accustomed to "bone" his campaigns, i.e., study them hard from morning till night.
>
> General Thomas furnished them the ammunition of knowledge, positive and abundant, of the surrounding regions of East Tennessee and Northern Georgia. General Grant appeared to listen with pleasant interest, and now and then made a pointed remark. Thomas was like the solid judge, confident and fixed in his knowledge of law; Sherman like the brilliant advocate; and Grant, rendering his verdicts like an intelligent jury.[6]

Grant's complete confidence in Sherman was obvious for all to see. Yet his friend was not himself. His soul ached from a deep personal tragedy that had shattered his facade of gritty manhood. In late September, after learning that he was to march his army to Rosecrans's succor, Sherman had hastily packed his family aboard a steamer at Vicksburg bound for Ohio; he would accompany them as far as Memphis. As the boat prepared to cast off, Sherman noticed that his son, ten-year-old Willie, was missing. The general had supposed Willie to be with his wife, Ellen; she assumed he was with the general. An officer of the Thirteenth United States Infantry, which had given Willie a sergeant's uniform and adopted him as one of its own, disembarked to look for him. A few minutes later he returned, leading the young boy who, all smiles, was carrying a small double-barreled shotgun with the pride of a soldier about to sail off on a grand adventure.

As the steamer puffed languidly up the hot, malarial river, Sherman passed the time pointing out to his family old campsites along the bank that his troops had occupied during the Vicksburg campaign. Glancing at Willie, he noticed the boy's face looked strangely pallid. Ellen hurried the child off to bed and army surgeons were summoned. Their diagnosis: a life-threatening case of typhoid fever.

Willie died twenty-four hours after the boat docked at Memphis. It was the most painful emotional blow of Sherman's life. His marriage had long been strained; he and Ellen had stayed together largely for the sake of their children. And of all their children, Willie was the general's favorite. He was "that child on whose future I based all the ambition I ever had." To Halleck, Sherman wired: "His loss is more to me than words can express."

The Thirteenth United States escorted the boy's body to the steamer *Gray Eagle* and Sherman watched the casket and the rest of his family cast off for home. That night he gave voice to his grief in a note of thanks to the commanding officer of the Thirteenth: "The child that bore my name and in whose future I reposed more confidence than I did in my own plan of life, now floats a mere corpse, seeking a grave in a different land, with a weeping mother, brother and sisters clustered about him. For myself I ask no sympathy. Oh, on I must go, to meet a soldier's fate." And on he went, but all the way to Chattanooga he was haunted by his dead son's face. "Sleeping, waking, everywhere I see poor little Willie," he wrote Ellen in one tortured letter. And in another: "Why was I not killed at Vicksburg and left Willie to grow up to care for you?" Such was the emotional state of the man upon whom Grant now placed all his hopes for victory.[7]

The conference adjourned with an agreement that Grant, Rawlins, Sherman, Thomas, and Smith would meet at dawn and ride out to the hill opposite South Chickamauga Creek from which the latter two generals earlier had "spied out the land."[8]

The quintet plus a few hangers-on departed Chattanooga as planned on the morning of 15 November. Leaving Grant and Thomas at the base of the hill, Smith and Sherman climbed to the top. Together they crept down the opposite slope to a fringe of trees along the riverbank, so near they could almost make out the conversation of the Rebel pickets on the far side. Smith pointed out the portion of Missionary Ridge that Sherman was to seize. Could the Ohioan carry it before Bragg was able to concentrate a force to resist him? Smith wondered. And, assuming he was over the river before daybreak, by what hour could he attack? Sherman swept the country with his field glass. For nearly half an hour he studied the land. Yes, he said at last, snapping the glass shut, he could take the ridge; what's more, he could seize it by 9:00 A.M. on the appointed morning.[9]

The party returned to headquarters. From points raised during the previous night's conference and the morning's ride, the general plan of battle was modified and the details fixed. Perhaps swayed by Sherman, who of course wanted every unit he could possibly muster to carry out his mission, Grant withdrew his support for Thomas's plan to take Lookout Mountain. "The possession of Lookout Mountain was of no special advantage to us now," Grant concluded. Besides, he later confessed, he failed to see the logic in Bragg's having occupied it in strength in the first place. "A hundred men could have held the summit against the assault of any number of men from the position Hooker occupied." Consequently, Grant assigned Howard's corps a supporting role. Howard was to cross the river at Brown's Ferry and hold himself in reserve north of the city, ready to reinforce either Sherman or Thomas. That would leave Hooker with Geary's small division and two brigades of Brigadier General Charles Cruft's division from the Army of the Cumberland for his now drastically diminished role of holding Lookout Valley.[10]

Sherman's successful crossing of the Tennessee River north of Chattanooga necessarily depended on great secrecy, preceded by exacting preparations. For the latter, Grant and Sherman looked to the architect of Brown's Ferry: Baldy Smith. Once again, he was up to the task. The Vermonter laid out for Sherman his concept of the operation. Sherman's command was to go into camp among the forested foothills north of Chattanooga, neatly hidden from view. One brigade was to encamp beside the mouth of North Chickamauga Creek. There Smith would assemble his flotilla of pontoons. Drawing upon the success of the Brown's Ferry operation, he would float this brigade downriver to secure a landing just below the mouth of South Chickamauga Creek. There engineers would throw across a bridge over which the rest of Sherman's force would cross.

As stated before, Sherman's immediate objective was to turn Bragg's flank, which meant seizing that portion of Missionary Ridge between Tunnel Hill and South Chickamauga Creek. If successful, Sherman also would gain control of the two railroads leading east out of Chattanooga. Loss of the rail lines would compel Bragg "either to weaken his lines elsewhere or lose his connection with his base at Chickamauga Station," said Grant. At best, it would force him to withdraw altogether.

The importance of the railroads hardly can be overstated. They were the arteries that pumped supplies critical to the survival of the Army of Tennessee from East Tennessee, northern Georgia, and beyond. The Chattanooga and Cleveland Railroad passed through Tunnel Hill by way of a passage that had been blasted through the rocky interior of Missionary Ridge in 1849. The track crossed South Chickamauga Creek about a mile and a half east of Missionary Ridge and continued east twenty miles to Cleveland. From there, the strategic line ran northward to Knoxville and then into southwestern Virginia. Even more significant was the Western and Atlantic Railroad, which threaded its way between the northern flank of Missionary Ridge and the bank of South Chickamauga Creek. It crossed the creek at nearly the same spot as the Chattanooga and Cleveland Railroad. Turning abruptly to the south and running through the Rebel commissary depot at Chickamauga Station, it continued on to Dalton, Georgia, then to Atlanta, and from there to the Southeastern seaboard.[11]

The ultimate goal of dislodging Bragg was momentarily buried under the weight of preliminary tasks. As Baldy Smith later explained it: "Roads had to be laid out among the hills, which were secure from the enemy's observation, the North Chickamauga Creek had to be cleared of trees, and made navigable and capable of holding all the boats; and the whole country put under guard to prevent information from being conveyed to the enemy."[12]

Well satisfied with the Vermonter's ability to pave the way for his command, Sherman hastened to return to his two corps, then closing in on Bridgeport. He galloped out of Chattanooga as soon as the high-ranking party returned from their ride of inspection, hoping to catch the steamboat on its return trip from Kelley's Ferry that evening.

He just missed it. Undaunted, he hunted up the nearest boat, which happened to be a large canoe. Sherman applied to the commanding officer at the ferry for four men to man it. With them, he started down the river at nightfall. He took a turn himself at the paddle to spell the tired soldiers, and about midnight they pulled ashore at Shellmound. There General Whitaker furnished him a fresh crew, and Sherman continued on through the frosty, fog-dampened night. He stepped aground at Bridgeport on the morning of 16 November, where he found his brother-in-law, Brigadier General Hugh Ewing, waiting for him with his, the lead division of the Army of the Tennessee.[13]

Not surprisingly, given Bragg's innate pessimism, the departure of the bothersome Longstreet did little to improve either his mood or his clarity of thought. Colonel Brent's counsel to the contrary notwithstanding, Bragg had decided to hold onto his line around Chattanooga, the strength or tactical value of which, now that Federal supplies and troops were flowing into the city unimpeded, was largely illusory. To do so, he had slightly under forty thousand infantry and only five hundred cavalry, which ruled out rapid reconnaissance beyond his flanks.[14]

Having at last given up Lookout Valley as lost, Bragg opted to defend the mountain itself. On 9 November, Hardee examined the mountain with Brigadier General John Jackson, temporarily in command of Cheatham's division while the Tennessean was on leave. It had fallen to Jackson to defend Lookout Mountain. Hardee, Jackson, and their staffs rode along the narrow bench that wrapped around the mountain below the jagged summit, searching for a defensible position.

Their reconnaissance gave them little comfort. On the bench, a few hundred feet southeast of the point of Lookout and near the base of the summit, stood the whitewashed frame house of Robert Cravens, the prosperous manager of the East Tennessee Iron Manufacturing Company. A few years before the war, Cravens had moved his family out of the city and, clearing a few acres, built his home on the mountain to escape the congestion and sooty smoke of his own iron foundries. Gathering near the long porch of the Cravens house, the two generals and their aides discussed what they had seen and groped for a solution. "No line to fight on was recommended by anyone present," recalled Jackson. "Indeed, it was agreed on all hands that the position was one extremely difficult of defense against a strong force of the enemy advancing under cover of a heavy fire."[15]

That fire would come from the Federal batteries on Moccasin Point, which had already torn a few holes in the Cravens house during their regular duels with Confederate artillery on the point. It was clear to Jackson, at least, that those same batteries could also sweep with impunity most of the bench. "In my judgment there was no place northwest of the Cravens house at which our infantry force could be held on the slope [i.e., bench] of the mountain," he declared. With the bench so vulnerable, Jackson saw no value in placing artillery there either. "If we were defeated on the slope the guns, as I thought, must inevitably be lost, from the impossibility of removing them under fire from their positions." As he saw it, the only hope—and it was a small one—for protecting the forces on the bench was to "place a gun in every available position on Lookout Point, and to sink the wheels or elevate the trails, so as to command the slope of the mountain. In addition to which I respectfully suggested that on the point a sharpshooter be placed wherever a man could stand, so as to annoy the flank of the enemy."[16]

Brigadier General John C. Moore, whose three Alabama regiments of Vicksburg parolees had come to Chattanooga with Hardee and been assigned to Cheatham's division, was even more skeptical than Jackson that the mountain could be held. "This position was a greatly exposed and badly protected key to General Bragg's whole line of operation . . . the weakest and most dangerously exposed point in his whole line of investment."[17]

Jackson at least had the satisfaction of being relieved of responsibility for defending the seemingly indefensible. On 12 November, Carter Stevenson and his division were transferred from the right of the Missionary Ridge line to Lookout Mountain, with orders to report to Hardee. Two days later, Bragg rode over the mountain himself to formally place Stevenson in command of the overall defense of Lookout and to clarify personally the line he expected to be taken up. "The line, as I understood it, passed from Lookout Point a little in rear of the Cravens house and Cravens house road, and thence to the precipitous rocks near the mouth of Chattanooga Creek," remembered Jackson, now a supernumerary on the mountain. "The engineers were put to work under someone's orders, whose I do not know, and fatigue parties furnished to them from my command, at their request."[18]

Stevenson placed his own three brigades, led by Brown, Pettus, and Cumming, atop the summit itself. As Jackson had suggested, sharpshooters were shaken out along the western edge, from the point southward for two miles; most of the division, however, made camp among the resort hotels and cottages of Summertown. To Jackson's division—which consisted of his own brigade and those of Walthall and Moore—went the thankless task of manning the line from the Cravens house down the side of the mountain to the mouth of Chattanooga Creek. Walker's reserve division was arrayed across the valley, from the mouth of the meandering creek to its west bank, a distance of one mile.

Looking at the pitiable state of his troops, Moore quickly gave up all hope of holding his part of the line near the Cravens house against a serious attack. After their exchange at Vicksburg, his Alabamians had been supplied with cast-off rifle-muskets, shoddy uniforms, and little else. All lacked tents, and few had even blankets. They shivered away the nights on the exposed northern slope of Lookout Mountain, where cold winds swirled among the slick, limestone boulders and frost shimmered on the crisp, rocky soil. Being newcomers to the army, the Alabamians also got the poorest rations, mostly rice and beans. Nearly a week passed before Moore was able to secure ammunition. That proved yet another bitter disappointment. "When we secured ammunition we found the cartridges either too large or too small for a number of the guns," he recalled thirty-three years later, none of his disgust mellowed with time. "When too small they could be inserted in the barrel and held in place by ramming leaves on top as wadding; but when a snugly fitting cartridge was inserted into a gun with a worthless lock spring the soldier frequently discovered it had become permanently lodged in the barrel, and some of those guns may remain loaded to this day."

Moore applied to corps and even army headquarters for better arms and ammunition and protested "against being assigned such an important and poorly protected position. All my efforts resulted only in an unfulfilled promise that the matter would be immediately attended to."[19]

Elsewhere along Bragg's tenuous front, his generals felt ample if not equally poignant reasons to complain. Breckinridge, in command of the center and right, was left to defend a position five miles long with just over sixteen thousand troops. After a bit of shuffling about, Stewart's division finally settled into position in the soggy fields of Chattanooga Valley, from the east bank of Chattanooga Creek to the base of Missionary Ridge. Bate's division and that of Patton Anderson were arrayed behind breastworks of logs and earth along the western base of the ridge. Cleburne's division, nominally under the command of Hardee, held the right just south of Tunnel Hill. Pickets from each command were shaken out a mile closer to the Federal entrenchments. A few batteries were left up on the ridge itself, but no one thought to dig them in.

Anderson was appalled at the sorry state of his sector. "This line of defense, following its sinuosities, was over two miles in length—nearly twice as long as the number of bayonets in the division could adequately defend."[20] One of his brigade commanders, Brigadier General Arthur Manigault, marveled at the steady buildup of Federal forces across the valley:

Such prisoners as we from time to time captured, gave a much worse account of matters for us than was agreeable to hear. They represented their supplies as ample, and the quality of their subsistence as good. Their works had long since been completed, and were of a most formidable character. Most of the timber on the ridge had been, by this time, cut away, used for fuel, building purposes, and breastworks at the foot of the hill. Such trees as were left standing had completely lost their leaves, and in the valley or level land below, the same condition of things existed, so that our view was uninterrupted. . . . At night just after dark, when all the camp fires were lighted, the effect was very grand and imposing, and such a one as had seldom been witnessed. Over and over again I spent an hour or more in the quiet of the evening on a large, prominent rock that jutted out from the face of the ridge, admiring this grand illumination, thinking of home, family, and friends, or speculating as to the future.[21]

Watching the ever-growing number of Federal campfires, many Confederate troops did more than just ruminate—they gave up the game as lost and walked across the valley under the cover of darkness to surrender. Desertions were a matter of grave and growing concern at army headquarters, but neither Colonel Brent, who noted the phenomenon with alarm in his journal, nor Bragg could think of any solution beyond issuing orders increasing the frequency of unit inspections and drills. Rather than discourage desertion or improve accountability, the morning formations only served to dishearten the stalwart by revealing new gaps in the ranks.[22]

The Federals received the line crossers with amazed delight. "The rebels manifested no disposition to fire on our pickets, but were soon anxious to know what treatment they would receive if they came over and gave themselves up," wrote the historian of the recently arrived Sixtieth New York, which picketed the west bank of Lookout Creek. "Desertions from their ranks soon became very frequent . . . they ranged from ten to seventy-five per day across our line alone, during the twenty days our regiment was on duty there. They were very anxious to see and converse with our officers, and manifested more confidence in their representations than they did in the statements of their own commanders. At night our men constructed rafts, which they would swing across the creek, and before morning would draw them back again, loaded with deserters."[23]

In Chattanooga Valley, the going was a bit tougher for prospective deserters. Recalled Levi Wagner of the First Ohio: "Our pickets and the Rebel pickets occupied the same field, perhaps forty rods apart. Our guns would easily carry that far, but we never molested each other, though after night, there were frequent shots from the Rebel pickets, though not intended for us. It always meant: 'Look out for a deserter,' for sometimes deserters from the Rebel army numbered a good many every night."[24]

The slow going of Sherman's army gave wavering Rebels ample time to contemplate desertion. The Ohioan had started promptly enough. He lost no time in pushing Ewing's division toward Trenton to make the agreed-upon demonstration against the Confederate left rear in Lookout Valley. Sherman's instructions to Ewing, which he issued just a few hours after stepping ashore at Bridgeport on 16 November, reflected the importance he and Grant attached to the movement:

> The Fifteenth Corps is destined for Chattanooga for offense, but an object is gained by threatening Trenton, as though this corps meditated to attack the enemy on Lookout by ascending at Trenton. But as soon as the other divisions have passed Whiteside's, I will send you an order quietly to retire and follow the other divisions of the corps.
>
> In the meantime, act as though you were the head of a strong column, waiting for the rear to close up. By this device, the enemy will strengthen that flank and weaken the other, of which we propose to take advantage. Do what you can to accomplish this end, using the head of your column, but leaving the rear at the head of the mountain, by which you descend to Trenton, and make plenty of fires on the mountain, as though a heavy force were collecting behind you.[25]

Sherman trusted Ewing implicitly. Although he had dropped out of the Military Academy on the eve of graduation in 1848 after failing his engineering exams, the thirty-seven-year-old Ohioan had distinguished himself in every engagement of the war to date. More important, he and

Sherman were intimate friends and foster brothers. When Sherman's father, then a justice of the Ohio Supreme Court, died suddenly in 1829, the family had been broken up and the children cared for by friends and relatives. Young William Tecumsah, then nine years old, was taken into the household of United States Senator Thomas Ewing. Although never formally adopted, he was raised as one of the family, growing up with Hugh. As adults, their relationship was cemented when Sherman married one of the Ewing girls.[26]

Ewing did not disappoint his brother-in-law. He had his entire division across the Tennessee River before the afternoon of 17 November, and his lead brigade reached Trenton the next morning. From there, Ewing sent heavy parties to reconnoiter up and down the valley and make as much of a commotion as possible. That night, his remaining brigades built campfires enough for a corps on the table of Sand Mountain and in the two gaps leading into the valley near Trenton.[27]

To Sherman's chagrin, the march of the main column from Bridgeport to Chattanooga did not proceed apace. Struggling along through cold rains and bitter winds over icy wagon roads, his three other divisions made miserable time between Winchester and Bridgeport. "This is perhaps the heaviest marching for the length of time on record," opined an Indiana soldier in a letter home. The "men were but scantily clothed, and hundreds of them without shoes or stockings, with the ground frozen and our marches usually commencing at daylight and ending at 8 or 9 o'clock at night."[28]

The division of Brigadier General John E. Smith—a former resident of Galena, Illinois, who had helped rescue Grant from obscurity by recommending him to Governor Yates for a regimental command at the outbreak of the war—trudged into Bridgeport shortly before noon on 15 November. Smith made camp there for two days, while foraging parties combed the area in an unrewarded search for forage for the famished mules and artillery horses, and a few fortunate units drew new clothing from the sadly depleted stock at the Bridgeport depot.[29] Brigadier General Morgan Smith's division reached Bridgeport on the afternoon of 17 November. Brigadier General Peter Osterhaus's division lagged even farther behind; at best, it was at least two days away from Bridgeport.[30]

Not until the morning of 18 November did the first regiments of John Smith's division cross the Bridgeport pontoon bridge over the Tennessee River. The going was slow. Narrow and shaky, the bridge consisted of scow boats anchored at sixteen-foot intervals with stringers laid between them. Twelve-foot planks were placed over the stringers. Infantry could cross safely at regular march time, but the artillery limbers, caissons, and supply wagons had to move at a crawl to avoid upsetting the boats. It was noon before all were over. The division covered just eleven miles more that day, halting for the night in the neighborhood of Shellmound under a drenching rain.[31]

Morgan Smith fared little better. After getting across the bridge on 19 November, he made only eight miles on the muddy road toward Shellmound. Osterhaus took his turn the next day, as the rains continued.[32]

Nature surely favored the Confederates at this juncture, but part of the blame for the delay during the final leg of the march rested squarely on Sherman's shoulders. Three weeks earlier, Thomas wisely had suggested to Hooker that he leave his wagons while he marched from Bridgeport to Chattanooga; whatever Hooker's shortcomings, he in turn had had the good sense to act on Thomas's recommendation. Sherman, however, decided to march with his trains.

It was a terrible miscalculation. As Dana reported to Washington with his usual candor: "A lamentable blunder has been committed in moving Sherman's forces from Bridgeport, with the enormous trains they brought from west Tennessee following in usual order in rear of each division, instead of moving all the troops and artillery first. Grant says the blunder is his; that he should have given Sherman explicit orders to leave his wagons behind; but I know that no one was so much astonished as Grant on learning they had not been left, even without such orders."[33]

Grant was beside himself. Burnside had fallen back onto his defenses at Knoxville with Longstreet in close pursuit. Although Burnside himself was confident he could resist at least a few days longer, the War Department was frantic for Grant to act. That, of course, he could not do without Sherman. James Wilson, newly promoted to brigadier general, saw Grant's frustration close up. "As everybody else had already reached the place assigned him, within striking distance of the enemy, Sherman's delays gave Grant great annoyance at the time, and had they not been warm friends might have led to sharp criticism and censure."[34]

Grant had hoped to begin offensive operations on Saturday, 21 November. By Friday evening, however, only one brigade of John Smith's division had crossed the pontoon bridge at Brown's Ferry; his other two brigades were strung out for six miles across Lookout Valley. Morgan Smith was a good fifteen miles short of the ferry, and the rains had forced him to bivouac early. Now, too, even Ewing disappointed, albeit through no fault of his own. The Ohioan, who was to have recalled his forces from around Trenton and marched down the valley on the twentieth, failed to receive the recall order until the morning of 21 November. The couriers bearing the order had stumbled upon Confederate picket posts and, in their haste to escape, had lost their way and ridden about aimlessly for nearly twelve hours.[35]

Bowing to the inevitable, Grant rescheduled the attack for 22 November. Nightfall of the twenty-first, however, found Sherman still unready. All of John Smith's division had crossed the Tennessee and gone into camp among the foothills north of Chattanooga, but Morgan Smith was only partially over, and Ewing's division had barely reached Hooker's line north of Wauhatchie.

Again nature played the role of spoiler. It had rained all day, churning the Tennessee River into a fast-rising, bubbling maelstrom. Waves lashed at the rickety pontoon bridge at Brown's Ferry, splitting it apart here and there. Columns of infantry, artillery, and wagons stacked up on the valley road while engineers patched up breaks amid the downpour. Grant's patience with his friend snapped. "I am directed by the general commanding to say that, in order to avoid delay, you will have your troops pass your transportation and move at once, leaving only a sufficient force to guard your trains," Rawlins wrote Sherman late in the day.[36]

Sherman's footsore and soaked soldiers found little in the greeting they received as they passed Hooker's camp that would encourage them to greater efforts. "Some of the men acted as if they were very glad we had come to help them and behaved themselves like gentlemen," remembered a member of the Fifth Iowa. "Others were very insulting. The worst of this class was the Thirty-third New Jersey (or as our boys call them from the trimming on their Zouave jackets, 'the red tape men'). One of them would say 'Now Grant expects to do big things as his Vicksburg gophers have come.' Another would say 'Yes, but how dirty and ragged they look, they ain't fit to be seen' (little thinking we were just getting in from one of the hardest trips of the whole war) and many other such remarks. To be sure we did not look well," conceded the Iowan, "our clothes were soiled and ragged and all were very weary." The contrast to the tidy rows of white tents, cleanly brushed coats, and fresh paper collars of the Eastern troops was painfully evident. Tired though they were, Sherman's men matched insult for insult. They derided their detractors as tin soldiers. "Oh look at their little caps. Oh how clean you look, do you have soap," they laughed. "What elegant corpses they'll make in those good clothes," sneered one Illinoisan as he passed a squad of Easterners.[37]

The Westerners of Hazen's brigade, however, saluted Sherman's veterans as kindred spirits. "Sherman's troops . . . all begrimed by their long march, came filing through our camps. To say they received a hearty welcome from the Army of the Cumberland is drawing it mildly. They were no paper collar soldiers," said Captain George Lewis of the One

Hundred Twenty-fourth Ohio.[38]

When Grant wrote Thomas that the attack would again have to be postponed—this time until Monday, 23 November—the Virginian took the opportunity to renew his earlier plea that Hooker be allowed to keep Howard's corps and attack Lookout Mountain in force. Thomas was worried that Sherman's three days of floundering about in Lookout Valley may have tipped Grant's hand, and that Bragg consequently would move to strengthen his right flank. Thomas argued also, and not unreasonably, that an attack against the Rebel left flank, if pushed beyond Rossville, would have the same effect of cutting off Bragg from his line of retreat.[39]

Grant had no interest in hearing Thomas's suggestion again: Sherman would make the main attack against the Rebel right, regardless of how long it took him to come up. He rejected Thomas's plan outright, and instead directed him to call Howard over the river and into his own lines south of the city quickly and ostentatiously, "thus attracting the attention of the enemy, with the intention of leading him to suppose that those troops he had observed were re-enforcing Chattanooga, and thereby concealed the real movement of Sherman," as Thomas himself explained the order.[40]

Grant and Thomas were to have their share of disagreements during the course of the campaign, leading Grant ultimately to slight Thomas's role in the climactic battles, but in this instance Grant's judgment was the more sound. Bragg had done nothing to strengthen his right; Ewing's display in the upper Lookout Valley had deceived him. On 18 November, as the first of Ewing's Federals showed themselves atop Sand Mountain, Bragg directed Hardee to hurry John C. Brown's brigade southward from its camp near Summertown to watch the mountain passes near Trenton, and he sent three hundred of his five hundred available cavalry galloping ten miles farther south to watch Johnson's Crook.[41]

Two days later, Bragg wrote President Davis of his conviction that Lookout Mountain was in peril: "Sherman's force has arrived, and a movement on our left is indicated." Despite the obvious accretion of Federal arms, Bragg had no intention of withdrawing. Instead, he asked Davis to coerce Joseph Johnston into sending him reinforcements from Mississippi. He closed his note with a pathetic bit of posturing: "Our fate may be decided here, and the enemy is at least double our strength."[42]

Meanwhile, Bragg asked his commander on Lookout Mountain, Carter Stevenson, to do the impossible. Stevenson, with his three brigades on the summit, was to build rifle pits to cover the entire twenty miles from the point of the mountain to Johnson's Crook. Hardee and Stevenson quietly pocketed the order, and instead parceled out reconnaissance parties from Brown's brigade and the cavalry into the upper valley. Not until midafternoon on 22 November, when the scouting parties reported the movement of Ewing's division away from Trenton and down the valley toward Brown's Ferry, did Bragg conclude that the threat to his left was a mere feint.[43]

Next came reports of the crossing of Sherman's main body and of Howard's corps at Brown's Ferry. Again, Bragg misjudged the Federal objective. He did not, as Grant had hoped he would, mistake Howard's troops marching into the Chattanooga entrenchments for Sherman's army. Bragg knew full well that the Ohioan's column had disappeared into the hills north of the city. Where he erred was in divining their objective. He assumed correctly that Grant was trying to drive a wedge between his army and Longstreet's corps, but he guessed wrong as to where it would be driven. Swayed by Longstreet's incessant demand for more troops to battle Burnside and by rumors (perhaps generated by Longstreet's own scouts) of a movement against the Georgian's left and rear, he concluded that Grant was sending Sherman against Longstreet, rather than to strike his own right flank. Acting on this assumption, Bragg weakened his attenuated lines even more. Late on the afternoon of 22 November, he surprised Pat Cleburne by ordering him to withdraw his own and Buckner's divisions from the line at once, march over Missionary Ridge to Chickamauga Station, and there board cars to join Longstreet.[44]

In a word, Bragg had opted to slice away eleven thousand more men from his small army at precisely the moment Sherman was reinforcing Grant with nearly twice that number.

## CHAPTER TEN

# A VERY GALLANT THING

COLONEL Aquila Wiley of the Forty-first Ohio squinted through the fast-gathering twilight at a surprising sight. Hazen's brigade recently had returned from Brown's Ferry to its proper place in the division line near the large redoubt named Fort Wood, in honor of division commander Thomas J. Wood. As commander of the brigade grand guard, on 22 November, it was Wiley's duty to visit the picket posts regularly and to report anything out of the ordinary. What he now descried certainly qualified as odd. "There is a general movement perceptible in our immediate front," he wrote Hazen. "Three columns are visible moving up Missionary Ridge on three different roads. One column is followed by a train of about fifteen wagons. I should think the columns consist of at least a brigade of 1,000 men each." Wiley also personally reported the movement to General Wood, who chanced to be General Officer-of-the-Day. Wood too had been watching the "singular and mysterious" movements across the valley.[1]

Wood and Wiley had witnessed the withdrawal of Cleburne's division. They reported the sighting through the chain of command to Grant's headquarters, although neither had an inkling of the destination of the departing Rebels; Wiley conjectured that they merely were going into camp behind the crest of the ridge. Two war-weary deserters from Cleburne's division wandered into Wiley's lines at midnight with a possible—and, if true, most welcome—answer. The Confederate army was falling back, they told him; the troops he had seen passing over the ridge were going to Chickamauga Station. Camp rumor mongers, they added, had speculated that nothing but picket posts would be left along Missionary Ridge by sunset on 23 November. At 3:30 A.M., Wood reported their story.[2]

Back in Chattanooga, Grant and his staff were awake to read the reports. They took them seriously. Wood's messages were the last—and strongest—of several mutually corroborating bits of intelligence received at headquarters during the past forty-eight hours that suggested something was in the air across the valley. The first came on the evening of 20 November, when under a flag of truce Bragg sent Grant an odd exhortation. It read as follows:

> Headquarters Army of Tennessee
> In the Field, November 20, 1863
>
> Maj. Gen. U. S. Grant,
> Commanding U.S. Forces, &c, Chattanooga:
> GENERAL: As there may still be some non-combatants in Chattanooga, I deem it proper to notify you that prudence would dictate their early withdrawal.
> I am general, very respectfully, your obedient servant.
>
> BRAXTON BRAGG,
> General Commanding

"Of course I understood that this was a device intended to deceive; but I did not know what the intended deception was," remembered Grant. He got a good clue on the morning of the twenty-second, when Phil Sheridan forwarded the statement of a lieutenant of the Thirty-seventh Tennessee Infantry, who had deserted the night before. According to the Rebel subaltern, Buckner's and Anderson's divisions had left on 20 November for McLemore's Cove, south of the old Chickamauga battlefield. (That, Sheridan added parenthetically, would be a logical destination for a force moving to cut off Sherman in Lookout Valley.) A general move was in the offing, the Tennessean went on: baggage was being reduced and cooked rations issued.[3]

Grant was interested but not yet convinced. Wood's reports, however, induced him to act. If the Rebel army was withdrawing, Grant reasoned, it was imperative that he disrupt Bragg's movement to prevent him from reinforcing Longstreet. Before dawn, he instructed Thomas to drive the enemy pickets from his front in order to force the Confederates to reveal the strength of their main line. "The truth or falsity of the deserters who came in last night, stating that Bragg had fallen back, should be ascertained at once. If he is really falling back, Sherman can commence at once laying his pontoon trains, and we can save a day," Grant explained.[4]

Since the best evidence of the enemy's departure had come from Wood's sector, Thomas charged him with conducting the reconnaissance. Wood's instructions were unambiguous: They "directed a reconnaissance in force—nothing more. It was not expected there would be a collision with the enemy. Furthermore, the verbal instructions from General Thomas and General Granger directed the return of my division to its fortifications of Chattanooga when the reconnaissance was completed."[5]

Daylight on Monday, 23 November, revealed the immediate objective of Wood's reconnaissance: a steep, craggy knoll, two thousand yards east of Fort Wood, known as Orchard Knob. Rising sharply one hundred feet above the Chattanooga Valley, the knob was covered with a liberal growth of small trees and a line of rifle pits occupied by Rebel picket reserves. A patchwork of little earthen mounds, thrown up to cover the enemy's most advanced picket posts, checkered the base of Orchard Knob. A belt of timber, extending from the foot of the knob nearly a quarter of a mile west into the valley, partially concealed the mounds, which one Federal staff officer likened to "an over-grown prairie dog village." Between the edge of the timber and Wood's own lines, however, the ground was open. Not a tree, fence, or other obstacle—except the bed of the Western and Atlantic Railroad—stood in the way of an advance.

Orchard Knob was the strongest but by no means only improved position along the Confederate picket line. To its right (from the Federal perspective), a rocky, wooded ridge ran a few hundred yards toward the southwest. Not quite as high as the knob, it too bristled with breastworks and rifle pits. To the left of Orchard Knob, a long line of rifle pits extended northeast across the valley all the way to the Tennessee River. As Wood put it, "Orchard Knob was the citadel of this line of entrenchments."[6]

The order to fall in found Wood's men anxious to advance. After nearly two months of hunger, cold, and boredom, any movement was welcome. Although a bit weak, as most units were still on partial rations, the soldiers looked forward to proving themselves to Grant; camp gossip held that Grant despised the men of the Army of the Cumberland as fought out and afraid to take the offensive.

In expectation of Sherman's arrival, three days' cooked rations and one hundred rounds of ammunition had been distributed two days earlier, allowing units now to assemble rapidly. Shortly before noon, "the drums beat, the bugles blew three 'fall in' calls, company and regimental officers appeared among the men with but one sentence on their lips, 'fall in, men; fall in at once.' In a moment we were ready, the lines were formed, and we moved out upon the plain," marveled an Illinoisan.[7]

Wood called together his brigade commanders. He told Brigadier General August Willich to go straight for Orchard Knob, Hazen to charge the rifle pits along the low ridge to the right of it, and Sam Beatty to follow in reserve to support whichever of the two lead brigades might run into trouble. At the signal to advance, all were to move "with the utmost rapidity, so as to get as near as possible to the enemy's entrenchments at the earliest possible moment," he explained to his lieutenants, "for on this depended the success of the reconnaissance."

Wood looked on proudly. Under the chill but crystal blue autumn skies, his eight thousand infantrymen marched out of their entrenchments and formed ranks with parade-ground precision. Phil Sheridan's division, under orders to protect Wood's right flank in the event the enemy counterattacked down the Moore road, lined up with equal exactitude. Howard's Eleventh Corps marched out onto the plain to the left of Wood, stretching the Federal line to the bank of Citico Creek.[8]

Thomas was putting on a grand show. By 1:15 P.M., nearly twenty-five thousand bluecoats stood at attention in the broad, open valley between the opposing picket lines. Grant, Hooker, Howard, and Dana all came out to watch the first performance of the Army of the Cumberland under Thomas's command. They stood atop the parapet of Fort Wood. Lieutenant Colonel Joseph Fullerton, assistant adjutant general on the staff of Major General Gordon Granger, to whose Fourth Corps belonged the divisions of Wood and Sheridan, was with them. None had ever seen so large an assemblage of troops on one field. In the anxious, almost surreal minutes before the advance, as ranks were dressed and alignment corrected, Fullerton shared their awe at the majesty of the spectacle:

> It was an inspiriting sight. Flags were flying; the quick, earnest steps of thousands beat equal time. The sharp commands of hundreds of company officers, the sound of drums, the ringing notes of the bugles, companies wheeling and counter-marching and regiments getting into line, the bright sun lighting up ten thousand polished bayonets till they glistened and flashed like a flying shower of electric sparks—all looked like preparations for a peaceful pageant, rather than for the bloody work of death.[9]

The Rebel pickets on and around Orchard Knob had no idea what to make of the display. A few tried to walk their beats calmly, but their furtive glances toward the Federal lines betrayed their uneasiness. Others, caught up in the grandeur of the moment, came out of their rifle pits to watch what some thought was simply a grand review. They sat transfixed atop their little mounds of dirt.

On Missionary Ridge, senior Confederate officers huddled together and peered through their field glasses, trying to divine the meaning of all this martial pomp. Bragg dismissed it as a review staged in honor of Grant. Breckinridge, who stood apart from the commanding general and his lieutenants, disagreed. He slammed shut his field glass abruptly, strode over to the group, and retorted: "General Bragg, in about fifteen minutes you are going to see the damnedest review you ever saw. I am going to my command." That remark broke up the session, and Bragg's generals abandoned him to hasten to their units.[10]

All doubt was removed at 1:30 P.M., when brigade buglers blew the command "Forward!" Regimental buglers answered it, swelling the sharp notes across the valley, and Wood and Sheridan's long lines sprang forward at the double-quick time.[11]

The Yankee skirmishers were astonished. Nearer and nearer they drew toward the Rebel pickets, yet not a shot greeted them. Even then, the Confederates seemed unable to comprehend what was happening. Over on the right, in the Thirty-sixth Illinois of Francis Sherman's brigade, the regimental mascots opened the fight. Three white greyhounds darted ahead of the skirmish line and chased down a family of rabbits that had strayed across their path.[12]

Wood's infantry had covered nearly eight hundred yards and was within easy range of the advanced picket posts in a fringe of wood west of Orchard Knob when the Rebels opened fire. Before the Southerners could reload, the Federal skirmishers were upon on them, rounding up prisoners and firing on the rest, who dashed madly toward the rifle pits at the base of the knob where their startled reserves were falling in.[13]

The crackle of skirmish fire brought the batteries on Missionary Ridge to life. Federal artillery answered from Forts Wood and Negley—thirty-three guns massed in the latter redoubt alone. Out on the plain, recalled a Kansan, "a quick race through the woods ensued, and meantime the heavy guns let loose their thunders; the ugly whiz of their shells . . . tearing and crashing through the forest overhead and around."[14]

The unfortunate Rebel pickets caught in the whirlwind belonged to the Twenty-fourth and Twenty-eighth Alabama regiments of Manigault's brigade; six hundred bewildered Southerners confronting an advance of nearly fourteen thousand Federals. The Twenty-fourth Alabama covered the ground in front of and atop Orchard Knob; the Twenty-eighth had formed in front of and along the ridge next to the knob, its left flank opposite the right of Sheridan's division. Through inexcusably poor coordination, a gap of nearly three hundred yards yawned between the two regiments, so that each fought on its own.[15]

The colonel of the Twenty-fourth allowed his men to trade a few volleys with Willich's brigade as it closed on Orchard Knob, then prudently gave the command to withdraw toward Missionary Ridge. The

Yankees surged up the knob and instinctively set to work digging in. They threw the logs and stones of the Rebel breastworks to the opposite side of the abandoned rifle pits and in a matter of minutes were firmly entrenched. The assault had cost Willich just four killed and ten wounded.[16]

The commander of the Twenty-eighth Alabama, Lieutenant Colonel William Butler, was more obstinate, and it nearly cost him his regiment. Someone (General Manigault knew not who) apparently had told Butler that he would be supported, and so the Alabamian stood firm in the rifle pits at the base of the ridge, squarely astride the path of Hazen's advance.[17]

Hazen had arrayed his brigade in a unique fashion. To better control his nine badly depleted regiments, he consolidated them into five battalions. Covering their advance was the Fifth Kentucky, deployed as skirmishers. The unexpectedly severe resistance of Butler's Alabamians caused the Kentuckians to fall to the ground one hundred yards short of the rifle pits. Behind them came Hazen's First Battalion, composed of the Forty-first and Ninety-third Ohio, under the command of Colonel Wiley, who had helped set the whole affair in motion with his sighting the night before.

Recalling Wood's orders not to bring on a general engagement, Wiley halted two hundred yards short of the Rebel line and sent for instructions. The Alabamians kept up their fire. Wiley fast grew frustrated; men were falling around him while he waited for a response from Hazen. His patience evaporated, and Wiley gave the command to fix bayonets and charge. Major William Birch, in charge of the Ninety-third Ohio on the left of the line, imitated Wiley, and the entire battalion pressed forward through the tangle of underbrush and timber toward a thirty-yard strip of open ground in front of the breastworks.[18]

Both regiments hesitated at the fringe of the forest. The color guard of the Forty-first ventured into the open but was quickly driven back by a murderous volley. Lieutenant Colonel Kimberly grabbed the national flag and spurred his horse into the clearing. A dozen bullets cut down the animal, and Kimberly tumbled to the ground. Colonel Wiley galloped out next and screamed at his men to follow. Inspired by their leaders' courage or perhaps ashamed of their own reticence, the Ohioans charged.

The Confederate fire weakened. Many of the Alabamians were lying on their backs to escape the return volleys, thrusting their rifle-muskets over the low breastwork and shooting blindly. Jogging along with the men, Lieutenant Colonel Kimberly recalled the first frenzied moments when the Forty-first hit the Rebel works:

As they mounted it, most of the enemy were lying flat; a few were standing, some of these having thrown down their guns, and fewer still were running through the brush toward Mission Ridge. One or two of the fellows who had been lying on their backs and firing over their heads, did this after the Union troops were on the breastworks and over it, and a man of the Forty-first was killed by a wild shot of this kind. The man who fired that shot was crazed with the fight, not seeing what was going on, for at the moment the men of the Forty-first were over the breastwork and the rest of its defenders had surrendered. It was said that the brother of the Forty-first man who was thus killed after the surrender was maddened at the sight, and with his bayonet pinned the fear-crazed Southerner to the ground as he lay.[19]

The Forty-first had taken its share of the ridge, but at a horrible price. Sixty men—nearly one-quarter of the regiment—were killed or wounded, most of them gunned down while sprinting the last thirty yards to the knob.

The Ninety-third Ohio had met with resistance equally heavy and suffered commensurate losses: twelve killed and forty-five wounded. While the regiment consolidated its hold on the ridge, Lieutenant Colonel Langdon rode forward to check on the Ninety-third. He paused beside Major Birch, who was staggering up the slope through the smoke, his features lost in a stream of blood. A bullet had gored his face. Langdon jumped off his horse and grabbed Birch's hand. "Are you badly hurt, Major Birch?" he asked. "Good-bye, Colonel," Birch whispered, then he sank to the ground, dead.[20]

Manigault's Alabamians ran nearly four hundred yards before collapsing midway between the knob and Missionary Ridge. A quick count told the cost of their brief encounter: the two regiments had lost nearly 175 men, mostly from the Twenty-eighth Alabama, which also had surrendered its colors.[21]

General Wood had ridden behind the second line during the assault, in the interval between Willich's and Hazen's brigades. As soon as they swept their front of Rebels, he galloped to the summit of Orchard Knob and sent an order to Beatty to deploy his brigade to the left of Willich and carry the picket posts there. Beatty accomplished the work in a matter of minutes, extending Wood's line to the west bank of Citico Creek. A few minutes before 3:00 P.M., Wood signaled to General Thomas, who was standing atop the parapet of Fort Wood: "I have carried the first line of the enemy's entrenchments." What were Thomas's instructions?

Grant and Thomas consulted briefly. They ignored Granger, who was lost in his peculiar habit of sighting artillery pieces during the height of combat. Both hesitated: Wood had done far more than conduct a mere reconnaissance; should he be recalled as planned? Sensing their indecision, Rawlins pressed his way between the two and spoke to Grant sharply: "It will have a bad effect to let them come back and try it over again." Grant took the advice. "Intrench them and send up support," he told Thomas. The Virginian waved Bridges's Illinois Battery forward. As it bounced across the plain toward the knob, he signaled Wood: "Hold on; don't come back; you have got too much; intrench your position."[22]

On Wood's right, Sheridan had played well his less spectacular but nonetheless important supporting role. His brigade commanders had faced little opposition. Brigadier General George Wagner's brigade had advanced in echelon on the division left. The brigade of the brilliant young Colonel Charles Harker, one of the few Union heroes at Chickamauga, had moved in echelon to the right of Wagner. Colonel Francis Sherman's brigade had followed in reserve. Coming within range of the Rebel pickets shortly after Wood closed on the knob and ridge, Wagner and Harker had had little trouble clearing their fronts. At Thomas's direction, they halted in the open field from which they had expelled the enemy, a mere three hundred yards beyond their own line of departure, and threw up breastworks. Sheridan anchored his right on the Moore road.[23]

On Wood's left, Howard's Eleventh Corps embarrassed itself. After sending word to Wood to dig in on Orchard Knob, Thomas told Howard at 3:30 P.M. to push forward the divisions of Schurz and Steinwehr and close up on Wood's flank. The Easterners encountered resistance no heavier than that which Hazen and Willich had overcome, but they faltered badly in the autumn twilight. Perhaps the gloaming was to blame, obscuring as it did the Rebel pickets. Whatever the reason, both divisions ground to a halt short of the enemy. In a few units, the behavior of the men bordered on the craven. Over on the far left, between the Chattanooga and Cleveland Railroad and the south bank of Citico Creek, George Metcalf of the One Hundred Thirty-sixth New York watched the untried Thirty-third New Jersey (which had heaped such abuse on Sherman's veterans the day before) fall apart as it came under fire for the first time in its three months of service:

A little to our left was a large barn, and when a regiment of New Jersey Zouaves came marching in column, the center of their line came upon the barn. The soldiers in this regiment were all new men, and a cowardly set too, although they looked fearfully brave in their queer-looking pants, hats and tasseled belts. The soldiers, protected by this barn, stopped under its shelter and refused to move, and presently the whole of that regiment doubled up and packed themselves behind it like a flock of frightened sheep. Do all they could, the officers could not budge them. They refused to go further and the column on either side moved on without them, leaving a gap of some twenty rods open.[24]

Neither could Metcalf in good conscience praise his own regiment. His fellow New Yorkers managed to work their way across the railroad tracks, only to be driven to the ground in a field of corn stubble by a spattering of pickets' bullets:

> We lay here over an hour. During all the time the bullets kept zipping over our heads. Close to me lay a member of my company with his nose flattened to the ground. Out of sport I got hold of a dry stalk of a weed and hit him on his ear. He jumped as if shot and put his hand up to feel the blood that wasn't there. Others began to toss little stones, without exposing themselves to danger, onto the heads of their comrades that dared not look up and did not understand that we were safe if we only kept down below the range of the rebel rifles. I saw one of our officers lying with one foot purposely stuck up in the air, as I believe, hoping to be shot in this non-vital spot and so have an excuse not to go into the main fight.[25]

Howard had ridden contentedly into Fort Wood after giving Steinwehr and Schurz their orders, unaware of the muddle into which they had fallen. Gordon Granger waved him down. Exhilarated by Wood's success and by the fun he was having firing cannons, Granger good-naturedly chided Howard. "How are you, Howard? This looks like work," he laughed. "Your troops on the left haven't squared up." A surprised Howard hurried off: "I entered a thicket to the left, and, finding my troops too much retired, went from brigade to brigade and dressed up the lines to Granger's satisfaction."[26]

Perhaps, but Wood saw matters differently. Growing weary of the Easterners' bungling, he told Sam Beatty to detach two regiments and with them sweep to the left to take the Rebel pickets in the flank and relieve the pressure on Schurz. Beatty wheeled the Nineteenth Ohio and Ninth Kentucky perpendicular to his main line, and they drove off the startled Southerners just as the last gray light of day melted into blackness. Confident that Schurz could take matters from there, Beatty withdrew the two regiments, only to learn later that night that the Easterners had failed to move into the rifle pits, which the Rebels reoccupied under the cover of darkness.[27]

The handful of pickets lingering near Howard's front and Wood's flank were like gnats on a buffalo. Everyone was too elated either to pay them much notice or to chastise Howard. As night fell, Grant and Thomas galloped across the plain to congratulate the men of Wood's division. Thomas was unusually effusive. Calling together the officers of the

Forty-first Ohio, the Virginian dismounted and told Lieutenant Colonel Wiley to pass along his profound thanks to the men of the regiment for the fight they had made: "A gallant thing, Colonel, a very gallant thing."[28]

Everyone was pleased, said Assistant Secretary Dana. Rawlins agreed. "I never saw troops move into action in finer style than Thomas's did today," he wrote that night. "They are entitled to the highest praise for their soldierly bearing and splendid bravery." Grant too was impressed with the Army of the Cumberland. As the last echoes from Wood's fight faded from the valley, he sent a message to Halleck in Washington praising the army's success and imparting his own resolve for the morrow: "General Thomas's troops attacked the enemy's left . . . carried the first line of rifle-pits running over the knoll . . . and the low ridge to the right of it. The troops moved under fire with all the precision of veterans on parade. Thomas's troops will entrench themselves, and hold their position until daylight, when Sherman will join the attack from the mouth of the Chickamauga, and a decisive battle will be fought."[29]

From their natural grandstand on the crest of Missionary Ridge, the high command of the Army of Tennessee had dumbly watched the Federals sweep over the plain. Perhaps they could have done no more, mused Manigault, whose brigade had taken the belly punch: "Whilst this combat was going on, all remained silent spectators. No effort to reinforce our advance posts was made, and as our lines were very weak and we had not men enough to man them, and not knowing what was the ulterior intention of the enemy, I do not know that it would have been wise to risk more men to the front. Our skirmish line was lost and to recover it a general engagement would have to be fought."[30]

As the sun set and a deep chill fell over the valley, Bragg and his lieutenants emerged from their daze and groped for a response. Giving in to wishful thinking, they tried to shell Wood and Sheridan from their freshly turned earthworks. At dusk, the batteries along Missionary Ridge roared and for the next two hours kept up a steady bombardment. "Such a spectacle I shall never forget," Sergeant-Major Lyman Widney of the Thirty-fourth Illinois wrote his sister. "The dusky form of the mountain, encircling our position for three miles, seemed in the dim twilight like some dense thunder cloud looming against the heavens, and shooting forth unceasing flames of lightning, while its thunder made the earth tremble beneath our feet [and] innumerable shells fell, bursting above and around our lines." For all the racket and expenditure of precious ammunition, the Confederate gunners caused little damage. "I have not learned that any considerable injury was received from this terrific bombardment of the enemy," Widney assured his sister.[31]

The manic reaction of General Manigault's immediate superior, Patton Anderson, to Wood's thrust was in marked contrast to the South Carolinian's quiet contemplation of the setback. At dusk, a courier startled Manigault with an order from Anderson for him to retake Orchard Knob with what was left of his brigade. Never in his two and a half years of service had Manigault received a command so preposterous. He galloped back to division headquarters to confront Anderson. What troops were to support him? asked the South Carolinian. "My own brigade on your left, and General Deas on your right, and the orders have been given them to advance with you and to conform to your movements. They are in readiness, and as soon as you are, communicate with them, and then move forward," explained Anderson. Manigault's contempt blazed into anger. He realized Anderson was setting him up: should the assault fail, the Floridian plausibly could deny having given the order to attack.

Seeing no alternative short of open insubordination, Manigault turned on his heels and walked out of Anderson's tent. Mounting to return to prepare his brigade for its suicide mission, Manigault noticed Anderson strolling off to take his supper.

Manigault got his men in line. "It was now dark, and only a few prominent objects visible against the gray sky, but the country was familiar to us, and I doubted not but that I could conduct our center straight to the point indicated. As to our ability to recover it, that was another matter," he recalled. Manigault sent couriers to Deas and Colonel W. F. Tucker (in command of Anderson's brigade) letting them know he was ready to move forward.

The couriers returned with news that pushed Manigault to the brink of mutiny: Deas and Tucker both reported that their orders had been changed; instead of advancing their whole brigades, only their skirmish lines were to move with Manigault.

The South Carolinian was incredulous. His brigade was being sent to certain slaughter: fourteen hundred men against a Federal corps. Manigault dashed off to division headquarters to confront the author of this "madness and most reckless stupidity." Anderson was enjoying his supper. On seeing Manigault, he strode from his tent, demanding to know why the South Carolinian had not attacked as ordered. Why? Because his tiny brigade could not possibly drive eight thousand Yankees from entrenchments, Manigault snarled. Anderson rebuked him in a tone that implied cowardice on the South Carolinian's part. Manigault dropped all pretense of subordination. Shouting loudly enough for every staff officer within earshot to hear, Manigault protested "the rashness and recklessness of his order, which would cost so many lives and men, to no purpose, and which I regarded as perfectly impracticable." He spun his horse around to return to his command. Before riding off, Manigault caught a glimpse of Lieutenant Colonel James Barr, the division Officer-of-the-Day, whispering something to Anderson.

Back with his brigade, Manigault gave the final instructions to his regimental commanders. As the word "Forward" swelled in his throat, Anderson's adjutant galloped up alongside Manigault and told him that Anderson had countermanded the order to attack. The troops could return to their quarters. "There was a general sigh of relief, and many a 'Thank God!' coming from the heart," said Manigault.

The South Carolinian learned later that the agent of his salvation had been Colonel Barr. Barr had convinced Anderson that the Federals did indeed outnumber Manigault, probably by at least six to one. "But for the timely appearance of Colonel Barr . . . on that night our brigade would have pretty much ceased to exist," averred Manigault years after.[32]

While Anderson and Manigault played out their duel of nerves, Bragg busied himself readjusting his lines and recalling units to meet what he now realized was a serious threat against his unprotected right. Ironically, as Baldy Smith astutely observed after the war, Thomas's very success at Orchard Knob worked against the larger interests of the Federal offensive. Until that moment, Bragg had been convinced that the Yankee objective was to turn his left on Lookout Mountain, precisely as Grant had hoped. Not only did Bragg now better understand the true purpose of the Federal movements of the past few days, but he was sufficiently roused to send for Cleburne's division, which, had Thomas not sallied forth on 23 November, would have been well on its way to Longstreet the next day, beyond recall.[33]

Cleburne was on the platform at Chickamauga Station early on the afternoon of the 23 November, watching the last of Buckner's division board the cars, when a messenger thrust at him the following order from army headquarters: "The general commanding desires that you will halt such portions of your command as have not yet left at Chickamauga; such as may have left halt at Charleston. Do not, however, separate brigades; if parts of brigades have gone, let the remaining portion of the brigade go, but halt at Charleston."

Seeing nothing alarming in this note, Cleburne allowed the train carrying the remaining regiments of Bushrod Johnson's brigade to go on its way. He had, however, pulled the first troops of A. W. Reynolds's brigade off the cars of the follow-on train.

Just minutes later, he received a second, decidedly frantic dispatch

The "Suck"

Williams
Island

Tennessee
River

Raccoon
Mountain

OSTERHAUS

CRUFT
XX

Brown's
Ferry

Moccasin
Point

Kelley's Ferry

GEARY
XX

Creek

WALTHALL

MOORE

Wauhatchie

Lookout

Lookout Mountain

0 miles       1       2

STEVENSON
XX

Summertown

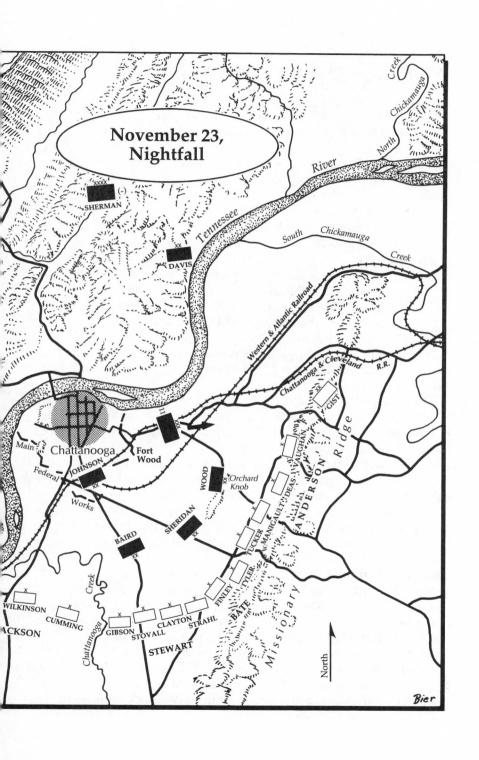

November 23,
Nightfall

SHERMAN

DAVIS

Tennessee River

North Chickamauga Creek

South Chickamauga Creek

Western & Atlantic Railroad

Chattanooga & Cleveland R.R.

GIST

Anderson's Ridge

Chattanooga

Fort Wood

Main

Federal

JOHNSON

Works

Orchard Knob

WOOD

VAUGHAN

DEAS

MANIGAULT

TUCKER

SHERIDAN

BAIRD

TYLER

FINLEY

BATE

WILKINSON

CUMMING

Chattanooga Creek

GIBSON

STOVALL

CLAYTON

STRAHL

STEWART

JACKSON

Missionary

North

Bier

from headquarters telling him to recall Johnson and return to Missionary Ridge at once with his own division and whatever remained of Buckner's. A third note followed, signed by Bragg himself: "We are heavily engaged. Move rapidly to these headquarters."

Cleburne's division filed up the reverse slope of Missionary Ridge behind army headquarters after dark. Bragg told the Irishman to rest his division near the Moore house; he was to act as the army reserve and take his orders directly from Bragg. The North Carolinian took personal control of Reynolds's brigade, which he sent on to support the overwrought Patton Anderson.[34]

Bragg called in every unit within a day's march. He recalled from guard duty at Chickamauga Station and returned to its beloved corps commander, John C. Breckinridge, the Kentucky Brigade of Brigadier General Joseph Lewis—these were the "Orphans" that Bragg so despised as to care little whether any of them survived the war. Bragg then ordered Marcus Wright's Tennessee Brigade—another unit that had earned the commanding general's disdain for its unabashed loyalty to Cheatham—to return from Charleston by rail immediately.[35]

For the moment, Bragg used the troops at hand to shore up his right, shuffling units and flip-flopping command relationships. To some, it must have seemed like the old Chickamauga game of eleventh-hour changes replayed.

Bragg stripped his left over the protest of Carter Stevenson, who still believed that the real threat was against Lookout Mountain. Watching Wood's capture of Orchard Knob, Stevenson concluded: "The movements of the enemy and his demonstrations against our right center were such that in my own mind I had not the slightest doubt that his purpose was to attract our attention, induce us to concentrate on our right, thereby weakening our left, and thus render the acquisition of Lookout Mountain practicable for him." Stevenson sent Bragg a dispatch telling him as much. The North Carolinian, of course, had too few troops to concentrate against threats to both flanks. He wisely ignored the advice of Stevenson and, shortly before 5:00 P.M., ordered Walker's division to withdraw from its position between the northeast base of Lookout Mountain and the west bank of Chattanooga Creek and move up along Missionary Ridge to the far right. There it was to take up a line a quarter mile south of Tunnel Hill and a mile and a half east of the ground Howard's Eleventh Corps was trying to occupy.[36]

To command this now critical sector, Bragg turned to his most reliable corps commander, William Hardee. While Wood's Federals dug in on Orchard Knob, Bragg told the Georgian to turn command of the extreme left over to Stevenson and accompany Walker's division to the right—adding, to Stevenson's dismay, that he felt a brigade was sufficient to hold the top of Lookout Mountain. As if to mock Stevenson's fears, Bragg removed Garrity's Battery from the mountain and relocated it on Missionary Ridge.[37]

Stevenson reluctantly assumed command of affairs west of Chattanooga Creek. Setting up headquarters in the shot-pocked Cravens house, which at least offered relief from the biting winds that blew over the mountain, he tried to make do with the two divisions left him. The forty-six-year-old Virginian sent a brigade of Jackson's division and Cumming's brigade of his own command off the mountain to close the gap in the valley that Walker's departure had opened. He set a detail from Walthall's brigade to work deepening a rifle pit near the Cravens house. Then he asked Walthall to deploy his fifteen hundred Mississippians so as to both picket the mountain (from a point about a mile south of the mouth of Lookout Creek all the way up the western slope to the foot of the palisades) and retain a reserve sufficient to help Moore hold the main line near the Cravens house. Stevenson spent the night feeling his way along the bench of the mountain and down the rocky road into the valley, trying to acquaint himself with the line he was to hold. The blackness blinded him, increasing his sense of impending doom. Brigadier General Alfred Cumming, whose brigade was charged with defending a mile-long front, shared Stevenson's doubts: "In consequence of the great length of the line, when compared with the smallness of the force on hand for its defense, I considered the position to be exceedingly weak."[38]

Having done what he felt he could for the left and right, Bragg turned his attention to the center of the army, which he had entrusted to Breckinridge. After two months in front of Chattanooga, day after day looking on with contempt at what they assumed to be a starving army incapable of moving out of its entrenchments, the two generals finally realized that it might be prudent to fortify the crest of Missionary Ridge. Breckinridge ordered Bate to organize details to begin digging at daybreak. Hardee, who for the moment was responsible for Anderson's division, told him to do likewise. Both Hardee and Breckinridge recalled their cannon from the valley, while their chiefs of artillery tried in the dark to select the firing positions they should have reconnoitered weeks earlier.

Neither Bragg, nor Breckinridge, nor Hardee apparently was ready to commit himself entirely to the defense of the crest of Missionary Ridge should an attack come against the center. Unable to decide between holding the existing rifle pits at the foot of the ridge or withdrawing to the unfortified crest, they settled on a peculiar compromise: Bate and

Anderson were ordered to recall half their divisions for duty on the crest and to leave the remainder in the rifle pits along the base.[39]

In their sudden excitement, Bragg and Breckinridge seem to have forgotten about "Old Straight" Stewart's division down in the valley east of Chattanooga Creek. With about four thousand men, the Tennessean was manning a front nearly two miles long, with nothing between him and half of Granger's Fourth Corps but scattered timber, soggy fields, and a ragged line of log-and-stone breastworks. Not until 9:00 P.M. did Breckinridge bother to communicate with Stewart, and what he had to offer was hardly constructive. Stewart was to stretch his already attenuated line a bit farther to the right, so as to rest at the foot of Missionary Ridge about a half mile south of Bragg's headquarters. Stewart too was to begin work on trenches on the crest, which loomed a mile to his rear. And, as if that were not enough to exhaust his limited resources, Breckinridge ordered Stewart to "organize any excess of men which this new disposition may give you into a reserve, subject to move in any direction required, at short notice."[40]

Bragg may have gone to bed that night satisfied with his dispositions. In part, his instincts had been correct. The right needed reinforcing, and quickly. In his zeal to do so, however, he had left Stevenson with far too few troops to hold the left, especially the vulnerable Chattanooga Valley. And although he at last had begun to strengthen the crest of Missionary Ridge, Bragg's and Breckinridge's decision to split the Kentuckian's corps between the top and the base negated any advantage the high ground might offer.

All this was of little moment to the Rebels shivering out in the valley. As night fell, the opposing pickets arranged their posts to accommodate the movements of the day. Before long, they were again near enough to hear one another cough. Forgiving the bluecoats for the grand review turned bloody that had sent them running, the Rebel pickets along Wood's front struck up a conversation with their counterparts in the dark.

"Hello, Yanks, what's got the matter with you all over there?" asked a Confederate curious to know why the Federals had pushed out onto Orchard Knob.

"We're out of wood," a Yankee called back.

"If you wanted wood why didn't you say so?" retorted the Rebel. "We have more than we need out here, and if you had only asked us you might have sent out your teams and got all the wood you wanted without kicking up such a damned fuss about it."[41]

# CHAPTER ELEVEN

# THE ADVANTAGE WAS GREATLY ON OUR SIDE NOW

O N THE whole, Grant was satisfied with the events of 23 November: "The advantage was greatly on our side now, and if I could only have been assured that Burnside could hold out ten days longer I should have rested more easy. But we were doing the best we could for him and the cause." Although Grant was reluctant to hurry Sherman's exhausted men to the attack, no one at headquarters really doubted the outcome of the impending battle. With some eighty thousand troops on hand, Grant's conglomerate command outnumbered Bragg's Army of Tennessee nearly two to one. The normally cautious John Rawlins summed up the prevailing optimism that night in a cheerful letter home: "With Bragg thus deflated by the absence of Longstreet, and General Thomas augmented by Sherman's splendid fighting corps, I am hopeful of the result."[1]

Thomas too was quite pleased. Not only had his army proven to Grant that it could fight, but he had won a concession, small though it might be, from the commanding general. Hard use and rising waters during the day finally had torn a hole in the pontoon bridge at Brown's Ferry too wide for the engineers to patch. Hugh Ewing had gotten his division over before the rickety structure snapped, but Brigadier General Peter Osterhaus, yet another of the German-born and Prussian-trained generals serving under Grant, was stranded in Lookout Valley with his two brigades. When in the early morning hours of 24 November it became evident that Osterhaus would be unable to cross the river for at least twelve hours, Grant ordered him to report to Hooker. The brigades of Walter Whitaker, which had been guarding Shellmound, and of William Grose, on similar duty at Whiteside's, had been told to abandon their now superfluous posts on the morning of the twenty-third and rejoin the army, with orders to pause at Hooker's headquarters during the day to receive further instructions. Division commander Brigadier General Charles Cruft found his march delayed by Osterhaus's column, which was stacked up along the muddy road around Raccoon Mountain, so that it was nearly sunset before he reported the two brigades to Hooker.

The three divisions now congregating in Lookout Valley obviously were more than sufficient for a simple diversion against the Confederate left, so Grant finally acceded to Thomas's persistent demand that a more serious effort be made against Lookout Mountain. He stopped short of giving permission for a full-scale assault; Hooker, he cautioned the Virginian, should "take the point only if [his] demonstration should develop its practicability."[2]

Such subtleties were lost on Hooker. Thirty-six hours earlier, disgusted at the prospect of sitting out the forthcoming battle, he had begged Thomas to allow him to ride into the city in order to play some active role. Full of fight, Hooker now was determined to make the most of his sudden opportunity. In his orders to Geary for 24 November, Hooker said nothing of a mere demonstration; the Pennsylvanian was to *take* Lookout Mountain, plain and simple. He was to set off at dawn, cross Lookout Creek just above Wauhatchie, and march down the valley, "sweeping every Rebel from it." Whitaker's brigade would accompany him. Meanwhile, Grose's brigade and Osterhaus's division would cross the creek simultaneously, near its mouth. The two forces then were to converge on the point of Lookout, linking up during the ascent. Once he controlled the mountain, Hooker intended to drive his united command through Chattanooga Valley against Bragg's extreme left near Rossville.[3]

Sherman, of course, was still the principal actor in the impending drama. Despite his misgivings over Burnside at Knoxville, Grant apparently told Sherman that he was willing to delay the offensive one day more, should the Ohioan feel he needed Osterhaus to ensure the success of his flanking maneuver. Sherman declined Grant's offer; he was confident he could succeed with the three divisions then on hand.

Sherman's certainty was bolstered by outside help. For several weeks, Jefferson C. Davis's division of the Army of the Cumberland had been scattered from the mouth of North Chickamauga Creek, where Dan McCook's brigade lay encamped, over thirty miles in a number of small posts along the north bank of the Tennessee River as far as Smith's Ferry, where Davis's line connected with Burnside's right. A few regiments were even back on duty at Stevenson and Bridgeport. On 19 November, Thomas had ordered Davis to concentrate the division at the Caldwell farm, opposite the mouth of South Chickamauga Creek. Davis assembled his command swiftly, and by the afternoon of the twenty-third, it stood ready to support the Army of the Tennessee.[4]

Colonel Dan McCook, the action-craving Ohioan who had so hungered for a brigadier general's star at Chickamauga, already had been of immense help to Sherman. On 17 November, Baldy Smith had enlisted McCook and his troops to help make ready the river crossing. Although it offered little promise of promotion, McCook threw himself into the job with commendable energy. To keep the expedition secret, he arrested every civilian living among the hills on the north side of the river between Williams Island and North Chickamauga Creek on the excuse that he had been bushwhacked. He even posted strong guards at the assembly point to keep away those of his own troops not involved in the work. On 18 November, details from his brigade joined Smith's engineers in cutting a three-mile stretch of road behind the foothills, to allow pontoons to be transported beyond the view of inquisitive soldiers in Rebel signal stations. Others cleared protruding limbs and debris from North Chickamauga Creek. Still others were organized by Captain John Kennedy of the Eighty-fifth Illinois into a launching party to push off the troop-laden boats on the night of the operation. The remaining members of the Eighty-fifth, along with the entire Eighty-sixth Illinois, were chosen to man the oars.

By nightfall on 20 November, Smith and McCook had opened the road, cleared the creek, and brought over the pontoons. One hundred sixteen boats floated in North Chickamauga Creek, four hundred yards from the Tennessee River. Crews stood ready on the creek bank. Nearby were secreted the materials needed to bridge sluggish South Chickamauga Creek.[5]

Sherman had issued a detailed operations order to his division commanders on the evening of 22 November. He modified it on the twenty-third only to the extent of scratching out Osterhaus. "The Fifteenth Army Corps, re-enforced by one division of the Army of the Cumberland, is to cross the Tennessee at the mouth of [South] Chickamauga Creek, advance and take possession of the end of Missionary Ridge, viz. from the railroad tunnel to Chickamauga, hold, and fortify. The Army of the Cumberland and General Hooker's command are to assist by direct attacks to their front," the order began.

During the afternoon of 23 November, Sherman's three divisions were to march from their concealed camps to their assigned staging areas. The brigade of Brigadier General Giles Smith (younger brother of Morgan L. Smith, his division commander) was to take to the boats in North Chickamauga Creek. Lightburn's brigade, Morgan Smith's division, and

Ewing's division were to march according to a precise timetable over carefully surveyed routes to the northern slopes of the high hills opposite South Chickamauga Creek.

The operation was to begin at midnight. Two regiments from Giles Smith's brigade were to float down the Tennessee River, hugging its northern bank. A half mile above South Chickamauga Creek, they were to land and disarm the Rebel pickets posted near its mouth. The other seven regiments would splash ashore below the creek at the foot of a low ridge, the summit of which they were to secure and fortify at once.

After Smith's men disembarked, the empty boats would begin bringing over the remainder of the army. Lightburn's brigade would cross north of South Chickamauga Creek and John Smith's division south of it, each to entrench along the east bank of the river. Smith's engineers simultaneously would begin work on a pontoon bridge to span the sixty-yard-wide creek, in order to open communications between the two divisions.

All this was to be accomplished by daybreak on 24 November, when the empty pontoons were again to cross the river and start transporting Ewing's division. Baldy Smith had arranged to have the recently pumped-out and repaired ex-Rebel steamboat *Dunbar* join in the operation. As soon as the *Dunbar* came up, it was to take over the duty of ferrying troops, freeing up the remaining pontoons for use in bridging the Tennessee. Ewing was expected to be across no later than 7:00 A.M.

Once everybody was organized on the east bank, the three divisions would advance in brigade columns on their objectives. Morgan Smith was to cross the pontoon bridge and follow the south bank of South Chickamauga Creek to the slope of what Sherman and his staff thought was the northernmost hill of Missionary Ridge, which he was then to ascend. Occupying the center, John Smith would move cross-country to seize the next hill to the south. Ewing, on the right, was to head for what everyone assumed to be the hill through which ran the track of the Chattanooga and Cleveland Railroad. Davis's division would cross the river on Smith's pontoon bridge and support whoever ran into trouble.

Sherman closed his operations order with a few strong words of caution: "The utmost silence, order, and patience must be displayed. . . . Very great care must be taken by division commanders that the routes of march do not cross each other. . . . Except in the case of orders, muskets must not be loaded until the troops are disembarked on the other side of the Tennessee."[6]

At 4:00 P.M., at the same time Wood's men were congratulating themselves on their capture of Orchard Knob, the first of Sherman's troops filed out of camp en route to their staging areas. Through the waning hours of the afternoon and deep into the night, the long columns trudged into position. Around midnight, as Giles Smith's troops stepped gingerly into their swaying pontoons, a fog settled over the river valley and a light rain began to fall. Baldy Smith may have smiled at the irony; nature had handed him the same cover it had four weeks earlier, on the eve of the Brown's Ferry expedition.

With a shove, McCook's detail launched the first pontoon, containing Captain Kennedy of the Eighty-fifth Illinois and a squad from the lead regiment, the Eighth Missouri.[7]

Levi Ross of the Eighty-sixth Illinois strained at the oars in the second boat. "Every man rowed as though his own life and that of his country was at stake," he recalled. "Many of the boys could not help manifesting considerable fear at this extremely perilous undertaking. Many acknowledged that they would rather be excused from facing the foe while in a position on the broad Tennessee." But there was no encounter. Remembered the chaplain of the One Hundred Sixteenth Illinois: "We could see the fires of the enemy on the other side, the sparks flying up when they were stirred, and at some points could even hear the voices of the pickets as they talked with each other. A drizzling rain was falling. Thus we drifted down the river for three miles without creating any alarm."

At the designated point on the north bank a signal fire was lit, and the lead pontoons swung away toward the opposite bank. "The moment was full of excitement," said a passenger. "Should we land unmolested? Or should we meet a deadly fire and be compelled to engage in a hand to hand struggle? For we were to land with fixed bayonets and unloaded guns. It would seem that we should have crouched down so as to derive some protection from the sides of the boats, in case we were fired on; but instead of that, as we approached the bank, every man of us stood up with muscles braced ready for a spring. To our surprise, no enemy appeared."[8]

The men of the Eighth Missouri reassembled silently on the riverbank above South Chickamauga Creek. Working their way down toward its mouth, they quickly and quietly disarmed the unsuspecting Rebel pickets. In the angle between the mouth of the creek and the south bank of the Tennessee River, the Confederates had dug a short rifle pit. The Missourians crept around behind it and pounced on its twenty occupants, all of whom were drowsing over a smoldering fire. The Missourians sent their groggy prisoners across the river with the empty pontoons and fanned out to cover the bridgehead. The One Hundred Sixteenth Illinois arrived a few minutes later. The critical first phase of the operation passed without the loss of a man.[9]

Lightburn's troops took their places in the pontoons and began crossing at about 1:30 A.M. Within an hour, the brigade was over and entrenching on the low ridge north of the creek.[10]

Colonel Jesse Alexander's brigade was the first across from John Smith's division. The Fourth Minnesota Infantry took the lead. By 2:30 A.M., the Minnesotans were fanned out in a skirmish line along the south bank of the creek.

As the soldiers of Matthies's and Raum's brigades waited their turn in the pontoons, their anxiety was eased by the sight of Lieutenant Colonel David Coleman of the Eighth Missouri, proudly leading his captured Rebels along their line. A few calming words from a dark figure as they entered the pontoons helped even more. Recalled an officer of the Fifth Iowa: "Quietly, two by two, we slipped down to the water's edge and stepped into the rude flatboats that waited there. `Be prompt as you can, boys; there's room for thirty in a boat,' said a tall man in a long waterproof coat who stood on the bank near us in the darkness. Few of us had ever before heard the voice of our beloved commander. Sherman's kind words gave us all cheer, and his personal presence, his hearing the danger we were about to undertake, gave us confidence."[11]

All through the predawn hours of Tuesday, 24 November, the pontoons plied back and forth across the river. Dawn broke gray at 5:30 A.M. Gone were the clear skies that had sharpened the spectacle of Wood's advance the afternoon before. A light drizzle peppered the waters of the Tennessee and deepened puddles in fields already soggy. Inevitably, delays arose. Ewing's division did not begin to cross until 8:00 A.M., an hour after it was to have been dug in on the opposite bank. Nonetheless, things were going exceedingly well for Sherman. By 6:30 A.M., he had two divisions—nearly eight thousand men—assembled less than two miles from Missionary Ridge. A mile and a half to the south, General Howard was preparing to send Bushbeck's brigade north along the river road to open communications with Sherman's right flank. Smith's engineers were hammering away at the bridges, and the steamboat *Dunbar*, with the young General Wilson riding along in the pilot house, showed up just as the first of Ewing's troops were entering the pontoons. They cheered the arrival of the sidewheeler, with its two battered smokestacks belching black smoke from the patched-up furnace, and began pouring aboard.

It was a critical moment for Sherman. Shortly after sunrise, John Smith had discovered a second, more commanding ridge five hundred yards east of the one he had fortified. He seized it without opposition. Not a single Rebel could be seen in the fields beyond Smith's new position. At a minimum, a strong reconnaissance into the woods beyond seemed in order. Yet Sherman hesitated, unwilling to move until Ewing's division was in place. He told Smith to fortify the ridge, and the morning slipped quietly away.[12]

On the road leading toward the foothills of Missionary Ridge, Frank De Mars and J. N. Bradford of Company B, Fourth Minnesota, slogged along through the mud. Smith had ordered Lieutenant Colonel John Tourtellotte to push his Minnesotans, who still manned the skirmish line, out beyond the second ridge. De Mars and Bradford left the fields behind them and entered the damp forest. From just out of sight they heard the squishing of horses' hooves in the pasty road. De Mars panicked and ran off, but Bradford ducked behind a tree stump. Two Rebels, an enlisted man and a lieutenant, rode into view. Bradford stood up and leveled his rifle. The soldier threw up his hands and cried, "Don't shoot, I surrender!" but the lieutenant wheeled his horse and made a dash back up the road. Bradford and a few comrades who had joined him fired and missed, and the officer galloped away to spread the warning that the Yankees were across the river.[13]

General Bragg was in the saddle shortly after daybreak. He and Colonel Brent rode north along Missionary Ridge to make sure Brigadier General States Rights Gist had gotten Walker's reserve division into position south of Tunnel Hill. Gist had, and Bragg and Brent were examining his lines with satisfaction when the black smoke of the *Dunbar*, steaming upriver, distracted them. Riding on through the lifting fog, they saw, two miles across the valley, the divisions of John Smith and Morgan Smith digging in at the mouth of South Chickamauga Creek and Bushbeck's brigade filing north to join them.[14]

No doubt Bragg was stunned. He had expected a movement against his right, but not one emanating from a point so far to the north. Bragg seems to have assumed that Thomas would launch the main Federal attack from Orchard Knob, against the divisions of Gist and Anderson.[15]

Even now, with proof of Federal intentions there before him, Bragg faltered; perhaps Sherman's crossing was merely an elaborate feint. The measures he took during the morning were halfhearted stopgaps, reflecting a groping uncertainty as profound as that of Sherman. Bragg had ample troops at hand with which to check—or at least seriously retard—Sherman's advance: Cleburne's division, which had been augmented by the Orphan Brigade during the night, lay bivouacked behind his headquarters. Bragg however, told Cleburne to send only Lucius Polk's brigade toward the far right; the rest of the division was to stay put. Suspecting that the Federal objective might be the supply depot at Chickamauga Station, Bragg told Cleburne to deploy Polk on the east bank of South Chickamauga Creek to cover the railroad bridges. When the trains carrying Marcus Wright's brigade chugged into Chickamauga Station at 8:30 A.M., the Tennessean was greeted with a note from Colonel Brent directing him to march at once to the mouth of South Chickamauga Creek to "resist any enemy attempt to cross"— a bizarre order since Sherman already had five times as many troops over as Wright had in his brigade.

That was all. Bragg did nothing more. Only two brigades, neither within supporting distance of the other, moved to resist a possible advance by four divisions.[16]

Bragg had handed Sherman the chance to destroy his army; the Ohioan let it slip through his fingers. As the morning passed, he kept the two Smiths busy digging in while waiting for Ewing to get his entire division across the river. Down in Fort Wood, Grant was growing impatient with his friend. Still, reflecting both his confidence in and unwillingness to offend his touchy compatriot, Grant stopped short of peremptorily ordering him forward. Instead, at 11:20 A.M., he wrote him a solicitous note:

> Thomas' forces are confronting enemy's line of rifle pits, which seem to be but weakly lined with troops. Considerable movement has taken place on top of the ridge toward you. Howard has sent a force to try and flank the enemy on our left, and to send through to communicate with you. Until I do hear from you I am loath to give any orders for a general engagement. Hooker seems to have been engaged for some time, but how I have not heard. Does there seem to be a force prepared to receive you east of the ridge? Send me word what can be done to aid you.[17]

Nothing, short of a kick in the pants, would start Sherman on his way before he was ready. The normally compassionate James Wilson, who had gotten off the *Dunbar* to watch the attack, was both mystified and angry with Sherman. With or without Ewing, Wilson believed,

> there was nothing left for him to do but to move against the enemy. The country was entirely open, and, while the ground was high and rolling, the way both to the enemy's flank and rear lay straight out from the river. Nothing could have been more favorable to a direct attack or to a turning movement against the enemy's right flank and rear, but from the first . . . Sherman's movements were slow and ineffective. Instead of pushing resolutely to the attack he lost several hours in digging rifle pits to cover the brigade. . . . The simple fact is that Sherman, with all his brilliancy, was not the man for such bold and conclusive operations.[18]

Oliver O. Howard cantered up to the head of Bushbeck's column shortly after noon. He waved down Sherman, who was on the north bank of South Chickamauga Creek watching the engineers ease the last pontoon into place. Sherman dismounted and jumped across the gap in the bridge and shook Howard's hand warmly. The two had never met, but Howard was at once struck by Sherman's "frank, hearty confidence of manner" as the Ohioan expressed his intention to advance as soon as the last of his troops were across the river. Sherman put their brief acquaintance to the test: Would Howard be so good as to leave Bushbeck's brigade with him, so that he might better communicate with Thomas's left on Orchard Knob? Howard agreed and turned back with his cavalry escort to rejoin his corps.[19]

At 12:20 P.M., the bridge over the Tennessee River was completed. Ten minutes later, the *Dunbar* landed the last of Ewing's division. Nearly an hour more passed while Ewing assembled his men and John Smith and Morgan Smith dressed their lines to Ewing's left. At 1:30 P.M., with slightly less than four hours of gray daylight remaining, Sherman gave the order to advance. A heavy line of skirmishers jogged ahead through a light, cold drizzle into the open fields. The three divisions stepped off in column, with Ewing hanging back a bit in echelon, "prepared to deploy to the right on the supposition that we would meet an enemy in that direction," said Sherman. Bushbeck trailed along to the right and rear of Ewing. Back at the landing, Jefferson C. Davis stood by, waiting for word from Sherman to come forward.[20]

Less than a mile and a half of fields, forest, and swamps stood between Sherman and the high hills. Displaying uncommon trepidation, Sherman moved at a snail's pace, constantly looking to his right for any sign of Rebels bounding down from Missionary Ridge to take him in the flank.

But there was not a Confederate within two miles of Sherman's flank. Before noon, Bragg had ridden off toward Lookout Mountain without taking any further action to strengthen his right. Nor did Hardee act on his own until Sherman's massed Federals left their breastworks and marched out into the fields, at which time he sent a courier galloping down Missionary Ridge to tell Cleburne to move his remaining three brigades and batteries with all haste toward the right of the ridge, "near the point where the [railroad] tunnel passes through." There, "I would find an officer of Hardee's staff who would show me my position," recalled Cleburne, whom the courier found at 2:00 P.M. Bragg, meanwhile, had gotten wind of Sherman's movement as well. He directed Colonel Brent to tell Cleburne that he must "at all hazards" prevent the Feder-

als from pushing through to the railroad bridges across South Chickamauga Creek.[21]

Brent's message reached Cleburne at the same time Hardee's winded
courier arrived. Thoroughly aroused, Cleburne spurred ahead of his
command. As Hardee had promised he would, Cleburne found Major
D. H. Poole waiting for him at the tunnel. With Sherman's skirmishers only a mile away, Poole explained as best he could the complex series
of hills and ravines that Hardee expected Cleburne to defend. The nex-
us of the line Hardee hoped to hold with Gist and Cleburne was Tunnel Hill (so named by Cleburne in his report). The highest point along
the northern stretch of Missionary Ridge, Tunnel Hill rose 250 yards
north of the Chattanooga and Cleveland Railroad tunnel. The next piece
of ground Poole showed Cleburne was a detached, U-shaped eminence
immediately north of, and much higher than, Tunnel Hill. It consisted
of two distinct hills, connected by a saddle that opened toward the
south. The southern slope of the eastern hill and the northern slope of
Tunnel Hill met in a deep ravine. A half mile separated the tops of the
two elevations. Poole hastily pointed out to Cleburne two other elevations. Paralleling the detached hills and Tunnel Hill was a long, narrow,
north-south ridge. A deep valley intervened. Through the valley ran a
wagon road that curled around the eastern base of Tunnel Hill and continued upward to the crest of Missionary Ridge. The other high ground
of note was a long spur that extended eastward for one thousand yards,
parallel to and just north of the railroad. Tunnel Hill and the spur formed
a right angle that opened toward South Chickamauga Creek and the
Confederate rear.

Cleburne and Poole rode their reconnaissance with dizzying speed.
After pointing out the last important terrain, Poole told Cleburne that
Hardee expected him to occupy the detached hills with one brigade and
stretch out his other two so as to cover the ground from the top of Tunnel Hill to Gist's right flank. It was nearly 3:00 P.M. when Poole finished
his recital. At that very moment, Sherman's skirmishers were feeling
their way across the tracks of the Western and Atlantic Railroad, a mere
half mile away.[22]

Cleburne protested. By no means could he cover such a long line with
three brigades; Poole had better ride at once to tell Hardee as much.

Events moved rapidly to a climax. No sooner had Poole started back
along the ridge then a private from the division signal corps, whom
Cleburne had sent ahead to inspect the detached hills, galloped back in
wide-eyed fright: the Yankees were marching up the far slope of the
eastern hill in line of battle. Before Cleburne could absorb the shock,
the crunching of brittle fallen leaves heralded the arrival of the first of

his own troops: the Texas Brigade of Brigadier General James A. Smith, as hard a fighter as there was in the Army of Tennessee. Cleburne yelled at the thirty-two-year-old West Point graduate to keep his column moving at the double-quick to seize the eastern hill. He halted Lieutenant H. Shannon, commanding Swett's Mississippi Battery, also known as the Warren Light Artillery, and told him to unlimber his four Napoleon twelve-pounders atop Tunnel Hill.[23]

Over the summit of Tunnel Hill and down its long northern slope ran the Texans. Smith hustled his skirmishers on ahead. Sprinting across the muddy ravine, they ran headlong up the near slope of the detached hill. A few yards from the summit, the flashes of hundreds of rifles lit up the gray woods. Bullets buzzed through the line of Texans from in front and both flanks. They stumbled back into the ravine, where Smith was on hand with the rest of the brigade. Together they retired back up Tunnel Hill. With Cleburne's help, Smith deployed his command around Swett's Battery: half fronting the detached hill and the rest thrown back to guard against an approach from the east.[24]

The Texans had stumbled upon the Fourth Minnesota, Thirtieth Ohio, and Sixth Iowa regiments. The Minnesotans were covering the advance of John Smith's division, the Ohioans that of Morgan Smith, and the Iowans that of Ewing's column. The three divisions converged on the detached hill at roughly the same time, each from a slightly different direction, so that the Texans were caught in a cross fire they could not possibly hope to return.[25]

Smith barely had time to throw out his Texas skirmishers from the summit of Tunnel Hill before the Thirtieth Ohio came whooping toward the ravine from the northeast. The Texans sent them darting for cover, and the two sides traded fire at a range of perhaps two hundred yards.[26]

Cleburne, meanwhile, was exhibiting the keen instincts and decisiveness that made him Hardee's most reliable subordinate. As Smith kept the Federals occupied, Cleburne deployed the remainder of his division. He arrayed Mark Lowrey's Alabama and Mississippi brigade to the left of Smith, and was about to place Daniel Govan's Arkansans on Lowrey's left, to complete the connection with Gist, when the volume and direction of the firing from Smith's front convinced him that the Federals might try to envelop the Texan's right flank. Responding to the threat, he sent Govan to the long east-west spur just north of the railroad. There, fronting northward, Govan was to protect Smith's flank and rear. With a few troops to spare, the Arkansan stretched out a line of skirmishers all the way to South Chickamauga Creek.[27]

Hardee came on the ground a few minutes later, at 4:00 P.M. No more than an hour of daylight remained. Hardee approved Cleburne's dispositions. Tinkering a bit, he took two of Lowrey's regiments and a section of Semple's Alabama Battery out of the line and moved them in front of Govan's right, up onto the southern edge of the ridge east of Tunnel Hill. That strengthened Cleburne's right flank, but it left Lowrey with no artillery and only two regiments of infantry to man the nearly one-mile front between Cleburne's left and Gist's right.[28]

Sherman's actions in the first crucial minutes after contact was made were hardly comparable to those of Cleburne. Simply stated, the Ohioan was dumbfounded. He had made a terrible error. Through an apparent combination of poor maps and egregiously negligent reconnaissance, Sherman had marched out from the river convinced that the detached hills were the northern extreme of Missionary Ridge. Not until the lead brigades of his three divisions consolidated on the summit of the eastern hill did Sherman, looking toward Smith's Texas brigade drawn up on Tunnel Hill, realize his mistake. Fumbling with his maps, he tried to orient himself and cope with this unforeseen turn of events. Neither Sherman nor his cozy trio of division commanders were inclined to risk taking. Though only Smith's three Texas regiments were visible through the naked trees to their front, they were unwilling to gamble on what might lie behind them. With fifty minutes of daylight remaining—enough time to have driven Cleburne's badly attenuated line across the railroad and probably forced Bragg to abandon his entire Missionary Ridge position during the night—Sherman chose the safe course: he ordered his generals to dig in.

In his report, the Ohioan explained away his blunder: "From studying all the maps, I had inferred that Missionary Ridge was a continuous hill, but we found ourselves on two high points, with a deep depression between us and the one immediately over the tunnel, which was my chief objective point. The ground we had gained, however, was so important that I could leave nothing to chance, and ordered it to be fortified during the night."

Writing years later in his capacity as the first official historian of the Chickamauga and Chattanooga National Military Park, Henry Boynton, a lieutenant colonel in Thomas's army during the battle, criticized Sherman unmercifully. His analysis merits relating, if only to spread a bit of deserved tarnish on the lustrous image of Sherman's genius:

> The astonishing error, an error which caused utter failure to the whole movement against Bragg's right, and which ever since has been covered thick in official reports and misleading histories, was the first day's occupation of a range of detached hills north of Missionary Ridge, and completely separated from it. Since the plan of battle turned on

occupying the north end of the ridge, it was certainly one of the most remarkable oversights of the war that this position was not thoroughly identified. Even the . . . method of preliminary reconnoitering, namely, when roads, distances, and positions were not known, or had been omitted from his notes, to stop at a farmhouse and ask a citizen, would have answered the purpose, since every field-hand in the vicinity could have given the needed information.[29]

Certainly there was plenty of time to knock on farmhouse doors during the two hours Sherman's troops plodded across the two miles of fields and open forest between the river and the hill.

Baldy Smith reached the same conclusion as Boynton: "Finding this unexpected break in the hills, Sherman, though he had met no resistance, and was expected by Grant to seize the ridge from the tunnel to the Chickamauga, determined to halt for the night and fortify his position. This was the blunder of the battle."[30]

Although he neglected to avail himself of it in his own report, there was one small mitigating factor in Sherman's favor. About the same time the brigades of Lightburn, Corse, and Alexander carried the hill, Giles Smith's brigade, trailing Lightburn in close column along the south bank of South Chickamauga Creek, ran into Marcus Wright's Tennessee Brigade marching in the opposite direction along the north bank on its quixotic quest to prevent Sherman from crossing the river. It is unclear who got the jump on whom, as both Wright and Smith seem to have been equally surprised by the encounter.

Not known for his veracity or his steadiness under fire, Wright claimed to have been hurrying westward in march column when his brigade "was suddenly assailed with a galling fire from the opposite bank of the creek, at a distance not exceeding one hundred yards," by an enemy concealed in the thick underbrush that lined the creek. Wright said he ordered his brigade to deploy to the left into line. Then, he said, he advanced smartly down to the creek bed and drove the enemy back behind the embankment of the Western and Atlantic Railroad. For good measure, Wright called up Kolb's Alabama Battery and began shelling the Federals.[31]

So Wright tells the story. John Anderson, commander of the Eighth Tennessee and Wright's senior colonel, had a very different recollection of things. When the brigade took its first fire from the Federals, Wright gave the order: "Get your men into line, Colonel Anderson! I'll go and order up the artillery." Kolb's battery came up, but that was the last Anderson or anyone from the brigade saw of Wright. Later that night, long after the fighting had sputtered out, Wright sent word to Anderson giving him command of the brigade, saying that he was indisposed.

"The next we heard of him he was commanding the Post at Atlanta, a post we were willing he should fill, as it gave us a brigade commander," sneered a Tennessee veteran.[32]

Wright had the last laugh on his detractors. In 1878, the War Department appointed him agent to collect Confederate records for inclusion in the massive government publication *War of the Rebellion: Official Records of the Union and Confederate Armies*. Wright worked assiduously at the task until 1917 and lived until the age of ninety-two, allowing him ample time to leave his imprimatur on the Southern record of the war and to weave his own version of events through countless books and articles.[33]

One thing is certain about the events that November afternoon, however. Far from lying in wait for Wright and his Tennesseans, Smith's Federals were scattered about at rest. Remembered Chaplain N. M. Baker of the One Hundred Sixteenth Illinois:

> It was late in the evening [Baker is mistaken here; the time was about 4:00 P.M.] and misting. A few shells came over us from a point back of the ridge occupied by Lightburn, but we did not mind these. The arms were stacked, the artillery horses were taken to the rear, and the men . . . prepared their supper.
>
> While we were thus somewhat off our guard, a detachment of the enemy, accompanied by a battery of artillery, advanced on our front, and approached pretty near before they were discovered. Our men were called to arms, but were so scattered that some time elapsed before they could get in line, and in the meantime the enemy poured a brisk fire both of artillery and musketry.[34]

Startled soldiers surrounded Baker. Instead of their rifle-muskets, some ran about toting sticks strung with half-cooked bacon. Others fell into line gulping coffee. Through the throng pushed Giles Smith and two of his staff on foot. They stepped out onto a dirt road that paralleled the railroad tracks, pausing just across the lane from Baker. Suddenly the unmistakable whir of a charge of canister caught their ear, and the three dove for shelter behind a tree. The two staff officers found cover in time, but not Smith. "I heard the ball strike the general as plainly as one would hear a ball of putty thrown against a wall, and it sounded much as that would, too. The general was staggered, but did not fall, and was supported by his companions and led from the field."[35]

Brigade command passed to Baker's colonel, Nathan Tupper, but at that moment he was nowhere to be found. Lieutenant Colonel James Boyd, trying to bring some order to the One Hundred Sixteenth Illinois, stormed back and forth along its tenuous line of battle shouting: "Where is Colonel Tupper? Where is Colonel Tupper? Where in hell is Colonel Tupper? He is in charge of this whole thing, and does not know it."

Lieutenant Colonel Oscar Malmborg could have benefited from Tupper's leadership as well. He had led his Fifty-fifth Illinois infantry away from the railroad and halfway up the slope of the detached hill, which only made his men easier targets for Kolb's gunners. Even the regimental chaplain could see that. "It was very plain, if we were lower down, the artillery could not reach us, but the men were kept at the best point for slaughter, till it looked as if not many would be left. It was an agony to endure it," remembered Chaplain Milton Haney, who finally cried out: "Colonel, why don't you take the men to the bottom of the hill?" Malmborg acceded, and the regiment eased itself into the underbrush at the base, having mercifully lost only three men to flesh wounds.[36]

Finally Tupper came up and restored order. Two three-inch rifle-guns from Battery A, First Illinois Light Artillery, unlimbered behind the One Hundred Sixteenth Illinois and opened on Kolb's guns. By now it was nearly dark, and Colonel Anderson had grown tired of the fight. With the evidence all too plain that Sherman had already crossed the river, he withdrew behind some low hills out of range of the Yankees.[37]

Certainly this unexpected clash in his rear was enough to give Sherman pause and lessen any inclination, however slight, he might have had to push on toward Tunnel Hill. By sunset, the Federals were fortifying the detached hills as if they intended to hole up there for the duration of the battle. Details of infantrymen strained to haul cannons up the slippery slopes with ropes. Those with spades worked feverishly overturning soil for breastworks. One regiment from each brigade on the hill was thrown forward to picket the ravine and surrounding valleys.

Sherman deployed his command oddly, in a manner suited to neither attack nor defend. Lightburn's brigade held the northeastern crest of the hill won from Smith's Texans. Once Tupper sorted out his brigade, he arrayed it to cover Sherman's left flank, from the base of the hill to the bank of the creek. Alexander's brigade of John Smith's division entrenched to the right of Lightburn. Matthies and Raum stood at the base of the hill in reserve. John Corse's brigade of Ewing's division held the western hill. Colonel Joseph Cockerill fell in on the slope to Corse's right, and Colonel Adolphus Bushbeck's brigade extended the line westward into the valley. Colonel John Loomis stood in reserve. Sherman made no use of Jefferson C. Davis's division that evening. He told the Indianian to spread out his command, leaving one brigade at the bridge, one midway across the valley, and one close to Sherman's extreme right.[38]

Night fell. The pop-pop of the skirmishers' blind shots died out. On the wooded hilltops and down in the muddy ravine and narrow valleys, the soldiers trembled through the long hours of darkness. Recalled an officer of the Fifth Iowa: "That night my regiment stood picket at the front. The ground was cold and wet, none of us slept a wink, and we were almost freezing and starving. We had not slept, indeed, for a hundred hours. It had been one vast strain, and now a battle was coming on."[39]

# CHAPTER TWELVE

# THE MOST CURIOUS BATTLE
# OF THE WAR

JOE HOOKER and John Geary had much in common. Both were vain and ambitious. They reveled in a good fight, particularly one that was likely to enhance their reputations. Geary had gotten a fair share of glory at Wauhatchie but was always on the alert for a chance at more. Hooker, on the other hand, had yet to prove himself to Grant. Thomas's amended orders to Hooker to demonstrate against and—if practicable—take Lookout Mountain whetted the martial appetites of both Hooker and Geary, exciting a hunger that drove caution from their minds.

Hooker had not the slightest doubt that he could take Lookout Mountain, its imposing appearance notwithstanding. Scouts, deserters, and simple observation had given him an excellent feel for Confederate dispositions, numerical strength, and vulnerabilities. From Lookout Valley the long, thin picket line of Walthall and Moore was visible to the naked eye, as were Walthall's reserves, encamped in a hollow halfway up the northwestern slope. Deserters confirmed the reports of loyal citizens that Stevenson held the summit itself with three brigades. Hooker also was aware of the labyrinth of Rebel rifle pits and earthworks on the bench, thrown up to repel attacks from the direction of the river, Chattanooga, or Lookout Valley.

Hooker dismissed any direct attempt at dislodging Stevenson from the summit: "The only means of access from the west, for a distance of twenty miles up the valley, was by two or three trails, admitting of the passage of but one man at a time, and even those trails were held at the top by rebel pickets." Besides, he reasoned, once he swept around the bench, Stevenson's position above him would be untenable. "On the Chattanooga side, which is less precipitous, a road of easy grade had been made communicating with the summit by zig-zag lines running diagonally up the mountainside, and it was believed that before our troops should gain possession of this, the enemy on top would evacuate his position, to avoid being cut off from his main body."[1]

Hooker and his staff worked until after midnight perfecting their plans for what one participant later called "the most curious battle of the war." Attention to detail was imperative, as Hooker's force consisted of three divisions from three different corps, none of which had fought together before.[2]

At 3:00 A.M. on 24 November, Geary received his orders to "cross Lookout Creek and to assault Lookout Mountain, marching down the valley and sweeping every rebel from it." He was to break camp at daylight. The Pennsylvanian summoned his brigade commanders to his headquarters at once. An hour later, they returned to their respective units, which were spread out across Lookout Valley from Smith's Hill to the Cumming farm, covering the ground previously held by Howard's entire corps. Shortly after 4:00 A.M., the strident notes of reveille shattered the frigid predawn blackness. Breakfast fires were kindled, and in minutes the acrid aroma of burning wood and boiling coffee filled the valley. Ordnance sergeants reported to their trains to draw cartridges in the number of one hundred rounds per man.[3]

Lieutenant Colonel Eugene Powell, commander of the Sixty-sixth Ohio and division officer-of-the-day, had been startled awake by the hoofbeats of a galloping rider approaching his tent. Powell's sentinel halted the shadowy messenger, who sang out: "I have orders for Colonel Powell." The Ohioan threw on his greatcoat and stepped outside. General Geary wished to see him at once, the orderly announced.

Together they rode to division headquarters. As they neared, "I noticed that the general's tents were lighted up, which to my mind, indicated that a movement for us was at hand," remembered Powell. He dismounted and entered the headquarters tent. "The General sat there, surrounded by a number of staff officers, in addition to his own; these were from Grant's and Hooker's headquarters, and had undoubtedly brought Geary his orders and were waiting to see the movement begin. It struck me, as I stepped into Geary's tent, that I had seldom looked upon a more silent, solemn party." Geary broke the silence with a hearty, confident greeting: "Colonel, I have sent for you. I have orders to make a demonstration upon Lookout Mountain. I wish to know where and how I can cross that creek with my command." In apparent deference to Grant's staff officers, Geary had been careful to say "demonstration." However, recalled Powell, he quickly added "that he intended to show the world what his ideas of a demonstration meant."

Powell was ready with an answer. On the evening of the twenty-third, while making his rounds, he had come upon a point near the extreme right of Geary's picket line, along the west bank of Lookout Creek, where supports had been laid across the creek to build a small dam to power a nearby gristmill belonging to Joseph Light. Light's Mill stood a half mile southeast of Wauhatchie. Light hadn't finished the dam, but the wooden supports projected above the water in such a manner that Powell was sure he could lash rails and boards to them to make a good footbridge.

Geary accepted Powell's proposal at once. He told the Ohioan to take his own picket reserve, a detail from the Twenty-ninth Pennsylvania, and the few pioneers on hand and begin building a bridge; the division would break camp at 6:00 A.M. and concentrate behind a tall ridge north of the Light farm, there to wait until Powell had finished his bridge and secured the east bank.[4]

"I withdrew at once, mounted my horse and was soon moving with my pickets to carry out the orders," said Powell. "When I reached the open space at the dam, the moon was shining, making it quite light, but soon thereafter clouds of mist settled down upon the mountain side, and it grew quite dark." Powell dismounted and gathered his men about him. He told them what their mission was and called for volunteers to cross the creek. None came forward. All were aware that Confederate pickets lurked in the underbrush on the far bank. In fact, they knew their enemy intimately, having met at a shallow and rocky spot midway across the creek every day for the past month to swap stories and merchandise.[5]

Finally a man stepped forward and said he would go over, then another, until the whole group took Powell's challenge. That was a better response than Powell had expected, so he divided the men into two parties, one to crawl across the supports and dislodge the enemy pickets from the east bank as quietly as possible, the other to begin carrying boards, rails, and ropes from the mill to lay the bridge.

The Yankee pickets from the first party felt their way across and reassembled on the far bank. Fanning out, they found not a single Rebel. Pleasantly surprised, Powell started his other party to work. To keep them from waking up the entire mountain, he told the men to lash the boards to the supports with rope rather than pound them together with nails.[6]

Colonel Whitaker (of Cruft's division of the Army of the Cumberland) got his orders about the same time as Geary. His men lay bivouacked in utter exhaustion near Hooker's headquarters—they had marched twenty-four miles that day over a road "indescribably bad" just to reach

Lookout Valley. Moreover, someone had foolishly issued the men new shoes before they set out, so that they all lay down that night with swollen feet and blisters. But orders were orders, and the Kentuckian roused his men at 4:00 A.M., with instructions to march in two hours to Wauhatchie, there to join up with Geary.[7]

Colonel Grose—Cruft's other brigade commander—reported to Hooker just before dawn to receive his orders in person. He was to move his command down to Lookout Creek and effect a lodgment on the far bank near the mouth, at a point where the wagon road to Chattanooga ran alongside the tracks of the Nashville and Chattanooga Railroad. The bridge over which the road crossed was known to be damaged, but Hooker counted on Grose to ford the creek.[8]

To General Osterhaus went a supporting role. Williamson's brigade was to protect the artillery that Hooker was gathering on the hills near the mouth of Lookout Creek; Woods's brigade would cover Grose and cross the creek after him, then ascend the slope and form a junction with the left of Geary's division as it worked its way around the mountain.[9]

Despite his confidence, Hooker was leaving little to chance. During the night, he brought forward all available artillery to pulverize the Rebel pickets and cover the advance of his own infantry. By daybreak, he had nine batteries situated between Light's Mill and the mouth of Lookout Creek. One section of Knap's Pennsylvania battery unlimbered on the hill beside Light's Mill. The rest of the battery set up on a swell beside the Kelley's Ferry road, from which it could range the western slope of the mountain. One section of the First Battery, Iowa Light Artillery, was posted on Tyndale's Hill to command the railroad crossing and to range the northwest slope of the mountain. Two twenty-pounder Parrott rifles from the Fourth Battery, Ohio Light Artillery, came into line in the open field between Tyndale's and Smith's hills. On the latter eminence, Major John Reynolds (Geary's timid chief of artillery who had found himself in command of the remnants of Knap's battery during the Wauhatchie fight) posted two sections from Battery I, First New York Light Artillery. He pushed four Napoleon guns from Battery K, First Ohio, onto Bald Knob between Smith's Hill and the mouth of the creek. The remaining sections of these batteries, along with Battery F, Second Missouri Light Artillery, and Battery K, Fifth United States, were scattered over the best available high ground farther to the rear.

The artillery of the Army of the Cumberland lent its support to Hooker's effort as well. From Moccasin Point, the Tenth Indiana and Eighteenth Ohio batteries commanded the northern slope of Lookout Mountain and the bench below the point. Two twenty-pounder Parrotts were loaned them during the night to add punch to their fire support. At the same time, the Eighth Wisconsin Light Battery and a section of the

Seventh Indiana Light Artillery left the city and set up behind the extreme right of Thomas's entrenchments to cover the mouth of Chattanooga Creek and harass any Confederate force that might try to move
across the valley to reinforce the mountain.

It was to be the grandest gathering of Federal artillery in the theater
of operations since Captain John Mendenhall had blasted Breckinridge
to bits with massed cannon at Stones River.[10]

General Walthall had no idea that nearly a quarter of Grant's artillery force was to be trained on his tiny brigade at dawn, but he could
feel the cold tingle of impending calamity in the misty night air. To
carry out his standing orders to observe the Federals in Lookout Valley
and guard against a surprise attack on the mountain, Walthall had
stretched nearly half of his fifteen hundred Mississippians in a picket
line from the partially destroyed turnpike bridge near the mouth of
Lookout Creek up the slope of the mountain to the palisades. Part of
the Thirty-fourth Mississippi picketed that portion of the line nearest
the creek; the rest of the regiment bivouacked a few hundred yards to
the rear at the base of the mountain. About half of the Twenty-ninth
and Thirtieth Mississippi regiments were strung out up the slope. Their
uncommitted companies encamped among slimy boulders and slippery
ravines a stone's throw from the cliff. Walthall held the Twenty-fourth
and Twenty-seventh Mississippi regiments, less those on picket duty,
in reserve on the bench just west of the point, about five hundred yards
from the Cravens house.[11]

Walthall feared for his brigade. While his men worked feverishly
through the night of the twenty-third to construct defensive works on
his front and improve those near the Cravens house, which had been
sadly ignored during the preceding week, the Mississippian contemplated his predicament:

> From the creek up to the bench of the mountain the surface was so
> broken that the rapid and orderly movement of troops was impossible.
> The batteries on Moccasin Point commanded at easy range the only
> route by which troops could come to my support or my own could re-
> tire upon the main army. These batteries were trained to sweep the
> slope of the mountain from the wagon road to the palisades. Commu-
> nication with my superiors on the mountain top was difficult and slow,
> the route by which messengers must travel being circuitous, as well
> as rugged. Such was the isolated and exposed position of this outpost
> brigade.[12]

Walthall's regimental commanders and soldiers shared his gloom.
"We had been lying for many days among the rocks without shelter, and
the regiment and command was much (I may say completely) exhaust-

ed by the heavy details constantly made upon it for picket and fatigue duty," grieved Colonel W. F. Dowd of the Twenty-fourth Mississippi. Rations were miserable and scarce. On a typical day, complained a member of the Twenty-seventh, the men were issued three crackers and two tablespoons of sugar.[13]

General Moore was even more pessimistic than Walthall. Under the original scheme, Walthall and Moore were to defend a mixed line of rifle pits, crude breastworks, and stone walls extending from the northeast base of the palisades past the Cravens house and down to the mouth of Chattanooga Creek. Walthall was to hold the line from the cliff to the house, while Moore was to man the remainder with his paroled Alabamians. Then Walthall went off to watch the Yankees in Lookout Valley, leaving the works to Moore's left undefended. Next, several hundred of Moore's own men were sent out to picket Lookout Creek from Walthall's right to the northern base of the mountain. Moore remonstrated with the acting division commander, John Jackson, against such a drastic depletion of the forces manning the main line. Jackson ignored Moore's pleading. Having done all he felt he could, Moore wrote off any chance of success and lost himself in cynical self-pity. He dismissed the half-finished fieldworks near the Cravens house as a joke: "No serious effort had been made to construct defensive works for our forces on the mountain. It is true some of the timber in front of Walthall's brigade had been cut down and a narrow, shallow, but worthless, line of trenches (unworthily called rifle pits) extended from Walthall's left to the Cravens house, and from the extremity of a short line of stone fence at this point to the mouth of Chattanooga Creek a still more abortive pretense had been made."[14]

Having resigned himself to the worst, Moore was unaffected by the ominous events of 23 November. While Walthall fretted the night away, Moore retired to his headquarters tent on the bench trail, about a quarter mile in rear of the line his brigade was to hold. General Jackson, even less interested in what might emerge from the valley at daybreak than Moore, passed the night at his headquarters, which were a quarter mile farther in the rear, on the eastern slope of the mountain beside a road leading up to the resort community of Summertown.[15]

The man in overall command, Carter Stevenson, could offer little in the way of constructive advice to his subordinates. Late on the afternoon of 23 November he had been ordered to defend ground that was unfamiliar; moreover, Stevenson was not even sure that Bragg really wanted him to stay on the mountain. As dawn broke drearily over the mountain on 24 November, Stevenson received orders from army headquarters to send his heavy batteries down into the Chattanooga Valley and to hold his infantry "in readiness to move in any direction." When Colonel D. R. Hundley, the division officer-of-the-day, reported to the Cravens house for orders a few minutes later, Stevenson could only shrug. "I know of my own knowledge that on the morning of the fight General Stevenson was in hourly expectation of having to send his division down into the valley in contemplation of an attack on our right. At least such was the information given me at the time I received my instructions," averred Hundley.[16]

Still, Stevenson put up a good front for Moore and Walthall. In the event of an attack, he told Walthall to fall back fighting to the trenches at the Cravens house and to hold on there until he could reinforce the Mississippian from the summit. Moore was to do the same on Walthall's right. Unfortunately, the only reinforcing unit Stevenson felt he could offer was Edmund Pettus's Alabama brigade. He deemed it essential to keep the rest of his division on the summit: "This would expose the enemy to a flank fire at short range from the crest of the mountain on which I proposed to deploy the remainder of my force not engaged in guarding the passes on the western side as sharpshooters." Stevenson briefed Moore on his plan, then began the slow ride up the rocky slope. It was 6:30 A.M. Off to the west, hidden behind the cold, damp palisades, the sun rose, poking a few furtive rays through the low mist that blanketed Lookout Valley.[17]

Lieutenant Colonel Powell was proud of his handiwork. He met General Geary near the Light farm about thirty minutes after sunrise and reported the bridge ready and not a Rebel in sight. Geary was at the head of the division column. While his troops filed off the mill road to rest behind the ridge and await the order to cross Lookout Creek, he and Powell rode down to the mill. There they dismounted and walked to the bank. Geary was impressed. "He thanked me heartily for the good work that the pickets had been able to accomplish, as until then he had no idea as to how or where he would be able to cross that creek," boasted Powell. In his exuberance, however, the Ohioan had neglected one key point: the waters of Lookout Creek, although receding, were still dangerously high. They boiled and gurgled among the logs and rails of his footbridge, threatening to rip it apart. Geary decided to wait an hour before trying to cross. Hooker happily endorsed the Pennsylvanian's recommendation in a note to Thomas at 7:30 A.M. He too was unready to begin the movement: Grose had gotten a late start breaking camp and Hooker had only just received final confirmation from Grant that Osterhaus was his to use as he saw fit.[18]

By 8:30 A.M., the current had calmed and the water level of Lookout

Creek had dropped. Better yet from the Federal perspective, the mist had thickened. Observed Geary with satisfaction: "Drifting clouds enveloped the whole ridge of the mountain top, and heavy mists and fogs obscured the slope from lengthened vision." Neither Walthall's pickets, who stood their beat nearly a mile and a half to the north, nor John Brown's Tennesseans fanned out along the western edge of the summit would have a clue of what was going on at the mill. With nature's apparent benediction, Geary gave the word to begin the crossing.

More orders followed. Horses were to be left on the west bank; the mountain was too treacherous to trust their footing. Colonel George Cobham was the first to file across Powell's footbridge. He had with him the Twenty-ninth and One Hundred Eleventh Pennsylvania regiments; his third regiment, the One Hundred Ninth Pennsylvania, had had the good fortune to draw camp-guard duty. Up the steep, slick slope clambered the Pennsylvanians, their field officers trudging along beside them. Colonel Rickards, who had helped save Geary at Wauhatchie by his adroit handling of Knap's battery, now had the dubious honor of guarding the extreme right of the line. The soldiers of his Twenty-ninth Pennsylvania, rejoined by their comrades who had helped build the bridge, climbed the slope until they ran squarely up against the perpendicular wall of the palisade. There they halted and faced to the front. The One Hundred Eleventh fell in on their left.[19]

Next over the creek was Colonel Ireland's New York brigade. It faced to the front midway up the slope to form the center of Geary's line of battle. While the 130 men of the One Hundred Second New York deployed as skirmishers to cover the brigade front, Ireland arrayed the rest of his command with the Sixtieth New York on the right, the One Hundred Thirty-seventh New York in the center, and the One Hundred Forty-ninth New York on the left.[20]

Colonel Charles Candy's brigade, which had missed the Wauhatchie fight, crossed the creek next and extended Geary's left down to the base of the mountain. Candy's line began about fifty yards to the left of and slightly behind that of Ireland. Candy lined up with the One Hundred Forty-seventh Pennsylvania on the right. Next came the Seventh Ohio, then the Twenty-eighth Pennsylvania, and finally, anchoring the left, Lieutenant Colonel Powell's Sixty-sixth Ohio. Fifty soldiers from the Fifth Ohio showed up at the last minute and fell in on Powell's left; the rest of their regiment and the entire Twenty-ninth Ohio had been left behind to guard the division's camp.[21]

Walter Whitaker, every bit as vain and ambitious as Geary though not nearly so adept at self-promotion, brought his brigade over Lookout Creek last and reluctantly formed three hundred yards to the rear of and in support of the Pennsylvanian's line of battle. As Geary's tiny division was only slightly larger than the Kentuckian's six regiments, he deployed his command in two lines, with his right resting against the palisades and his left ending behind that of Ireland. He tucked the Eighth Kentucky beneath a rough, protruding crag of the cliff on the right of his first line. Next came the Thirty-fifth Indiana, then the Ninety-ninth Ohio, and finally the Fortieth Ohio on the left. One hundred yards to the rear of the right regiments, he posted the Ninety-sixth Illinois and Fifty-first Ohio. Despite his disappointment at not being in the front line of the assault, Whitaker saw from the nature of the mountain slope that, as Geary swept to the northeast, his own line, hugging the palisades, would move faster than and eventually overtake the Pennsylvanian's left, giving him the satisfaction of at least being close to the fight.[22]

By 9:00 A.M., everyone was across Lookout Creek—everyone, that is, but General Geary and his staff. As soon as lines were dressed and the men ready to move forward, Geary sent staff officers over to summon his brigade and regimental commanders back to "the safe side of the creek." Recalled Lieutenant Albert Greene of Ireland's staff derisively: "He made a speech, in which he expatiated on our undertaking, told us of the dangers we would undoubtedly encounter, said something about success and glory, directed us to sweep along the slope and push the enemy off, observed cheerfully that he was not going up then but would come up later, shook hands with us all, and bade us goodbye." The colonels returned to their commands amid a good deal of angry grumbling. "Some remember that when Geary's division was in sore straits at Gettysburg, he was miles away on the Taneytown road, and they thought of it then, and remembered too that less than a month ago, in that dark and bloody wood at Wauhatchie, there was no word from Geary till the firing had ceased and the only sounds on the field were the digging of entrenchments and the cries of the wounded," sneered Greene.[23]

When Geary finally did go over, he and his staff hiked along behind Whitaker's second line, safe from Rebel bullets and far too distant to give any meaningful instructions to the Pennsylvanian's three brigade commanders.[24]

Whitaker gave a speech of his own that, if not more inspirational, was certainly more spirited. He faced his front line to the rear and, riding between the two lines, addressed his troops under the brooding palisades of Lookout Mountain. Whether the men understood a word he said is questionable. Not only did the Kentuckian speak with a lisp, but he had a notorious habit of drinking himself silly during a battle. On the second day at Chickamauga, while his brigade clung desperately to Horseshoe Ridge, he absented himself from the front in a search for whiskey. Here on Lookout Mountain, he decided to drink his fill before the action began, and so was in a jovial mood as he addressed his troops. "Gentlemen," he stammered, "we are to storm and carry the enemy's works on Lookout. You will of course whip the enemy, and then we will all assemble at my quarters and take a drink."[25]

A little after 9:30 A.M., the bugles sounded "Forward" and Geary's skirmishers disappeared into the thick fog and dense timber. Spruce and cedar trees abounded, their coniferous coats masking the way ahead. Huge rocks and limestone outcrops blemished the complexion of the mountainside. Countless ravines of varying depths and lengths sliced across the line of march, forcing the bluecoats to look down constantly to keep their footing.

When the skirmishers had had time enough to cover about three hundred yards, Cobham, Ireland, and Candy started their main line. For nearly a mile they marched unopposed through the forest. Only the squashing of damp leaves, snapping of twigs, and panting of the soldiers broke the morning silence. The sergeant-major of the Ninety-sixth Illinois contemplated the early going: "Much of the ground over which we advanced was rough beyond conception. It was covered with an untouched forest growth, seamed with deep ravines, and obstructed with rocks of all sizes which had fallen from the frowning wall on our right. The ground passed over by our left was not quite so rough; but, taking the entire stretch of the mountain side traversed by our force . . . it was undoubtedly the roughest battle field of the war."[26]

As yet, of course, there was no battle. General Walthall had not an inkling of the tempest brewing far down the western slope. Walthall was in the saddle and out on the bench beyond the Cravens house early. Shortly after daybreak, he had detected movement in Geary's camp, but the mist obscured the valley before he could ascertain in which direction the Yankees were headed.

The fog infuriated the Rebel leaders. Indeed, recalled Colonel Hundley, the division officer-of-the-day, the morning broke "more than foggy. The atmosphere was thick almost to darkness with vapor." Through a momentary gap in the mist Colonel W. F. Dowd of the Twenty-fourth Mississippi caught a glimpse of the rear of Geary's column marching up the valley toward Light's Mill. He sent word of his sighting to Walthall, who ordered him to reinforce the picket reserves of the Twenty-ninth and Thirtieth Mississippi with four companies.

Where was the advanced Rebel picket post that Lieutenant Colonel Powell had expected to encounter the night before at the creek and that should have provided early warning of the Yankee crossing? Powell

*In Reserve.* Brigadier General Charles Woods waits with the Thirteenth Illinois Infantry as Federal artillery shells the Confederate position on Lookout Mountain.

learned the answer two days later. There had, indeed, been some two dozen Confederates on the east side of the creek, hidden in the underbrush near the bank. They had seen Powell's pickets gather to lay the footbridge, but assumed them to be a mere scouting party. The lieutenant in command of the Rebels led his detachment back to the cover of some bushes farther up the slope, planning to pounce on and bag Powell's party after daylight. Before he could act, however, Geary's division appeared and began to cross the creek. Shocked and frightened, the Rebels watched the blue line of battle form on the mountainside and march off. For the next forty-eight hours the little Southern band shivered in the bushes until, worn down by exposure and uncertainty, they left their hiding place and walked over the footbridge to give themselves up.

Walthall sent a courier to Jackson at 8:00 A.M. with news of Dowd's sighting, not because he had any confidence in Jackson as a general but because, until Cheatham returned, he was Walthall's immediate commander. Moore had an equally low opinion of Jackson, whom the brigade commanders called "Mudwall" behind his back to contrast his lack of talent with the great ability of the late Stonewall Jackson.[27]

The slick ground forced the messenger to walk his horse, so that Jackson, in his tent on the Summertown road, did not receive Walthall's note until 9:00 A.M. Mudwall took the news calmly. He passed the note on to Stevenson, who had transferred his headquarters to the summit, and sent a staff officer back to Walthall to tell the Mississippian to hold his command "under arms ready for action," which Walthall of course had been doing for nearly two hours. After that, Jackson went for a walk—in the wrong direction. Instead of heading toward the point of Lookout, he wandered off toward Chattanooga. Of course he saw nothing alarming. "I walked out on the road toward the Cravens house to a favorable point and could distinguish the enemy's troops in the plain in front of Chattanooga—all quiet, no massing, no movements of any kind," he recalled. "From this point I sent another staff officer to the Cravens house to report to me immediately anything of interest, and returned myself to my position at the fork of the road."[28]

At that moment, Walthall's full attention was given over to the Federals assembling opposite his picket line along the creek, near the railroad crossing. Moore was with him. Together they watched the Yankees throw forward a regiment and begin skirmishing with troops from both their picket lines. Moore dashed off a note to Jackson apprising him of this development and asking when he should place his brigade, which still lay encamped on the east side of the mountain, in line of battle behind its breastworks, then rode back to await a response.

Walthall prepared himself as best he could, given his uncertainty as to whether the main Federal thrust would come along the western slope beyond his left or over the creek opposite his right. He sent forward the remainder of the Thirty-fourth Mississippi to strengthen his picket line near the railroad crossing, ordered the Twenty-ninth and Thirtieth Mississippi to stand ready to repel an attack from the left, and held the Twenty-fourth and Twenty-seventh Mississippi in reserve to move to the right or left as needed.[29]

What had caught the attention of Walthall and Moore was the arrival of Grose's brigade near the west bank of Lookout Creek at 9:00 A.M.—ninety minutes behind schedule. The delays had not been of Grose's making. He had ridden far ahead of his column after daybreak to examine the crossing site personally. Riding up through the mist, he "found the enemy's pickets on the east bank and ours on the west, within thirty paces of each other, enjoying a friendship" that he quickly broke up. Like Geary, Grose found the creek swollen and turbulent, and he ruled out an attempt at fording it. As he saw it, the only way over was to repair a space in the center of the bridge about fifteen feet wide. And, as Grose noted, the bridge was covered by enemy pickets tucked in rifle pits and behind the railroad embankment near the east bank.

Because Hooker's staff had assured him that the bridge was in far better repair than it was, Grose had brought along only a handful of tools with his brigade. When he discovered the error, Grose reluctantly halted his brigade near the Parker farm and hastily sent back for more. An hour slipped away. When Grose finally neared the creek with his troops and tools, Walthall's pickets peppered his work party with rifle fire, keeping them well away from the damaged structure.

Grose reacted swiftly to protect his work party. He ordered the Eighty-fourth Illinois, supported by the Seventy-fifth Illinois, to form a skirmish line and sweep down to the edge of the creek. There, they were to open a steady fire on the Mississippians; with luck, it would compel them to keep their heads down long enough for the work party to repair the bridge.[30]

At 10:00 A.M., the Illinoisans raised a yell and charged toward the creek, splashing through a four-foot-deep swamp under a constant hail of sharpshooters' bullets. For seventy-five yards they endured the chill muck and rifle fire. At the fringe of underbrush along the west bank, they fell to the ground. After gathering together loose branches and fallen trees for a crude line of breastworks, they returned the Rebel fire. The Illinoisans forced a handful of Walthall's exposed sharpshooters to scamper back into the rifle pits, but they were unable to silence the Rebel fire altogether. For the next thirty minutes, the two sides popped away at one another.[31]

Meanwhile, Osterhaus had come up along the Brown's Ferry road a half mile to the rear of Grose. By then, Hooker had grown tired of the largely ineffectual efforts of Grose to cross the creek at the bridge. Standing with his staff atop a high hill beside the Parker farm, Hooker had a clear view of the muddle down at the bridge. When he saw the remainder of the Thirty-fourth Mississippi file off the mountain to reinforce the Confederate pickets behind the railroad embankment, Hooker abandoned the idea of effecting his main lodgment there. Instead, he decided to try to cross the creek eight hundred yards farther to the south. He told Osterhaus to leave Williamson's brigade behind to support the massed artillery batteries and to take Woods's brigade upstream to attempt the crossing. At the same time, Hooker ordered Grose to leave the Eighty-fourth and Seventy-fifth Illinois where they were to divert the Rebels' attention and with his remaining four regiments fall in to the rear of Woods. To keep Walthall's pickets occupied and their commander's attention away from Woods, Hooker commanded his artillery to hammer the Mississippians at the railroad embankment.[32]

For nearly an hour Geary's bluecoats had slipped and stumbled along the craggy western slope of Lookout, the heavy mist wetting the outside of uniforms already soaked with sweat from the inside. Finally, at 10:30 A.M., the rattle of musketry from the skirmish line announced that contact had been made. The firing became louder and more regular, and the main line halted expectantly. Out of the fog came a stretcher bearing the bloody remains of Major Gilbert Elliott. In command of Ireland's skirmish line, Elliott foolishly had gone into the fight in full dress uniform with a red-bordered cape on his overcoat. A conspicuous target, he was the first man in the division to be hit.

Elliott and his skirmishers had struck Walthall's pickets one mile southwest of the point. Even with the addition of the remaining companies of the Twenty-ninth and Thirtieth Mississippi, the Rebel line was stretched far too thin to offer prolonged resistance. At least six feet, probably more, separated each soldier from his nearest comrade. Crouched behind boulders and crude log breastworks along the sixty-degree slope, each Mississippian fought largely on his own, holding out for as long as he felt it prudent.[33]

Geary's main line came up without much trouble, and the pressure on the Mississippians rapidly became unbearable. Cobham's One Hundred Eleventh and Twenty-ninth Pennsylvania regiments, moving along a narrow ledge at the base of the palisades, got a little ahead of Ireland and engaged them, pouring a sharp fire down the slope into the left flank of the Twenty-ninth Mississippi. Ireland's New Yorkers fixed bayonets and pushed forward with a yell. Passing over their skirmish line, they

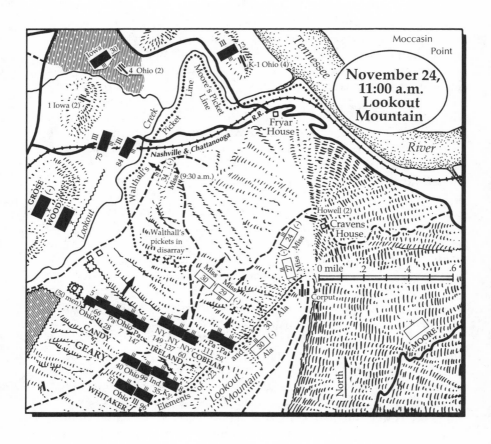

Iowa 30
4 Ohio (2)
III 13
K-1 Ohio (4)

Moccasin
Point

**November 24,
11:00 a.m.
Lookout
Mountain**

1 Iowa (2)

*Tennessee*

Moore's Picket Line
Picket Line
Creek

R.R.
Fryar
House

*River*

III III
75 84

*Nashville & Chattanooga*

GROSE
WOOD
x
x

Lookout

Walthall's

Miss (9:30 a.m.)
34 (-)

Walthall's
pickets in
disarray

Howell (2)
Cravens
House

24 (-)
Miss

27
Miss

0 mile     .2     .4     .6

Miss
30
Miss
29 (-)

Corput
x

(50 men)
5
66
Ohio
28
CANDY
GEARY

Pa Ohio
7    Pa
147

NY  NY  NY
149  137  29
COBHAM
IRELAND
60

Pa  Pa
111

30
Ala (-)

30
Ala

x
MOORE

North

40 Ohio 99 Ind
51
Ohio  III  96
WHITAKER

35 Ky
8

*Lookout Mountain*

Elements of 23

dashed toward the pickets from in front. Candy, meanwhile, swept along in good order between the creek bed and the lower stretches of the mountainside, his front clear.[34]

As the New Yorkers closed to within a few yards, most of the Mississippians chose to break for the rear. They, ironically, were the brave ones. "This was one of the few times in battle that it took a braver man to run than it did to stand; because those who remained behind the rocks could surrender in safety, and those who ran would draw the fire of the heavy Yankee line," averred one who elected to flee. "Many of our boys were captured that day on account of our line holding its position until the enemy were so near that it was almost certain death to run," he added in sympathy for those of his comrades who held the line.[35]

Captain George Collins of the One Hundred Forty-ninth New York vividly described the scene from the Federal perspective, as his regiment chased the Rebels out of their works and northward along the timbered slope:

> As the boys pressed forward, the enemy fired a volley or two into their ranks and then made a desperate struggle to get away. When the boys had him running, they kept him going, so that it was a pure question of courage, muscle and personal endurance. When the men were fatigued and their breaths so hot as to scorch their throats, they dropped on the ground for a few moments and then got up and went at it again. The course up and down the gullies and ravines was so rugged that the men had to work themselves along hanging to the bushes and by clambering over rocks on their hands and knees.[36]

Dozens of Confederates were hit, and scores more surrendered. The Mississippians' ragged volleys were not without effect, however, confessed Collins:

> Close behind the advance line came the surgeons, hospital stewards and stretcher-bearers. When the boys dropped out of line from injuries, their immediate wants were cared for by the medical officers and then they were carried back to the field hospital by the stretcher-bearers. Once on the stretcher, then came the tug of war to hang on and get safely down to the crossing over the creek. The men when injured were reeking with sweat and their clothes drenched with perspiration, consequently when relieved from exertion they were chilled to the bone by the bleak November air. Part way up the mountain the long line of stretcher-bearers were met by chaplains with large bottles of whiskey to keep up the strength of the men and ward off the effects of the terrible chill.[37]

As Geary's line came in sight and the Rebel pickets began trickling from their breastworks, Hooker ordered his artillery to shift its fire from the railroad embankment and saturate the enemy's line of retreat along the mountainside. Hooker's intentions were good but, up in the dusky forest toward which his cannoneers trained their pieces, the opposing lines were on top of one another. Gunpowder smoke and fog effectively hid the action from those in the valley, so that the aim of the artillerymen was uncertain at best. "The shriek of shells came up from the valley below, passing parallel with our line, and now and then a shell would burst in our front," recalled Lieutenant Greene of Ireland's staff.[38]

Around 11:30 A.M., the wild pursuit of Ireland and Cobham came to an abrupt halt some three hundred yards southwest of the point of Lookout. Suddenly, said, Greene, the "work became sharp and hot. At every tree and rock and log in front of us was the flash of a rebel musket; from the palisades above the rebel bullets fell thickly. We could see the men on the rocks above us and in our front." New Yorkers began to drop in alarming numbers. Puffing along with his troops, thoroughly exhausted, was Colonel Henry Barnum of the One Hundred Forty-ninth New York. Declared unfit for duty by the regimental surgeon because of wounds sustained at Wauhatchie, he nonetheless had joined the regiment in its climb up the mountain. Barely able to put one foot before the other, he mustered what little strength he had left to exhort his men forward until a bullet ripped through his right arm and he collapsed from the shock. Instinctively, Ireland's entire line took cover among the rocks and ravines, while he and his officers, running about on foot, tried to restore order.[39]

Ireland and Cobham had run into Walthall's two reserve regiments, the Twenty-fourth and Twenty-seventh Mississippi, posted between the base of the cliff and the Cravens house road. Though badly outnumbered, the Mississippians gave a good account of themselves, throwing back Ireland's first attempt at storming their works. While the Federals regrouped, Walthall hastily prepared a fallback position. He told Colonel W. F. Dowd to detach three companies from his Twenty-fourth Mississippi as sharpshooters and deploy them three hundred yards to the rear, from the ledge above and just west of the Cravens house on up a narrow ravine to the very base of the palisades. A moment later, Walthall yelled at Dowd to reinforce them with a fourth company and, if the need arose, to defend that line "till hell froze over." That left the Mississippi colonel, who had sent out four companies before dawn to reinforce the picket line, with just two companies and a few stragglers from the Twenty-ninth Mississippi to resist the next Federal charge.

The Twenty-seventh Mississippi, holding onto Dowd's left, was in similar straits. At daybreak, Walthall had ordered its commander, Colonel William Campbell, to assume responsibility for the brigade picket line. Campbell had posted himself near the railroad bridge, and so was cut off from his regiment by Geary's assault. Now Lieutenant Colonel A. J. Jones was busy realigning ranks of the Twenty-seventh, badly mangled after survivors from the picket line had stampeded through it.

Walthall was getting precious little help from either his immediate superior or the troops atop the mountain. Mudwall Jackson had yet to respond in a meaningful way to the developing crisis down on the bench, and Carter Stevenson's efforts at harassing the Federals from above proved to be but a temporary irritant. Stevenson instructed General Brown, in temporary command of his own division, to reinforce the line of sharpshooters along the western edge of the summit and open fire on the Yankees below. While the Twenty-third and Thirtieth Alabama shot down through the fog at Cobham's Pennsylvanians, Brown hurried the Thirty-second Tennessee to the point to cover Walthall's left flank from above. At the same time, Captain Max Van Den Corput brought his two-gun reserve section up to the western edge of the precipice. His Georgia cannoneers raised the trails of their guns, depressed the barrels as low as possible, and began shelling Ireland's prone line.[40]

With Geary and his staff on foot far to the rear, Ireland, Cobham, and their regimental commanders acted on their own to meet this unexpected vertical resistance. Although they were momentarily surprised, the result was never in doubt. Calm thinking, sheer weight of numbers, the peculiarities of the terrain, and the fog all worked in the Federals' favor.

Just as he had at Wauhatchie, Colonel William Rickards of the Twenty-ninth Pennsylvania now contributed decisively to the outcome. By hugging the palisades, his men escaped the fire from the sharpshooters above, who could neither aim low enough nor see their targets clearly. Rickards edged his small command forward, past Walthall's left flank and toward Dowd's sharpshooters, who were hastily forming to Rickards's right front.[41]

Cobham's One Hundred Eleventh Pennsylvania, meanwhile, charged down off the ledge at the left front of the Twenty-seventh Mississippi. Moments later, Ireland resumed the attack along the rest of the line. Whether any orders were given is open to debate. Lieutenant Greene swore that the regimental color-bearers, "as by a common impulse, rushed ahead, and with a great shout the whole line broke cover and followed them."[42]

It was the same story all over again. Outnumbered four to one and outflanked on both the right and left, Walthall's second line of resistance disintegrated. "We were simply crushed by numbers," explained Robert Jarman of the Twenty-seventh Mississippi. Walthall rode about shouting at the men to rally, but few paid him any attention. All order was lost as the Mississippians ran rearward, past Walthall, around the point of the mountain, and back toward the Cravens house. Some clawed at the slick walls of the palisades in a futile effort to climb them before the Federals shot or grabbed them; Jarman got away by leaping off a twenty-foot ledge just ahead of his Federal pursuers.

Lieutenant Colonel Jones tried to obey Walthall's order to regroup, but in so doing lost nearly half of his Twenty-seventh Mississippi. "In one or two minutes the enemy pointed their guns over logs and rocks within eight or ten paces of us, and I ordered [the regiment] to fall back again," reported Jones. By then it was too late, and 163 of his men dropped their rifle-muskets and surrendered. Jones tried to rally the few score still with him on the bench a couple hundred yards in front of the Cravens house, but the incessant pounding from Hooker's cannons in the valley and the demonic pursuit of Ireland's New Yorkers at last convinced him all hope was lost.[43]

So too, momentarily, were the regimental colors. When the Twenty-seventh Mississippi broke for the last time, the color-bearer was shot dead. Glancing over his shoulder, a fleeing private saw the colors go down and ran back to grab them. He bent down into the path of an incoming bullet and collapsed across the body of the color-bearer, the standard wedged between them. Another soldier tried his luck. With the Yankees only a few yards away, he darted for the colors. He yanked them free from the corpses, snapped the staff off short, and sprinted after the regiment, waving the banner and yelling madly. A score of Federal rifles were trained on him, but he escaped unscathed, a hero among the survivors of the Twenty-seventh.[44]

Colonel Dowd fared no better than Jones. He waited until Ireland's New Yorkers were thirty feet away before ordering his two companies to fall back from the first line of breastworks. By the time he reached the line of sharpshooters near the point, only a handful of men were still with him. Dowd tried to marshal them, but the murderous fire from the Federal artillery across Lookout Creek and on Moccasin Point nearly wiped them out. Those not killed or wounded, lamented Dowd, collapsed from exhaustion. The storm of shot and shell was wrecking his line of sharpshooters as well, and the Yankees were within pistol range and closing fast. Reflecting on Walthall's order to "hold my post till hell froze over," Dowd concluded that "the ice was about five feet over it." He ran up the crevice toward the cliff, yelling to the company commanders to retire firing and rally in the works at the Cravens house.[45]

But time had run out for the Twenty-fourth Mississippi. Lieutenant Colonel Rickards crashed through the timber with the Twenty-ninth Pennsylvania. Changing front, he moved by the right flank, then reformed his line of battle to take the sharpshooters cowering behind the rocks in the flank. A few squeezed off a round, a few—including Dowd—escaped, but most threw up their hands in surrender. Rickards ordered his men to cease firing and waved at the Mississippians to come down. Nearly 150 gave themselves up. Rickards sent them rearward and resumed his march along the ledge toward the point. The One Hundred Eleventh Pennsylvania fell back in on his left.

Down on the bench, Ireland's New Yorkers were having a fine time chasing the Mississippians. "The Rebels broke and ran and we ran after them, heedless of the bullets from the summit," said Lieutenant Greene. "Into holes, over rocks and stumps and logs, through a camp of hut and shelter tents, and over fires where rebel breakfasts were cooking, on, capturing squads of the fleeing enemy, till the dense fog shut in again over and around us, and we must stop and feel our way."

At 12:10 P.M. Ireland and Cobham rounded the point of Lookout Mountain and drove eastward along the bench toward the Cravens house. Through the thickening fog, less than one hundred yards away, the Federals descried two Rebel cannons, standing unprotected in the farmyard near the very doorstep of the house. Cannon, like unit colors, were coveted battlefield trophies. Men would gamble their lives on a reckless bid for a bit of cloth or a touch of cold bronze. Ireland's New Yorkers were no different. Raising a yell, his center two regiments threw aside caution and broke into a run, both eager to lay claim to the prize.[46]

The coveted cannons were two six-pounder howitzers belonging to Howell's Georgia Battery. Commanded by Second Lieutenant R. T. Gibson, the section had been placed there eight days earlier and the horses sent down into Chattanooga Valley to graze. Gibson and his men waited patiently for a chance to fire, but Walthall's fleeing Mississippians blanketed their front. By the time the last of them had staggered past the guns, the Yankees were too near to be stopped. As Lieutenant Gibson put it: "My supports having fallen back, and my horses being at the foot of the mountain, I considered it best to march off my men, as there was no possibility of either moving my guns or repulsing the enemy."[47]

The right flank company of the One Hundred Thirty-seventh and the left flank company of the Sixtieth New York reached the abandoned guns simultaneously; for decades after the war, survivors of both regiments would claim exclusive rights to their seizure. At that moment, however, no one stopped to haul off the pieces. The Sixtieth New York kept on to the right of the Cravens house after Walthall's survivors, who were fast disappearing into a fog now so thick as to render invisible anyone more than fifty yards away. From clouds hovering between the summit and the bench a chilling drizzle had begun to fall. Sprinting ahead through the rain, the soldiers of the One Hundred Thirty-seventh New York swarmed around the Cravens house. The One Hundred Forty-ninth New York hopped over the stone wall to the left of the house, the left companies of the regiment extending off the bench and down the northern slope of the mountain. A handful of skirmishers from the One Hundred Second New York, overtaken in the rapid advance of the main line, were sent by Ireland to the left of the One Hundred Forty-ninth. More slowly now, uncertain of what lurked in the mist-shrouded trees beyond the farm, Ireland's New Yorkers wheeled to the right and trod southeastward along the slope. Off to their left, faintly visible through the seams of the rolling fog, were Chattanooga Valley and the entrenchments of the Army of the Cumberland.[48]

# CHAPTER THIRTEEN

# GO IN AND GIVE 'EM HELL

GEARY'S appearance below the point of Lookout Mountain at noon was the signal for Hooker to set in motion the brigades of Charles R. Woods and Grose, which were poised on the west bank of Lookout Creek and ready to cross a narrow footbridge laid down by the pioneers. While Cobham and Ireland cleared the upper reaches of the mountainside, Candy's brigade swept the ground between the base of Lookout Mountain and the east bank of the creek.

Shortly before noon, Candy passed through the marshy field opposite the bridge, clearing the way for Woods and Grose. When Candy wheeled his brigade to the right to ascend the slope and reestablish contact with Ireland's left, Woods sent the Seventy-sixth Ohio across the creek and into the field to deploy as skirmishers. With gentlemanly deference, he allowed Grose to march his four regiments over next. Grose formed a double line of battle to the right of the Ohio skirmishers, with the Thirty-sixth Indiana and Fifty-ninth Illinois in the front line. Woods got the rest of his brigade across and fell in on Grose's left. Together the two commands stepped off up the mountain. Woods advanced eastward, with his left on the river road to Chattanooga. Grose ascended the slope obliquely, trying to catch up with the left flank of Whitaker, which had passed him on his right while he was forming his line of battle.[1]

The belated advance of Grose and Woods spelled doom for the last of Walthall's regiments. Crouched behind the railroad embankment and in the rifle pits opposite the turnpike bridge, the men of the Thirty-fourth Mississippi were giving their full attention to the Eighty-fourth and Seventy-fifth Illinois directly across Lookout Creek. When they realized that Federal units had slipped over the creek beyond their left and gotten in their rear, the Mississippians abandoned any hope of resistance. Virtually the entire regiment gave up. After ten days with little food or sleep, many soldiers welcomed the ignominious denouement. Lieutenant Chesley Mosman of the Fifty-ninth Illinois was surprised at the cheerfulness of the captives. "We soon met [prisoners] coming back in squads of from five to forty, disarmed, hurrahing for Yankee Doodle and shaking hands with us." A few score tried to escape up the slope under the cover of a ravine, but theirs was a largely empty effort. When two sergeants from the Seventy-sixth Ohio sprinted ahead of their own regiment and caught up with one band of fourteen Mississippians, the Rebels meekly stopped, laid down their rifles, and raised their hands. J. E. Reynolds was one of the few who ran the gauntlet successfully. Ducking into a crevice with four comrades, he scrambled on hands and knees up the mountain. Halfway to the bench, a bullet cut into his chest, but he kept climbing. Gasping and bleeding, he reached the Cravens house in time to witness the collapse of Walthall's line. "I turned around to my right to see what caused the commotion and disorder, when, to my astonishment, I beheld our men . . . contesting every inch of ground that the enemy, numbering twenty-five to one, were taking," he recalled with a forgivable bit of embellishment. "I forgot all about the rattle of bullets and cannonballs plowing the ground under me, and my eyes filled with tears when I saw them mashed to the ground."[2]

The surrender of the Thirty-fourth Mississippi allowed the Eighty-fourth and Seventy-fifth Illinois finally to cross Lookout Creek. The Illinoisans threw logs across the gap in the turnpike bridge and hurried over on the double-quick. Climbing feverishly, they caught up with and fell in on the left flank of Woods's brigade, extending the Federal line across the Chattanooga road to the banks of the Tennessee River. Their reward for a morning of patient skirmishing was a hand in the capture of nearly two hundred men from Moore's picket line (mostly members of the Fortieth Alabama), whom the Illinoisans and Woods's left regiments took from behind.[3]

General Moore had caught a glimpse of his picket line withering. At that moment, however, up on the bench four hundred yards south of the Cravens house, he had more pressing concerns. Ninety minutes had passed before Moore received an answer from General Jackson to his inquiry (sent at 9:30 A.M. after he and Walthall had watched Grose march toward the railroad crossing) asking where he should deploy his brigade. Jackson was incredulous: Did Moore not recall the plan of the previous night to defend the line at the Cravens farm? He sent a division staff officer to repeat the standing order—Moore was to form behind the stone wall and rifle pits on Walthall's right. Moore, whose enthusiasm for the enterprise was none too great, was still reluctant to move. He applied to Walthall for reassurances that the Mississippian would be on his left when he brought his own brigade forward. With a vague notion that Walthall was doing battle somewhere on the far side of the mountain, Moore dispatched a messenger to apprise him of Jackson's response and to ask where his right then rested. Walthall, of course, was at that moment being overwhelmed too quickly to say with certainty where any of his command stood. "I could get no definite answer, he merely stating that he intended to fight first beyond the entrenchments and then fall back if he found it necessary to do so, and desired that I leave vacant on the left space for his command," asserted Moore.[4]

Moore hesitated. He accepted the offer of Major John Ingram of the division staff to find Jackson and get more definite instructions. Ingram rode off, and Moore held his brigade on the edge of its encampment, while around the point, Walthall was watching his reserve regiments crumble.[5]

Moore clearly needed a kick in the pants. Mudwall Jackson, however, was not the man to apply it. There was bungling aplenty among the Confederate commanders on Lookout Mountain that day, but no one displayed greater negligence than did Jackson. He remained glued to his headquarters at the intersection of the Summertown and Cravens house roads, near the base of the cliff. He was nearly a mile from the line he had been charged to defend. In his report of the battle, Jackson tried to excuse his dereliction of duty by arguing that his headquarters was a good spot from which to receive both commands from Stevenson on the summit and reports from the front line. That may have been true, but his presence was badly needed nearer the Cravens house.[6]

Jackson lacked even the presence of mind to call for reinforcements; Stevenson had to offer them. Stevenson, for his part, had first become aware of the impending Federal push against the mountain at 10:00 A.M., when he received Walthall's note of two hours earlier warning of Geary's movement up the valley. A few minutes later, he learned from sharpshooters along the summit that the Yankees were maneuvering to cross Lookout Creek. He rode to the point, confirmed the reports with his own eyes, and then sent word to Jackson to form his division. There matters rested until 12:30 P.M., when the roll of rifle volleys announced Walthall's clash with Geary. The fog was far too thick to distinguish precisely what was happening down on the bench, and Corput's cannons had to cease fire for fear of hitting their own men. Nonetheless, the growing roar and sporadic glimpses of rifle flashes were evidence enough to Stevenson that Walthall was sorely pressed. He ordered Pettus to take three of his regiments down from the summit and report to Jackson.[7]

By then, Moore had finally rustled up the will to move. "The firing on the left becoming quite heavy, I thought it advisable to place my command in position without further orders," he later reported blithely. The Tennessean placed in line of battle the Thirty-seventh, Forty-second, and those companies of the Fortieth Alabama not lost while on picket duty and started forward through the gray forest.

The Alabamians met with an unnerving reception as they approached the stone wall. "Just as our rear files turned out of the bench road near the Cravens house we met the remnant of Walthall's brigade rushing to the rear in inextricable disorder. The officers seemed to be using every effort to arrest their flight, but the men rushed past them in spite of threats and even blows," said Moore, who at first was not unduly concerned, thinking he merely had come upon the inevitable skulkers that fled any hard fight: "When members of Walthall's brigade passed to the rear I had no idea that the balance had been killed or captured, but supposed them in line beyond the Cravens house; but it soon became evident that such was not the case."[8]

Instead of finding the stone wall to their front, Moore and his men glimpsed a line of Federals through the drizzle. It was the One Hundred Forty-ninth New York and the handful of skirmishers from the One Hundred Second New York. Behind and to the right of these Yankees were the One Hundred Thirty-seventh and Sixtieth New York; Walthall's last, pathetic stand in the timber at the eastern edge of the Cravens yard had been enough to cause the latter regiments to pause behind the stone wall and in the abandoned rifle pits.

A few minutes before 1:00 P.M., Ireland's lead regiments and Moore's Alabamians met at a range of perhaps one hundred yards. In the thick mist, no one hit much of anything. Its density, however, disguised Moore's small numbers and made an unexpected volley, even a weak one such as he delivered, take on ominous significance for an unsuspecting foe. "At this time it was impossible to distinguish clearly the movements of the enemy or of our own troops on account of the fog and rocks," repined Lieutenant Colonel Charles Randall of the One Hundred Forty-ninth New York. His men, startled by the rifle flashes, quickly retired over and beyond the stone wall, and Moore settled his men in behind it and the rifle pits it screened. The One Hundred Thirty-seventh and Sixtieth New York regiments fell back as well, largely out of confusion over what had caused their comrades to take flight. Moore had his own explanation for the ease with which he dislodged the Yankees: "Due to the fact of having gotten a closer view of the miserable burlesque on rifle pits they did not consider their possession worthy of a serious struggle."[9]

Neither did Moore, but he put up a good fight nonetheless. He stretched his one thousand men as thin as he felt he could behind the entrenchments from the Cravens house down the mountainside and awaited the Yankee counterattack.[10]

It was slow in coming. Ireland's New Yorkers were not only dazed but tired. While their officers tried to assess the foe to their front, the men lay down along the western fringe of the Cravens yard, protected from Moore's fire by the fog and a slight dip in the ground.[11]

Relief came most opportunely to the New Yorkers. Whitaker's brigade arrived behind Ireland's stalled line a little after 1:00 P.M. His men were spoiling for a fight. They had had to endure stray shots from Walthall's Mississippians that missed Geary's line as well as sharpshooter's bullets from the summit without the satisfaction of shooting back. Whitaker was still deep in his cups, which left his regimental commanders to act largely as they chose.

Fortunately Colonel Jacob Taylor, whose Fortieth Ohio held the left of the line, needed no orders. His regiment had gotten well ahead of the rest of the brigade, in part because Whitaker had formed his regiments in echelon to the right at the start of the day to conform to the grade of the slope. As the Buckeyes passed over the One Hundred Forty-ninth New York in the peach orchard at the edge of the Cravens yard, the New Yorkers shamed Taylor into action. "Here come fresh troops to relieve us," they yelled. "Go it boys, we have chased them for you; pour it into them, give them hell."[12]

Taylor urged his men into the field. Unable to see the enemy, they instinctively paused and began to shoot into the mist. In the open ground, the Ohioans were easy marks, even for the blind return fire of Moore's Alabamians. Indeed, in its brief foray into the yard, the Fortieth suffered eleven soldiers killed—exactly half the number killed in Geary's entire division during the day. As men began dropping to no good end, the field officers of the Fortieth tried to nudge the line forward. Lieutenant Colonel Nimrod Jones got the right of the regiment going, and Colonel Taylor pried loose the center. Major Thomas Acton stepped forward to do the same on the left. Kneeling beside him, Sergeant Isaac Doan looked on with respect and dread. Acton's "light blue overcoat presented a conspicuous mark; and I could hear the cruel zip of the bullets that sought his life; and pulling his coat told him to get down." Doan tugged too late. "At this instant I heard the fierce whack of the bullet that pierced his heroic heart. He threw up his hands, and his cry of mortal anguish rings in my memory still. I sprang to my feet and caught him in my arms, easing him down; as his body sank upon my knee, I felt his form quiver and become rigid in death agony, and saw his face receive the seal of the king of terrors."[13]

Gradually the Ohioans worked their way across the yard toward the stone wall. They passed over the two guns of Howell's battery, which Ireland had neglected to remove from the field. For years after the battle, a spirited war of words raged between the survivors of the Fortieth Ohio and Ireland's brigade as to who seized the guns. For the moment, however, the cannons were on no one's mind. The Fortieth was taking a beating around the Cravens house from the left companies of Moore's brigade crouched behind the stone wall. When the advance of the Fortieth stalled, the Ninety-ninth Ohio hurried forward toward its right in an effort to complete a line across the length of the narrow yard. Whitaker, who had regained a semblance of lucidity, was reluctant to commit his brigade to the fray. He tried to stop the men of the Ninety-ninth as they stepped over Ireland's New Yorkers. "Steady! Steady! Steady!" he hollered. No one listened. Whitaker gave up. "If you will go, go! go! go! and give them hell!"[14]

The largely Irish Thirty-fifth Indiana paid him no heed either. For a moment, the men halted and took cover behind Ireland's line. Then Colonel Bernard Mullen sprang forward: "Up bullies with a cheer. Charge at a run!" he bellowed. "Steady! Steady! Thirty-fifth," countered Whitaker, repeating the only command he seemed capable of articulating. "But the 'Faugh a ballach' (leave the way), the Irish war cry, had been given and there was no stopping," remembered the adjutant. Whitaker again conceded the game: "If you won't stop, then go in and give 'em hell."[15]

Moore was now woefully outnumbered—Whitaker alone had five hundred more men than he did—and the odds were about to get worse. Indeed, the Federals seemed ubiquitous. To Moore's right front, Candy's brigade was clambering up the mountainside to regain its connection with Ireland's left. For Candy's men, the battle thus far had been a lark, despite the hard climbing. They had seen scores of Rebel prisoners trudge past to the rear and had had scarcely a shot fired at them in anger. A few shells from the summit were hurled their way, but they did no harm; "their greatest efficiency was secured by shooting off the tops of the trees to fall upon the heads of the men," quipped a member of the Seventh Ohio. The only real casualty was Candy himself, who tripped and fell during the ascent, bruising his hip so badly that he had to leave the field and turn brigade command over to Colonel William Creighton.

To Creighton's left and rear were the brigades of Woods and Grose. Although they were not yet near enough to make an attack against Moore, it was evident to him that the Federal line extended far beyond his right flank. And to Moore's left, most of the Ninety-ninth Ohio and all of the Thirty-fifth Indiana were marching toward the rifle pits that

Walthall was supposed to have defended. If all this were not enough, his men—as Moore had pointed out repeatedly to his superiors before the battle—only had thirty rounds in their cartridge boxes and were armed for the most part with cast-off rifle-muskets that other units had condemned as unfit for combat use.[16]

The accuracy of the Federal fire was improving as well. In Company I of the Thirty-seventh Alabama, seventeen men fell dead or wounded in a matter of minutes. Those who remained stood their ground, thanks to the example of their company commander, Lieutenant Thomas Carlisle. Just before going into battle Carlisle had filled and lit his pipe. Now, as the fighting reached a crescendo, the deliberateness with which he smoked it had a calming effect on all who saw him—including General Moore. As his regimental commander, Lieutenant Colonel A. A. Greene, recalled: "Lieutenant Carlisle was rushing here and there among the men, with sword in right hand and pipe in his left. For a moment he would stop, take a pull or two at his pipe, then renew it, and shout at his men to stand firm. A little later, when the pipe had been exhausted, we saw him deliberately dust out the ashes and replace the pipe in his pocket and again rally the men, all the time just as cool and apparently unconcerned as if out for a picnic frolic, when men were falling about him."[17]

For a few excruciating minutes the outcome of Moore's seemingly hopeless stand appeared in doubt. Neither the Ninety-ninth Ohio nor Thirty-fifth Indiana had managed to close up on the right of the Fortieth Ohio, and Taylor's unsupported troops mingled around the Cravens house and began to give ground. Some of Moore's Alabamians sallied forth from their cover to press the Fortieth. At this instant, Whitaker made his one real contribution of the day. Having for no good reason halted the Eighth Kentucky at the base of the palisades just before reaching the point of Lookout Mountain, Whitaker now had no front-line regiment far enough to the right to maneuver against Moore's left flank and rear. Consequently, he called up his supporting regiments, the Ninety-sixth Illinois and Fifty-first Ohio, to execute the movement. He assigned the duty to Colonel Thomas Champion of the Ninety-sixth, as ranking colonel in the brigade.[18]

Champion was well positioned to carry out the order, and he responded handsomely. His regiment and the Fifty-first Ohio were on the wooded ledge to the left of and about one hundred feet above the Cravens yard. Through rifts in the mist, they could make out both the imperiled Fortieth Ohio and the exposed end of Moore's line. Champion ordered the regiments to wheel to the left and charge. They did so eagerly, "the men scrambling down the rocks, many of them falling as they sought to reach the margin of the field," boasted the sergeant major of the Ninety-sixth. Moore saw them coming. "It became evident we must either fall back or be surrounded and captured," he surmised. The Tennessean chose the former course and passed the word to retire southward toward the Summertown road. Moore got most of his command off in good order, but a few companies on the extreme left were cut off and captured by Champion's Illinoisans.[19]

Their front clear, Colonel Taylor's Ohioans whooped and hopped over the stone wall. Whitaker was content to stop there. Once again, however, his regiments acted on their own. "Steady, there! Steady!" came the tiresome refrain. "Hold what you have!" he implored, while tottering among the men, waving a ramrod in lieu of a sword.

Off they went. The Fortieth Ohio led the way, engaging in a stumbling battle with Moore through the vaporous, rock-cluttered woods. The Ninety-ninth Ohio and Thirty-fifth Indiana followed to its right and rear. The Ninety-sixth Illinois resumed its original line of march, as did the Fifty-first Ohio, which during the melee had traded places with the Illinoisans and now was on their right. About all Whitaker himself accomplished was to distract Colonel Mullen long enough to convince him to detach a small detail to take possession of the two Rebel cannon, which the Irishman subsequently had the decency to turn over to the Fortieth Ohio.[20]

Ireland was on the move again as well, to the left and rear of Whitaker. Geary and Ireland contended vociferously in their reports that Whitaker's brigade not only had not passed by the New Yorkers, but took no real part in the fight around the Cravens house. According to the two, Whitaker trailed Ireland throughout the fight. Ireland's brigade, they maintained, dislodged Moore and pursued him alone; Whitaker's brigade halted at the stone wall and, Geary and Ireland added, the very drunk Kentuckian refused to send even one regiment forward to relieve Ireland. The only shred of truth in these allegations was with regard to Whitaker's lack of sobriety; the eighty-two casualties suffered by the Kentuckian's brigade—only fifty-six fewer than Geary's total losses— sufficiently demonstrate the fiction that blemished the reports of Geary and Ireland. A burning thirst for glory and the mutual loathing that had set in between the Easterners and their ragged Western compatriots lay behind the falsehoods.[21]

Geary could take honest satisfaction in being ahead of Whitaker, but not in the manner he claimed. While the Kentuckian's regimental commanders were busy driving Moore from the Cravens house, Colonel Cobham had slipped his two small Pennsylvania regiments quietly around the palisades by means of a trail that skirted the base, so near the wall that the men could reach out and touch its moist, smooth surface. The path was narrow and could accommodate men moving only in single file; the ledge it traversed was too precipitous to risk even a column of twos. Nevertheless, by the time the Fortieth Ohio waved its banner atop Moore's vacated fieldworks, Cobham's men were a good two hundred yards farther to the south than Whitaker's brigade.[22]

Whitaker was not alone in wanting to call a halt at the Cravens house. As the battle unfolded and the weather worsened, Hooker was content merely to see Geary round the bench and had given Osterhaus and Cruft positive orders to halt beneath the point. Fearful that the enemy might be reinforced and his own lines disordered by the rugged ground and fog, he had sent word to Geary to stop for the day before reaching the Cravens house. Geary, of course, was on foot and too far behind his troops to stop them, and so, as Hooker put it, "fired by success, with a flying, panic-stricken enemy before them, they pressed impetuously forward." By then, the combatants were invisible from the valley, and Hooker had to rely on messages brought down from the mountain to learn how the fight was progressing.[23]

It was nearly 2:00 P.M. The drizzle continued, becoming colder and more annoying as the short autumn day wore on. The clouds thickened. They floated down from the summit and settled over the forests on the mountainside. Visibility had been as good as one hundred yards at times; now it was virtually nil. "Wrapped in a seamless mantle of vapor, we became confused as to locality, direction and distance. Some of our men became entangled in the felled timber, which, at this point, obstructed the slope, and were separated from their command," said a Union veteran. The mist, he may have added, was a source of both perplexity and protection.[24]

It certainly saved Federal lives, blinding Brown's skirmishers and Corput's gunners on the summit. "The fog was so dense that we could not see the enemy, although we could hear his march, and guided by this and the report of his musketry ours was directed," said Brown. Hearing the slippery tread of Cobham's file along the eastern base of the palisades, Brown moved his largest regiment, the Thirty-second Tennessee, to the edge of the summit to try to pick off the Yankees before they could glide by the left flank of Walthall's tenuous new line. Unable either to see their targets or to point their rifles straight down from the precipice, the Tennesseans resorted to rolling rocks and tossing lighted shells and grenades down on Cobham's men. The noise was terrifying to those below, but the Rebel aim was awful. Cobham's Pennsylvanians dodged the debris by standing with their backs up against the palisades wall. They were uncomfortable but well protected—the One Hundred Eleventh Pennsylvania, which led the single-file procession, lost only one man killed and eight wounded.

Mostly, the fog aided the Confederates. While it shielded Cobham, it also stopped him. It caused Whitaker's men to slow instinctively. It allowed Moore to withdraw in reasonably good order, firing into the fog as he fell back. And it gave Walthall the time he needed to piece together a scratch line of six hundred men—all that remained of his brigade—some three hundred yards south of the Cravens house and, mercifully, out of range of the Yankee artillery on Moccasin Point.[25]

Walthall, perhaps, was the most relieved man on Lookout Mountain at that moment. Although he had yet to lay eyes on the elusive Mudwall Jackson, a division staff officer had assured the Mississippian that reinforcements were on the way. On that promise, Walthall's men crouched behind boulders and fallen trees and kept up enough of a fire to halt Whitaker. Thirty minutes later, they heard the tramp of Pettus's column coming up behind them along the Cravens house road. Walthall wasted no time on pleasantries: Many of his men had been captured, those left were down to their last rounds and could not hold out any longer, he told the former Alabama judge.

Pettus understood. He had met Jackson upon coming off the mountain but, like Walthall and Moore, found him singularly unhelpful. His only instruction had been to go forward and support the two beleaguered brigadiers. That Pettus proceeded to do. He filed his three Alabama regiments off the road to the left and into line of battle. Marching forward, he relieved Walthall and fell in behind a natural breastwork of limestone outcrop. His line was engaged instantly. When he learned that a gap of 150 yards yawned between his right and Moore's left, Pettus rode down the slope to consult with the Tennessean. Moore begged him to extend intervals to connect with his line. Pettus agreed, although it left a space between his own left and the base of the palisades. "These facts were communicated by me to Jackson with the request that he would come forward, look at the line, and give us orders, but he did not come in person, but sent orders that the position must be held." Such was service under Mudwall Jackson, mused the Alabamian.[26]

For the rest of the afternoon and well into the night, the six Alabama regiments of Pettus and Moore traded volleys with their invisible foe. In some places, the two lines were only thirty yards apart. At points of collision, the smoke of battle hung in blue sheets among the naked branches of the trees until beaten into nothing by the falling rain. The racket was tremendous, the lead expended prodigious, but hardly anyone was hurt. Everybody kept their heads down. Soldiers squeezed off rounds haphazardly, hoping to forestall forays that neither side had the will to make, but which both imagined were happening. Lieutenant Chesley Mosman of the Fifty-ninth Illinois saw his own bewilderment and that of his men reflected in the addled activity of their mascot:

> We had to shoot at the flash of their guns, the mist or cloud was so heavy. The fog and smoke were so thick we could not see a man two paces from us, but the Rebel bullets flew over us in showers and it was necessary for us to keep firing to keep them from advancing. Some men fired from fifty to eighty rounds each. A big cur dog followed the regiment in and stood with his head sticking over a log some fifteen inches in diameter that protected his body very well, and when the Rebels gave us a volley he could not understand what it was all about. The balls would hit the log and he would look to see what it was. The bullets hitting the rocks were flattened into all sorts of shapes and they would whistle all sorts of tunes or shrieks, and the dog just kept looking everywhere, in every direction to see what was making the noise. It was comical to see him. We kept things roaring for the next two or three hours.[27]

Mosman's claim to the contrary notwithstanding, it was the Confederates who were being showered with bullets. Even Geary later admitted this: "Some of the regiments of my relief . . . and others on the left, unnecessarily fired continuous volleys in the fog, without response, save from secreted sharpshooters who were busy in front, and from the cliffs." The Rebels had no rounds to waste, especially Moore's Alabamians, who had started the day with half a basic load. The Yankees, on the other hand, had the luxury of feeding fresh units with full cartridge boxes into the fight. Geary consolidated his front at 3:00 P.M. He brought two regiments from Creighton's brigade, which hadn't fired a round, over to relieve Ireland. Shortly thereafter, Grose moved from the left of the line and began to detail regiments to replace those of Whitaker and Cobham on the firing line on a one-for-one basis as needed.

The fighting degenerated into a series of weak, half-blind punches and counterpunches in the foggy twilight. Someone thought they saw troops gathering near the palisades and imagined the phantom forms to be the harbingers of a Rebel buildup there. In response to the spurious threat, Geary sent the Twenty-eighth Pennsylvania to the extreme right of his line. The Pennsylvanians filed into place and started shooting into the fog. Reacting to the added firepower of the Pennsylvanians and of Grose's well-supplied regiments on his left, Pettus called on Walthall to close the gap between his flank and the palisades. Wearily, the Mississippian complied. He gathered together the remnants of the Twenty-ninth and Thirtieth Mississippi, augmented by a few squads from the Thirty-fourth, and sent them toward the bluff. A small hole remained, which in the gathering twilight took on disproportionate import, and so Walthall led forward the last, exhausted survivors of his brigade. Collapsing behind the chilly boulders and wet logs, they found themselves in the fight until well after nightfall. Pettus contributed to the defense of his left with the one serious counterattack of the evening, a spirited advance by the Twentieth Alabama against Federal reinforcements congregating near the palisades.[28]

Lieutenant Mosman had excellent company in his personal fight with fog-shrouded chimera. Throughout the afternoon, Hooker, Geary, and Whitaker all were plagued with doubts that limited their enjoyment of their apparent victory. Hooker had moved his headquarters forward along the Chattanooga road simultaneous with the advance of the Eighty-fourth and Seventy-fifth Illinois. Setting up within sight of Chattanooga Creek, Hooker sent off a boastful dispatch to General Thomas at 1:25 P.M.: "In announcing the fact of our great success this morning I had no time to state its results. The conduct of all the troops has been brilliant, and the success has far exceeded my expectations. Our loss has not been severe, and of prisoners I should judge that we had not less than 2,000. The bulk of my infantry is now assembling on the east side of Lookout Mountain."

Having little faith in the author of the message, nobody at headquarters took it at face value; Grant later berated Hooker for claiming to have taken more prisoners on Lookout Mountain than the army captured during the entire campaign, and all knew that Hooker had expected not only to take the mountain but then to descend gloriously into Chattanooga Valley.

Few were surprised when, less than ninety minutes later, Hooker answered a casual message from General Palmer, made via the Fourteenth Corps signal station in Chattanooga Valley, asking "Do you want help?" with a frantic: "Can hold the line I am now on; can't advance. Some of my troops out of ammunition; can't replenish." In fact, Grant and Thomas were primed for the appeal. At 2:00 P.M., after settling into the Cravens house, Whitaker forgot to whom he had been detailed and sent desperate appeals directly to his own corps commander and to army headquarters for reinforcements: "I have established my headquarters in the white house, on Lookout Mountain. The enemy are massing rapidly on my right. Support me." Thomas shrugged and approved the transfer of Palmer's nearest brigade—that of William Carlin—to Hooker.[29]

Actually, Geary was largely responsible for Hooker's humiliating volte-face. Although neither Pettus nor Moore had given any indication that they wanted trouble, at 2:45 P.M. the Pennsylvanian scribbled an appeal for help to Hooker: "We are pressed heavily, and need re-enforcements. We must have ammunition; I have sent for some, but it does not come. My rear should be well looked to."[30]

Hooker's confidence returned an hour before sunset. To Geary, whom he had told a short time earlier to dig in for the night along the eastern slope, Hooker now announced his intention to descend into Chattanooga Valley as soon as the fog lifted, unless he received orders to the contrary. "Our communications on the left with Chattanooga is established. In all probability the enemy will evacuate tonight. His line of retreat is seriously threatened by my troops."

The fog never lifted, so Hooker was not put to the test. Hooker may have embarrassed himself to superiors and subordinates alike with his alternate whimpering and blustering, but he had correctly guessed Bragg's intentions.[31]

# CHAPTER FOURTEEN

# THE SHIPWRECK OF THEIR HOPES

DOWN IN Chattanooga Valley, near the base of Missionary Ridge, General Stewart, Colonel J. T. Holtzclaw (in temporary command of Clayton's brigade), and their staff officers stood, field glasses in hand, contemplating the fighting up on Lookout Mountain, two miles to the west. It was a few minutes after 2:00 P.M. on 24 November. We "watched with deep interest and astonishment this evident attack in heavy force along a line deemed so nearly impregnable that earth-works there seemed almost unnecessary," said Captain J. W. Wright of Holtzclaw's staff. "Suddenly, as a cloud rolled away, we saw our line of breastworks swarming with men for nearly half a mile and flags waving there." "What flag is that," everyone wondered aloud. "Try the field-glass," someone answered. "There, it is plain enough. It is the stars and stripes."[1]

It was plain enough to Bragg as well, who on hearing the rumble of Hooker's artillery barrage had ridden down from Missionary Ridge to the rear of Stewart's division. He was furious—at a loss to understand how Stevenson, with six brigades at his disposal, could have failed to hold the bench and slope of Lookout Mountain. Now Stevenson was begging for another brigade in order to avert total defeat, "though it appeared [all] his forces had not been brought into action," reported Bragg disgustedly. The North Carolinian granted the request conditionally—the brigade sent over was to be used to cover Stevenson's withdrawal. He selected Holtzclaw's Alabamians for the job and told Stewart to dispatch them to the base of the mountain at once. Bragg would not do more than that. As far as he was concerned, the battle effectively was over and Lookout Mountain lost. At 2:30 P.M., he had Colonel Brent write Stevenson explicit instructions: "The general commanding instructs me to say that you will withdraw your command from the mountain to this side of Chattanooga Creek, destroying the bridges behind. Fight the enemy as you retire. The thickness of the fog will enable you to retire, it is hoped, without much difficulty."[2]

As Bragg had left the timing and manner of the withdrawal to his discretion, Stevenson decided not to risk breaking contact with the Federals on the eastern slope until the troops on the summit made good their escape. Walthall, Pettus, and Moore would have to hold on—all night if necessary—to keep open the vital Summertown road, the only means of egress into Chattanooga Valley. Since it had grown too cloudy for his artillery to do any good, Stevenson sent them off the mountain at 4:00 P.M. He told Brown to recall his brigade, which was scattered for ten miles over the summit, and descend into the valley with the division trains at 7:00 P.M.

Jackson showed up at Stevenson's headquarters as Brown's column was moving out. Mudwall had done nothing more during the waning hours of the afternoon than tell his harried brigade commanders to hold on at all costs. As he had from the start of the fight, Jackson sent his latest exhortation through a staff officer, sticking close to the Summertown road himself. Stevenson told Jackson of Bragg's withdrawal order. Breckinridge, he added, had arrived at the base of the mountain with Holtzclaw's brigade and offered to help him in any way possible. Also, Cheatham had returned to the army that afternoon and sent word to Stevenson to meet him at the Gillespie house in the valley, where they would make final arrangements for extricating Jackson's command. Together, Stevenson and Jackson (the latter probably relieved that his tenure as division commander was about to draw to a close) galloped down the Summertown road past Brown's demoralized infantry.[3]

Meanwhile, the senseless firing on the mountainside continued, alternately sputtering and swelling. Union regiments were moved in and out of the line throughout the night, so that everyone on the mountain eventually had a hand in the fight. Units from Williamson's and Woods's brigades were called forward and inserted wherever the need seemed greatest.[4]

Carlin reported to Geary at 7:00 P.M. He had been delayed several hours in crossing Chattanooga Creek while his men fashioned a floating bridge. Carlin found Geary and his staff huddled around a fire near the Cravens house. Rubber ponchos stretched over poles protected them from the drizzle and whipping wind. Although nearly five hours had passed since either side had moved, Geary was still nervous and fearful of a counterattack—but not so afraid as to prevent him from regaling Carlin with his complete military history upon their meeting. "I had heard of him as Governor of Kansas and occasionally through the newspapers. I knew but little of his history during the war. He told me he was the only Federal general who had ever beaten Stonewall Jackson.

This interested me very much, as I had never heard of it before," remembered Carlin. The conversation of two of his staff interrupted Geary's soliloquy. One had just asked another to wake him up if anything should occur needing his attention. Geary spun around and snarled at the sleepy officer: "If any officer of my staff falls asleep tonight, I'll brain him, by the Eternal." Carlin walked off to deploy his brigade near the palisades; "What a lovely chief for staff officers to serve, was my silent reflection."[5]

Sleep, of course, was impossible out on the firing line. As soon as it grew still enough for the men to drowse, a snapping twig or some tumbling stones would set off the shooting anew. "About 10:00 P.M. quiet reigned, and I got under a big rock for part protection from the cold, when all at once the whole Rebel line opened fire, and seemingly very close, yet not directly in front of us, as we were to near the top," wrote a startled Private A. M. Brinkerhoff of the Fourth Iowa. "It seemed as though the fire from the guns almost met, and for about ten minutes the whole side of the mountain was lit up by the flashes of thousands of muskets. Finally the firing ceased on the left, and while I was wondering whether the rebs had driven our men back, a voice called out down the line: 'Hey rebs, don't you want to charge again.'"[6]

Sleep eluded even those fortunate enough to come off the line. "We retired from the line and build fires but the wind blew hard all night . . . it got very cold so that we lay shivering all night on the mountain side without supper for the officers as we had all gone into a common mess, but the cook couldn't find us," bemoaned Lieutenant Mosman of the Fifty-ninth Illinois. Grouped in close column of regiments in the yard of the Cravens house, with arms stacked, Ireland's New Yorkers fared no better. "If the men had anything to eat they ate it. I know that the brigade officers had nothing to eat, nor even blankets or overcoats," Lieutenant Greene wrote. He continued:

> Occasional shots were exchanged through the fog between our men and the sharpshooters on the palisades, but few of us had either strength or animation enough to feel much interest in that. The fog was very penetrating, it had rained some, we were wet through, and ached with fatigue. Night shut in about us and the darkness was almost impenetrable. A cold rain commenced to fall, freezing as it fell, and our outer clothing was coated with ice. It seemed as if our blood was cold and the last spark of vitality frozen within us. At the slightest attempt to make a fire the sharpshooters on the palisades would open on us, and all attempts were forbidden.

Except, apparently, among Geary's circle.[7]

The clatter that had awakened Private Brinkerhoff had been the jousting of Carlin's and Holtzclaw's brigades, both of which settled into line at roughly the same time and had ammunition to burn. Holtzclaw's Alabamians replaced Walthall's zombie-like troops and two of Pettus's three regiments. Moore's Alabamians, though they probably had fewer than five rounds left per man, were held in place.

The Mississippians staggered back through the dreary forest. The private who had saved the colors of the Twenty-seventh Mississippi jammed the snapped-off flag staff into the nearly frozen ground. "The boys crowded around it with saddened hearts and recounted the eventful and dangerous scenes of the day, telling where Tom, Jack or Jim had fallen and others had surrendered," reminisced a survivor sadly. "Many of them showed where minié balls had cut their hats, coats or blankets. The meeting at that flag was one never to be forgotten, and many of us joined hands around it and pledged that no Yankee should ever lay hands on it without passing over our dead bodies. Strong men unused to tears, although accustomed to the cruel scenes of war, cried like children."[8]

Breckinridge, Cheatham, Stevenson, and Jackson met at the Gillespie house around 8:00 P.M. When Cheatham arrived, Breckinridge yielded the floor to him and returned to Missionary Ridge. Cheatham may not have cried as did the Mississippians, but he had good reason to feel anguish—Jackson nearly had destroyed two of his brigades. Given Cheatham's volatile temper, one can well imagine the words that passed between the two that night.

Cheatham concluded the business rapidly. He told Stevenson to remove both divisions from the west side of Chattanooga Creek. Brown's brigade, which was already huddled in the icy flats near the creek, was ordered to cross at once. Cumming was to follow at 1:00 A.M., and the remnants of Cheatham's own division, along with Pettus's brigade, were to come off the mountain afterward. All were to stand by on the east side of the creek while Cheatham searched out Bragg for further orders. The burly Tennessean turned command back over to Stevenson and strode out of the house.[9]

Bragg, meanwhile, was deeply absorbed in a meeting of his own. Breckinridge had ridden directly from the Gillespie house to army headquarters. There he, Bragg, and Hardee fell into a somber but largely futile discussion of how they might recoup their losses of the day. The situation was grim. With Lookout Mountain lost and Sherman menacing Tunnel Hill, both flanks were in danger. Another setback on either flank clearly threatened the whole army. Outnumbered two to one, Bragg had barely enough troops to reinforce one flank. Finally, South Chickamauga Creek was swelling rapidly from the steady rains, jeopardizing Bragg's line of retreat.[10]

Bragg had no idea what to do. He turned to Hardee and Breckinridge for advice. "Old Reliable" was all for conceding Chattanooga. The army, Hardee said, should cut its losses and withdraw across South Chickamauga Creek. Once over, it could defend the east bank or consolidate at Chickamauga Station and fall back by rail farther into Georgia. Breckinridge disagreed vehemently. There was no time that night for such a move, which certainly would be discovered. In falling back, he continued, the army would be subject to defeat in detail after daybreak. Furthermore, Missionary Ridge was an inherently strong position. Filled with bravado and, perhaps, with liquor, Breckinridge concluded that if troops could not fight there, they could not fight anywhere.

Bragg later claimed that Breckinridge had been on a binge since the day before and was drunk during their meeting. That the Kentuckian's thinking was cloudy, whatever the source of his muddle, is beyond dispute. If his plan was adopted, Breckinridge would be left to defend most of the ridge—a four-mile stretch from Rossville Gap to a point a mile shy of Tunnel Hill—with only three divisions. In other words, he would be holding two-thirds of the line with less than half of the army, or about one soldier spaced every three or four feet along the line.

Nonetheless, the Kentuckian's enthusiasm was contagious. Bragg warmly endorsed Breckinridge's petition to hold fast on Missionary Ridge, which seems to belie his later assertion that the Kentuckian was drunk. Hardee argued a bit longer for a withdrawal, but finally acceded. He eventually convinced himself—or allowed Breckinridge to convince him—that the natural strength of Missionary Ridge was sufficient to deter a direct assault against the center and left. Hardee decided that the real threat would come from Sherman against the right flank, which he argued was also the most vulnerable part of the Confederate line.

Bragg agreed. He promised to send Cheatham and Stevenson to reinforce the right during the night. Hardee would command the four divisions on the right—those of Cleburne, Walker (commanded by Brigadier General States Rights Gist), Stevenson, and Cheatham. Anderson's division had been under his orders, but it was too far to the left for Hardee to devote adequate attention both to it and to the expected fight around Tunnel Hill. Consequently, it was reassigned to Breckinridge, which gave him his third division. The Kentuckian was to order Stewart up from Chattanooga Valley and onto the ridge at once; responsibility for guarding the extreme left at Rossville Gap would rest with the Tennessean.[11]

Captain Irving Buck rode up to army headquarters as the meeting was breaking up. It was midnight. Unable to restrain his anxiety, Pat Cleburne had told his assistant adjutant general to go to corps headquarters to find out if he was to fight the next morning or fall back that night. From corps headquarters, Buck was directed to that of Bragg, where Hardee had gone. Buck dismounted and met Breckinridge sauntering out of the house. "I never felt more like fighting than when I saw those people shelling my troops off Lookout today," he told Buck. Hardee came out next, considerably more restrained. "Tell Cleburne we are to fight, that his division will undoubtedly be heavily attacked, and that he must do his very best."[12]

Stevenson and Jackson waited patiently for Cheatham to return. It was well after midnight when a courier from Bragg galloped up in the dark. All the troops west of Chattanooga Creek were to start at once for the far right of the army. No one could find Cheatham, he told Stevenson, so the Virginian must take responsibility for the move.[13]

Up on the frigid slope of Lookout Mountain, the firing died out a little after midnight. The clouds parted, and the sky cleared, as sharp and radiant as the heart of a diamond. The moon was full. Its brilliant beams glittered on the icy rocks and cast weird shadows in the deep crevices. At 2:00 A.M., Holtzclaw and Pettus were handed their orders to march off the mountain. Then, suddenly, the night turned black. The moon had slipped into a total eclipse. The blackness hid the Rebels' departure from prying Yankee eyes and spared most the more lurid scenes of gore that lay along their line of battle, but it made the descent treacherous, and "many a man received a stunning tumble," recalled Moore. For Captain Wright of Holtzclaw's staff, the eclipse came an instant too late: "A grim sight, never to be forgotten, greeted the eyes of some of us as we left that rocky ridge in the dead of night. In a small open ravine some of our poor fellows lay stark and cold, one with outstretched arms. Those pallid faces, those staring eyes, upturned to the bright moon, how startlingly distinct! No time to bury them; no time for weary men to bear these bodies with them over that rugged, rocky trail."[14]

A sadder lot seldom had abandoned a position. To the Alabamians, the eclipse was a divine portent of immutable disaster. A Confederate veteran captured the scene in all its poignancy:

As quietly as possible, but with stiffened limbs, they went stumbling and falling and rolling down those rough declines, cold and chilled to the bone. Getting into column as best they could, they passed across the valley and Chattanooga Creek. The men, wet and cold and tired and hungry, were disheartened by defeat. . . . Disappointment had succeeded disappointment, and incapacity had turned victories into defeats. It was expected that similar lines would be followed, and they were not in good humor. The moon . . . went into an eclipse and shrouded everything in almost total darkness, which to many was an omen of evil.

The Alabamians did not brood alone. During the early morning hours of 25 November, nearly every soldier in the army was gripped by a strange ennui, rendered more sinister by the eclipse. Said a member of Cleburne's division:

> Their minds were filled with doubt, and their hearts burdened with misgivings. . . . They had seen nothing but blunders and defeats, and expected nothing else today. . . . They knew they would fight only with the strength left from the shipwreck of their hopes; that they were standing on the embers of their ruined edifice, and with this knowledge the eclipse produced an effect that was unaccountable, were it not for the gloom that paralyzed their hope. They discussed the situation— the loss of Lookout Mountain, the foothold the enemy had obtained on our right; of Hooker to follow from Lookout Mountain and envelop our left, and no force to stop him; of the opportunity thrown away to capture Chattanooga and destroy the Federal army; and the infatuation that determined a general engagement with the risk of ruin to the army. They were in a poor state of mind to loan any confidence to General Bragg; he had expressed a want of confidence in the army, and they returned the want of it in him with interest.[15]

# CHAPTER FIFTEEN

# TIME IS EVERYTHING

TUESDAY, 24 November, had been a day unique in the history of the Army of the Cumberland. The army had played the role of bystander while a battle was fought out within earshot. Not only were they not engaged, but the Cumberlanders were spectators to a drama the likes of which they had never witnessed. Accustomed to combat at close quarters, amid deep forest and suffocating smoke that limited a soldier's span of vision to a few yards, they found themselves instead in a grand natural amphitheater that afforded a view of the entire field of operations. The fighting on Lookout Mountain, toward which all devoted their undivided attention, had an almost surreal quality. Instead of searing flame, deafening racket, and gore, they were treated to a battle from a safe distance, and they reveled in it. This was war on a heroic scale, the way they had all imagined it would be when they had enlisted in the innocent days of 1861 and early 1862. The fog only added to the mystique. One historian eloquently conveyed the essence of the experience: "Here the smoke billowed upward, soft and beautiful as a cloud. Gun flashes winked harmlessly, the noise was muted to a rumbling or a small crackling, men fell down as if they were tired and wanted rest."[1]

As the clouds parted and merged teasingly throughout the afternoon, troops gathered atop their breastworks to catch a glimpse of the contest. Officers fixed their field glasses on Lookout Mountain. "Men of excellent imagination could see a great deal" through the clouds that enveloped the mountainside, said the chaplain of the Fifty-eighth Indiana, but all saw enough to know that, by midafternoon, the battle was won. The cheers of Geary's and Whitaker's men swarming past the Cravens house removed any doubt. "Finally faint cheers came down to us from the mountain. It was the signal of victory and we took it up," an Indiana soldier wrote to his hometown newspaper. "The glad cry spread from camp to camp and we listened to its echoes far up the majestic Tennessee River. We shook hands, we danced, we cried, we threw our hats in the air, and we shouted our victory again and again, as the faint voices above us came down." Even General Thomas was rumored to have tossed his hat in the air at the moment the first Federal flags poked through the mist on the eastern slope.[2]

None of this had been of great interest to Grant. From his headquarters in Fort Wood, he had watched impatiently the ponderous march of Sherman against Bragg's right. This was the real battle, in his view, and it was upon this effort that he pinned all his hopes. As darkness drew a curtain across the northern reaches of Missionary Ridge, Grant believed his faith in his friend vindicated. Sherman assumed he had carried Tunnel Hill. How he reached this conclusion remains something of a mystery. In the uncertain light of the late afternoon, Sherman may have convinced himself that he really had carried his objective and that Smith's Texans occupied an eminence of lesser consequence farther down the ridge, and reported his own position accordingly. That he willfully misrepresented his lack of success to Grant is unlikely. Or, Grant may have misunderstood the situation on the left due to an absence of reports from Sherman. In either case, Grant based his planning that night on the mistaken impression that the Ohioan had carried his immediate objective and that he need only press his advantage at daybreak to roll up Bragg's flank and complete his victory.[3]

Assuming Sherman knew where he was and thought Grant did as well, there was nothing in Grant's written orders to him that would have alerted Sherman to his commander's misconception; the operative sentence instructed Sherman simply to "attack the enemy at the point most advantageous from your position at early dawn." In his order to Thomas, who was to continue to play a supporting role, Grant articulated what he presumed that position to be: "General Sherman carried Missionary Ridge as far as the tunnel, with only slight skirmishing. His right now rests at the tunnel and on top of the hill; his left at Chickamauga Creek," Grant assured the Virginian. "I have instructed General Sherman to advance as soon as it is light in the morning, and your attack, which will be simultaneous, will be in co-operation. Your command will either carry the rifle-pits and ridge directly in front of them or move to the left, as the presence of the enemy may require."

The role Hooker was to play on 25 November was even less clearly defined. Grant had no serious part for him in what he imagined would be the climactic struggle of the morrow. At best, Hooker was to divert the enemy's attention from his right flank by a further display on Lookout Mountain. "If Hooker's present position on the mountain can be maintained with a small force, and it is found impracticable to carry the top from where he is, it would be advisable for him to move up the valley with all the force he can spare and ascend by the first practicable road," was all Grant had to say to Thomas on the matter.[4]

Thomas, who undoubtedly bristled at the cavalier treatment accorded his own Army of the Cumberland, had even less regard for Grant's intended use of Hooker's powerful column. Consequently, he chose to flout Grant's directive. Rather than leave Hooker to try to scale the summit of Lookout, which Thomas assumed already to be vacant, he decided to call him down to the valley, where he could make a more tangible contribution by demonstrating directly against Bragg's left flank on Missionary Ridge. Also, Thomas wanted to ensure that his own right, held by Palmer's Fourteenth Corps, was supported. In the event there still were Rebels on the mountaintop, Thomas did not want them sweeping down on his flank. To guard against this, Hooker was to confirm first that the summit was clear, and then stand ready to advance "as early as possible in the morning into Chattanooga Valley and seize and hold the Summertown Road, and cooperate with the Fourteenth Corps by supporting its right."[5]

That suited Hooker and his men just fine. They were equally anxious to verify their presumed control of the mountain. Besides, 25 November broke even colder than the day before, so that everyone was ready to move, if only to shake off the chill. In fact, Hooker's lieutenants were so ready that he never had a chance to give the order to reconnoiter the summit. At dawn, a sober General Whitaker walked into the bivouac of the Eighth Kentucky, which had relieved the Twenty-eighth Pennsylvania at the eastern base of the palisades long after the Rebels had quit the field. "Colonel Barnes," he yelled to its commander in the clear, crisp air, "I want a few volunteers to climb that cliff and see if the enemy are still there." "The whole regiment, General, if you wish it," replied the Kentuckian melodramatically. No, a squad would do fine. Barnes turned to the regiment and asked for volunteers. Captain John Wilson, commander of the color company, jumped up and begged to be allowed the honor. Barnes granted his request. Wilson turned to the color-bearer and asked him to follow with the flag. The bearer hesitated, glancing at the sheer, hundred-foot wall of rock and contemplating the weight of the flagstaff. Wilson grabbed the flag and handed the reluctant sergeant his sword. Six enlisted men volunteered to join Wilson. Gripping with one hand a long wild grapevine that dangled from the summit, Wilson started up a natural stairway of broken rock. His Kentuckians followed him. They clutched at rocks and bushes, grasped limbs and vines, and shoved one another upward. "At every step they expected to be greeted with deadly missiles of some sort from the enemy," recalled Wilson.[6]

General Geary had had the same idea as Whitaker. While the squad of Kentuckians picked their way upward on the east side of the palisade, he told Colonel Rickards to send a party up the west side with the colors of the Twenty-ninth Pennsylvania. The ascent became a contest between Easterners and Westerners, and everyone eagerly awaited the result.

The Kentuckians won. "Just as the king of day came peeping up over Missionary Ridge, Captain Wilson stepped out on the projecting brow of Lookout Mountain, and unfurled to the morning breeze that dear old emblem of light and liberty," recalled the regimental historian with unabashed pride. General Cruft was equally delighted at his boys' daring. "As the morning sun rose it discovered the national banner floating out in the mountain air from Lookout Point, and the soldiery below caught up a shout from the regiment on the summit which rang through the crags and valleys and was borne to their comrades below, who were standing to arms behind the defenses of Chattanooga," he wrote admiringly in his report.

Geary was angry but too clever to feel discomfited. Anyone could claim to have planted the national colors first; what was needed was a distinctive unit banner. "Captain," he barked at his aide-de-camp, W. L. Stork, as the young officer stumbled from his bedroll. "Take our division flag and hurry up and plant it on the top." Stork called to an orderly to bring the banner and then climbed up a crevice toward the Stars and Stripes planted by the Eighth Kentucky. He shoved the flag of the White Star division into the dirt beside it. With that act, Stork planted the seeds of a controversy that engaged the interest of aging veterans from both commands for decades to come: What unit reached the summit first? Stork personally was too honest to claim an honor that was not rightfully his. The Kentuckians had won the game, he admitted: "The planting of the Stars and Stripes on the palisades was more from the fact that the lucky planter got up little earlier than the rest of us, and got a furlough for his early task. It was a marvelous feat of early rising. The early bird catches the worm."[7]

Hooker maintained the momentum. Colonel Barnes had sent his entire regiment up the craggy stairway to the summit after Captain Wilson had unfurled the flag. Whitaker immediately pushed it forward along the mountaintop. The Kentuckians moved in a strong skirmish line, scooping up a few dozen sleepy Rebel stragglers before reaching the deserted Confederate camp at Summertown. Meanwhile, Hooker personally ordered the Eighty-fourth and Seventy-fifth Illinois, which guarded the left flank of his line on the Chattanooga road, to conduct a reconnaissance into the valley. The Illinoisans likewise found nothing but stragglers and discarded equipment. Convinced beyond a doubt that both the mountain and that part of the valley between it and Missionary Ridge were free of Rebels, Hooker assembled his command and awaited the order to move.[8]

It came shortly before 9:30 A.M. At daybreak, Grant had moved his headquarters from Fort Wood to Orchard Knob to better watch Sherman's progress on the northern end of Missionary Ridge. Thomas had ridden forward with him. Although the two generals and their staffs were huddled shoulder to shoulder on the little knoll, they may as well have been miles apart. Grant's gaze was toward Tunnel Hill, that of Thomas in the direction of Lookout Mountain. The atmosphere was heavy with ill will and mistrust. Rawlins and the other officers of Grant's staff looked to Sherman not only to deal the decisive blow of the battle, but to humiliate the Cumberlanders in the bargain. Thomas's chief of staff, Major General Joseph Reynolds, and his colleagues shared with the Virginian the strain of uncertainty regarding their own, relatively humiliating role, and all still felt the sting of Grant's comments to the War Department that the Army of the Cumberland was too sluggish to leave its trenches.

Thomas fretted and, as he did when he worried, withdrew into a sullen silence. He had far less faith in Sherman than did Grant. The Virginian foresaw disaster if his army—which had been reduced to fewer than twenty-five thousand men, after detachments to Hooker and Sherman—was ordered across the valley to storm Missionary Ridge before both Bragg's flanks were crushed; thus his eagerness for Hooker to roll up the Rebel left.

Baldy Smith was in the saddle beside Thomas when the flag went up atop Lookout Mountain. That clinched it. "I shall send Hooker at once across the ridge at the Rossville Gap," announced Thomas. Smith wholeheartedly seconded Thomas's desire to apply added pressure on Bragg, and he encouraged him to send a staff officer to Hooker at once. At 8:00 A.M., General Reynolds scribbled a terse command: "Leave Carlin's brigade at Summertown road, to rejoin Palmer," he wrote Hooker. "Move with the remainder of your force, except two regiments to hold Lookout Mountain, on the Rossville road toward Missionary Ridge, looking well to your right flank."[9]

Hooker drafted marching orders at 9:30 A.M., ten minutes after receiving Reynolds's note. He directed Osterhaus's division, which had done the least fighting the day before, to take the advance. Cruft was to follow with Grose and Whitaker. Carlin would march next and break off as ordered upon reaching the intersection with the Summertown road. Geary would bring up the rear. To the Eighth Kentucky and Ninety-sixth Illinois went the comfortable honor of holding the summit of Lookout. A few minutes after 10:00 A.M., Hooker rode off the mountain and out onto the Rossville road, his gaze fixed on Rossville Gap and Bragg's left flank.[10]

By then, Thomas was feeling much relieved, perhaps even a bit smug. A stunning revelation had compelled Grant not only to endorse Thomas's orders to Hooker (which he later claimed as his own), but to postpone the Virginian's own advance toward Missionary Ridge. Three and a half hours earlier the sun had risen above the eastern crest of the ridge, flooding the valley with a cold, sharp light that dissolved the last traces of haze that had lingered overnight. As the fog burned off, Grant and his staff stared in amazement toward Tunnel Hill. Not only did Sherman not hold it, but the hill bristled with Confederate cannon and long lines of Rebel infantry. Although the infantry were not entrenched, heavy columns appeared to be marching northward along the ridge to reinforce them. They kept coming until 9:00 A.M., some settling on the high ground south of the hill, others drawing up behind it. With the task before Sherman obviously greater than Grant had expected, he yielded to Thomas's conviction that a movement against the center of Missionary Ridge before the Ohioan had shaken loose Bragg's right flank would be a pointless slaughter. So Grant, Thomas, and their staffs waited with ill-concealed impatience for Sherman to go into action.

But nothing happened. The hours slipped away, with only a few ragged volleys echoing from the narrow valley between Sherman's lines and Tunnel Hill. It was 10:00 A.M. By then, Sherman should have been sweeping away Bragg's right and linking up victoriously with Thomas along Missionary Ridge. Instead, the only blue forces in motion were those of bit player Joseph Hooker descending Lookout Mountain.[11]

Sherman was in the throes of indecision. Dawn found him and his cozy coterie of generals no more capable of grasping the reality of the Confederate presence on Tunnel Hill—or of overcoming it—than they had been at sunset the day before. Neither did they appreciate the overwhelming superiority of numbers they enjoyed.

To recapitulate, Sherman had on hand the divisions of Morgan Smith, John Smith, and Hugh Ewing, plus Bushbeck's brigade on loan from Howard—a total of about 16,600 men. Jefferson C. Davis's division was back near the river, within easy supporting distance. To oppose Sherman at dawn, when the Ohioan was to have attacked, Cleburne could muster only three of his four brigades (Polk's was on detached duty guarding the railroad crossings over South Chickamauga Creek) for a total of perhaps 4,000 men. Of that number, only Smith's Texas brigade actually stood atop Tunnel Hill.

Yet Sherman hesitated. Throughout the long, bitterly cold night he had compelled his men to dissipate what remained of their strength in digging entrenchments and hauling cannon up the soggy slopes of the detached knolls they held north of Tunnel Hill. Not until 8:00 A.M., ninety minutes after Sherman should have launched his attack, did some of his weary men finally receive orders to quit fortifying their fronts. Hardly anyone had slept—those fortunate enough to escape fatigue duty found their blankets stiffen with frost only a few minutes after they laid them out on the ground. Most gave up any thought of rest and walked around in the dark to keep warm.[12]

How had Sherman passed the night and early morning? By his own account, he received his attack orders from Grant at midnight. "Accordingly, before day, I was in the saddle, attended by all my staff." They assembled near South Chickamauga Creek, on the extreme left of Sherman's line, and from there rode up the steep hill held by Lightburn's brigade. They continued along the thin ridge that connected Lightburn's Hill with that occupied by Alexander and Cockerill, "catching as accurate an idea of the ground as possible by the dim light of morning," said Sherman. Down its western slope rode the general, through the damp fields where Corse and Loomis rested, all the way to the far right, anchored by Bushbeck's Easterners. During the entire ride, Sherman's gaze never strayed far from Tunnel Hill. From Corse's front, he sized up his objective through the slowly receding darkness. "Quite a valley lay between us and the next hill of the series, and this hill presented steep sides, the one to the west partially cleared, but the other covered with the native forest. The crest of the ridge was narrow and wooded. The farther point of the hill was held by the enemy with a breastwork of logs and fresh earth, filled with men and two guns."[13]

By 5:00 A.M., he had made up his mind to strike Tunnel Hill primarily—and simultaneously—from the north and northwest. Although he had at his disposal nine brigades, Sherman decided to make his main effort with only two: those of Corse and Loomis of his brother-in-law Hugh Ewing's division. Corse would come at Tunnel Hill with as much of his brigade as he could bring into play through the narrow valley between the eminence held by Alexander (commonly known as Alexander's or Ewing's Hill) and Tunnel Hill. Loomis, on his right, was to approach Tunnel Hill through the open fields between the railroads. To John Smith and Morgan Smith went loosely defined supporting roles. The former was told to move the brigades of Matthies and Raum forward from their bivouac behind Alexander's Hill out into the valley, where they were to wait in the woods behind Loomis, "ready to act in any emergency that circumstances might require." Morgan Smith was instructed to detail one regiment from Lightburn's brigade to cooperate with Corse on his immediate left. The brigade of his younger brother, Giles Smith, was to march eastward, following the tracks of the Western and Atlantic Railroad until it had cleared the base of Lightburn's Hill, at which point it was to wheel to the south and gradually move against the eastern face of Tunnel Hill. Cockerill and Alexander, along with the remaining regiments of Lightburn's brigade, were to remain behind their entrenchments, as good an indication as any that Sherman went into the attack halfheartedly.[14]

Such was Sherman's plan, as neatly summarized in his report of the battle. Its execution, however, was halting and horribly coordinated, a reflection of the extent to which the confusing contours of the northern extreme of Missionary Ridge beguiled Sherman. The Ohioan seems to have set no precise time for the movement to commence, Grant's demand for a dawn assault notwithstanding.

At sunrise, he turned to his brother-in-law and, feigning indifference, said: "I guess, Ewing, if you're ready you might as well go ahead." He puffed on his cigar, then continued: "Keep up formation till you get to the foot of the hill." Ewing retorted, "And shall we keep it after that?" Sherman pushed his brother-in-law gently away. As he did, he rephrased the order so that it sounded more like a weak plea than a dictate. Ewing might go up the hill, "if you like—if you can"; but, Sherman warned, "don't call for help until you actually need it."[15]

The uncertain tenor of Sherman's instructions led Ewing to issue his subordinates orders that lacked conviction or clarity. He told Corse first to dislodge the enemy skirmishers who could be seen strung out across the narrow valley south of Alexander's Hill and then to drive their supports from a line of breastworks that crowned a low ridge just north of Tunnel Hill. Only after he accomplished these tasks would Corse be free to go after Smith's Texans and the battery on Tunnel Hill itself. Perhaps doubting that Corse, with only 920 men, could accomplish even these first two limited goals, Ewing urged restraint on Loomis: He was to advance southward through the level forests in his front, with his left hugging the western base of the rolling hills, until he reached the edge of the first open field, a half mile west of Tunnel Hill. There Loomis was to wheel to the left, form line of battle, and "push the enemy's skirmishers." But, Ewing cautioned, "under no circumstances" was he to bring on a general engagement.[16]

Brigadier General John Corse was a fiery, wiry little man. He stood five foot eight and weighed less than 125 pounds, so small as to escape notice. "To look at him, a stranger would not think his mind and body much out of proportion," observed a contemporary, who was quick to add, however, that the twenty-eight-year-old Iowan "has more ability than he seems to have." Behind his sharp features, large dark eyes, and long black hair, there burned an ambition that more than compensated for his diminutive stature. Before the war, a story made the rounds in his hometown of Burlington that, although probably apocryphal, pretty well summed up his character. When young John became a partner with his father in the family book and stationery business, a new sign had to be made. The father, then mayor of Burlington, suggested it read "J. L. Corse and Son." The future general retorted that it should read "John M. Corse and Father."[17]

"Boisterous and blasphemous," was how one Illinoisan described Corse. Some delighted in his profanity, others forgave it. However, virtually all of his men loved Corse, for both his gallantry under fire and his concern for their welfare and comfort on the march. Here at Chattanooga the Iowan's initial actions sustained their faith. Constrained by numbers (he had only three and a half regiments) and the vagaries of the ground, Corse arrayed his small command carefully in what amounted to two skirmish lines supported by the remainder of the brigade pulled together in double column. The first line consisted of five companies of the Fortieth Illinois under Major Hiram Hall—130 men in all. The second was composed of the Forty-sixth Ohio, deployed single file with six paces between each man. Trailing the Ohioans in reserve were the One Hundred Third Illinois and Sixth Iowa. Corse placed himself between his two Ohio regiments and turned control of the brigade reserve over to Colonel Charles Walcutt. So methodical was the Iowan in his preparations—and so remiss were Ewing and Sherman in seeing that the attack moved according to the timetable laid down by Grant—that it was nearly 8:00 A.M. before Major Hall waved his Illinoisans down the slope of Alexander's Hill and into the heavily forested valley, from which, less than one hundred yards away, a handful of Smith's Texans watched their approach.[18]

The lone regiment of Lightburn's brigade selected to support Corse's left had moved out more promptly, and, sadly, it was to suffer for its alacrity. Bypassing Morgan Smith, Sherman had ridden over to Lightburn's Hill and given Lightburn oral orders to "send forward two hundred men to occupy Tunnel Hill." Lightburn summoned Colonel Theodore Jones, commander of the Thirtieth Ohio, and repeated the oddly simplistic instructions to him. Sherman interjected a few word of clarification: "I wish you to go up the point of the hill and assist Corse who is coming up the side, and the sooner you get off the better as Corse is ready to start." Jones protested that he had only 170 men in his regiment. Lightburn promised to loan him 30 men from the Fourth West Virginia. A bit placated, Jones returned to his command and in a few minutes started off over the brigade breastworks on his quixotic mission. Even assuming Corse was ready to start, which he was not, Sherman had committed only slightly over 1,100 men to the direct assault on Tunnel Hill, whose Texas defenders numbered perhaps 1,300. The Ohioan had begun what was to be a pattern that day. Through sheer temerity, he repeatedly negated his overwhelming advantage in numbers.[19]

Halfway down the southern slope of Lightburn's Hill, Jones's Ohioans ran into skirmishers from the Twenty-fourth Texas, under the command of a hot-blooded Yankee-hater, Captain Samuel Foster. Foster and his men had been standing watch since 3:00 A.M. Shivering, hungry, and bored, they were eager for something to shoot at. "I see one of them. Can I shoot him?" an elated private whispered to Foster after the first blue uniform became visible through the naked forest. Foster told him to wait until it was a bit lighter and the man drew nearer, then to blast away. The man curbed his impatience long enough to satisfy his captain, then fired. The rest of Foster's men opened up as soon as they caught Ohioans in their sights.

Jones's skirmishers replied. Foster saw one of his men spin to the ground, his throat ripped open by a minié bullet. Blood bubbled and hissed from his torn windpipe. Tiring of the pointless exchange, Jones ordered a charge. Foster passed the word down the line "to fall back slowly, but to keep firing. We began moving back tree to tree."

The Ohioans matched them, tree for tree, across the valley and up the northeastern slope of the narrow ridge north of Tunnel Hill. There, said Foster, "the undergrowth deserted us, but there was still plenty of large trees around." Although outgunned, Foster's Texans continued to make him proud. "I was able to see most of my men from where I stood. This was something which I had not been able to do before. They were in a very good line, backing up from tree to tree, stopping and loading, shooting two or three times before falling back some more. We killed several Yanks. We could see them fall. But they kept pressing us very hard. Whenever one of my men saw a Yank, he hid behind a tree and waited. He killed the Yank every time. He then moved on, seemingly satisfied with what he had done."

By then Foster was satisfied enough to concede the ground to the Ohioans, and he yelled at his Texans to follow him back to Tunnel Hill.[20]

Jones swept up the ridge and took the Rebel breastworks, which consisted of logs indifferently piled atop one another, from the right and rear. He shot or captured a few men from the Rebel picket reserve who had not gotten off with Foster.

Jones was within 250 yards of the open crest of Tunnel Hill. The four twelve-pounders of Swett's Mississippi Battery stood on the hilltop like candles on a cake, waiting to be plucked off. In front of the guns, nearest Jones's Ohioans, were the men of the Seventh Texas, only partly protected by their own low breastworks. Midway between the ridge and Tunnel Hill, where the slopes from the two rises met, was a long, narrow east-west ravine. Tempted by the nearness and apparent docility of the Rebel battery, which had yet to fire a shot, and expecting to be joined momentarily on his right by Corse's brigade, Jones coaxed his men over the breastworks in a charge. They made it through the ravine and a few steps up the opposite slope, before a sudden blast of canister swept them back to the relative safety of the abandoned Rebel works on the ridge.[21]

Jones was furious—Corse had not come up. He sent his adjutant down the western side of the ridge, from which direction he had expected Corse. The lieutenant returned empty handed. Alarm over his isolated position fueled Jones's anger. He sent to Lightburn for reinforcements. Nearly an hour passed before the Thirty-seventh Ohio showed up and fell into line on Jones's left.

About the same time that the Thirty-seventh Ohio arrived, the snapping of twigs and pop-pop of skirmish fire heralded the approach of the dilatory first line of Corse's brigade. Up the northwestern slope of the ridge came Major Hall and his 130 Illinoisans, gaily chasing a few Texan skirmishers. Like Jones, Hall became immediately enamored of the four cannons on Tunnel Hill. He led his little band over the logworks a few dozen yards to the right of the Thirtieth Ohio and on toward the hill. Miraculously, his men made it to within a few feet of Smith's works. Two Illinoisans hopped over them, only to be cut down quickly. Like Jones, Hall had expected support. Swearing a blue streak when the second line of his own brigade failed to follow him, he withdrew his five companies, now reduced to fewer than one hundred men, to the breastworks on the low ridge. A few of Smith's Texans foolishly followed, only to be driven back to their own works by a determined volley from the Illinoisans.[22]

It was 9:00 A.M. Although not yet in contact with one another, Hall and Jones were keeping their troops busy sharpshooting at Swett's gunners. Finally Corse came up at the head of the Forty-sixth Ohio. He sought out Hall. "What did you see?" he asked breathlessly. Hall described the Rebel works and the relative position of the battery. Could they be taken? Corse wondered. With a strong force, yes, replied Hall testily, but not with his depleted skirmish line. "Get your men in readiness and we will support you with the brigade and we will charge and take that battery," Corse announced.[23]

Corse settled the Forty-sixth Ohio in behind the breastworks. Back down in the valley, Colonel Walcutt waited with the One Hundred Third Illinois and Sixth Iowa. With his men out of harm's way, Corse sought out Colonel Jones. He proposed to charge Tunnel Hill and asked the colonel to join him in the effort. Jones inquired as to the formation. Corse's reply led to an animated debate. "He said that I should move to the left and let his men in on the right and form a line and charge," said Jones. "I opposed the formation as we had to make a right wheel in the charge, my men being on the left would be under a cross fire as soon as they left the works, and suggested that we form in column and charge to position occupied by the enemy's artillery on the high ground." Corse disagreed. "He thought we would lose too many men in that way, and his order was carried out," Jones later recalled. Corse rode away to bring up his brigade, and Jones filed to the left to make room for the additional troops. No sooner had Jones gotten ready than the Iowan reappeared. Suddenly transformed, Corse now had considerably less confidence in the wisdom of an attack of any sort with their small force. Might not Colonel Jones report back to Sherman the situation on their front and seek further instructions?

Jones found Sherman atop Lightburn's Hill at 10:00 A.M. The general had just been told of Grant's impatience at his delay. Displeasure from his friend was something to which Sherman was unaccustomed. He was thus in no mood for excuses when Jones made his report. "Go back and make that charge immediately; time is everything," he snarled. "If you want more men, I will give you all·you want; if you want artillery, I will give you that. General Grant is on Orchard Knob waiting for your assault in order to send up a column from the Army of the Cumberland." The ill-used colonel saluted and started back to his command.[24]

# CHAPTER SIXTEEN

# THIS WAS BUSINESS

S HERMAN'S dawdling had been Cleburne's salvation. Every minute
that the Ohioan delayed his assault had brought the Irish immigrant
vital reinforcements. The first came just after sunrise, when Brigadier
General John Brown's Tennesseans staggered into position on Cleburne's
left after their all-night march from Lookout Mountain. Carter Stevenson and Hardee each tinkered a bit with Brown's brigade before finally
agreeing to place it on the ridge between the left flank of Smith's Texans and the railroad tunnel. No sooner had his men filed into position
than Brown sent skirmishers down into the partially cleared fields—
known as the flat—north of the Chattanooga and Cleveland Railroad.
They deployed several hundred yards west of the ridge, covering the
ground from the tracks to the Glass farm, with their left thrown forward so as to enfilade any force moving across the fields toward Tunnel Hill. With infantry now on hand to support them, the batteries of
Calvert and Goldthwaite were wheeled into place above the tunnel,
their guns similarly trained to enfilade the approach to Tunnel Hill from
the flat.[1]

Cumming's brigade showed up at 9:30 A.M. Hardee and Stevenson fed
it into line to the left of Brown. About the same time, Lewis's Orphan
Brigade reported to Cleburne for duty, having been sent to the right by
Bragg. The Irishman asked Lewis to hold himself a few hundred feet
behind Smith, on the eastern slope of Tunnel Hill, and be ready to move
as exigencies might require.

The detachment of Lewis from the center to duty on the right reflected not only Bragg's concern for that sector but his confidence in Cleburne. Bragg had visited Tunnel Hill at daybreak and after an inspection of Cleburne's lines had returned to his headquarters. Though deeply
troubled by the strength of Sherman's force, he had faith enough in
Cleburne to reinforce him without meddling in his affairs.

So too did Hardee, who gave his favorite subordinate license to manage the extreme right as he saw fit. While Cleburne prepared for the inevitable attack against Tunnel Hill, Hardee rode away to superintend the placement of the remaining brigades of Stevenson's division and those of States Rights Gist.[2]

At 10:30 A.M. the mud-streaked cannon on Lightburn's Hill unleashed an artillery barrage that forced Smith's Texans to duck low. Behind the exploding shells came Corse's infantry. Again Major Hiram Hall's Fortieth Illinois, deployed as skirmishers, led the way. The Illinoisan was burning mad. He was sure he could have taken Swett's Battery, had Corse been on hand to support him in his first attempt. To assuage Hall's ire and compensate for his losses, Corse gave him three companies of the One Hundred Third Illinois. These Hall placed thirty paces behind his five depleted companies. The Forty-sixth Ohio lined up close behind Hall. The remainder of the One Hundred Third Illinois and the Sixth Iowa trailed in support, still under the command of Colonel Walcutt.[3]

Corse placed himself in the front rank, among Hall's Illinoisans. At the sound of the bugle, they jumped the breastworks and started for Tunnel Hill. Hall glanced over his shoulder to make sure the Ohioans were with him; they were. Through the ravine and up the scrubby slope of Tunnel Hill charged Corse's Federals. True to his word, Colonel Jones joined them on their left with his Thirtieth Ohio. Lieutenant H. Shannon, in command of Swett's Battery, wheeled his four pieces to face the oncoming bluecoats. He shredded their ranks with canister, but the Yankees kept coming. They charged to within fifty feet of Smith's line before breaking. Then, recalled Captain Foster, "the fun commenced in earnest. The Yanks . . . began falling back, and in bad order. In other words, they ran back. I enjoyed it hugely. We all just laughed and hollered."

Not all the Texans shared Foster's exuberance. Cleburne had waited until the Yankees were a stone's throw from Smith's line before launching a perfectly timed counterattack with the right companies of Colonel Roger Mills's mixed regiment of infantry and dismounted cavalry and the left companies of Colonel Hiram Granbury's Seventh Texas. They drove the enemy handily back the eighty yards down the slope, but Hall's Illinoisans and the Forty-sixth Ohio took cover in the ravine and refused to budge. They picked off Smith and Mills, both of whom tumbled from their saddles dangerously wounded. Their men fell back to their breastworks, and Cleburne assigned brigade command to Colonel Hiram Granbury.[4]

Corse's attack was over before the One Hundred Third Illinois or Sixth Iowa could join the fight. Before trying again, the Iowan decided to bring them forward. Aware of Sherman's guarantee of reinforcements to Ewing, reluctant though it might have been, Corse called for help.

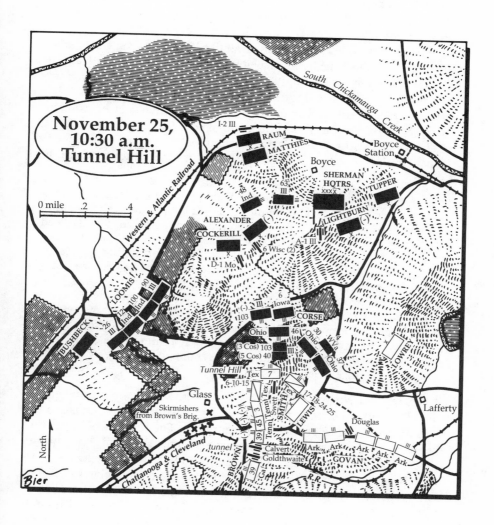

November 25,
10:30 a.m.
Tunnel Hill

South Chickamauga Creek

0 mile    .2    .4

Western & Atlantic Railroad

I-2 Ill

RAUM

MATTHIES

Boyce
Station

Boyce

SHERMAN
HQTRS.

TUPPER

48
Ind

63
Ill

LIGHTBURN

ALEXANDER

COCKERILL

(-)

6 Wisc (2)

A-1 Ill

D-1 Mo

LOOMIS

90
Ill

(-)

6
Iowa

26
Ill

120
Ind

100
Ill

1103

CORSE

4
W Va.

30
Ohio

6
Ohio

BUSHBECK

Ohio  46
Ill

(3 Cos) 103
Ill

(5 Cos) 40
Ill

LOWREY

Tunnel Hill

6-10-15

Tex  7

Lafferty

Glass

Skirmishers
from Brown's Brig.

(-)

3

45

39

Tex
Tenn

Tenn
Swett

17

18-24-25

SMITH

LEWIS

Douglas

Ark

Ark

Ark

Ark

Ark

North

Chattanooga & Cleveland

tunnel

BROWN

39
Ga.

Calvert
Goldthwaite

GOVAN

R.R.

Bier

The impetuous Iowan, however, had no intention of waiting for reinforcements that may or may not come before attacking a second time. He formed the One Hundred Third Illinois and Sixth Iowa behind the logworks on the narrow ridge (later called Corse's Hill in his honor) and told their commanders, when the bugle again sounded charge, "to move rapidly to the front, and halt for nothing, but go directly into the enemies' works."

They followed his instructions literally. At 11:30 A.M., Corse ordered the advance. Once again, he placed himself in the front line. Hall's decimated command edged only a few yards out of the ravine, preferring to sharpshoot from behind trees and rocks. The rest of the brigade charged over them with abandon. Shannon's cannon spewed canister as fiercely as before, but this time some of the Yankees made it over the Rebel breastworks. The fighting became brutally—and sometimes almost comically—personal. Recalled a soldier of the One Hundred Third Illinois:

> A member of Company F, Joe S. Walters, getting a little too near, a lean, lank, hungry-looking Johnnie sergeant jumped over the works and demanded of him, "gimme that gun, and come in hur, you damned Yankee coward." Joe replied, "Here, take the gun, it ain't worth a cuss anyway." It had been hit with a bullet, and was bent and spoiled; at this time a little corporal sprang over the works and grabbed Joe's other arm and with much bluster and many big oaths, ordered that "you come over here, you Yankee coward," but Isaac Harn and another comrade were just at the right, and heard the conversation. Harn gave the big sergeant the contents of his gun, bringing him to the ground, and Joe gave the little corporal a blow that brought him to the ground and turning, ran down the hill under a shower of bullets, escaping with the loss of one finger. Harn was killed.[5]

Dozens fell within a few feet of the enemy works, their bodies riddled by minié bullets or ripped apart by canister. Among those to fall was Corse, his knee bruised by a spent shot. The severity of his wound became a source of speculation among his men. Corse had gone into the fight full of bluster, "declaring his ability to lick the Confederacy, with other manifestations of lunacy," remembered an iconoclastic lieutenant. Apparently, however, his vaunted courage failed him there before the Rebel breastworks. Borne from the field on a stretcher, still cursing the Confederacy, he was greeted by a team of concerned surgeons. They gently removed his clothing, expecting, since there was no blood, to find a severe contusion. Instead, confessed the division surgeon, there was only "a little blue spot."[6]

While Corse was carried to the rear, his troops kept up the pressure on the Texans, holding onto the slope with a rabid tenacity. From a range of less than fifty yards they turned their rifle-muskets on the Confederate gunners. Shannon was already down, hit by a shell fragment that broke his collarbone, punctured a lung, and came out near his backbone. A few minutes later his successor, First Lieutenant Joseph Aston, who had been promoted only two days before, was shot dead. Shannon, who was sitting under a tree nursing his wound, saw Ashton fall. Struggling to his feet, he walked back to the battery and resumed command, cheering his men as the blood gurgled from his chest and streamed down his jacket. Cannoneers fell all around him. Shannon grew woozy and had to leave the field. As he staggered off, the last officer in the battery, Second Lieutenant H. H. Steele, was shot. Eventually all the sergeants were gunned down, and command of the battery devolved on a corporal, one F. M. Williams. Colonel Granbury pulled troops from his Seventh Texas out of the line to man the cannon.[7]

Cleburne, meanwhile, worked feverishly to dislodge the Federals. He positioned Douglas's Battery near Granbury's right flank to enfilade Corse's left, then called forward the Ninth Kentucky and Second Kentucky to extend his line of infantry far enough eastward to pry loose Jones's Thirtieth Ohio.[8]

Even the sadistic Captain Foster was worried now. The fun had gone out of the fight. "This was business," he admitted. "We could see what we were doing. When we killed a man, we knew it. We saw him fall. Two Yanks achieved to get killed but a few yards from our breastwork."[9]

Edward Schwietzer of the Thirtieth Ohio marveled at the slaughter. "The fire we was under was terrible. The leaves was flying up as the bullets would strike them. Everything seemed to be flying but the Rebels, and they was busy shooting at the Yanks."[10]

Finally the Federals began to give way. Caught up in the horrible thrill of the moment, the Texans followed them instinctively from behind the cover of their breastworks. "Our men did not wait for orders. They jumped over the works, yelling as only Texans can yell," said Foster, who made no effort at stopping his own company. "I jumped atop the logs and yelled like an Indian. Then some deluded Yank . . . not knowing the fear of the Confederacy when he saw it before his eyes, shot me in the leg." The bullet caught Foster just below the knee, and he crumpled up on the logs. "Captain, are you hit?" several of his men shouted above the din. "The captain's hit," confirmed others. "Some of my men came over to help me off the logs. At first, I did not realize that I had been shot," Foster recalled. "It felt as if someone had struck me with a ramrod or a stick. It also burned somewhat." One of his men yelled for a litter. Another ripped open his pants leg. "I then saw it. The leg was bleeding freely. It was not a mistake. I was wounded," said Foster. His men laid him on the stretcher and the bearers went off at a jog, taking him down off the hill and out of range of the bullets. There Foster was loaded onto an ambulance for the jarring ride to a field hospital.[11]

Colonel Walcutt was present to greet the survivors of the brigade as they fell back to Corse's Hill. After repelling Granbury's counterattack and restoring a semblance of order, Walcutt sent to Sherman for orders.

Sherman had had enough. Corse's setback convinced him that the northern approach to Tunnel Hill was bankrupt, and so he refused to send Walcutt reinforcements. Instead, he told him simply to hold his ground. Hall's Illinoisans and an intrepid few from the other regiments ventured out into the ravine, keeping up a harassing fire from behind trees until nearly sunset. For all practical purposes, however, the first Federal effort to take Tunnel Hill was over at noon.[12]

How was it that Cleburne had been free to turn his undivided attention to pulverizing Corse's brigade? Largely because Colonel Loomis had taken literally Ewing's admonition that he "under no circumstances" bring on a general engagement. In fact, Loomis evinced no interest in bringing on a fight of any kind. Unlike Corse's men, who later claimed to have been hurried into action on empty stomachs, Loomis's bluecoats enjoyed a leisurely breakfast before they were ordered into line a little after 8:00 A.M. What they saw as they dressed ranks, however, did little to aid their digestion. A mile to the southeast, Tunnel Hill was visible above the valley, as were the Rebel reinforcements hurrying to join Granbury's Texans in its defense. "It was still foggy on the lowland, where we formed, but it was clear and the sun shone brightly on the top of Missionary Ridge so that the Confederates could not look down into the fog and see us, but we could look up through it and see one long column of Rebels after another moving . . . to their right and being massed directly in our front," attested one fidgety Indianian. "We looked up through the fog and saw the thousands of bright gun barrels of the Rebel soldiers flashing in the sunshine."[13]

Loomis formed his command in a level forest west of Alexander's Hill, apparently with the Ninetieth Illinois on the left, the One Hundredth Indiana on the left center, the Twelfth Indiana holding the right center, and the Twenty-sixth Illinois anchoring the right. Ewing gave Loomis a section of artillery and told him that he could call on Bushbeck's brigade for help as needed. With that, Loomis moved out southward through the woods, his left protected first by the western base of Alexander's Hill, then by the slope of a lower rise, behind which General John Smith was shortly to form the brigades of Matthies and Raum in support of Ewing, as Sherman had ordered. (For want of a better name, we will call this eminence Smith's Hill.) After half a mile, at a point where the Western and Atlantic Railroad intersected a dirt lane known later as the Tunnel Hill road, Loomis wheeled his brigade to the left and resumed the march, now directly toward the hill. The Midwesterners had gone no more than a few hundred feet before they suddenly ran out of forest. At the timber's edge, behind a worm-rail fence, Loomis halted the brigade and ordered the men to lie down while he pondered the situation.

It was not encouraging. Nearly half a mile of meadows and soggy fields lay between him and the black, beckoning mouth of the railroad tunnel. The flat, said a captain of the Twelfth Indiana, was "shaped like a smoothing iron—the little or peaked end went up to the mouth of the tunnel and the big end lay to the west or where the Twelfth lay concealed in the timber." Once Loomis's brigade left the woods, it would be at the mercy of the Rebel artillery atop the tunnel. One deep and narrow ditch, two lesser ones, and three more fences lay astride their path of advance as natural impediments—or as cover if they faltered; the only other cover to be had out on the flat came from a few tree stumps. On the far side of the flat, tucked nearly under the western slope of Tunnel Hill and blocking the final two hundred yards to the tunnel, stood the white frame house, barn, and handful of slave cabins that made up the Glass farm. General Brown's Tennesseans already had come off the ridge and were nestled into place south of the farm, ready to skirmish with the Yankees.[14]

Not surprisingly, particularly in light of his orders, Loomis hesitated to challenge the Tennesseans For nearly half an hour his troops lay nervously in limbo, contemplating the open ground before them and the steep slopes of Missionary Ridge beyond, while Loomis procrastinated. He brought up his two cannon and tried to shell the Rebels from the Glass farm. All the gunners accomplished, however, was to set fire to the farmhouse and send its occupants—three frightened women, a few children, and two yelping dogs—fleeing across the field toward Loomis's lines.[15]

At 10:30 A.M., an aide from Ewing shoved unexpected orders into Loomis's hands—certainly the product of Grant's prodding Sherman into action. Corse was about to assault Tunnel Hill, the instructions read; Loomis was to advance at once in cooperation. Loomis made a good-faith effort at complying, but with Smith's Hill standing between him and Corse, the Indianian had no idea where his fellow brigade commander's flank lay or precisely when or in what direction Corse might attack. Consequently, Loomis moved out blindly. He guided on the mouth of

the tunnel, which he presumed to be his objective. In doing so, however-
er, he opened a yawning gap of some four hundred yards between his
left and Corse's right.[16]

Loomis never had a chance. The instant his men felled the fence to
their front and stepped into the clearing, they were easy marks for the
two batteries atop the tunnel. Captain Irving Buck of Cleburne's staff
watched the slaughter from beside the cannon:

> The Napoleon guns posted over the tunnel, which had been rapidly and
> continuously served, were turned upon this advancing brigade with
> deadly precision; every discharge plowed huge gaps through the lines,
> which were promptly closed up, as the troops moved forward with a
> steadiness and order that drew exclamations of admiration from all who
> witnessed it. The brigade advanced to an old fence row, where plant-
> ing their colors and lying down they opened and kept up a damaging
> fire, and held their position with a tenacity which seemed proof against
> all efforts to dislodge them.[17]

Buck flattered Loomis. What he took for gallant perseverance was
really the product of the continued irresolution of Sherman and his
generals. Loomis had stopped less than halfway across the open ground
because word had reached him that Corse had been repelled. Unwilling to go forward alone and lacking orders to fall back, he chose to remain where he was. And contrary to Buck's claim about the Yankees'
good aim, most of Loomis's men were ordered not to fire; those who
were allowed to shoot could do so only when crouching or standing up,
and few were willing to expose themselves to the murderous pounding
from the ridge for a chance at squeezing off a long-range rifle shot.[18]

It was noon. Nearly six hours had passed since Sherman was to have
launched his decisive daylight assault, yet all he had done was bloody
two of his brigades in badly coordinated, unsupported charges. There
was a brief lull on the field, punctuated only by the occasional boom
of Calvert's and Goldthwaite's batteries. Cleburne put the time to good
use, patching the weak spots in his defenses. He peeled off Govan's left-
flank regiment—the Second and Fifteenth Arkansas (Consolidated)—and
placed it in direct support of the guns above the tunnel. Next, Cleburne
retired two guns of Swett's Battery and their skeleton crews from Tunnel Hill and replaced them with four light cannon from Lieutenant
Thomas Key's battery, turning command of the whole over to Key.

General Hardee, who was still superintending affairs on Stevenson's
front, lent the Irishmen a hand. To help check any further advance by
Loomis, he told Alfred Cumming to hurry two regiments from his Georgia brigade down from Missionary Ridge to seize the Glass farm. Should

the Federals compel them to fall back, Hardee added, they were to set fire to the buildings. Cumming ordered out the Thirty-ninth and Fifty-sixth Georgia.[19]

Although he offered him no such support as Hardee gave Cleburne, Sherman compelled Loomis to push on. Through Ewing, he directed the hapless colonel to advance to the foot of Tunnel Hill. Once there, he was to place his left on the road that wrapped around its base and hold his ground. What he expected to happen after that, Sherman did not specify.

Loomis tried again to obey, and the senseless killing went on—only at closer range. Instinctively seeking cover, the Yankees made for the railroad embankment at a point where it curved south, away from the tunnel, creating an even larger gap between their left and Corse's right. Behind the embankment, still nearly four hundred yards shy of the tunnel, the men of the One Hundredth Indiana, Twelfth Indiana, and Twenty-sixth Illinois buried their heads in the dirt and held on, without understanding why. "We did not advance beyond the railroad nor even attempt to charge up the hill, but I saw men in the ranks shed tears because they were denied the privilege of going forward," Major J. B. Bruner of the Twenty-sixth Illinois complained bitterly. As they soon discovered, the protection of the embankment was largely illusory. "We lay there in plain view of the enemy and watched them shooting at us, while we were unable to return the fire on account of their elevation," said Bruner.[20]

A short distance behind the embankment was the deep ditch that had tripped up Loomis's men when they crossed the field. Now it began to fill with wounded soldiers seeking a measure of protection from the hail of gunfire or, in the more desperate cases, simply a quieter place to die. Captain Noble King, commander of the color company of the Twenty-sixth Illinois, was forced to turn down the request of his badly wounded color sergeant that he detail two soldiers to carry him off the field. He had no men to spare, King told the sergeant—too many had fallen. "I told him he better crawl back and lie in the ditch until the battle was over."

Huddled in the ditch were two brothers from the Twelfth Indiana, nineteen-year-old James Vanscoy and his older brother, Jacob, age twenty-three. Together they had enlisted in Company B a year earlier. And together, shoulder to shoulder, they marched out onto the flat here at Chattanooga with their regiment. They splashed through the ditch, which was knee-deep with rain water, and slogged on toward the railroad embankment. A few yards beyond the ditch, a bullet ripped through Jacob's chest, and he dropped to the ground. James threw aside his rifle and, with the aid of another man, dragged his brother back to the ditch. Its side was slippery and they lost their balance. Jacob pitched forward into the muck. James recalled, "The man that was helping me left me there and the ditch was so deep and narrow that I could not get [Jacob] out and all I could do was to hold his head out of the water." James cradled Jacob in his arms and listened intently to the ramblings of his frightened and dying brother. Both were deeply religious farm boys, and, with James's gentle coaxing, Jacob's fevered mind eventually found solace in their faith. Wrote James to their parents:

> Shortly after he was wounded he told me, yet while he was on the field, that he had to die. I spoke to him about his soul and he did not seem at first to be satisfied to die, but shortly the Lord powerfully blessed him and he was enabled to shout although he suffered intensely. He took from his pocket a Testament and gave it to me and told me to read it and meet him in Glory. He also told me to tell his wife to train up his children in the nurture and admonition of the Lord and meet him in Heaven. He then said "Tell father and mother and all the boys to meet me in Heaven."[21]

Loomis was in deep trouble. The three regiments behind the embankment were leaking wounded rearward at an alarming rate. The Ninetieth Illinois, Loomis's left-flank regiment, had the unenviable duty of trying to make the connection with Corse, across the field from the tracks to the foot of Tunnel Hill. It was an impossible task. The brigade had strayed too far south and the Ninetieth Illinois had lost so many men that it covered a front barely the width of two normal-sized companies. Worse yet, Cumming's Georgians still owned the Glass farm. From there, they were in a position to roll up the left flank of the Ninetieth.

After thirty minutes in this untenable position, Loomis summoned Bushbeck. At 12:30 P.M., he asked the German to send forward two regiments to roust the Confederates from the farm, thereby offering a measure of protection to his left.

Bushbeck obliged him at once. He passed the mission on to Lieutenant Colonel Joseph Taft, commander of the Seventy-third Pennsylvania. With his own regiment leading and the Twenty-seventh Pennsylvania following some two hundred yards in his rear, Taft broke out of the safety of the timber at the double-quick. As the cannoneers on Tunnel Hill turned their attention to him, Taft ordered his men into a run. Through bursting shells the Pennsylvanians dashed, bearing straight for the Glass farm. In front of the farm, the Rebels had thrown up a line of rude breastworks. Skirmishers from Cumming's two regiments knelt behind them. They waited until the Pennsylvanians closed to within fifty yards before letting loose a volley and then falling back to join their comrades around the house and outbuildings. Taft's men fell down on the opposite side of the vacated works and opened fire on the Georgians, who dodged the bullets from behind the buildings, stepping out only long enough to squeeze off their own rounds.

Seeing little to be gained from this cat-and-mouse exchange, Taft decided to try to outflank the Rebels. He called first for one company of the Twenty-seventh Pennsylvania, which quite sensibly had sought cover in the long ditch to his rear, then another to extend the left flank of the Seventy-third Pennsylvania. Taft's tactic worked. Finding himself now open to an enfilading attack against his right and his men dangerously low on ammunition, Cumming recalled the Thirty-ninth and Fifty-sixth Georgia to the ridge. Cumming was happy to see them return largely intact but annoyed at the haste of their departure. "Owing to some misconception of orders, the troops withdrew without setting fire to the houses," he rued. Colonel J. T. McConnell begged permission to go out again and make amends. Cumming refused. McConnell persisted, and Cumming relented. Hastily stuffing their cartridge boxes with fresh ammunition, four companies of the Thirty-ninth Georgia sprinted back down to the farm and set fire to those buildings not already aflame, getting off just ahead of the Federals.[22]

As the Georgians disappeared up the timbered slope for the second time, Taft grew reckless. He urged the remainder of the Twenty-seventh Pennsylvania to come up and further extend his left. They did and together with the Seventy-third Pennsylvania charged into the stinging smoke, surging around the flames and past the farm. At the base of Tunnel Hill, Taft called a halt. In the confusion, however, the order was missed by the left half of his line. Company B of the Seventy-third, together with the entire Twenty-seventh Pennsylvania, kept on up the six-hundred-foot western slope of Tunnel Hill. With no threat from Corse on the north end of the hill, Lieutenant Key was free to turn his six guns against the Pennsylvanians. Charge after blistering charge of canister shredded their ranks, but still the Pennsylvanians came on. They clawed their way upward through the mud, brush, and trees. Thirty yards short of the hilltop, they collapsed, exhausted. Once they regained their strength, the Pennsylvanians opened an uphill fire on Key's gunners so surprisingly precise that it forced them to abandon their cannon and scamper out of sight. Neither could Granbury's Texans fire without exposing their heads to the volleys of the Pennsylvanians. Out of frustration, they began to hurl rocks blindly over their breastworks and down the hill. They kept up this anachronistic form of warfare at intervals the rest of the afternoon, bashing in the heads of a number of luckless Federals as effectively as if they had been struck by shrapnel.[23]

Unfortunately, Taft's well-intentioned maneuvering had done little to relieve Loomis's concern for his left. In climbing the hill, the Twenty-seventh Pennsylvania had pulled so far away as to be of no help to his exposed flank. Even the Seventy-third Pennsylvania, though nine of its companies still clung to the foot of Tunnel Hill near the farm, had veered too far to the left. Loomis's Ninetieth Illinois, which was to lose 117 men by the day's end, simply could not stretch itself thin enough to close the gap. And the largely Irish regiment had lost its commander, the recklessly gallant Colonel Timothy O'Meara, who had acted as though he were on some Napoleonic field of glory. "He went into the battle dressed in his best uniform, his famous sword at his side, his crimson sash across his breast, a foreign medal won in some other war above it, and last but not least a little amulet or charm hung by a cord around his neck. This, he said, would keep him from all harm," remembered an admiring courier from Ewing's staff. "But the bright sash was his undoing. Some sharpshooter's ball pierced his body, and after a few hours of suffering, while faithfully attended by the Catholic chaplain of his regiment, he gave his life for the country he called his own."[24]

Now, too, Loomis imagined the Confederates were preparing to sally forth down the Tunnel Hill road in strength, straight into the feeble line of the Ninetieth and the void to its left. Desperate to forestall them, he personally rode across the shot-riddled field to the reverse slope of Smith's Hill to beg General John Smith for support.[25]

What Loomis had descried through the smoke was actually the movement of the Thirty-ninth Georgia, its ammunition replenished, along the ridge behind Brown's brigade to shore up Cleburne's left flank on Tunnel Hill. Hardee had asked Stevenson to send a regiment to Cleburne's succor a little after 1:00 P.M. A few minutes later, he told him to dispatch another, and Cumming withdrew the Thirty-fourth Georgia from his line of battle. Although Cumming had not ventured back into the valley, his lateral movement on the summit toward Loomis's left understandably frightened the Indianian, whose nerves were fast fraying.[26]

Loomis came upon Matthies's brigade lying in the long field behind Smith's Hill, but its division commander was nowhere to be found. At 11:00 A.M., Smith had bowed to a request from Ewing that he move Matthies there to be within easy supporting distance of Loomis. An hour later, Ewing again called on Smith, this time to advance Raum's brigade. Again Smith obliged. Having spent the morning up on Lightburn's Hill with Sherman, the crusty Swiss emigré had not paid much attention to what Ewing was doing with his two brigades. A few minutes after Raum moved off, Smith decided to find out. He discovered Raum's brigade drawn up in an open field in front of the rifle pits previously held by Corse and Loomis. Having far more lucrative targets closer at hand, the Rebel artillery had ignored Raum. Nonetheless, Smith was furious at seeing Raum's brigade exposed while Cockerill's brigade of Ewing's division was safely tucked behind its breastworks. In his pique, he forgot to check on Matthies and instead rode off to demand an explanation from Ewing. Ewing paid him no heed, so Smith galloped off to complain to Sherman, who gave him no satisfaction either. Trusting to his brother-in-law's judgment, Sherman approved the disposition of Raum's brigade.[27]

Loomis, meanwhile, had taken matters into his own hands. The lives of his men were too precious to waste time on protocol. When Matthies proved reluctant to move without higher authority, Loomis sought out Ewing, who told Loomis to order Matthies forward in his name. (As this sorry little affair reveals, the Union effort against Tunnel Hill continued to be improvised from below rather than orchestrated from above. Someone in authority—preferably Sherman himself or at the very least his senior staff officers—should have been on hand to see that troops were put to better use and not deployed piecemeal to plug gaps in what had become a static defense on untenable ground.)

But such was not to be, and so back to Matthies galloped Loomis. Together they rode to the top of Smith's Hill. "The order for you is to move your brigade up and take that white house," Loomis announced, pointing toward the brightly burning remains of the Glass farm.[28]

Matthies put up no more resistance. Born Karl Leopold Matthies, the thirty-nine-year-old emigré was too deeply schooled in Prussian standards of obedience to question the order. (In the higher ranks of the Western Federal armies, Prussian emigrés were as common as Tennessee lawyers in the Army of Tennessee.) The son of an affluent peasant family, Matthies had entered the Prussian army and fought ably in the Polish insurrection, winning a commission for his good conduct. In the spring of 1849, Matthies quit the service and set out for America. He settled in Burlington, Iowa, where he opened a liquor business, prospered, and most certainly came to know young John Corse, whose father, it will be recalled, was seven-time mayor of the town. Sherman's generals were indeed a close-knit group.

Despite his austere Prussian upbringing, Matthies was a genial man. Wrote a native-born Iowa officer admiringly: "General Matthies . . . is one of those men whom to know is to like. His sanguine temperament, and earnest, open-hearted disposition enables him, in his happy moods, to talk and laugh with extreme good nature. . . . He was always on kind and familiar terms with every soldier in his command, and his familiarity in no way interfered with his discipline. The soldiers loved 'Old Dutchie,' he was so good and brave." Like most Midwesterners who had foreign-born commanders, though, Matthies's men smiled at his odd speech. "To look at him, you would not take him for a foreigner," wrote the same Iowan, "but he no sooner speaks than he betrays his nativity. He has never been able to master the accent of our language."[29]

Nevertheless, his command to fall in, given shortly after 1:00 P.M., was clearly understood by all. Matthies's regimental officers formed their lines of battle hastily, impelled by the obvious suffering of Loomis's brigade. Any lingering doubts that they were needed, or that they faced a hard fight, were quickly dispelled. "We marched out on quick time . . . but little distance till we commenced meeting the wounded coming in . . . some on litters and others not wounded so bad limping along as best they could. . . . We soon came in sight of the dreaded mountain that we was to charge," remembered Aaron Dunbar of the Ninety-third Illinois.[30]

As his brigade emerged from the timber, Matthies called a halt to study the ground. The men threw off their blankets and lay down. Although still a half mile from Tunnel Hill, they caught the attention of the Rebel gunners. "Our broad sabre bayonets glittering in the sun made an excellent mark for the enemy's artillery," lamented Colonel Jabez Banbury of the Fifth Iowa. "The first shot struck close to my line, ricocheted and skipped over the men; the second struck directly in the ranks of the regiment on my left, several others plowed the ground immediately in our front and rear."[31]

Fortunately, the pause was brief. After fifteen minutes, Matthies ordered his men to their feet and started them forward at the double-quick. He advanced with the Tenth Iowa on the left, the Ninety-third Illinois on the left center, and the Twenty-sixth Missouri and Fifth Iowa completing the line. Opposite his right flank, on the far side of the fields, stood the Glass farm.

With each step the Rebel barrage became heavier and more accurate. "By this time all the cannon in the Rebel army were brought to bear on the field we had to cross . . . and the storm of shot and shell became terrific," marveled Lieutenant Samuel Byers of the Fifth Iowa. The cacophony shattered nerves, the bursting shells and fences unraveled unit lines, and the long ditch tempted the fainthearted. Byers vividly described the feeling of helplessness and terror, out there in the open:

> In front of us was a rail fence, and, being in direct line of fire, its splinters and fragments flew in every direction. "Jump the fence, men! Tear it down!" cried the colonel. Never did men get over a fence more quickly. Our distance was nearly half a mile to the Rebel position.
> We started on a charge, running across the open fields. I had heard the roaring of heavy battle before, but never such a shrieking of can-

nonballs and bursting shell as met us on that charge. We could see the enemy working their guns, while in plain view other batteries galloped up, unlimbered, and let loose at us. Behind us our own batteries were firing at the enemy over our heads, till the storm and roar became horrible. It sounded as if the end of the world had come. Halfway over we had to leap a ditch, perhaps six feet wide and nearly as many deep. Some of our regiment fell into this ditch and could not get out, a few tumbled in intentionally and stayed there. I saw this, and ran back and ordered them to get out, called them cowards, threatened them with my revolver; they did not move. Again I hurried on with the line. All the officers were screaming at the top of their voices; I, too, screamed, trying to make the men hear. "Steady! Bear to the right! Keep in line! Don't fire! Don't fire!" was yelled till we all were hoarse and till the awful thunder of the cannon made all commands unheard and useless.[32]

Byers engaged in a bit of forgivable hyperbole—every cannon in the Army of Tennessee was not trained on his brigade. He was right, however, in his impression that fresh Confederate batteries joined in the barrage. At virtually the precise moment Matthies motioned his men forward, William Carnes, the young Tennessee captain who had lost his own battery at Chickamauga and now commanded the artillery battalion of Stevenson's division, unlimbered the batteries of Corput, Rowan, and Baxter along the ridge just south of the tunnel. Carnes gave the word and his guns roared into action.[33]

Byers and his fellow officers may have felt they were losing control of their men, but from the viewpoint of the Confederates defenders, their advance looked menacing enough. "Our artillery opened upon the dense masses a well-directed and destructive fire. I could see great gaps and lanes cut through their ranks; but on they moved, and be it said, to the honor of the Federals, that they never faltered one instant under this murderous and fearful fire," attested Colonel Dowd of the Twenty-fourth Mississippi. And certainly the enemy's counter-battery fire was taking a toll. "Shells from the Federal artillery were bursting on the ridge, and I saw one of them explode behind our lines, destroying several men. One soldier's head was blown into a tree, where the hair held it suspended on the limbs," said Lieutenant Key.[34]

Matthies's roughed-up brigade gradually settled in behind a fence along the wagon road at the foot of Tunnel Hill, a few hundred feet to the left of the Glass farm. There it was surprisingly well sheltered. The confounding contours of the ridge prevented either the cannon atop the tunnel or Carnes's batteries from firing on the Federals, and the survivors of the Twenty-seventh Pennsylvania on Tunnel Hill were keeping Key's gunners from accurately aiming their pieces. Also, the road had been worn down by heavy usage and recent rains to a depth of nearly five feet. Into its muddy bed the Yankees gravitated.[35]

As his brigade sorted itself out at the foot of the hill, about 250 yards from the enemy above, Matthies realized that, like Colonel Taft before him, he had veered too far to the left to cover Loomis's flank. During its frenzied advance, the Fifth Iowa, on the right of the line, had come upon the fragments of the Seventy-third Pennsylvania crouched behind a fence near the flaming remains of the Glass house. In their eagerness to gain cover, the Iowans had shoved their way past the Pennsylvanians and dashed through the farmyard to the base of Tunnel Hill. By then, the Seventy-third was in no shape to offer them much help anyway. The Pennsylvanians had shot off their last rounds and were simply clinging to the fence because the alternative—recrossing the open ground—was too horrible to contemplate. Nor did they any longer have the will to advance. Colonel Taft was dead, and what was left of the regiment was now led by a captain. Three times Taft had sent runners to the rear for a resupply of ammunition. None returned. Finally he decided to go himself. Scarcely had he stood up when a bullet cut him down. Clutching the hand of a nearby company officer, he pleaded: "Hold the position at all hazards." Over and over he repeated the phrase, until it faded into a dying whisper.[36]

Matthies tried to close the gap. He ordered the Tenth Iowa out from under the foot of Tunnel Hill, on the brigade left, and over to the far right. It deployed on the right of the Fifth Iowa, which itself was cut off from the rest of brigade by a gap of nearly fifty yards. The Prussian was contemplating further adjustments in that direction when Colonel Holden Putnam, the commander of the Ninety-third Illinois, came up beside him. A band of Pennsylvanians clinging to the slope above his regiment had sent down for reinforcements, he reported breathlessly. They were convinced, as was he, that with support the hill could be held. Not pausing to consider what merely clinging to the slope would accomplish, Matthies acceded to Putnam's request, with the admonition that he move up cautiously. At the same time, Matthies sent an aide rearward to apprise his superiors of his predicament: The Glass farmhouse and outbuildings were fire-gutted ruins; he was sending one regiment up Tunnel Hill to succor the Twenty-seventh Pennsylvania; and he believed he could hold on to the hillside and that, with further support, perhaps clear the Rebels from the top. Matthies directed the Twenty-sixth Missouri to edge over by the left flank to occupy the ground along the road that Putnam's advance would open up, and told the commanders of the Fifth and Tenth Iowa to keep close to the foot of the hill. Then he waited.[37]

*Never Forsake the Colors.* Colonel Holden Putnam urges the Ninety-third Illinois up Tunnel Hill.

Matthies's words of caution were lost on Colonel Putnam. With more courage than prudence, he ordered his regiment up the hill at full tilt. Displaying greater common sense than their commander, a few of the Illinoisans ripped rails from a fence before leaving the road and carried them along to lie behind when the regiment halted.

It was a wise precaution, because Cleburne continued to anticipate Federal moves with an uncanny exactness and counter them effectively. A few minutes before Putnam got started, he had thrown the Second and Fifteenth Arkansas Regiment of Govan's brigade, commanded by Lieutenant Colonel E. Warfield, a few yards forward of Granbury's breastworks. The Arkansans were now lying in wait, ready to greet Putnam's Yankees.

Up the slope struggled the Illinoisans. They paused to catch their breath a moment, then pushed on, negotiating a high fence in their ascent. As they neared the Twenty-seventh Pennsylvania, some of Putnam's officers realized that the Pennsylvanians had hoodwinked them. Where they had expected to find a resolute regiment, mere disordered fragments of the unit remained, scared handfuls of soldiers trying to bury themselves in the dirt near the crest before they were shot. "I remember . . . they were in a disorganized condition," recalled an Illinoisan. "Some fell into rank and moved with us." Exhaustion, compounded by the obvious hopelessness of their task, overcame Putnam's men as well, and they fell to the ground perhaps sixty feet from Warfield's Arkansans, who were tearing their ranks with a brutal fire. Directly behind the Arkansans and opposite the right companies of the Ninety-third were Key's six cannon. "The deadly missiles was flying on and in every direction . . . the roar of muskets was incessant . . . men was falling on every side of me," said a survivor. After fifteen minutes, men began leaking rearward from the center of the line. With them went several of the demoralized Pennsylvanians.[38]

Putnam was undeterred. Conspicuously mounted on a black horse ("How that horse got up there, I will never tell," a captain of the Twenty-sixth Missouri later mused), he grabbed the colors and began waving them in broad sweeps. Never forsake them, he yelled above the racket. A bullet in the brain put an end to his histrionics, and Putnam tumbled to the ground, dead. The adjutant crept forward to retrieve his body, and the rest of the regiment settled into a short-range slugging match with the Second and Fifteenth Arkansas.[39]

Regrettably, General Matthies chose to reinforce what already had become a losing proposition. Still down on the road himself, Matthies sent the Twenty-sixth Missouri forward to bolster the Ninety-third Illinois as the first stragglers from the regiment stumbled down the hill.

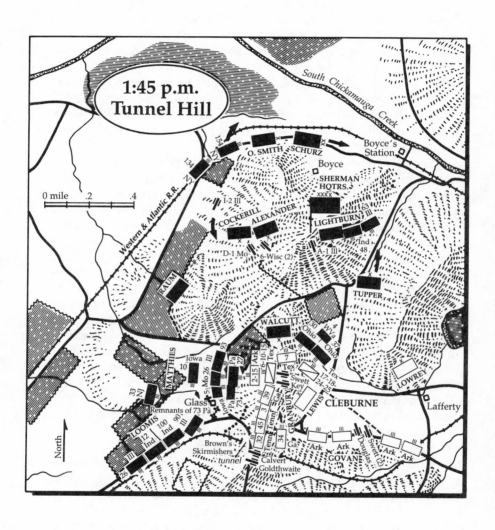

**1:45 p.m. Tunnel Hill**

South Chickamauga Creek

Boyce's Station

154 NY

O. SMITH  SCHURZ

Boyce

134 NY

SHERMAN HQTRS.
xxxx

Western & Atlantic R.R.

0 mile   .2   .4

1-2 Ill

COCKERILL   ALEXANDER

LIGHTBURN   63 Ill

D-1 Mo   6-Wisc (2)   A-1 Ill   Ind 48

RAUM

TUPPER

WALCUTT   30 Ohio   4 W.Va   37 Ohio

93 Pa   Ark   7 Tex   Tex   LOWREY

Iowa 10   MATTHIES   5 Mo 26 Ill   Pa   2-15 Tex   6-10-15 Tex

33 NJ   73 Iowa   Swett Key   17-18 24-25 Tex

Glass
Remnants of 73 Pa   GRANBURY   CLEBURNE   Lafferty

LEWIS

LOOMIS   12 Ind   100 Ind   90 Ill   Iowa   32   45 Tenn   3 Tenn   Cal   34 Ga   Ark   Ark   Douglas   Swett (2)   Ark   Ark

North

Brown's Skirmishers   tunnel   Calvert   GOVAN

26   Goldthwaite

The Missourians began by walking and ended up crawling into position just behind the right companies of the Ninety-third. Next, Matthies drew in the Tenth Iowa, which broke his tenuous link with Loomis's left. He directed the Tenth up the hill with instructions to fall in on the right of the Illinoisans. However, its commander, Colonel Paul Henderson—who before the war had climbed the ladder from tanner, to sheriff, to county judge, and finally to state senator—lost his bearings and instead came up on the left of the Ninety-third Illinois. There, stunned by a blast of canister, the Iowans hit the ground.[40]

Matthies went up the hill himself. Though surprised to find the Tenth Iowa out of place, he set about encouraging his men. His stay was brief. "I was turning round to caution my men to fire low and sure," he reported after the battle. "I was struck by a bullet in the head, which felled me to the ground. I regained consciousness in a few minutes, sent for Colonel Dean of the Twenty-sixth Missouri, he being the senior officer on the hill, turned over to him command of the brigade, and the orders I had received, showed him the position of the brigade, the safest route to fall back on, also the line of troops advancing to our assistance, and left the field for the hospital."[41]

The troops that the bleeding and dazed Matthies had pointed out to Colonel Dean belonged to Green Raum's brigade. Some thirty minutes earlier, Raum and his staff had been watching the fight with keen interest from atop Smith's Hill. "It is an interesting and exciting spectacle to witness the movements of the troops in a great battle and see the struggle for mastery—the roar of artillery, the rattling of musketry, the impetuous charge, the shouts of the men, the sturdy resistance of the assailed. All this I saw and heard, knowing full well that in a short time my own command would be in the midst of the fray," reflected Raum.[42]

That time came later than he expected or thought prudent. Generals Smith and Ewing rode forward from Sherman's headquarters on Lightburn's Hill to join Raum at 2:00 P.M. The two apparently had reconciled their differences, but Smith still was a bit confused. He had sought out Ewing just minutes before, after seeing Federals whom he supposed to be Loomis's brigade charging up Tunnel Hill. Noticing that the enemy was massing fresh troops on the hilltop, he had told Ewing of the danger to his troops. Ewing appreciated Smith's concern, but gently pointed out the Illinoisan's error: the troops in danger were Smith's—Matthies's brigade to be precise—and, yes, they obviously were in trouble. Startled and unsure what to do, Smith rode to Sherman to seek his advice; Ewing accompanied him. Sherman agreed that Matthies should be reinforced. Sherman's concurrence seemed to rouse Smith, and he galloped off with Ewing to find Raum and regain control of his division.[43]

Drawing rein beside Raum and his staff, Smith announced that Sherman had directed the brigade to succor Matthies. Rather sarcastically, Raum replied that he "had for some time felt that Matthies needed help."

Smith took no umbrage at Raum's impudence. The thirty-three-year-old Illinoisan, a former lawyer and Douglas Democrat, had a well-deserved reputation as a rock-solid combat commander. Indeed, when Raum asked Smith and Ewing for instructions as to how he should move, they demurred, requesting his opinion on the matter instead. Having studied the field for some time, Raum was ready with a reply. He proposed forming his brigade in two lines, facing them to the left into close column, and then moving the columns diagonally across the valley to a point directly behind Matthies. Once there, he would send the two regiments of his first line (still in column formation)—the Eightieth Ohio and Seventeenth Iowa—up the hill to reinforce Matthies, while keeping his second-line regiments—the Tenth Missouri and Fifty-sixth Illinois—down in the road.

Smith and Ewing concurred readily. Raum called together his regimental commanders. He pointed out the route of march and called their attention to the batteries above the tunnel, which he warned would certainly open on them the moment they stepped into range. Raum assigned command of the first line to Colonel Clark Wever of the Seventeenth Iowa; he would remain with the second line and deploy it as circumstances dictated.

Wever was an odd character, certainly out of place among his more cultivated peers. Just twenty-eight years old, he had left his home state of New York at the age of twenty-one and wandered through Texas and Mexico for two years. In 1858 he settled in Burlington, Iowa (home of Matthies and Corse), where he opened a brokerage firm. Here is how he struck a fellow officer: "Colonel Wever is about six feet in height, and has a slender, but not an elegant form: there is an awkward twist about his shoulders. He has dark hair and complexion, and piercing black eyes. Considering his age and opportunities, he is rather a remarkable man. His education is limited; but, in spite of that, he has worked his way up above many who in that respect were greatly his superiors. He is recklessly brave in the face of the enemy, and one of the most ambitious men I ever met."[44]

At 2:30 P.M., Raum and Wever started their columns forward, keeping a sharp eye on the Rebel batteries. For two hundred yards their men traipsed unmolested. Then Raum spotted white puffs of smoke rising from the ridge. "Instantly I gave the order to double-quick, and galloped forward followed closely by the troops, who maintained their lines intact," he said. This time the Confederate cannoneers overshot their mark. "The shells flew thick and fast, and many exploded, but fortunately the guns were trained too high; not a man was killed, and only two or three slightly injured," continued Raum.[45]

His brigade got across the field in good order. Raum reached the foot of the hill before Wever and was pleased to find the wagon road so deeply cut. He told Wever to take his column on up the slope at once and halt when he reached the rail fence behind the Ninety-third Illinois, there to await further instructions. Wever and his field officers wisely dismounted in the road and started up on foot with their troops. Raum likewise dismounted, and helped shepherd his reserve regiments into a line of battle along the road.[46]

Wever got up the hill with little trouble—Warfield's Arkansans and Granbury's Texans had their hands full holding off Matthies's Federals, and Key's cannoneers were kept from their guns by the accurate though dwindling fire of the Yankees. The head of his column reached the fence, seventy-five yards from the Rebel works, a few minutes after 3:00 P.M. The Eightieth Ohio filed to the left into line and lay down; the Seventeenth Iowa turned off smartly to the right. Wever barely had come up when he met Matthies, stumbling rearward. The bleeding Prussian paused long enough to sketch for Wever his own and the enemy's dispositions and warn him that his men were almost out of ammunition. Matthies's adjutant jogged up a few minutes later with the same story—the men on the firing line, he told Wever, had rounds enough for fifteen minutes more. Recognizing the need for haste, Wever sent his own adjutant down the hill to Raum for orders.

Raum was on his way up. While standing in the roadbed with the Tenth Missouri and Fifty-sixth Illinois—two hundred yards behind Wever's regiments—the Illinoisan had run into Matthies as well. "He had received a painful wound in the head, and was quite bloody, but able to walk," said Raum. "We conversed a moment. He stated that his brigade was almost out of ammunition; that their losses had been very heavy, including Colonel Putnam."[47]

By the time Raum reached Wever, the situation along Matthies's line had deteriorated almost beyond repair. The Ninety-third Illinois had all but ceased to exist as an effective force. Though they clung to the ground they had gained, the Illinoisans could go no farther. Their colors, which Colonel Putnam had stained vainly with his blood, had passed from one color-sergeant to another until only a corporal remained unhurt from the color guard to bear them. By then, there was little left for him to carry. "The staff that supported its shining folds was splintered and shivered and shot in twain. The banner itself was riddled and tattered and torn into shreds. Not a twentieth part of it remained upon the broken staff. Carried away by shot and shell, its fragments were scattered on the mountain side among the dead and bleeding heroes who followed it there," lamented the adjutant of the Ninety-third. To add to the Illinoisans' torment, the Rebels, also low on ammunition, had resorted to their earlier trick of tossing large rocks at the Yankees. The bluecoats found an abundant supply along the slope too, but throwing uphill was infinitely harder than hurling stones downward. The sergeant-major of the Ninety-third attested to the good aim of the Arkansans: "I had one eye brow peeled down over my cheek with a rock." No one could stand such a beating indefinitely, and at 4:00 P.M., after nearly three hours under fire, the Illinoisans, individually and by squads, began slipping away. Soldiers from the Twenty-sixth Missouri followed their example, and a wholesale collapse appeared imminent.[48]

In hopes of reversing the tide, Raum gave Wever the go-ahead to charge the summit. With a yell, the men of the Seventeenth Iowa rose up and jumped the fence. The color-bearer slumped over the rails; another sergeant grabbed the flag and was instantly shot down. But the Iowans kept on. They ran forward through the underbrush toward the supine forms of those Illinoisans still to their front. To their left, the Eightieth Ohio had gone forward as well, although its commander, Lieutenant Colonel Pren Metham, had no idea who had given the order to charge. "The roar of musketry and artillery was so great that you could scarcely hear yourself holler," he remembered. The Ohioans climbed the fence and advanced to relieve the Tenth Iowa, ducking low amid the thick bushes and twisted vines.

Warfield's Arkansans were in trouble. With two fresh Federal regiments about to hit their front, Walcutt's Federals plunking away at their right flank from behind their breastworks on Corse's Hill, and their own ammunition supply down to only a handful of cartridges, it was just a matter of time before they would have to give way. For the first time that afternoon, it looked as though Cleburne's salient might be broken.[49]

But fortune favored the Irishman. After watching Raum cross the flat, General Hardee had seen to it that reinforcements were sent Cleburne's way, knowing his protégé would use them wisely. With the advantage of interior lines and fairly easy ground to traverse, the Rebels could marshal troops on and near Tunnel Hill far faster than Sherman's disorganized generals could bring units to bear against it. At Hardee's behest, Carter Stevenson shortly after 1:00 P.M. had told Cumming to detach again the Thirty-ninth Georgia for duty with Cleburne. The regiment filed into line on the left of Granbury's brigade, to cover a weak spot caused by the detachment of so many of Brown's Tennesseans as skirmishers. Nearly half of Brown's brigade had gone down off the ridge to keep Loomis at bay, so Stevenson offered up another of Cumming's regiments—the Thirty-fourth Georgia—to further shore up the line over the tunnel. As the Georgians settled into place, the senior colonel present, J. T. McConnell of the Thirty-ninth, rode to the edge of the ridge to have a look into the valley. It proved a costly reconnaissance; a bullet plowed through his head, killing him instantly.

Meanwhile, Matthies's attack had intensified the pressure on Granbury's tired Texans. Once again, Cleburne benefited from timely help. With no threat to his own front, Cumming pulled the last two regiments of his brigade—the Thirty-sixth and Fifty-sixth Georgia—out of his portion of the line and marched them to the rear of Tunnel Hill. There he reported to Cleburne shortly after Raum had made his appearance in the valley. Cleburne welcomed the thirty-four-year-old Georgian and bade him take the Fifty-sixth Georgia to the top of the hill and fall in as near to the breastworks as possible. Cumming moved the regiment up the rear slope smartly, though he lost its commander to a shell fragment that slashed open his leg the instant he and his horse popped up on the crest.[50]

Cleburne found himself with more troops than he had room for on the hill. Despite nearly five hours in action, Granbury's Texans had no desire to cede their place to reinforcements. As one Rebel lying in reserve put it, the Texans "declined to be relieved, saying that it was the first time they had ever had a chance to fight the Yankees from behind breastworks and that they were rather enjoying it." So, when George Maney reported with his Tennessee brigade from Gist's division about the same time as Cumming, Cleburne simply posted him behind Granbury "with instructions to support the brigade behind the works and the artillery at the angle." Understanding, however, that the battle-crazed Texans could not hold on forever, Cleburne, before riding back to the front line, beseeched Maney: "When I send for reinforcements, send me the best regiment you have."[51]

Cleburne called for them ten minutes later, just as Raum signaled Wever to charge past Matthies's brigade (now under Colonel Dean) toward the summit. Warfield's Arkansans were down to their last rounds, a panting messenger from the division staff told Maney, and Granbury's men were little better off. Recalling Cleburne's appeal, the former Nashville lawyer waved forward his premier regiment—the First and Twenty-seventh Tennessee under Colonel Hume Field. Up the rear slope they charged. On the crowded hilltop they were greeted "with a shower of bullets which came as though they were sifted." Cleburne was there to feed them into the line, in the thick of the fight then as he had been all afternoon. He yelled at Colonel Field to go over the breastworks and fall in to the right of Warfield's Arkansans. The Tennesseans leapt over the logs and fell to the ground less than a hundred feet from the Yankees. "We were hugging the ridge so closely that nothing but our heads peered over, so it was not so easy to see us, as the bushes were quite thick and many large trees were on the ridge," said a private from the First Tennessee. Nonetheless, attested another member of the regiment, the fighting was fierce, with a frenzy unequaled even at Chickamauga. "Stones were thrown into our lines, and we threw them into the lines of the enemy, at a distance so short that they had an effect. A man immediately to the right of the writer, raising himself up to fire, received a bullet in his cheek before he could pull the trigger. A hat raised . . . on the point of a bayonet was riddled in less time than it takes to write it, and the writer distinctly remembers brushing fragments of bark from his own hat which were clipped off logs in front by bullets."[52]

Field's appearance eased the pressure on Lieutenant Colonel Warfield's flank, but the Arkansan knew that the fight was still going against him. Drastic action was needed to turn the tide, he reasoned. Leaving his men in the midst of their fight with Dean's Federals, Warfield searched out Cleburne and, as the Irishman recalled, "suggested to me that our men were wasting ammunition and becoming disheartened at the persistency of the enemy, and proposed a charge down upon them with the bayonet."[53]

Others felt as Warfield did that the time had come to do more than merely resist the Yankees. As he ascended Tunnel Hill with the Fifty-sixth Georgia, General Cumming was surrounded by the commanders of Granbury's regiments, all of whom begged him to counterattack. Their men were being shot down by an enemy "who was completely under shelter" (few of the badly exposed survivors of the Ninety-third Illinois would agree with this assertion by Granbury's officers, which shows how relative one's perspective is in combat). A "brisk, effective charge would probably succeed in driving him from the front of the works," the colonels added. What's more, there was a gap in the breastworks to the right of Sixth and Tenth Texas Infantry and Fifteenth Texas (Dismounted) Cavalry Regiment, through which a charge could be made with ease. And, they argued, Cumming's Georgians were the men for the job.

Cumming was persuaded but felt he needed both another regiment and the consent of Cleburne before acting. He dispatched one messenger to bring up the Thirty-sixth Georgia and another to get Cleburne's approval. The Thirty-sixth Georgia came up at once, and he placed them ten paces behind the Fifty-sixth. While he waited for word from

Cleburne, Cumming called together the field officers of his two regiments to explain what they were about to do. "This was, substantially, to push forward, on the word being given, at the double-quick, passing over every obstacle that they might encounter, breaking over the breastworks and the men that lined them when they should reach that point, and engage the enemy with the bayonet, not opening fire until he should commence to give way."[54]

Cleburne, of course, heartily approved Cumming's proposal for a charge, which he in any event was about to order. Word of the Irishman's concurrence came just as Cumming completed his preparations. "Immediately the word was given, the men stood up in their ranks, and at the word forward rushed on with a cheer, one regiment following in rear of the other."

When he reached the breastworks, Cumming discovered that Granbury's regimental commanders had grossly understated the obstacles that stood in the way of a successful counterattack. The opening in the line through which he was expected to pass was far smaller than they had represented it to be; so narrow, in fact, that only about one-third of a regiment could pass through it at a time. The men on either flank were forced to step over the recumbent Texans and their logworks. Confusion was inevitable, and the Fifty-sixth Georgia unraveled as it passed to the front. Before Cumming could reform the regiment to charge, a withering volley from Dean's Yankees sent the Georgians reeling back toward the breastworks.[55]

The setback, however, was fleeting. Everyone, from Cleburne to the lowliest private, was seized with a will to drive away the Yankees and put an end to the fight. When Cumming started a second time through the gap in the breastworks, he had plenty of support. Warfield's Arkansans and Field's Tennesseans picked themselves up off the ground and fell in on Cumming's right, no more than sixty feet in front of the Tenth Iowa and Ninety-third Illinois. Cleburne, meanwhile, had galloped to the left of his line, held by the wounded Colonel Mills's Sixth, Tenth, and Fifteenth Texas Regiment, and given its officers orders to attack the Federal right flank the instant Cumming charged the Yankees in front.[56]

The effect was electric. With the equivalent of a brigade front, the Rebels bounded down the slope at 4:00 P.M. So spontaneous did the effort seem that some participants swore no order was ever given to charge. "The men knew the only hope of ending the conflict was to charge. We had the advantage of position, and this we well knew. The order to charge came from no general officer. It came from the men themselves. It meant death to many, but perhaps safety to the majority," asserted a Tennessee private.[57]

After three nerve-wracking hours with their heads in the dirt, unable to advance, Dean's Federals had neither the strength nor the ammunition to resist. In a matter of seconds, the First and Twenty-seventh Tennessee was on top of the Tenth Iowa. "We got so close to them that Colonel Field hit a Federal on the head with a rock, and Comrade John Branch grabbed at the colors, tearing out a piece, but the sergeant got away with them," said a soldier from the First Tennessee. "The issue of the conflict at this point was not, for an instant, doubtful. Numbers of the Federals dropped their guns, and with hands overhead, rushed through our lines to surrender. Those who manfully stood their ground were, for an instant, unable to fire, for fear of shooting their own men, who had rushed forward in surrender," added another. Similar scenes were played out between Cumming's Georgians and the Ninety-third and Fifty-sixth Illinois and the remnants of the Twenty-seventh Pennsylvania.[58]

What doomed Dean's line was not the foe to their front, however, but the startling appearance of the Texans on their right flank. As Colonel Raum later put it: "This front attack could, and no doubt would, have been resisted; but the movement upon the right flank was pushed with such energy and determination that there was no time to make a change of front to meet it. Our right flank was practically in the air."

The unfortunate unit on the right flank was the Fifth Iowa. Most of the regiment was strung out as skirmishers, holding a long line from the Glass farm as far northward as the right flank of the Twenty-seventh Pennsylvania. Due to an odd fold in the hill, it looked to the men of the Fifth as though the enemy had burst forth from the tunnel itself. In truth, the Texans had used the cover of the fold and the element of surprise to charge down the hill undetected. Near the base, they wheeled to the right and crashed into the Iowans' flank. The result was devastating. Lieutenant Byers, who had had such a hard time getting the men of his company across the field earlier that afternoon, was one of those who thought the Confederates had come out of the tunnel. Though mistaken as to their point of origin, he accurately and vividly related the utter confusion into which the Iowans were thrown:

> Someone cried, "Look to the tunnel! They're coming through the tunnel." Sure enough, through a railway tunnel in the mountain the graycoats were coming by hundreds. They were flanking us completely.
>
> "Stop them!" cried our colonel to those of us at the right. "Push them back." It was but the work of a few moments for four companies to rise to their feet and run to the tunnel's mouth, firing as they ran. Too late! An enfilading fire was soon cutting them to pieces. "Shall I run over there too?" I said to the colonel. We were both kneeling on the ground close to the regimental flag. He assented. When I rose to

my feet and started it seemed as if even the blades of grass were being struck by bullets. As I ran over I passed comrades stretched out in death and some were screaming in agony.

Instantly it seemed as if a whole Rebel army was concentrated on that single spot. For a few moments I lay down on the grass, hoping the storm would pass over and leave me. Lieutenant Miller, at my side, was screaming in agony. He was shot through the hips. I begged him to be still; he could not. Now, as a second line of the enemy was upon us, and the first one was returning, shooting men as they found them, I rose to my feet and surrendered. "Come out of that sword," shrieked a big Georgian, with a terrible oath. Another grabbed at my revolver and bellowed at me "to get up the hill quicker than hell." I took a blanket from a dead comrade near me, and at the point of the bayonet I was hurried up the mountain.[59]

Byers had plenty of company going up the hill. "The Fifth Iowa is almost annihilated," a survivor wrote sadly that night. The regiment had gone into action with 227 men and had lost 106, 82 of whom were captured. Among those taken were the entire color company and the colors.[60]

The collapse of the Fifth Iowa allowed the Texans to roll up the rest of Dean's right with ease. The Twenty-seventh Pennsylvania got away with only 13 men captured, but it too lost its colors. Attacked by Cumming's screaming Georgians in front and Granbury's ecstatic Texans on their right, those of the Ninety-third Illinois who had not drifted rearward earlier now ran down the hill as well—less 27 captured, 66 scattered dead or wounded on the bushy slope, and the colors that Colonel Putnam had so ostentatiously waved before his death. The Twenty-sixth Missouri, tucked behind the Ninety-third, got off largely intact.[61]

Where did all this leave Raum? The Illinoisan, it will be recalled, had given Colonel Wever permission to take the Eightieth Ohio and Seventeenth Iowa and charge past Dean's line toward the summit at the same moment Cumming's men were filtering through the gap in the breastworks to counterattack. Wever was about to lead his own Seventeenth Iowa over the Ninety-third Illinois when it broke and fled through his ranks. Behind them came Cumming's Georgians. Suddenly, Granbury's ubiquitous Texans hit his flank. "A yell from our right flank and rear caused us to look that way," related Christopher Kiser of the Seventeenth. "The Rebels were making desperate efforts to cut us off, and came on in a big force crying: 'Surrender, you Yankee devils.' The cry was met with derision, I remember, as I hastily loaded my gun and looked at their heavy mass approaching."

Defiant shouts and a few lucky shots were hardly enough to stop the

Texans, and Colonel Wever quickly gave the command: "Fall back, Seventeenth." Already there were Rebels sneaking in behind the regiment, firing into the backs of the Iowans. Wever repeated the command at the top of his voice: "Fall back, save yourselves." His call was taken up by the company officers: "For God sake, get out of this." The men were eager to oblige. Spilling down the hill, they ran headlong into their tormentors. There was more yelling and shoving than harm done at this point, said Private Kiser: "It was now a hand to hand fight, no time for loading. I remember how funny it looked to see so many of our men—as well as Rebels—without hats or caps. And then my hat went off. Making a grab, I recovered it and dashed through the line of yelling Rebels, down the slope. It seemed to me I would never get down that field alive; but the Rebel guns as well as ours were empty, and in the hurry and excitement and shooting down the slope, their bullets did not hit many."[62]

The Eightieth Ohio had a bit more warning, but it too had to fight its way through a few of the more intrepid and fleet-footed Texans, while taking volleys from Field's Tennesseans and Warfield's Arkansans bounding down the slope behind them. Lieutenant Colonel Metham had heard from neither Raum nor Wever nor any of the brigade staff, so was left to react on his own. He of course gave the order to change front to the rear, intending to slip away through the narrow valley toward Ewing's Hill. The regiment, however, crumbled in the confusion. Every member of the color guard was gunned down except Sergeant Jacob Darst, the bearer of the national colors. Darst's son was captured, and he himself was shot through the left arm. Although the bullet shattered the bone, he managed to drag the heavy banner with him all the way to the road, where, dizzy from loss of blood, he turned it over to a comrade.[63]

Colonel Raum, who was standing behind the Seventeenth Iowa, certainly lost no time in getting down the hill. "I must confess I did not stand upon the order of my going. The question was whether I should be killed, captured, or escape," he wrote. "I went at once, followed by an eager line of the enemy. I ran as fast as my legs would carry me. The ground was rough and rocky. I fell twice, but hurriedly scrambled to my feet and rushed on to keep out of the way of the determined men who were close on my heels. I could not see my reserve line, but I knew that the Fifty-sixth Illinois and Tenth Missouri were in the road at the foot of the hill, and would be there when I arrived."

They were, and they did not disappoint him. As soon as Raum and the men of his front-line regiments ducked safely through their ranks, the Tenth Missouri and Fifty-sixth Illinois let loose a simultaneous volley at the Rebels, who were no more than thirty yards away. Despite the shock of the sudden opposition, Cumming, Warfield, and Field managed to hold their men in line long enough to trade four or five volleys with the Yankees. Then, herding their prisoners before them, the Confederates slowly started back up the hill. The commanders of the Tenth Missouri and Fifty-sixth Illinois sent forward their skirmishers but made no real effort to hurry the Rebels on their way. Neither did they keep firing after the enemy broke contact, for fear of hitting the hundreds of blue-clad wounded who blanketed the slope above them.[64]

There was no point to another charge, nor was Raum in any condition to lead one. While he was standing behind his reserve regiments, admiring their stand, a bullet gored his left thigh. Caught up in the excitement of the fight, Raum did not even realize he had been hit until after the shooting died down and he felt a hot pool of blood rising in his left boot. The stoic Illinoisan pulled a bandage from his pocket, bound his thigh, then sat down against a tree to catch his breath. He sent for Colonel Francis Deimling of the Tenth Missouri. Raum told Deimling that Wever had been hit as well, ordered the Missourian to take command of the brigade, then allowed himself to be carried to the rear.[65]

Among the other Federal casualties inflicted by the Confederate counterattack were nearly half of those soldiers of the Seventy-third Pennsylvania still on their feet after four hours in action around the Glass farm. The regiment had started the day three-hundred strong. A quarter of that number were dead or wounded by the time the left companies of the Sixth and Tenth Texas Infantry and Fifteenth (Dismounted) Texas Cavalry slammed into their flank. Clinging to the fence in the farmyard, the Pennsylvanians were captured by the dozen. Some tried to resist, but stragglers from the Fifth Iowa pouring over the fence made it impossible for them to change front. Nearly every officer was wounded or captured, and eighty-five enlisted men also surrendered. In the confusion, the senior captain, John Kennedy, tore the regimental colors from their staff and stuffed them in his blouse. Through long months of confinement at Libby Prison he carefully hid them from the prying eyes of Rebel guards, bringing them safely back to Pennsylvania after the war. While Kennedy and his men were marched up the hill by their Texan captors, the pitiful remnant of the regiment that got away found itself under the command of a lieutenant.[66]

Neither Cleburne nor Cumming was content to allow the Federals even their tenuous foothold at the base of Tunnel Hill. After permitting his men fifteen minutes' rest, Cumming called them to their feet and prepared to charge one last time. Cleburne brought up the Fiftieth

Tennessee from Maney's brigade to support him. Mills's Texas regiment reformed on the Georgian's left, Field and Warfield fell in again on his right, and shortly before 5:00 P.M. they started down the slope.[67]

They met little resistance. The lull between attacks had given Dean's brigade and the two front-line regiments of Raum time to slip back toward the safety of Smith's Hill. General John Smith was there to greet them, "smoking a pipe as calmly as he would in camp," reflected a begrimed survivor. "Well, boys, that's a tough place up there," he laughed. His joke fell flat, and the men drifted past in sullen silence. Colonel Wever, injured but still in the saddle, reported to the general with the Seventeenth Iowa and Eightieth Ohio. With no further effort at humor, Smith waved him back to the cornfield where the brigade had first formed.

With Dean and Wever on their way to the rear, Colonel Deimling saw no need to sacrifice more lives on Tunnel Hill. After a few well-aimed volleys, one of which toppled Colonel Cyrus Sugg of the Fiftieth Tennessee, grievously wounding him, Deimling drew his two regiments off by the left flank. The Rebels stopped in the road, and the long, strange struggle for Tunnel Hill was over.[68]

Almost. General Smith might crack jokes; his troops were out of danger. General Ewing, however, still had one brigade out on the bloody flat. Loomis's all-but-forgotten Federals were pinned down exactly where they had been for the past four hours—behind the embankment of the Chattanooga and Cleveland Railroad. With Cleburne's victorious troops mingling about on the wagon road just four hundred yards behind Loomis's brigade, it clearly was time to withdraw it. Ewing motioned to his staff officers. In the gathering twilight, he carefully studied the faces of each, reluctant to send any one of them on what probably would be a suicide ride. Finally his gaze settled on his assistant adjutant general, Captain Ira Bloomfield. He must ride into the valley and recall Loomis, Ewing told the captain. Bloomfield knew the odds—"to do that I had to go down over the open field across three ditches and four rail fences"—but started promptly on his way. Wisely, he made for the right of the brigade line, which was shielded from the Rebel fire. He rode along the line behind the embankment and gave the order to the commanders of each regiment. After imparting it to Colonel Reuben Williams of the Twelfth Indiana, Bloomfield readied himself to ride back into the open to the Ninetieth Illinois, which was still trying to extend the brigade left toward the Glass farm. Williams told him not to bother; it was certain death to try to reach the Illinoisans on horseback—he would send an officer on foot to pass the word to them. Though grateful for the reprieve, Bloomfield was horrified to watch first one, then a second staff officer gunned down as each started across the tunnel road. A third officer ran the gauntlet successfully. As the brigade made ready to pull out, Bloomfield began the return ride. Although the sun had set, the Rebel cannoneers managed to land a few rounds dangerously close to the captain; "they made it pretty warm for me," he reminisced sardonically. Bloomfield put the spurs to his horse. Over the ditches and fences he galloped. Nearing the fourth and tallest fence, Bloomfield grew worried: "When I was coming to the last fence I thought my horse could not jump it. Though I was well mounted, my horse disliked to turn his broad side to the firing. However, when I was within three or four rods of the fence a shell burst near his side, frightening him so that he took the fence and went clean over it, but he jumped so high that he threw me out of the saddle." The captain lunged for the saddle blanket. Grabbing it, he yanked himself back onto the animal. Ruffled but unhurt, he reported to Ewing. "My God, I am glad to see you sir," exclaimed the general. "I never expected to see you come back alive."[69]

So ended one of the sorriest episodes in this or any other battle of the war. Sherman's failure to turn Cleburne's line defies explanation. That he had the forces needed to do it is undeniable. Present were the divisions of John Smith, Morgan Smith, and Ewing. Back near the river, within easy supporting distance, was Jefferson C. Davis's division, which idled away the day as spectators. And by 2:00 P.M., Sherman had on hand yet a fifth division, that of Carl Schurz. Alarmed by the repulse of Corse and the apparent absence of any other effort against Tunnel Hill, Grant had told Howard at 9:45 A.M. to hurry with Schurz's division to succor the Ohioan. Grant assumed that Sherman's lack of headway stemmed from a need for reinforcements; he could not conceive that his friend simply was in over his head and unable to construct a coherent plan of action.[70]

In his assault on Tunnel Hill, Sherman exhibited an egregious lack of imagination. He attacked Cleburne's salient head on, and with only a fraction of his force, rather than look for a way to outflank Tunnel Hill. That it could have been done, Baldy Smith had no doubt. "Sherman should have put in all his force to turn Bragg's right, instead of attacking the strongest place on the right, for Bragg had given to the right every man that he could safely spare," he complained.[71]

No one in Giles Smith's brigade would have contested the Vermonter's conclusion. Waved off on an ill-defined foray along the Western and Atlantic Railroad, they had come within rifle range of cracking the fragile shell of Cleburne's defenses to the right of Tunnel Hill. Neither Sherman nor Morgan Smith gave any serious thought to the brigade or what it might accomplish, and it was recalled before the men had a chance to fire a shot.

Morgan Smith had told his younger brother to set off at shortly before 9:00 A.M. What his precise instructions were is unknown. In any event, Giles Smith's brigade advanced eastward along the line of the Western and Atlantic Railroad. The creek to the north and the slope of Lightburn's Hill to the south left Smith three hundred yards of soggy bottomland suitable for maneuvering. He placed the Fifty-fifth Illinois and Sixth Missouri in line of battle—the left-most soldier standing over the bank of the creek, the right-most well up against the edge of Lightburn's Hill—and funneled his remaining five regiments and one battalion of regular infantry in column behind them. A few minutes after 9:00 A.M., while Corse's small brigade was being torn apart three-quarters of a mile to the south, Smith's Federals started out at a leisurely pace along the railroad tracks. Where they were going or why seemed an open question to all who left a record of the day.[72]

Past Boyce's Station they tramped, upsetting a few stray chickens that were quickly snatched by the hungry soldiers. For a half mile they marched. The gummy mud of the creek bottom sucked at their shoes, making each step an effort. The men were tired but unscathed. Not a Rebel came out to challenge them. When his right flank came up even with the northernmost edge of Missionary Ridge, Smith ordered the brigade to swing suddenly to the right. Up the ridge and onto the first hilltop they scrambled. It was nearly 11:00 A.M. A quarter of a mile to the west rose Lightburn's Hill. A half mile to the southwest lay Tunnel Hill and the right flank of Granbury's Texas brigade, distracted by its savage fight with Corse. A handful of enemy pickets squeezed off a few badly aimed shots at Smith's Federals, and some misdirected shells tore through the trees above them, but otherwise they were unmolested. Most seemed to know they had gotten behind the enemy lines, and everyone could see clearly the blue smoke hanging in the treetops above Tunnel Hill and hear the roar of battle. "We were far in rear of the Confederate lines and were still advancing, meeting no opposition, when we were hurriedly recalled," said Lieutenant George Bailey of the Sixth Missouri. Who gave the order is unclear, but Smith's men retraced their steps toward Lightburn's Hill at the precise moment when their well-timed appearance on Corse's left might have changed the outcome of the fight.[73]

Of course, there had been Confederates nearby. Tucked in a narrow draw no more than two hundred yards south of the hilltop where Smith's Federals had stopped was Lowrey's brigade. Lowrey's pickets had given him fair warning of the Yankees, who were unaware of their presence. Whether Lowrey would or could have swept away Smith, had Smith crossed the valley to Corse's assistance, is open to debate; that Smith was not permitted to try is unconscionable.[74]

The troops of Smith's brigade were not the only Federals who felt they had been cheated out of a chance to turn the tide. Schurz's division lined up at 2:00 P.M. in front of Smith's recalled brigade and did nothing. Alexander's brigade fidgeted away the day on its hill. Most in the brigade were baffled at their inactivity and, with so many suffering comrades a short distance away, anxious to contribute something. Summing up their frustration, one young Indianian complained in a letter to his father: "I felt all the time that if they had sent our brigade to assist General Corse we could have walked the [Rebels] out of their chosen position." Regrettably, Sherman had seen things differently.[75]

# CHAPTER SEVENTEEN

# AN UNUSUAL SOLEMNITY PERVADES OUR RANKS

FIGHTING Joe Hooker was having a tough go of it. His jubilant march off Lookout Mountain and along the Rossville road had been stopped abruptly at Chattanooga Creek, one mile short of the gap in Missionary Ridge at Rossville that was the key to the Confederate left flank. Retreating Rebels had burned the bridge behind them. It was 1:25 P.M. when the Twenty-seventh Missouri, the advance guard of Peter Osterhaus's division column, bumped up against the bank of the creek.[1]

Hooker was dismayed but determined to push on. Once again, fate had handed him a chance to play a prominent role in the battle. As earlier related, Sherman's delay in getting underway against Tunnel Hill had convinced Grant to acquiesce in Thomas's desire to send Hooker against Bragg's left. To recapitulate, Thomas was absolutely convinced that both of the enemy's flanks must be crushed before he dare send his Army of the Cumberland—reduced by detachments to Sherman and Hooker to slightly under twenty-five thousand men—against the enemy rifle pits at the base of and atop Missionary Ridge. Thomas had no reserves on hand; every soldier was in the battle line of four divisions, and the Rebels across the valley enjoyed numerical parity—bad odds for an attack across a partially open, mile-wide valley. So, while Grant placed his hopes for victory in his friend Sherman, Thomas, who shared little of Grant's enthusiasm for the Ohioan, looked southward to Hooker for decisive results.

Thomas's anxiety was apparent. At 10:00 A.M., just as Hooker was starting down Lookout Mountain, Thomas amended his order of two hours earlier, which had told Hooker simply to move across the valley over the Rossville road toward Missionary Ridge, while taking care to protect his right flank. Now, with the enemy evidently long since off the mountain, Thomas threw caution aside. He exhorted Hooker to "move forward firmly and steadily upon the enemy's works in front of Missionary Ridge." Palmer's Fourteenth Corps would cooperate in the assault once Hooker came up.[2]

Hooker tried hard to obey. He scribbled a note apprising Thomas that his march had stalled, then importuned Osterhaus to improvise a way over the creek at once. The Prussian was equally conscientious. He got the men of the Twenty-seventh Missouri to throw together a log footbridge, then sent them over it and out the road toward the Rossville Gap to reconnoiter. The rickety contrivance sufficed for a regiment but would never do for three divisions. As the Missourians stepped across in single file, Osterhaus set his detail of pioneers to work repairing the main bridge. While they did, the remainder of the division stacked arms and awaited their turn. The rest of Hooker's column clogged the road for two miles behind them. A few enterprising members of the Seventy-sixth Ohio diverted themselves with an attack on a cluster of beehives, laughing and licking at the honey while shadows of the late-autumn afternoon lengthened in the valley.[3]

Seldom did the war witness a more anxious gathering of surly senior officers than Grant, Thomas, and their staffs atop Orchard Knob. Shells burst overhead as Rebel batteries on Missionary Ridge answered the continuous volleys of Federal cannon in Fort Wood. The shells were a danger, the racket deafening, but both were scarcely noticed. Churned by fears that Sherman had failed in his attack and that Hooker was fatally stalled along Chattanooga Creek, all present were absorbed in a tension more palpable than the rain of shell fragments. Grant fidgeted and sucked short, hard puffs from his cigar. Thomas stood in brooding silence a few yards distant. Baldy Smith, James Wilson, and John Rawlins huddled together and, as Wilson put it, "exchanged opinions freely and frequently on every point worthy of notice," but as yet they offered no advice to their superiors. Gordon Granger, whose corps would bear the brunt of any assault against Missionary Ridge, was busy working a nearby cannon. He, at least, was enjoying himself, but his idiotic act at so critical a moment, while perhaps therapeutic for Granger himself, only sharpened Grant's annoyance. Granger's star, which had soared after Chickamauga, was fast falling in the estimation of Grant.[4]

The generals had an unparalleled view of the arena of battle. Bragg's headquarters were in plain sight. Grant recalled watching staff officers come and go from the white frame Moore house. From Orchard Knob, said Sylvanus Cadwallader, a favorite at Grant's headquarters, "the semicircular sweep of the entire Union line from the river above to the river below Chattanooga was distinctly visible, as well as the corresponding heights of Missionary Ridge." Continued Cadwallader:

We could overlook the belt of cottonwood timber next in front of our line (nearly a half mile in width), see the open cotton fields across which our troops must advance to reach the strongly prepared line of rifle pits at the foot of the ridge, could see plainer even than all others the second line of rifle pits halfway up the face of the ridge (for the sunlight fell directly upon them), and could see the frowning earthworks bristling with heavy ordnance on the crest of the ridge, and back of these could often catch glimpses of rebel battle flags, troops in line or movement, and Confederate officers scanning us through their field glasses.[5]

Their unusually clear view of the fight for Tunnel Hill in particular and of the length of Missionary Ridge in general did not prevent Grant and his staff from misinterpreting what Bragg was up to. Perhaps because he could not conceive that Sherman could fail unless the odds were stacked against him, Grant construed the morning movements of Stevenson's division along the ridge and into place beside Cleburne as part of a general shifting of forces by Bragg toward his right flank. Some pointless marching and countermarching by Bate's division in the early afternoon only served to cement Grant's conclusion that Bragg was weakening his center to reinforce his right.

Neither did seeing Sherman's setback on the left help the generals respond to it. By midafternoon, Grant had run out of ideas. Sherman's delay in attacking had caught him by surprise. And when his attack stalled, Grant's only solution was to feed the Ohioan more troops. He hastened Howard to the left. Shortly before noon, he told Thomas to detach his left division, that of Absolom Baird, to reinforce Sherman as well. That reduced Thomas's force to three divisions. Baird obediently filed down the river road toward the rear of the Army of the Tennessee, only to be met by a messenger who told him to return at once to his original place in the line of battle; in a moment of candor, Sherman had confessed to Grant that he had more troops on hand than he knew what to do with.[6]

After watching Raum's brigade stall on Tunnel Hill, Grant wandered over to General Wood. It was a few minutes past 2:30 P.M. Grant and Wood had been roommates at West Point, and the Ohioan felt at ease with Wood.

"General Sherman seems to be having a hard time," Grant said absently.

"Yes, General, he does seem to be in a warm place," answered Wood, not quite sure how to respond to Grant's statement of the obvious.

Grant was groping for a solution: "It does seem as if he is having a hard time, and it seems as if we ought to help him."

Wood followed the tentative flow of Grant's thinking. "I think so too, General, and whatever you order we will try to do," he said.

Wood's gentle nudge helped Grant make up his mind. "If you and Sheridan advance your divisions to the foot of the ridge, and there halt, I think it will menace Bragg's forces so as to relieve Sherman," Grant speculated.

"Perhaps it might work in that way; and if you order it, we will try it, and I think we can carry the intrenchments at the base of the ridge," answered Wood.[7]

Grant approached Thomas. The burly Virginian had his field glasses trained on the ridge. In a conversational tone, Grant suggested that Thomas move against the rifle pits at the foot of Missionary Ridge. Thomas never lowered his glasses. He was walking the tightrope of his temper. What precisely Thomas told Grant is unknown, but he made clear his objection to an attack. His reluctance seemed sound. Baird had yet to return, which meant Thomas had only nineteen thousand troops present. Moreover, he had heard nothing from Hooker since 1:30 P.M., when Hooker had reported his delay at the creek and estimated it would take him about an hour to cross. Thomas had no intention of sending his paltry command against the center of the Rebel defenses without proof that at least one of the enemy's flanks had been crushed.[8]

Grant did not press the point but walked away quietly. Watching Grant yield to Thomas, Rawlins grew livid. And Granger's puerile display only fueled his fury. He vented his spleen on Wilson and Smith. When thirty minutes passed with no action, Wilson suggested Rawlins do something to break the impasse. He did. Striding over to Grant at 3:00 P.M., Rawlins shamed him as only he could into silencing Granger and peremptorily ordering Thomas to move. Embarrassed, Grant dropped his easy demeanor and barked loudly enough for everyone to hear: "General Thomas, order Granger to turn that battery over to its proper commander and take command of his own corps. And now order your troops to advance and take the enemy's first line of rifle pits."[9]

Thomas did not answer, but he knew an order when he heard one. He motioned Granger to his side. The two talked briefly. Granger walked off.

The minutes passed. Not a single soldier from the Fourth Corps stirred. Again Rawlins broke the silence with a scolding. "Why are not those men moving on the rifle pits. I don't believe they have been ordered forward," he snapped at Grant accusingly.

"Oh, yes, I think the order must have been given," Grant replied defensively. To be certain, though, he called to General Wood: "Why is not your division in motion?"

"We have received no such orders, sir," answered Wood.

Grant turned to Thomas. "General Thomas, why are not these troops advancing?"

"I don't know. General Granger has been directed to move them forward."

Grant looked about for Granger. He was back among the artillerymen of Bridges's Illinois battery, aiming cannons. "General Granger, why are your men waiting?"

"I have no orders to advance," Granger lied.

"If you will leave that battery to its captain, and take command of your corps, it will be better for all of us," snapped Grant.

The rebuke brought Granger back to the reality of his larger responsibilities. He "obeyed promptly and rushed into the fight like a wild Irishman," observed Sylvanus Cadwallader.

Granger pulled Wood aside. "You and Sheridan are to advance your divisions, carry the intrenchments at the base of the ridge, if you can, and, if you succeed, to halt there," he explained. "The movement is to be made at once, so give your orders to your brigade commanders immediately, and the signal to advance will be the rapid, successive discharge of the six guns of the battery." Wood acknowledged the order and called for his brigade commanders. Baldy Smith rode off to General Baird, who was only then returning from his abortive march to the left, to give him the order. Aides were dispatched to pass on the command to Sheridan and Richard Johnson. Thomas stood apart, watching their going with profound trepidation. To Thomas's way of thinking, Grant was about to sacrifice what little of the Army of the Cumberland he had left in a quixotic effort to salvage Sherman.[10]

The Confederate fortifications opposite Thomas's four divisions certainly looked menacing enough. Arrayed along a front slightly less than three miles long were the better part of four Rebel divisions and nine batteries of artillery—approximately sixteen thousand men defending seemingly impregnable heights against an attacking force of some twenty-three thousand that had nearly a mile of largely open ground to cross.

Opposite Baird's division and extending nearly half a mile beyond its left front were Walthall's, Moore's, and Jackson's brigades of Cheatham's division; Wright's brigade was still on detached duty helping Lucius Polk guard the railroad crossings over South Chickamauga Creek. Next in line was Hindman's division, under the command of Patton Anderson. Alfred Vaughan's small Tennessee brigade held the right of the division. Next came Zachariah Deas's brigade, then that of Arthur Manigault. On the division left lay Anderson's own brigade, temporarily led by Colonel William F. Tucker. Tucker's left flank rested along the Bird's Mill road. To the left of Anderson's division was that of Breckinridge, commanded by the recklessly ambitious William Bate. A gap of some four hundred yards had been opened between Anderson's left and Bate's right the night before, after Bragg ordered Lewis's brigade out of the line to reinforce Cleburne. That left Bate with just his own brigade, under Colonel R. C. Tyler, and Jesse Finley's Florida brigade. The right two brigades of Stewart's division, commanded by Randall Gibson and Otho Strahl, were the southern-most units of the Confederate center and stood roughly opposite Richard Johnson's Federal division. To their left, stretched over nearly two miles, were the brigades of Marcellus Stovall and Henry Clayton; the latter, like so many other units, was also under a temporary commander, Colonel J. T. Holtzclaw.[11]

Imposing at first glance, the Confederate defenses were in reality a horribly improvised, sadly neglected patchwork. Their sorry state stemmed largely from the misplaced faith of both Bragg and Breckinridge that any serious Federal attack would come *only* against the army's flanks. The daring Federal assault on Lookout Mountain and Sherman's crossing of the Tennessee River on 24 November had seemed to confirm their suspicions. All this Federal activity on the army's flanks could not, however, excuse the blatant disregard for affairs along the center. A host of problems plagued the defenders in this sector, some inherent to the strange sinuousities of the ridge, others created through the negligence of their commanders. For the latter shortcomings, Bragg and Breckinridge were to blame. Breckinridge's overconfidence in the strength of the center—so contagious during the conference at army headquarters on the night of the twenty-fourth, when the decision was reached to stay and fight it out on the present line—was a major impediment to rational thought. (Hardee, too, must share a measure of the guilt for having acceded to Breckinridge's claim that the position was a strong one.) His anger at having lost Lookout Mountain led Breckinridge to make wild promises that he failed to back up with careful preparations; as will be recalled, he reputedly had boasted that if his men could not hold Missionary Ridge, with its great natural strength, they could not hold any position: "I never felt more like fighting than when I saw those people shelling my troops off of Lookout Mountain," he purportedly told Captain Buck after the council of war.

Was Breckinridge's bravado fed by liquor? His biographer, William C. Davis, assiduously examined the question and declared the evidence inconclusive. Whether or not he was inebriated on Missionary Ridge, Breckinridge's detractors contended that he took to the bottle during periods of stress. Although there was no evidence that liquor had impeded his performance to date, some whispered that his drinking worsened as Confederate war prospects grew more bleak. By the time of the army's surrender in 1865, Breckinridge's defamers were slandering him as an irresponsible, two-fisted drinker.

The following story—probably apocryphal, since its supposed author, Joseph Johnston, subsequently denied any recollection of the incident—was later circulated at Breckinridge's expense. After the war, so the story went, Johnston related to a friend an episode during the final negotiations with General Sherman for the surrender of the Army of Tennessee that conclusively proved Breckinridge's dependency. "You know how fond of his liquor Breckinridge was," Johnston began. "Well, nearly everything to drink had been absorbed. For several days Breckinridge had found it difficult, if not impossible to procure liquor. He showed the effects of his forced abstinence. He was rather dull and heavy that morning. That is until Sherman suggested a drink." Breckinridge, said Johnston, lit up with a look almost "beatific." When the bottle came his way he poured out a deep drink, which he swallowed ardently. Breckinridge grew animated and cheerful. "See here, gentlemen, who is doing the surrendering anyhow? If this goes on, you'll have me sending a letter of apology to Jeff Davis," said Sherman, surprised by the Kentuckian's lightheartedness during the interment of the Confederacy. Time passed and Sherman poured himself a second drink but forgot to offer the bottle to the Southerners. Breckinridge turned morose. "From pleasant hope and expectation the expression on Breckinridge's face changed successively to uncertainty, disgust, and deep depression. He took little part in the remainder of the interview," said Johnston. On the ride back to camp, Johnston asked Breckinridge his opinion of Sherman. "He is a bright man, and a man of force," answered Breckinridge. "But General Johnston, General Sherman is a hog! Yes sir, a hog! Did you see him take that drink by himself? No Kentucky gentleman would ever have taken away that bottle. He knew we needed it and needed it badly."[12]

Character flaws aside, however, what were the weaknesses in the Confederate defenses? To begin with, neither Bragg nor Breckinridge had ordered that the ridge itself be fortified until the last possible moment. They seemed content with the line of rifle pits along its base. Even if they seriously believed an attack could be halted on the flat, fall-back positions should have been laid out atop the ridge. There was time aplenty during the long, dreary weeks of the siege to do so, and a little hard work might have been an effective antidote to the inveterate drinking and gambling that debilitated the idle ranks of the army.

Not until the night of 23 November did Breckinridge direct that work begin. Bedding down at Anderson's headquarters after an inspection of Lookout Mountain, Breckinridge hastily drew up a plan for entrenching the crest of Missionary Ridge. He enjoined his engineer officer, Captain John Green, to lay out breastworks and Anderson to supply the troops to construct them. The Kentuckian also told Anderson to bring the four batteries of his divisional artillery battalion up from the base to the crest. Then, apparently with Bragg's concurrence, he issued an order that took Anderson by surprise. The Floridian was to leave half of his division in the trenches at the foot of Missionary Ridge and withdraw the remainder to defend the crest. Zachariah Deas was to command the former troops, Anderson those on top of the ridge.

Oddly, Breckinridge gave no such instructions to Bate or Stewart. He made no provision to withdraw any part of Bate's two brigades—those of Tyler and Finley—then entrenched at the base, or to remove his artillery. To Lewis's Kentuckians, who were encamped near Bragg's headquarters at the Moore house in reserve, went the task of digging rifle pits on the summit above Bate. Bate's artillery battalion was left encamped behind the reverse slope of the ridge. Stewart stayed in the valley with his entire division.[13]

Neither Anderson, nor Deas, nor Manigault cared for Breckinridge's plan. Anderson called the proposed disposition the worst he had even seen. He and his brigade commanders barely had troops enough to cover a single line along their front; splitting the division between two lines, one from four hundred to eight hundred yards behind the other, struck them as the height of folly. During the next thirty-six hours, their concerns would sharpen and, when ignored by higher headquarters, recede into glum resignation.

For the moment, Anderson and Manigault were preoccupied with scraping together enough tools to throw up the works that Captain Green was trying to lay out in the dark of night. Manigault fast grew disgusted. "Details were made to construct breastworks; some forty entrenching tools were furnished for this purpose but were taken away by superior authority, after having had the use of them for two or three hours," he complained. "There were but four axes in the command, the consequence was that the work progressed slowly and the protection obtained against the enemy's fire in this new line was poor and insufficient."[14]

Nor was the line chosen appropriate. The harried Captain Green, scurrying about in a single-handed effort to lay out three miles of breastworks, placed them too far back to be of practical use. Grumbled Man- igault's adjutant, Captain Cornelius Walker: "Defective engineering located the breastworks so far back on the crest of the ridge as not to command the slope in their front." Green, apparently under Breckin- ridge's instructions, was entrenching the topographical crest—in other words, the highest elevation at each point of the ragged ridge. From there, defending infantrymen would be silhouetted and badly exposed to enemy fire. At the same time, blind spots would be created in the ravines and contours just below the crest. If Breckinridge demanded a single line, then the logical location was the military crest on the for- ward slope of the ridge. Even that, however, was not wholly satisfacto- ry. There simply were too many odd undulations, sharp projections, abrupt descents, and deep ravines for a single line of works to provide an adequate field of fire along the whole ridge; as one student of the battle put it, "no single location at the crest gave both infantry and artillery an unobstructed sweep of the entire slope."[15]

Manigault saw the folly in Green's scheme and questioned him. "He appeared to be in a great hurry, and said he had much to do," recalled the South Carolinian, who offered to relieve him of the responsibility of laying out the line on his own front. Green happily accepted, but cautioned Manigault that his orders had been to "run the line on the highest point or outline of the hill." That, of course, was precisely what Manigault hoped to avoid. After mulling over the consequences of dis- obedience, he decided to flout the order and dig in wherever the terrain offered the best coverage of the slope to his front. As he later related his thinking: "I noticed that at many points, an intervening projection or irregularity of the downward slope prevented the fire of the defend- ers from playing on the enemy, after their reaching the foot of the ridge and when they ascended. The same obstacle protected them until within fifteen, twenty, or thirty yards of our works. The only way in which this difficulty could be obviated was by selecting the ground when such was the case, below the crest." Sadly, even when correctly situated, the works were rendered deficient by the lack of proper tools, both on Manigault's front and elsewhere along the ridge. "The works were of very inferior quality, were low, and only afforded protection to the lower part of the body, and against the fire of artillery were rather a disadvan- tage than otherwise, when struck by a solid shot or shell," he noted. Colonel Dowd of the Twenty-fourth Mississippi concurred: "The breast- works were formed of logs, stone, earth, etc., and were scarcely suffi- cient to protect the men, when lying down, from the enemy's rifles."

Manigault offered his solution to Anderson and to the commanders of neighboring brigades, but it "was not deemed worthy of notice."[16]

For the artillery, the problem was even more serious. As one historian has observed:

> The battery emplacements on the crest were prepared too close to the edge. Consequently, the gun barrels could not be depressed enough to sweep the slope. This in effect created an obtuse angle: A represented the pieces on the crest, B the foot of the ridge, and C a point about two hundred yards in front of the ridge base. The artillery would thus be delivering what General Bate termed a "plunging fire" between points A and C, and thus creating a blind spot. . . . The open plain over which the Yankees would need to advance was also deceptive. Those moving on the double-quick could be out of the artillery fire zone within ten minutes.[17]

Not only were the cannon run too far forward, but they were too widely dispersed. In an apparent effort to command every possible knoll or rise along the ridge, Breckinridge and his division commanders split their batteries. Individual sections often were separated by several hundred yards, and thus left to fight on their own. The litany of the cannoneers' woes seemed endless. Their half-starved battery horses were nearing exhaustion, so that infantrymen had to help drag the guns up the slope with ropes and pulleys. And there were few avenues of rapid escape. Only five trails led down the reverse slope of Missionary Ridge in Breckinridge's sector. The artillery generally was posted too far from these roads to have any hope of using them, in the event the ridge was overrun. Behind most sections was tangled forest and a sheer, rocky drop. Finally, many of the guns were positioned at the last minute and consequently deprived of protective earthworks of any sort. For example, Captain Cuthbert Slocomb's Washington Artillery was moved into position north of Bragg's headquarters only minutes before the Federal attack began on the afternoon of 25 November. And it had not been until early evening of the twenty-fourth that the batteries of Stewart's division began the ascent from Chattanooga Valley; Dawson's Georgia Battery did not come into line until 3:45 P.M. the next day, after Thomas's Federals already were on the move.

Once they were up, little attention was given to the placement of Stewart's batteries. While Anderson's cannon were too widely scattered, Stewart's four batteries were left tightly packed precisely where they had been hauled to the crest, which happened to be just to the left of Bragg's headquarters. It fell to Stewart to defend the two miles of ridge between there and Rossville Gap with four small brigades of infantry. Nearly two months of benign neglect gave way to a few hours of frenzied improvisation.[18]

One final, potentially fatal flaw existed in Breckinridge's attenuated sector: he had no reserves with which to plug any hole that the Federals might punch into the narrow crest. Every man was committed, either to the rifle pits at the foot of Missionary Ridge or the breastworks atop it.

Bragg's and Breckinridge's double-line defense scheme ignored unit integrity and opened ominous holes. Only Cheatham had his division united on the ridge. Anderson's division was a hodgepodge. Vaughan was in the trenches on the flat with a portion of his brigade, resulting in a considerable gap between Anderson's right and Cheatham's left. Manigault's two largest regiments—the Tenth and Nineteenth South Carolina and the Thirty-fourth Alabama—also were at the foot of the ridge, leaving him with only a third of his effective force to man a brigade front along the crest. Half of Deas's and Tucker's brigades similarly were down below. So too was all of Reynolds's brigade, which was charged with manning the rifle pits across Bate's front. That opened a yawning breach between Anderson's left and the right of Bate's division on the ridge. When Breckinridge learned that Reynolds had too few troops for the job, he convinced a reluctant Bate to send three of the five regiments of Finley's small Florida brigade to man the rifle pits from Reynolds's left to the Moore road.[19]

As officers and men contemplated their thin lines, morale plummeted. "An unusual solemnity pervades our ranks," wrote a member of the Fifth Tennessee with remarkable understatement. "The men were over three feet apart in line!" snarled General Anderson. "Thus the front rank was not strong enough to hold its position, nor could it retire to the top of the ridge so as to be of any service to the line there." The distance between soldiers in the two regiments of the Florida Brigade that remained on the crest was nearly eight feet. To disguise their paltry numbers and create the illusion of reinforcements, Colonel Finley marched and countermarched a portion of the men behind the works.[20]

No one was more distraught than General Deas. After inspecting the rifle pits at the base of Missionary Ridge during the afternoon of 24 November, he came to the inescapable conclusion that his mission was suicidal. Wrote Deas: "This position was very disadvantageous . . . for the reason that if the men made a stubborn resistance as ordered and were overpowered by numbers, capture or annihilation were the alternatives, as retreat, with the enemy close on us, up the steep ascent of the hill behind, would have been impossible." Deas took his concern to Anderson. He begged the Floridian to order his troops from the flat to the crest, where he was convinced that "a much better fight could be made."

Anderson consoled Deas but could do nothing more without approval from Breckinridge. That he failed to get. "No, remain as you are," came the curt reply from corps headquarters. Anderson urged Deas to reassure his men, who were grumbling over the prospect of having to clamber up the steep slope behind them under enemy fire, and with that bit of fatuous advice the two parted company for the night.[21]

On the morning of 25 November, Breckinridge accompanied Anderson on a tour of Deas's line. Anderson seized the moment to renew Deas's request. Again, Breckinridge denied it. He promised, however, to consult with Bragg on the question.

So matters stood until 10:30 A.M., when Thomas pushed forward his skirmishers to test the strength of Deas's defenses. The Federals drove in the Rebel pickets, who came from Manigault's ill-fated brigade, then pressed on to within rifle shot of the trenches. They were repulsed after a sharp fight, but their probe demonstrated that the Yankees might consider doing what Bragg and Breckinridge had thought unimaginable: attack the center in force. The two still were unwilling to abandon the flat, but they struck a bizarre compromise with Deas. Should the enemy advance in force, Deas's troops—and all others on the flat—were to hold their position until the Yankees approached to within two hundred yards, then deliver a single volley and retire up the slope of Missionary Ridge, skirmishing as they climbed. What such a tactic might accomplish, short of blocking the line of fire of those at the top and exhausting the men at the bottom, neither Bragg nor Breckinridge ventured to explain.[22]

In keeping with the chaotic improvisation that characterized the Confederate high command's management of affairs along the center of Missionary Ridge, Breckinridge's latest order was muddled in the transmission. Deas and Manigault understood the intent, but Tucker and Vaughan didn't know how close they were to allow the Yankees to come before falling back. Neither Reynolds nor Bate mention even having received the order. And, oddly, only regimental commanders and above were brought in on the plan; company officers and the rank and file were kept in the dark. Perhaps the generals felt it would demoralize those in the trenches to learn that they were there for no good purpose; if that was their fear, however, it should have caused them to evaluate the advisability of any plan that, if revealed, would blast morale.[23]

By noon, Bragg and Breckinridge recognized that at least a strong demonstration might be made against the center. The Federals were coming out of their entrenchments across the valley, said Manigault, and massing in column. Atop the ridge, Breckinridge scrambled to close the gap between Anderson and Bate. At 1:00 P.M., he ordered both Bate and Stewart to move to the right to connect "with the general line of battle on the ridge. Bate being on the right will touch Anderson's left."[24]

The errors continued with the inevitability of a Greek tragedy. When he received the order to move to the right, Bate waved a staff officer off the ridge to bring up Finley's Floridians, contrary to Breckinridge's desire that they stay put until attacked. Bate also found that he could not close on Anderson's left, as Gibson's brigade of Stewart's division stood between his division and that of Anderson. Bate informed Breckinridge of Gibson's location—something that the Kentuckian, had he had a better grasp of his sector, already should have known. In any event, Breckinridge told Gibson to withdraw, face about, march behind the ridge, and come back up on Bate's left. Bate resumed his movement to the right. No sooner had he done so than a courier summoned him to corps headquarters.

By the time Bate galloped the mile to the cabin that served as Breckinridge's headquarters, the Kentuckian was mounted and ready to ride to Rossville. A member of his staff returning from a visit to Holtzclaw's brigade, posted a mile north of Rossville, had reported the ominous congregation of bluecoats under Hooker at Chattanooga Creek. With his left flank in danger, Breckinridge decided to supervise its defense—and that of the vital Rossville Gap—himself. Bragg concurred and agreed to assume command of the center. This was a logical arrangement, reasoned Breckinridge's biographer, but one that also reflected the Kentuckian's misplaced confidence in the invulnerability of the center. After he rode off, Breckinridge made one final error in judgment that Bragg obviously endorsed. He sent a member of his escort back to tell Bate, whose right had just come into contact with Anderson's left, to reverse himself and march the length of one brigade to the left to make room for Reynolds, should he be forced out of the trenches at the foot of the ridge. The Kentuckian also forbade Bate from withdrawing Finley's men from the flat.

Away Breckinridge galloped, accompanied by his son Cabell; his adjutant, Major James Wilson; and a few troopers from his headquarters escort. It was a three-mile ride to the gap. Breckinridge was tired, tense, and, perhaps, a bit drunk. The jarring ride along the ragged ridge compounded his irritability. When the courier returned and the Kentuckian learned that he had misconstrued his order, Breckinridge flew into a rage. He called for a second courier, repeated the order, and sent him off to Bate, who got the message and moved, partially reopening the very gap he was to have filled. "It was wholly unlike Breckinridge to vent anger on a soldier," observed the historian William C. Davis. The Kentuckian's bad day was about to get worse.[25]

# CHAPTER EIGHTEEN

# WE ARE ALL OFFICERS TODAY

THOMAS'S probe of the Confederate rifle pits along the foot of Missionary Ridge had exacted a heavy toll on the Sixth Ohio Infantry. Hopping over their own entrenchments a few minutes after 10:00 A.M., the Ohioans had deployed as skirmishers and stepped off into a belt of leafless, open timber. They stumbled upon a few startled Rebel pickets, who fired a quick volley and ran. The Ohioans gave chase. Two hundred yards short of the Rebel rifle pits the Ohioans found themselves in a field chopped clear of trees. The Confederates opened fire, and the Ohioans dove for cover behind stumps and logs that lay scattered over the flat. For a while, they got on all right. Amidst the sharpshooting, the regimental postmaster sprinted from man to man, delivering letters received that morning from home. Finally, a few minutes before 2:00 P.M., the purpose of the reconnaissance having been achieved—that is to say, proof gained that the Rebels held the foot of Missionary Ridge in force—the Sixth was ordered to fall back. By then, Southern guns on the summit had ranged the regiment. As the men made for the timber, the guns boomed. A shell fragment split the skull of the major. Bursting shells cut down eighteen others.

While the Ohioans regrouped in the wood, orders came for them to return to their entrenchments. An audible sigh of relief rose from the ranks. "As we knew nothing of the intended attack, we congratulated ourselves upon our good fortune in being relieved so soon," remembered the regimental historian. "But the moment we reached our fortifications on Orchard Knob we saw that something was up."[1]

Something indeed. Troops by the thousands were rising to their feet. Anxious company officers shepherded them to their stacked arms. Color-bearers unfurled and shook out their flags. Field and staff officers took their places toward the front, and in the rear, surgeons mustered their stretcher-bearers. Regiment after regiment passed out of the fortifications and onto the flat. The troops of the Sixth Ohio promptly faced about and—instead of spending a restful afternoon in their field-works—found themselves in the front line of Hazen's brigade.

Just as they had two days earlier before sweeping Orchard Knob, the Federals marched with parade-ground precision toward the near edge of the cottonwood timber. When a regiment reached its designated line of departure, the men were ordered to lie down, leaving its general guides standing so that the next regiment coming up could align itself. All the while, the Rebel cannons on Missionary Ridge kept up a slow and steady rumble. Their range was poor and virtually no one in the gathering tide of blue was struck, but the possibility of a chance hit lent an urgency to the whole affair.[2]

As long as they were in the timber, the Federals knew they were fairly safe: the woods would provide at least a modicum of shelter for half the distance of their advance. Over the final three hundred to seven hundred yards of the flat, however, the Rebels had chopped down every last tree, both to provide firewood during the long siege and to open a clear field of fire. As the soldiers of the Sixth Ohio had discovered, only a few stumps and logs dotted this last stretch of the flat. Just in front of the rifle pits, the ground swelled. From the pits themselves to the physical base of the ridge was a plateau about one hundred yards wide, upon which the Confederates had built clusters of huts. Because of undulations in the ridge and variations in the starting points of the assaulting troops, the distance to the rifle pits would vary from brigade to brigade.[3]

Granger claimed he interrupted his cannon play long enough to instruct his division commanders to deploy with all their brigades on line. Each brigade was to cover itself with a double line of skirmishers and maintain a strong reserve of one or two regiments massed in close column, he added. This formation was adopted more or less throughout the Fourth Corps. All was ready by 3:00 P.M. (some said thirty minutes earlier, some thirty minutes later—the recollection of precise times, always uncertain during the war, was especially bad here at Chattanooga).

Baird's division had returned from its hike toward Sherman and assembled on the left of Wood. Phelps's brigade was arrayed on the extreme left of Baird's line, opposite Vaughan's brigade of Anderson's Rebel division. Van Derveer held the center, Turchin the right.

Wood deployed his division with Sam Beatty on the left, August Willich in the center, and the hot-tempered, hard-fighting William Hazen on the right of his division. Gazing up at the summit, the Army of the Cumberland's consummate careerist may have noted with giddy anticipation that the gap in the Rebel defenses created by Reynolds's detachment to the base of the ridge lay in front of his brigade's route of advance.

Phil Sheridan had George Wagner, Charles Harker, and Francis Sherman lined up from left to right. The youthful Harker's command assembled a mile west of Bragg's headquarters.[4]

On Granger's right, Palmer's Fourteenth Corps was represented solely by Richard Johnson's division. Johnson formed the brigades of William Stoughton and the recently returned William Carlin in line of battle, leaving that of Starkweather behind to man the fortifications.[5]

The soldiers were in position to move, though few believed the rumor swirling through the ranks that they were to make an assault. "We deployed our line and lay down and were in comparative safety. It soon began to be rumored among the officers that we were to charge the rifle pits at the foot of Mission Ridge. We could hardly credit it for there was a mile of level ground to cross before we reached the rifle pits," recalled a member of the Thirty-sixth Illinois.[6]

Then came couriers to confirm the worst. Captain George Lewis of the One Hundred Twenty-fourth Ohio remembered the moment he learned that they were to attack. His commander, Colonel James Pickands, "came to the officers of the regiment with the order that 'at the firing of six guns from Fort Wood [actually, Orchard Knob], and the sounding of the forward, we must face to the front, and not suffer ourselves to be checked until we put ourselves into the rebel works at the base of the ridge.'" A brief, tense silence followed. Said Lewis:

> No emotion was visible in the soldierly face of our brave colonel, save, perhaps, a little more violent chewing of a large quid of the weed that added rotundity to his bronzed weather-beaten cheek. His further order was that we inform each man in the ranks of what was expected of him. Commanding at the time Company B, it was my painful duty to break the news to those that I had known from boyhood, and that I had learned to love as brothers. No one that I communicated the order to, but turned pale.
>
> Now there was nothing to do but wait. Now the time hung heavy. Now the soldier's thoughts were filled with home and the loved ones left behind, and what would become of them if he should fall in the terrific charge that he knew would soon have to be made. It is the dreadful waiting that is more terrible than the shock of battle.[7]

At least Lewis and his men knew their mission. Several senior officers in both the Fourth and Fourteenth corps were confused about what was expected of them. They were unsure how far they were supposed to advance or what to do when they got to where they were going. Indeed, Grant's order to halt at the rifle pits at the base of the ridge was misunderstood by far too many of the generals charged with executing it. Some doubted the order because they thought it absurd to stop an attack at the instant when the attackers would be most vulnerable both to fire from the crest and to a counterattack. Others apparently received garbled versions of the order.

Absalom Baird got the correct version; Baldy Smith brought it to him personally. He simply couldn't believe it. "And when I have captured the rifle-pits, what then?" he asked. Smith shrugged. "I have given you the order in the exact words of General Grant." Smith rode away. A few minutes later, General Wilson arrived bearing the same instructions, but with a slight twist, apparently an extrapolation of his own. General Thomas, Wilson said, intended the advance to be "preparatory to a general assault on the mountain, and that I should take part in this movement, so that I would be following his wishes were I to push on to the summit," said Baird.

Major James Connelly, the division inspector general, reported a few moments later, having been away on an errand to Wood's division. Baird had decided to incorporate Wilson's speculation as to the ultimate objective into his orders to his subordinates. "When six guns are fired in quick succession from Fort Wood, the line will advance to storm the heights and carry the ridge if possible. Take that order to Colonel Phelps and tell him to move forward rapidly when he hears the signal," Baird barked at Connelly. Off the major galloped. Baird himself started off to Van Derveer. Just as he gave Van Derveer his orders, the signal guns boomed. Baird spurred his horse toward Turchin, while the rest of the division moved forward. Most of Phelps's and Van Derveer's regimental commanders dismounted, preferring to go it on foot with their men rather than be silhouetted on horseback on the broad open flat. Baird's staff scattered along the division line to superintend the movement.[8]

Matters were equally muddy in Wood's division. Wood admitted to having gotten the correct order directly from Granger and said he then called together his brigade commanders to repeat it to them verbatim. "I directed them to give the orders to their regimental commanders in person, who, in turn, were to give the orders to their company commanders in person. I was thus careful in having the orders transmitted, because I desired commanders of every grade in the division to fully understand what the movement was to be, and that there might be neither misconception nor confusion."[9]

Laudable intentions, but something went wrong. Hazen and every man in his brigade understood the task at hand. Sam Beatty may have understood the order as well, but his front-line regimental commanders, at least, were unsure where they were supposed to stop. And the redoubtable August Willich, as honest an officer as there was, swore in his report that it was several days after the battle had been fought that he learned that the order had been "to take only the rifle pits at the foot of the ridge." He maintained, "By what accident, I am unable to say, I did not understand it so; I only understood the order to advance." Oddly, Colonel John Martin, commander of the Eighth Kansas in Willich's brigade, claimed that Willich "distinctly stated that we were directed to take the line of Confederate works at the foot of the ridge." On the other hand, Major John McClenahan, in command of the brigade skirmishers, said he asked Willich where they were to stop. "I don't know, at Hell, I expect," the Prussian told him. At least one of McClenahan's company officers was equally perplexed. "First a shot was fired from headquarters, and then all along the line came the bugle call to go forward. That is all the order we had, all we got," he insisted.[10]

No one was more befuddled—or more fearful of the outcome of his uncertainty—than Phil Sheridan. After receiving his orders from a corps staff officer, he rode forward to get a better look at his presumed objective. What he saw troubled him. "While riding from right to left, and closely examining the first line of pits occupied by the enemy, which seemed as though they would prove untenable after being carried, the doubt arose in my mind as to whether I had properly understood the original order, and I dispatched Captain Ransom, of my staff, to ascertain from General Granger whether it was the first line that was to be carried, or the ridge. He had scarcely left me when the signal was given, and the division marched to the front," lamented Sheridan.[11]

Of course Sheridan's confusion trickled down through the division. Hopeful that Ransom would return in time, he had passed on the order not as given to him but rather as he wished it to read. Granger's chief of staff, Joseph Fullerton, said the only instruction given in the Irishman's division was that, "as soon as the signal is given, the whole line will advance, and you will take what is before you." Sheridan's subordinates went forward blindly. "I knew nothing of an order to halt at the first rifle pits, neither do I believe any colonel on the line did," said Colonel Allen Buckner of the Seventy-ninth Illinois of Harker's brigade. Colonel Emerson Opdycke, in charge of one of Harker's two demi-brigades, said Harker told him simply "to be governed by the movements of the troops next on my left, and if they advanced up the ridge, I was to move up also and maintain my relative position." Wagner adopted a similar, wait-and-see approach. He told his regimental commanders "to advance slowly and steadily in line until ordered to halt."

At the same time, however, he told them that he thought the objective was the crest. "It was intended," he went on, "to take all before us to the top of Missionary Ridge."[12]

Richard Johnson had only a vague idea what was about to happen, which left his brigade commanders largely on their own. "My instructions were not very definite," said William Carlin. So he proceeded to come up with his own. Riding along his line of battle, he shouted: "Boys, I don't want you to stop until we reach the top of that hill." The Illinoisan dismounted, slapped his horse in the rump to send it away, and prepared to sally forth on foot with his men.[13]

When did the first signal gun roar? Estimates vary widely, from as early as 3:00 P.M. to as late as 4:00 P.M. Gordon Granger says it was 3:40 P.M. Since the only thing that really interested him that afternoon was working cannon, he probably paid close attention to the signal shots. His guess thus may be accepted as a good compromise.[14]

Twenty-three thousand officers and men lay in line of battle in Chattanooga Valley, waiting for the inevitable six-gun volley that would sound the march to whatever awaited them. William Morgan of the Twenty-third Kentucky raised his head to cast furtive glances at his surroundings. "Time moves slowly," he noted. "Here and there a soldier readjusts his accouterments or re-laces his shoes. All know that many will never reach the enemy's works. . . . The delay is becoming unendurable. At last the first boom of the signal is heard. Men fall in and dress without command. Another gun, and nervous fingers play with gunlocks. Another and another, and each man looks into the eyes of his comrades to ascertain if he can be relied upon." As the echo of the last shot melted into the valley, hundreds of bugles sounded the advance, and the four divisions stepped off into the timber at the quick time.[15]

Walking behind his company, Lieutenant John Shellenberger of the Sixty-fourth Ohio marveled at the spectacle of thousands of men moving together over so huge an expanse. Wrote the Ohioan:

Far and near could be heard the bugle notes and the voices of the officers calling the men to attention, and as they sprang to their feet there was a great rustling of dead leaves and a snapping of dried twigs. I cast a hurried look to the right and the left, and on either hand, as far as I could see, stood two lines of blue coats with beautiful flags waving and bright arms gleaming in the pleasant afternoon sunshine. It was a splendid sight that sent the blood tingling to the finger tips. The moral effect which it produced upon the enemy must have contributed greatly to our success. We were standing in a stretch of open timber, but the leaves were all off the trees, and we were in plain sight. As we advanced, every Confederate soldier along the crest of the ridge in our front could take in our entire array with one sweeping glance, while looking to the right or left along their own line, on account of the inequalities of the ridge and other obstructions, he could see but a small number of his own comrades. He would naturally get the impression that they were being attacked by overwhelming numbers.[16]

Shellenberger was right. From the ridge, the Rebels could see far more than could the Yankees who marched among the trees, and their fear was commensurately greater. "Every movement in the plains below was visible to us, and a sublime scene was presented to our view, when the massive columns began their onward march," said Colonel James Cooper of the Twentieth Tennessee. And, as Shellenberger guessed, the Confederates wildly exaggerated the number of Yankees coming at them. Wrote an Alabamian whose regiment lay opposite Johnson's division: "There was Grant's army, formed and forming in battle array, at least eighty thousand men in the valley below, in full view. It was a most uncommon sight even to veteran soldiers—those brigades and batteries, with glittering rifles and burnished cannon, wheeling steadily into line, one after another, from our right to left."

A brooding melancholy touched many who never before had displayed anxiety prior to a battle. Lieutenant Colonel B. F. Moore of the Nineteenth Tennessee, whose boyhood home was serving as Bragg's headquarters, sat on a log, lost in some private misery. One of his men, who watched him with compassionate curiosity, thought the colonel was "holding communion with his own heart, utterly oblivious to what was going on, unconscious of the excitement that was moving and agitating Bragg's whole army." Moore was a brave man, the soldiers of the Nineteenth knew from experience, and "if Colonel Moore had thought there was one drop of cowardice blood coursing his veins, he would have severed every artery to let it out. If there be such a thing as premonition of coming danger, the soul of Colonel Moore must have been heavily pressed by such an unseen power." Moore's father came to him before the shooting started. The lieutenant colonel emptied the contents of his pockets into his father's hands—his knife, comb, money, watch—everything. His precautions proved wise; Moore did not live out the day.

A few Rebels in the ranks lost their nerve and slipped out of their trenches. Of one member of Manigault's brigade who sneaked away it was later said that "he was willing to fight the Yankees two to our one, but when he heard old Grant command 'Attention World! by Nations right and left wheel,' he thought it was about time for him to retire."[17]

Spellbound by the exhibition in the valley, General Manigault only half saw the tension that was building among his men. He too overestimated the number of Yankees on the plain, guessing their number to be fifty thousand. Said Manigault:

> The sight was grand and imposing in the extreme, and I was much struck by the order and regularity of their movements, the ease with which they preserved their line, and the completeness of all arrangements. Such a sight I never saw either before or after, and I trust under the same circumstances never to see again; and yet I felt no fear for the result, even though the arrangements to repel the attack were not such as I liked. Neither did I know at the time that a column of the enemy was at that moment on our left flank and rear, or that our army numbered so few men. I think, however, that I noticed some nervousness amongst my men as they beheld this grand military spectacle, and heard remarks which showed that some uneasiness existed amongst them.[18]

At least one young Rebel was so moved with admiration that he forgot that the troops he was watching were the enemy. Wrote Charles Hemming of the First Florida:

> We looked out on the plain, and with the precision of a dress parade their magnificent army came in view.
> The officers, all superbly dressed, pranced out on their high-mottled chargers; the bands played, and to the music came the most wonderful array of splendidly equipped soldiers I ever saw. The old flag waved beautifully at the head of each regiment and the smaller flags were in their places with the brigade and division commanders. The atmosphere was perfectly still excepting just breath enough to straighten out the banners.
> I loved the old flag dearly when I was a boy, and when the Fourth of July came, I had my miniature cannon lined up on small entrenchments in our game to cannonade the fort and salute the flag. When I looked upon the old flag at the head of that wonderful army, I confess that it drew my silent admiration, as I suppose it did that of many others of our Confederate soldiers.
> However, we had a duty to perform and a new flag to serve; so we lay down on the top of the hill, waiting for the coming foe.[19]

And come they did. The first moments of the advance passed in silence. Then, through the branches of the naked trees, the Federals saw bright flames spew from the ridge and strands of dull gray smoke curl upward. An instant later, a crash like a thousand thunderclaps shook the valley. Attackers and defenders alike were deafened. None had ever heard such a cannonading in mountainous country before. A single discharge, swore a Union captain, would echo five or six times between Missionary Ridge and Lookout Mountain. So fast did the Rebel gunners fire that it "was like the rattle of musketry," marveled a private.

The air was sibilant with screaming shells. "The first effect of that tremendous discharge of artillery was stunning," recalled Lieutenant Colonel Kimberly of the Forty-first Ohio, "but in a moment it was plain that no harm was being done." The Confederate artillerymen were hopelessly overshooting their targets. Said General Hazen: "As we moved across the plain before coming to the works at the foot of the hill, although the fire of the mass of guns on Mission Ridge seemed terrific, it had but little effect, on account of the great depression of fire, which made the angle with the plain we were crossing so great that the zone of danger from each shot was very narrow." Private Levi Wagner agreed. The range was wrong, but the timing was perfect; indeed, he remembered, "the explosions took place at about the proper time to have annihilated us if they had had as accurate elevation."[20]

Some regiments lost not a single man to the cannonade; most, fewer than a dozen. There were, however, a few hits, the results of which were sickening. An Illinois soldier watched a shell spiral earthward and obliterate the head of an Indiana sergeant in the regiment directly in front of him. The headless corpse reeled backward against him.

For the overwhelming majority of Yankees, who bore witness to no such gore, fear gave way to exhilaration. "The much-talked-of moral effect of big guns was missing; there was no wavering in the lines," said Lieutenant Colonel Kimberly. "Rather, a feeling of new confidence came upon the men as they moved on, always too fast for the Confederates' depressing of their pieces."[21]

As the Federals emerged from the timber, they caught sight of the Rebel rifle pits. They looked to Lieutenant Shellenberger like a raised, yellowish streak of dirt along the base of the ridge. A grand, spontaneous cheer swept along the long Union line. Just as spontaneously, it seems, the Yankees accelerated their pace from the quick time to the double-quick time. Some regiments burst into an uncontrolled run. No one seems to have recalled who gave the original command to pick up the pace, if indeed it came from anyone. For instance, Colonel Harker said he ordered his men into the double-quick after he saw Wagner's brigade on his left do so. Within Wagner's brigade itself, the men had taken it upon themselves to surge forward. The punctilious commander of the Twenty-sixth Ohio, Lieutenant Colonel William Young, whose regiment held the right of Wagner's first line, said the regiment to his left quickened its pace without instructions. Young tried to resist the impulse but eventually gave up. "After endeavoring for some time to preserve the prescribed pace, finding my men were falling to the rear and chafing under the restraint, I quickened their step, regained my place in the line, and double-quicked," he reported.[22]

That the men would want to cover the open plain between them and

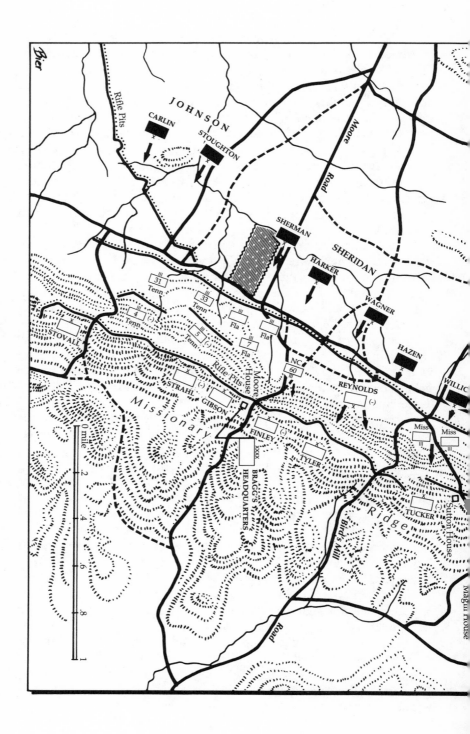

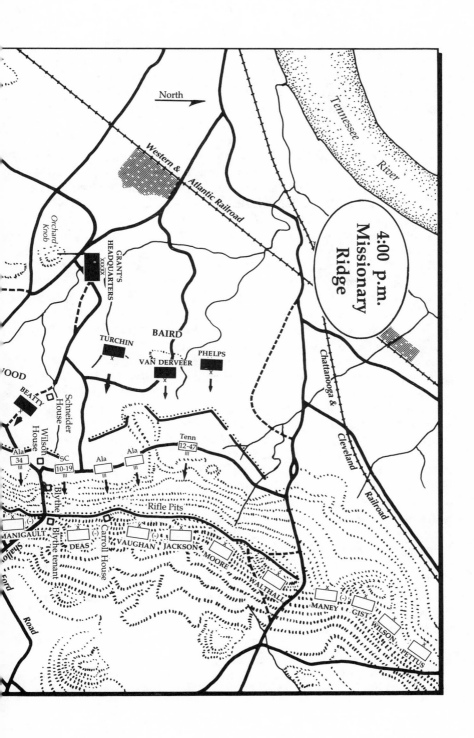

North

Tennessee River

Western & Atlantic Railroad

4:00 p.m.
Missionary Ridge

Orchard Knob

GRANT'S
HEADQUARTERS
xxxxx

Chattanooga & Cleveland Railroad

TURCHIN

BAIRD

VAN DERVEER

PHELPS

WOOD

BEATTY

Schneider House

Wilson House

Tenn
12-47
III

Ala

Ala
III

SC
10-19
III

Ala
34
III

Blythe

Rifle Pits

MANIGAULT

Blythe tenant

Carroll House

DEAS

VAUGHAN

JACKSON

MOORE

WALTHALL

MANEY

GIST

WILSON

PETTUS

Shallow Ford

Road

the rifle pits as fast as possible is easy to comprehend. Every moment they spent on the flat increased the odds that the Rebel cannoneers on the crest would correctly range them. Also, the order had been given not to fire during the advance—a typical shock tactic but one that certainly heightened the soldiers' sense of vulnerability. And, finally, said a member of the Eighty-sixth Indiana, the mere sight of the enemy works "seemed to act as an electrifier."[23]

General Turchin had no choice but to let his men loose. By the time Baird had reached him with the command to move forward, Van Derveer's brigade on his left and Sam Beatty's on his right already were well on their way. Breathlessly, Baird bade him "push to the front, and without halting to take the rifle pits; then conforming his movements to those of the troops on his right, to endeavor to gain the summit of the mountain along with them."[24]

Turchin knew he would have a hard time catching up with the rest of the line. The ground to his front was probably the worst faced by any Federal brigade. Dense underbrush blanketed most of it, Citico Creek crossed his path, and two smaller streams paralleled Turchin's flanks. Off his men went as fast as they could through the snarled thicket.[25]

The Confederate withdrawal from the rifle pits was even more ragged than the Federal advance toward them. It was a classic case of indecision, confusion, and last-minute changes in orders. After Breckinridge rode away to superintend the defense of Rossville Gap, Bragg thought better of the Kentuckian's decision to leave Reynolds's brigade at the foot of the ridge. The gap between Bate's right and Anderson's left was of deeper and more immediate concern to him than it had been to Breckinridge. Consequently, at 2:00 P.M., he directed Reynolds to return to his earlier place in the line on the crest. A seemingly reasonable command, it ignored one cardinal fact: Reynolds's position at the foot of Missionary Ridge did not correspond precisely to the gap above him. His brigade was stretched across the front of Bate's division; so, when Reynolds's men started up the slope, half of them made for Bate's entrenchments rather than the gap to Bate's right that they were to have filled. The Sixtieth North Carolina, which had held the left of Reynolds's line, stumbled into the trenches of Finley's troops, "breaking and throwing [them] into slight confusion as they passed through," complained Bate. Bits of other regiments retired with the Sixtieth and were reorganized behind Finley astride the Moore road. To plug the gap between Bate and Anderson, Reynolds found himself with fewer than half his troops.[26]

The removal of Reynolds from the foot of Missionary Ridge revealed the utter bankruptcy of Bragg and Breckinridge's improvised scheme for the defense of the center. First and foremost, the timing was terrible. Reynolds abandoned the rifle pits at precisely the instant the Federals burst forth, cheering and running, from the timber to his front. The sight of Rebels fleeing without firing a shot excited the soldiers of Hazen's, Wagner's, and the left regiments of Harker's brigades, who were bearing down on Reynolds's front. Although still three hundred yards away from the enemy, Levi Wagner of the First Ohio watched in delight as the Rebels "at once vacated their lower works and went scurrying up the ridge like a flock of sheep with dogs at their heels. And to accomplish all this we had not fired a gun." In equal measure, Reynolds's departure perplexed and disheartened the already jittery soldiers under Deas who held the rifle pits to Reynolds's right and the Floridians from Finley's brigade who held those to his left.[27]

Not privy to Bragg's and Breckinridge's order that they fire one volley and then retreat, the Floridians tried to hold their small portion of the works to the right of the Moore road. Their misguided effort cost them dearly. The right regiments of Harker's brigade swept down on them with an inevitability not lost on the defenders. "We held our fire until they were within about three hundred yards of us and then poured a deadly fire into them and made many of them bite the dust, but [we] were very few in number, merely a line of skirmishers in single rank and scattered at that. We mowed them down until they were within thirty yards of us and then we retreated up the hill," said Robert Watson of the Seventh Florida. Watson exaggerated both the accuracy and quantity of his regiment's volleys. In truth, hardly a man in Harker's brigade was hit. The Forty-second Illinois, which covered the brigade front as skirmishers, managed to keep most of the Floridians pinned down with a well-directed fire, allowing their comrades in the subsequent lines of battle to cross the flat virtually unmolested. So effective was the Illinoisans' harassing fire that dozens of Floridians were captured lying face down behind their rifle pits. For many, surrender seemed preferable to trying to scale the sheer ridge with their backs to the oncoming Federals. Watson decided to run, and for most of the way up wondered why he had: "The hill was dreadful steep and the enemy kept up a continual fire and threw a continual shower of bullets among us and I only wonder that they did not kill all of us. Many a poor fellow fell exhausted and was taken prisoner." With the skirmishers of the Forty-second Illinois following the Floridians up the slope, Watson expected to share the fate of his comrades. Burdened with a heavy knapsack, a haversack stuffed with three days' rations, and a full canteen, he found each step upward a hellish struggle. "I stopped several times and took a shot at the damned Yankees and at the same time it rested me. The bullets flew around us so thick that it seemed impossible to escape unhurt," he said. At one point, Watson wrestled to discard his knapsack, but could not get it off. And, in spite of its bulk, it was good that he hadn't, confessed Watson, as "a bullet struck my knapsack at the right shoulder and came out at the left shoulder, making twenty-three holes in my blanket." Watson made it. "When I reached the top of the ridge, I was so much exhausted that I fell down and lay there for several minutes to recover breath."[28]

All along the foot of the ridge, the feebleness of the Rebel resistance both mystified and delighted the Yankees. Recalled Lieutenant Shellenberger of the Sixty-fourth Ohio, which charged toward Reynolds's portion of the rifle pits: "I was commanding Company F, and was running a little in advance of my company with my eyes intently fixed upon the breastworks. We had approached near enough to see that there were no head logs, and I was wondering why I could see no heads showing above the works, when I remembered what I had read of the orders given by General Putnam to his men at Bunker Hill, and almost with a groan I mentally exclaimed: 'They are waiting till they can see the whites of our eyes.' It was a tremendous relief to discover that the breastworks were not occupied."[29]

The works in front of Stoughton's and Carlin's brigades were defended by just two regiments, the Thirty-first and Thirty-third Tennessee of Strahl's brigade. Most of the Tennesseans scampered off to a second line of rifle pits that Strahl had dug partway up the slope. The few who elected to stay and fight were killed or captured by Federal skirmishers, who seized the rifle pits entirely on their own. Giddy with his easy success, Private Billy Butler of the Nineteenth Illinois confronted a lone Rebel officer on the reverse side of the works. He loudly demanded his surrender. The indignant Confederate retorted that he would surrender only to a fellow officer. "You damned Rebel, we are all officers today," laughed Butler. "Take off that sword, double-quick, or I will let daylight through you!" The Rebel obliged.[30]

On Anderson's front, the men on the plain resisted more stubbornly, but only because they failed to follow the order to fire one volley and then retire. It was not a case of willful disobedience but sheer ignorance of the order, which Breckinridge had insisted be kept secret. As the Federals closed to within two hundred yards, Deas and his regimental commanders gave the word to fire. The volley ripped through the Yankee ranks, spilling a good number in the first line of attackers. Only in Van Derveer's brigade were the losses negligible. Wishing to minimize casualties during the advance, the quietly competent colonel had covered his front with the 185 men of Lieutenant Colonel Judson Bishop's

Second Minnesota. The first line of the brigade trailed the Minnesotans by nearly three hundred yards. Bishop, in turn, had strung out his troops with at least five paces between men, so that the Rebel bullets breezed past the Minnesotans and fell harmlessly to the ground before they could find other targets.[31]

There is no telling what a few more such volleys from Deas's line might have done to the other brigades of Wood's and Baird's divisions. Lieutenant Shellenberger, speculating from a vantage point farther to the south, thought the result might have been another Fredericksburg. But Deas and his regimental commanders yelled out the command to fall back before the smoke had cleared from the first volley. That should have been the end of it. Instead, as a horrified General Manigault observed from the crest, there "followed a scene of confusion rarely witnessed." In the terrific racket raised by their own cannon on the ridge, many company officers, none of whom had been privy to the secret order, failed now to hear it. Others thought the units around them were fleeing and refused to permit their own men to do likewise. Among the enlisted men, a few, certain they would be shot in the back if they tried, feared to make the climb. Manigault penned this portrayal of the final moments down in the rifle pits: "All order was soon lost, and each, striving to save himself, took the shortest direction for the summit. The enemy seeing the confusion and retreat, moved up their first line at a double quick, and went over the breastworks, but I could see some of our brave fellows fighting to the last, firing into the enemy's faces, and at last fall, overpowered by numbers."[32]

Only the Twelfth and Forty-seventh Tennessee (Consolidated) of Vaughan's brigade seems to have managed a coherent withdrawal. The Federals attacking the Tennesseans belonged to Phelps's brigade, which had more ground to cover than did Van Derveer's brigade to its right. The Tennesseans fell back not because of any pressure on his front, but because Deas's Alabamians had come apart on their left flank. Vaughan consequently was able to pull his troops up the ridge in a fairly even line, skirmishing as they retreated.[33] But even Vaughan's men were spent by their long climb, and at least a quarter of an hour passed before Vaughan could coax them into the entrenchments along the crest.[34]

Elsewhere in Anderson's division, the situation bordered on the uncontrollable. Not only were the men from the base of the ridge exhausted, but their wild pushing and shoving as they tried to get to the rear frightened and demoralized their comrades on the crest. Their primary desire, said Manigault, was to place "the ridge itself between them and the enemy." This, of course, was intolerable, and Manigault set up to restore order:

It required the utmost efforts of myself, staff, and other officers, to prevent this, which we finally succeeded in doing. Many threw themselves down on the ground, broken down from over-exertion, and became deathly sick, or fainted. I noticed several instances of slight hemorrhage, and it was fifteen minutes before most of these men were so recovered as to be made use of, or their nervous systems so restored as to be able to draw trigger with any steadiness.[35]

The Federals below were only slightly better off. Panting and coughing, they collapsed in the abandoned rifle pits. Compounding their exhaustion was a gnawing hunger. Despite boastful telegrams by Grant and Thomas to the War Department to the contrary, most of the men of the Army of the Cumberland were not yet on full rations. Just five days earlier, an Illinois private wrote home that he would spend four months' pay on food if only he could find some to buy. The day after, the chaplain of the Fifty-eighth Indiana noted with concern in his diary: "Rations are exceedingly scarce: relief must come soon, or we will be starved out." The historian of the Seventy-fourth Illinois told of one soldier who, contemplating the forbidding heights of Missionary Ridge as the regiment emerged from the timber, sighed: "Oh, hell, boys, there is no use to try that on an empty stomach," then turned back into the woods and complacently watched the rest make the effort.[36]

The skirmishers got to the rifle pits first. In about ten minutes the first-line regiments of each brigade joined them, creating a momentary jumble of jaded bluecoats two miles long. Brigade commanders halted their subsequent lines out on the flat. They did so reluctantly, understanding that the Rebel artillery fire, until then ineffectual, would improve in accuracy with each minute their men lay in the open.

Meanwhile, the rifle pits themselves were proving death traps. As soon as the last of their comrades cleared their front, the Confederates on the crest began sending volleys down into the midst of the clustered Yankees. Then the greater portion of the Confederate artillery turned its attention from the flat to the rifle pits, changing their ammunition from shot and shell to canister. "The fire was terrific," reported Sheridan laconically. As far as offering protection, the rifle pits were worse than worthless, explained a member of Hazen's staff: "They were so constructed as to be under cover and protection of the Confederate artillery placed along the heights; and when our troops reached these rifle pits they found themselves enfiladed from both directions by a murderous cross-fire of shot, shell, and grape, which not only made the rifle pits of no protection to us, but made them, if anything, more dangerous than the open plain itself." Lieutenant Colonel Bishop of the Second Minnesota agreed: "When we got possession of the first line we found that while to the enemy, standing in a ditch on their side of the work, it was a breast high protection, to us on the other side, it was only knee high and not protection at all against the musketry and canister that rained down upon us from the crest of the ridge."[37]

So, in every mind there arose one thought: get out of the rifle pits immediately. For some commanders, of course, there really was no decision to be made; they incorrectly had understood Grant's order to be to seize the summit. For others, a continued advance at least to the base of the ridge—from two hundred to four hundred yards away—seemed the only alternative to universal slaughter. There the contours of the slope would provide some cover from the rain of bullets, and its steepness would prevent the Rebel artillerymen from depressing their cannon tubes sufficiently to hit anyone. For those whose units were near the clusters of Rebel huts that dotted the plain between the rifle pits and the ridge, the clapboard shelters offered at least the semblance of safety until further orders came.[38]

In those first critical moments after taking the rifle pits, then, Thomas's four divisions moved independently of one another. Even brigades splintered as regimental commanders instinctively took the course of action that seemed most promising.

To the headstrong Prussian, August Willich, went the honor of reaching the rifle pits first. It was probably a few minutes after 4:00 P.M. when the four companies of the Fifteenth Ohio that comprised his skirmish line leapt over the nearly empty works. The Ohioans kept running until they got to the log huts. There they scattered and collapsed for a few minutes. After catching their breath, they picked themselves up and darted to the foot of the ridge. The Rebels aimed lower, and bullets began to pepper the dirt around the skirmishers. The Ohioans then took what seemed the only rational course of action: they started up the ridge itself a few yards to the left of the Bird's Mill road to silence the enemy riflemen. Halfway up, Sergeant Alexis Cope paused to rest. Glancing over his shoulder, he was stunned to find that his little group was alone. The rest of the brigade was still in the rifle pits. "What are we going to do up here? Why don't they send us support?" he yelled over the clatter to a nearby comrade.[39]

Cope worried unduly; help was on the way. Willich had every intention of joining the Ohioans on the ridge. Contemplating the rifle pits in which his men were milling about, Willich later wrote, "It was evident to everyone that to stay in this position would be certain destruction and final defeat; every soldier felt the necessity of saving the day and the campaign by conquering, and everyone saw instinctively that the only place of safety was in the enemy's works on the crest of the ridge."[40]

Commendable sentiments, but the going would be hard. Willich had come up against a particularly tough segment of the ridge. Before him, the slope curved like a horseshoe, and his men would have to advance up its interior. That would expose both flanks to an enfilading fire from Tucker's brigade and Garrity's Battery, which had split so that one section was posted on each edge of the horseshoe.[41]

Nevertheless, Willich called together his staff to disseminate the order to charge. His adjutant went to the extreme left. He sent two aides to the other regiments of the first line. Willich himself made for the Eighth Kansas.

Virtually everyone had anticipated his command. Colonel Frank Erdelmeyer of the Thirty-second Indiana decided to advance the moment his men hit the rifle pits. Major Samuel Gray, whose Forty-ninth Ohio held the center of the front line, at first sought cover amid the Rebel shanties, then edged his men toward the base of the ridge. "The fire to which we were now exposed was terrific beyond conception, and from the position we occupied we were unable to check it by firing; our only hope was to charge the hill." Up went the Forty-ninth. On the brigade left, Lieutenant Colonel William Chandler of the Thirty-fifth Illinois told his color sergeant to fix his gaze on a two-gun section of Garrity's Alabama Battery that fumed from the second summit south of the Shallow Ford road. The regiment would guide on him toward the cannon.[42]

Sam Beatty's brigade had reached the rifle pits a few minutes after Willich. Above it loomed a high knob graced by a two-gun section of Dent's Battery. Captain Dent had placed the other two sections of his six-gun battery on a high hill north of this knob, near a ramshackle house rented out to a tenant farmer by the Blythe family. Between Dent's detached left section and the remainder of his battery there ran an improved cow path that diverged from the Shallow Ford road below the eastern slope of Missionary Ridge, coursing first northward and then due west, over the ridge and down onto the flat as far as the Wilson house.[43]

Colonel Frederick Knefler was in charge of the first line of Beatty's brigade, consisting of his own Seventy-ninth Indiana and the Eighty-sixth Indiana. He assessed the situation in an instant. "Not having received any order to remain in the Rebel works, I ordered my command to advance upon the mountain side." He aimed for Dent's detached left section. While his front line sprinted across the plain, Beatty himself fretted in the rifle pits. His left was entirely uncovered, as Turchin's brigade was still several hundred yards in the rear. Beatty shook out the Ninth Kentucky to cover the exposed flank, then sent to Wood for instructions. None came. Despairing of help and seeing Knefler already halfway up the ridge, Beatty waved forward his second line. Like Willich, he was now fully committed to an assault on the crest.[44]

On the division right, Hazen took his cue from Willich. Like Willich and Beatty, he had heard nothing from Wood. His brigade was horribly compacted—the skirmishers, front line, and second-line regiments lay virtually on top of one another in and near the rifle pits. Hazen himself hugged the ground on the extreme left of the brigade, just behind the First Ohio. The roar was deafening; no command could be heard farther than a company front. Major Joab Stafford of the First Ohio crawled over to Hazen to ask what to do. Lieutenant Colonel Bassett Langdon, who lay a few yards away, looked toward Hazen and Stafford expectantly. Hazen waved his arm frantically. Langdon got the message. He jumped up, drew his sword, and bellowed "Forward." The men of the First were happy to comply; in fact, they had been yelling at him for permission to go on. "Was a command ever more promptly obeyed," asked Levi Wagner rhetorically. "Instantly every man was on the move and going up that ridge like a herd of stampeded cattle."

On Langdon's right, Lieutenant Colonel Foy crouched panting in the trench. The soldiers of his Twenty-third Kentucky already were starting forward. "Unable to return the enemy's fire, the delay drives the men to desperation," explained one of the Kentuckians who set out on his own. Foy got up and went forward with the remainder.[45]

Behind the supine Hazen was the Forty-first Ohio. Colonel Aquila Wiley, in command of the second line, was nearby. By now, every mounted officer had dismounted—whatever course was taken, it was evident that the horses could go no farther. The animals were set loose, and most galloped rearward. But Wiley's horse, bewildered by the din, lingered about the prostrate soldiers. His hooves stomped dangerously near them. Wiley rose to turn the horse's head to the rear and drive him off. As he grabbed the bridle, a canister shot shattered Wiley's knee, and he crumpled to the ground. Command of the line devolved on Lieutenant Colonel Kimberly, who inched toward Hazen for instructions. Hazen screamed at him to advance. Kimberly assembled a few officers and men around him, and together they jumped over the logs and sprinted toward the shanties. "This movement instantly spread right and left, and the whole battalion dashed forward to the ascent of the ridge," said the Ohioan. "It was the intention to gather the men behind the shanties for a better beginning of the ascent, but this could not be done. The oblique fire of the Confederate artillery knocked the shanties about the heads of the men, while the infantry riddled them with bullets. So the start was made as it could be."[46]

Where was Wood when his division began to claw its way up the ridge? He had been riding behind the second line of the division, as doctrine dictated. He watched the first line sweep out of the rifle pits before he could issue a command to halt. When he pulled rein amid the troops of the second line, those nearest him implored his permission to go on as well. "General, we can carry the ridge," they yelled. "Can you do it?" asked the Missourian. "We can," they replied. "Men, go ahead," Wood shouted.

Wood knew he had exceeded his orders. "Speaking for myself, individually, I frankly confess I was simply one of the boys on that occasion," he later wrote. "I was infected with the contagion of the prevailing enthusiasm. I was conscious from the moment the skirmishers of my division commenced the ascent of the steep acclivity, that the movement was in direct contravention of positive orders, and that nothing but success could excuse this palpable disobedience of orders." Wood had acted rashly in pulling his division out of the line on the second day at Chickamauga, setting in motion a chain of events that ended in disaster for the army. Yet he escaped with both his reputation and rank intact. Perhaps his luck would hold.[47]

Wood's lurching and uncertain assault on Missionary Ridge was a model of parade-ground precision compared to that of Sheridan. By most accounts, Sheridan was at least five minutes behind Wood in reaching the rifle pits.[48]

Wagner's brigade hit the pits a few moments before Harker and Sherman. The works were empty; Reynolds's Rebels already were well on their way to the crest. In keeping with his assumption that Missionary Ridge was the objective, Wagner encouraged his entire brigade to push on beyond the rifle pits at the run. Atop the ridge, two batteries—those of Mebane and Stanford—hammered at Wagner's command with an accuracy uncommon among Southern artillery that afternoon. The Federals charged over the plain to the bottom of the ridge. There, momentarily safe from the cannonading, they collapsed. "By the time we reached the foot of the hill, the men having already run near one mile, and that with their blankets, rations, and eighty rounds of cartridges, besides equipment, on them, they were almost perfectly exhausted," said the commander of the Fifty-eighth Indiana.[49]

Clutching at the rough, muddy face of the ridge, Wagner's men began to take hits from Mebane's and Stanford's batteries, which were able to depress their gun tubes to a greater degree than other batteries. Phil Sheridan, who had paused momentarily behind the prone second line of the brigade to talk to Wagner, didn't help matters. Either to flaunt his contempt for the bursting shells or to steel his nerves against them, Sheridan drew out his hip flask, filled a cup with whiskey, and yelled

toward the cannoneers on the summit, "Here's to you, General Bragg."
Of course nobody except those unfortunate soldiers lying near him heard
Sheridan's toast, but the enemy artillerymen couldn't miss the sight of
a mounted officer of obvious rank and questionable sanity making such
a target of himself. They rammed home fresh charges and aimed at the
Irishman. The shower of shot missed him. "That is damned unkind,"
remarked Sheridan of their answer to his gesture. What was later hailed
as a heroic act struck the soldiers around him as sheer idiocy. Sergeant
Ephraim Wagley, in temporary command of the company of the Fifteenth Indiana behind which Sheridan had paused, recalled: "I did not
know the act was to become so historically famous, I saw, and heard,
the whole performance, but instead of thinking it a grand and heroic
act, I only wished he would quit his foolishness, drawing down the rebel
cannon on us." He did, riding off to make his feisty little presence felt
elsewhere along the line.[50]

Beside the brutal artillery pounding, there was little letup in the rifle fire. So, tired or not, the men of Wagner's brigade began to climb the
ridge. Lieutenant Colonel Young of the Twenty-sixth Ohio, who a half
hour earlier had tried to restrain his men from moving too quickly across
the flat, now found himself directing the advance of the first line upward. Characteristically, Young was determined to maintain discipline.
"I ordered my men to move slowly, advancing firing as skirmishers,
availing themselves of every shelter available, avoiding undue exposure,
but to keep a forward movement. The latter I found extremely difficult
by reason of the great exhaustion of officers and men, both behaving
with the utmost gallantry, but in a number of cases falling at my feet
completely undone." Stumbling and wheezing, Young's bluecoats
lunged in a ragged line toward a long dip in the slope, about 150 feet
up, that offered a haven from the Rebel fire.[51]

The mood sparked by Wagner's impetuous push toward the ridge was
infectious, spreading through the regiments of Harker's brigade as they
came up. Harker could not have stopped the men had he tried. His skirmishers from the Forty-second Illinois raced ahead to keep pace with
Lieutenant Colonel Young's men in their ascent. Colonel H. C. Dunlap,
commander of the Third Kentucky, which was the left-flank regiment of
Harker's front line, had been told to "conform exactly to the movements
of the troops on [his] left," and that is precisely what Dunlap did. Without waiting for confirmatory orders from Harker, the Sixty-fourth Ohio
tried to follow suit, but the men were too tired to make the climb with
Dunlap's Kentuckians, and their colonel permitted them to rest in a thin
belt of timber at the base of Missionary Ridge. Lieutenant Shellenberger
availed himself of the pause to take in his surroundings:

On reaching the timber line, we threw ourselves flat against the face of the ridge, panting for breath. Those of our men who had strength enough left to pull a trigger now opened fire on the enemy. On looking around, I could see, by the way the bullets were striking the ground behind us and barking the trees above us, that while lying close the enemy could not reach us with their fire; and on rising up high enough to peep over the top of the stump behind which I had taken shelter, I could dimly see through the battle smoke some of the Confederates rising above their low breastworks and trying to search us out. These men made good targets, with their heads and shoulders outlined against the sky, for our men hugging close to the face of the ridge. Where the Sixty-fourth went up, we were under a direct fire only.

Shellenberger was quick to acknowledge that this advantage was not shared by Wagner's brigade, which faced both a direct fire and enfilading volleys against its flanks.[52]

Like Wagner on the division left, Francis Sherman on the right faced a challenge greater than did Harker. Here the slope was sheerer. Also, troops from Strahl's Fourth and Fifth Tennessee were ensconced in the additional rifle pits that Strahl had constructed a third of the way up the ridge. Although the two regiments were stretched out for nearly a half mile, well beyond Sherman's flank and across the front of Johnson's division, their comparative nearness to the Federals gave them a distinct advantage over their comrades on the crest, many of whom were badly overshooting their targets. The Tennesseans found easy marks among the Yankees who had dropped into the rifle pits out on the plain. It was imperative, then, that Sherman seize the portion of the entrenchments to his front. After sweeping the right-flank companies of the Thirty-third Tennessee off the plain, Sherman personally started up the ridge with his lead regiments.[53]

Perhaps because of the nearer, more accurate fire to his front, Sherman had a harder time motivating his men than did Wagner or Harker. An alarming number of men from his front line either dropped behind or refused to leave the first line of rifle pits, so Sherman sent his aide-de-camp back down the slope to urge the laggards forward. At the same time, the commanders of Sherman's follow-on regiments were finding it nearly impossible to pry their own men out of the rifle pits. Admitted Colonel Jason Marsh of the Seventy-fourth Illinois: "After a very brief rest, an effort was made to move the men forward, which it was found a very difficult thing to do. The long, steep ascent in front covered with the enemy, the top lined with numerous batteries and breastworks, was well calculated to appall the stoutest hearts. It was, therefore, not strange that men required much urging to induce them to brave the danger."[54]

Sheridan himself was helping induce the men forward in his own, inimitable way. Cursing and swinging his sword, he rode along the edge of the rifle pits on a big black horse, slapping at skulkers. Despite his bravado, the Irishman was racked by doubt. Sheridan still had no answer to the question that had perplexed him when the signal guns had sounded: Had Granger meant for him to take only the rifle pits at the base or those at the top of the ridge as well? He now sent an aide, Captain J. S. Ransom, galloping back to Orchard Knob to get a positive answer. While awaiting an answer, Sheridan, like General Wood a two-star supernumerary, watched Wagner and Harker lurch up Missionary Ridge.[55]

On Sheridan's right, Richard Johnson was equally frustrated. Compared to the divisions of Wood and Sheridan, his two brigades were giving a poor accounting of themselves. Determined resistance in the first line of rifle pits by the Thirty-first and Thirty-third Tennessee, supported by an effective cannonade from Oliver's Alabama Battery on the summit, impeded Johnson's advance for a good ten or fifteen minutes. Not until the Tennesseans voluntarily abandoned the works were Johnson's men able to seize them. Stoughton's small brigade of Regulars, which had performed miserably at Chickamauga, did little to redeem itself now. Facing the steepest portion of the ridge, the Regulars edged forward tentatively, preferring the cover of the Rebel huts on the plain to the uncertainties of the slope.[56]

To Stoughton's right, Carlin was having no greater success. In the initial advance, his well-dressed lines of battle had unraveled upon crossing a deep, vine-snarled tributary of Chattanooga Creek. Precious minutes were lost as regimental commanders restored order at the edge of the flat. By the time they seized the rifle pits, at 4:00 P.M., Carlin's Yankees had neither the strength nor inclination to push on. A few made for the huts, but most clung to the rifle pits. Neither place was safe. Colonel Benjamin Scribner, in command of the second line of the brigade, made a dash for the one of the shelters, which, he said, was no more than a few clapboards laid loosely on sticks, just high enough to crawl under for protection from the dew or the sun. Scribner felt fairly secure, until the coming and going of regimental staff officers drew the attention of the Rebels to his refuge. "They directed their fire upon my shed and caused it to rattle as if in a hailstorm. Many of the bullets passed through the thin boards and rousted me out of this trap," said the Indianian. Back to the rifle pits he ran. As he dove behind the earthworks, a solid shot plowed the ground in front of him, "and had it been an explosive shell, this story would not have been written."[57]

On the Union left, Baird too had run into trouble. The brigades of

Phelps and Van Derveer—preceded by Judson Bishop's Minnesotans—reached and cleared the lower rifle pit perhaps ten minutes after Wood's division had done the same on their right. Turchin's brigade, however, was still hurrying across the flat, trying to catch up. Perhaps because the "Mad Russian" was lagging behind, Phelps and Van Derveer elected to halt their first line at the rifle pits. Both also directed their second-line regiments to lie down back on the flat. Fortunately, neither line suffered much. Vaughan's Tennesseans were still retreating, masking their comrades on the crest, so that their fire at Phelps was erratic. Similarly, those of Deas's brigade opposite Van Derveer on the summit had their field of fire blocked by fellow Alabamians clambering up the ridge. (For nearly thirty minutes, the men of Phelps and Van Derveer's front-line regiments hid behind the long mound of dirt that skirted the reverse side of the entrenchments; yet, in several units, not a man was hit.) The batteries of Waters and Scott were also having a hard time ranging the prone Federals on the flat. Colonel Milton Robinson, whose Seventy-fifth Indiana was among the commands lying in the open, called the artillery fire "harmless but annoying."[58]

Harmless or not, Turchin had no intention of stopping at the rifle pits. His men reached them even more winded than their comrades to their left, but Turchin urged them on; he would obey Baird's order to seize the crest of Missionary Ridge, with or without support. Up the log-strewn slope they went, guiding on the high knob just north of the trail to the Wilson house that was defended by the two right sections of Dent's Alabama Battery and the right regiment of Manigault's brigade.[59]

Lieutenant Colonel C. D. Bailey was delighted to see Turchin's Federals puffing up the ridge to his left and rear. At that moment, Bailey was with the left companies of his Ninth Kentucky, which Sam Beatty had parceled out to protect his flank in the absence of Baird. By then, the Kentuckians had clawed halfway up and were hiding behind some rail pens. As Turchin and his staff, who elected to stay mounted, galloped along the Wilson house trail behind their men, they ran into General Wood. Wood, who was at the foot of the ridge directly behind the Ninth Kentucky, spoke briefly with Turchin. Like Bailey, he was pleased finally to have his flank covered, and he encouraged Turchin to make the ascent. In fact, he had just sent a staff officer to coerce Van Derveer into moving.[60]

Baird, on the other hand, was more worried than pleased that Turchin was obeying his orders so assiduously. Until Baird could get Van Derveer and Phelps moving, Turchin was in grave danger of having his left flank decimated by an enfilading fire from Waters's battery, which glowered from the Carroll house knoll (later renamed De Long Point). The highest and most pronounced projection along that part of the ridge, the knoll jutted out toward the valley. The abruptness of its slope, which dropped off at a nearly ninety-degree angle, prevented the gunners of Waters's Alabama Battery from engaging targets to their immediate front, but the lightly timbered spur offered them a sweeping command of the ground up which Turchin was pushing.

At the base of the ridge, Baird spun his horse about and spurred back to the rifle pits to start Van Derveer and Phelps forward. Just as he prepared to give the order, a messenger from corps intercepted him. Baird was not, under any circumstances, to allow his men to go farther, nor to permit them to become engaged. Baird was nonplussed. Looking upward, he glimpsed two of Turchin's regimental banners, each surrounded by a handful of men, waving tantalizingly near the crest. That they would float there much longer, or that the gallant few guarding them would survive, seemed doubtful, yet Baird had no clue how to withdraw either them or the rest of Turchin's brigade.[61]

It was now 4:10 P.M., just thirty minutes after the signal guns had barked.[62] Baird, Wood, Sheridan, and Johnson all wrestled with their own worries, giving little thought to the problems of the others. Each was fighting his own battle along the long, disorderly sweep of Missionary Ridge. A guiding hand was urgently needed.

# CHAPTER NINETEEN

# ALMOST UP, SIR

BACK ON Orchard Knob, General Grant watched the divisions of Wood and Sheridan inch their way up the side of Missionary Ridge. His incredulity fast gave way to fury. "Thomas, who ordered those men up the ridge?" he barked.

"I don't know; I did not," the Virginian answered. His quiet, measured tone masked a fear that the Army of the Cumberland was about to be obliterated.

Grant sought a new target. "Did you order them up, Granger?"

"No, they started without orders. When those fellows get started all hell can't stop them," Granger replied with characteristic brusqueness.

Grant was not amused. "Well, somebody will suffer if they don't stay there," he announced.

Grant's anger subsided. He bit down on his cigar and stared quietly at Missionary Ridge, resigned to letting events unfold as they might.[1]

With his corps seemingly dangling on the edge of destruction, Granger at last showed an interest in the battle beyond the barrels of the cannon on Orchard Knob. To Joseph Fullerton, his chief of staff, he shouted: "Ride at once to Wood, and then to Sheridan, and ask them, if they ordered their men up the ridge, and tell them, if they can take it to push ahead." Granger sent a staff officer to Baird to give him the go-ahead as well.

Fullerton found Wood at the base of the ridge. No, he had not ordered his men up, Wood told Fullerton, but he "would like to know who in hell was going to stop them." Wood added, "Tell Granger, if we are supported, we will take and hold the ridge!"[2]

At that moment, Fullerton made a costly error. Instead of continuing on to Sheridan to relay Granger's approval of the attempted ascent of Missionary Ridge, he first—and needlessly—galloped back to Granger to report Wood's reply. At a minimum, Fullerton should have recognized that his detour would cost minutes, and that minutes were precious when everything was in a jumble. Especially so, since Sheridan was unwilling to commit his second-line regiments without confirmatory orders. All Fullerton's return to Orchard Knob accomplished was to give Grant a scapegoat, should he need one. "If Wood fails, by God he'll pay for it," Grant muttered.[3]

Tragically, Fullerton's mistake cost far more lives than minutes. While Fullerton galloped back across the flat to Orchard Knob, Captain Ransom hurried in the opposite direction. To Granger, the captain had reported Sheridan's inquiry as to whether the original order to take the rifle pits "meant those at the base of the ridge or those at the top." Those at the base, Granger answered. What more he told Ransom is an open question, because the captain left the knob believing that Granger wanted Sheridan's division to fall back to the first line of rifle pits. Perhaps Granger realized he had misled Ransom, because shortly after Ransom left, he told his own aide-de-camp, Captain William Avery, to go to Sheridan to repeat the exhortation he had charged Fullerton with delivering.[4]

Avery rode hard, but Ransom had too much of a head start. Ransom reached the division first. He had taken the shortest route across the flat, which brought him to the left of Wagner's second line. There he met General Wagner. Breathlessly, he told Wagner that only the first line of rifle pits was to have been carried. Wagner took Sheridan's young aide-de-camp at his word. Although his lead regiments were nearly halfway up the ridge, Wagner dispatched staff officers to pass the word to his colonels and ordered the recall sounded.

Few who heard the bugle call could believe it. "This we felt to be [a] mistake, as we could have gathered some protection from stumps and stones from the infantry fire, and the artillery, though terrific in sound, was doing our front line comparatively little damage, from the inability to depress the guns sufficiently. If we had been ordered to lie down and wait there would have been fewer casualties, and a little breath gained that would have enabled the line to move in unison," observed Private E. T. Hibbard of the Twenty-sixth Ohio. Lieutenant Colonel Young concurred with Hibbard's assessment. Only two officers and a few men had been lost in the ascent, recalled Young, and at that moment most of the rest were protected by a horizontal roll in the ridge. Though they were tired, confidence was high. Reluctantly, Young gave the order to fall back. Whether out of disobedience or ignorance, nearly a fifth of the regiment disregarded it and instead clung to the slope.[5]

Young relayed the command to Lieutenant Colonel Lennard, whose soldiers of the Fifty-seventh Indiana, as brigade skirmishers, were scattered even farther up the ridge. Lennard was sickened. "This order, though doubtless given for the best of military reasons, was very unfortunate, as then . . . the enemy's artillery could do us no harm, and his musketry but little. Most of the men obeyed the order reluctantly, as it would subject them to that murderous cross-fire which had killed and wounded so many of their comrades."[6]

Lennard was right. As the Federals broke contact and turned their backs to their tormentors, the Rebels, no longer afraid to expose themselves above their breastworks, leapt up and poured volley after volley into the retreating Yankees. Dozens fell. The survivors were taunted with gleeful shouts of "Chickamauga, Chickamauga," from the Tennesseans of Tyler's brigade. Recrossing the plain, Wagner's men took a horrible pounding from the Rebel artillery before they reached the rifle pits. By the time the last Yankee had rolled over the parapet, nearly a quarter of the brigade had been shot down.[7]

The unexpected withdrawal of Wagner startled the commanders of Harker's left regiments and made the young colonel's hold on the ridge unsupportable. The reaction of Colonel Dunlap, whose Third Kentucky lay alongside Wagner's right, was typical. His men, he said, were "almost within range of the crest, when I discovered the line to my left falling back and heard a mounted officer, whom I did not recognize, give the order to fall back." Dreading the consequences should his men be exposed a second time to the horrors of the open plain, Dunlap at first declined to obey the order. Then he noticed the Sixty-fourth Ohio, to his right, beginning to retire. Seeing that he would be left without support on his flank if he stayed, Dunlap acceded to the inevitable and told his men to pull back. Still mounted, he worked his way off the slope and galloped to the rifle pits ahead of them. "I ordered those near to me to form at the ditch, but gave no command, for in the clamor of battle it could not be heard; about forty or fifty of the regiment remained on the hillside."[8]

Lieutenant Shellenberger of the Sixty-fourth Ohio was lying in the dirt, dizzy and dazed, when he saw his commander, Colonel Alexander McIlvain, walking along the line toward him. As McIlvain neared, Shellenberger noticed the troops he had passed "rising up and running back in a straggling manner to the rear." Bending down beside Shellenberger, the colonel explained: "Lieutenant, you must take your company and go back to the breastworks." Shellenberger refused to credit his senses. "The order was so manifestly a blunder, and my social relations with the colonel were of such a character, that I ventured to violate the military proprieties by remonstrating against it," he confessed. "I pointed out how the enemy were overshooting us, and declared my decided conviction that we could inflict far more damage upon them, and with much greater security to ourselves, by remaining where we were." Shellenberger had struck a nerve. "I know all that very well," replied McIlvain with a pained impatience, "but the orders are to go back to the breastworks, and we must obey orders." Shellenberger went, but, as in the Third Kentucky, many decided to disregard the order and hold what they had won. So too did part of the One Hundred Twenty-fifth Ohio—one angry company commander simply took his forty men under an outcrop to wait out the storm while the rest of the regiment fell back.⁹

When Shellenberger and the others of Opdycke's demi-brigade who had heeded the command reached the rifle pits, they found barely room enough to squeeze in. The rifle pits, said Shellenberger, were "packed on the outside with our second line, which had stopped there, and with the men of the first line who had run back, all of them hugging the ground as closely as possible." As if to mock their discomfiture, they noticed that Walworth's demi-brigade, which had not received the order to retire, was still climbing the ridge to its right and that Wood's division, on its left, though moving very slowly, was more than half-way to the top.¹⁰

This state of affairs clearly was intolerable. Honor alone demanded a return to the front. General Wagner sent a messenger to Sheridan begging permission to make a second run at the ridge, "as I saw we must do that or we could not remain in the works, the enemy having complete control of them with his artillery." That Hazen, on his left, was within striking distance of the crest only fed his frustration. Without waiting for a reply from Sheridan, Wagner brought up his reserve regiments, the Fifteenth Indiana and Ninety-seventh Ohio. He told them to pass over the badly intermingled regiments in the rifle pits and storm the ridge. Within fifteen minutes, he had restored order sufficiently to send the rest of the brigade out over the plain—for the third time—in support.¹¹

Sheridan shared Wagner's contempt for the order that had allowed Wood to outdistance them. Watching the demoralized retreat of Wagner's brigade and Opdycke's demi-brigade, Sheridan decided to act. Even before Ransom found him, he had made up his mind to go forward again. He called over Harker and Opdycke and told them to make ready to charge. Along the rear slope of the rifle pits he rode with a staff officer, shouting words of encouragement to the jaded men. Pausing behind the One Hundred Twenty-fifth Ohio, he promised: "It's all right, boys; when you catch your breath, you can go on again." To the men of the Seventy-ninth Illinois, who as members of the brigade reserve had missed out on the first assault, he called: "Boys, when I say go, will you go?" A universal cry of "Yes" rose from the regiment. Pressing on to Sherman's brigade, he swung his hat as a signal to the commanders of the second-line regiments, which were still in the trenches, to move up. By the time Captain Avery tracked Sheridan down, his division was again on its way to the ridge, the men intent on closing the distance between themselves and Wood's division.[12]

With Wood more than halfway to the crest, Sheridan beginning his second lunge, and Baird and Johnson starting up for the first time, the assault up Missionary Ridge lost any semblance of order. The texture of the craggy, ravine-laced slope saved hundreds of Federal lives by preventing the Confederates along the summit from getting a good aim at the ascending enemy. At the same time, it made a burlesque of unit integrity among the attackers. Regiments broke up, but "the men formed and fought under any commander who was near and who was headed towards the enemy," said an Ohioan. "All regular formations were soon lost," agreed a Kansan. "Great masses of men, who had crowded together in the places easiest of ascent, were climbing the steep at intervals and vying in their efforts to be first." "In making the ascent of the ridge, the men naturally sought shelter of the ravines and avoided the backbone of the projecting ridges in order to shelter themselves, as far as possible, from the enemy's cross-fire," added another survivor. "Every man took the route in ascending the ridge that at the time seemed to him to be the easiest and safest."

At the head of each cluster of soldiers were regimental or national colors, so that, instead of one long line, the Federal assault gave the appearance of a series of arrowlike sorties. Said a member of the Twenty-third Kentucky: "Each battalion assumed a triangular shape, the colors at the apex surrounded by the strongest men, the flanks trailing to the rear." His brigade commander, William Hazen, agreed: "Not much regard to lines could be observed, but the strong men, commanders and color-bearers, took the lead in each case, forming the apex of a triangular column of men. These advanced slowly but confidently, no amount of the fire from the crest checking them."[13]

Not everyone shared Hazen's confidence. The good-natured and honest Colonel Benjamin Scribner agreed that it had become a soldier's battle—"This was their fight; their officers had nothing to do with the advance"—but he feared for the outcome. "As I assisted myself over the obstacles of the way with my heavy sabre as a lever, I would exclaim to myself, 'Good-bye, my brave boys! Good-bye; you will gain the top, but it will be your last success; it will be the last of the first brigade!' I felt like a lamb led to the slaughter, helpless and hopeless."[14]

Scribner might have been more sanguine, had he known the enemy soldiers atop the ridge were beset by problems that struck many of them as fatal. Breckinridge's generals could have recited a litany of woes. First, friendly troops continued to disrupt fields of fire, as scores of frightened Rebels from the base of the ridge were still struggling for the safety of the crest, many stumbling upward less than fifty yards ahead of the Yankees. Second, smoke blanketed the front of the defenders on the crest and settled in the ravines up which the Yankees were snaking. (General Bate's solution was to push two regiments of Finley's brigade a few hundred feet below the crest after Wagner's withdrawal, hoping they might break clear of the smoke and provide him some warning of any subsequent Yankee approach.) Third, as dozens of Federals later attested, those Rebels who did fire were badly overshooting their mark. Fear of hitting their own men, the blinding smoke, and a reluctance to expose themselves above the trenches caused many to squeeze off their shots haphazardly. Said Jeremiah Donahower of the Second Minnesota: "We had but to watch the men with rifles who had just as much difficulty in seeing our men as we had in seeing them, and we found but little trouble after one half the ascent had been made, in preventing the enemy from seeing us long enough to take sight and pull the trigger." Then there was the utter exhaustion of the Confederates who survived the climb. Manigault may have gotten most of his men into line, but Colonel William F. Tucker found a dangerously large number of his Mississippians unfit for further duty. "Many had to be carried off by the infirmary corps, while numbers of others who remained were so sick they could scarcely stand." Finally, most of the batteries could no longer depress their cannon tubes to engage the Yankees. Exasperated cannoneers resorted to hurling lighted shells down the slope.[15]

Nearer came the Federals. Puffing and perspiring, crawling on hands and knees where the incline was too steep or rugged to walk, they dragged themselves upward. Color-bearers toppled by the dozen. The noise was terrific. "Orders could not be heard ten feet, so almost all orders of officers were given by the motion of the hand or sword," said Major Stafford of the First Ohio. Among the men there was no cheering, no strength even for words of encouragement to one another. Each moved as his courage and endurance dictated. Soldiers threw themselves down behind trees stumps or fallen logs to catch their breath, then heaved forward again.[16]

Back on Orchard Knob, every gaze was fixed on Missionary Ridge. General Wilson and Sylvanus Cadwallader stood on top of an earthwork, too enthralled by the spectacle to pay heed to repeated warnings that they come down before a Rebel shell shredded them. "My own experience and observation is probably that of most men similarly situated.

Personal danger was forgotten till the excitement was over," recalled Cadwallader.[17]

General Howard told the following story, perhaps apocryphal, that circulated among the high-ranking spectators. Four soldiers were seen carrying a badly wounded sergeant to the rear. They stopped beside Orchard Knob to rest. One E. P. Smith, a dignitary from the Christian Commission, left the gathered generals and bent down beside the stretcher. "Where are you hurt, sergeant?" he asked solicitously.

"Almost up, sir," wheezed the man.

"I mean in what part are you injured," persisted Smith.

The sergeant stared hard at Smith. "Almost up to the top," he said.

Then Smith noticed the man's mangled arm. The sergeant looked at it too. "Yes," he sighed. "That's what did it. I was almost up; but for that I should have reached the top."[18]

# CHAPTER TWENTY

# CHICKAMAUGA, DAMN YOU!

P ATTON Anderson watched the approach of Wood's division with
deep misgiving. Mounted with his staff behind Manigault's brigade,
he appreciated the difficulties faced by his thin line of riflemen in the
entrenchments. "Owing to the conformation of the ridge, from which
several spurs projected along my front, affording cover to the attacking
forces, and protecting them from any but a direct fire and in some places
even from that—he was enabled to advance to within a short distance
of the crest with comparative impunity," rued the Floridian. With Willich's and Beatty's Federals a stone's throw from the brigades of Tucker
and Manigault, Anderson galloped south along the ridge, beyond Tucker's left flank and across the Bird's Mill road to the right section of Slocomb's battery of the Washington Artillery. He begged its commander,
Lieutenant J. A. Chalaron, to swing his three pieces to the right in a
desperate bid to rake the flank of the enemy. In his haste to return to
his own division, Anderson may not have noticed the strange absence
of infantry support around Chalaron's section. But both Chalaron and
Captain Slocomb, who was then with the left section a hundred or more
yards to the south, were impressed with their own vulnerability. Reynolds claimed to have rallied most of his brigade on the crest and
plugged the gap between Anderson's left and Bate's right. Nonetheless,
most of his men either had regrouped behind Bate's division or disappeared over Missionary Ridge and out of the battle altogether. Slocomb,
who traduced the "unusual timidity" of Reynolds's troops in his report,
resigned himself to holding off Hazen's brigade with his own six cannon and the handful of infantrymen his section commanders had co-
erced into making a stand beside the guns.[1]

Anderson met Tucker on his return ride. The colonel "was entirely
confident of his ability to hold his position against all odds, and so ex-

pressed himself on parting with me," said Anderson. Indeed, Tucker seemed to have the situation well in hand. "At this time the utmost coolness and composure appeared to pervade the ranks. I rode within a few yards of the breastworks and could hear expressions of confidence from the men, as they loaded and fired with the greatest deliberation." His fears somewhat allayed, Anderson galloped off to check on Deas, who was having trouble holding back the Yankees gathering in ever-increasing numbers on the precipitate slopes of the Carroll house knoll.[2]

At the foot of the ridge, General Wood endured a strain as palpable as that which was enervating Anderson; "a moment of such intense anxiety I will not probably be called to pass through again," he reflected. Wood worried that Willich's and Hazen's men would be swept off the ridge by a ferocious Confederate counterattack just before they touched the top. In fact, he had convinced himself that the enemy was about to "pour in a heavy volley, bound over their intrenchments, lower their bayonets, and come down on us at the double-quick, with that famous 'rebel yell' with which we, who were at the front, were so familiar. This, by all the rules of battle, is what the Confederate should have done." That his command could survive the onslaught seemed impossible. "Fagged and blown as the men were by the exhausting effort they had already made, they could have interposed but a feeble resistance to such a countercharge," he estimated.

Wood hardly bothered to conceal his dread. Colonel Thomas Baylor, a brash young staff officer from army headquarters, showed up to convey Thomas's reluctant approval of the assault while Wood was absorbed in his brooding. His message did little to boost Wood's spirits. "Since you are committed to this attack, go on," was all Thomas had had to say on the matter, a foretelling that Wood's luck would not see him through a second fiasco.

"All right, Baylor," answered Wood.

Baylor loitered a moment. "General Wood, I have never been in battle before during the whole of this war. I have been kept at the ordnance depot in the east, and just now have got an opportunity to go into battle, and I want to go through this battle with you," he pleaded.

"All right, Baylor, join the lines and bawl as loud as you can bawl. The men are not going now as they did when they started at the base of the ridge; I want them to think it is reinforcements coming up behind them," answered Wood, who then told his entire staff to fan out behind the lines and do the same.[3]

It is unlikely that any of his men near the crest paid much attention to Wood's deception, if indeed they heard it above the racket. Huddled in small groups, the soldiers of Willich's and Hazen's brigades looked no further than the nearest regimental officer for guidance. Willich was climbing the ridge a few dozen yards behind his men, waving his hat to inspire anyone who might glance backward but otherwise resigned to letting matters run their course. Hazen was trudging up the Bird's Mill road, close to the action but also unable to contribute much to its outcome.[4]

It was a few minutes before 5:00 P.M. The sun had dipped below the horizon and a chill was setting in. Amid the lengthening shadows, Lieutenant Colonel Frank Erdelmeyer of the Thirty-second Indiana and his men lay behind a dirt embankment that bordered the north side of the Bird's Mill road. Sprinkled among them were members of the Fifteenth Ohio who had started the day as the brigade skirmishers. Raising his head above the abutment, Erdelmeyer saw the left section of Garrity's battery and its infantry support from Tucker's brigade, blazing away at a distance of less than fifty yards. He paused an instant to let his men regain their strength, then motioned them forward. The men surged over the embankment. A bullet plowed into the forehead of the color-bearer. Climbing, crawling, and clutching branches, Erdelmeyer and his men pulled themselves to within a few yards of the Mississippians before stopping behind a roll in the ground for one final rest. There they were screened from the enemy along the crest. Tucker's Mississippians had no inkling of the force gathering just below them.[5]

Falling in on Erdelmeyer's right were the equally winded soldiers of the Sixth Kentucky and the Sixth Ohio of Hazen's brigade. Other troops trickled in to swell the ranks of resting Yankees. Junior officers and soldiers from the Sixth Indiana and Fifth Kentucky, all looking for a safe spot amid the slaughter, turned now to Erdelmeyer for guidance.

The Indianian rose to the occasion. As his men regained their wind, Erdelmeyer told them to fix bayonets. Down the line of the Sixth Ohio, officers repeated the command.[6]

The two regiments and their strap hangers rushed forward, piercing the smoke. Over the log breastworks they leapt before the startled Mississippians could fire a shot. Panic gripped the Rebels. They ran from the works by the score. Nearly as many surrendered, most of them only too happy to give themselves up. Peeking over the breastwork, one private yelled at an officer of the Sixth Ohio: "H'yer, cap'n; I want to surrender—what shall I do?" "Get over them logs to this side," answered the captain; "you'll be in the United States then." A private in Company E ran up against five other Rebels peering above the logs, tentatively aiming their rifles at him. The Yankee called their bluff. "Surrender, you God damned fools," he shouted, "or I'll shoot every one of you." They laid down their arms and started down the ridge, helping to carry wounded Federals.

The Indianians and Ohioans, who so carefully had conserved their

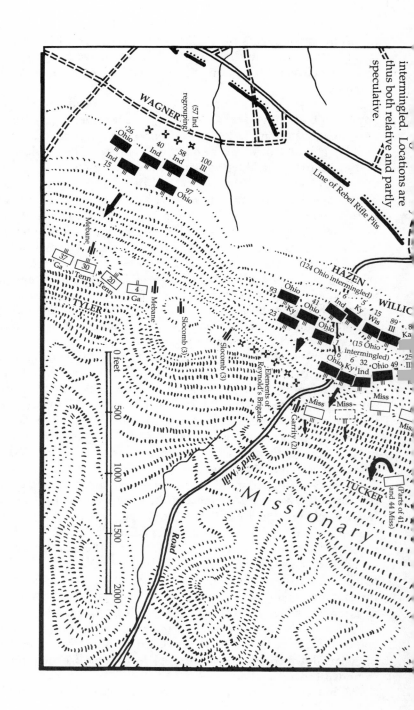

intermingled. Locations are
thus both relative and partly
speculative.

WAGNER

(57 Ind
regrouping)

'26
Ohio

40
Ind

58
Ind

100
Ill

15
Ind

97
Ohio

Line of Rebel Rifle Pits

Mebane

37
Ga

30
Tenn

20
Tenn

4
Ga

Mebane

(124 Ohio intermingled)

HAZEN

WILLIC

93
Ind

Ohio

41
Ohio

6
Ind

5
Ky

15
Wis

89
Ill

8
Ka

23
Ky

Ohio

(15 Ohio
intermingled)

25
Ill

6
Ohio

32
Ky

Ohio

Ind

49
Ohio

TYLER

Slocomb (3)

Slocomb (3)

Elements of
Reynold's Brigade

Miss

Miss

Miss

Miss

Garrity (2)

Bird's Mill

Road

M i s s i o n a r y

TUCKER

(Parts of 41
and 44 Miss)

0 feet

500

1000

1500

2000

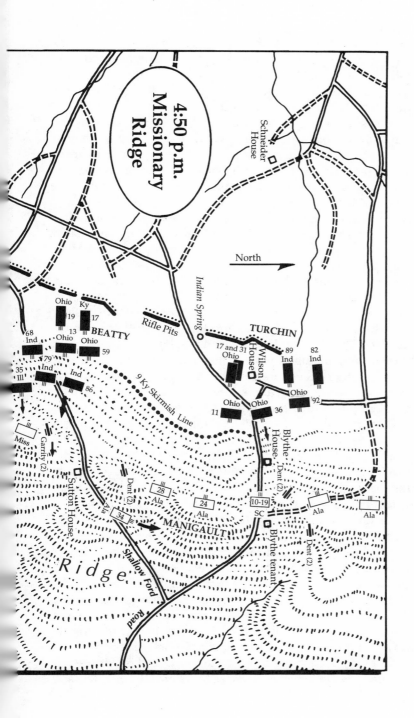

4:50 p.m.
Missionary
Ridge

Schneider
House

North

Indian Spring

Rifle Pits

Ohio
19

Ky
17

68
Ind

13
Ohio

Ohio
59

BEATTY

TURCHIN

17 and 31
Ohio

Wilson
House

89
Ind

82
Ind

35
Ill

79
Ind

Ind
86

Ohio
11

Ohio
36

Ohio
'92

9 Ky Skirmish Line

Miss

Garrity (2)

Sutton House

Ala

Dent (2)

28
Ala

24
Ala

10-19
SC

Blythe House

Dent (2)

Ala

Ala

34
Ala

MANIGAULT

Blythe tenant

Dent (2)

Shallow Ford

Road

R i d g e

strength throughout the long climb, now let loose with whoops of joy and cries of vengeful derision. "Chickamauga! Chickamauga!" they taunted their captives. When one Mississippi captain refused to start down the hill, the teenaged Ohio private who had captured him snarled "Chickamauga, God damn you" and kicked him in the behind. Down the slope tumbled the stubborn Southerner.[7]

It was strictly a losing proposition for the Mississippians: those few who stayed and fought were bayoneted where they stood; many who ran were shot in the back. "Such a confused mass I never saw, nor expect to see again," said an officer of the Sixth Ohio. "Here were officers trying to rally their men, and everywhere masses of running Rebels—fellows 'lighting out' for dear life—and our men popping them over as if they were quails. I saw many a poor fellow bayoneted, but it was all fair play. You have no idea of the spirit of our troops in making the attack. Every man tried to be the first on the hill, and such enthusiasm I never saw. It was glorious!"[8]

Colonel Tucker was among those trying to restore order and close the breach before it widened. He frantically rode back to bring up his only reserve—a few companies of the Forty-first and Forty-fourth Mississippi regiments. But before they could come into line, Erdelmeyer had reorganized part of the Thirty-second Indiana and faced it northward across the narrow ridge. A cannonball passed three feet from his head. Undaunted, he got together enough men to open a ragged flanking fire that helped drive the rest of Tucker's Mississippians from their breastworks. Part of the Sixth Ohio joined him, while the rest went after the two Napoleon twelve-pounders belonging to the left section of Garrity's battery. They shot down all the horses and swarmed around the guns. A squad from Company A of the Sixth, joined by a few men from the One Hundred Twenty-fourth Ohio, swung them northward and made ready to rake the flank of the fleeing Mississippians. The cannon were loaded and plenty of ammunition lay about, but nobody could find friction primers. A quick-thinking member of the One Hundred Twenty-fourth solved the dilemma. Yelling "Stand back," he placed his rifle over the vent of one of the cannon and fired it. The cannon roared. Others followed his example, and soon both guns were booming away.[9]

Toward the breastworks clambered the remainder of Willich's brigade. Crowding Willich's left, having scurried for the shelter of a deep ravine, was Beatty's brigade. So intent were Beatty's men in availing themselves of the ravine to avoid the horrendous fire from the crest that the brigade contracted to a front nearly as small as that of a normal-sized regiment.[10]

For an instant, the issue hung in doubt. Sixty feet short of the entrenchments, the Federals wavered—stopped by a fierce Rebel volley and their own fatigue. Piles of logs and snarled brush, cut by the Rebels to trip up the Yankees, also played a part. As the attack slowed, casualties mounted. Five color-bearers from the Thirty-fifth Illinois were shot down in rapid succession. Seeing that the slaughter of the color guard was about to demoralize his whole regiment, Lieutenant Colonel William Chandler stepped forward and grabbed the colors, just as the sixth man to carry them was hit. Thirty bullet holes had peppered the flag. Looking about him, Chandler saw the Twenty-fifth Illinois coming up on his right and the Eighty-sixth Indiana of Beatty's brigade struggling ahead on his left. Nearer still, so completely intermingled with his command as to escape his notice as an independent unit, was the Seventy-ninth Indiana, also of Beatty's brigade. Behind Chandler, the Sixty-eighth Indiana was hurrying forward from the second line to bolster his tired soldiers.[11]

This timely arrival of support restored Chandler's confidence, and he made a run for the breastworks, yelling to his men to follow. They did, and in a moment were over, grappling briefly with the Mississippians before the mad panic that had struck Tucker's left center infected his entire line. Chandler and his men, joined by eager members of the Twenty-fifth Illinois, Sixty-eighth Indiana, and Beatty's front-line regiments, spilled over the breastworks but missed the chance to bag the right section of Garrity's battery, which had limbered up and slipped away in the confusion.

The rest of Willich's command swarmed into the works. Color-bearers rammed their regimental banners into the dirt atop the parapets (survivors of every regiment of the brigade claimed their flag to have been the first to wave from the summit), and the Yankees paused to enjoy their sudden triumph. "The Rebels were completely routed and we had more fun laughing over it than we have had since the battle of Pea Ridge. They ran like sheep, and threw their guns, knapsacks and everything that would hinder them from running and lots of them ran downhill and gave themselves up," remembered one delighted Illinoisan. "It was one grand bushwhack as our men entered their trenches. They, many of them, threw down their arms and gladly surrendered," affirmed a captain of the Thirty-fifth Illinois.[12]

Tucker could do nothing. His entire brigade was on the run—the reserve companies of the Forty-first and Forty-fourth Mississippi regiments had stampeded without firing a round. In their defense, it must be said that the ridge simply was too narrow to permit the Mississippians the space they needed to back away from their foe far enough to regain their courage and regroup. Seeing no other alternative, the frightened Confederates sprinted and tumbled down the reverse slope. Tucker and his staff turned their horses and rode after them. The Confederate line had endured its first breach—a brutal gash nearly a quarter mile long.[13]

With Willich's brigade in possession of Tucker's line, the amateur gunners from Company A of the Sixth Ohio and the One Hundred Twenty-fourth Ohio swung the two pieces of Garrity's left section southward to help the comrades of their own (Hazen's) brigade. They began blasting away at the nearest Rebel cannon, which happened to be the three-gun section of the Washington Artillery under Lieutenant Chalaron, posted on a rise two hundred yards away.[14]

Chalaron turned two cannon northward to answer the challenge. There were few Rebel infantrymen along the ridge to impede his field of fire: most of Reynolds's remaining soldiers were now quietly slipping away down the eastern slope.[15]

Unbeknownst to Chalaron, he faced a nearer—and graver—threat. Between the rise on which his guns stood and the knoll formerly held by Garrity's left section the ridge dipped and curved. A handful of stalwart men from Reynolds's brigade manned the breastworks along this lower stretch of the ridge. Just beneath them, hiding behind a roll in the slope, were a few hundred men from the First Ohio, Forty-first Ohio, and Twenty-third Kentucky. The guiding presence among them was Lieutenant Colonel Bassett Langdon. As Frank Erdelmeyer had done a few minutes before along the Bird's Mill road, Langdon was availing himself of this slight bit of protection—a mere twenty yards away from the Rebel works—to rest the men of his own First Ohio and assemble enough others to make a final rush at the enemy.[16]

Lieutenant Colonel Foy of the Twenty-third Kentucky lay beside Langdon. Foy was happy to follow his lead. When Langdon told his Ohioans to fix bayonets, Foy repeated the order to his own regiment. Lieutenant Colonel Kimberly, watching from a few yards behind and to the right of the First Ohio, passed the word to his Forty-first Ohio. Scabbards clanked. Color guards huddled together. Langdon stood up to lead the charge. A bullet smashed into his face, and he fell hard on his stomach. No one moved, not even Foy. All looked hopefully for some sign of life from Langdon. Slowly, he rose to his knees. As the blood streamed down his jacket, he yelled out, "I am not killed yet!" Langdon turned his bloody face to Foy. He calmly asked the Kentuckian to select a few good marksmen and have them pin down the Rebels who were hiding behind the log from which the bullet that disfigured him had come. Foy consented, and in a moment the Confederates were burrowing for cover. Langdon stood up and waved the men on. Foy sprinted ahead. Major Stafford grabbed the colors of the First, which had passed through the hands of six color-bearers, and darted forward.

A fortuitous undulation in the slope helped shelter the Federals until they were three yards from the breastworks. By then Reynolds's Rebels had fired their final volley and had no time to reload. Over the logs climbed the Federals. "We were up the hill in a very few moments, and some of the Rebels who had been murdering our men to the last moment, rolled over on their backs and looked up in a very pitiful attitude," said Foy. Others threw away their rifle-muskets and hopped over to the Federal side for safety. Langdon braced himself on a log, emptied his revolver at some fleeing Southerners, then staggered back down the ridge, his duty done.[17]

Foy was now in charge. He halted all the men he could from his own Twenty-third Kentucky and the First Ohio at the breastworks and rallied them in a line of battle fronting southward to challenge Chalaron's cannon and a line of infantry hurrying to their succor. Lieutenant Colonel Kimberly prodded his Forty-first Ohio into line on Foy's right. Major Stafford was with Foy, still waving the colors of the First Ohio; the indomitable Levi Wagner was not.[18] He had an interest more personal and immediate than seizing Rebel cannon—to replace the equipment he had lost at Chickamauga. "At this time my mind was fully set on this task which might, or might not, be an easy one," recalled Wagner. Continued the Ohioan:

When we struck the crest I never halted, for my mind was set on some Rebel knapsack, so down the opposite side of the ridge I went. As I got part way down a Rebel soldier jumped up from behind a log in front of me and said "don't shoot, I surrender." I asked him where his gun was, to which he replied that it was behind the log. I looked back, and seeing an officer told him to go back and report to him. I might have fixed my bayonet on my gun, marched him back to the colonel and delivered him up after telling a long story of how I had captured him, but honors of any kind I never cared for. Besides was he not a voluntary prisoner? At all events, I never saw him again. I got his gun, fired out the cartridge, threw it on the ground and started in search of a knapsack. In the narrow valley at the eastern slope of the ridge I found an opportunity to make a good choice of knapsacks, as the ground was literally covered with them as though the Rebels had been perfectly panic-stricken, and in their haste to get away had divested themselves of every pound of weight they could possibly spare. After looking over a few I chose one which I thought would supply all my needs. Upon examining my prize I found a good government blanket, two shirts, two pairs of drawers, a pair of light summer pants, a night cap, a plug of tobacco, and a cornpone.

Wagner trotted back up the ridge to rejoin his company, quite pleased with himself.[19]

Wagner's company had had a brief but hard fight in his absence. General Bragg, his staff, and Governor Isham Harris of Tennessee—an implacable Bragg foe—had been on horseback behind Bate's division when word reached them of the collapse of Tucker's brigade and the growing force of Yankees that Foy and Kimberly were assembling perpendicular to the crest near the Bird's Mill road.

Bragg was dumbstruck; he had at that very moment been congratulating Bate's men for having sent the brigades of Wagner and Harker recoiling down the ridge. Now he felt keenly the absence of a tactical reserve. Lacking such, he implored Bate to spare whatever troops he could from his own breastworks to drive away the Federals and restore the break on Anderson's front. At the same time, he yanked Massenburg's Georgia Battery from its position in the line of Finley's brigade and sent it galloping toward the Bird's Mill road to help steady the wavering remnants of Reynolds's brigade.[20]

Bate already knew of the Yankees' presence beyond his flank. Just before the second charge of Wagner and Harker, one of Bate's officers called his attention to "some scattered troops a few hundred yards to my right, making their way, apparently without resistance, to the top of the hill." The Tennessean assumed them to be friendly troops who were a bit tardy in abandoning the rifle pits on the plain. Consequently, he forbade his men to fire on them. To be certain of their identity, he asked a staff officer to go take a closer look.

Bate got his answer sooner than he expected. "In a few moments, I saw a flag waving at the point in the line of Anderson's division, beyond the depression in the ridge, where a section of artillery of [Garrity's] battery had been firing and was then located." The Tennessean hoped it was a Rebel banner, but as it drew nearer he realized it was the United States colors.

Bate felt mortified but unable to respond. Wagner and Harker were on the move and almost halfway up the ridge to his front, "advancing in such numbers as to forbid the displacement of any of my command."

Bate sought out Bragg to remonstrate with him: he had no troops to spare. Bragg insisted. The Tennessean must do something to thwart the penetration. Bate thought a moment. He remembered Major Weaver's Sixtieth North Carolina and the other dispossessed soldiers of Reynolds's brigade who earlier had reassembled on the Moore road behind his left. Bate galloped to Weaver, and with the North Carolinian and his few hundred men rushed five hundred yards to the knoll where Slocomb's left section stood. Together they tried unsuccessfully to coax the men closer to the Yankees. Then Lieutenant Chalaron made an effort. He grabbed the battery flag and rode out in front of Weaver's men, offering to lead them in a charge at least as far north as his own section. "The troops did not respond," he lamented. Bate and Weaver contented themselves with throwing together a scratch line behind the guns, a quixotic move meant to halt the Federals long enough for Tucker to rally his brigade and resume his place in the line. Bate watched Weaver fire his first volley, than returned to his own command, which by then was being hard pressed by Sheridan.[21]

Weaver's infantrymen gave a sorry account of themselves. Captain Slocomb had been helping to carry armfuls of ammunition along the ridge, from his left section to his imperiled right, when a well-placed Yankee shell exploded the limber chests of Chalaron's two Napoleon guns simultaneously. Huge splinters of wood spiraled skyward. Horses collapsed in their harnesses, their bodies torn. The roar and flash thoroughly unnerved the North Carolinians, and they fled in panic. Behind them, unfurled in the mud, were their colors. Chalaron dismounted, grabbed them, and shoved them into the arms of a fleeing infantrymen.[22]

Alone now with his guns, Chalaron knew it was time to leave. He no longer had the means to resist. Captain Slocomb had brought ammunition from the left section but had forgotten friction primers. Under a pelting fire from Foy's fast-approaching Yankees, he told his men to spike the two Napoleon guns and shove them down the ridge, then try to save themselves.

They didn't quite succeed. Foy's little band was only a few yards away. Some of the gunners sprang forward and swung sponges and rammer staffs at the Federals, but they were instantly gunned down or bayoneted. "Hey you Yanks, stop your shooting," begged a Rebel cannoneer. "Get away from that gun!" yelled a sergeant from the First Ohio, waving them off. The Rebels stepped aside, leaving one gun to the sergeant and his squad and the other to a party from the Forty-first Ohio. Firing their rifle-muskets over the vents of the cannon, they began shelling Tyler's brigade on the right of Bate's line with their trophies. The first shell skimmed the ground and burst on the front porch of the Moore house, less than half a mile away from Foy's delighted Federals.

That loud knock on his headquarters door was a harbinger of doom for Bragg.[23]

# WE'VE GOT 'EM IN A PEN

CAPTAIN Slocomb was scurrying to save what remained of his once-proud Fifth Company of the Washington Artillery Battalion of New Orleans. While lugging shells to Lieutenant Chalaron's two Napoleon twelve-pounders, he had ordered the three guns of the battery's left section off the ridge while there was still time. This, he complained, "could be accomplished only by plunging down the slope in my immediate rear." Chalaron similarly had ordered the third cannon of his section off the knoll. After the loss of Chalaron's Napoleons, Slocomb and the lieutenant rode down the slippery eastern slope to discover the four other guns foundering in a hollow. Two were stuck axle-deep in mud; the limbers pulling the other two were straining up a low hill. As they began to slip backward, Slocomb added the horses from the caissons to the limber teams of all four pieces. Still the guns refused to budge. Slocomb was livid: "The men were at their posts, yet the exhausted condition of both made them unequal to the task. Could I have collected sufficient infantry their assistance would have enabled me to have saved some of these pieces." But his appeals went unheeded. Reynolds's men streamed past with no interest in Slocomb's dilemma. "The enemy were now within forty yards, and my struggling men and teams were the only targets left to the volleys. Longer delay would have encompassed in a common loss, men, horses, and guns. I gave the order to unlimber the pieces, thereby saving my men, horses, and limbers." Off Slocomb and Chalaron rode, over the rolling hills and deep ravines toward South Chickamauga Creek.[1]

Slocomb's fury at the infantry was excusable. He had lost his cannon to a mere handful of Yankees. With fifteen men of his own regiment and an equal number from other units who had fallen in with him, Major Stafford had charged into the hollow toward the guns at the double-quick. "It seemed incredible, nevertheless it is true, that our thirty men went at them with a right good will. The enemy broke and retreated in every direction, leaving their four guns and a great number of prisoners in our hands," reported an amazed Stafford.[2]

Major Stafford's surprising success was about to be repeated on a far grander scale. The division of "Fighting Billy" Bate, buckling on both flanks and pressed hard in front, was on the brink of collapse.

The pressure came first and hardest against Bate's right flank, near which Hazen, now on the summit himself, had succeeded in reforming his brigade, less the few hundred men who had turned north with Willich. Hazen drove his command relentlessly southward. Colonel Tyler tried to pull back his right-flank units to meet Hazen, but a bullet cut him down before he could put together an adequate firing line. On the extreme right of the brigade, the Fourth Georgia Battalion fronted slightly to the northeast to conform to the curve of the ridge. As Hazen's Yankees neared, the Georgians broke and ran. Their path of retreat led them toward the right flank of the Twentieth Tennessee, the next regiment in line. The Tennesseans were powerless to help their comrades or halt the foe. "Our regiment could only look on; we could not fire to the right oblique, for that would endanger our Georgia battalion," said a private of the Twentieth. On his own authority, the commander of the regiment, Major W. M. Shy, ordered his men to retire. Seeing that they were about to be enveloped, the rest of Tyler's leaderless Tennesseans began sneaking off the ridge. That only emboldened Hazen's Federals, who closed to within a few dozen yards of the Rebels. J. J. Turner of the Thirtieth Tennessee assumed brigade command, but by then it was too late. The men were scattering like chaff. "The Federals [ran] over us like a herd of wild cattle," confessed a frightened Tennessean. "The Rebels were completely routed, scuttling in every direction—utterly demoralized," an Ohio lieutenant boasted.[3]

The defection of Turner's right regiments exposed Mebane's Tennessee Battery to a withering cross fire from Hazen's Yankees on their flank and Wagner's men to their front, who had climbed to within thirty yards of the crest. Captain Mebane, however, was not about to repeat Slocomb's mistake. He wheeled his four howitzers to the right, fired a few rounds of canister at the Yankees on his flank, then limbered his pieces and bounded down the reverse slope toward the east.[4]

In the rapidly gathering twilight, the sudden blasts from Mebane's battery seem to have shaken the confidence of Hazen's men, who until then had easily swept everything in their path. They paused long enough for Colonel Turner, at Bate's command, to withdraw the rest of his bri-

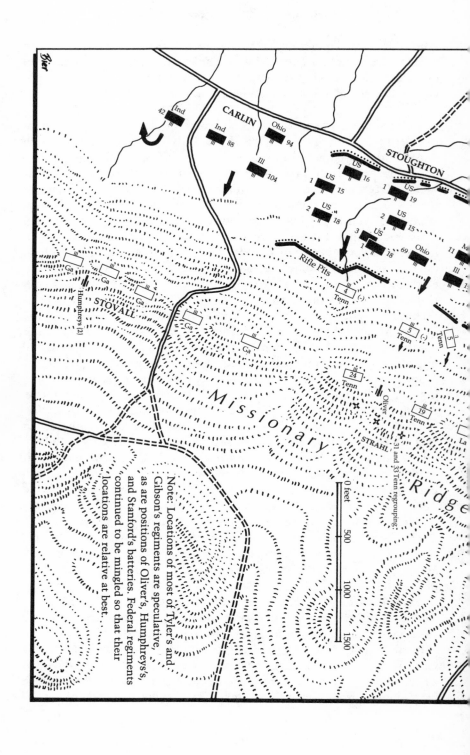

Bier

CARLIN

STOUGHTON

42 Ind

Ind 88

Ohio 94

Ill 104

1 US 16

1 US 15

1 US 19

2 US 18

2 US 15

3 US 1 18 69 Ohio

11 M

Rifle Pits

4 Tenn (-)

5 Tenn (-)

5 Tenn

5

Ga

Ga

Ga

Humphreys (2)

STOVALL

Ga

Ga

Missionary

24 Tenn

Oliver

19 Tenn

La

STRAHL

31 and 33 Tenn regrouping

Ridge

0 feet

500

1000

1500

Note: Locations of most of Tyler's and Gibson's regiments are speculative, as are positions of Oliver's, Humphreys's, and Stanford's batteries. Federal regiments continued to be mingled so that their locations are relative at best.

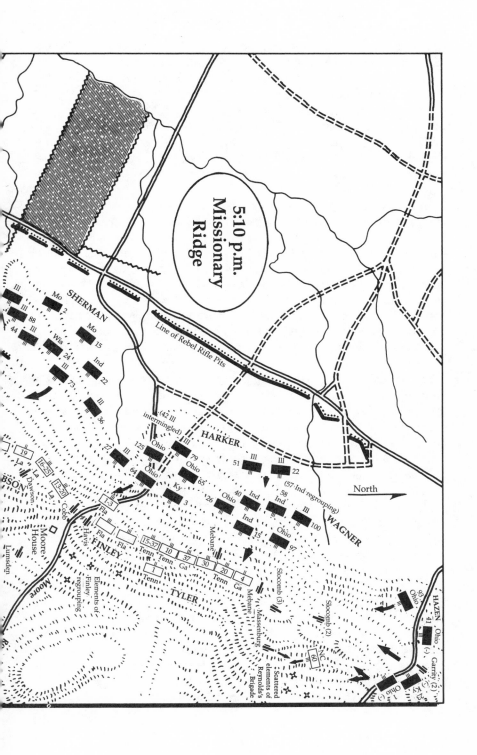

5:10 p.m.
Missionary
Ridge

Line of Rebel Rifle Pits

III
III
88 III
44 III

Mo
2
Wis
24
III
73
III
36

SHERMAN

Mo
15
Ind
22

(42 III intermingled)

HARKER

III
51
III
22

North

27 III
125 Ohio
64 Ohio
III 79
Ohio
Ky
3
65
26
40 Ind
Ohio
Ind
15

58
Ind

(57 Ind regrouping)

III
100
Ohio
97

WAGNER

19 La
La
16-23
15-23 La
Dawson
Cobb
1-3 Fla

Moore House

Havis
Fla
Fla
15-37
Tenn
10
Tenn

Lumsden
MOORE

Elements of
Finley
regrouping

FINLEY

37
Ga
30
20
Tenn
1
Tenn

4
Ga

Mebane

Slocomb (3)

Slocomb (2)

N C
60

Scattered
elements of
Reynolds's
Brigade

TYLER

Massenburg

93
Ohio

HAZEN

41
Ohio

Garrity (2)

Ohio (-)

1
Ohio (-)

93
Ky
(-)

gade in good order; one regimental commander swore that his Tennesseans marched off the ridge and into the gloaming at a leisurely pace.[5]

Turner withdrew moments before Wagner's brigade crowned the crest. Thanks to the idiotic order that had resulted in their recall forty-five minutes earlier, no brigade suffered more in ascending Missionary Ridge than did Wagner's. He lost 730 men. In the Fifteenth Indiana alone, 195 of 334 engaged were killed or wounded. Wagner lost three times more than did Sam Beatty and endured more than twice the casualties sustained by Sherman, Harker, or Willich. Only Hazen's losses of 522 came close.[6]

Having suffered so much, the disappointment of Wagner and his troops at finding the summit virtually abandoned was almost unbearable. Everyone wanted a chance to sink his bayonet into a Rebel. The soldiers' rage found expression in the report of Lieutenant Colonel Young of the Twenty-sixth Ohio. Of the final push up the slope, he wrote: "My color sergeant was already severely wounded, the senior corporal had been killed, another had fallen down exhausted, a fourth and the last seemed scarcely able to climb farther, when, feeling the moment had come for the crowning and final effort, I took the colors and led the advance of my command the remaining one hundred fifty yards into the enemy's works."

But nearly all the Rebels were gone, despite the claims of several of Wagner's regimental commanders to the contrary. Lieutenant Colonel Young shoved the colors into the dirt and spurred his horse to the far side of the ridge to try to find someone for his men to shoot at. He saw wagons bouncing through the ravine and speeding along the Moore road. He watched Major Stafford's Ohioans gobble up Slocomb's four guns in the hollow off to his left. Impatiently, he waited a moment for the men with him to catch their breath and the rest of his regiment to come up, then pushed off the ridge without orders, hoping to stampede a wagon train still in sight. But the train slipped away, and Young halted on a knob east of Missionary Ridge to allow those men yet with him to catch their breath. In a few moments, Young led his men forward again, still intent on taking the wagons. After pushing three hundred yards, Young halted again to rest his weary troops; the wagon train continued to elude him. While he contemplated further pursuit, Young was joined by the Fifteenth Indiana, which also had pushed forward from Missionary Ridge. Together the two regiments resumed the pursuit. The train eluded them, but they were rewarded by the sight of the six guns of Massenburg's Georgia Battery struggling through a ravine. As the Federals sprinted toward them, the Rebel artillerymen cut loose the horses from their limbers and rode off, leaving all six pieces to the enterprising Young.

Back on the ridge, Wagner's other regiments found some solace in two cannon they had seized from Havis's Georgia Battery.[7]

On Wagner's right, Charlie Harker and his brigade enjoyed a more stirring climax to their ninety-minute ordeal. They crossed the rifle pits where Finley's thin line of Floridians had been standing—eight feet apart by one survivor's reckoning—a minute or two before Wagner reached the summit.

Like Turner's Tennesseans, the Floridians retreated without waiting for a hand-to-hand encounter. In his haste to depart, Finley had forgotten to recall the First and Third Florida Regiment, which Bate had sent partway down the slope after Sheridan's first repulse to keep an eye out for the enemy. Among those left behind was young Charles Hemming. He had been crouching behind a rock a few yards in front of Havis's Georgia Battery, slowly going deaf as the cannon boomed over his head. Suddenly the guns stopped firing, and he heard a man nearby shout: "For God's sake, men, don't give up the field!" Hemming looked up and saw the brigade back away from the breastworks.[8]

Hemming and his comrades dashed toward the crest. "I do not think I exaggerate when I say that from seventy-five to a hundred men of the Union army, just climbing the crest of the hill, were to my right not over twenty or thirty feet away. It seemed to me that they all fired at me at once. The blaze from their gun barrels scorched my face, and one bullet barely reached my right cheek," remembered Hemming. "I was not frightened in the least. I held my gun and had my cartridge box, but I certainly was running faster than a young deer before the hounds. When I reached the decline of the hill on the other side, which could not have been more than two hundred yards from the crest upon which we fought, I saw there was no road leading down and, balancing my body with my gun, I sailed out into the air and lit at the bottom squarely upon my feet." Pushing through the brush toward his right, Hemming came out on the Moore road. The going was easier on the road, and the Floridian broke into a sprint.[9]

Harker's Federals may have been denied the chance to cross bayonets with the Floridians, but a finer trophy awaited them beyond the breastworks. There, on the narrow crest beside the Moore house, struggling to bring off their four Napoleon twelve-pounders, were the Kentuckians of Cobb's Battery. Finley's brigade had deserted them before their commander, Lieutenant Frank Gracey, was able to call up his limbers. His was a proud though ill-starred battery; already it had the dubious distinction of having lost more men and horses during the war than any other battery in the army. That count was about to go up dramatically.[10]

Raising a yell, the ubiquitous Lieutenant Shellenberger and several members of the Sixty-fourth Ohio broke into a race with Colonel Buckner's Seventy-ninth Illinois and the One Hundred Twenty-fifth Ohio for the guns. Two cannon in particular caught their attention. Shiny brass pieces fresh from an Atlanta foundry, they had painted on their trails the names "Lady Breckinridge" and "Lady Buckner." As the Federals surged toward them, most of the gunners prudently ran off. Gracey walked away "slow and sullen, as though he didn't know exactly whether he had as soon live as to die." One young artilleryman, a mere boy, sat on a battery horse and cried. Wounded in the leg, he begged the Yankees not to shoot him. Some kindly Federals lifted him from the horse and led him away. A spirited Irishman, who gripped a rammer, was at first inclined to fight the Yankees with it at close quarters. Then he thought the better of it. Tossing the rammer aside and throwing up his hands, he snarled: "This bathery was niver caphthured [sic] before."[11]

"The men went wild with joy over their splendid success," said Shellenberger. Colonel Harker sprang from his horse and jumped astride the breech of the "Lady Breckinridge," but just as quickly he jumped off—the barrel was still hot enough to fry an egg. As the excitement wore off, Colonel Buckner examined his uniform; it was riddled with bullet holes.[12]

Well could the men of the Sixty-fourth Ohio, One Hundred Twenty-fifth Ohio, and Seventy-ninth Illinois feel proud. With a little timely help from Walworth's demi-brigade and the left regiments of Sherman's brigade, they not only had seized four guns with their limbers and caissons, but had come within a few yards of capturing the Rebel commanding general himself.

Bragg—the general who lacked the charisma to inspire even the most simpleminded private—had been shuttling along the ridge, trying with almost comic desperation to rally first Tucker's broken brigade, then Finley's Floridians, and finally Gibson's Louisiana brigade, which crumbled before Francis Sherman's Federals. Near the front yard of the Moore house, Bragg sat astride his horse holding a large flag, imploring men who detested the sight of him to hold their ground. At one point, so the story was told around army campfires, he dismounted and walked among them. But Bragg was no Napoleon and his soldiers were no Old Guard. One burly private heard Bragg shouting. He threw down his rifle-musket and walked up to him from behind. Grabbing Bragg by the waist, he spun the haggard general about, yelled in his face, "General, here's a mule for you," then calmly went on his way. Even then, with all lost, no one else apparently had the nerve to physically assault his commanding general, and the angry and frustrated soldiers took their pleasure in hooting at Bragg as they passed by.[13]

With an assistant adjutant general already in Federal hands and nothing but blue to be seen on the summit, Bragg turned his horse rearward and joined the retreating throng. In any meaningful sense, the center of his supposedly impregnable Missionary Ridge line had ceased to exist.[14]

There was still killing and running aplenty going on along the doomed sector. Francis Sherman's largely Illinois brigade had endured a climb as torturous and touched with pathos and heroism as that of Harker and Wagner. With some opportune assistance from the foul-mouthed Sheridan, who cursed and swung his saber at timid troops, Sherman had managed to get his men out of the rifle pits at the foot of the ridge and on their way toward Strahl's lightly defended second line partway up the slope. While cowering in the rifle pits, Sherman's regiments had become hopelessly tangled, probably more so than those of any other brigade in the corps. "We struggled up the hill as best we could, each man for himself," reported the commander of the Fifteenth Missouri. Yes, agreed Colonel Jason Marsh of the Seventy-fourth Illinois, "the entire charge up the hill was pretty much every man on his own hook, without regard to regiments or companies." So officers took charge merely of those men who happened to be nearest them, and all ascended in a promiscuous mass.[15]

Once they got started, Sherman's men had no trouble rolling over Strahl's weak intermediate entrenchments. The Tennesseans put up a commendable fight against the Illinoisans in front of them, but far too many Federals were clambering unopposed uphill beyond their right flank. One company of the Fifth Tennessee even sallied forth in a brave but foolish charge against a column of Yankees snaking up a ravine to their right. The Tennesseans caught the enemy by surprise but inevitably were repulsed, losing a score of brave men to no good end.

By then, the regiment and its compatriots in the Fourth Tennessee were being raked by a cross fire from their flank. Watching the madness from the crest, General Stewart mercifully ordered their recall; only half, however, were left to respond to the summons.

Stumbling into the breastworks at the top, the survivors joined their fellow Tennesseans, Gibson's Louisianians, and Dawson's battery in one final, furious attempt to stop the Yankees.[16]

Sherman gave his men ten minutes to recover their strength. Then, with a rush, they swarmed out of the abandoned second trench. They quickly expended their initial burst of energy in scaling the ridge, which rose abruptly in front of them at a forty-degree angle. Felled trees and thick brush checkered the way between them and the top. Huddled in small groups around the nearest stand of colors, Sherman's men grabbed at tufts of sod or took hold of bushes to pull themselves along. Caught up in a race with their counterparts from other regiments to be the first to the summit, only the color-bearers seemed to find the strength to stay on their feet.[17]

The Rebels fought like fiends for as long as they could. A member of the Thirty-sixth Illinois said that with each step he and his comrades took nearer, the men "defending the heights grew more and more desperate. . . . They shouted 'Chickamauga' as though the word itself were a weapon." But it wasn't. Here as elsewhere, the terrain betrayed the defenders. The same sharp incline that winded the Yankees also kept the Rebels from getting a clear shot without showing themselves above their low works. So, instead, the Tennesseans lay down and hurled rocks and lighted shells randomly downhill.[18]

Over the top came the Federals. Incredibly, Dawson's Georgia Battery managed to limber up and bounce away intact. The Rebel infantry ran off, taunted by the same cries of "Chickamauga, Chickamauga!" they had so desperately been hurling at their foe.

As they did everywhere else along the ridge that afternoon, Federal color-bearers vied for the honor of planting their regiment's banner on the Rebel works first. And, as elsewhere, they paid dearly for their dedication. In the Seventy-fourth Illinois, Sergeant George Allen was hit twenty feet from the crest. Corporal S. C. Compton seized the colors and made it another ten feet before being killed. Private Frederick Hensey snatched them and finally jammed them into the breastwork.

Sergeant John Cheevers of the Eighty-eighth Illinois had outpaced his comrades the entire way up, determined to get his flag on the crest first. He was so anxious, in fact, that he vaulted into a rifle pit while it was still full of Rebels. Cheevers stuck the banner into the ground, and in the excitement of the moment was more worried that the Rebels would make off with it than that they might shoot him. Neither happened. Cheevers was invisible to the frightened Rebels, who shoved past him in retreat.

In the Twenty-fourth Wisconsin, the color-bearer was shot, the next man to take the flag was bayoneted in Stahl's breastworks midway up the slope, and the third was decapitated by a shell. Then the eighteen-year-old adjutant of the regiment, Lieutenant Arthur MacArthur, Jr., took the flagstaff. Screaming "On Wisconsin," he waved the colors high in the air. His conduct won the praise of his regimental commander. And, as his son, General Douglas MacArthur, was fond of boasting, it earned him the praise of Sheridan as well. As the younger MacArthur told it, Sheridan saw the act, dismounted beside his father, embraced him, and told the young lieutenant's troops to "Take care of him. He has just won the Medal of Honor." Perhaps. But MacArthur's act was no more intrepid than that of the dozens of long-forgotten soldiers who lost their lives carrying their unit colors to the crest. It is more likely that political connections forged during a subsequent illustrious military career enabled MacArthur finally to procure his medal, twenty-seven years after the fact.[19]

Throughout Sherman's brigade, exhaustion gave way to ecstasy. The men crowded around four guns of a Rebel battery—probably Stanford's Mississippi Battery—abandoned in the melee. "Cheer after cheer is heard," said an Illinois captain. Pumping the hand of a friend, Colonel Wallace Barrett of the Forty-fourth Illinois marveled: "Look back over the ground, think of the deadly fire that was poured upon us; it is a miracle, and this will be looked upon as the greatest military charge ever made since the world began." Even the lightly wounded forgot their agony for an instant. In the Thirty-sixth Illinois was a young private, a mere boy, who had infuriated his comrades at Chickamauga by some particularly offensive display of cowardice. Colonel Silas Miller, however, took pity on him. He threatened to court-martial the soldier, recalled the adjutant, "but permitted him to go into this fight to redeem himself, with the understanding that if his cowardice was repeated, he would suffer. He went in; stood his ground, and was wounded in the hand. He was so overjoyed that he ran to the colonel and showed his wound with all the pride he might have felt if he had been promoted."[20]

William Corzine of the Seventy-third Illinois did his commander proud as well. Before the assault began, Colonel James Jaquess, perhaps to distract their thoughts from what looked like a suicide mission, had jested his men: "Besides whipping the rebels thoroughly, and paying them up fully for what they did at Chickamauga, I want you to capture, besides many prisoners, one horse—a good one—for me. They—the rebs—got both my fine horses at Chickamauga, as you know, and I want one now in return, and another later on." As the regiment passed over the breastworks, Jaquess noticed Corzine run ahead and disappear into some bushes. A moment later, Corzine emerged, smiling broadly and leading a fine-looking gray pacing horse. "Here, Colonel, I have brought you your horse." Jaquess learned later that it had belonged to a member of Breckinridge's staff and was named, appropriately enough, Breckinridge.[21]

Most of the plundering was of the more base sort. Gnawing hunger and a thirst for revenge overcame the average soldier. The Ohioan Levi Wagner had not been alone in his quest for spoils. "We were after something to eat, and we got it too," said Sergeant Thomas Ford of the Twenty-fourth Wisconsin, speaking of the predominant feeling—besides terror—that had prevailed in the ranks when the signal guns sounded. "The first thing I did after the rebels skedaddled was to grab a full haversack and jerk it off a wounded rebel captain's neck. He was shot in the shoulder and his hand lay on the mouth of the haversack on the down-hill side. I opened it and divided its contents with my comrades in the immediate vicinity. It was saturated with the rebel captain's blood, but we ate it all the same."[22]

Some showed commendable restraint. Captain Lyman Bennett noticed a member of his company arguing with a Confederate captain he had just prodded out from behind a log. With bayonet fixed, he was poking lightly at the officer and demanding his surrender. The Southerner hopped from side to side, dodging the thrusts and snapping back: "Call an officer." "I'm officer enough for you; surrender, or I will put the bayonet through you," countered the private. Bennett intervened and took the officer's sword. "You Yankees are rough on prisoners," the Rebel bristled indignantly. His remark almost cost him his life. Bennett grew angry: "The soldier should have bayoneted you," he snapped back. "Why, sir, what do you mean," answered the startled Rebel. "I have had prisoners in my charge and never treated them in this way." "Then take off that overcoat you have stripped from some of our shivering, wounded comrades on Chickamauga," retorted Bennett. Suddenly contrite, the captain threw it aside, muttering that "we attacked them so suddenly that he forgot to take it off."[23]

Sherman's appearance on the summit, although as dramatic as that of any other Union brigade, was anticlimactic insofar as the defeat of Bate was concerned. It did, however, make an important contribution to dislodging Stewart, whose division at 5:15 P.M. was the only Confederate force left on the ridge south of Bragg's headquarters.

Stewart was holding on because Richard Johnson's two brigades were making no headway against the thread of a line held by Strahl's left regiments and Stovall's brigade. Stoughton's mixed brigade of regulars and volunteers was repulsed in its first effort at clearing out the Tennesseans from the rifle pits on the slope. By the time it took them, Sherman's men were going over the top. Stoughton rested his men, then drove hard to make up the lost ground. His effort halted abruptly. Though Strahl's troops on the crest were putting up a gallant resistance, their numbers alone were too few to stop the Yankees; what caused Stoughton to lag behind was the almost perpendicular wall formed by the ridge over the last two hundred or so feet to his front. Those few officers still on horseback left their animals in the entrenchment and with their troops crawled upward.

The maddeningly slow progress of Stoughton's soldiers gave Strahl's handful of Tennesseans ample time to select their targets. In the Nineteenth Illinois, three color-bearers were cut down in rapid succession. The commander of the color company, Captain David Bremner, chose to take them himself. "We could not spare a rifle in that battle; if I ordered a man from the ranks to take up the flag it would silence his musket; and as I carried only a sword, I took it up and bore it on." Bremner survived to count fourteen bullet holes in his coat.[24]

Stoughton might have languished on the dizzying incline longer had Sherman's success on his left not compelled Strahl finally to give up his line along the crest. Indeed, the order to depart came so suddenly that many Tennesseans, intent on the enemy before them, didn't realize it had been given until they were cut off. Five members of the Twenty-fourth Tennessee color guard fell dead in a heap defending their flag to the last. "Our squad kept shooting, fully confident that we could hold the position for some time if not definitely, unconscious of the fact that the Southern line had given way on our right and that the Yankees were sweeping down the ridge in our rear," said John Gold of the Twenty-fourth Tennessee, who was among those picking apart Stoughton's brigade. "In fact we did not know that our own regiment had left the ridge. When our captain realized what had happened the squad of eighteen or twenty was surrendered as it would have been suicidal to attempt to get away at that late stage of the fight."

Private Goodloe of the Fourth Tennessee likewise missed the order in the din. Catching sight of a man to his left falling back, he snarled: "Here's the way to gain your independence," and fired a deliberate shot at the Yankees. His comrade paused to tell Goodloe that the word had been given to retreat. Goodloe rammed down another cartridge, fired hastily, then sprinted to catch up with the man, muttering: "I'll gain my independence that way too."[25]

It was the Forty-fourth Illinois of Sherman's brigade and Stoughton's own left-front regiment, the Eleventh Michigan, that had finally made Strahl's position untenable. Reaching the summit simultaneously with their flank companies commingled, the two regiments advanced to the south along the crest. One by one they pried the Tennessee companies from their earthworks, allowing Stoughton's regiments to scale the final few yards largely unmolested.[26]

Brigadier General William Carlin was having an even more exasperating afternoon than Stoughton. In fact, the fight seems to have swirled about him and his second-in-command, the affable Benjamin Scribner, without either ever comprehending fully what was going on. Scribner had just rolled back into the rifle pit near the foot of the ridge after almost being bowled over by a solid shot when Carlin grabbed him. The Illinoisan was the picture of despair. The enemy was coming down off the ridge to outflank their right, he had learned; would Scribner take a company out and confirm the veracity of the report?

Out of the rifle pit went Scribner a second time. He and his detail combed the ground south of Carlin's flank and found only tree stumps. Jogging back to the rifle pit, Scribner beheld Sheridan's and Wood's divisions swarming up the ridge; "the whole line, as far as the eye could reach, was steadily climbing the hill." Carlin had been too distracted to notice. When Scribner pointed out the movement to him, the Illinoisan wailed, "My God, who will take the responsibility of this?" The two conferred briefly amid the bursting shells and bullets that rained down on their huddled men. They decided to let the brigade go forward as well. Explained Carlin in later years: "I started up the ridge because I saw the troops on my left going up, but who gave the original impulse it would be hard to ascertain. It was the inspiration of genius and courage and also of plain common sense."[27]

Carlin and Scribner had made the only choice possible, but their decision was irrelevant: the men already had taken matters into their own hands. "They were like a headstrong horse with a bit in his teeth, beyond holding in. The troops on the left had moved, and they did too," said Scribner. Carlin sent his mount rearward and jogged on after his brigade.[28]

The attack that Carlin was powerless to direct seemed destined to fail. On the brigade left, the One Hundred Fourth Illinois took its portion of the rifle pit partway up the slope with ease. By then, Stoughton had forced a lodgment in it, so that Strahl's outflanked Tennesseans were quick to oblige the charging Illinoisans. "As we neared it the terrified Rebels rushed up the hill in wild confusion, casting away guns, cartridge boxes, blankets and everything that impeded their speed," said an Illinoisan, repeating what had become a familiar refrain.[29]

Matters, however, were far different on the brigade right. There it was the Federals who were in danger of being outflanked, or so Colonel Anson McCook, commander of the Second Ohio, thought. As he climbed the ridge, he glimpsed the line of Marcellus Stovall's Georgia brigade, trending a half mile along the crest off toward the south. A section of Rebel artillery (probably from Humphreys's Arkansas Battery), posted with the Georgians a mere seventy-five yards away, was trained on his exposed right.

The guns boomed, and Stovall sallied forth—half seriously at best— to envelop McCook. But the sight of even a few Rebels sliding down the slope toward their flank was enough to trigger panic in the ranks of the Second Ohio and the regiments near it. "I attempted to stop it, but only partially succeeding, I deemed it best, under the circumstances, to order the men around me, composed of members of several regiments, to fall back to the works near the base of the ridge, which I did, accompanying them myself," explained McCook. Most of the rest of the brigade followed McCook's example. Only the One Hundred Fourth Illinois and a few stray companies from other regiments that had attached themselves to the Illinoisans stuck it out on the slope.[30]

At the foot of the ridge, buglers blew "Halt" and "To the Colors." The men rallied and officers restored order. Carlin came looking for McCook. None too sure of himself, Carlin readily accepted McCook's rationale for retreating. He knew he had to attack again, however, and cautioned McCook to swing his regiment obliquely to the right the moment the brigade carried the ridge and to occupy the first knoll it was able, so as to guard against another Rebel counterattack.[31]

Up went Carlin's brigade a second time. By then, Stewart had ordered Stovall to give up the ridge. Around 5:30 P.M., some thirty minutes after sunset, Carlin's Yankees carried the summit, at the cost of more perspiration than blood. McCook immediately formed a line of battle across the ridge and started southward. He called a halt astride a knoll three hundred yards beyond the brigade right and waited. Nothing happened. Where Stovall's brigade had stretched for half a mile there was now only a tattered canvas of empty trenches and discarded equipment. McCook and his men could hear the clatter of musketry and the throaty chorus of cheers rolling up from the south over the dips and knolls of the crest. The sound drew steadily nearer.[32]

General Breckinridge may or may not have been sober when he drew rein behind Holtzclaw's brigade shortly before 3:30 P.M., but what he learned after speaking with the Alabama colonel certainly would have justified at least a healthy swig. When Breckinridge arrived, Holtzclaw was huddled with a group of his brigade officers near the western crest of Missionary Ridge, about a mile north of Rossville. All were peering anxiously through their field glasses toward the southwest. For the past two hours, they had watched Hooker methodically lay bridges across Chattanooga Creek. By the time Breckinridge joined Holtzclaw, Hooker had Osterhaus's division over the creek and on the march toward the undefended gap. Not only was Rossville Gap critical as the break in the ridge through which passed the Ringgold road, an easy avenue into the Rebel rear, but in the tiny hamlet of Rossville itself were gathered substantial stores and a large supply train.[33]

Breckinridge probably had heard the echo of the signal cannon booming on Orchard Knob a few minutes later, and may have inferred that the center was about to be attacked, but for the moment, his only concern was the visible threat to his left flank. With no artillery on hand—except perhaps one section of Humphreys's Arkansas Battery—and Stovall's brigade too far away to be of any help, the Kentuckian realized he would have to fend off Hooker's three divisions with Holtzclaw's five under-strength Alabama regiments. For better or worse, during the next two hours, the former vice president of the United States and the man, after Bragg, most responsible for the fate of virtually all of Missionary Ridge south of Tunnel Hill would play the role of brigade commander at a point two miles from the vortex of the impending struggle.[34]

The Alabamians, exhausted after their bone-numbing ordeal on Lookout Mountain the night before, had been dozing under the late-autumn sun, but Breckinridge got them on their feet and into ranks. Groggy and stiff, they deployed according to the Kentuckian's wishes. The Thirty-second and Fifty-eighth Alabama, which had been consolidated under Lieutenant Colonel John Inzer two days earlier, and the Eighteenth Alabama stepped off into an open field choked with knee-high weeds, fronting west toward the valley. Breckinridge, his son Cabell, and his adjutant, Major Wilson, rode another four hundred yards farther south at the head of the Thirty-sixth and Thirty-eighth Alabama regiments.

The general placed the Thirty-eighth Alabama in line of battle fronting west on the last eminence before the ridge tapered off down into the gap. The Thirty-sixth Alabama filed to the left and faced south, forming an "L" with the rest of the brigade. Lacking the troops needed to hold the gap itself, Breckinridge sent four companies of the Thirty-sixth Alabama down the end of the ridge toward a bald knob that rose in the gap at precisely the point where the Ringgold road intersected the Lafayette road. Presumably, from there these Alabamians were to provide early warning of a Federal approach.[35]

They never got the chance. Osterhaus already had marched through the gap, brushing aside the handful of Rebels who had been guarding the supplies and wagons at Rossville, and was resting his men in some overgrown fields nearly a half mile to the east. There he had paused to report his success to Hooker and to tell him of a rare opportunity. Where his division had halted, a passable dirt road split off from the Ringgold road and ran north up and along a lower ridge that paralleled the eastern face of Missionary Ridge. A narrow valley intervened. In the receding light of the late afternoon, it looked to Osterhaus like the ideal route by which to slip unnoticed behind the Confederate left.[36]

Hooker not only endorsed Osterhaus's suggestion but deftly expanded on it. He sent Dan Butterfield to tell Cruft, who had halted Grose's and Whitaker's brigades in the gap itself, to swing north, get onto the ridge, and then "engage the enemy vigorously in case he should be met, pressing the line rapidly northward along the ridge until the enemy was encountered." To John Geary, who was closing in on Rossville, he gave orders to leave the road short of the gap and march northward along the western base of the ridge.[37]

It was a brilliant plan, the more so for its simplicity. Cruft would take the Confederates in the flank; Geary would feel for an opportunity to strike a weak point from in front; and Osterhaus would net any Rebels trying to flee the field from behind.

The youthful Cabell Breckinridge was the first to stumble upon the Federals. Coming through the gap at a gallop, perhaps in search of his father, he rode to within rifle shot of Osterhaus's reposing ranks before it dawned on him that they were the enemy. The Kentuckian stopped, whirled his mount around, and put the spurs to it, hoping to make his escape up the ridge. Unfortunately, the Fourth Iowa was patrolling the woods into which he hoped to disappear. In the murky shadows of the timber he came upon two Yankees with leveled rifle-muskets. He freely confessed his identity. Dismounting, Breckinridge walked back down the ridge with his captors, who presented both Cabell and his horse, a beautiful Kentucky mare named Fannie, to General Osterhaus. The Prussian asked Cabell a few questions but seemed more interested in his animal. After a brief conversation Osterhaus told the Iowans to take Cabell to the rear; he would keep the horse. Cabell threw his arms around the horse's neck, kissed her, and said softly: "Fannie, you have taken me through many a dangerous place, but we must part at last. Good-bye."[38]

Osterhaus mounted his prize and gave orders for the division to fall in. He formed his command in an oblique line of two echelons, facing northwest, with the left retired slightly. Williamson, with four regiments, was to edge his left flank up against the eastern face of Missionary Ridge and array the remainder of his force across the narrow valley and over the secondary ridge, linking his right flank with Woods's brigade, which would continue the line down the opposite slope of the low ridge. As soon as Cruft uncovered the Rebels, Osterhaus intended to wheel his division to the left and up the eastern slope of Missionary Ridge to support him.

Osterhaus expected an easy denouement to the afternoon. "We've got 'em in a pen," he yelled gleefully to the men of a Missouri regiment, behind which he and his staff assembled for the advance.[39]

Osterhaus's analysis was endorsed by an unlikely source. As the Federals stood in line and waited for the word to move out, a family that had been living in a cabin between the ridge and Osterhaus's division, comprehending the suddenly unenviable location of their home, darted out the door and made straight for the Thirteenth Illinois. The Illinoisans opened ranks to let them through: a man, a grandmother, a younger woman, and three children. All but one, a boy seven or eight years old, looked terrified. He, on the other hand, took in the situation quite casually and astutely for one so young. Dressed in a miniature uniform of Southern Butternut, he stuffed his hands in his pockets and, addressing the Illinoisans, sighed: "Well, I think you have got them this time."[40]

That they did. Some of the skirmishers from the Thirty-sixth Alabama that General Breckinridge had sent toward the gap spotted Osterhaus's long line as it stepped off. The incredulous Alabamians presumed they were fellow Confederates; when their company commander ordered them to open fire on the Federals, they refused. Then Osterhaus's skirmishers, taking the Alabamians for deserters, began to call out: "Come over boys; we won't hurt you." The two lines edged closer to one another, neither firing but both suspicious. At last the Alabamians saw that the uniforms of the unknown troops were blue. They let go a volley and scampered off toward their regiment.[41]

Meanwhile, the remaining companies of Alabama skirmishers had run into Cruft's column, which was ascending the ridge from the gap. It was an encounter neither side expected. Cruft and his staff, riding complacently at the head of the column in search of a spot wide enough to form line of battle, bore the brunt of the first Rebel volley. The aim of the startled Alabamians was bad, and after the bullets whizzed by, Cruft and his officers rode clear of their own front.

The Ninth Indiana of Grose's brigade sprang forward and deployed from column into line at the run. They charged the Alabamians while the rest of the brigade struggled to catch up. "It was hard enough to make the movement on that rough ground, up hill at a walk let alone on a run under fire," recalled Lieutenant Mosman of the Fifty-ninth Illinois, which somehow caught up with and fell in on the left of the Ninth Indiana. With the ridge too narrow to allow for a full brigade front, Grose contented himself with placing the Eighty-fourth Illinois and Thirty-sixth Indiana in the second line and the Seventy-fifth Illinois and Twenty-fourth Ohio in the third. Whitaker's brigade sent two regiments forward to help, but they were not needed. Indeed, even before the men of Grose's second line had dressed ranks, their anxious comrades from the Ninth Indiana and Fifty-ninth Illinois already were wreaking havoc on Holtzclaw's brigade, leading one member of the Eighty-fourth Illinois to remark: "It was more like a frolic than a battle to me. I never enjoyed myself better in my life, than while that fight was going on."[42]

At the first fire from the skirmish line, Breckinridge withdrew the Thirty-sixth and Thirty-eighth Alabama a hundred yards to take advantage of the cover afforded by some old log breastworks thrown up by the Federals two months earlier to cover their retreat from Chickamauga. Unfortunately, instead of fronting directly to the south, the breastworks ran diagonally across the ridge toward the advancing Federals, exposing the Alabamians' right flank to a withering enfilading fire from Grose's left wing. After submitting to a few volleys, the two regiments fell back a couple hundred yards and reassembled under the watchful eye of Breckinridge. Unbeknownst to the Kentuckian, who had come close to falling captive himself, his adjutant, Major Wilson, was taken prisoner during the melee.[43]

The two regiments fought on for another thirty minutes, before the sudden appearance of Williamson's left regiments coming up the eastern slope of the ridge opposite their left flank caused them finally to give way. Once again, Breckinridge barely got away with his life.[44]

Meanwhile, Holtzclaw was coming forward with the remaining two regiments of the brigade, the Eighteenth Alabama and Thirty-second and Fifty-eighth Alabama (Consolidated). Regrettably, he had chosen to move them by the left flank—the most expeditious means, but one that left them strung out and helpless in the event of a collision, which is precisely what occurred. Out of the forest came the frightened fragments of the Thirty-sixth and Thirty-eighth Alabama. The head of Holtzclaw's column fell into disorder. Men ducked and tumbled out of the way. Lieutenant Colonel Inzer tried to restore order. He snatched his regiment's colors, sprinted to the center of the ridge, stuck the flag into the dirt, and yelled at his men to form a firing line behind the loose logs of yet another line of old Federal breastworks. "The line, I must say, was a poor one," confessed Inzer; many of the men ignored his plea to fall in and instead opted for cover behind nearby trees. Still, Inzer and Holtzclaw scraped together enough men to bring Grose to a halt.[45]

Inzer had just settled into the fight when he saw Williamson's persistent Iowans flanking him on the left. They were coming up the narrow hollow between Missionary Ridge and the low ridge to the east and were less than one hundred yards away. Inzer tried a partial change of front under fire. "I never worked so hard in my life as I did at this time to rally my command," he remembered. "I stood there until every man left me, begging them to come back and fight the enemy."

Inzer was not quite ready to give up the game. He ran back a hundred yards to where the men were milling about. Among them was Colonel Holtzclaw, sitting in a daze astride his horse. He implored the colonel to help him form another line. Holtzclaw, however, was inconsolable. He told Inzer to face his men about and march to the rear in column of squads. Breckinridge punctuated the order in unmilitary but more practical terms. "Boys, get away the best you can!" he cried, then galloped north to check on the center of his sector, drawn by the horrendous racket of Thomas's assault.[46]

Few escaped. It was nearly 6:00 P.M. The lingering bit of twilight had receded before the rising gray smoke of battle. The Alabamians were hopelessly hemmed in. Osterhaus was climbing the ridge to the east. Geary's division had skirted beyond them along the western base and had skirmished briefly with the left wing of Stovall's brigade, which General Stewart, having learned of the collapse of Bate, was then withdrawing. And Cruft continued to hammer Holtzclaw relentlessly from the south.

Thanks to Stewart's ability both to recognize a lost cause and to react to it in time, Stovall came off the field in good order and regrouped on a hill a half mile to the east after dark, having lost only eighty-four men. Holtzclaw's brigade, however, all but ceased to exist. Many Alabamians, tired of trying to outrun Cruft's Federals, stopped and allowed Osterhaus's men to take them. They were, recalled a Federal, by then little better than "a whirling, struggling mass of panic-stricken men, signalling frantically to make us understand they surrendered."[47]

Most, however, kept on, only to run headlong into a very surprised Anson McCook and his Second Ohio. Finding Federals now on all four sides, nearly all the Confederates gave up. The Second Ohio took the colors of the Thirty-eighth Alabama; the Eighty-eighth Indiana got the banner of the Thirty-sixth Alabama. Further resistance was useless, Lieutenant Colonel Inzer concluded. He stuck his sword in the ground and surrendered to McCook, with whom he fell into a congenial conversation. McCook introduced Inzer to General Carlin, with whom he also had a pleasant talk.

Inzer was no turncoat, just tired and glad to be alive. He was far from alone. "They were anxious to surrender for the protection it gave them," said Benjamin Scribner. "Many officers would deliver up their swords to an orderly, or to anyone who would take them." Carlin was amused to see one of his orderlies laden with seventeen officers' sabers and revolvers. And he was deeply moved by the sight of one proud young Rebel "who halted when his officers were being taken prisoners, and came to 'order arms.' I rode up to him and asked him if he had surrendered. 'No, I have not,' was his reply. I said to him: 'Your officers have surrendered, and the best thing you can do is to surrender immediately, for you may be shot down if you don't.'" The soldier looked around him and, seeing the truth in Carlin's kind words, laid down his rifle. All told, 27 officers and 679 men gave themselves up.[48]

General Osterhaus urged his horse up the rocky incline and cantered over to greet Carlin and Scribner. Throwing his cap into the air, he exclaimed: "Two more hours of daylight and we'll destroy this army!"[49]

## SAVE YOURSELF! THE YANKEES ARE ON YOU!

ARTHUR Manigault was as serene as one could be amid screeching shells and buzzing bullets. Despite having voiced his disgust the day before over the shoddy construction and poor location of the rifle pits along the crest, he watched Thomas's massed brigades move across the valley certain that the Confederate lines would hold. Manigault's surety seemed vindicated when the Federals climbing the slope to his immediate front floundered, halted, and then melted away. "They were unable to make any progress. . . . The fire from the breastworks swept the ascent from top to bottom. A few of the more daring spirits of the attacking force succeed in gaining some fifty or sixty yards of the slope but this force was much scattered, without order and in no way dangerous," Manigault observed. As these few Yankees ducked behind tree stumps or fell to the ground, Manigault ordered his men to cease firing; he saw no need to waste ammunition against an attack that had spent itself.[1]

The South Carolinian was sadly self-deluded. The situation on his front was under control, it is true, but that was simply because the only serious opposition he had faced—Beatty's brigade—had veered to the south and channeled itself into a ravine to avoid the Rebel fire. At that moment, Beatty's bluecoats were nearing the crest with Willich just beyond Manigault's left flank. The disordered blue line that remained to distract Manigault's men was the Ninth Kentucky, which Beatty had stretched thin to close the gap with Turchin on his left, and the Kentuckians had no intention of going up alone.

Manigault was shaken from his complacency not by the impending disaster beyond his left, but by the sudden appearance of a United States flag directly beneath the precipitate, protruding southern slope of the

Carroll house spur, a quarter mile to his right. Around the flag huddled a growing cluster of Federals, men of the Second Minnesota and the right flank regiments of Van Derveer's brigade.

Although these Federals were the problem of General Deas, whose brigade defended the spur, Manigault doubted that the Alabamian knew of their existence, and it was obvious to him that Waters's battery could not depress its guns enough to dislodge them, given the abrupt descent. In the spirit of mutual support, he therefore ordered Captain Dent to turn the cannon of his right section against the massed Yankees. For good measure, he added the fire of the two right companies of his brigade. When the smoke cleared, the Yankees seemed to be gone (although they too merely had found a ravine in which to shelter themselves), and Manigault returned to contemplate his quiescent front.[2]

Manigault's gaze turned next to the left. The Federals, he noticed, were edging surprisingly close to Tucker's rifle pits. Still the South Carolinian was unmoved; Tucker "had sent word to Anderson that his position was secure, and that the enemy could not move him, [so] I thought little more of it."[3]

What finally roused Manigault was the unexpected appearance of his own Thirty-fourth Alabama—the largest regiment in the brigade—double-quicking northward behind his line. Manigault collared its commander, Major John Slaughter, and demanded to know by whose authority he had left his place in the line. By order of General Anderson, who had directed him to go and reinforce Deas, replied the major. Manigault was about to return the regiment to its rightful place on the brigade left when his adjutant, Cornelius Walker, showed up and confirmed Slaughter's story. Manigault waved the regiment on, "much annoyed at so unusual a proceeding and the want of courtesy shown me." First the foolish order to retake Orchard Knob on the twenty-third, now this. Not only had Anderson treated Manigault contemptuously twice in as many days, but this time he had opened a gap on Manigault's left that the South Carolinian could close only by stretching out his already thin line.[4]

Manigault rode to the right of his brigade to see whether Deas at least would put the Thirty-fourth Alabama to good use. He had been there fewer than ten minutes when Captain Walker galloped up with incredible news: the enemy had shattered Tucker's brigade and was swarming over the rifle pits along the North Carolinian's entire front. From where Manigault and Walker sat, an intervening knoll blocked their view to the south, so they rode rapidly toward the breach. Drawing rein atop the knoll beside Dent's left section, they saw the painful evidence of a rout. Two Federal flags waved defiantly where Tucker's Mississippians had stood. Jubilant Yankees gathered in fast-increasing numbers around the flags and the two abandoned guns of Garrity's battery. The only sign of Tucker's brigade was "the rearmost of the men, making good their escape down the back slope" of Missionary Ridge, scoffed Manigault.[5]

With his attenuated left flank in the air, Manigault saw at once that his predicament was "critical in the extreme." He sent Walker to tell Anderson, who was then behind the South Carolinian's right regiment, of the disaster. Walker rode north to deliver the message, Manigault south to his left companies to see what, if anything, he could do to salvage the situation.

Anderson greeted Walker with disdainful incredulity—his old brigade could not possibly have broken. Walker lost his temper. Perhaps the general commanding should take the trouble to ride the hundred yards to the knoll where Manigault and he had been and see the Yankees for himself. Anderson did. Badly shaken, he again called on Manigault to do the impossible. Off the knoll to Manigault rode Walker. Anderson, the captain told him, wanted Manigault to draw half his force out from behind their breastworks, form them into a line fronting south, and counterattack to drive off the Federals. By then the South Carolinian had lost both his patience and whatever residue of respect he may have retained for his division commander. "It is much more easy to give an order than to have it executed, and to do so with half a brigade what a whole one had a short time before failed to do—that is, to beat the Yankees under much less favorable circumstances—was not a thing so easily done," he recalled.[6]

Nevertheless, Manigault sent word to his left regiment, the Twenty-eighth Alabama, to prepare to execute Anderson's desperate command. He also asked Lieutenant D. L. Southwick, commanding Dent's left section, to open on the Yankees. While he waited for the Twenty-eighth to change front, Manigault watched the Federals form a line of battle three hundred yards away that he guessed contained no fewer than three thousand men. Simultaneously, the Yankees began shelling his position with the captured guns of Garrity's battery.

The shells flew over the Twenty-eighth Alabama and crashed among the astonished soldiers of the Twenty-fourth Alabama, who held the center. Although only the scattered skirmishers of the Ninth Kentucky challenged them in front, the men began to abandon their breastworks. This caught Manigault's eye, and he momentarily turned his attention from his imperiled left to the strange disorder brewing in his center. He was at a loss to explain it. "There was at the time no pressure in my front by the enemy and indeed no force of the enemy within one hundred yards of the breastworks. I can only account for the confusion here to the fact that this was the most elevated point within my line, the men here could see all that took place to their right and left, and saw that their left was threatened," he opined. In a red-hot flare of temper, Manigault told his provost marshal to shoot down any man seen heading for the rear who wasn't wounded. "But in a moment I noticed that instead of an occasional individual, groups of four, five, and ten were roving in a like manner. . . . Every effort to check the fugitives in their mad flight proved abortive." When his center snapped, Manigault gave up on his left and looked instead to saving the four guns of Dent's battery on his right, near the Blythe tenant house, where the Tenth and Nineteenth South Carolina and Deas's left regiment were still holding firm against Turchin's Federals.

Manigault had problems aplenty, but at least he was no longer troubled by Anderson. All the Floridian's staff officers were off on errands. Left with a single orderly, Anderson gave up the game as lost in Manigault's sector and made his way north toward Vaughan's brigade, the only unit in his division that had not yet given way or shown signs of faltering.[7]

Isolated by the defection of the Twenty-fourth Alabama on its right, the Twenty-eighth Alabama was doomed. The Federals whom Manigault had watched forming to drive north against the Twenty-eighth were Willich's left regiments, for whom Lieutenant Colonel Chandler of the Thirty-fifth Illinois continued to be the guiding spirit, and the Eighty-sixth and Seventy-ninth Indiana of Beatty's brigade. They surged forward and the Alabamians delivered a few ragged volleys into their ranks. Meanwhile, Beatty's second-line regiments—the Fifty-ninth and Thirteenth Ohio—had filed to the left along the face of the ridge and, taking advantage of the unexpected collapse of Manigault's center, poured into the empty breastworks behind and on the right flank of the Twenty-eighth Alabama.[8]

Hit from front and rear, the regiment disintegrated. Its collapse was hastened by the panicked firing of Lieutenant Southwick's section of Dent's battery. As Willich's Yankees lunged toward the Alabamians, Southwick's gunners depressed their pieces in a frantic effort to stave off the enemy ranks. But they lowered their guns too much, and instead let loose a blast of canister into the backs of Manigault's Alabamians, ripping several to shreds. "This action created a panic in their ranks that would have demoralized the best soldiers in the world," wrote a sympathetic Yankee, who with his comrades in Willich's left regiment spilled over the breastworks. Lieutenant Southwick was gunned down along with nearly half his men and most of his horses before he could

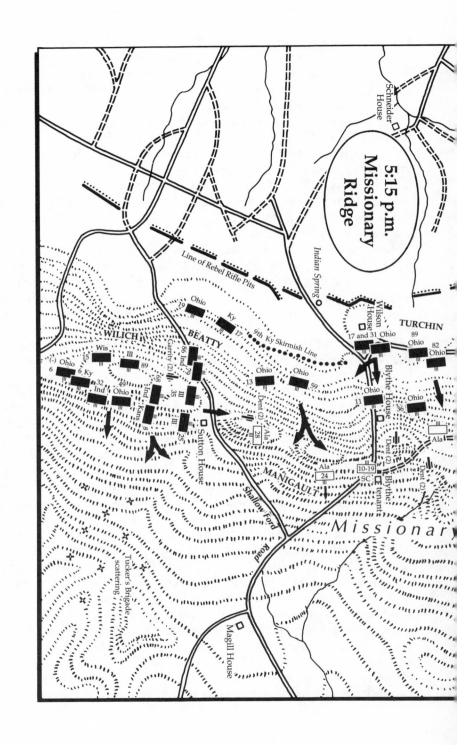

5:15 p.m.
Missionary
Ridge

Schneider House

Line of Rebel Rifle Pits

Indian Spring

9th Ky Skirmish Line

Wilson House
J. House
TURCHIN

WILICH

BEATTY

17 and 31 Ohio    89 Ohio    82 Ohio

Ohio    19

Ky    17

Blythe House

86 Ind    Ohio    Ohio    Ohio
Wis    15    Ill    Garrity (2)    79    13    59
(-) Ohio    89    68    Ohio    11
6    6 Ky    32    49    Ill
Ind    Ohio    Ind    Kans    35    Ala    Dent (2)    36
25    28    Ala    Ohio

Sutton House    Ala    24    Dent (2)
Dent (2)    10-19    Blythe
MANIGAULT    SC    tenant

Shallow Ford    Missionary

Tucker's Brigade scattering

Magill House

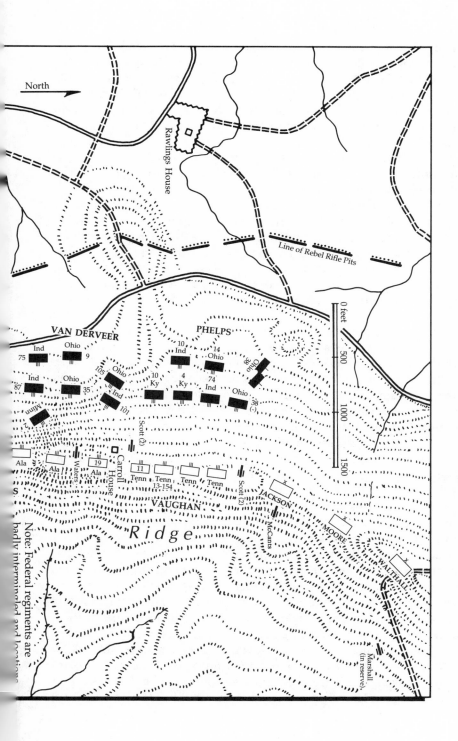

North

Rawlings House

Line of Rebel Rifle Pits

0 feet

500

1000

1500

VAN DERVEER

PHELPS

Ind
75

Ohio
9

10
Ind

14
Ohio

Ohio 38

Ind
87

Ohio
35

105

Ohio

Ind
101

10
Ky

4
Ky

74
Ind

38
(-)
Ohio

Minn

Scott (2)

Ala

Ala

Ala
19

Carroll House

11
Tenn

Tenn
13-154

Tenn

Tenn

Scott (2)

JACKSON

McCants

x

Waters

VAUGHAN

R i d g e

MOORE

x

WALTHALL

x

Marshall
(in reserve)

Note: Federal regiments are
badly intermingled and locations

limber his two Napoleons. The jubilant Federals swarmed toward the cannon, with soldiers from the Fifty-ninth Ohio, Thirty-fifth Illinois, Sixty-eighth, Seventy-ninth, and Eighty-sixth Indiana converging on the guns. While their commanders tried to restore order and continue the advance, a lieutenant from Company B of the Seventy-ninth Indiana got his men to turn the two cannon northward, load, and fire them in the direction of Dent's remaining sections.[9]

The aim of the Hoosier infantrymen was atrocious. As their shots flew wide of their mark, one of Dent's cannoneers shouted defiantly: "The old guns know whom they are shooting at and do not hurt us."[10]

It was small consolation. Southward as far as Dent could see, the ridge was alive with Yankees "sweeping over our position in pursuit." And in front of his four remaining cannon, the Tenth and Nineteenth South Carolina was beginning to leak men rearward as the soldiers of Turchin's brigade, inspired by the success of Beatty on their flank, steeled themselves for a final push at the crest. North of Dent, Deas's left regiment also began to buckle under the weight of Turchin's resuscitated attack.[11]

Dent took the only rational course left to him: he tried to escape with his cannon and caissons via the Shallow Ford road. Dent ran one gun past the gauntlet of Yankees, onto the road and down the eastern slope. But before the second and third pieces reached the road, the Tenth and Nineteenth South Carolina collapsed, as did Deas's left. Terrified infantrymen blocked the path of Dent's caissons. As Dent tried to force a way through the throng, Beatty's and Willich's Yankees picked off nearly all his horses and toppled several of his crew. Those artillerymen not shot either surrendered to the Yankees, who came whooping down on them, or ran down the ridge with the infantry. One angry young cannoneer, a mere boy, threw rocks at the bluecoats until they gunned him down. The two cannon disappeared in a swirl of blue.

With the road closed to him, Dent tried to take his last gun straight down the steep slope to his rear. Limber, cannon, and caisson bounced off the crest and slid down the slope. The caisson smashed into a tall tree stump, snaring an axle. Dent and his men worked feverishly to free it. General Manigault scraped together some seventy infantrymen to form a line to screen the cannoneers while they worked. As they strained to lift the caisson over the stump, one of the gunners yelled: "Look out, Captain." Glancing over his shoulder, Dent saw a Yankee color-bearer waving his flag only fifty yards away. On either side of him soldiers were falling in and capping their muskets. Dent warned Manigault. "Leave the gun, General, and save yourself! The Yankees are on you!" Manigault saw them too—soldiers of Turchin's Eleventh, Thirty-first, and Thirty-sixth Ohio regiments pouring over his vacant breast-works. Before Manigault or Dent could react, the Federals let go a volley. "To this day I do not understand why nearly all of us were not killed," remembered Dent. But enough bullets found their mark. A man next to Dent was shot through the jugular vein. Several fell near Manigault, around whom "the bullets whistled like a swarm of bees."

Enough was enough. Manigault yelled at his inspector general to ride for it. "I thought my chance of escape doubtful in the extreme, but determined not to be taken if I could possibly help it." Manigault and the staff officer parted company. "Putting spurs to our horses, we dashed down the rough and rugged slope at nearly full speed, and at imminent risk of our necks, the balls pattering against the trees and rocks around me like hailstones." Dent was not far behind. He too had told his men to leave the gun and run for their lives. While the Confederates fled, men from the Eleventh and Thirty-first Ohio vied with Beatty's troops for the honor of claiming the cannon.[12]

Despite the seemingly intractable jumbling of units as they neared the crest and the lack, in any meaningful sense, of a guiding hand, the Federals' assault against Anderson's division followed a discernible pattern. The Floridian's brigades folded from south to north, as Union forces pushed them from in front and rolled up their flank. First the left regiments of Willich's brigade and right regiments of Beatty's brigade, after clearing Tucker's Mississippians from their front, had turned Dent's left two cannon on the enemy and swept northward. Their pressure on Manigault's left flank hastened his collapse and eased the pressure on Turchin, allowing his right regiments and the remainder of Beatty's brigade to reach the crest. They, in turn, wheeled north and similarly used enemy artillery to cover their advance. All of the above events—from the rout of Tucker to the defeat of Manigault—lasted no more than fifteen or twenty minutes.

Just as it had Manigault, the unexpected pressure on Deas's flank doomed the Alabamian. Deas sensed his position was lost the instant the captured cannon of Dent's right sections began to enfilade his line. Then, a staff officer breathlessly told Deas that enemy colors were waving on the crest to his left, where Manigault's right had been. Deas went to have a look. What he saw confirmed his fear. "Riding a few paces, I became convinced of the painful fact [that] resistance now had ceased to be a virtue. I gave the order to fall back," he reported. His left regiments retired from the Blythe tenant house, permitting the last of Turchin's men to reach the crest. With their comrades and the inter-mingled regiments of Beatty's brigade, they regrouped and swung to the left. As they drove northward, they poured a merciless flanking fire into Deas's right regiments, which wanted only to break contact with Van Derveer's Federals to their front and escape.[13]

The fiercest fighting on Deas's line occurred on the southern face of the Carroll house spur, near where it joined the main crest of the ridge. Huddled below and inching upward were Van Derveer's men. Lieutenant Colonel Bishop and the 150 members of the Second Minnesota still in the fight continued to lead the way as brigade skirmishers.

After half an hour of hard climbing, the Minnesotans paused a few dozen yards below the log breastworks that crowned the point. Crowding them from behind was a disorganized mass of "gallant and enthusiastic men," the troops of the front-line regiments of the brigade. Despite the pressure to keep on, Bishop briefly halted his Minnesotans, determined that the regiment make the final rush with some semblance of order. While Bishop readied the men of the four companies on the right, Captain Jeremiah Donahower steadied those of the four companies on the left, including the color company.

Already the color guard had been decimated; six of eight noncommissioned officers had been shot on the way up. The flag was in tatters. A shell fragment had knocked off the color lance and a solid shot had torn out the field of stars. In command of the company was a sergeant, Axel Reed. Donahower ducked down and ran behind his four companies, urging their commanders to restore their alignment and close distance toward the shredded colors; everyone must "reach the works on the crest and cross at the same moment," he urged.[14]

With the men aligned to his satisfaction, Donahower waved his sword, and the line crept through the yellowed grass and muddy, shell-plowed earth, around blasted trees, until "at last the crest is reached and hands are placed on the lower logs." Down the line went the word "All ready! Over!" A sergeant who had braced a foot on a projecting rock extended Donahower his hand and lifted him to his side. Together they jumped across the barricade. Their men were with them. "We are inside their works and in the arena of strife we stand for just one moment," recalled Donahower of the surreal instant when the opposing lines, trying to absorb the reality of the situation, merely gawked at one another. The Alabamians, who had been withdrawing, broke the silence with a rattling volley delivered at sixty feet. Lieutenant William Hamilton and his artillerymen of Waters's battery were straining to pull off their four guns, hoping the infantry would buy them time to get off the spur.[15]

They did, barely. "We have you now," one of the Minnesotans shouted at the wounded commander of a Rebel cannon toward which he and his comrades were rushing with bayonets fixed. "Yes, but only because my thigh is broken," retorted the sergeant, who at least had the satisfaction of denying the Minnesotans the gun, as his men shoved it over the side of the spur.

Through the smoke and receding daylight, Axel Reed caught a glimpse of another cannon, just limbered, that was trying to get away. He leveled his rifle-musket at a Rebel who was swinging onto a caisson horse and fired. The man tumbled to the ground. Feverishly Reed rammed home a cartridge for a second shot. As he capped his rifle, a minié bullet struck his right arm just below the elbow, shattering the bone nearly down to the wrist. With the help of another man, Reed ripped the strap from his haversack. He stanched the flow of blood with a handkerchief and trudged off the Carroll house spur in search of the regimental surgeon. Reed was the seventh noncommissioned officer from the color company to be hit that afternoon. At the field hospital, after his arm had been sliced off and laid beside him on a table, Reed is said to have muttered to those around him: "I had rather have that, that way, than to have been whipped by the rebels up there."[16]

After ten minutes, the Alabamians broke. The Minnesotans gave chase, while behind them the rest of the brigade clambered over the logworks. By then, Lieutenant Hamilton's three remaining cannon had disappeared from view below the eastern slope of the ridge. The Minnesotans strove madly to catch them, but were deprived of their spoils. Coming along the slope from the south were Turchin's Federals, with the burly Ukrainian himself puffing along behind the Seventeenth Ohio. As they caught sight of Hamilton's teams, the cry went up, "Shoot the leaders!" Horses shrieked and fell by the dozen. "The whole outfit roll[ed] up into a conglomerate mass of men and horses," marveled a sergeant of the Thirty-first Ohio, who was in on the kill. Hamilton and most of his men ran off, but their cannon had become the property of Turchin.[17]

Cheated out of the capture, Captain Donahower led the colors and some eighty men over the ridge and into a wide ravine that trended toward the north, while Lieutenant Colonel Bishop tried to reassemble the rest of the men, who had spilled recklessly down the slope after Hamilton's guns. Once Bishop had gotten them together, he drove them north past the Carroll house. Turchin kept his men moving north as well on the east side of the ridge, while back up on the spur, Van Derveer was sorting out his front-line regiments. He too intended to form a line of battle perpendicular to the crest and charge north.[18]

Turchin, Van Derveer, Donahower, and Bishop all were heading toward the last of Anderson's brigades still clinging to the crest behind its breastworks: the four Tennessee regiments of Brigadier General Alfred Vaughan. "A better officer and nicer gentleman never lived," wrote his inspector general. "I would rather be with him than any man I know of."[19]

The thirty-three-year-old Tennessean was about to have that estimate tested. General Anderson, who was with him, clung to his hope of hurling the Yankees off the ridge. During his ride from Manigault's doomed line to that of Vaughan, the Floridian had paused to try to help Deas restore order to his crumbling brigade. He failed, but did manage to gather about him some 150 men from the Nineteenth Alabama. These he now handed over to Vaughan, along with orders to retake the Carroll house spur.[20]

To Vaughan, who was holding off Phelps's Federals to his front with little difficulty and who had not seen Anderson's quixotic side the way Manigault had, the order did not seem unreasonable. He at once commanded the Eleventh Tennessee to pull out from behind the breastworks and, with the survivors of the Nineteenth Alabama, charge toward the spur.

They barely had gotten started when they collided with the Second Minnesota and Turchin's brigade. In the uncertain light of the late afternoon, both sides felt confused and outnumbered. "We soon found that our mixed up line had its hands full," said a surprised soldier from Turchin's brigade. So too did the commander of the Eleventh Tennessee, who called to Vaughan for help.[21]

Vaughan responded promptly, peeling away a second regiment, the Thirteenth and One Hundred Fifty-fourth Tennessee, from the entrenchments. Over on the Carroll house spur, Van Derveer was feeding troops into the fray as rapidly as they could be brought onto the summit. He directed the One Hundred First Indiana forward on the left of Bishop's detachment and the Thirty-fifth Ohio down into the swale to the right of Donahower's band of Minnesotans. Before reinforcements could reach them, the Eleventh Tennessee was overwhelmed by the Federals, who were again on the move. The majors of both the Eleventh and Thirteenth Tennessee were shot from their saddles. Vaughan, realizing the impossibility of checking an enemy "who came in overwhelming numbers," withdrew his two regiments out of range.

Despite the presence of Phelps on his front, Vaughan pulled another regiment from the breastworks and launched a second counterattack at Van Derveer and Turchin. The two lines blazed away at a hundred yards until the Tennesseans ran out of ammunition. Vaughan conceded the contest, retreating by the left flank off Missionary Ridge. So too, finally, did Anderson, who rode away with the Tennesseans.[22]

Unfortunately, in their zeal to defeat the enemy that was flanking them, Anderson and Vaughan had neglected to provide for the security of either section of Scott's Tennessee Battery, both of which continued to blaze away with four guns at Phelps's brigade. Suddenly, the few infantrymen in the trenches in front of the left section broke and streamed past its position. Since none of Phelps's Yankees had evinced a desire to charge the crest, the Tennessee artillerymen stood by their pieces. It was a brave act but a grave miscalculation. Through the tall grass to their left and rear came the Second Minnesota and Thirty-fifth Ohio, the Minnesotans whooping with delight at having a second chance to capture Rebel cannon. The Yankees opened fire, horses fell in their harnesses, and the artillerymen scattered. The right section was overrun moments later, and three of the four guns of the battery were left to the enemy.[23]

The loss of Scott's battery was the pathetic denouement to the battle for the Confederate center and right. As twilight deepened into a purple and gun-smoke gray darkness, every unit of Anderson's, Bate's, and Stewart's divisions was either tentatively reforming among the innumerable foothills and low ridges east of Missionary Ridge or else in headlong retreat toward Chickamauga Station. Only Cheatham's and Cleburne's divisions of Hardee's right wing remained of what Bragg and Breckinridge had deemed to be an impregnable line. And, with the Federals still on the move north, the future of these two divisions looked bleak.

# WE ARE FIGHTING THE WORLD

FRANK Cheatham was a study in contradictions. In combat, he seemed to have only very good or very bad days. No one questioned his courage or competence. What infuriated Bragg and troubled even Cheatham's most loyal Tennessee lieutenants was his notoriously heavy drinking. When sober, no division commander in the Army of Tennessee—save Cleburne—fought better. But if a battle happened to coincide with a binge, Cheatham's drink-fogged judgment led him to erratic and often capricious acts.

Thankfully for the men of his own and Cleburne's divisions, Cheatham was cold sober here on Missionary Ridge—fully cognizant of the disaster unfolding to his left. Shortly after Thomas's long line started across the valley, Cheatham had surmised correctly that few if any of the attacking Federals would strike his portion of the line on the ridge. Consequently, he rode to the extreme left of his division to watch the fight unfold on Anderson's front. The Tennessean sat behind Jackson's brigade. To Jackson's right were the decimated commands of Moore and Walthall. The moment Vaughan began to flounder, Cheatham ordered Jackson and Moore to change front to the left. Only McCants's Florida Battery stayed put to hold the line against Phelps's left regiments, which, contrary to Cheatham's earlier estimate, were climbing the ridge in front of Jackson.[1]

Despite this threat to his front, Cheatham's instincts were sound. The execution of his order, however, left much to be desired. Jackson got his brigade out from behind its breastworks and in line of battle across the ridge in relatively good order while the Yankees were still at least 150 yards away. As they drew closer, however, Jackson's men grew panicky. At the first Federal fire they turned and shoved their way through Moore's Alabamians, who at that moment were double-quicking by the flank behind Jackson in an effort to come up on his left. Still fuming over Jackson's inept handling of the division atop Lookout Mountain two days earlier, Moore eyed his former superior's crumbling ranks with grim satisfaction, despite the havoc it temporarily wrought on his own brigade. As his men filed to the left behind Jackson, Moore noticed "a lank, six-foot Georgia 'cracker' . . . gazing over his front file's shoulder with open mouth and bulging eyes. Just at that moment a pretty heavy volley was poured into us. This was more than the Georgian could stand. He wheeled about, rushed through our ranks with gun at a trail, went down a slope half-bent, looking back over one shoulder exclaiming: 'Good Lordy, how they is shootin!' In a few yards he reached a large fallen tree, and as he tumbled over it headforemost he was heard to cry out: 'Now I lay me down to sleep.'"[2]

In the fast-fading light, the Federals failed to realize their opportunity, and Cheatham and Jackson managed to restore order and drive their men back into line. By the time the enemy had closed to one hundred yards, Jackson and Moore were able to present a formidable-looking front that extended down the eastern slope of the ridge and well across the wide swale through which Captain Donahower and his Minnesotans were jogging.

One volley from Moore's Alabamians was enough to bring Donahower's little band to an abrupt halt. Squinting at the murky line of Rebels behind the rifle flashes, Donahower decided that, "standing shoulder to shoulder, [they] presented an impassable barrier to the further advance" of his ragged and winded skirmish line. He motioned to his sergeants to hold their ground while he sought help back up on the ridge.

Donahower stepped back onto the crest. Before him was a confused swirl of blue. It was Van Derveer's front-line regiments, all inextricably entangled. Somewhere among them was Lieutenant Colonel Bishop with the rest of the Second Minnesota. Although the brigade managed to return the fire of Jackson's Rebels, Donahower saw that it was going no farther and that, in its present condition, the brigade could offer him no relief.[3]

Not that Van Derveer's Federals weren't fighting hard. On the brigade left, Lieutenant Colonel William Tolles had his One Hundred Fifth Ohio whipped into a frenzy. A "lean, dyspeptic old fellow," Tolles was a martinet in camp but a soldier's salvation in combat. On the day of battle, said Lieutenant Hartzell, then in command of Company H, Tolles "grew mild and gracious." As the regiment charged up Missionary Ridge, Tolles had kept an eye out for men who showed signs of tiring— not to chastise, but to ease their burden. Mounted conspicuously on a large, coal-black horse, Tolles "in gentle pity reached down and took a gun from any lagging, panting fellow, until he had a bundle of muskets across his horse's withers, and he could scarcely reach over" the crest, continued Lieutenant Hartzell.

Once the regiment was over the breastworks, he ordered the men to lie down and engage Jackson as best they could until reinforcements arrived. While the men lay flat, he remained mounted. "He looked over us in a sort of motherly solicitude, and roared out with all the wind he had 'Keep your heads down there, men, or you will be shot.'" Lieutenant Hartzell watched the colonel closely, expecting at any moment to see him topple from his horse. When Tolles drew beside to him, Hartzell dared to suggest that he too lie down. "Lieutenant, when I want my advice from you, I'll let you know," Tolles replied stiffly. Another line officer, overcome with anxiety, rose to his feet and waved his sword at the lieutenant colonel. "Lie down," roared Tolles. "But, Colonel, you—," the subaltern began. Tolles cut him off: "It is my duty to stand, and your duty to lie down!"[4]

Colonel Phelps shared Tolles's contempt for taking cover. He had dismounted at the base of the ridge and, placing himself in front of his brigade, led the men up the steep incline, lashing the smoky air with his sword and yelling for all he was worth. He had crossed Vaughan's abandoned breastworks and motioned the Tenth Kentucky into line on the left of Tolles's Ohioans. When they ran up against Jackson, Phelps decided the Tenth Kentucky could contribute more by extending Van Derveer's right flank, and so ordered the regiment down into the swale at probably the same instant Donahower was climbing out of it, looking for help. Phelps watched the Fourth Kentucky plant its colors on the crest, taking the spot abandoned by the Tenth Kentucky. The commander of the Fourth could see Phelps, still conspicuous on the summit, trying to urge forward his remaining two front-line regiments, which McCants's Florida Battery was keeping at bay just below the crest. Phelps's exhortations were lost in the racket, and in a few moments, he fell, shot down a few dozen yards in front of Jackson's line.[5]

Federal field officers seemed intent on outdoing one another in tempting fate. Shortly after Phelps dropped, General Baird was swept into the vortex of his scrambled division. Undaunted, he rode along the line, trying to restore order and calm the men while aides brought up Van Derveer's reserve regiments, the Ninth Ohio and Seventy-fifth Indiana. "Hold the hill, men," he said over and over, "the Ninth Ohio is coming." Captain Donahower flagged him down to relate his own woes; Baird responded by telling the Minnesotan to help shepherd Colonel Gustave Kammerling's Ninth Ohio into action.[6]

The recklessly brave Kammerling, whose proclivity for acting before thinking had been confirmed at Chickamauga, needed little encouragement. No sooner had four of his ten companies gotten over the breastworks than he wheeled them to the left and ordered them to open fire over the heads of their prone comrades from Tolles's, Bishop's, and assorted other regiments of the division. The sudden, well-aimed volley from the Ninth Ohio sent a shudder down Jackson's line. Kammerling kept up the pressure until his regiment had settled into place. The Confederates began to give ground. Kammerling moved toward the enemy. Baird and Van Derveer saw their chance. They fed the Seventy-fifth Indiana into the fray behind the Ninth Ohio the instant it came up. The Ohioans in turn lay down to allow the Seventy-fifth to charge over them.[7]

That broke Jackson. After nearly thirty minutes in action, the Georgians and Mississippians turned and fled, just as "the half light of evening deepened into darkness," recalled Lieutenant Hartzell. It was 5:30 P.M. With his flank exposed, Moore ordered a withdrawal as well. Both brigades fell back toward the northeast, off Missionary Ridge and up and over the next ridge to the east. Most of Phelps's brigade was on Missionary Ridge now, and his and Van Derveer's men rose to their feet and surged northward.[8]

In keeping with the pattern of the afternoon, McCants's Florida Battery was forgotten by the Rebel infantrymen in their haste to distance themselves from the charging Federals. Twenty-six-year-old Lieutenant Andrew Neal was the unfortunate commander of the battery. Neal had been intently watching the hazy blue targets in front of his battery. Their battery colors hoisted and fluttering defiantly, Neal's gunners were "giving them fits." Then a shower of balls rained down on the battery from the left. Whirling in the saddle, Neal saw the Stars and Stripes waving above a mass of Federals, just a hundred yards beyond his flank. Between his cannons and the Yankees thronged Jackson's men. Neal could limber up or try to hold his ground; he chose the latter option. He barked at the commander of his left section to swing his two guns to meet the threat, but in his zeal, the sergeant ran the two guns into one another. While Neal struggled with the gun crews to separate the locked axles, Jackson's troops "came rushing along through our [battery] in utter panic. My men stood steady as veterans, but in vain. The infantry rushed over us pell mell and we could do nothing."[9]

Neal now tried to save his guns. He gave the order to retire firing, but the ridge was too steep to get the horses up to the guns. Yielding to the inevitable, he ordered the limbers away and told his men to save themselves, content with having gotten off two of his four pieces.[10]

The Seventy-fifth Indiana claimed one of the guns; half the regiments in the division seem to have claimed the other. Colonel Milton Robinson grabbed the flag of the Seventy-fifth and waved it in the air beside his trophy, yelling at his men to stand by the colors. "Not that there was any danger of our deserting them," quipped a member of the regiment, "but it was to—and did—cheer us up to the verge of insanity."[11]

While the Federals regained their composure, General Cheatham scrambled to place another obstacle before their further advance northward along Missionary Ridge. Baird was just one mile from Tunnel Hill. All Cheatham had left to stop—or at least slow—him was Walthall's fragment of a brigade. This he now brought into play. He told the phlegmatic Mississippian to change front to the south. Walthall, who was about to suggest the movement himself, obeyed with alacrity. He stayed close to his men as they filed out of their rifle pits, admonishing them to keep quiet and not worry. Cheatham was right beside him. The eastern slope of the ridge behind the generals was gentle and open. As Cheatham and Walthall watched the brigade wheel into line across its expanse, a withering volley from out of the purple twilight cut through the Rebel ranks. In the dark, the Federals were firing by feel, and their aim was bad. Their bullets missed most of the men in ranks but found targets aplenty amid the mounted officers. A minié bullet ripped open Walthall's heel. Sacrificing his agony to the danger of the moment, Walthall made light of what was a horrid wound and stayed on the field. "Colonel, they have hit me," he remarked in a lighthearted voice to the commander of the Twenty-fourth Mississippi. "It must have been very painful, but he never left the saddle," recalled Dowd.[12]

Also hit was Hardee's horse. The general had showed up just after Cheatham gave Walthall the word to move. Having seen the last of Sherman's Federals shooed away from Tunnel Hill, Hardee was drawn to the fighting on his left flank by the rapidly rising volume of rifle fire. While riding to the sound of the guns, he paused behind Stevenson's division and told General Brown to follow him with his brigade. After recovering from his spill, Hardee turned Brown's brigade over to Cheatham, who in turn directed Brown to come into line on Walthall's left.[13]

Brown hastened to comply, but his presence proved superfluous. Walthall's Mississippians, few though they were, proved sufficient for the task at hand. A few volleys halted the Yankees, who came no nearer than two hundred yards, and after several more minutes of frenetic shooting by both sides, they ceased fire and backed out of range. It was about 6:00 P.M.

Darkness, more than the Mississippians, had put an end to Baird's advance. "It was too dark to discern forms at any distance, and we fired mainly at the blaze of their guns," confessed Colonel Dowd. And, despite their superior numbers, the Yankees were badly disorganized and thoroughly exhausted. Everyone from General Baird to the lowest private in the division seemed content to let the fighting sputter out and the Confederates leave the field at their leisure.[14]

Baird and his men were hardly unique in their desire to let night draw a curtain on the fighting. Hardly anyone on the ridge at nightfall gave serious thought to a pursuit. Generals Wood and Johnson gave orders to bivouac in place atop the ridge; so too did Hooker. Their tired troops yanked logs from the Rebel rifle pits and carried them to the opposite side of the narrow crest where they built breastworks of their own and settled in for the night.[15]

Not surprisingly, Phil Sheridan had ideas distinctly different from those of his fellow generals. The free-thinking Irishman had climbed the crest of Missionary Ridge just behind Harker's front-line regiments. A few yards from the top, Colonel Joseph Conrad of the Fifteenth Missouri had run up to Sheridan and begged him to dismount, as he was about to expose himself to a blast of canister from Cobb's Kentucky Battery, which stood squarely across his path. Sheridan recalled, "I accepted his excellent advice, and it probably saved my life, but poor Conrad was punished for his solicitude by being seriously wounded in the thigh at the moment he was thus contributing to my safety."[16]

Sheridan ached for revenge. Pausing for a moment between the captured cannons "Lady Buckner" and "Lady Breckinridge," he called for Wagner and Harker and told them to take up the pursuit along the Moore road, which Sheridan knew led to Bragg's supply depot at Chickamauga Station. He placed Wagner in command of the pursuit.

Sheridan's men wanted only to rest and eat. As they caught sight of Sheridan, their jubilant cries of "Chickamauga, Chickamauga!" gave way to lusty demands for food and whiskey. A cluster of hungry troops gathered expectantly around the general. Sheridan raised his hat, and the men fell silent. "Boys, in less than two hours' time you will have all the hardtack, all the sow belly, and all the beef you want; as for the whiskey, I can't say yet for sure," he said. For the moment, however, he expected them to push on after the fleeing Rebels.[17]

Wagner got most of his brigade together and started down the ridge. Harker had a harder time restoring order. His men were still "wild with joy over their splendid success. They shook hands and hugged each other, tossed their hats in the air, danced, sung, cheered, and some of them whooped and yelled like of a lot of drunken demons." After a few minutes of trying futilely to gather all his scattered men, Harker told Colonel Opdycke to take what he could of his demi-brigade and move over the Moore road on Wagner's right. Walworth in turn formed his demi-brigade on Opdycke's right. As soon as Wagner and Harker were off the ridge, Sheridan moved Sherman's brigade by the left flank along the crest and then down the road behind them in support.[18]

The Federals netted dazed and demoralized Rebels by the dozen, along with more cannons and limbers—all part of "the debris which had sloughed off from the first line," as the Confederate General Bate put it.

Among those taken was the young Floridian, Charles Hemming, who had run a gauntlet of bluecoats on the western slope of Missionary Ridge and then leapt off its steep eastern side. Regaining his footing at the base of the ridge, Hemming, it will be recalled, had pushed through the brush until he reached the Moore road. Down the road he sprinted until he met a wounded friend, who had paused to apply a tourniquet to his leg. "Charlie, don't leave me!" the man begged. Hemming glanced at the wound and saw it was not dangerous. "It's no time to stop now," he replied, and kept on running. The soldier limped along behind him. Suddenly from a dense thicket to their left they heard the command "Attention! Attention!" ring out in German. Through the underbrush, Hemming saw what looked like two Union regiments of German-Americans (probably the Second and Fifteenth Missouri). "Right then flashed across my mind: 'We are fighting the world! Here on this battlefield are foreigners who do not speak English and yet are fighting for the American flag." Hemming looked for a place to hide. Nearby was a small hut. Hemming and his comrade ducked into it. Peering through the cracks in the puncheons, his blood chilled: the Germans were shooting several Confederates who had thrown up their hands in surrender. "All at once I made a decision, and that was to load up and fight it out," he resolved. Hemming slammed a round into his rifle-musket. "What are you doing, Charlie?" asked his friend. "I am going to sell out here and now." Just then a Federal mounted on a captured horse came into range. Hemming's moment had arrived:

> He was a Union soldier and was making directly for the cabin door. I was ready and my gun loaded; I peeked through the cracks; I looked at him closely. He was a handsome fellow and looked to be about twenty-two. He was not coming rapidly but steadily. I knew I could kill him as soon as he got close enough. I looked at him again. He had ruddy cheeks and dark brown hair, and was a soldier of whom either side would have been proud. I said to myself, "I cannot kill that boy!" I thought of his mother at once; a strange thing that she came into my mind; but that is just as it happened.

When he got within fifteen feet of the door, he sang out a violent oath and told us to come out. I am sure I surprised him more than he ever was surprised in his life, for with my gun pointed at his breast, I was within five feet of him in a moment and shouted, "Throw up your arms!" They went up, and his gun went down.

He said, "What do you mean? You are surrounded and cannot get away."

I answered, "I want to be treated as a soldier and not murdered, as your men have murdered all around us in the last few moments. Promise me that and I will surrender."

He said, "I will protect you," and I said, "Here's my gun."

Out of the hut hobbled Hemming's friend, and the two walked away with the Yankee, who proved true to his word.[19]

A thousand yards east of Missionary Ridge, General Bate was working feverishly to prevent his entire division from being shot down or captured like Hemming. There, on the north side of the Moore road, the ground swelled into a high hill. On the hilltop and down across the road, Bate resolved to make a stand. His decision was endorsed by Bragg, who with his own staff was trying to rally the broken units of Bate's and Stewart's divisions. Bragg was having no more success here than he had had on Missionary Ridge. "He had lost the confidence of the army, and officers and men dashed by without heeding his commands or appeals," commented Lieutenant Colonel J. J. Turner of the Thirtieth Tennessee. Bragg returned their scorn. The men, he later wrote, "were in rapid flight, nearly all the artillery having been shamefully abandoned by its infantry support. A panic which I had never before witnessed seemed to have seized upon officers and men, and each seemed to be struggling for his personal safety, regardless of his duty or his character." Bragg at last gave up the effort and yielded to Bate, whom the men still respected. He told the Tennessean to hold out as long as possible and cover the retreat of Stewart's division and Reynolds's hopelessly scattered brigade, then fall back fighting, if necessary, to Chickamauga Station, where Bragg would set up headquarters. He sent staff officers to tell Hardee and Breckinridge to retire as best they could to the supply depot at Chickamauga Station as well. With that, Bragg took to the road, which was littered with abandoned equipment and angry soldiers.[20]

Bate succeeded where Bragg had failed. Tyler's brigade had fallen back from Missionary Ridge in relatively good order, and around it Bate formed a line. Colonel Tyler had been shot coming off the ridge and the next ranking officer had fallen a moment later, leaving J. J. Turner in charge of the brigade. Turner drew up his Tennesseans on the hill north of the road. He sent the First Tennessee Battalion of Sharpshooters forward to cover his front. His brigade acted as a magnet, attracting some five hundred lost soldiers whom Turner fed into his line. The remaining guns of Cobb's battery rumbled up out of the twilight and were placed astride the road, along with Mebane's battery. Finley's brigade rallied and deployed south of the road.

In less than twenty minutes, Bate had fashioned a respectable delaying position that stood in sharp contrast to the pandemonium on either side of his division. Not content with that, Bate turned command of his force over to Finley. He wisely withdrew the Sixth Florida from the line and led it a few hundred yards to the rear. In a large meadow east of the hill held by Turner, near the junction of the Bird's Mill and Moore roads, he halted the Floridians, intending to use them as the nucleus around which to form a second delaying position, should the Federals breach his first line.[21]

Wagner and Harker stumbled onto Bate's position at dusk. Though outnumbered, the Rebels knew the terrain. They opened on the Federals at such close range that, even in the dark, their bullets couldn't miss. Wagner's Yankees fell to the ground on the slope of the hill in front of Turner, and Opdycke ground to a halt across the road opposite Finley. For nearly an hour the two sides blasted away at one another with no appreciable effect, save a few dozen more dead and wounded.

Groping for a way to break the stalemate, Sheridan told Wagner to try to outflank Turner by coming at him from a high hill to the Tennessean's right. Wagner detailed the Fifteenth Indiana and Twenty-sixth Ohio for the mission.

"When the head of the column reached the summit of the hill, the moon rose from behind, and a medallion view of the column was disclosed as it crossed the moon's disk and attacked the enemy, who, outflanked . . . fled," reported Sheridan with a flourish. "This was a gallant little fight."

The reality was neither as decisive nor as colorful for the men on the front line as Sheridan maintained. "The exceeding and unexpected roughness of our route, comprising steep acclivity, dense thicket, and thickly tangled swamps, made the undertaking one of no little difficulty," said Lieutenant Colonel Young of the Twenty-sixth Ohio.[22]

The Confederates did fall back, but not simply because of Wagner's flanking movement. John C. Breckinridge had ridden into Finley's lines at about the same time Young's Ohioans were feeling their way through the dark. For the past two hours, it seems, the Kentuckian had been wandering among the foothills and ravines east of Missionary Ridge, caught up in the flotsam of his ruined corps and lost in grief. Drunk or sober, Breckinridge was profoundly depressed. General Stewart had run into him at dusk. "He was in a great state of distress, and informed me that he had fallen into Hooker's column that passed through the gap and turned our flank—that [Clayton's] brigade had been cut to pieces and captured and he had lost his son."

Stewart continued on with Breckinridge through the woods to Finley's position, the two drawn there by the sharp cracks of gunfire ringing through the twilight. Breckinridge was in no better frame of mind when he met Lieutenant Colonel Turner. He asked Turner what command he belonged to and what it was doing there. Turner explained. Breckinridge seemed not to hear him. Instead, he poured out the same litany of woes to Turner that he had related to Stewart: the whole corps had been shattered and was in retreat, and Turner was surrounded on three sides by overwhelming forces; he must retire at once. Turner acknowledged the order and issued the necessary instructions. "Nothing but the darkness and our knowledge of the roads enabled us to get out, as some of the regiments on the right of the line came out to the roads within a few yards of the Federal line," conceded Turner. Breckinridge gave the same command to Finley, then—after tipping his hat to some of the regiments of Finley's rear guard, placed himself at the head of the column as it withdrew.[23]

There he met Bate, who was riding forward from the field where he had left the Sixth Florida. Breckinridge told the Tennessean what he had done; Bate countered by relating Bragg's order that he hold on as long as possible before falling back to Chickamauga Station. The Kentuckian may have realized that he had exceeded his authority in ordering off Finley, but by then it was too late to about face. He bade Bate carry out Bragg's instructions, then rode rearward into the darkness with Stewart to find the commanding general. Bate shrugged and superintended the passage of Finley's and Turner's brigades through the Sixth Florida. That done, he led the Floridians out onto the Bird's Mill road and off in the direction of a pontoon bridge across Chickamauga Creek near the mill, two miles to the east, toward which the remnants of Breckinridge's corps were converging.[24]

Sheridan ascended the hill abandoned by Turner at about 7:30 P.M. His success had not satiated him; the dark of night notwithstanding, the Irishman believed that a momentous opportunity was being lost. "Having previously studied the topography of the country thoroughly, I knew that if I pressed on my line of march would carry me back to Chickamauga Station, where we would be in rear of the Confederates that had been fighting General Sherman, and that there was a possibility of capturing them by such action." But no troops beside his own had ventured from Missionary Ridge, and Sheridan, brash though he could be, was too good a general to try to push on alone. Reluctantly, he called a halt on the hill and rode back to Missionary Ridge to plead his case to whomever he might find in command there.[25]

# WHIPPED, MORTIFIED, AND CHAGRINED

THE NIGHT of 25 November 1863 was the saddest to date in the largely depressing history of the Army of Tennessee. A deep chill set in after sunset, blanketing the woods with a bright hoarfrost, the very brilliance of which seemed to mock the misery of the retreating soldiers. Over three rough country lanes—the Bird's Mill road, the Shallow Ford road, and a nameless trail that paralleled the Chattanooga and Cleveland Railroad—the heartbroken troops of Bragg's widely dispersed divisions moved with the labored gait of somnambulists toward South Chickamauga Creek, on the far bank of which they might find at least temporary safety.

The degree of confusion varied greatly from unit to unit. Thanks to Bate's deft delaying action, Stewart was able to piece his division back together and withdraw to Bird's Mill in relatively good order, Breckinridge's doomsday predictions notwithstanding.

Matters remained unsettled in Anderson's division, where each brigade commander found himself acting largely on his own. Arthur Manigault and his inspector general both had managed to escape from Missionary Ridge. After riding separately and frantically for five hundred yards, they were reunited on a hill that commanded the Shallow Ford road. There Manigault scraped together about two-thirds of the survivors of his brigade. His manner of restoring order was drastic but effective. "To stop the men in their mad flight, even after leaving the enemy hundreds of yards in their rear, was almost impossible," Manigault confessed. "The officers generally seemed to lose their presence of mind. Threats and entreaties alike proved unavailing, and I only succeeded by telling them to reach the brow of a hill still further to the rear, and there to throw themselves upon the ground behind the crest, assuring them that in this way only could they be saved. Collecting the most resolute and authorizing them to shoot down all who went beyond that point, I at last succeeded in forming the nucleus of a line."

A little later Manigault was joined by Tucker with what men he had rallied. Deas showed up on Manigault's right with the thoroughly demoralized remnant of his brigade. With Anderson nowhere to be found, Manigault took charge. He understood the importance of keeping open the Shallow Ford road and was confident he could do so: "The men again shoulder to shoulder, they moved forward promptly at the word of command and advanced . . . and I believe would have made a creditable resistance if again the Yankees had attacked them." Manigault's certainty was shaken somewhat when Deas marched away at sunset without bothering to tell either him or Tucker. Nevertheless, he was determined to try to hold his ground until he received orders to the contrary.

Shortly after dark, one of Bragg's staff officers chanced upon Manigault's makeshift force while searching for Hardee. He related to Manigault the commanding general's orders to Hardee: the army was to fall back across South Chickamauga Creek and regroup around Chickamauga Station. Manigault extrapolated from the order that he too should retire, and at 8:00 P.M. he led his column down the Shallow Ford road toward the creek.[1]

General Anderson had been looking for Manigault ever since moving off Missionary Ridge with Vaughan. As soon as Vaughan's brigade was out of harm's way, he handed it over to Cheatham and ventured into the murky forest to find the rest of his division, accompanied only by a lieutenant from Vaughan's staff. At first, they headed for Missionary Ridge, still impelled by the bizarre hope that the division might have retaken it. That illusion was quickly dispelled. "We returned to within about 250 yards of the position at which Dent's battery had been camped, encountering many stragglers through the woods, many looking for their commands, and some appearing indifferent as to their fate. All were ordered to cross the Chickamauga, and whenever an officer was found he was placed in command of a squad of these stragglers." Someone finally told him that Deas, Manigault, and Tucker already had taken up the march for Shallow Ford. Anderson cleared the woods of all the stragglers he could find, then galloped off to overtake his division.[2]

In marked contrast to the almost comic confusion in Anderson's division was the near textbook precision of Hardee's disengagement and withdrawal. To Hardee and his lieutenants must go great credit for keeping their heads amid the chaos. After dark, Cheatham told Walthall and Brown to shake out a line of skirmishers in the direction of Baird's Federals and then sneak off the field. They executed the movement flawlessly. "After everything became still General Walthall gave a whispered order along the line to move by the left flank. This was done in silence and perfect order," averred Colonel Dowd of the Twenty-fourth Mississippi.[3]

Walthall, despite the dolor his mangled heel caused, and Cheatham stayed close to the men on the march and spoke to them as they crossed the creek, a far from pleasant prospect in the frigid night air. Recalled a Tennessee private:

> General Cheatham stood on the bank and as each file passed going down the bank, he would say, "Boys, keep quiet! If you make the least noise, we are lost." File after file plunged into that icy flood four feet deep struggling to reach the opposite shore. The men held their guns and accoutrements on top of their heads. With bated breath and chattering teeth they waded waist deep in that ice cold water. Oh! how I dreaded my turn! As my file reached the edge of the water, we plunged in with clinched teeth for fear our breath would come out in such force that it would end in a scream. It proved to be too severe an ordeal for one of my file who was a great big fellow. As we stepped into the icy water to our waists, he hollered out to the top of his voice, "Jesus Christ! God Almighty!" However, with few exceptions, we passed over very quietly and struck the mountain trail. . . . Safe from capture at last![4]

Cleburne also executed his withdrawal skillfully in the face of Sherman's huge force, aided in no small measure by the timidity of the Ohioan, who had no stomach for renewing the contest, even after Thomas had seized Missionary Ridge. To mask his retreat, Cleburne ordered General Mark Lowrey to launch a brief but spirited sortie. Lowrey swept the Federal skirmishers from his front, then retired into his breastworks. To Granbury's tired Texans fell the task of staying on Tunnel Hill until the rest of the division had moved off.

All went as planned. "By 9:00 P.M. everything was across [South Chickamauga Creek] except the dead and a few stragglers lingering here and there under the shadow of the trees for the purpose of being captured, fainted-hearted patriots succumbing to the hardships of the war and the imagined hopelessness of the hour," reported Cleburne with a mixture of compassion and censure.[5]

Most who had not experienced the terror of the rout from Missionary Ridge had far less patience with the weak willed than did Cleburne. Resting beside the road near Shallow Ford, Private Sam Watkins of Maney's brigade, which Cleburne had loaned to Cheatham and Anderson to help screen their withdrawal, watched the dispirited pass by the thousands. First came Deas's brigade. "They were gunless, cartridge-boxless, knapsackless, canteenless, and all other military accoutermentsless, and swordless, and officerless, and they all seemed to have the 'possum grins, like Bragg looked, and as they passed our regiment, you never heard such fun made of a parcel of soldiers in your life," said Watkins. "Every fellow was yelling at the top of his voice, 'Yaller-hammer, Alabama, flicker, flicker, flicker, yaller-hammer, Alabama, flicker, flicker, flicker.' I felt sorry for the yellow-hammer Alabamians, they looked so hacked, and answered back never a word."

Like Cleburne, Private Watkins found it hard to blame the fainthearted. Almost to a man, he said, they felt betrayed by their superiors. Rising to his feet to join in forming a line of battle across the Shallow Ford road with his comrades from the First Tennessee, Watkins had ample time to study the shuffling stragglers:

> I remember looking at them, and as they passed I could read the character of every soldier. Some were mad, others cowed, and many were laughing. Some were cursing Bragg, some the Yankees, and some were rejoicing at the defeat. I cannot describe it. It was the first defeat our army had ever suffered, but the prevailing sentiment was anathemas and denunciations hurled against Jeff Davis for ordering Longstreet's corps to Knoxville, and sending off Generals Wheeler's and Forrest's cavalry, while every private soldier in the whole army knew that the enemy was concentrating at Chattanooga.[6]

At Chickamauga Station, Braxton Bragg was trying to summon the strength to deal with the disaster he had done precious little to prevent. He was as badly shaken as his men. One soldier who saw him that night thought he looked utterly "scared . . . hacked and whipped and mortified and chagrined at defeat." The first thing Bragg did after setting up temporary headquarters near the supply depot was to send a laconic message to Richmond informing the War Department of the defeat. Just four sentences long, its brevity probably reflected both Bragg's bewilderment at what had transpired and a heartsickness that prevented him from writing more:

Chickamauga, November 25, 1863—7 P.M.

General S. Cooper:
> After several unsuccessful assaults on our lines to-day, the enemy carried the left center about 4 o'clock. The whole ground gave way in considerable disorder. The right maintained its ground, repelling every attack. I am withdrawing all to this point.

Braxton Bragg[7]

Bragg understood that the army's stay at Chickamauga Station must by necessity be brief. The Federals were sure to pursue—and soon. "After arriving at Chickamauga and informing myself of the full condition of affairs, it was decided to put the army in motion for a point farther removed from a powerful and victorious army, that we might have some little time to replenish and recuperate for another struggle," he reported.[8]

The "condition of affairs" was desperate in the extreme. By 9:00 P.M., flames were licking skyward as the rear guard fired the railroad bridges over South Chickamauga Creek. Around Chickamauga Station, bedlam reigned. To call the forces congregating there an army would, with the exception of Hardee's four divisions, be crediting them with a semblance of discipline that they completely lacked. It was more a milling, maddened mob that marched about aimlessly outside Bragg's headquarters. Said Captain Buck of Cleburne's staff: "The scene of disorder and demoralization at the station beggars description; it can only be realized by one who has seen a beaten army. Regiments were separated from brigades, brigades from their divisions, and in a large part of the army organization had completely disappeared. The staff officers of the various commands spent the remainder of the night in endeavoring to bring order out of chaos."[9]

One who proved of little immediate help to Bragg was his perennial nemesis, John C. Breckinridge. The Kentuckian staggered into Bragg's headquarters sometime between nightfall and midnight. As Bragg later told it, Breckinridge collapsed on the floor in a drunken stupor. More probably, the effects of whatever liquor he might have consumed earlier in the day had long since worn off, and he simply was exhausted from worry over the fate of his son Cabell and the defeat of his corps. Also, the Kentuckian had an unfortunate habit of pushing himself too hard during active campaigning, often going two or more nights without sleep. In any case, shortly after midnight, Breckinridge awoke and went off to set up his own headquarters.[10]

Lost to Bragg for the upcoming retreat was one of his favorite subordinates, General Walthall. The Mississippian reached the station that night, having seen his brigade safely over the creek. Bragg took one look at his bloody heel and peremptorily ordered Walthall to relinquish his command and go at once to Atlanta for treatment. The Mississippian went. He spent the next eight weeks recuperating.[11]

Bragg chose as the immediate objective of his retreat Ringgold, Georgia, a town that lay ten miles southeast of Chickamauga Station astride the strategically vital Western and Atlantic Railroad. A half mile southeast of Ringgold, the railroad passed through a gap in a long, narrow eminence that was even more imposing than Missionary Ridge. Beginning ten miles below the town as Taylor's Ridge, the elevation resumed north of the gap and continued for another twenty miles. The long northern stretch was known as White Oak Mountain.

From Ringgold, Bragg planned to retire along the line of the railroad at least as far as Dalton, which lay another fifteen miles to the south and east. Bragg calculated that he must abandon Chickamauga Station no later than 2:00 A.M. on the twenty-sixth. To tarry until daylight would be to invite certain destruction, should the Federals attack. So, during the early hours of the night of 25 November, Colonel Brent penned the following circular to Bragg's senior lieutenants:

> Headquarters, Army of Tennessee
> Chickamauga, Tenn., November 25, 1863

> I. Corps commanders will immediately put their commands in motion toward Ringgold, keeping their trains in front. They will move in two columns.
> II. Hardee's corps will move by the west or Graysville road. Breckinridge's corps will move by the eastern road.
> III. All quartermaster's, commissary, and ordnance stores will be sent to Dalton.
> IV. Col. J. W. Grigsby will divide his cavalry and protect the rear of the two columns.
> V. Corps commanders will call in their detachments and guards when they are ready to move. Cleburne will serve as a rear guard to Hardee, and Gist to Breckinridge.
> VI. Three days' rations of hard bread and salt meat will be carried.

> By command of General Bragg:

> George Wm. Brent
> Assistant Adjutant General[12]

With only four or five hours to prepare for the march, it was evident that vast quantities of commissary stores at the station would have to be left behind; only a small portion could be loaded and gotten off in the wagons at hand. Bragg ordered the rear guard to burn the rest.

That command was taken lightly by soldiers who had suffered through several weeks of near starvation while vast stockpiles had accumulated just three short miles to their rear. Their anger at discovering the stores was predictable, and it grew hotter when they were told to torch them. Instead, those who could plundered supplies, often with the connivance of their officers. The experience of the Twenty-seventh Mississippi was typical. A fellow named Tom Farr was detailed to draw rations for Companies F and K, which had been consolidated after their severe losses on Lookout Mountain. Returning to the unit bivouac, he allowed someone to "steal" the whole three days' rations. His company commander knew full well what Farr was up to but played along nonetheless. He sent a detail of six men to draw—or steal—more rations. They did their job well, recalled Private Robert Jarman of Company K, coming back laden with more supplies than the entire regimental entitlement. When the commander of Company L learned of their profligacy, he complained to the regimental commander, Lieutenant Colonel Jones. Jones merely laughed and told the captain to requisition enough supplies for a division, which he did, and got. Having been on short rations for two weeks, the men were almost giddy with delight. Gluttony, then, helped ease the pain of defeat. Private Jarman swung onto the road for Ringgold loaded down with a full haversack, five pounds of bacon, and a half-bushel sack of crackers.[13]

Those of the rear guard fared best. Related Sam Watkins: "Before setting fire to the town, every soldier in Maney's and Polk's brigade loaded himself down with rations. It was a laughable looking rear guard of a routed and retreating army. Everyone of us had cut open the head of a corn sack, emptied out the corn, and filled it with hard-tack, and, besides, everyone of us had a side of bacon hung to our bayonets on our guns. Our canteens, and clothes, and faces, and hair were all gummed up with molasses. Such is the picture of our rear guard."[14]

Where were the Yankees during the long, cold night of 25 November, while Maney and his comrades were helping themselves to commissary stores? Why did no columns of jubilant bluecoats come bursting through the dark forest west of South Chickamauga Creek to consume the weary Rebels, or at least double-quick down the very roads over which they were escaping to nip at the rear of the whipped army?

Phil Sheridan learned the reason when he returned to Missionary Ridge. In essence, there was nobody in charge of the victorious Federals. Grant, Thomas, Granger, Baldy Smith, and their staffs had ridden out from Orchard Knob to the ridge at dusk, just in time to duck a ragged volley from a few Confederates who were retreating down the opposite side. Grant later claimed that he ordered Granger to follow the enemy with Wood's division after seeing Sheridan start down the eastern slope in pursuit, but that Granger "was so much excited, and kept up such a roar of musketry, in the direction the enemy had taken, that by the time I could stop the firing the enemy got well out of the way." Grant's assertion, however, doesn't ring true, particularly in light of his intended use of Granger's corps as expressed later that night. Also, Grant already had come to loathe Granger for his sharp tongue and preoccupation with shooting cannon, so his memory of events may have been clouded by lingering acrimony. More likely, neither Grant nor Thomas issued any orders of consequence while on Missionary Ridge; they probably tarried there only long enough to offer a few words of congratulations to the soldiers—who, as their jubilation subsided, were more interested in a hot meal than adulation—before leaving for the return ride to Chattanooga at about 7:00 P.M.[15]

On the ridge, then, Sheridan found only Granger, who was tucked comfortably into bed in Bragg's former headquarters. Sheridan spoke passionately. He related his skirmish with Bate and his conviction that an immediate pursuit by the entire Army of the Cumberland would most certainly complete the destruction of Bragg. According to Sheridan, Granger at first declined to take any action; the army had done well enough for one day, he thought. Sheridan pressed the point, and Granger relented a bit. He authorized Sheridan to advance to Bird's Mill but not to cross the creek. He promised to send Sheridan reinforcements should the Irishman encounter resistance. Frustrated but full of fight, Sheridan started back to his division. Along the way, he may have pondered Granger's reluctance to commit at least the remainder of his own corps to a pursuit. The men may have been tired, but if any unit had an excuse for halting, it was Sheridan's division. It had suffered over thirteen hundred casualties in the day's assault—nearly a quarter of the total Federal casualties during the three days' battles for Chattanooga—yet was still pressing the enemy.[16]

Sheridan was unduly hard on Granger, and in fact seems to have misrepresented their conversation. Indeed, Granger saw the opportunity as clearly as did Sheridan, but he lacked the audacity to pursue the Rebels without permission from Thomas, who by then was on the way back to Chattanooga. At 7:15 P.M., probably a good hour before Sheridan came to wake him, Granger had scribbled the following request to Thomas:

> Headquarters Fourth Army Corps,
> Bragg's Vacated Headquarters,
> Missionary Ridge, November 25, 1863—7:15 P.M.

Major General Thomas,
Commanding Department of the Cumberland:

General: It is probable that we can cut off a large number of the enemy by making a bold dash upon the Chickamauga, either upon the Rossville road or the one to the north of it, or upon all of the roads leading from our present front to the Chickamauga. The enemy evidently are badly demoralized. Our men are in great courage and in spirits. I am ready for any orders or dispositions you may be pleased to make.

We have captured about forty pieces of artillery and about 2,000 prisoners, small-arms, &c., in proportion, besides 50 wagon loads of forage.

G. Granger
Major-General, Commanding[17]

Sheridan got his division underway at midnight. The head of his column reached South Chickamauga Creek two hours later, gathering up scores of stragglers and wagons and limbers by the dozen along the way. He met no resistance. Sheridan of course wanted to go on but was afraid to cross the creek without help. So he tried a little ruse. Said Sheridan: "I caused two regiments to simulate an engagement by opening fire, hoping that this would alarm Granger and oblige him to respond with troops, but my scheme failed. General Granger afterward told me that he had heard the volleys, but suspected their purpose, knowing that they were not occasioned by a fight, since they were too regular in their delivery."

Sheridan finally called it a night. "I was much disappointed that my pursuit had not been supported, for I felt that great results were in store for us should the enemy be vigorously pursued," he complained years later. "Had the troops under Granger's command been pushed out with mine when Missionary Ridge was gained, we could have reached Chickamauga Station by 12 o'clock the night of the 25th; or had they been sent even later, when I called for them, we could have got there by daylight and worked incalculable danger to the Confederates."[18]

Sheridan was correct in his assessment of the damage the Federals could have inflicted. They easily would have swept up hundreds of stragglers and perhaps shattered the outnumbered brigades of Cleburne's rear guard. At a minimum, Grant would have been poised to cross South Chickamauga Creek at dawn. It is true, as Cleburne's disastrous evening attack at Chickamauga had demonstrated, that night fighting was something to be avoided, especially in the heavily forested and hilly terrain east of Missionary Ridge, but there was little chance that following the enemy at least as far as the bank of South Chickamauga Creek would precipitate a pitched battle.

Sheridan was wrong in his opinion of where the blame rested for the absence of an immediate and vigorous pursuit. The fault was not Granger's, nor Thomas's, but that of a man Sheridan was to come to revere— Ulysses S. Grant. Having won an obviously stunning though unexpected victory on Missionary Ridge, the general commanding seemed momentarily at a loss what to do next. The last Confederates scarcely had disappeared into the thick forests and rolling hills beyond Missionary Ridge before Grant felt compelled to turn the better part of his attention to a problem more vexing than how or even whether to try to finish off Bragg: what to do about General Burnside, who was reportedly besieged at Knoxville by Longstreet and running low on provisions. Personally, the Ohioan may have seen Burnside's plight as of secondary importance, but the administration's constant, often frenetic dispatches importuning Grant to relieve him made it seem as if that were his first priority. Both Lincoln and Stanton had grown even more solicitous of Burnside since Longstreet had cut the telegraph line from Knoxville across the Appalachians.

The pressure from Washington and the doubts Grant himself held rendered him unable, or unwilling, to fashion a fast, coordinated pursuit of Bragg during the night of 25 November. Thomas went to see Grant bearing Granger's request for permission to give chase. Grant, however, had other plans for Granger. Far from authorizing Granger to press on, Grant told Thomas to recall him to Chattanooga and have him prepare to move upriver to reinforce Burnside. Thomas returned to his own headquarters. Five hours after Granger had requested instructions, the Virginian replied:

> Department Headquarters
> Chattanooga, November 25, 1863—12 M.
>
> Major General Granger,
> Missionary Ridge:
>
> Your dispatch of 7:15 P.M. was duly received. Please accept my hearty congratulations on the splendid success of your troops, and convey to them my cordial thanks for the brilliant style in which they carried the enemy's works. Their conduct cannot be too highly appreciated. I have just seen General Grant, who desires that you make preparations to move up the river as soon as possible.
>
> Geo. H. Thomas,
> Major-General, U.S. Vols., Commanding.[19]

Sometime during the night, Grant fashioned a compromise strategy. At daylight, he would pursue Bragg with Sherman's troops and part of Thomas's forces; Granger, meanwhile, would go to succor Burnside. His directives to both Sherman and Thomas were tentative and somewhat contradictory in tone and content. To Thomas, he urged a vigorous pursuit, which he implied Sherman would support with a rapid advance due east to sever the East Tennessee and Georgia Railroad, Bragg's most reliable link with Longstreet. To Sherman, however, he suggested a more cautious approach—perhaps no more than a reconnaissance in force to find out if Bragg had gone north to the aid of Longstreet. Both orders are worth relating in full, if only to show the uncertainty that plagued

Grant during that cold, dark night of missed opportunities. To Sherman, he wrote:

Chattanooga,
November 25, 1863.

Maj. Gen. William T. Sherman,
Near Chattanooga:

No doubt you have witnessed the handsome manner in which Thomas' troops carried Missionary Ridge this afternoon, and can feel a just pride, too, in the part taken by the forces under your command in taking, first, so much of the same range of hills, and then in attracting the attention of so many of the enemy as to make Thomas' part certain of success. The next thing now will be to relieve Burnside. I have heard from him to the evening of the 23d. At that time, he had from ten to twelve days' supplies, and spoke hopefully of being able to hold out that length of time. My plan is to move your forces out gradually, until they reach the railroad between Cleveland and Dalton. Granger will move up the south side of the Tennessee with a column of 20,000 men, taking no wagons, or but few, with him. His men will carry four days' rations with them, and the steamer *Chattanooga*, loaded with rations, will accompany the expedition. I take it for granted that Bragg's entire force has left. If not, of course the first thing is to dispose of him. If he has gone, the only thing necessary to do to-morrow will be to send out a reconnaissance to ascertain the whereabouts of the enemy.

U. S. Grant,
Major General.

Then to Thomas, he had Rawlins write:

Maj. Gen. George H. Thomas,
Chattanooga:

I am directed by the general commanding to say that you will start a strong reconnaissance in the morning at 7 A.M., to ascertain the position of the enemy.

If it is ascertained that the enemy are in full retreat, follow them with all your force, except that which you intend Granger to take to Knoxville. This will make sufficient force to retain here. I have ordered Sherman to pursue also, he taking the most easterly road used by the enemy, if they have taken more than one.

Four days' rations should be got up to the men between this and morning, and also a supply of ammunition. I shall want Granger's expedition to get off by the day after to-morrow.

By order of Major-General Grant:

Jno. A. Rawlins,

Brigadier General, and Chief of Staff[20]

The grand irony in all this is that both the War Department and Grant were more worried about Burnside's welfare than was Burnside himself. During the second week of November, that general had conducted a commendable withdrawal to Knoxville under pressure from Longstreet. By 17 November, Burnside was comfortably ensconced behind a formidable ring of forts, earthworks, and abatis. He had supplies enough to last at least another two weeks and some 12,000 troops to oppose Longstreet, who had at his disposal approximately 18,500 men. The Confederates were in even greater difficulty than the besieged. Not only did they suffer from shortages, but they were among a hostile population—the same loyal mountain folk of East Tennessee whose deliverance from Confederate depredations Lincoln had been determined to ensure since the opening of the Tullahoma Campaign—and they were far from their nearest base. Finally, of course, Longstreet had started from Chattanooga with fewer supplies and less transportation than he had thought essential to success.[21]

Grant's dilemma and Burnside's suffering—or lack of it—were of no concern to the tired, hungry, and cold Federal soldiers bivouacked atop Missionary Ridge. The thrill of victory was no substitute for hot food or a warming fire. As the excitement of the fight wore off and the temperature plummeted, the men looked to their comforts. In the arduous climb that afternoon, many had flung aside their blankets and greatcoats to lighten their load. They now deeply regretted their shortsightedness. They huddled close to their campfires, both for warmth and to cook their rations, which Thomas had the quartermaster corps carry to the men on the ridge after dark. Under the light of a full moon, brightened by the flickering brilliance of hundreds of fires, recalled a grateful soldier, "you could see men as far as the eye could reach, several lines of them, with boxes of crackers on their shoulders."[22]

His stomach full, Lieutenant Hartzell of the One Hundred Fifth Ohio curled up beside his campfire and quickly fell into a deep sleep. He awoke only once, when the flames escaped the confines of the campfire and kindled the grass near him. They licked at the feet of the man beside him, and the sickly sweet smell of roasting human flesh brought Hartzell out of his dreams. "I raised up and pulled the man next to me, whose feet were burning, back a bit. He wore the gray, and his feet were burning sadly, but he never knew it," remembered the Ohioan, who soon fell fast asleep again, untroubled that his closest companion was a corpse.[23]

Frustrated by the uncertain warmth of his campfire, Sergeant Thomas Ford of the Twenty-fourth Wisconsin got up and wandered off in search of a blanket:

I found nothing to suit till I came to a rebel colonel who had a fine, large, gray overcoat with large cape and trimmed with gold braid [probably the soul-sick Lieutenant Colonel Moore, who had fallen near his family farm]. I rolled him over and took it off; took it to camp under my arm thinking, "Now I will have something fine and warm to put about me"; but alas! When I got nicely settled down for sleep I could not sleep. The thoughts of lying under that rebel overcoat and taking it off him in that lonely battlefield, overcame me. The way he appeared to me in the bright light of the moon made me think that I was robbing my dead enemy, when he was helpless to defend himself, and no witness to the action but the sweet silver moon. My heart filled with emotion and I got up and took it back and laid it over him, then returned to my company and lay down under a part of my comrade's blanket, and immediately went to sleep with a full ration in my stomach.[24]

Few of the battlefield ghouls who picked their way along the dark ridge, shunning the accusatory light of the campfires, shared Ford's pang of conscience. Their antic errands sickened the chaplain of the Fifty-eighth Indiana. "I saw some parties of thieves prowling among the dead. I am in favor of leaving a detail of good men on such occasions to shoot down these cowardly scoundrels, who remain behind to rob the honored dead."[25]

Both sides were guilty of desecrating the dead. As Sherman's skirmishers crept toward the former Rebel position on Tunnel Hill after midnight to verify that the enemy had left, they found more than abandoned breastworks. To their horror, they found that nearly every Yankee who had fallen within arm's length of the works had been stripped naked by the Rebels; only those whose clothes were too saturated with blood or brains were spared. "It is my prayer that I may never behold another such sight," wrote a private who witnessed the wrong.[26]

Of more practical concern than the dignity of the dead was the survival of the wounded. Death from exposure was a danger in the biting cold, so the wounded were hurriedly carried down the ridge and placed in the rickety Rebel huts on the flat until they could be evacuated to field hospitals. When the huts filled up, the wounded were gathered together and laid on the ground around bonfires.[27]

Hospital stewards and litter-bearers were burdened beyond their means, and ambulances couldn't negotiate the treacherous slope in the dark, so many from the rank and file left their campfires to lend a hand, either individually or in details organized by their officers. One of the first to come back down the ridge was Frank Wagley of the Fifteenth Indiana. He had gotten permission to leave the regiment before it went chasing off after Bate's fleeing Confederates. A kindhearted soldier who inevitably ventured out to help the wounded after an engagement, Wagley had a more acutely personal motive for his ministrations now—his brother Ephraim was nowhere to be found among the survivors on the summit.

Twenty-eight-year-old Ephraim, who had been so annoyed by Sheridan's histrionics ninety minutes earlier at the foot of the ridge, was shot while negotiating the rugged slope. He had been fumbling in his cartridge box for a round when a minié bullet struck him in the left leg, midway between the knee and the thigh. "The first sensation was the same that I once felt when a boy, when a mink bit me just in that same place, a stinging sensation, as if a briar had been jabbed in the flesh," he remembered. "I put my foot down to make my step, and my leg would not hold me up, then I said to myself, I am wounded." Frightened musings rushed through Wagley's mind. Wondering if his leg was broken, he rammed the butt of his rifle in the dirt and let himself down easy onto the ground. Ephraim felt his leg. It wasn't broken, he decided. His next thought was of the horrors of the field hospital: Would the heavy-handed surgeons have to probe the wound? "I was about as afraid of them then as I was of the Rebs," he confessed. He touched the underside of his leg and found a bubbling hole large enough to thrust his fist into. The ball had gone clear through, he concluded.

The next thing Ephraim noticed was a group of Rebels who had climbed out of their rifle pits a few dozen yards to his right and were about to pour a flanking fire into his regiment. Wagley lay between the two lines. He watched them come to a front, halt, load, and aim. "Good gracious, they will get me, and that will be too bad, now that I am wounded," Ephraim thought. Still lucid despite the shock of his wound, he pulled his blanket roll and oilcloth from around his neck, pushed it in front of him, and lay as flat as he could. The Rebel bullets whistled overhead or splattered around him. His comrades drove the Southerners off with a volley, and Ephraim lay back to watch the rest of the battle.

Through the lengthening shadows and lingering wisps of gunpowder smoke, Ephraim caught sight of his brother treading gingerly down the slope, carefully examining each corpse he passed. Ephraim let loose a long shrill whistle. Frank cocked his head in surprise; he recognized his brother's whistle but couldn't tell where it came from. Ephraim whistled again; his brother spotted him and came toward him. By the time Frank reached him, Ephraim was laughing uncontrollably. Three times Frank had to ask where he was shot before Ephraim replied. "I told him I was laughing at the way he stuck up his ears, when I whistled, but if he had a drop of water in his canteen, I would stop laughing long enough to take a drink."

Ephraim gulped down the water while his brother tenderly bandaged his leg with a strip of cloth torn from his underwear. Comforted by Frank's presence, Ephraim began to take note of his surroundings. Nearby lay a friend, Dan Cox, who had been trying for some time to talk to Ephraim. Cox had been shot through the face and his tongue cut in two. His face was one large clot of dark blood. It clung to his heavy whiskers like syrup. Blood had gurgled from Cox's mouth, changing the shape of his face, recalled Ephraim, so much so that he didn't recognize his friend. Looking away from Cox's pleading eyes, Ephraim saw the body of a boyhood friend crumpled only an arm's length from him. The man had been shot three times, the fatal bullet piercing the heart. Two other friends lay together in a promiscuous death embrace.

Frank asked Ephraim if he could make it down the ridge on his own; he wanted to stay behind and help some other wounded men. Ephraim said he could, and did. Using his rifle-musket as a crutch, he staggered off the ridge and over the flat toward Chattanooga, thanking God that he was away from the carnage and still among the living.[28]

Captain Donahower of the Second Minnesota ventured into the gathering blackness with a few men, blankets, and tin cups filled with steaming coffee. He and his troops struck matches over the still forms that lay thick near their bivouac, searching the faces for dead or wounded members of their own regiment. They gave succor to Yankees and Rebels alike, but there were simply too many who needed care. Everywhere Donahower and his party turned, a sight seemingly more pathetic than the last greeted them. Recalled Donahower:

> One sad case was that of a Union soldier wounded in the head. [It] proved a trying case to our nerves. Surgeon Brown informed me that the man would die very soon, and that he was not conscious of pain, and that attention must first be paid to those to whom he could give relief from pain and whose wounds required prompt attention. Corporal Nicholas Sons secured two blankets which we wrapped around the dying man, who was subject to awful convulsions of the muscles and nerves and long drawn moans.
>
> We built a small fire near the man, and as sleep was out of the question sat near him until about two o'clock, when, following a relaxation of the muscles, a long drawn moan somewhat different to all others caused us to look at his face just when death came, and we saw that he was at rest.
>
> Another case was that of a sergeant, a young man probably twenty-five years of age, a cleanly clothed, fine-looking man, educated, intelligent, and certainly a gallant soldier, and as he informed Captain John Moulton and myself—a South Carolinian. His hip or thigh bone had been broken by a musket ball which disabled him to such an extent that he was unable to move his body, which we did for him to make

him less miserable. Assistant Surgeon Brown saw him for a moment and promised to give him the earliest possible care. In the course of an hour we gave the sergeant a pint of good strong coffee, a little fried bacon and a couple of crackers and he ate and drank and was thankful for the kindness shown him, and soon after the stretcher bearers came and placing him on the stretcher, carried him down the slope. We wished him speedy recovery.

When their extra coffee, rations, blankets, and last reserves of strength gave out, Donahower and his men returned to their bivouac. Wrapping himself in a blanket and lying down on a slick rubber poncho, Donahower shivered away the waning hours of darkness.[29]

The smoky, gray morning twilight of Thursday, 26 November, revealed the full extent of the carnage. The adjutant of the Sixty-fourth Ohio had spent the night checking on wounded members of the regiment who had been evacuated to Chattanooga. Riding out of the city, he struck Missionary Ridge at the base of Tunnel Hill. The vista overwhelmed him, and he dismounted and began wandering, half-consciously, amid the dead and dying. Said the adjutant:

I came upon the body of a young Confederate soldier that had been thus far overlooked. A solid shot had carried away the entire rear part of his head, leaving his face, like a mask, intact. Neither chin, mouth, cheeks, eyes nor forehead was disfigured. He lay upon his back, with the head up hill. The face had fallen back upon the stump of his neck in such a manner that if the body had been perpendicular the face would have been horizontal.

I called upon two of the stretcher bearers to come and remove the body. On seeing this strange feature of the corpse they stood back, apparently paralyzed with horror, for, indeed, it was a sight to appall the most unfeeling spectator. The large, glaring eyes, glazed in death, the colorless face, and the singular position gave the spectacle a frightful appearance. One of the bearers was almost frantic with amazement, uttering expressions such as, "My God, what an awful sight!" For several minutes not a hand touched him, but after waiting for his excitable companion to quiet his nerves, the other said: "Come, let us get him out of sight as soon as possible," but no movement was made to do it. A second appeal also failed. Becoming a little impatient, the cooler one said:

"Do take hold of him! You ain't afraid of him are you?"

"No," said the other. "I'd a good deal rather help bury him, bad as he looks, than fight him alive!"

Near the foot of the ridge I saw the remains of one from an Ohio regiment that showed how destructive had been the Rebel shot. Evidently the soldier was lying down, his head toward the enemy, and his body on a line with the passage of the missile, for it struck him on the head and passed the whole length of the body and limbs. From appearances that were but few whole bones left. I think a bushel basket would have held all that remained.[30]

Hardened to the horrors of war, the veteran adjutant was prepared for what he encountered on his walk. Not so Frank Wolfe. Wolfe was a civilian member of the staff of Brigadier General Montgomery Meigs, the Quartermaster General of the Union Army, who had been in Chattanooga helping coordinate the logistical aspects of the relief of the beleaguered Army of the Cumberland. Prior to the war, Wolfe had been Meigs's secretary when the latter, a talented engineer officer serving in the District of Columbia, supervised additions to the Capitol that included the House and Senate wings and the dome. He also had been Meigs's draftsman for the construction of the Potomac Aqueduct. Wolfe, however, was an innocent when it came to warfare; until now, the Philadelphian had never seen a shot fired in anger. He had watched the storming of Missionary Ridge from Fort Wood, at a distance from which falling soldiers looked like tiny toys and everything else appeared grand and bloodless. He went to bed thrilled with the excitement of it all.

Wolfe confronted the cold reality the next morning when he, General Meigs, and a friend named Tom saddled their horses and rode out to Missionary Ridge. They made for Tunnel Hill first. On the way they passed the smoldering ruins of the Glass farm, into which wounded soldiers had been dragged early in the fight. There they saw their first charnel curiosities. "The houses were fired (God forbid! by design), and the charred remains lay still unburied," Wolfe wrote a friend. "Most of the dead—perhaps in the death throe—had a singularly life-like position, the hands and arms being slightly raised, as though by a convulsive jerk of the muscles. Enough of this. I saw death in almost every conceivable form that could revolt humanity." Wolfe tried to conclude, yet morbid fascination compelled him to write on. "Most of the death wounds, except those torn to pieces by shell, were minnie [sic] balls through the head. On most of the countenances there was a rigid enthusiasm, showing that they died in the excitement of action, before pain could contract the features. I never care to see the like again."

Yet the small party rode on, up the slope and along the ridge. All the wounded they met, blue and gray alike, were being tenderly cared for. Such a fraternal sight cheered Wolfe, and with surprising ease he grew momentarily indifferent to the gore. He eagerly joined Meigs in picking up souvenirs. "The general made a regular curiosity shop of himself in the way of relics, such as bayonets, bullets, cartridge boxes, etc. I contented myself with a roll of music that lay near a rebel musician, a piece of rebel color, a hymn and a couple of grape shot." His callousness deepened. "We lunched on the supply of bread and meat designed for the wounded we expected to have met, and half emptied a bottle of prime Madeira. I regret now every mouthful of viands swallowed at that meal." For at the extreme end of Missionary Ridge, near the Rossville Gap, they met horribly wounded men to whom the litter-bearers had yet to come. One group of five caught their attention, and Meigs and his cohorts dismounted to render assistance. Wrote Wolfe:

> They proved to be five Alabamians, wounded the previous night, whom our men had hastily provided for, filling their canteens and wrapping them in their blankets beside fires of fence rails. Those who had left them thus, had been too busy advancing to think of the wounded in their rear, supposing the ambulance parties would look out for that. The loneliness and seclusion of the spot had prevented their being detected, and I cannot say how long they would have lain thus, had we not happened upon them.
>
> The young fellow wounded in the leg and arm, evidently the most intelligent of the party, certainly the handsomest, to one of Tom's sallies, as he bustled around, said "Well, we have received nothing, lived on nothing, been fighting for nothing, and could expect nothing from our enemies surely; but from this night I, for one, shall judge you all better."

Wolfe was impressed. "They bade God bless us as we left them; and I am sure I had rather done thus much for the relief of the suffering than won a dozen laurels," he continued, cheered by the noble words of the Rebel. Then he stepped over the fence rails and almost onto the "stark and cold" corpse of one of the Southerners' comrades, shot through the temple. That was enough for Wolfe. As a mist settled over the valley and a light drizzle peppered the ridge, he mounted his horse and rode hastily and heartsick back to Chattanooga. "I have seen enough of fighting to last me a lifetime," he closed his letter.[31]

# CHAPTER TWENTY-FIVE

# THEY ARE CROWDING US

PRESIDENT Lincoln lay in bed ill. Exactly one week earlier, he had spoken a few words at the dedication of the National Soldiers' Cemetery at Gettysburg. Back in Washington, he was stricken with what physicians at first thought to be a cold. Then a fever set in, and a nasty rash broke out over his body. After some stumbling misdiagnoses, the doctors correctly identified his malady as varioloid, a mild form of smallpox.

Ironically, several weeks before, while General Rosecrans was licking his wounds inside the Chattanooga fortifications and Burnside was wasting time in East Tennessee, Lincoln had decided to proclaim this very day, Thursday, 26 November 1863, as a special, national day of thanksgiving and praise "to our beneficent Father who dwelleth in the heavens." Lincoln had asked Secretary of State Seward to pen the proclamation in part to deflect public anxiety over the disaster at Chickamauga and to remind the nation of the victories won at Gettysburg and Vicksburg. The first draft, finished by Seward on 3 October, had noted, in part, that "order has been maintained, the laws have been respected and obeyed, and harmony has prevailed everywhere, except in the theater of military conflict; while that theater has been greatly contracted by the advancing armies and navies of the Union."

The stunning defeat of Bragg on Missionary Ridge the day before its promulgation had dramatically demonstrated the truth of that optimistic assertion. Whereas journalists from Boston to Chicago had spent the past week debating the merits of Lincoln's Gettysburg address, the newspapers suddenly spread before their readers the story of Grant's victory. "More good reason than expected had arisen for the Day of Thanksgiving proclaimed by the President weeks earlier. If he had wanted good news as he lay abed with varioloid in the White House, he had it with running-over measure," wrote Carl Sandburg.[1]

Now it remained to be seen how, or if, Grant would follow up his success; whether he would let it slip through his fingers as McClellan had after Antietam and Meade had after Gettysburg, or if he would aggressively pursue Bragg's battered army and clean Longstreet out of East Tennessee.

As might be expected given the irresolute tone of Grant's orders of the night before, the pursuit of Bragg got off to a disjointed and, in the case of Thomas's column, slow start.

Sherman acted on his instructions first. A mile east of his lines, the railroad bridges over South Chickamauga Creek were aflame, so the Ohioan decided to take a different, and definitely roundabout, route after the enemy. He turned to Jefferson C. Davis, who had chafed away the afternoon of the twenty-fifth anxious to play a part in the fight against the Confederate right, to lead the pursuit. Davis was to face his division about and march back to the mouth of South Chickamauga Creek. There he was to cross the pontoon bridge to the northern bank, then move cross country and sweep down on Chickamauga Station from the north. Howard's corps would follow Davis over the creek, and Sherman's own mangled divisions would bring up the rear.[2]

Davis got his division underway at once. Having seen no action, the men were well rested but reluctant to leave their campfires. "It was so cold we could not keep warm in any way," a regimental commander wrote his wife. "I thought of home and our comfortable beds, and how little the dear people know of the soldier's privations." Once the men were rousted out they marched quickly, largely to try to warm themselves. The division crossed the pontoon bridge at midnight. A thick fog rolled down the river valley and spread its drenching net over the countryside. Davis pushed on for about three miles, over frosty cornfields and scattered thickets, before yielding to the fog at 4:00 A.M. on 26 November, less than three miles from Chickamauga Station. The troops broke ranks, but sleep was impossible. Fires were forbidden. The men chewed on a breakfast of cold hardtack and pork and listened to the crisp strains of reveille from the enemy's drums and bands that pierced the night.[3]

At 7:00 A.M., General Howard overtook Davis's dormant column. The fog still lay heavy, "so dense that you could not discern a horse at one hundred yards," said Davis. The Indianian briefed Howard and yielded to him as the senior officer present; Howard told him to keep the lead and make whatever dispositions he thought appropriate.

Davis could make no dispositions until the fog lifted, so he and his men waited in the damp, bitter cold—a compact column of six thousand shivering soldiers. At 8:00 A.M. the fog began to dissipate, and Davis gave the order to advance. The road to Chickamauga Station was horrible, a sloppy paste overlaid with a thin sheet of ice that shattered under the feet of the marching men.

The fog parted to reveal Rebel cavalry in the fields ahead of the Yankees. Davis deployed his skirmishers and the horsemen fled. In their place, the Federals found dispirited stragglers from Bragg's infantry. Too tired and disgusted to dissemble, they freely volunteered that the Army of Tennessee was in retreat. Cheered by the news, the head of Davis's column picked up the pace. At noon, Chickamauga Station came into view. Clouds of smoke rose from the depot. The crackle of burning supplies confirmed the confessions of the stragglers.

Davis deployed his lead brigade, that of Brigadier General James Morgan, which had had the good fortune to miss the fighting at both Chickamauga and Chattanooga, and waved it forward. The Twenty-first Kentuckians covered the brigade front in a skirmish line and dashed ahead. On the northern edge of the little hamlet the Federal Kentuckians ran into a skirmish line from Lewis's Confederate Kentucky brigade, which had remained with Cleburne after the retreat from Missionary Ridge. The luckless Orphans found themselves bringing up the rear of the rear guard. They tried to hold off the Yankees long enough for their comrades to apply the torch to all the storehouses, but they were too few for the task. Morgan's men chased their Kentucky antagonists though the smoky byways of Chickamauga Station and into the fields beyond without the loss of a man.[4]

The Federals were ecstatic. Said Davis: "In this sharp encounter several of the enemy were wounded and captured, belonging to Kentucky regiments of the Confederate army. This fact was soon known to the gallant Twenty-first Kentucky. Kentucky loyal was now meeting Kentucky rebel face to face. The enthusiasm it created ran through the lines like an electric thrill."[5]

Tons of easy plunder didn't hurt either. The Rebels had been unable to burn everything, and the Yankees broke ranks and dashed into undamaged warehouses eager to augment their rations. Captain Allen Fahnestock of the Eighty-sixth Illinois tolerated this momentary lapse of discipline among his men, as did most other officers. "I here witnessed a laughable sight," he recalled. "The men rushed into some of the rebel store houses and filled their haversacks with what they thought was brown sugar, and when they came out began to taste the sugar and found it was brown salt. There was some swearing and emptying of haversacks." The official tally: two siege guns, one thousand bushels of corn, ten pontoons, and countless sacks of flour seized.[6]

The avarice of Davis's troops allowed most of Lewis's Kentuckians to escape, just as the early morning fog had allowed the main body of Hardee's corps to put a respectable distance between it and the Federals.

Sherman joined Howard and Davis at Chickamauga Station shortly after noon. He watched the generals restore order and resume the chase. Davis kept the lead. During the waning hours of daylight, he played a cat-and-mouse game with Cleburne along the Graysville road.

Cleburne's task was both difficult and crucial. Hardee's infantry had gone off alone, leaving the lumbering wagon trains and most of the artillery of the army not captured on Missionary Ridge to follow. Cleburne, if necessary, was to sacrifice his division to protect them. Captain Buck wrote admiringly of Cleburne's skillful handling of his rear-guard responsibilities:

> His division, intact from the disasters . . . was perhaps the only one in the army to which that responsibility could have been safely entrusted. The trains were toiling forward over a single narrow road, the artillery wheels cutting into the soft mud up to the axles, and requiring heavy details to prize them out, and the rear wagon was still in sight when the enemy, flushed with victory and pressing forward in energetic pursuit, appeared and opened on Cleburne with shells. Showing his men at all prominent points, to create an impression of greater force, Cleburne gradually fell back towards Graysville.[7]

The second tentacle of Grant's pursuing leviathan was slow to extend itself. Sherman had made a good-faith effort to get an early start after the enemy; the fog had been an unanticipated and legitimate barrier. Thomas had no such excuse, except perhaps a vague feeling that Grant himself was not wholly committed to the game. In any event, the only activity of consequence on his front during the early morning hours was the gradual withdrawal of Wood's division back to Chattanooga preparatory to going upriver under Granger to relieve Burnside.

A reconnaissance was made by Hooker soon after dawn, but whether it was at Thomas's direction or of Hooker's own volition is unclear. Hooker said that he took it upon himself to explore the ground to his front. Finding "the field as silent as the grave," Hooker sent Thomas a note at 10:00 A.M. suggesting that he be permitted to march on Graysville at once via the Rossville road to try to intercept the enemy and that Palmer's corps be ordered to accompany him. It was 1:00 P.M. before the Virginian responded, approving Hooker's suggestion and sending concomitant orders to Palmer to cooperate with him.[8]

By then, Grant had gotten wind of the delay. He was furious. Despite his own ambivalence about pursuing Bragg, an order was an order; here too was further proof that Thomas could be obstinately slothful. Grant rode out of Chattanooga to prod the Virginian along. As Rawlins put it in a note to Sherman, "the general commanding will be with the pursuing column, that he may give such general directions on the field as circumstances may suggest."[9]

The delay was less egregious than Grant had expected. Hooker, it seems, had started forward before getting written approval from Thomas. Unfortunately, when he reached the west bank of South Chickamauga Creek, Hooker found only smoldering ruins where the Ringgold bridge had stood. His chief of staff, the roundly detested but essentially competent Dan Butterfield, had requested three pontoons that morning from Thomas's headquarters to meet just such an exigency. They were not sent, however, and nearly half the precious daylight hours of the short, late autumn afternoon were lost while a new bridge was hammered together. Hooker used the time to clarify the objective of the pursuit (was he to give battle if challenged?) and his destination, both of which until then had been vague. Neither Grant nor Thomas seems to have told Hooker definitively what he was to accomplish, besides chasing the Rebels and perhaps cutting the Western and Atlantic Railroad near Graysville, so he fashioned his own objective. Hooker decided that Cruft's division, which was still serving under his command, would lead the way and push out over the Ringgold road directly for that town rather than Graysville. Palmer, meanwhile, was to divert his corps in the direction of Graysville, then rejoin Hooker the following morning for a lunge against the railroad in the neighborhood of Ringgold. Hooker would be striking the tracks five miles farther to the south than Thomas apparently had suggested, and, by aiming for Ringgold rather than Graysville, might have a better chance of cutting the Rebel rear guard off from Bragg's main body.[10]

It was a sound plan, but Cleburne and Gist had too much of a head start for Hooker to trap them. It was 3:00 P.M. before the first of the Federal infantryman stepped onto the makeshift bridge over South Chickamauga Creek. Hooker left his artillery behind to catch up as best it could and drove his infantry hard, but to no avail. After marching two miles, they found the bridge over Pea Vine Creek burned. Night had fallen before this second obstacle was overcome. Still Hooker drove on. Over the moon-bathed muddy road the Federals marched. "We went along slowly and could see along the road evidence that the rebs were in a considerable hurry. They left wagons, gun carriages, tents, blankets, old pieces of carpet, in fact everything that could lighten their loads and aid their flight," said a member of the Eighty-fourth Illinois. But these tokens of their own triumph were not enough to dispel the fatigue that fell over the Federals. "The boys began to grumble and want to stop, but didn't have the say so, and on we went," added the Illinoisan.[11]

Deep into the night they shuffled along the road. The men were exhausted. The eerie darkness and the soldiers' own profound fatigue transformed the real into the surreal, giving full play to the wildest imaginings of the Yankees. Remembered Lieutenant Mosman of the Fifty-ninth Illinois, which was near the head of the column:

> As we're moving slowly up a slope about 12 midnight there came a sound from the top of the hill. Everybody was tired out and sleepy with the slow movement and the late hour, and the only thought I had was that a caisson—the horses of which were running away—was coming down the road. We were in the center path, a field on our left fifty yards away. I very naturally jumped out of the road and by a common impulse every man jumped out of the road, knelt down and cocked his musket, facing the field. In half a second not a man could be seen. Every fellow lay down. It was done quicker than a flash and such a sound of cocking muskets I never heard before . . . but everybody seemed at once to get control of themselves and not a shot was fired and no one could tell two minutes later what it was all about. But it was ludicrous in the extreme when we got wide awake and tried to find out what caused it all. I think it was the caisson but it didn't get us. . . . The boys say that the same panic struck the Ninth Indiana, which was right behind our regiment; that General Hooker had dismounted and was walking up the hill in the road, with a file of the men on each side of him, and when the alarm came the men literally ran over him, knocking him down.[12]

Being nearly trampled to death convinced Hooker it was time to call it a night. He edged Cruft forward a little farther, to the crest of a low ridge just two and a half miles northwest of Ringgold, the sleepy seat of Catoosa County. The Federals bivouacked along the ridge. "If not otherwise directed, I shall move on Ringgold at daylight," Hooker announced in a note to Thomas before bedding down. Off on the horizon, enemy campfires flickered enticingly.[13]

Bragg was in trouble, and he knew it. The army that encamped that night near Ringgold was still little more than a dispirited mob. Its ability to resist an attack was minimal. Messengers brought nothing but bad news to Bragg at his headquarters at Catoosa Station, on the eastern side of Ringgold Gap.[14]

They told him of the near destruction of the division of States Rights Gist, which constituted half of his rear guard. Palmer's Federal division had marched to within a mile of Graysville at dusk from the west, stumbling upon the flank of Gist's own brigade. At about the same time, the lead elements of Davis's division came down the Graysville road from the north and ran into Maney's brigade. Howard brought up Steinwehr's division on Davis's right and massed that of Schurz in reserve.

Davis unleashed two brigades into the twilight. "Well, we quickly form line of battle, and the Yankees are seen to emerge from the woods about two hundred yards from us," recalled Private Sam Watkins of the First Tennessee. "We promptly shell off those sides of bacon and sacks of hard-tack that we had worried and tugged with all day long. Bang, bang, siz., siz. We are ordered to load and fire promptly and to hold our position." The racket was tremendous, and for a moment it looked as if the brigade would be swallowed up. Maney went down badly wounded. Bledsoe's Missouri Battery lost a gun before limbering up and escaping down the road, sending Tennessee infantrymen jumping for cover to avoid being run over. "They are crowding us; our poor little handful of men are being killed and wounded by scores," wrote Watkins. "We can't much longer hold our position. A minnie ball passes through my Bible in my side pocket."

Then, almost as quickly as it had begun, the fight was over. Davis was afraid to launch a general attack in the dark and so halted his men just as they prepared to charge Bledsoe's guns. Maney's brigade hurriedly fell back down the Graysville road toward the crossing over South Chickamauga Creek.[15]

Gist was not yet free from danger. Palmer's lead elements under Carlin were closing in on the Graysville road near the spot Maney's brigade would have to pass to make good its escape. Palmer recognized his opportunity to bag the fleeing enemy force. Riding at the head of his column with Generals Johnson and Carlin, he admonished his subordinates: "Gentleman, the success of this undertaking depends upon it being a surprise; therefore, send down the column and have the men cautioned not to speak above a whisper, and to move quickly and quietly, and above all, to keep well closed up."[16]

Carlin complied, turning over the advance guard to Colonel Benjamin Scribner. Scribner neared the road with his demi-brigade at a point just a few dozen yards from the bridge over South Chickamauga Creek; Maney's artillery and lead regiments were closing on the same point from the north. The creek had overflowed its banks during the heavy rains of November. The water had drained from the road, leaving in its wake a cracked, glazed surface, but the surrounding woods were a marshy mess. The flood proved Gist's salvation. The fastidious Federals, wrote Scribner, slowed down to keep from getting their feet wet. "I hastened to one of the regiments which was not closed up, to urge them forward, and found the men picking their way among the branches of the trees, which had been blown down and had so obstructed the drainage that water had collected about them. To avoid wetting their feet, the men were mincing their steps, thus impeding the rear and delaying the movement," recalled Scribner in anger.

Scribner wanted to scream at them to hurry forward, but he knew he had to keep quiet. So near the road was he that he "could hear the 'Gee-ups' and cracking whips of the artillery men and teamsters, and the slang and ribaldry of the rebel soldiers as they with unconscious abandon trudged along." Bursting with indignation, he grabbed the shoulder of the commander of the dilatory regiment, and shaking him violently, whispered hoarsely: "Will you convince me that you are fit to command men, that you have the stuff in you that influences men? If you have, prove it to me right here, and make your men walk through this water and close up the column."[17]

The officer got his men going and a moment later formed them into line of battle in the underbrush beside the road. "And now all was ready; the culminating moment had come," said Scribner, "a volley, a dash, one long explosive shout and all was still again." The Rebel infantry left the road and dashed into the woods on the far side, abandoning part of Ferguson's South Carolina Battery and several ordnance wagons to the Federals. In a few minutes, Scribner had his demi-brigade in line. He wheeled to the left, sweeping the forest into which the Southerners had disappeared. Rebels were gathered up by the dozen, most from the Sixteenth South Carolina.[18]

The few critical minutes lost while Scribner deployed his column into line gave Gist the time he needed to save his two brigades. Realizing he was hemmed in on the road between Palmer and Davis, Gist sent staff officers to look for a place to ford the creek out of reach of the Federals. They found it, along with a branch trail leading east away from the Graysville road. Into the water went the Southerners. Related a member of Maney's brigade: "We waded across, hip-deep. It was a cold, frosty night. We looked like a drove of cattle in the water, and we had to stand there until we nearly froze while scouts felt around to see if the enemy was over there. We were too sharp for them and slipped out of their trap."[19]

Gist's wet and weary men wandered into Ringgold at 2:00 A.M. on 27 November. They were too tired to be of further use as an effective rearguard, so Bragg waved them on through the Ringgold Gap to bivouac with the main body of the army. That left him with only Cleburne's 4,157-man division to hold off the inevitable dawn attack by Hooker, who had at least three times as many men, while the rest of the army resumed its march to Dalton, another fifteen miles to the southeast.[20]

Given the odds, it is not surprising that Bragg despaired. Privately, he told his staff that he considered his wagon trains and artillery, which trailed the main body of the army, to be as good as lost. Nonetheless, he rightly felt it imperative to try to protect them, even if it meant sacrificing Cleburne's fine division.[21]

By 10:00 P.M., Cleburne's footsore soldiers had staggered to the outskirts of Ringgold. Between them and the town itself was South Chickamauga Creek. Here the long, meandering creek was wide and deep, its waters frigid and rapid. Someone from army headquarters appeared out of the dark and handed Cleburne orders to cross and bivouac on the opposite bank, there to renew the march at 4:00 A.M., still acting as rear guard. A sharp wind whipped the paper as Cleburne read it. He shook his head emphatically. No, he would not cross the creek just then. Cleburne told the messenger "that if his troops waded the creek, waist deep, and went to sleep chilled he would lose more men by sickness than in a battle." He would take his chances with the Federals and camp on the northern bank for the night and then ford the creek just before 4:00 A.M., trusting that the morning sun and the march would help the soldiers shake off their chill before they took ill.[22]

At midnight, a second messenger, this one from Bragg, tracked down Cleburne. He brought different, though ultimately more disturbing, instructions. Cleburne, he said—having nothing in writing to give the Irishman—was to cover the rear of the retreating army, taking position on the high ground on either side of Ringgold Gap and holding the enemy in check until the trains, artillery, and rest of the army could get away safely. Cleburne balked. He told the staff officer he was not in the habit of disobeying orders, but as these might well spell the end of his division, he wanted them in writing.

He got them. They were brief but comprehensive: "Tell General Cleburne to hold his position at all hazards, and to keep back the enemy until the transportation of the army is secured, the salvation of which depends upon him."

As Cleburne contemplated the words, his men lay down all around him for a few hours of fitful sleep.[23]

# A SAD AFFAIR

THE COLD predawn hours of Friday, 27 November, augured another frigid and frosty sunrise. As the black of night yielded to a purple twilight, the troops of Cleburne's division arose from their brief bivouac and walked stiff-legged through a light, damp vapor—the mere ghost of a fog—toward the bank of South Chickamauga Creek. On the far side, huge bonfires roared and crackled, casting a weird, crimson gleam over the icy waters.

The men appreciated Cleburne's consideration in readying fires for them, but that did little to palliate their dread of the crossing. Remembered an Alabamian from Lowrey's brigade: "We took off our shoes, socks, pants, and drawers, tucking the lower ends of our shirts under our belts, clothing and cartridge boxes up under our armpits, waded the creek, this ford being about waist deep, while there was ice along the edges of the water, but we hurriedly got into the water after stripping. The cold was stinging our exposed anatomy."[1]

Once over, the men gathered around the fires and hastily dressed. Their officers allowed them to linger near the flames long enough to warm themselves, but not to dry their clothing; impatient lest the Yankees catch up, they herded their troops back onto the Ringgold road. Through the town of some two thousand slumbering inhabitants they marched toward their designated defensive positions.

By the time the first of Cleburne's infantry passed through Ringgold, it was light enough to make out the long, stark outlines of Taylor's Ridge and White Oak Mountain that rose abruptly half a mile to the east. Between them was Ringgold Gap, about a thousand feet wide and four thousand feet long. It was a cramped passage. The Western and Atlantic Railroad and the wagon road to Dalton passed through the gorge, as did the sinuous South Chickamauga Creek. The road bridged the creek a half mile east of the gap. Should the Federals penetrate the gap or flank either end of the position Cleburne was about to assume on the ridges, they could easily block his route of retreat by capturing or burning any one of these bridges.

The terrain around Ringgold Gap was almost a mirror image of Rossville Gap and Missionary Ridge. A small patch of saplings and bushes stood before the western entrance to Ringgold Gap. White Oak Mountain rose gradually from the north side of the gap to a height of 350 feet along the stretch that Cleburne intended to defend. At the base of the mountain, a fringe of virgin timber ran northward for four hundred yards. Taylor's Ridge jutted up precipitately on the south side of the gap to an altitude of 400 feet. The western slopes of both elevations were steep and lightly forested.[2]

Cleburne posted his troops with great care to prevent a repeat of the Missionary Ridge disaster, placing units so as to anticipate every possible Federal move. He studied the lay of the land as carefully as time permitted. He planned to use every stand of timber, every hill, every roll in the ground—in short, every natural obstacle, no matter how insignificant it might appear—to stop an attack.

He gave Granbury's Texans the mission of defending the ground to the right of the Ringgold Gap. Behind the long fringe of trees at the base of White Oak Mountain, Cleburne personally positioned the Sixth, Tenth, and Fifteenth Texas (Consolidated) and the Seventeenth, Eighteenth, Twenty-fourth, and Twenty-fifth Texas Dismounted Cavalry Regiments (Consolidated). Cleburne dispatched the Seventh Texas to the top of the ridge. He told the Texans to keep out of sight but to watch the right flank of the regiments at the foot of the mountain.

To cover the ground to the left of the gap, Cleburne relied largely on a single regiment, the Sixteenth Alabama of Lowrey's Brigade, which he ordered onto Taylor's Ridge. As he had with the Seventh Texas, Cleburne told the Alabamians to conceal themselves; they were to keep a weather eye out for the left flank. To help them, he detailed three companies of the Sixth and Seventh Arkansas (Consolidated).

To the remainder of Lowrey's Alabama and Mississippi and Govan's Arkansas brigades, Cleburne entrusted the defense of Ringgold Gap. He availed himself of its narrowness to fashion a defense of four short lines, thus compensating with depth what he lacked in numbers. He ushered the Fifth and Thirteenth Arkansas (Consolidated) into a small ravine that traversed the mouth of the gorge from the edge of White Oak Mountain to the railroad embankment. The Eighth and Nineteenth Arkansas (Consolidated) formed line of battle five paces to the rear. Next came the other seven companies of the Sixth and Seventh Arkansas

(Consolidated). The fourth line was comprised of the Second, Fifteenth, and Twenty-fourth Arkansas (Consolidated). From these latter regiments Cleburne sent skirmishers forward into the patch of young trees at the mouth of the gap.

Cleburne concentrated two of Lowrey's remaining regiments in reserve in the center of the gap. The Irishman ordered Polk's brigade to take position near the eastern mouth of the gap to keep an eye on the White Oak Mountain line and to reinforce Granbury's Texans, should the enemy make a serious effort to turn his right flank.

In front of the gap, supported by Govan's Fifth and Thirteenth Arkansas (Consolidated), which lay in a ravine to the right, Cleburne had Lieutenant Richard Goldthwaite unlimber his section of two Napoleon guns from Semple's battery. Continuing his careful supervision, Cleburne told the artillerymen to build screens of withered branches in front of the cannon, which nicely camouflaged them. Goldthwaite's gunners rammed home a charge of canister into one gun and a shell into the other, then lay down themselves to wait. There, at what was sure to be the storm center, Cleburne stayed on to direct the impending fight.[3]

A mile to the west, on the near bank of South Chickamauga Creek between the ford where Cleburne had crossed and a covered bridge through which the Ringgold road passed over the water, two hundred troopers from the Ninth Kentucky Cavalry sat quietly scanning the horizon for Yankees. The Thirty-third Alabama Infantry had drawn the duty of supporting them. Their vigil had begun just before dawn, but "the Yankees were quite obliging, for they did not put in an appearance for two hours. This gave us ample time for rest and to feed," recalled a grateful cavalryman.[4]

Their repose ended abruptly at 7:30 A.M., when pickets galloped across the bridge to report that the head of Hooker's long column was only a short distance off, tramping along the road toward the creek.[5]

Hooker had awakened his men at 5:30 A.M. Thirty minutes later they were on the road. Osterhaus's division led the way, followed by those of Geary and Cruft. Woods's brigade served as advance guard, its front screened by 170 mounted infantrymen commanded by Captain W. T. House. Woods's march was delayed by a steady stream of Rebel stragglers who waved down House's little band to give themselves up and by several frustrating twists and turns in the road as it neared the creek. Finally, House and a dozen of his men who had ridden on ahead came within sight of the creek and the two hundred Kentucky troopers arrayed behind it. What looked like certain slaughter for the Federals turned into a laughable, bloodless little triumph. The Kentuckians delivered a single, long-range volley, then turned their horses and fell back into town. Knowing Hooker with his thousands of infantry was close behind House, explained a member of the Ninth Kentucky Cavalry, "we had no desire to exchange compliments with that gentleman at that time." Actually, there was a sound tactical reason for their seemingly disordered departure. Cleburne intended for them to take to their heels at the first sign of blue so as to create the impression that only a small force of cavalry guarded Ringgold Gap.[6]

On seeing the Kentuckians spin around in their saddles, the Thirty-third Alabama about-faced and made for Ringgold as well. In their haste to get away, neither the Kentuckians nor the Alabamians took time to set fire to the covered bridge. Calculated though their ragged retreat might have been, it certainly didn't excuse this blunder; burning the bridge would have delayed the Federals at least a good half hour, putting that much more time between them and Bragg's lumbering trains.

House galloped across the bridge with his tiny contingent and rode recklessly into Ringgold after the Rebels, who showed no interest in pausing to eliminate the pesky Yankees. The rest of House's mounted men caught up with him, and the reunited command drew rein on the eastern edge of town a few minutes before 8:00 A.M., just as the last of the Confederates filtered into the gap, sixteen hundred yards away.[7]

Cleburne was there beside Goldthwaite's guns to offer a few words of reassurance to the Kentuckians as they trotted past. He yelled to their commander to dismount his men to the right of Cleburne's second line, adding that he intended to "salivate" the Yankees when they came up. To the Thirty-third Alabama, he gave orders to fall in with Lowrey's other two regiments in the center of the gap.[8]

Cleburne's ruse at the creek and the carefully camouflaged lines of infantry completely baffled Hooker and Osterhaus. Encouraged as well by the talk—a bit of it dissembling—of townspeople who had watched Bragg's army drag itself through their streets the day before, Hooker decided to launch a direct attack against Ringgold Gap. And he determined to launch it at once, even though his formidable force of artillery, which could have softened up any Rebels who might happen to be hiding in the area, was still miles behind, trailing Cruft's division. In his report, Hooker, while explaining the basis of his decision, also unwittingly revealed the extent to which Cleburne had taken him in:

It was represented by citizens friendly to our cause, and confirmed by contrabands, that the enemy had passed through Ringgold, sorely pressed, his animals exhausted, and his army hopelessly demoralized.

In a small portion of it only had the officers been able to preserve regimental and company formations, many of the men having thrown away their arms. A still greater number were open and violent in their denunciations of the Confederacy.

In order to gain time, it was the intention of the rear guard to make use of the natural advantages the gorge presented to check the pursuit. The troops relied on for this were posted behind the mountain and the trees, and the latter were also used to mask a couple of pieces of artillery. Only a feeble line of skirmishers appeared in sight.

The only way to ascertain the enemy's strength was to feel of him, and, as our success, if prompt, would be crowned with a rich harvest of material, without waiting for my artillery, the skirmishers advanced.[9]

Cleburne watched their approach from his close but concealed vantage point, fully appreciating the weight of the task that rested upon his shoulders. "The valley in front was clear of our troops, but close in rear of the ridge our immense train was still in full view, struggling through the fords of the creek and the deeply cut up roads leading to Dalton, and my division, silent, but cool and ready, was the only barrier between it and the flushed and eager advance of the pursuing Federal army," he reported with scarcely exaggerated drama.[10]

The thick line of Yankee skirmishers moved steadily across the open valley north of the railroad tracks toward the long fringe of timber near the foot of White Oak Mountain. Behind the trees Granbury's Texans crouched in wait. It was a few minutes after 8:00 A.M.

The Yankees belonged to the Seventeenth and Thirty-first Missouri regiments of Charles Woods's brigade. The first clues they had of the Texans' presence were hundreds of muzzle flashes and the roar of a concentrated volley. The stunned Missourians recoiled instinctively. Woods sent forward the Twenty-ninth Missouri at once to steady them, but the added numbers only gave the Texans more targets.

For a moment it looked as if the Twenty-ninth Missouri might slip past the right flank of the Texans crouched in the timber. But Major W. A. Taylor, the commander of the Seventeenth, Eighteenth, Twenty-fourth, and Twenty-fifth Texas Dismounted Cavalry Regiments (Consolidated), adroitly bent back his right flank and deployed skirmishers up the slope of White Oak Mountain at right angles to his line. More important, he placed two companies atop a swell that jutted from the mountain at a point due east of Ringgold; like Cleburne, Taylor appreciated the opportunities that the sinuous high ground offered a defending force. So too did Colonel Granbury, who reinforced Taylor's men on the swell with two companies from the left of the brigade line.

By the time the Missourians began to climb the rocky ridge, which

*The Rear Guard.* Major General Patrick Cleburne watches the advance of Hooker's Federal infantry against Ringgold Gap. Cleburne sits to the side of the cannon of Lieutenant Richard Goldthwaite.

rose before them at an imposing incline of forty-five degrees, Taylor, who had climbed the slope himself, was ready for them. He led three companies off the swell in a wild, stumbling charge down on the Twenty-ninth. His little band seized the colors of the Missourians, who gave way abruptly before the unexpected counterattack. Their fright was contagious. In a matter of minutes, all three Missouri regiments were in frantic retreat back over the open fields toward the protection of Rock Depot and the neighboring houses on the eastern edge of Ringgold.[11]

There General Woods made ready to advance his remaining regiments. He allowed his defeated Missourians to pass to the rear—not realizing that they would resist all subsequent attempts to rally them—then sent forward in their stead the rest of the brigade. The Twelfth and Third Missouri marched straight ahead toward ground already littered with dead and dying men from their home state. To avoid a repeat of the senseless slaughter on the flat, Woods ordered the Seventy-sixth Ohio to skirt the northern limit of the fringe of timber and climb the mountain, with an eye toward turning the Rebel right flank. The Thirteenth Illinois, meanwhile, filed out from behind the depot and, forming line of battle to the right of the Missourians, aimed for the mouth of the gap.[12]

Although they had witnessed the destruction of Woods's front-line regiments, the men of the Thirteenth Illinois were confident of success. The little clump of trees ahead of their right flank looked innocuous enough, and the gorge behind it appeared empty. "The boys were chipper as could be, and hardly expecting so much danger so near at hand," confessed the regimental historian.

But Cleburne, dismounted now, had kept a sharp eye on the Illinoisans through his field glasses. Now they were near enough to make out the stars on their regimental colors with the naked eye—just fifty yards away. The Illinoisans faced to the front and their right flank swung around as if to offer itself in sacrifice to Goldthwaite's gunners. Cleburne was beside himself with glee. A private from the Thirteenth Arkansas, lying in the ravine nearby, watched Cleburne release the tension of the morning: He "almost sprang into the air, clapped his knee, and shouted in a strong Irish accent, 'Now, Lieutenant, give it to 'em, now!'"[13]

Goldthwaite obeyed. The first horrible blast of grape and canister shredded the soldiers of the right files of the Thirteenth Illinois. The Fifth and Thirteenth Arkansas (Consolidated) opened fire simultaneously from the ravine. "This was a surprise and a severe test of our nerve and power of concession as a regiment; at a word from the officers, all the men lay flat on the ground but stayed in place," continued the chronicler of the regiment.

To the Arkansans, squinting through the smoke, it seemed as if every Federal had been killed. "Every man hit the ground and, from the way their hats, caps, guns, and accouterments went flying the air, I had not a doubt that the entire line was annihilated and exclaimed, 'By Jove, boys, it killed them all,'" recalled a young Rebel private. Cleburne overheard him. He "smiled at my boyish incredulity [and] said to me good naturedly, 'If you don't lie down, young man, you are liable to find that there are enough left for you to get the top of your head shot off."

It was sound advice. There were still plenty of Illinoisans alive, and their commander, Lieutenant Colonel Frederick Partridge, was reacting as well as could be expected to the short-range hammering. He called on Companies A and B to move out beyond their prone comrades and open fire on the gunners in the trees, then rode along to keep them from faltering. With the copse blanketed in smoke, the Illinoisans could only guess at their targets, and their blind shots did nothing to silence Goldthwaite's guns, which continued to mangle the right companies of the regiment.

Partridge tried a different tack. He sent orders back to Major Bushnell to call the entire regiment to its feet and have it charge straight for the cannon. Dazed by the din, the men seemed not fully to comprehend what Partridge expected of them, but they stood up, executed a half right wheel, and made for the trees nonetheless.

All that this movement accomplished, however, was to expose the entire regiment to the effects of the Rebel fire. The color sergeant collapsed with a grapeshot through the chest. His blood splashed the silk of the national colors—and years later visitors to the Illinois State House in Springfield would gawk at the faded stains in the folds of the banner. Corporal Joseph Sackett of the color guard grabbed the colors and ran on, heedless of what was happening around him.

While Sackett sprinted off with the flag, Partridge called a halt near the north bank of the creek. He screamed at his men to take cover behind a log farmhouse, barn, pigpen, and a stack of railroad ties. There, on the Jobe family homestead, the Illinoisans opened up a well-intentioned but largely ineffectual fire that drained their cartridge boxes.[14]

Their futile three-hour struggle cost the Thirteenth dearly. Lieutenant Colonel Partridge had his left hand shredded while standing next to the barn. Before departing for the rear to have the wound dressed, Partridge asked a nearby soldier to let Major Bushnell know he was temporarily in command.

But Bushnell was beyond hearing. With a handful of men he had sought cover behind the pile of railroad ties. A bullet found him nonetheless. It grazed the end of a tie and bored into his forehead, coming to rest in the back of his neck. Command passed to Captain Walter Blanchard of Company K. His tenure too was brief. As he stood next to the farmhouse shouting orders that no one could possibly hear, a grapeshot shattered his knee. Blanchard died a week later.[15]

Corporal Sackett, at least, was still alive. When it dawned on him that no one had followed him, he dropped the flag through the forked branches of an apple tree and threw himself to the ground beside it. There the banner dangled for the rest of the battle, swinging temptingly in the breeze sixty yards from the Rebel lines.

The temptation was more than some of Govan's officers could bear. They begged Cleburne to allow them to rush out with a detail to grab the colors, but the general, who had little regard for trophies and a high regard for the lives of his men, forbade it. One captain from the Second Arkansas persisted so vehemently that he had to be physically restrained from violating Cleburne's sensible prohibition.[16]

Like the Illinoisans on their right, the soldiers of the Third and Twelfth Missouri were shedding blood to no good end. Granbury's Texans had them pinned down in front of the long line of timber.

For a time, it appeared as if the Seventy-sixth Ohio might save them. Fewer than 250 strong, the regiment made its way around the right flank of Major Taylor's Texans and started up the mountain. Its ascent followed a course that, if successful, would take it to the summit at a point far beyond the right of even the Seventh Texas, which, because of an intervening spur, was unaware of the climbing Ohioans. Behind the Seventy-sixth, the Fourth Iowa of Williamson's brigade trailed in support. As the two Federal regiments passed beyond the brigade right, Major Taylor sent word of the threat to Colonel Granbury.[17]

Up the slope toiled the Ohioans. Large rocks, smaller loose stones, and a fine covering of shale made the ascent slippery and slow. The men naturally gravitated toward the path of least resistance, which happened to be a wide draw flanked by two spurs. It was also an ideal spot in which to be ambushed, which is precisely what happened.

Cleburne had had plenty of warning of the Federals' approach, as they were clearly visible marching across the flat, and he had dispatched messengers to Lucius Polk and Mark Lowrey to tell them to put their brigades in motion to meet the threat. Neither general needed nudging. Both were acting splendidly on their own. Seldom, in fact, was a unit commander in the Army of Tennessee better served by his subordinates than was Cleburne here at Ringgold Gap.

Polk had been on his way to confer with the commander of the Seventh Texas when a breathless straggler stumbling off the mountain warned him of the Yankee movement beyond Granbury's right.[18]

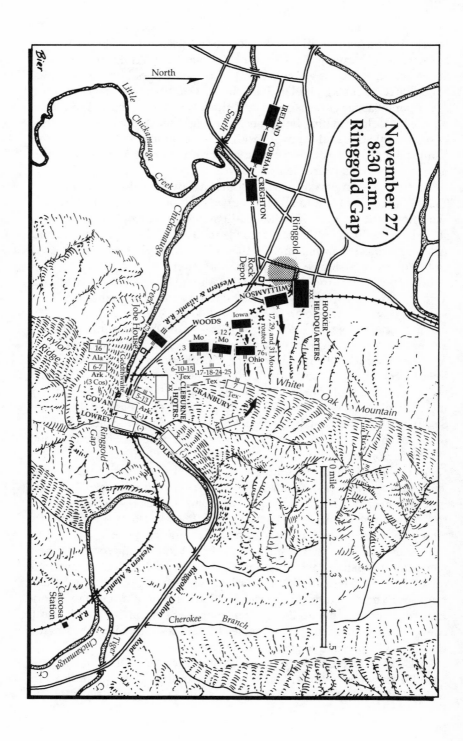

*Bier*

North

November 27,
8:30 a.m.
Ringgold Gap

*Little Chickamauga Creek*

*Chickamauga Creek*

IRELAND

COBHAM

CRECHTON

South

Ringgold

Rock
Depot

WILLIAMSON

HOOKER
HEADQUARTERS

Western & Atlantic R.R.

Jobe House

WOODS

Iowa

Mo

4

12
Mo

3

17, 29, and 31 Mo.
routed

76.
Ohio

Taylor's Ridge

16
Ala

6-7
Ark.
(3 Cos)

Goldthwaite

6-10-15
Tex

17-18-24-25

White

5-13
Ark

Tex

7

Tex

Oak

Mountain

GOVAN

CLEBURNE H.QTRS

GRANBURY

LOWREY

Ringgold
Gap

POLK
(-)

Ark

1

(-)

0 mile

1

2

Western & Atlantic

Ringgold-Dalton Road

3

Tiger

Catoosa
Station

R.R.

E. Chickamauga Cr.

Cherokee Branch

4

5

Polk instantly ordered up the First Arkansas. It climbed the reverse slope in column, reaching the summit atop the spur opposite the left companies of the Seventy-sixth Ohio, with the enemy's skirmishers a mere twenty paces away. The Ohioans began shooting before Polk had a chance to deploy his Arkansans in line of battle. They came into line on the run and returned the fire. The Ohioans backed away a few yards and took cover.

General Lowrey showed up just after the First Arkansas deployed. He had heard the racket over on the mountain and ridden out from the gap to see what it meant. Assuming the worst, he brought his brigade with him. Arriving at the summit ahead of his troops, Lowrey assured Polk's Arkansans that help was on the way. He spun about in the saddle and hurried back to his brigade, which was puffing up the steep reverse slope at the double-quick. "The bullets from the enemy's guns already [were] flying down the line," said Lowrey, who well understood the threat. "I knew that nothing but the most prompt and rapid movement could save the position, and that I could not take time to put the whole brigade in position before moving upon the enemy."

So, as soon as Lowrey reached the head of the column, which consisted of the Fifteenth Mississippi Sharpshooters and the Thirty-second and Forty-fifth Mississippi Infantry, he yelled: "By company into line." Like the Arkansans before them, the men sprinted into line, deploying on their tenth company. While Lowrey shepherded them into place, his aide rode down the slope to hurry forward the Thirty-third Alabama, which lined up on the left of the Mississippians, then the Forty-fifth Alabama, which rounded out the brigade front and closed the gap with the Seventh Texas. Lowrey was delighted. "Our spirited fire, the sight of reinforcements, and a terrific 'Rebel yell,' combined to strike terror to the foe, and he fled in confusion.'"[19]

Not quite. In truth, the men of the Seventy-sixth Ohio, although now painfully outnumbered, held on for perhaps ten minutes more, encouraged a bit by the Fourth Iowa, which was coming up the hill behind them. With each passing minute, however, the Confederates grew stronger. Polk brought up the Third and Fifth Confederate Infantry and the Second Tennessee to extend his line far beyond the left flank of the Ohioans. No longer could the Seventy-sixth endure the volleys that raked its lines from in front and both flanks. As the Ohioans began to break contact, Polk waved forward the First Arkansas, which bounded down the ridge intent on taking the colors of the Seventy-sixth.

Eight color-bearers and two officers were shot down while shielding the national colors, which the Ohioans brought safely off the ridge. The First Arkansas got the regimental flag, however. With the opposing lines only one hundred feet apart and the momentum clearly with the descending Arkansans, Major Willard Warner had given the word to retreat. A bullet struck Silas Priest, who was carrying the blue regimental banner, before he could turn around, and he fell facing the enemy. The flag tumbled into a narrow gully. Several men sprang forward to rescue it, but all were shot.

Major Warner reassembled the regiment on the slope just above the foot of the mountain and hung on. Of the 250 who had gone into action, 18 had been killed outright and another 46 wounded. The Fourth Iowa had come onto the scene too late, and it also retreated. Adroitly using the advantages of high ground and jutting spurs in a way Breckinridge's corps had failed to two days earlier on Missionary Ridge, Lowrey and Polk had swept their front clean of Federals.[20]

Although Woods's brigade was fought out, the threat against Cleburne's right flank had only begun. Watching the brave but doomed ascent of the Seventy-sixth Ohio and Fourth Iowa and the gathering host of Rebels under Polk and Lowrey, General Osterhaus had ordered Colonel Williamson to send the rest of his brigade up the ragged slope of White Oak Mountain farther to the left.

Williamson deployed his command in two lines and moved out from Ringgold toward the mountain. He never had a chance. By the time Williamson got his forward two regiments to the slope, the First Arkansas had returned from its counterattack and Polk and Lowrey had eight regiments along the summit. Nevertheless, Williamson tried to succor the Seventy-sixth Ohio and his own Fourth Iowa. Up the ridge went his front-line regiments—the Ninth and Twenty-sixth Iowa—only to be stopped a few yards short of the crest.

A vicious, short-range struggle ensued. It was Tunnel Hill repeated. Officers used their pistols, rocks were tossed, and insults were exchanged as the opposing lines settled into a tense stalemate that both Williamson and Polk hastened to break to their advantage.

Williamson acted first. The Iowa colonel climbed toward the crest with his reserve regiments, the Twenty-fifth and Thirtieth Iowa, intending to come in on the left of his front line and outflank the enemy. Slowly and purposefully the Iowans moved, skirmishing as they climbed.

The stalled attack of Williamson's brigade was about to end Osterhaus's contribution to the battle but it did not dissuade Hooker from trying to seize Ringgold Gap. As soon as the lead brigade of Geary's division showed up at Rock Depot, Hooker told the Pennsylvanian to send it against White Oak Mountain to the left of Williamson. He was determined to outflank Cleburne and confident that he could feed troops to that sector faster than could Cleburne.[21]

Hooker was wrong. Cleburne's careful dispositions would continue to pay handsome dividends.

At about 9:00 A.M., Colonel William Creighton started across the valley with his brigade of Ohioans and Pennsylvanians deployed in two lines, all cocky and contemptuous of the Rebels. They had driven them from the seemingly impregnable heights of Lookout Mountain and had refused to believe that this attack would be any more difficult. The men of Creighton's front-line regiments ascended the slope, stepping through the ranks of the cautious soldiers of the Twenty-fifth and Thirtieth Iowa regiments. As they moved past, they jibed Williamson's exhausted Iowans that they would soon teach "Western troops a lesson" in fighting.[22]

But it was they who were to learn a bloody lesson. Polk had watched them come out of Ringgold. As they marched confidently across the flat, Polk deftly shifted the Second Tennessee and First Arkansas northward along the summit to meet them and called on Lowrey for additional reinforcements.

From the base of White Oak Mountain, Colonel Williamson watched the Easterners go up. Their whole way of attacking was wrong, he mused, partly in sympathy for the men who were about to die and partly in disgust at the arrogance of their commanders. Instead of climbing cautiously, with skirmishers thrown forward, he said, "they tried to go up as if on parade where the men could barely have gone up by clinging to the rocks and bushes."[23]

Williamson's judgment was vindicated. Creighton's troops, winded before they were halfway to the top, halted and opened fire. "We were tired and our fire was not delivered with that accuracy and effect that might have been hoped for," confessed a member of the Twenty-eighth Pennsylvania. "It was as much as we could do to climb the rough and steep mountain-side without having to fight a larger army in front of us."[24]

In truth, the Easterners were not outnumbered, but outgeneraled. Polk and Lowrey again made excellent use of the jagged spurs on the crest to deliver enfilading volleys against the flanks of the four Yankee regiments, which were naturally channeled into the intervening draws. Lowrey contributed the Forty-fifth Alabama to the fight on the left of the First Arkansas, and Polk threw the Second Tennessee down the hill against the left flank of the Yankees. The slaughter was terrific.[25]

None was harder hit than Creighton's old regiment, the Seventh Ohio. The Ohioans moved from their position on the right of the second line to ascend the slope to the left of the two front-line regiments, already engaged. As they passed by, Creighton shouted to the men the same quixotic command that had Colonel Williamson shaking his head:

"Boys, we are ordered to take that hill. I want to see you walk right up it."

They did. Between the open arms of two spurs they struggled toward the crest. Suddenly Confederates popped up on both flanks, pouring volley after volley into the Seventh. Officers pushed among their troops, now a scared mob, pleading with them to keep going. The regimental commander, Lieutenant Colonel Orrin Crane, was shot dead early on. Then one officer after another fell, until only a single commissioned officer was left. Men dropped at the rate of one in every two. In Company C, fourteen of twenty troops were lost. With few troops still on their feet and virtually no one to lead them, there was no alternative but to retreat. "It was a sad affair for the regiment. Its glory seemed to have departed it," remembered a survivor sadly.

Colonel Creighton too was saddened. "There goes poor Crane," he moaned, on hearing of his old friend's death. An instant later, Creighton was down, mortally wounded. "Tell my wife I died at the head of my command," he whispered as he was carried from the field.[26]

Colonel Williamson had watched the brief struggle of the Easterners intently. "They stood manfully for a minute or two, then they gave way and came down like an avalanche, carrying everything before them, and to some extent propagating panic among my regiments," he reported of that, the last effort by Hooker to envelop Cleburne's right flank.[27]

During the two hours that Cleburne was countering Hooker's moves against White Oak Mountain, he also had to watch his left, where the Sixteenth Alabama and three companies of the Sixth and Seventh Arkansas (Consolidated) stood alone on Taylor's Ridge. Shortly before 10:00 A.M., the Federals made their first serious move against Cleburne's left flank. Colonel George Cobham's small brigade of three Pennsylvania regiments, which Geary had been holding in reserve behind Rock Depot, charged across the flat, past the left of the Thirteenth Illinois to the railroad embankment, where Goldthwaite's cannon and Govan's infantry stopped them. Cobham ordered his men to lie down, return the fire, and wait for reinforcements.[28]

Back in Ringgold, Generals Hooker and Geary were standing behind Rock Depot, watching the head of Geary's last brigade, that of Colonel David Ireland, march up. Hooker happened to step out from behind the building and look toward the front at the very instant Cobham's brigade began to waver. Turning to Geary, Hooker gave vent to his frustration. "Have you any regiments that will not run?" he snapped. "I have no regiments that will run," retorted Geary, seeming to have forgotten about Creighton's debacle. Hooker forgave the hyperbole. "Then send some men into that gap and hold it until my artillery arrives," he commanded. Out of Ringgold and over the same fields streaked with the blood of Woods's and Cobham's brigades charged Ireland's New Yorkers.

It was 10:40 A.M. As Ireland advanced, the Thirteenth Illinois fell back, having fired its last rounds. The New Yorkers charged past the Illinoisans and made for the bank of South Chickamauga Creek at the double-quick, all the while taking a terrific pounding from Goldthwaite's seemingly omnipresent cannon. Lieutenant Albert Greene, the young brigade staff officer who had watched his father fall at Wauhatchie, went down when a solid shot ripped through his horse and severed Greene's right leg.

The New Yorkers reached the creek and prepared to ford. A few skirmishers splashed across before Cleburne stopped the entire brigade with a counterattack launched by a detachment from the Sixteenth Alabama and an accurate, concentrated fire from Govan's own skirmishers. Ireland commanded his men to take cover behind the creek bank and the buildings of the Jobe farm that the Thirteenth Illinois had just abandoned. From there, a few minutes after 11:00 A.M., they opened up a fire that drove the Sixteenth Alabama back up Taylor's Ridge.[29]

A deadly stalemate settled over the gap. "The firing on both sides soon resolved itself into sharp-shooting. The men fired upon the enemy whenever he showed himself, and he returned the compliment whenever an opportunity was afforded him," explained a New Yorker.[30]

It was a stalemate that Cleburne obviously could not sustain indefinitely. He had all but exhausted his reserves in checking the moves of two Federal divisions. From his vantage spot at the vortex of the fight, Cleburne could see more Federal infantrymen tramping through the streets of Ringgold and congregating behind Rock Depot. It was Davis's division, just arrived. By noon, Hooker's artillery at last had begun to come up and was maneuvering east of town into position to shell both ridges and the gap. Hooker, speculated Cleburne, was "doubtless preparing to throw an overwhelming force on my flanks."[31]

The Irishman gave Hooker credit for an aggressiveness he no longer possessed. Indeed, Hooker had told Geary not to press an attack with Cobham or Ireland, but simply to have them hold their ground near the mouth of the gap. Far from deploying his artillery to cover an attack, Hooker wanted simply to silence Goldthwaite's section and then let the fighting sputter out. Two hours earlier, Hooker had sent off Cruft's division with orders to cross the creek several miles to the south near Catoosa Station and get behind the Rebels there, rather than commit it to the struggle for Ringgold Gap; it was a movement that easily would take the rest of the afternoon to complete. In addition to Davis's division, Palmer's corps was up as well. The streets of Ringgold thronged with Federals that Hooker had no interest in deploying.[32]

Knowing none of this, Cleburne was deeply relieved to receive a dispatch from Hardee at noon telling him that the army trains were now well on their way and that he could withdraw as he pleased. For the first time since the Federal attacks had begun four hours earlier, Cleburne left the clump of trees and rode back into the gap. There he consulted with Generals Breckinridge and Wheeler, who had remained with his division to offer their advice and moral support. The three agreed that the division should withdraw as soon as possible to take up a new line on Dick's Ridge, one mile east of Ringgold Gap.

Cleburne returned to Goldthwaite's guns. He had the screen of branches rebuilt in front of them. Availing themselves of this ragged camouflage, the Alabama artillerymen proudly dragged off their two pieces by hand. Next, Cleburne ordered his infantry off the ridges and out of the gap simultaneously, as Hooker's artillery at last came to life. Over the ruts of the wagon road to Dalton they trudged. Shortly after 2:00 P.M., Cleburne pulled back his skirmishers, and the field belonged to the Federals.

Hooker was glad to see the Rebels leave and made no effort to continue the pursuit. Five hundred nine killed and wounded in four hours of futile fighting had satiated his appetite for spoils.

Grant had ridden into Ringgold at about 11:30 A.M. The roar of battle still echoed through the streets. The Ohioan and his staff shoved through crowds of idle soldiers. Lacking anything better to do, the men were catching pigs and poking chickens from under sheds and house porches with their ramrods. Grant reached Rock Depot to find Hooker sitting atop a large barrel, eating a sandwich and drinking a cup of tea. Grant's first inclination was to order Hooker to reinforce the aborted attack against Cleburne's south flank on Taylor's Ridge. He then thought better of it and confirmed Hooker's decision to break off the fight and allow Cleburne to leave.

In saving the trains and artillery of the Army of Tennessee, Cleburne had lost 221 men, only 20 of them killed, when the night before he had resigned himself to sacrificing his entire division to the purpose.[33]

# THE FRUITS ARE BITTER

T HE NASTY affair at Ringgold Gap marked the end of the Chattanooga campaign. It also brought down a rain of censure on Hooker. In a dispatch to Stanton, Assistant Secretary Dana derided Hooker's assault as "the first great fault in this admirable campaign. It was a very dangerous defile to attack in front, and common sense plainly dictated that it should be turned."

Most of the officers and men of the army agreed with Dana's dismal assessment. Colonel Oscar Harmon of the One Hundred Twenty-fifth Illinois wrote his wife in disgust: "General Hooker, to maintain his reputation as a fighting man, pushed his pursuing column against the enemy at Ringgold and lost very heavily." A member of the decimated Seventh Ohio pondered: "For what purpose this handful of men were ordered to storm the enemy's position on the hill has never been explained. There was no artillery used to cover the assault, without which it was impossible to carry the position with such a force, and hazardous to attempt it with any. But thus far Hooker and his almost invincible corps had carried everything before them. This success seemed to bring with it a contempt for the rebel soldiers, which finally resulted in the great disaster at Taylor's Ridge."[1]

Among the few who refrained from fustigating Hooker was Grant. Perhaps he recognized that the criticism was largely unjust. Hooker, in fact, had performed capably. The tons of discarded weapons and equipment and hundreds of disheartened stragglers his column scooped up as it marched toward Ringgold were ample evidence that the Rebel army was on the verge of collapse. Where the opportunity so obviously existed to destroy an entire army, every tenet of military science dictated an aggressive pursuit. Risks were warranted; lives might of necessity be sacrificed to keep the pressure on the fleeing foe. And Hooker did try to flank Cleburne out of his position. His decision to attack without waiting for his artillery also was reasonable; had Ringgold Gap not been so well defended, the four hours lost awaiting the arrival of his guns might have cost Hooker his chance at bagging Bragg's trains. Hooker's only error, it seems, was in calling off his assault when he did, and in this decision he was seconded by Grant.

Grant may have reasoned similarly, but more probably he let Hooker off easy because he already had made up his mind to halt the pursuit. He simply saw no alternative but to accede to Lincoln's insistence that he save Burnside. Grant had gotten a not so gentle nudge the very day Missionary Ridge fell. On 24 November, he had sent the president a buoyant telegram reporting (incorrectly as it turned out) that Hooker had captured two thousand prisoners on Lookout Mountain and that Sherman had carried the northern end of Missionary Ridge. "Well done. Many thanks to all. Remember Burnside," was all Lincoln had to say the next day in response to the first really good battlefield news he had received since the fall of Vicksburg.[2]

Grant took the point. On the afternoon of 27 November, he, Hooker, and Sherman conferred at Ringgold. Sherman explained that he had detached Howard that morning to march east from Graysville to Red Clay to cut the East Tennessee and Georgia Railroad, as Grant had previously ordered. Grant approved of the move but told Sherman to halt Howard once he had destroyed the tracks. Grant already had made up his mind to quit the chase of Bragg. As he explained in his report: "Had it not been for the imperative necessity of relieving Burnside, I would have pursued the broken and demoralized retreating enemy as long as supplies could have been found in the country. But my advices were that Burnside's supplies would only last until about the third of December. It was already getting late to afford the necessary relief."[3]

Grant passed the night with Sherman in Graysville. To his friend, he confided his doubts about Granger's ability to manage the relief expedition. In a word, Grant was fed up with Granger, who had not yet started for Knoxville, and told Sherman as much. He felt the need to return to Chattanooga at once to prod Granger along. In the meantime, Sherman was to concentrate his command, augmented by Howard's corps and Davis's division, in the neighborhood of Cleveland to block any lateral movement between Bragg and Longstreet.[4]

On 28 November, with Granger still frittering about Chattanooga, Grant gave up entirely on him. Although Granger got started that afternoon, Grant decided to turn over the expedition to Sherman. "Granger is on the way to Burnside's relief, but I have lost all faith in his energy and capacity to manage an expedition of the importance of this one," he wrote Sherman the next day. "I am inclined to think, therefore, that I shall have to send you. . . . In plain words, you will assume command of all the forces now moving up the Tennessee, including the garrison at Kingston, and from that force organize what you deem proper to relieve Burnside." Sherman drove his force relentlessly northward over sloppy roads and through a numbing cold.[5]

Granger's men were utterly worn out, wearing the same tattered uniforms with which they had suffered through the long weeks of siege in Chattanooga; most wore shoes that were more holes than leather, and some went barefoot. Sherman's own troops were in similar straits, having come all the way from Mississippi and fought a major battle without a change of clothing. Yet they marched, hard and fast, for eighty-five miles to save what they thought was a starving army on the verge of being overrun.[6]

One can imagine their shock when they learned that their efforts had been wasted. On 5 December, while riding with the head of his column just fifteen miles short of Knoxville, Sherman was handed a dispatch from Burnside. It said, in essence, that Sherman's services were no longer needed. Longstreet had launched a savage but stupid frontal attack on the city's formidable fortifications on 29 November over the protest of his chief lieutenant, Lafayette McLaws. McLaws had argued that, if the unconfirmed reports of Bragg's defeat at Chattanooga were indeed true, prudence dictated that Longstreet lift the siege and retreat toward Virginia before Grant turned his entire victorious army against him. Longstreet dismissed McLaws's counsel and attacked. His troops were massacred. A half hour after the repulse, couriers brought Longstreet two messages from Davis confirming the disaster at Chattanooga. Bragg, said the first, "had retired before superior numbers"; the second, that he "had retired to Dalton, and General Longstreet must depend upon his own resources." Scouts reported the approach of Sherman at about the same time. His resources being far more limited than those of the Federals whom he had besieged, Longstreet disappeared from the city and melted into the cold, desolate mountains of easternmost Tennessee.[7]

On 6 December, Generals Sherman and Granger rode into Knoxville ahead of their men. Thinking of his own famished soldiers, Sherman was unamused by what he discovered. "Approaching from the south and west, we crossed the Holston on a pontoon-bridge, and in a large pen on the Knoxville side I saw a fine lot of cattle, which did not look much like starvation. I found General Burnside and staff domiciled in a large fine mansion, looking very comfortable."

Burnside told Sherman he had already given orders to follow Longstreet, then took him on a tour of his lines. Later, the generals and their staffs sat down to a sumptuous dinner of roast turkey. Sherman was dumbfounded. "There was a regular dining-table, with clean table cloth, dishes, knives, forks, spoons, etc. I had seen nothing of this kind in my field service, and could not help exclaiming that I thought they were starving." Between mouthfuls, Burnside explained offhandedly that his army never had been completely invested; that his cavalry had kept open communication with the friendly Unionists of the region, from whom he received a supply of beef, bacon, and cornmeal sufficient to keep his men decently fed. Sherman gave free play to his ire over having driven his tired troops to the point of collapse to relieve what he thought was a starving garrison. After giving Burnside the two divisions of Granger to join in the pursuit of Longstreet, he was only too happy to turn his own troops around and begin a leisurely march back to Chattanooga.[8]

Sherman's expedition to Knoxville may have been superfluous, but Grant had calculated correctly the anxiety in Washington over the fate of the Tennessee city. Lincoln had no words of praise for Grant in the immediate wake of his triumph at Chattanooga. In his mind, so long as the fate of Knoxville remained in doubt, the battle was only half over. Consequently, the president waited until 7 December, after he got official confirmation of Longstreet's retreat, to tell the nation of the triumph of Union arms in eastern Tennessee. The announcement read: "Reliable information being received that the insurgent force is retreating from East Tennessee, under circumstances rendering it probable that the Union forces can not hereafter be dislodged from that important position; and esteeming this to be of high national consequence, I recommend that all loyal people do, on receipt of this, informally assemble at their places of worship and tender special homage and gratitude to Almighty God, for this great advancement of the national cause."

The next day—almost two weeks after the victory at Missionary Ridge—Lincoln got around to sending Grant a congratulatory message. Like his public pronouncement, it reflected more his relief that the loyal Unionists in East Tennessee had been delivered, once and for all, from Southern subjugation than an appreciation of Grant's triumph at Chattanooga. "Understanding that your lodgment at Chattanooga and Knoxville is now secure," Lincoln began, "I wish to tender you, and all under your command, my more than thanks—my profoundest gratitude—for the skill, courage, and perseverance, with which you and they, over so great difficulties, have effected that important object. God bless you all."[9]

Grant had no need of presidential praise to convince him he had won a great victory. A week before Lincoln acknowledged his achievement,

Grant had written to his friend and political patron, Congressman Elihu Washburn, his assessment of the Chattanooga campaign. The uncommonly florid prose flowed from Grant's simple sincerity. "Last week was a stirring time with us and a magnificent victory was won," he wrote. "I am sorry you could not be here. The spectacle was grand beyond anything that has been, or is likely to be seen, on this continent. Hooker on our right soon carried the point of Lookout Mountain and Sherman the north end of Missionary Ridge thus shortening the line by five or six miles and bringing the whole within our view. Our troops behaved most magnificently, and have inflicted on the enemy the heaviest blow they have received during the war." Quite a statement, coming from the man who had humbled Vicksburg.[10]

The South indeed had been dealt a devastating blow. Counting those of Cleburne's division who fell at Ringgold Gap, the Army of Tennessee reported to Richmond casualties of 6,667 in the battles for Chattanooga, that is to say, Orchard Knob, Lookout Mountain, and Missionary Ridge. For a major campaign, the number of killed and wounded had been relatively light: 361 killed, and 2,180 wounded. Many of the latter could be counted on eventually to return to the ranks. Irreplaceable were the captured. The army's official report placed the number missing at 4,146. Grant, however, insisted that he sent 6,142 men northward to Union prison camps. His count probably is more reliable, reflecting as it does the hundreds of stragglers netted during the brief pursuit from Chickamauga Station to Ringgold.

Equally serious was the loss in artillery. Forty cannon and sixty-nine limbers and caissons had been surrendered or abandoned. Whole batteries ceased to exist, although the men were kept together in anticipation of procuring guns that the South's few remaining foundries would be hard pressed to supply.[11]

By way of comparison, Grant had suffered 684 killed, 4,329 wounded, and just 322 captured or missing. Sheridan's division had sustained nearly a quarter of these casualties: 1,346, nearly all in the assault on Missionary Ridge.[12]

Although volunteers were virtually nonexistent in the war-weary Confederacy and able-bodied conscripts as scarce as hard currency, it was still easier to replace men than regain territory. The South had lost—this time for good—the state of Tennessee. The late-autumn offensive of John B. Hood's ragged, barefoot, and sick remnant of an army a year later could not change that reality. Hood's pitiful band could have marched to Cincinnati without having materially changed the outcome of the conflict; most would have died or fallen ill from exposure in the frigid North in any event. From 25 November 1863 until the end of the war, the South would be on the strategic defensive in the West. The loss of Tennessee deprived it of a rich source of supply; the loss of Chattanooga robbed it of a staging area for offensive operations.

Not that the South would again be able to muster in the West anything approaching a force sufficient to take the offensive against a Union army that was to grow even stronger during the winter of 1863/64. The concentration of forces under Bragg prior to Chickamauga had given the Confederacy temporary numerical superiority over the Federals in the Southern heartland, an advantage that Bragg let slip through his hands in the aftermath of that bloody but barren victory.

Obviously, Bragg had had his best chance to crush the Army of the Cumberland and reverse the tide of the war in the West—perhaps irrevocably, given the deepening war weariness in the North—during the first hours following the Federal flight into Chattanooga. But even after Grant had brought together his formidable command beneath the gun barrels of the dormant Army of Tennessee, Bragg still was in a fair position to displace the Federals from the city. Notwithstanding the added manpower of Sherman's and Hooker's divisions, the final Federal victory at Chattanooga had been far from certain. What sealed the Confederate fate on Missionary Ridge was not, as some have speculated, a loss of confidence in Bragg on the part of the common soldier— the tenacious fighting of Cleburne's veterans on Tunnel Hill and of Walthall's already decimated brigade beyond their left disproves that notion. Rather, it was the absence of a strong, mobile reserve with which to plug gaps along the ridge. Had President Davis not suggested and Bragg not acceded to sending Longstreet off on his quixotic expedition toward Knoxville, Bragg could have disposed his forces—if not along the narrow ridge then behind it—so as to have such a reserve. Even allowing for the acrimony between Bragg and Longstreet, it is inconceivable that the two or three brigades needed to break the initial, tentative Federal foothold on the crest of Missionary Ridge would not have been on hand.

Had Grant's attempt to break out of Chattanooga failed, the onset of winter would have postponed any further effort until the following spring; indeed, the miserable weather that came on shortly after the Federal triumph worked to cut short active campaigning in East Tennessee.

With little to fear from the timorous Burnside on his flank—that general early on had demonstrated to the disgust of both Lincoln and Grant that a few brigades of Rebel infantry and a handful of intrepid cavalry were enough to hold him at bay—Bragg perhaps could have kept Longstreet with him long enough to compel Grant to evacuate Chattanooga in favor of more secure lines of communication and supply farther north.

But any such hope was lost when Longstreet set off for Knoxville. Bragg was driven from Missionary Ridge and into northern Georgia, ultimately to be replaced by Joseph Johnston, who had a penchant for avoiding pitched battle and whose primary talent rested in his ability to manage retreats. With a timid commander and too few troops, the Army of Tennessee after Chattanooga was left to play out a seventeen-month-long, bloody anticlimax to a drama that effectively had ended on the heights of Missionary Ridge.

That they had lost not only a battle but the war in the West was evident to most of the stunned Southern soldiers who shuffled along the trails winding away from the battlefield on the night of 25 November. "Captain, this is the death knell of the Confederacy," a subaltern whispered to his company commander during the march. "If we cannot cope with those fellows with the advantages we had on this line, there is not a line between here and the Atlantic Ocean where we can stop them." "Hush, Lieutenant," warned the captain, though certainly in agreement. "That is treason you are talking."[13]

Of course, the South's loss was the North's gain. Union armies now had secure lines of communication, free from the danger of depredations by Rebel cavalry, from the Ohio River to Chattanooga. The city became a giant storehouse, where supplies stockpiled during the winter months made possible Sherman's spring 1864 offensive against the last virgin reaches of the Confederate heartland—the interior of Georgia.

The Chattanooga campaign also cemented the triumvirate that would win the war: Grant, Sherman, and Sheridan. Grant's star, which had faded briefly after Vicksburg, was to burn brightly from then on, illuminating a path to the White House. That he had made several questionable tactical decisions during the battles went unnoticed in the adulation that followed the lifting of the sieges of Chattanooga and Knoxville. He never satisfactorily explained his foolish order to Thomas to seize only the rifle pits at the base of Missionary Ridge. Instead, Grant chose to lie. In both his report of the battle and his memoirs, he insisted that he had given Thomas express authority to carry the ridge itself, and implied that he fully expected that to be done. General Thomas died just four years after the war, and in any case was not the sort to engage in egotistical bickering. Few chose to dispute Grant's version of events while Grant lived.

More serious was Grant's dissembling regarding the performance of his friend Sherman. By any objective reckoning, Sherman handled the attack against Bragg's right flank, which was supposed to have been the main effort of the Union arms, with a degree of incompetence that bordered on gross negligence. His myopic fixation on Tunnel Hill blinded him to greater—and potentially less bloody—opportunities to turn the Rebel flank. Equally egregious was his piecemeal and only partial employment of his three divisions. Augmented by those of Howard and Davis, he should have been able to crush Cleburne, terrain constraints notwithstanding.

Grant forgave the Ohioan his missteps. He appreciated Sherman's loyalty and his larger, strategic talents. And, of course, given Grant's icy relations with George Thomas, he had little interest in giving the Virginian credit for any more than he had to. In fact, Grant went out of his way to assure Sherman that no blame would be cast his way. Only minutes after Thomas's troops crowned Missionary Ridge, he began rewriting history. "No doubt you witnessed the handsome manner in which Thomas' troops carried Missionary Ridge this afternoon," he wrote Sherman. Quick to mitigate Sherman's failings, Grant added: "and [you] can feel a just pride, too, in the part taken by the forces under your command in taking, first, so much of the same range of hills [which Sherman never did], and then in attracting the attention of so many of the enemy as to make Thomas's part certain of success [which, as we have seen, was also untrue]." In his report of the campaign and later in his memoirs, Grant puffed this praise almost to outright mendacity, implying that Sherman's attack had been a mere feint to draw troops away from Thomas's front, where the real effort to crush Bragg was to have been made all along.[14]

Among the three, the most deserving of praise was Phil Sheridan. Until Missionary Ridge, he had been merely one of several talented division commanders in the Army of the Cumberland, neither better nor worse than Baird, Johnson, or—his despicable behavior at Chickamauga notwithstanding—Tom Wood. And Sheridan himself had been under a cloud since that battle for having left the field hastily on the second day and then making only a halfhearted effort to return with his rallied troops. But Sheridan's aggressiveness during the waning hours of 25 November erased all that. His enthusiastic pursuit of the enemy down the eastern slope of Missionary Ridge, when everyone else seemed content to bivouac, had impressed Grant. In the little Irishman he saw a natural fighter. When Grant went east to accept his third star, Sheridan went with him.

Thomas lost more than he gained at Chattanooga. Grant came away with an impression of him as slow and argumentative, an opinion that time would not mellow. The Virginian kept the Army of the Cumberland, but until Hood's invasion of Tennessee the honor was largely empty, as he would be subordinated to Sherman, whom he liked personally but whose ability he thought no greater than his own.

Gordon Granger was the greatest loser. A popular hero after marching to Thomas's rescue on Horseshoe Ridge at Chickamauga, he found himself, less than three months later, the laughingstock of the officer corps. Grant came to Chattanooga assuming him competent and went east despising him as an imbecilic blowhard. It took a lot to rile the normally tolerant Grant, but Granger had managed to do so. First there was his silliness during the Battle of Missionary Ridge. As James Wilson, who both liked Granger and considered him equally as brave as and far more intelligent than Sheridan, wrote sadly: "His behavior on that day was a great disappointment to all. It was not only trivial, but brought upon him a severe rebuke from Grant for wasting his time on a battery and leaving his army corps to take care of itself. From that day forth his fortune was on the wane."

It sank farther when he was slow in starting for Knoxville. It disappeared altogether after he arrived there. A bit of Christmas merrymaking gone awry sealed his fate. Grant had given instructions for the Federal forces then congregated in that theater to pursue the enemy and to destroy him or at least drive him from East Tennessee. Instead, the yuletide found Granger's corps snugly quartered in Knoxville and Longstreet's command shivering in rough winter quarters in extreme northeastern Tennessee, miserable but unmolested by the Yankees.

On Christmas Day, the ranking Federal officers assembled for a holiday dinner. Afterward, while they lounged about a roaring fire, Granger shouted with the animation of one obviously intoxicated: "Let's send a telegram to Grant." He called for a blank sheet, then scribbled: "We are in Knoxville and will hold it till hell freezes over." Granger shoved it into the hands of Major General John Foster, who had replaced Burnside two weeks earlier and was thus the senior officer present. "How will that do?" Granger asked. Foster glanced at the message. Realizing it to be both superfluous and in bad taste, he added the word "Tight" at the end of it, meaning that Granger was drunk and that the message should not be sent. Unfortunately, the telegraph operator didn't get Foster's point, and tapped out Granger's festive foolishness with Foster's extra word added.

General Wilson was on duty at headquarters when the telegram came. He missed Foster's point as well. When Grant returned to Chattanooga a few days later, Wilson handed him the message. Grant too was puzzled, then indignant, in part because of the rude tone of the note, and also because he had thought Foster and Granger were in close pursuit of Longstreet. That was the last straw. Foster was trundled off to command the backwater Department of the South, and Granger thereafter bounced between corps and division commands in unimportant theaters. From that day on, the only campaigning of consequence he was to see was the capture of Mobile during the closing weeks of the war.[15]

There remains one great imponderable in the Chattanooga campaign, a "what if" that some have raised rhetorically, often to traduce Grant: What would have been the outcome had Grant kept up his pursuit of Bragg beyond Ringgold? Thomas Robson Hay, the distinguished historian of the Army of Tennessee, summarized the views of those who believe Grant let slip a unique chance to eliminate an army:

> An aggressive pursuit of Bragg's defeated army might have been productive of large and immediate results. Bragg was certainly, at the moment, in no condition to offer effective resistance. His troops were disheartened as a result of being defeated and driven from what were considered impregnable positions. But the same hesitancy and uncertainty as after Shiloh characterized Grant's actions. Hooker's pursuit was stopped and he was ordered to return to Chattanooga. Except perhaps at Vicksburg, and until pitted against Lee before Richmond, Grant does not seem to have realized that, always, the organized forces of the enemy, not geographical positions and territory, should be the primary objective of an army in the field.[16]

That the Army of Tennessee was incapable of resisting a determined attack in the days immediately following Missionary Ridge is indisputable. On the cold, rain-swept night of 27 November, the populace of Dalton, Georgia, witnessed a scene of confusion nearly as complete as that which had disheartened the townspeople of Ringgold the evening before. With stragglers strung out all over the countryside, only 27,987 officers and men answered roll call at Dalton. And the reliability of even these was dubious. Not only had Bragg lost whatever shred of support within the army that he may have enjoyed before Chattanooga, but the chain of command was in disarray. That night, Lieutenant Colonel Brent confessed the confusion in a circular to corps commanders that sounded more like pleading than directing: "So many errors having occurred in the transmission of dispatches, it is ordered that, during the march, at the end of a day's journey, all commanding officers will inform the officer next in rank of the exact locality of their headquarters." Brent also begged Breckinridge and Hardee to have their troops both "in readiness to move in any direction at a moment's notice and well in hand for an engagement."[17]

The generals grumbled. With what were they to fight? Over a third of the army's artillery was gone, and thousands of men had thrown away their rifles while bounding down Missionary Ridge; Grant claimed that his army picked up over seven thousand weapons strewn over the battlefield. Major General William Bate, a cold-blooded martinet, lashed out at those who had lost their arms as "cowardly traitors" who ought to be "promptly and summarily punished, in addition to being charged with the value of their guns."[18]

A Union prisoner took note of the sorry state of the Rebel army as he was hurried through the streets of Dalton that night: "The Rebels have a line of infantry deployed here in the rear of their army to pick up stragglers. It does not appear that their men are very willing to fight, or they would not try to get to the rear, at least I never knew of our men having skirmish lines in the rear of the army to pick up stragglers."[19]

There is no disputing Thomas Hay's final point that, as a military axiom, a general's primary objective should be the destruction of an enemy army rather than the conquest of territory. But Lincoln was not Clausewitz, and such was not his thinking at the time. Grant ultimately had to bow to the wishes of the president and look to the relief of East Tennessee.

Could Grant have both succored Burnside and destroyed—or at least more profoundly disrupted—the Army of Tennessee? Probably not, even if he had pursued vigorously from Ringgold. The departure of Sherman and Granger for Knoxville left him with only about thirty thousand troops. Despite their high morale, they were hungry and poorly clothed. Even Dana, always anxious to press field commanders to greater efforts, confessed to Secretary Stanton on 29 November that bad roads and uncertain supplies ruled out serious campaigning in the theater beyond 6 December. A move against Rome or Atlanta could not even be considered, he added, until six months' supplies for troops and animals were accumulated at Chattanooga.[20]

As rain rilled the roof of his headquarters at Dalton, Bragg fixed the next destination of the army's retreat as Resaca, fifteen miles deeper into Georgia along the Western and Atlantic Railroad. All trains—except the ordnance and ammunition wagons—were to start for there at once and keep moving all night long. For the next day and a half, Bragg gave his limited energy over to ensuring the escape of his army.[21]

When on 29 November reliable reports confirmed that the Federals, far from pursuing, actually were withdrawing toward Chattanooga, Bragg began to give vent to his characteristic post-battle truculence, which over the course of nearly fourteen months had reduced the high command of the Army of Tennessee to a gaggle of conspiratory neurotics, and the rank and file to fatalistic drones or embittered deserters.

Two days earlier, in a laconic note to Joseph Johnston, he had called the "disastrous panic" at Missionary Ridge "inexplicable."[22] Bragg expanded on that theme in his draft report of the battle, written on 30 November. In it, he castigated not only his generals but, for the first time in his troubled tenure, the common soldiers of his army. That part of his report is worth relating in full, if only to reveal the fevered meandering of a dazed and depressed mind. Wrote Bragg:

> No satisfactory excuse can possibly be given for the shameful conduct of our troops on the left in allowing their line to be penetrated. The position was one which ought to have been held by a line of skirmishers against any assaulting column, and wherever resistance was made the enemy fled in disorder after suffering heavy loss. Those who reached the ridge did so in a condition of exhaustion from the great physical exertion in climbing, which rendered them powerless, and the slightest effort would have destroyed them. Having secured much of our artillery, they soon availed themselves of our panic, and, turning our guns upon us, enfiladed the lines, both right and left, rendering them entirely untenable.
>
> Had all parts of the line been maintained with equal gallantry and persistence no enemy could ever have dislodged us, and but one possible reason presents itself to my mind in explanation of this bad conduct in veteran troops who had never before failed in any duty assigned them, however difficult and hazardous. They had for two days confronted the enemy, marshaling his immense forces in plain view, and exhibiting to their sight such a superiority in numbers as may have intimidated weak-minded and untried soldiers; but our veterans had so often encountered similar hosts when the strength of position was against us, and with perfect success, that not a doubt crossed my mind. As yet I am not fully informed as to the commands which first fled and brought this great disorder and disgrace upon our arms. Investigation will bring out the truth, however, and full justice shall be done to the good and the bad.[23]

Bragg's lack of information did not prevent him from lashing out at his lieutenants, who had so long plotted against him. Everyone was a potential scapegoat. "The warfare against me has been carried on successfully, and the fruits are bitter," he complained. Bragg accused Breckinridge of drunkenness so extreme that it had rendered him completely unfit for duty during the crucial days of 23 to 27 November. For no other reason than their longstanding mutual antipathy, he also lashed out at Cheatham, in writing, as "equally dangerous" to the well being of the army.

In a short letter to Davis on 1 December, to cover his draft report, however, Bragg confessed a measure of his responsibility for what had happened. "The disaster admits of no palliation and is justly disparaging to me as a commander. I trust, however, you may find upon full

investigation that the fault is not entirely mine." Despite his equivo-
cating, Bragg did pen one painfully true line. Ruminating on the dark
days of conspiracy after Chickamauga, he confessed: "I fear we both
have erred in the conclusion for me to retain command here after the
clamor raised against me."[24]

Davis, at last, agreed. As he had done after Stones River and Chickamauga, Bragg again submitted his resignation. While complaining directly to Davis of his errant subordinates, Bragg on 29 November wrote
the Adjutant General of the Confederacy, Samuel Cooper, of the sorry
state of the army, saying that his "first estimate of our disaster was not
too large, and time only can restore order and morale." Whether out of
his growing awareness that he bore some responsibility for the disaster
or because he believed Davis would sustain him in command, thus once
again freeing him to attack his enemies in the army, Bragg concluded:
"I deem it due to the cause and to myself to ask for relief from command and an investigation into the causes of the defeat." Two days later,
Cooper replied with unseemly haste that the president had accepted
Bragg's offer.

Sick and depressed, Bragg had skulked about headquarters after sending in his resignation. Once it was accepted, he tried to make a digni-
fied exit. On Wednesday, 2 December, he released what he probably
thought was a gracious farewell message to the army, but memories of
draconian discipline and summary executions gave it an almost comic
ring. "Upon renewed application to the President, his consent has been
obtained for the relinquishment of the command of this army. It is accordingly transferred to Lieutenant General Hardee," the message began. (Hardee declined permanent command before it could be proffered.)
Continued Bragg: "The announcement of this separation is made with
unfeigned regret. The associations of more than two years, which bind
together a commander and his trusted troops, cannot be severed without deep emotion. . . . In bidding the army an affectionate farewell, they
have the blessing and the prayers of a grateful friend." In the dark of
night, without fanfare, Bragg and his personal staff boarded an eastbound
train out of Dalton.[25]

The regret Bragg deigned to feel was hardly reciprocal. Reflecting on
the battles for Chattanooga, a member of Brown's Tennessee brigade
wrote his family: "Since my connection with the army it has made no
movement so disastrous as this, nor which so much depressed the feelings of our troops." Then, turning to Bragg's recent departure: "This
depression, however, does not amount to despair, but is from a want of
confidence in our commanding general; but happily for us, this objection has at last been removed and with another commander there is

scarcely a doubt of our success. . . . [Bragg] has now left us and the confidence of our army has wonderfully revived."[26]

In view of the events of ten days earlier, such a swing of mood seems almost incomprehensible. But the officers and men of the Army of Tennessee, after long months of defeat, retreat, and lost opportunities under Bragg, had come to expect little. In their secret musings, most probably knew that the collapse of their cause was only a matter of time. Many nonetheless searched the horizon longingly for any ray of hope, however dim. Some, like Cheatham, took to the bottle. He passed the first night in Dalton taking deep drinks, cursing Bragg, and shaking his head, telling everyone who cared to listen: "I told you so." Others coped with the debacle that had been the Chattanooga campaign by ignoring it, as if it had never happened. No less a figure than General Hardee himself kept his balance by this last approach.[27]

St. John Liddell had missed the battles. He was on a leave of absence near Atlanta when the first whispers of defeat reached his ears. Hopping a train to Ringgold, he caught up with Bragg and Hardee and the retreating army. Bragg looked so dejected that Liddell could not find it in himself to "reproach him for his unmitigated follies." Hardee, on the other hand, was brimming with good cheer. He was lost in dreamy contemplation of Mary Lewis, the Mississippi belle with whom he had fallen in love two months earlier. Beckoning Liddell to his side, Hardee said excitedly: "I want to tell you a secret. I am engaged to be married to a most estimable young lady." Liddell was incredulous. "I am in earnest," Hardee insisted. "Goodbye."

Off he rode. Watching Hardee go, Liddell knew it was time to leave the Army of Tennessee.[28]

# APPENDIX

# THE OPPOSING FORCES IN THE CHATTANOOGA CAMPAIGN

The following list was assembled from *War of the Rebellion: A Compilation of the Official Records of the Union and Confederate Armies.* With respect to officer casualties, (k) signifies killed, (mw) mortally wounded, (w) wounded, and (c) captured.

## Organization of the Forces under Command of
Major General Ulysses S. Grant

### Army of the Cumberland
Major General George H. Thomas

*General Headquarters*
1st Ohio Sharpshooters   10th Ohio Infantry

FOURTH ARMY CORPS
Major General Gordon Granger

*First Division*
Brigadier General Charles Cruft[1]
*Escort*
92d Illinois, Company E
*Second Brigade*
Brigadier General Walter C. Whitaker
96th Illinois   35th Indiana   8th Kentucky

---

1. The First Brigade and Battery M, 4th U.S. Artillery, at Bridgeport, Ala.; the 115th Illinois and 84th Indiana, of the Second Brigade, and 5th Indiana Battery, at Shellmound, Tenn., and the 30th Indiana and 77th Pennsylvania, of the 3d Brigade, and Battery H, 4th U.S. Artillery, at Whitesides, Tenn.

40th Ohio  51st Ohio  99th Ohio
*Third Brigade*
Colonel William Grose
59th Illinois  75th Illinois  84th Illinois
9th Indiana  36th Indiana  24th Ohio

*Second Division*
Major General Philip H. Sheridan
*First Brigade*
Colonel Francis T. Sherman
36th Illinois  44th Illinois  73d Illinois
74th Illinois  88th Illinois  22d Indiana
2d Missouri  15th Missouri  24th Wisconsin
*Second Brigade*
Brigadier General George D. Wagner
100th Illinois  15th Indiana  40th Indiana
51st Indiana[2]  57th Indiana  58th Indiana
26th Ohio  97th Ohio
*Third Brigade*
Colonel Charles G. Harker
22d Illinois  27th Illinois  42d Illinois
51st Illinois  79th Illinois  3d Kentucky
64th Ohio  65th Ohio  125th Ohio
*Artillery*
Captain Warren P. Edgarton
1st Illinois Light, Battery M  10th Indiana Battery
1st Missouri Light, Battery G  1st Ohio Light, Battery I[3]
4th United States, Battery G[4]  5th United States, Battery H[5]

*Third Division*
Brigadier General Thomas J. Wood
*First Brigade*
Brigadier General August Willich
25th Illinois  35th Illinois  89th Illinois
32d Indiana  68th Indiana  8th Kansas
15th Ohio  49th Ohio  15th Wisconsin
*Second Brigade*
Brigadier General William B. Hazen
6th Indiana  5th Kentucky  6th Kentucky

2. Between Nashville and Chattanooga en route to join brigade.
3. Temporarily attached.
4. Temporarily attached.
5. Temporarily attached.

23d Kentucky  1st Ohio  6th Ohio
41st Ohio  93d Ohio  124th Ohio
*Third Brigade*
Brigadier General Samuel Beatty
79th Indiana  86th Indiana  9th Kentucky
17th Kentucky  13th Ohio  19th Ohio  59th Ohio
*Artillery*
Captain Cullen Bradley
Illinois Light, Bridges's Battery  6th Ohio Battery
20th Ohio Battery[6]  Pennsylvania Light, Battery B


ELEVENTH ARMY CORPS[7]
Major General Oliver O. Howard

*General Headquarters*
Independent Company, 8th New York Infantry

*Second Division*
Brigadier General Adolph von Steinwehr
*First Brigade*
Colonel Adolphus Bushbeck
33d New Jersey  134th New York
154th New York  27th Pennsylvania
73d Pennsylvania
*Second Brigade*
Colonel Orland Smith
33d Massachusetts  136th New York
55th Ohio  73d Ohio

*Third Division*
Major General Carl Schurz
*First Brigade*
Brigadier General Hector Tyndale
101st Illinois  45th New York
143d New York  61st Ohio
82d Ohio
*Second Brigade*
Colonel Wladimir Krzyzanowski

6. Temporarily attached from the Artillery Reserve.
7. Maj. Gen. Joseph Hooker, commanding 11th and 12th Army Corps, had under his immediate command the 1st Division, 4th Corps, the 2d Division, 12th Corps, portions of the 14th Corps, and the 1st Division, 15th Corps. Company K, 15th Illinois Cavalry, served as escort to General Hooker.

58th New York   119th New York
141st New York   26th Wisconsin
*Third Brigade*
Colonel Frederick Hecker
80th Illinois   82d Illinois
68th New York   75th Pennsylvania
*Artillery*
Major Thomas W. Osborn
1st New York Light, Battery I   New York Light, 13th Battery
1st Ohio Light, Battery I[8]   1st Ohio Light, Battery K
4th United States, Battery G[9]

TWELFTH ARMY CORPS[10]

*Second Division*
Brigadier General John W. Geary
*First Brigade*
Colonel Charles Candy (w)
Colonel William R. Creighton (mw)
Colonel Thomas J. Ahl
5th Ohio   7th Ohio   29th Ohio
66th Ohio   28th Pennsylvania   147th Pennsylvania
*Second Brigade*
Colonel George A. Cobham, Jr.
29th Pennsylvania   109th Pennsylvania
111th Pennsylvania
*Third Brigade*
Major General George Sears Greene (w)
Colonel David Ireland
60th New York   78th New York
102d New York   137th New York   149th New York
*Artillery*
Major John A. Reynolds
Pennsylvania Light, Battery E   5th United States, Battery K

FOURTEENTH ARMY CORPS
Major General John M. Palmer
1st Ohio Cavalry (Escort)

8. Temporarily attached to 2d Division, 4th Army Corps.
9. Temporarily attached to 2d Division, 4th Army Corps.
10. The 1st Division engaged in guarding the Nashville and Chattanooga Railroad from Wartrace Bridge, Tenn., to Bridgeport, Ala., etc. Maj. Gen. Henry W. Slocum, the corps commander, had his headquarters at Tullahoma, Tenn.

*First Division*
Brigadier General Richard W. Johnson
*First Brigade*
Brigadier General William P. Carlin
104th Illinois  38th Indiana  42d Indiana
88th Indiana  2d Ohio  33d Ohio
94th Ohio  10th Wisconsin
*Second Brigade*
Colonel Marshall F. Moore
Colonel William L. Stoughton
19th Illinois  11th Michigan  69th Ohio
15th United States, 1st and 2d Battalions
16th United States, 1st Battalion
18th United States, 1st and 2d Battalions
19th United States, 1st Battalion
*Third Brigade*[11]
Brigadier General John C. Starkweather
24th Illinois  37th Indiana  21st Ohio
74th Ohio  78th Pennsylvania  79th Pennsylvania
1st Wisconsin  21st Wisconsin
*Artillery*
1st Illinois Light, Battery C  1st Michigan Light, Battery A
5th United States, Battery H[12]

*Second Division*
Brigadier General Jefferson C. Davis
*First Brigade*
Brigadier General James D. Morgan
10th Illinois  16th Illinois  60th Illinois
21st Kentucky  10th Michigan  14th Michigan[13]
*Second Brigade*
Brigadier General John Beatty
34th Illinois  78th Illinois  3d Ohio[14]
98th Ohio  108th Ohio  113th Ohio  121st Ohio
*Third Brigade*
Colonel Daniel McCook
85th Illinois  86th Illinois

11. During the engagements on the 23d, 24th, and 25th was in line of battle holding fort and breastworks at Chattanooga.
12. Temporarily attached to 2d Division, 4th Army Corps.
13. Detached at Columbia, Tenn.
14. Detached at Kelley's Ferry, Tennessee River.

110th Illinois   125th Illinois   52d Ohio
*Artillery*
Captain William A. Hotchkiss
2d Illinois Light, Battery I   Minnesota Light, 2d Battery
Wisconsin Light, 5th Battery

*Third Division*
Brigadier General Absalom Baird
*First Brigade*
Brigadier General John B. Turchin
82d Indiana   11th Ohio   17th Ohio
31st Ohio   36th Ohio   89th Ohio   92d Ohio
*Second Brigade*
Colonel Ferdinand Van Derveer
75th Indiana   87th Indiana   101st Indiana
2d Minnesota   9th Ohio   35th Ohio   105th Ohio
*Third Brigade*
Colonel Edward H. Phelps (k)
Colonel William H. Hays
10th Indiana   74th Indiana   4th Kentucky
10th Kentucky   18th Kentucky[15]   14th Ohio   38th Ohio
*Artillery*
Captain George R. Swallow
Indiana Light, 7th Battery   Indiana Light, 19th Battery
4th United States, Battery I

ENGINEER TROOPS
Brigadier General William F. Smith
*Engineers*
1st Michigan Engineers (Detachment)
13th Michigan Infantry   21st Michigan Infantry
22d Michigan Infantry   18th Ohio Infantry
*Pioneer Brigade*
Colonel George P. Buell
1st Battalion   2d Battalion   3d Battalion

ARTILLERY RESERVE
Brigadier General John M. Brannan

*First Division*
Colonel James Barnett

---

15. Detached at Brown's Ferry, Tenn.

*First Brigade*
Major Charles S. Cotter
1st Ohio Light, Battery B   1st Ohio Light, Battery C
1st Ohio Light, Battery E   1st Ohio Light, Battery F
*Second Brigade*
1st Ohio Light, Battery G   1st Ohio Light, Battery M
Ohio Light, 18th Battery   Ohio Light, 20th Battery[16]

*Second Division*
*First Brigade*
Captain Josiah W. Church
1st Michigan Light, Battery D   1st Tennessee Light, Battery A
Wisconsin Light, 3d Battery   Wisconsin Light, 8th Battery
Wisconsin Light, 10th Battery
*Second Brigade*
Captain Arnold Sutermeister
Indiana Light, 4th Battery   Indiana Light, 8th Battery
Indiana Light, 11th Battery   Indiana Light, 21st Battery
1st Wisconsin Heavy, Company C

CAVALRY[17]
*Second Brigade (Second Division)*
Colonel Eli Long
98th Illinois (Mounted Infantry)   17th Indiana (Mounted Infantry)
2d Kentucky   4th Michigan   1st Ohio
3d Ohio   4th Ohio   10th Ohio

POST OF CHATTANOOGA
Colonel John G. Parkhurst
44th Indiana   15th Kentucky   9th Michigan

# Army of the Tennessee
Major General William T. Sherman[18]

16. Temporarily attached to 3d Division, 4th Army Corps.
17. Corps headquarters and the 1st and 2d Brigades and 18th Indiana Battery, of the 1st Division, at and about Alexandria, Tenn.; the 3d Brigade at Caperton's Ferry, Tennessee River. The 1st and 3d Brigades, and the Chicago Board of Trade Battery, of the 2d Division, at Maysville, Ala.
18. General Sherman had under his immediate command the 11th Corps and the 2d Division, 14th Corps, of the Army of the Cumberland; the 2d and 4th Divisions, 15th Corps, and the 2d Division, 17th Corps.

FIFTEENTH ARMY CORPS[19]

*First Division*
Brigadier General Peter J. Osterhaus
*First Brigade*
Brigadier General Charles R. Woods
13th Illinois  3d Missouri  12th Missouri
17th Missouri  27th Missouri  29th Missouri
31st Missouri  32d Missouri  76th Ohio
*Second Brigade*
Colonel James A. Williamson
4th Iowa  9th Iowa  25th Iowa
26th Iowa  30th Iowa  31st Iowa
*Artillery*
Captain Henry H. Griffiths
Iowa Light, 1st Battery  2d Missouri Light, Battery F
Ohio Light, 4th Battery

*Second Division*
Brigadier General Morgan L. Smith
*First Brigade*
Brigadier General Giles A. Smith (w)
Colonel Nathan W. Tupper
55th Illinois  116th Illinois  127th Illinois
6th Missouri  8th Missouri  57th Ohio
13th United States, 1st Battalion
*Second Brigade*
Brigadier General Joseph A. J. Lightburn
83d Indiana  30th Ohio  37th Ohio
47th Ohio  54th Ohio  4th West Virginia
*Artillery*
1st Illinois Light, Battery A  1st Illinois Light, Battery B
1st Illinois Light, Battery H

*Fourth Division*
Brigadier General Hugh Ewing
*First Brigade*
Colonel John M. Loomis
26th Illinois  90th Illinois
12th Indiana  100th Indiana

19. The 3d Division, Brig. Gen. James M. Tuttle commanding, at Memphis, La Grange, and Pocahontas, Tenn.

*Second Brigade*
Brigadier General John M. Corse (w)
Colonel Charles C. Walcutt
40th Illinois   103d Illinois
6th Iowa   15th Michigan[20]   46th Ohio
*Third Brigade*
Colonel Joseph R. Cockerill
48th Illinois   97th Indiana   99th Indiana
53d Ohio   70th Ohio
*Artillery*
Captain Henry Richardson
1st Illinois Light, Battery F   1st Illinois, Battery I
1st Missouri Light, Battery D

SEVENTEENTH ARMY CORPS

*Second Division*
Brigadier General John E. Smith
*First Brigade*
Colonel Jesse I. Alexander
63d Illinois   48th Indiana   59th Indiana
4th Minnesota   18th Wisconsin
*Second Brigade*
Colonel Green B. Raum (w)
Colonel Clark R. Wever (k)
Colonel Francis C. Deimling
56th Illinois   17th Iowa   10th Missouri
24th Missouri   80th Ohio
*Third Brigade*
Brigadier General Charles L. Matthies (w)
Colonel Benjamin D. Dean
Colonel Jabez Banbury
93d Illinois   5th Iowa
10th Iowa   26th Missouri
*Artillery*
Captain Henry Dillon
Cogswell's (Illinois) Battery
Wisconsin Light, 6th Battery   Wisconsin Light, 12th Battery

---

20. Detached at Scottsboro, Ala.

# Organization of the Army of Tennessee
### General Braxton Bragg, C. S. Army, Commanding
### 20 November 1863[21]
### *General Headquarters*
1st Louisiana (Regulars)  1st Louisiana Cavalry

## LONGSTREET'S ARMY CORPS[22]

### *McLaws's Division*
### *Kershaw's Brigade*
2d South Carolina  3d South Carolina  7th South Carolina
8th South Carolina  15th South Carolina
3d South Carolina Battalion
### *Humphreys's Brigade*
13th Mississippi  17th Mississippi
18th Mississippi  21st Mississippi
### *Wofford's Brigade*
16th Georgia  18th Georgia  24th Georgia
Cobb's Legion  Phillips's Legion
3d Georgia Battalion Sharpshooters
### *Bryan's Brigade*
10th Georgia  50th Georgia
51st Georgia  53d Georgia
### *Artillery Battalion*
Major Austin Leyden
Georgia Battery, Captain Tyler M. Peeples
Georgia Battery, Captain Andrew M. Wolihin
Georgia Battery, Captain Billington W. York

### *Hood's Division*
### *Jenkins's Brigade*
1st South Carolina  2d South Carolina Rifles
5th South Carolina  6th South Carolina
Hampton (South Carolina) Legion
Palmetto (South Carolina) Sharpshooters
### *Robertson's Brigade*
3d Arkansas  1st Texas
4th Texas  5th Texas

21. The artillery assignments indicated were made in circular of this date from General Bragg's headquarters.
22. Detached 4 November for operations in East Tennessee.

*Law's Brigade*
4th Alabama   15th Alabama   44th Alabama
47th Alabama   48th Alabama
*Anderson's Brigade*
7th Georgia   8th Georgia   9th Georgia
11th Georgia   59th Georgia
*Benning's Brigade*
2d Georgia   15th Georgia
17th Georgia   20th Georgia
*Artillery Battalion*
Colonel E. Porter Alexander
South Carolina Battery, Captain William W. Fickling
Virginia Battery, Captain Tyler C. Jordan
Louisiana Battery, Captain George V. Moody
Virginia Battery, Captain William W. Parker
Virginia Battery, Captain Osmond B. Taylor
Virginia Battery, Captain Pichegru Woolfolk, Jr.

HARDEE'S CORPS

*Cheatham's Division*
*Jackson's Brigade*
1st Georgia (Confederate)   5th Georgia   47th Georgia[23]
65th Georgia[24]   2d Georgia   5th Mississippi   8th Mississippi
*Moore's Brigade*
37th Alabama   40th Alabama   42d Alabama
*Walthall's Brigade*
24th and 27th Mississippi
29th and 30th Mississippi
34th Mississippi
*Wright's Brigade*
8th Tennessee   16th Tennessee   28th Tennessee
38th Tennessee   51st and 52d Tennessee
Murray's (Tennessee) Battalion
*Artillery Battalion*
Major Melancthon Smith
Alabama Battery, Captain William H. Fowler
Florida Battery, Captain Robert P. McCants
Georgia Battery, Captain John Scogin
Mississippi Battery (Smith's), Lieutenant William B. Turner

23. Assigned 12 November 1863.
24. Assigned 12 November 1863.

*Hindman's Division*
*Anderson's Brigade*
7th Mississippi  9th Mississippi  10th Mississippi
41st Mississippi  44th Mississippi
9th Mississippi Battalion Sharpshooters
*Manigault's Brigade*
24th Alabama  28th Alabama  34th Alabama
10th and 19th South Carolina
*Deas's Brigade*
19th Alabama  22d Alabama  25th Alabama
39th Alabama  50th Alabama
17th Alabama Battalion Sharpshooters
*Vaughan's Brigade*
11th Tennessee  12th and 47th Tennessee
13th and 154th Tennessee  29th Tennessee
*Artillery Battalion*
Major Alfred R. Courtney
Alabama Battery, Captain S. H. Dent
Alabama Battery, Captain James Garrity
Tennessee Battery (Scott's), Lieutenant John Doscher
Alabama Battery (Waters's), Lieutenant William P. Hamilton

*Buckner's Division*[25]
*Johnson's Brigade*
17th and 23d Tennessee  25th and 44th Tennessee
63d Tennessee
*Gracie's Brigade*
41st Alabama  43d Alabama
1st Battalion, Alabama (Hillard's) Legion
2d Battalion, Alabama (Hillard's) Legion
3d Battalion, Alabama (Hillard's) Legion
4th Battalion, Alabama (Hillard's) Legion
*Reynolds's Brigade*
58th North Carolina  60th North Carolina
54th Virginia  63d Virginia
*Artillery Battalion*
Major Samuel C. Williams
Mississippi Battery (Darden's), Lieutenant H. W. Bullen
Virginia Battery, Captain William C. Jeffress
Alabama Battery, Captain R. F. Kolb

25. Detached 22 November for operations against Burnside in East Tennessee.
Reynolds's brigade and the artillery were recalled.

*Walker's Division*[26]
*Maney's Brigade*[27]
1st and 27th Tennessee   4th Tennessee (Provisional Army)
6th and 9th Tennessee   41st Tennessee[28]
50th Tennessee[29]   24th Tennessee Battalion Sharpshooters
*Gist's Brigade*
46th Georgia   8th Georgia Battalion
16th South Carolina   24th South Carolina
*Wilson's Brigade*
25th Georgia   29th Georgia   30th Georgia
26th Georgia Battalion   1st Georgia Battalion Sharpshooters
*Artillery Battalion*
Major Robert Martin
Missouri Battery, Captain Hiram M. Bledsoe
South Carolina Battery, Captain T. B. Ferguson
Georgia Battery, Captain Evan P. Howell

BRECKINRIDGE'S ARMY CORPS

*Cleburne's Division*
*Liddell's Brigade*
2d and 15th Arkansas   5th and 13th Arkansas
6th and 7th Arkansas   8th Arkansas
19th and 24th Arkansas[30]
*Smith's Brigade*
6th and 10th Texas Infantry and 15th Texas (Dismounted) Cavalry
17th, 18th, 24th, and 25th Texas Cavalry (Dismounted)
7th Texas[31]
*Polk's Brigade*
1st Arkansas   3d and 5th Confederate
2d Tennessee   35th and 48th Tennessee
*Lowrey's Brigade*
16th Alabama   33d Alabama
45th Alabama   32d and 45th Mississippi
15th Mississippi Battalion Sharpshooters

26. Transferred from Longstreet's Corps, 12 November 1863, and regiments of Gregg's brigade distributed to Bate's, Maney's, and Smith's brigades.
27. Transferred from Cheatham's Division 12 November 1863.
28. From Gregg's brigade.
29. From Gregg's brigade.
30. Transferred from Smith's brigade, 12 November 1863.
31. Transferred from Gregg's brigade, 12 November 1863.

*Artillery Battalion*
Major T. R. Hotchkiss
Arkansas Battery (Calvert's), Lieutenant Thomas J. Key
Texas Battery, Captain James P. Douglas
Alabama Battery (Semple's), Lieutenant Richard W. Goldthwaite
Mississippi Battery (Swett's), Lieutenant H. Shannon

*Stewart's Division*
*Adams's Brigade*
13th and 20th Louisiana   16th and 25th Louisiana
19th Louisiana   4th Louisiana Battalion
14th Louisiana Battalion Sharpshooters
*Strahl's Brigade*
4th and 5th Tennessee   19th Tennessee
24th Tennessee   31st Tennessee   33d Tennessee
*Clayton's Brigade*
18th Alabama   32d and 58th Alabama[32]
36th Alabama   38th Alabama
*Stovall's Brigade*
40th Georgia   41st Georgia   42d Georgia
43d Georgia   52d Georgia
*Artillery Battalion*
Captain Henry C. Semple
Georgia Battery (Dawson's), Lieutenant R. W. Anderson
Arkansas Battery (Humphreys's), Lieutenant John W. Rivers
Alabama Battery, Captain McDonald Oliver
Mississippi Battery, Captain Thomas J. Stanford

*Breckinridge's Division*
*Lewis's Brigade*
2d Kentucky   4th Kentucky   5th Kentucky
6th Kentucky   9th Kentucky
John H. Morgan's Dismounted Men
*Bate's Brigade*[33]
37th Georgia   4th Georgia Battalion Sharpshooters
10th Tennessee[34]   15th and 37th Tennessee   20th Tennessee
30th Tennessee[35]   1st Tennessee Battalion (Sharpshooters)[36]

---

32. The *Official Records* incorrectly lists the 32d Alabama and 58th Alabama as separate units; they were consolidated just prior to the Battle of Missionary Ridge.
33. Transferred from Stewart's division, 12 November 1863.
34. Transferred from Gregg's brigade, 12 November 1863.
35. Transferred from Gregg's brigade, 12 November 1863.
36. Transferred from Gregg's brigade, 12 November 1863.

*Florida Brigade*[37]
1st and 3d Florida   4th Florida   6th Florida
7th Florida   1st Florida Cavalry (Dismounted)
*Artillery Battalion*
Captain C. H. Slocomb
Kentucky Battery (Cobb's), Lieutenant Frank P. Gracey
Tennessee Battery, Captain John W. Mebane
Louisiana Battery (Slocomb's), Lieutenant W. C. D. Vaught

*Stevenson's Division*
*Brown's Brigade*[38]
3d Tennessee[39]   18th and 26th Tennessee   32d Tennessee
45th Tennessee and 23d Tennessee Battalion
*Cumming's Brigade*
34th Georgia   36th Georgia
39th Georgia   56th Georgia
*Pettus's Brigade*[40]
20th Alabama   23d Alabama   30th Alabama
31st Alabama   46th Alabama
*Vaughn's Brigade*[41]
3d Tennessee (Provisional Army)   39th Tennessee
43d Tennessee   59th Tennessee
*Artillery Battalion*[42]
Captain William W. Carnes[43]
Tennessee Battery, Captain Edmund D. Baxter
Tennessee Battery, Lieutenant L. Y. Marshall
Georgia Battery, Captain Max Van Den Corput
Georgia Battery, Captain John B. Rowan

WHEELER'S CAVALRY CORPS[44]
Major General Joseph Wheeler

37. Organized 12 November 1863.
38. Transferred from Stewart's division, 12 November 1863.
39. In Gregg's brigade, 31 October 1863.
40. Reassigned to division, 12 November 1863.
41. Exchanged prisoners, but few reported.
42. According to Stevenson's return, his artillery battalion consisted at this date of Carnes's, Corput's, and Rowan's batteries, and the 20th Alabama Battalion, viz: Company A, Captain Winslow D. Emery; Company B, Captain Richard Bellamy; and Company C, Captain T. J. Key.
43. The *Official Records* incorrectly reports Captain Robert Cobb as in command of the battalion.
44. The 1st Brigade of Wharton's Division, Martin's Division, Armstrong's Division (the 5th Tennessee excepted), and all the artillery (except Huwald's Battery) detached under Wheeler's command.

*Wharton's Division*
Major General John A. Wharton
*First Brigade*
Colonel Thomas Harrison
3d Arkansas   65th North Carolina (6th Cavalry)
8th Texas   11th Texas
*Second Brigade*
Brigadier General Henry B. Davidson
1st Tennessee   2d Tennessee   4th Tennessee
6th Tennessee   11th Tennessee

*Martin's Division*
Major General William T. Martin
*First Brigade*
Brigadier General John T. Morgan
1st Alabama   3d Alabama   4th Alabama (Russell's)
Malone's (Alabama) Regiment   51st Alabama
*Second Brigade*
Colonel J. J. Morrison
1st Georgia   2d Georgia   3d Georgia
4th Georgia   6th Georgia

*Armstrong's Division*
Brigadier General Frank C. Armstrong
*First Brigade*
Brigadier General William Y. C. Humes
4th Tennessee (Baxter Smith's)   5th Tennessee
8th Tennessee (Dibrell's)   9th Tennessee   10th Tennessee
*Second Brigade*
Colonel C. H. Tyler
Clay's (Kentucky) Battalion   Edmundson's (Virginia) Battalion
Jessee's (Kentucky) Battalion   Johnson's (Kentucky) Battalion

*Kelly's Division*
*First Brigade*
Colonel William B. Wade
1st Confederate   3d Confederate
8th Confederate   10th Confederate
*Second Brigade*
Colonel J. Warren Grigsby
2d Kentucky   3d Kentucky   9th Kentucky
Allison's (Tennessee) Squadron   Hamilton's (Tennessee) Battalion
Rucker's Legion

*Artillery*
Tennessee Battery, Captain A. L. Huggins
Tennessee Battery, Captain Gustave A. Huwald
Tennessee Battery, Captain B. F. White, Jr.
Arkansas Battery, Captain J. H. Wiggins

RESERVE ARTILLERY[45]
Major Felix H. Robertson
Missouri Battery, Captain Overton W. Barret
Georgia Battery (Havis's), Lieutenant James R. Duncan
Alabama Battery (Lumsden's), Lieutenant Harvey H. Cribbs
Georgia Battery, Captain Thomas L. Massenburg

DETACHED
Roddey's Cavalry Brigade
4th Alabama   5th Alabama   53d Alabama
Moreland's (Alabama) Battalion
Georgia Battery, Captain C. B. Ferrell

45. Sengstak's (Alabama) Battery, assigned 10 November, noted accounted for.

# NOTES

## ABBREVIATIONS

| | |
|---|---|
| ADAH | Alabama Department of Archives and History |
| CCNMP | Chickamauga-Chattanooga National Military Park |
| ChiHS | Chicago Historical Society |
| CV | *Confederate Veteran* |
| CWC | Civil War Collection |
| CWRT | Civil War Round Table |
| CWTI | *Civil War Times Illustrated* |
| DLC | Library of Congress |
| DU | Duke University |
| InHS | Indiana Historical Society |
| IoHS | Iowa Historical Society |
| ISHL | Illinois State Historical Library |
| MDAH | Mississippi Department of Archives and History |
| MnHS | Minnesota Historical Society |
| NYPL | New York Public Library |
| OHS | Ohio Historical Society |
| OR | *War of the Rebellion: A Compilation of the Official Records of the Union and Confederate Armies* (all references are to Series 1) |
| PMHSM | *Papers of the Military and Historical Society of Massachusetts* |
| SHSP | *Southern Historical Society Papers* |
| TSLA | Tennessee State Library and Archives |
| UNC | Southern Historical Collection, University of North Carolina |
| USAMHI | United States Army Military History Institute |
| WRHS | Western Reserve Historical Society |

CHAPTER ONE / CHANGES OF VAST MOMENT

1. William S. McFeely, *Grant: A Biography* (New York: W. W. Norton, 1981), 137–38; Herman Hattaway and Archer Jones, *How the North Won: A Military History of the Civil War* (Urbana: University of Illinois Press, 1983), 435; Horace Porter, *Campaigning with Grant* (New York: Century Company, 1897), 14.

2. Hattaway and Jones, *How the North Won*, 428–36; Ulysses S. Grant, "Chattanooga," in *Battles and Leaders of the Civil War*, ed. Clarence Buell and Robert Johnson, 4 vols. (New York: Thomas Yoseloff, 1956), 3:679–80; James H. Wilson, *Under the Old Flag: Recollections of Military Operations in the War for the Union, the Spanish War, the Boxer Rebellion, etc.*, 2 vols. (New York: D. Appleton, 1912), 1:258.

3. McFeely, *Grant*, 140–41; Ulysses S. Grant, *Personal Memoirs of U. S. Grant*, 2 vols. (New York: Charles Webster, 1885–86), 2:16–17; Lloyd Lewis, *Sherman, Fighting Prophet* (New York: Harcourt, Brace, 1932), 309.

4. Grant, "Chattanooga," 681; McFeely, *Grant*, 141; Wilson, *Under the Old Flag*, 1:258–59; OR 30, pt. 3, 923.

5. McFeely, *Grant*, 141; Grant, "Chattanooga," 681; Wilson, *Under the Old Flag*, 1:259.

6. Wilson, *Under the Old Flag*, 1:259–60; McFeely, *Grant*, 141; William Wrenshall Smith, "Holocaust Holiday," *Civil War Times Illustrated* 18, no. 6 (October 1979): 31.

7. Grant, "Chattanooga," 681–82; McFeely, *Grant*, 141–42.

8. For a detailed treatment of the events precipitating Rosecrans's removal and Stanton's hand in it, see Peter Cozzens, *This Terrible Sound: The Battle of Chickamauga* (Urbana: University of Illinois Press, 1992), 522–28; McFeely, *Grant*, 142; Wilson, *Under the Old Flag*, 1:260; Grant, *Personal Memoirs*, 2:17–18.

9. Rawlins to Mary Hurlbut, 23 November 1863, John Rawlins Papers, ChiHS.

10. Wilson, *Under the Old Flag*, 1:261.

11. Ibid., 1:260–61; McFeely, *Grant*, 142; Grant, *Personal Memoirs*, 2:19.

12. McFeely, *Grant*, 85–87; Ezra Warner, *Generals in Blue: Lives of the Union Commanders* (Baton Rouge: Louisiana State University Press, 1964), 392; Porter, *Campaigning with Grant*, 15; Sylvanus Cadwallader, *Three Years with Grant, as Recalled by War Correspondent Sylvanus Cadwallader*, ed. Benjamin Thomas (New York: Knopf, 1955), 140.

13. Rawlins to Hurlbut, 23 November 1863, Rawlins Papers, ChiHS; Wilson, *Under the Old Flag*, 1:262.

14. OR 30, pt. 4, 479; McFeely, *Grant*, 143; Grant, *Personal Memoirs*, 2:26; James A. Hoobler, *Cities under the Gun: Images of Occupied Nashville and Chattanooga* (Nashville: Rutledge Hill Press, 1986), 115; William M. Lamers, *The Edge of Glory: A Biography of General William S. Rosecrans, U.S.A.* (New York: Harcourt, Brace and World, 1961), 389.

15. Wilson, *Under the Old Flag*, 1:262.

CHAPTER TWO / STARVATION CAMP

1. John Ely Diary, 19 October 1863, Thirty-sixth Illinois File, CCNMP; Isaac C. Doan, *Reminiscences of the Chattanooga Campaign, a Paper Read at the Reunion of Company B, Fortieth Ohio Infantry, at Xenia, O., August 22, 1894, by Sergeant Isaac C. Doan* (Richmond, Ind.: N.p., 1894), 8.

2. L. A. Simmons, *History of the 84th Reg't Ill. Vols.* (Macomb, Ill.: Hampton Brothers, 1866), 119; H. H. Hill, "The Second Minnesota: Reminiscences of Four Years' Service at the Front," *National Tribune*, 20 July 1899; Alfred D. Searles to his parents, Searles Family Papers, Bowling Green State University; B. L. T., "With the Wagon Train: Reminiscences of the Chattanooga Campaign," *National Tribune*, 27 December 1900; Chesley A. Mosman, *The Rough Side of War: The Civil War Journal of Chesley A. Mosman*, ed. Arnold Gates (Garden City, N.Y.: Basin Publishing Company, 1987), 105.

3. David B. Floyd, *History of the Seventy-fifth Regiment of Indiana Infantry Volunteers, Its Organization, Campaigns, and Battles* (Philadelphia: Lutheran Publishing Society, 1893), 201; Charles Partridge, *History of the Ninety-sixth Regiment Illinois Volunteer Infantry* (Chicago: Brown, Pettibone and Company, 1887), 254; Frederick W. Keil, *Thirty-fifth Ohio, a Narrative of Service from August 1861 to 1864* (Ft. Wayne, Ind.: Archer, Housh and Company, 1894), 162, 182.

4. George Kirkpatrick, *The Experiences of a Private Soldier in the Civil War* (Chicago: N.p., 1924), 32; Spillard F. Horrall, *History of the Forty-second Indiana Volunteer Infantry* (Chicago: Donohue and Company, 1892), 201.

5. Jeremiah Donahower, "Civil War Narrative, Volume 2," 170–71, in Jeremiah Donahower Papers, MnHS; B. L. T., "With the Wagon Train"; *History of the Organization, Marches, Campings, General Services and Final Muster Out of Battery M, First Regiment of Illinois Light Artillery* (Princeton: Mercer and Dean, 1892), 105; Wilbur F. Hinman, *The Story of the Sherman Brigade: The Camp, the March, the Bivouac, the Battle; and How the Boys Lived and Died during Four Years of Active Field Service* (Alliance, Ohio: Press of Daily Review, 1897), 447.

6. Alexis Cope, *The Fifteenth Ohio Volunteers and Its Campaigns, War of 1861–1865* (Columbus, Ohio: Press of the Edward T. Miller Company, 1916), 346; Silas S. Canfield, *History of the 21st Regiment Ohio Volunteer Infantry, in the War of the Rebellion* (Toledo: Vrooman, Anderson and Bateman, Printers, 1893), 160.

7. Levi Wagner Reminiscences, 90, *CWTI* Collection, USAMHI; Alfred Pirtle, "Three Memorable Days—A Letter from Chattanoga, November, 1863," in *Sketches of War History, 1861 to 1865. Papers Prepared for the Commandery of the State of Ohio, Military Order of the Loyal Legion of the United States, 1903–1908*, 6 vols. (Cincinnati: Monfort and Company, 1908), 6:36; B. L. T., "With the Wagon Train"; *History of Battery M, First Illinois Light Artillery*, 105; Canfield, *21st Ohio*, 160; Hill, "The Second Minnesota."

8. Canfield, *21st Ohio*, 160.

9. Allen Buckner Memoirs, 25, ISHL; Charles T. Clark, *Opdycke Tigers, 125th O.V.I, a History of the Regiment and the Campaigns and Battle of the Army of the Cumberland* (Columbus, Ohio: Spahr and Glenn, 1895), 140.

10. George W. Lewis, *The Campaigns of the 124th Ohio Volunteer Infantry, with Roster and Roll of Honor* (Akron: Werner, 1894), 78; Buckner Memoirs, ISHL, 25–26.

11. William F. Smith, "An Historical Sketch of the Military Operations around Chattanooga, Tennessee, September 22 to November 27, 1863," in *PMHSM. Volume VIII. The Mississippi Valley. Tennessee, Georgia, Alabama, 1861–1864* (Boston: Military Historical Society of Massachusetts, 1910), 188.

12. *Map of the Battlefields of Chattanooga: Wauhatchie and Brown's Ferry, September 27–28, 1863 [sic]. Prepared under the Direction of the Honorable Daniel S. Lamont, Secretary of War, by the Chickamauga and Chattanooga National Park Commission* . . . (1901); *The Eighty-sixth Regiment, Indiana Volunteer Infantry, a Narrative of Its Services in the Civil War of 1861–1865* (Crawfordsville, Ind.: Journal Company, Printers, 1895), 212–13; Hoobler, *Cities under the Gun*, 123, 139.

13. Smith, "Operations around Chattanooga," 186; Henry Cist, *The Army of the Cumberland* (New York: Charles Scribner's Sons, 1882), 233; *OR* 31, pt. 2, 73; Hoobler, *Cities under the Gun*, 121; Gilbert E. Govan and James W. Livingood, *The Chattanooga Country, 1540–1976: From Tomahawks to TVA* (Knoxville: University of Tennessee Press, 1977), 14–15.

14. *Map of the Battlefields of Chattanooga: Wauhatchie and Brown's Ferry, September 27–28 [sic], 1863*; Francis Nohrhardt, "Field Notes as an Army Engineer in the Tennessee Campaign During the Civil War," CWC, TSLA; *Military Map Showing the Theater of Operations in the Tullahoma, Chickamauga, and Chattanooga Campaigns. Prepared under the Direction of the Hon. Daniel S. Lamont, Secretary of War, by the Chickamauga and Chattanooga National Park Commission* (1896).

15. To get a true feel for the contemporary appearance of Missionary Ridge and Lookout Mountain, the reader should consult Hoobler's *Cities under the Gun*, in which is reproduced a spectacular series of photographs of the area taken by Alexander George Barnard and others in early 1864.

16. Govan and Livingood, *Chattanooga Country*, 11–12; William F. G. Shanks, "Lookout Mountain and How We Won It," *Harper's New Monthly Magazine* 37, no. 217 (June 1868): 5.

17. Edward C. Walthall, "Walthall on the Battle of Lookout," *CV* 6, no. 12 (December 1896): 562; Shanks, "Lookout Mountain and How We Won It," 3–4; *Map of the Battlefields of Chattanooga: Wauhatchie and Brown's Ferry, September 27–28 [sic], 1863*.

18. Shanks, "Lookout Mountain and How We Won It," 4.

19. *Military Map Showing the* . . . *Tullahoma, Chickamauga, and Chattanooga Campaigns*; George K. Collins, *Memoirs of the 149th Regt. N.Y.*

*Vol. Inft., 3rd Brig., 2d Div., 12th and 20th A.C.* (Syracuse: By the author, 1891), 196.

20. Lamers, *Edge of Glory*, 370; *Military Map Showing the . . . Tullahoma, Chickamauga, and Chattanooga Campaigns.*

21. Lamers, *Edge of Glory*, 370; Francis F. McKinney, *Education in Violence: The Life of George H. Thomas and the History of the Army of the Cumberland* (Detroit: Wayne State University Press, 1961), 268–69; Nohrhardt, "Field Notes," CWC, TSLA; *Military Map Showing the . . . Tullahoma, Chickamauga, and Chattanooga Campaigns.*

22. Lamers, *Edge of Glory*, 370; Thomas B. Van Horne, *History of the Army of the Cumberland, Its Organization, Campaigns, and Battles*, 2 vols. (Cincinnati: Robert Clarke, 1875), 2:393.

23. Lamers, *Edge of Glory*, 371; Thomas L. Livermore, "The Siege and Relief of Chattanooga," in *PMHSM*, 8:283.

24. Henry M. Cist, "Comments on General Grant's Chattanooga," in *Battles and Leaders*, 3:717; Lamers, *Edge of Glory*, 371–72; Livermore, "Siege and Relief of Chattanooga," 287–91; John P. Sanderson Letter Diary, 1 November 1863, OHS; William F. Smith, *The Re-Opening of the Tennessee River Near Chattanooga, October, 1863, as Related by Major General George H. Thomas and the Official Record* (Wilmington, Del.: Press of Mercantile Printing Company, n.d.), 4–5, and *Autobiography of Major General William F. Smith, 1861–1864* (Dayton, Ohio: Morningside, 1990), 76.

25. Lamers, *Edge of Glory*, 374–76; Van Horne, *Army of the Cumberland*, 1:387–89; H. V. Ashbaugh, "Captured by Wheeler in the Sequatchie Valley," *National Tribune*, 28 May 1903; George Brent Journal, 29 October 1863, William J. Palmer Collection of Braxton Bragg Papers, WRHS; Arthur Manigault, *A Carolinian Goes to War: The Civil War Narrative of Arthur Middleton Manigault, Brigadier General, C.S.A.* (Columbia: University of South Carolina Press, 1983), 129–30.

26. Smith, *Re-Opening of the Tennessee River*, 6–7; Livermore, "Siege and Relief of Chattanooga," 292–93; Lamers, *Edge of Glory*, 377.

27. Lamers, *Edge of Glory*, 377; Smith, *Re-Opening of the Tennessee*, 7–8; Van Horne, *Army of the Cumberland*, 2:393; Walter H. Hebert, *Fighting Joe Hooker* (Indianapolis: Bobbs-Merrill, 1944), 255–56.

28. Simmons, *84th Reg't Ill. Vols.*, 119–20; Evander Law, "Lookout Valley, Memorandum of Gen. E. M. Law, November 3, 1878," E. A. Carman Papers, New York Public Library; *OR* 31, pt. 1, 224.

29. John Patton Memoir, Book 17, DLC.

30. Patton Memoir, Books 16–17, DLC; James Lee McDonough, *Chattanooga—A Death Grip on the Confederacy* (Knoxville: University of Tennessee Press, 1985), 48.

31. John Duke, *History of the Fifty-third Regiment Ohio Volunteer Infantry, during the War of the Rebellion, 1861 to 1865* (Portsmouth, Ohio: Blade Printing Company, 1900), 220.

32. Patton Memoir, Book 17, DLC.

33. Kirkpatrick, *Experiences of a Private Soldier*, 47–48; Theodore Black-

burn, *Letters from the Front: A Union "Preacher" Regiment (74th Ohio) in the Civil War* (Dayton, Ohio: Morningside, 1981), 160; Albion Tourgee, *The Story of a Thousand, Being a History of the Service of the 105th Ohio Volunteer Infantry, in the War for the Union* (Buffalo: McGerald and Son, 1896), 252–53; William Bircher, *A Drummer Boy's Diary* (St. Paul: St. Paul Book and Stationery Company, 1889), 80–81; Peter Kellenger to "Friend Add," 19 December 1863, DLC; W. C. Black Diary, 26–27 October 1863, Kansas Historical Society.

34. Smith, "Operations around Chattanooga," 167.

## CHAPTER THREE / EVERYONE HERE CURSES BRAGG

1. Quoted in William C. Davis, *Jefferson Davis: The Man and His Hour* (New York: Harper Collins, 1991), 518–19, which gives a lively account of Davis's visit to the Army of Tennessee. For more on the anti-Bragg movement, see chapter 32 of Cozzens, *This Terrible Sound*, and chapter 10 of Thomas L. Connelly's outstanding *Autumn of Glory: The Army of Tennessee, 1862–1865* (Baton Rouge: Louisiana State University Press, 1971).

2. St. John Richardson Liddell, *Liddell's Record*, ed. Nathaniel C. Hughes (Dayton, Ohio: Morningside, 1985), 152–53.

3. Arndt M. Stickles, *Simon Bolivar Buckner: Borderland Knight* (Chapel Hill: University of North Carolina Press, 1940), 238–39.

4. Connelly, *Autumn of Glory*, 250–51; James Longstreet to Benjamin Franklin Cheatham, 21 October 1863, Cheatham Papers, TSLA.

5. *OR* 31, pt. 3, 685–86; Connelly, *Autumn of Glory*, 250–51; Christopher Losson, *Tennessee's Forgotten Warriors: Frank Cheatham and His Confederate Division* (Knoxville: University of Tennessee Press, 1989; Cheatham to George Brent, 31 October 1863, Cheatham Papers, TSLA; "Second Hand Pictures for Silly Southerners," *CV* 1, no. 12 (December 1893): 377–78; John C. Moore, "Battle of Lookout Mountain," *CV* 6, no. 9 (September 1898): 426.

6. Brent journal, 22–26 October, 1863, Palmer Collection of Bragg Papers, WRHS; Davis to Bragg, 29 October 1863, in Jefferson Davis, *Jefferson Davis, Constitutionalist: His Letters, Papers, and Speeches*, ed. Dunbar Rowland, 10 vols. (Jackson, Miss.: Mississippi Department of Archives and History, 1923), 6:68. For an excellent treatment of the Bragg-Buckner controversy, see Stickles, *Buckner*, 237–56, and for the complete correspondence between the two, see *OR* 31, pt. 3, 655–68.

7. For a convincing recital of Breckinridge's merits and worthiness for corps command, see William C. Davis, *Breckinridge: Statesman, Soldier, Symbol* (Baton Rouge: Louisiana State University Press, 1973), 380–84.

8. Connelly, *Autumn of Glory*, 250–52; Davis, *Breckinridge*, 384; Longstreet to Cheatham, 21 October 1863, Cheatham Papers, TSLA; James Longstreet, *From Manassas to Appomattox, Memoirs of the Civil War in America* (Philadelphia: J. B. Lippincott, 1896), 468–69; Judith Lee Hallock, *Braxton Bragg and the Confederate Defeat. Volume II* (Tuscaloosa, Ala.: University of Alabama Press, 1991), 107–8.

9. Connelly, *Autumn of Glory*, 251.

10. Ibid., 246; Davis, *Jefferson Davis*, 522; T. B. Roy, "Sketch of Lieut. [Gen.] W. B. Hardee," 12, William J. Hardee Papers, ADAH.

11. Nathaniel C. Hughes, *General William J. Hardee: Old Reliable* (Baton Rouge: Louisiana State University Press, 1965), 158–62; Roy, "Sketch," 12, Hardee Papers, ADAH.

12. Davis to Bragg, 29 October 1863, and Davis to Hardee, 30 October 1863, in Davis, *Jefferson Davis, Constitutionalist*, 6:69–72.

13. Peter Cozzens, *No Better Place to Die: The Battle of Stones River* (Urbana: University of Illinois Press, 1990), 33–35; Hughes, *Hardee*, 161–62.

14. Quoted in Hughes, *Hardee*, 164; John C. Brown to James Longstreet, 14 April 1888, Longstreet Papers, DU; Brent journal, 16 October 1863, Palmer Collection of Bragg Papers, WRHS; W. J. Milner, "Lieutenant General William Joseph Hardee," *CV* 22, no. 8 (August 1914): 361; Hallock, *Bragg*, 102–3.

15. Liddell, *Liddell's Record*, 155; June I. Gow, "Chiefs of Staff in the Army of Tennessee under Braxton Bragg," *Tennessee Historical Quarterly* 27 (1968): 355–59.

16. John Harris to "Dear George," 13 October 1863, Harris Letters, TSLA; "Maney's Brigade at Missionary Ridge," *Southern Bivouac* 2 (1883/84): 299.

17. Quoted in Losson, *Tennessee's Forgotten Warriors*, 116–17.

18. A. Doss to Sarah Doss, 13 November 1863, Nineteenth Alabama File, CCNMP; Brent journal, 19 November 1863, Palmer Collection of Bragg Papers, WRHS; Frank M. Phelps to "Dear Friends," 2 December 1863, Lewis Leigh Collection, USAMHI; *Record of the Ninety-fourth Regiment, Ohio Volunteer Infantry in the War of the Rebellion* (Cincinnati: Valley Press, 189–), 57.

19. Samuel R. Watkins, *"Co. Aytch," Maury Grays, First Tennessee Regiment; or, a Side Show of the Big Show* (Chattanooga: Times Printing Company, 1900), 100.

20. Ibid., 101.

21. James L. Cooper Memoirs, 37, Confederate Collection, TSLA; Frank Mixson, *Reminiscences of a Private* (Columbia, S.C.: State Company, 1910), 44; Johnny Williams Green, *Johnny Green of the Orphan Brigade: The Journal of a Confederate Soldier* (Lexington: University of Kentucky Press, 1956), 105; Moore, "Battle of Lookout Mountain," 426.

22. W. E. Preston, "Memoirs of the War, 1861–1865," 29, Thirty-third Alabama Infantry Papers, ADAH; H. W. Henry, "Little War-Time Incidents," *CV* 22, no. 7 (July 1914): 307; Larry J. Daniel, *Cannoneers in Gray: The Field Artillery of the Army of Tennessee, 1861–1865* (University, Ala.: University of Alabama Press, 1990), 107–8; William Ralston Talley Autobiography, 33, Havis's Georgia Battery File, CCNMP.

23. Manigault, *Carolinian Goes to War*, 125. Manigault was virtually alone in claiming that his troops were well provided for and comfortable. For a more typical rendering of affairs, see P. D. Stephenson, "Missionary

Ridge," *CV* 21, no. 11 (November 1913): 540, and Andrew Malone Hill, "Personal Recollections of Andrew Malone Hill," *Alabama Historical Quarterly* 20 (Spring 1958): 88.

24. Mixson, *Reminiscences*, 44; E. Porter Alexander, *Fighting for the Confederacy: The Personal Recollections of General Edward Porter Alexander* (Chapel Hill: University of North Carolina Press, 1989), 301.

25. *OR* 30, pt. 4, 713–14; Hallock, *Bragg*, 106–7.

26. Green, *Johnny Green*, 106–7. The veracity of Green's claims were borne out when, after the Confederate defeat at Chattanooga, pursuing Federals torched vast stockpiles of supplies at Chickamauga Station.

27. Quoted in Hallock, *Bragg*, 109.

28. Brent journal, 1–31 October 1863, Palmer Collection of Bragg Papers, WRHS.

29. Longstreet, *Manassas to Appomattox*, 463; *Map of the Battlefields of Chattanooga: Wauhatchie and Brown's Ferry, September 27–28 [sic], 1863.*

30. Alexander, *Fighting for the Confederacy*, 304; Daniel, *Cannoneers in Gray*, 105–6.

31. Daniel, *Cannoneers in Gray*, 106; Garrity's Alabama Battery Marker on Lookout Mountain, CCNMP.

32. Lewis, *124th Ohio*, 77–78; Floyd, *Seventy-fifth Indiana*, 203; Donahower, "Narrative, Volume 2," 176–77, Donahower Papers, MnHS.

33. Hill, "The Second Minnesota"; Benjamin Franklin Scribner, *How Soldiers Were Made; or, the War as I Saw It under Buell, Rosecrans, Thomas, Grant, and Sherman* (Chicago: Donohue and Henneberry, Printers, 1887), 173–74.

34. Daniel, *Cannoneers in Gray*, 107; Alexander, *Fighting for the Confederacy*, 334; Longstreet, *Manassas to Appomattox*, 463; *Record of the Ninety-fourth Ohio*, 556.

35. Quoted in Hallock, *Bragg*, 111; Van Horne, *Army of the Cumberland*, 1:389–91; Connelly, *Autumn of Glory*, 268–70; Manigault, *Carolinian Goes to War*, 130.

36. Van Horne, *Army of the Cumberland*, 1:391; Connelly, *Autumn of Glory*, 269–70.

37. Longstreet, *Manassas to Appomattox*, 464.

38. Ezra J. Warner, *Generals in Gray: Lives of the Confederate Commanders* (Baton Rouge: Louisiana State University Press, 1959), 174–75; William C. Oates, *War between the Union and the Confederacy and Its Lost Opportunities, with a History of the 15th Alabama Regiment and the Forty-eight Battles in Which It Was Engaged* (New York: Neale, 1905), 269.

39. Longstreet, *Manassas to Appomattox*, 464; *OR* 31, pt. 1, 224; Law, "Lookout Valley," Carman Papers, New York Public Library; Oates, *War between the Union and the Confederacy*, 270; Glenn LaFantasie to Peter Cozzens, 7 December 1991.

40. Oates, *War between the Union and the Confederacy*, 270.

41. *OR* 31, pt. 1, 216, 224; Law, "Lookout Valley," Carman Papers, New

York Public Library; Oates, *War between the Union and the Confederacy*, 280–81.

42. Connelly, *Autumn of Glory*, 254, OR 30, pt. 4, 745–46; Longstreet, *Manassas to Appomattox*, 468–69; Alexander, *Fighting for the Confederacy*, 305–6; OR 31, pt. 1, 43–44; William Ralston Talley Autobiography, 32, Havis's Georgia Battery File, CCNMP.

43. Alexander, *Fighting for the Confederacy*, 305–6.

44. Longstreet, *Manassas to Appomattox*, 469–70; Connelly, *Autumn of Glory*, 254, questions the veracity of Longstreet's account, pointing out that two weeks earlier Longstreet had proposed to Secretary of War Seddon the same sort of move into East Tennessee that Bragg now made at the council of war. Alexander's testimony, as well as a subsequent letter from Davis to Bragg lamenting the lost opportunity to strike at Bridgeport, would tend to bear Longstreet out. See Davis to Bragg, 29 October 1863, in Davis, *Jefferson Davis, Constitutionalist*, 6:69–70.

45. Bragg to Davis, 17 October 1863, and Brent journal, 21 October 1863, both in Palmer Collection of Bragg Papers, WRHS; Longstreet, *Manassas to Appomattox*, 470–71; Thomas Robson Hay, "The Battle of Chattanooga," *Georgia Historical Quarterly* 8 (1924): 122.

46. Launcelot I. Scott, "Brown's Ferry Expedition: Shortening the Ration Line and Helping Save the Starving Army at Chattanooga," *National Tribune*, 25 January 1912; Lamers, *Edge of Glory*, 387; Simmons, *84th Reg't Ill. Vols.*, 121.

47. Brent journal, 21–24 October, 1863, Bragg to Johnston, n.d., and Bragg to Davis, 21 October 1863, all in Palmer Collection of Bragg Papers, WRHS.

CHAPTER FOUR / AUDACITY MIGHT YET BRING US THROUGH

1. Warner, *Generals in Blue*, 462–63; Smith, *Autobiography*, ix.

2. Smith, *Autobiography*, 71–72.

3. Wilson, *Under the Old Flag*, 1:271; Smith, *Autobiography*, 72.

4. Smith, *Autobiography*, 72.

5. Ibid., 76; Lamers, *Edge of Glory*, 391.

6. Smith, *Autobiography*, 72–74, and "Operations around Chattanooga," 156, 166, 169, 186; Livermore, "Siege and Relief of Chattanooga," 319–20, 328. Lamers, *Edge of Glory*, 390–91, gives Smith virtually no credit for such creative thinking, but Lamers's arguments are unconvincing.

7. Smith, *Autobiography*, 74, "Operations around Chattanooga," 169, and *Re-Opening of the Tennessee*, 21; Lamers, *Edge of Glory*, 391; OR 31, pt. 1, 77; Livermore, "Siege and Relief of Chattanooga," 328.

8. Smith, *Autobiography*, 74, and "Operations around Chattanooga," 169; Charles E. Belknap, *History of the Michigan Organizations at Chickamauga, Chattanooga and Missionary Ridge, 1863* (Lansing: Robert Smith Printing Company, 1897), 179, 202, 204.

9. Smith, *Autobiography*, 74.

10. Ibid., 75; Smith, "Operations around Chattanooga," 169–70. Lamers,

*Edge of Glory*, 391, contends that Rosecrans visited Brown's Ferry later that same day, but offers no real evidence to support this claim. Neither does he explain Rosecrans's failure not only to appreciate the importance of Brown's Ferry but, apparently, even to have been aware of its existence. During the long weeks before his removal, he had had ample time to study the country around Chattanooga. Livermore takes Rosecrans to task on this oversight. Rosecrans, he wrote, had been "blind to, or neglectful of, the strategic control of the river below Brown's Ferry which a bridge at that point would give him, during all this period. . . . It is incredible that Rosecrans, in view of the distress of his command for food and forage, could have neglected this opportunity . . . if he had seen the strategic advantage offered him. . . . To contend otherwise would be an impeachment worse than that of the mental and temperamental weakness disclosed in Dana's dispatches." Livermore, "Siege and Relief of Chattanooga," 294, 309. What Livermore accurately assessed was but the most glaring example of Rosecrans's deepening despondency and growing inability to focus his efforts.

11. Lamers, *Edge of Glory*, 398; Grant, *Personal Memoirs*, 2:28; Wilson, *Under the Old Flag*, 1:265; John Alcott Carpenter, *Sword and Olive Branch: Oliver Otis Howard* (Pittsburgh: University of Pittsburgh Press, 1964), 59.

12. Carpenter, *Sword and Olive Branch*, 58; Hebert, *Fighting Joe Hooker*, 251; Warner, *Generals in Blue*, 238.

13. Carpenter, *Sword and Olive Branch*, 58; Oliver Otis Howard, "Grant at Chattanooga," in *Personal Recollections of the War of the Rebellion: Addresses Delivered before the New York Commandery of the Loyal Legion of the United States, 1883–1891* (New York: By the Commandery, 1891): 1:246.

14. Hebert, *Fighting Joe Hooker*, 250.

15. Mosman, *Rough Side of War*, 131.

16. Wilson, *Under the Old Flag*, 1:264; Hebert, *Fighting Joe Hooker*, 257; Howard, "Grant at Chattanooga," 246.

17. Howard, "Grant at Chattanooga," 247; Hebert, *Fighting Joe Hooker*, 257.

18. Wilson, *Under the Old Flag*, 1:268–69; Grant, "Chattanooga," 684.

19. Rawlins to Mary E. Hurlbut, 23 November 1863, Rawlins Papers, ChiHS; Grant, "Chattanooga," 684, and *Personal Memoirs*, 2:28; Howard, "Grant at Chattanooga," 247; Wilson, *Under the Old Flag*, 1:273.

20. Porter, *Campaigning with Grant*, 1–3; Hoobler, *Cities under the Gun*, 159; Grant, *Personal Memoirs*, 2:28.

21. Wilson, *Under the Old Flag*, 1:273–74; Porter, *Campaigning with Grant*, 4; McKinney, *Education in Violence*, 274.

22. Wilson, *Under the Old Flag*, 1:274–76; McKinney, *Education in Violence*, 273–74; Warner, *Generals in Blue*, 555.

23. Porter, *Campaigning with Grant*, 4–5.

24. Smith, "Operations around Chattanooga," 170, and *Autobiography*, 75; Wilson, *Under the Old Flag*, 1:277.

25. Grant, *Personal Memoirs*, 2:29; Porter, *Campaigning with Grant*, 4–5; Smith, *Autobiography*, 75; OR 31, pt. 1, 70.

26. Grant, *Personal Memoirs*, 2:29–30; Porter, *Campaigning with Grant*, 5–6.

CHAPTER FIVE / A MEDAL OF HONOR OR TWO EARS OF CORN

1. Lewis, *124th Ohio*, 81–82.
2. Donahower, "Narrative, Volume 2," 177, Donahower Papers, MnHS; John Calvin Hartzell, "The Autobiography of John Calvin Hartzell, Part 2, The Civil War Years," edited by Thomas M. Hartzell, 89 (unpublished manuscript in the possession of Thomas M. Hartzell).
3. Hartzell, "Autobiography, Part 2," 93.
4. Ibid.
5. Samuel F. Foster Diary, 54, *CWTI* Collection, USAMHI; R. M. Collins, *Chapters from the Unwritten History of the War between the States; or, Incidents in the Life of a Confederate Soldier, in Camp, on the March, in the Great Battles, and in Prison* (St. Louis: Nixon-Jones Printing Company, 1893), 170.
6. Hartzell, "Autobiography, Part 2," 95; Lewis, *124th Ohio*, 92.
7. Will F. Peddycord, *History of the Seventy-fourth Regiment Indiana Volunteer Infantry* (Warsaw, Ind.: Smith Printery, 1913), 123; Manigault, *Carolinian Goes to War*, 125; Foster diary, 54, *CWTI* Collection, USAMHI.
8. Thomas J. Wright, *History of the Eighth Regiment Kentucky Vol. Inf., During Its Three Years Campaigns, Embracing Organizations, Marches, Skirmishes, and Battles of the Command, with Much of the History of the Old Reliable Third Brigade, Commanded by Hon. Stanley Matthews, and Containing Many Interesting and Amusing Incidents of Army Life* (St. Joseph, Mo.: St. Joseph Steam Printing Company, 1880), 198–99; Clark, *Opdycke Tigers, 125th O.V.I.*, 141; Mosman, *Rough Side of War*, 100.
9. Hartzell, "Autobiography, Part 2," 88.
10. Hill, "Second Minnesota"; Bishop's easy-going attitude is reflected in his *The Story of a Regiment, Being a Narrative of the Second Regiment, Minnesota Veteran Volunteer Infantry, in the Civil War of 1861–1865* (St. Paul: N.p., 1890), 114–15.
11. Grant, *Personal Memoirs*, 2:31–32; Porter, *Campaigning with Grant*, 6.
12. Grant, *Personal Memoirs*, 2:32; OR 31, pt. 1, 77.
13. OR 31, pt. 1, 43–44; Grant, *Personal Memoirs*, 2:35–36; Livermore, "Siege and Relief of Chattanooga," 318, 328; Wilson, *Under the Old Flag*, 1:277.
14. OR 31, pt. 1, 71; Livermore, "Siege and Relief of Chattanooga," 315–16.
15. OR 31, pt. 1, 42–45, and pt. 2, 27–28; Hebert, *Fighting Joe Hooker*, 258; Livermore, "Siege and Relief of Chattanooga," 316.
16. OR 31, pt. 1, 77; William A. Morgan, "Brown's Ferry," in *War Talks in Kansas: Papers Read before the Commandery of Kansas, Military Order of the Loyal Legion of the United States*, vol. 1 (Kansas City, Mo.: Franklin Hudson Publishing Company, 1906), 344–45; William Hazen, *A Narrative of Military Service* (Boston: Ticknor, 1885), 154.

17. McDonough, *Chattanooga*, 77; Grant, *Personal Memoirs*, 2:35–36.

18. McDonough, *Chattanooga*, 77–78.

19. *OR* 31, pt. 1, 77, 82; 'Hazen, *Narrative of Military Service*, 154–56; Ebenezer Hannaford, *The Story of a Regiment, a History of the Campaigns, and Associations in the Field of the Sixth Regiment, Ohio Volunteer Infantry* (Cincinnati: By the Author, 1868), 487–88; Morgan, "Brown's Ferry," 344.

20. Hazen, *Narrative of Military Service*, 154–55; Robert L. Kimberly, *The Forty-first Ohio Volunteer Infantry in the War of the Rebellion, 1861–1865* (Cleveland: W. R. Smellie, 1897), 59–60.

21. *OR* 31, pt. 1, 82, 85; Hazen, *Narrative of Military Service*, 156; Charles Banks, "How Hazen's Brigade Floated Down in Pontoon Boats and Established the Cracker Line," *National Tribune*, 12 May 1892.

22. Kimberly, *Forty-first Ohio*, 60; Hazen, *Narrative of Military Service*, 155–56; *OR* 31, pt. 1, 82–83, and pt. 2, 27–28.

23. Connelly, *Autumn of Glory*, 255–56; Bragg to Joseph Johnston, n.d., Palmer Collection of Bragg Papers, WRHS.

24. George Brent, "Notes on the Investment and Operations around Chattanooga," 2–3, Longstreet to Brent, 26 October 1863, and Brent journal, 26 October 1863, all in Palmer Collection of Bragg Papers, WRHS.

25. Oates, *War between the Union and the Confederacy*, 280–81; Law, "Lookout Valley," Carman Papers, NYPL; Smith, "Operations around Chattanooga," 165.

26. Oates, *War between the Union and the Confederacy*, 274–75; Law, "Lookout Valley," Carman Papers, NYPL; Connelly, *Autumn of Glory*, 256–57.

27. Law, "Lookout Valley," Carman Papers, NYPL; *OR* 31, pt. 1, 224; Oates, *War between the Union and the Confederacy*, 276.

28. Wagner reminiscences, 91, *CWTI* Collection, USAMHI; Philip Dicks, "The Cracker Line," *National Tribune*, 30 April 1885; Hazen, *Narrative of Military Service*, 155; Hannaford, *Sixth Ohio*, 487–88; A. Brandley, "The Cracker Line," *National Tribune*, 28 May 1885; Banks, "How Hazen's Brigade Floated Down."

29. Hazen, *Narrative of Military Service*, 158–59, 177; Kimberly, *Forty-first Ohio*, 60.

30. Kimberly, *Forty-first Ohio*, 60; Morgan, "Brown's Ferry," 345; Wagner reminiscences, 91, *CWTI* Collection, USAMHI; *OR* 31, pt. 1, 84, 86; Banks, "How Hazen's Brigade Floated Down"; "Recollections of a Soldier of the First Ohio Infantry," 29, Federal Collection, TSLA.

31. *OR* 31, pt. 1, 88.

32. Morgan, "Brown's Ferry," 345; *OR* 31, pt. 1, 86.

33. Morgan, "Brown's Ferry," 345.

34. Hannaford, *Sixth Ohio*, 489; Kimberly, *Forty-first Ohio*, 61.

35. Morgan, "Brown's Ferry," 346; Brandley, "The Cracker Line"; Kimberly, *Forty-first Ohio*, 61; *OR* 31, pt. 1, 88.

36. *OR* 31, pt. 1, 84, 86, 88; Morgan, "Brown's Ferry," 347; Kimberly, *Forty-first Ohio*, 61; Hannaford, *Sixth Ohio*, 490.

37. Oates, *War between the Union and the Confederacy*, 275–77; Law, "Lookout Valley," Carman Papers, NYPL; Brandley, "The Cracker Line"; *OR* 31, pt. 1, 87–89.

38. Oates, *War between the Union and the Confederacy*, 277; *OR* 31, pt. 1, 49.

39. Wagner reminiscences, 92, *CWTI* Collection, USAMHI; Brandley, "The Cracker Line."

40. Oates, *War between the Union and the Confederacy*, 278–79, 281; *OR* 31, pt. 1, 50.

41. Morgan, "Brown's Ferry," 348–49; *OR* 31, pt. 1, 85.

## CHAPTER SIX / OUR LAGGING EFFORTS

1. Connelly, *Autumn of Glory*, 257–58; Longstreet to Brent, 26 October 1863, and Brent, "Notes on the Investment and Operations around Chattanooga," 3, both in Palmer Collection of Bragg Papers, WRHS; *OR* 31, pt. 1, 225; Law, "Lookout Valley," Carman Papers, NYPL; *Military Map Showing the . . . Tullahoma, Chickamauga, and Chattanooga Campaigns.*

2. Liddell, *Liddell's Record*, 155–56; Connelly, *Autumn of Glory*, 258–59.

3. Brent, "Notes on the Investment and Operations around Chattanooga," 3–4, Palmer Collection Bragg Papers, WRHS; Liddell, *Liddell's Record*, 156.

4. Longstreet to Brent, 27 October 1863, and Brent, "Notes on the Investment and Operations around Chattanooga," 4, both in Palmer Collection of Bragg Papers, WRHS.

5. Brent, "Notes on the Investment and Operations around Chattanooga," 4–5, and Longstreet to Brent, 27 October 1863, both in Palmer Collection of Bragg Papers, WRHS; *OR* 31, pt. 1, 217, 222.

6. Brent to Longstreet, 11:00 P.M., 27 October 1863, and Brent, "Notes on the Investment and Operations around Chattanooga," 5–6, both in Palmer Collection of Bragg Papers, WRHS; *OR* 31, pt. 1, 222.

7. *OR* 31, pt. 1, 42–48, 54.

8. Ibid., 45–46.

9. Ibid., 72; Hebert, *Fighting Joe Hooker*, 258.

10. *OR* 31, pt. 1, 49, 55, 115–17; Howard, "Grant at Chattanooga," 207–8; Simmons, *84th Reg't Ill. Vols.*, 128; Collins, *149th Regt. N.Y. Vol.*, 194–96; Albert R. Greene, *From Bridgeport to Ringgold by Way of Lookout Mountain* (Providence, R.I.: By the Society, 1890), 14–15.

11. *OR* 31, pt. 1, 55; Greene, *Bridgeport to Ringgold*, 14–15.

12. Liddell, *Liddell's Record*, 156–57; Longstreet, *Manassas to Appomattox*, 474; *OR* 31, pt. 1, 217.

13. Liddell, *Liddell's Record*, 157; Longstreet, *Manassas to Appomattox*, 474; Shanks, "Lookout Mountain and How We Won It," 12.

14. Longstreet, *Manassas to Appomattox*, 475; Liddell, *Liddell's Record*, 157; Alexander, *Fighting for the Confederacy*, 310–11.

15. Greene, *Bridgeport to Ringgold*, 18–19; George Metcalf Reminiscences, 125, Harrisburg CWRT Collection, USAMHI; Howard, "Grant at Chattanooga," 208.

16. Metcalf reminiscences, 124, Harrisburg CWRT Collection, USAMHI.

17. J. L. Coker, "Battle of Lookout Valley or Wauhatchie," *CV* 18, no. 10 (October 1910): 473; *OR* 31, pt. 1, 97, 101–2.

18. Kimberly, *Forty-first Ohio*, 63–64; Samuel H. Hurst, *Journal-History of the Seventy-third Ohio Volunteer Infantry* (Chillicothe, Ohio: N.p., 1866), 85–86; Andrew McCormick to his parents, 24 November 1863, Wiley Sword Collection, USAMHI; Howard, "Grant at Chattanooga," 208; Hartwell Osborn, *Trials and Triumphs: The Record of the Fifty-fifth Ohio Volunteer Infantry* (Chicago: A. C. McClurg, 1904), 120–21; Henry Henney Diary, 22 October 1863, *CWTI* Collection, USAMHI; Daniel Brinton, "Dr. Daniel Garrison Brinton with the Army of the Cumberland," *Pennsylvania Magazine of History and Biography* 90 (October 1966): 477.

19. *OR* 31, pt. 1, 41; William G. Le Duc, "The Little Steamboat that Opened the 'Cracker Line,'" in *Battles and Leaders*, ed. Buell and Johnson, 3:677–78.

20. Smith, *Autobiography*, 77.

21. Ibid., 77; *OR* 31, pt. 1, 72; John R. Boyle, *Soldiers True: The Story of the One Hundred and Eleventh Regiment Pennsylvania Veteran Volunteers, and of Its Campaigns in the War for the Union, 1861–1865* (New York: Eaton and Mains, 1903), 168.

22. *OR* 31, pt. 1, 57, 93, 97, 111; Douglas R. Cubbison, "Midnight Engagement: Geary's White Star Division at Wauhatchie, Tennessee, October 28–29, 1863," *Civil War Regiments* 3, no. 2 (1993): 100. Cubbison asserts that Hooker was correct in leaving Geary at Wauhatchie, arguing that possession of the junction was essential to holding open the road from Kelley's Ferry. Cubbison does not take into account the equally viable road from Kelley's to Brown's Ferry, over which supplies could be brought and which Hooker could control.

23. Warner, *Generals in Blue*, 170.

24. Greene, *Bridgeport to Ringgold*, 21–22; Jesse H. Jones, "Lookout Mountain: An Account of the Battle by a Fighting Parson," *National Tribune*, 21 October 1889; Warner, *Generals in Blue*, 169.

25. Greene, *Bridgeport to Ringgold*, 19–20; *OR* 31, pt. 1, 113; Jerry Korn, *The Fight for Chattanooga: Chickamauga to Missionary Ridge* (Alexandria, Va.: Time-Life Books, 1985), 92–93.

26. *OR* 31, pt. 1, 113, 123.

27. Ibid.; Collins, *149th Regt. N.Y. Vol.*, 197.

CHAPTER SEVEN / THE CHANCE OF SUCCESS MAY BE
CALCULATED AT ZERO

1. Connelly, *Autumn of Glory*, 259; Liddell, *Liddell's Record* 157; Brent journal, 28 October 1863, Palmer Collection of Bragg Papers, WRHS.

2. Longstreet, *Manassas to Appomattox*, 475; Law, "Lookout Valley," Carman Papers, NYPL; *OR* 31, pt. 1, 217.

3. Brent journal, 28 October 1863, Longstreet to Bragg, two letters dated 28 October 1863, Brent to Longstreet, 7:30 P.M.—28 October 1863, Brent, "Notes on the Investment and Operations around Chattanooga," 7, all in Palmer Collection of Bragg Papers, WRHS; Longstreet, *Manassas to Appomattox*, 475–76; Connelly, *Autumn of Glory*, 259–60; Cubbison, "Midnight Engagement," 97–99.

4. Longstreet to E. A. Carman, undated letter quoted in Adin Underwood, *The Three Years' Service of the Thirty-third Mass. Infantry Regiment, 1862–1865, and the Campaigns and Battles of Chancellorsville, Beverley's Ford, Gettysburg, Wauhatchie, Chattanooga, Atlanta, the March to the Sea and through the Carolinas in Which It Took Part* (Boston: A. Williams and Company, 1881), 158; Longstreet, *Manassas to Appomattox*, 475; *OR* 31, pt. 1, 217; Brent, "Notes on the Investment and Operations around Chattanooga," 7, Palmer Collection of Bragg Papers, WRHS; McDonough, *Chattanooga*, 92.

5. Alexander, *Fighting for the Confederacy*, 116–17; Oates, *War between the Union and the Confederacy*, 281; Longstreet, *Manassas to Appomattox*, 467–68.

6. *OR* 31, pt. 1, 217, 225–26; Law, "Lookout Valley," Carman Papers, NYPL.

7. Law, "Lookout Valley," Carman Papers, NYPL.

8. *OR* 31, pt. 1, 226–27.

9. Ibid.

10. Ibid., 98, 113, 122–23.

11. Ibid., 113, 123.

12. Oates, *War between the Union and the Confederacy*, 281–82; Longstreet, *Manassas to Appomattox*, 476; Brent, "Notes on the Investment and Operations around Chattanooga," 8, Palmer Collection of Bragg Papers, WRHS.

13. Mixson, *Reminiscences*, 44–45; Turner Vaughan, "Diary of Turner Vaughan, Co. C, 4th Alabama," *Alabama Historical Quarterly* 18 (Winter 1956): 599; Coker, "Battle of Lookout Valley," 473.

14. *OR* 31, pt. 1, 123, 231; Coker, "Battle of Lookout Valley," 473; Cubbison, "Midnight Engagement," 83–84.

15. Boyle, *Soldiers True*, 164–65; Collins, *149th Regt. N.Y. Vol.*, 197–98; *OR* 31, pt. 1, 114; Fergus Elliott to his family, 1 November 1863, Fergus Elliott Letters, CWTI Collection, USAMHI; Boyle, *Soldiers True*, 161–62; Cubbison, "Midnight Engagement," 84.

16. Greene, *Bridgeport to Ringgold*, 22–23; *OR* 31, pt. 1, 113, 123; George W. Skinner, *Pennsylvania at Chickamauga and Chattanooga: Ceremonies at the Dedication of the Monuments Erected by the Commonwealth of Pennsylvania to Mark the Positions of the Pennsylvania Commands Engaged in the Battles* (Harrisburg, Pa.: Wm. Stanley Ray, State Printer, 1900), 379.

17. Greene, *Bridgeport to Ringgold*, 23.

18. *OR* 31, pt. 1, 127–28; Greene, *Bridgeport to Ringgold*, 23–24.

19. *OR* 31, pt. 1, 231; Greene, *Bridgeport to Ringgold*, 24–25; John Bratton to his wife, 29 October 1863, John Bratton Papers, Robert W. Woodruff Library, Emory University.

20. Boyle, *Soldiers True*, 163; Skinner, *Pennsylvania at Chickamauga and Chattanooga*, 379; Greene, *Bridgeport to Ringgold*, 25; *OR* 31, pt. 1, 120, 123, 135; David Nichol Diary, 28 October 1863, Harrisburg CWRT Collection, USAMHI; Fergus Elliott to his family, 1 November 1863, Elliott Letters, *CWTI* Collection, USAMHI.

21. *OR* 31, pt. 1, 128–29, 132; Cubbison, "Midnight Engagement," 88–89.

22. Boyle, *Soldiers True*, 163–64; *OR* 31, pt. 1, 128–32.

23. *OR* 31, pt. 1, 124; Skinner, *Pennsylvania at Chickamauga and Chattanooga*, 379; Greene, *Bridgeport to Ringgold*, 25; K. J. Alban, "Charge of Mule Brigade," *National Tribune*, 22 February 1923.

24. Boyle, *Soldiers True*, 165; Greene, *Bridgeport to Ringgold*, 25; *OR* 31, pt. 1, 115, 231; Coker, "Battle of Lookout Valley," 473; Asbury Coward, *The South Carolinians: Colonel Asbury Coward's Memoirs* (New York: Vantage Press, 1968), 90; Cubbison, "Midnight Engagement," 93.

25. John Ryder, *Reminiscences of Three Years' Service in the Civil War by a Cape Cod Boy* (New Bedford, Mass.: Reynolds Printing, 1928), 42; *OR* 31, pt. 1, 142, 185.

26. *OR* 31, pt. 1, 164, 185–86, 207.

27. Warner, *Generals in Blue*, 427.

28. *OR* 31, pt. 1, 101–2, 144–45, 206–7; J. L. Locke to "Dear Lem," 9 January 1864, J. L. Locke Letters, ISHL; Hurst, *Seventy-third Ohio*, 86–87; Osborn, *Trials and Triumphs*, 123.

29. *OR* 31, pt. 1, 140–42, 185.

30. Hurst, *Seventy-third Ohio*, 87; *OR* 31, pt. 1, 227; Metcalf reminiscences, 126, Harrisburg CWRT Collection, USAMHI; Ryder, *Reminiscences of Three Years' Service*, 42; Osborn, *Trials and Triumphs*, 123.

31. Hurst, *Seventy-third Ohio*, 87; J. L. Locke to "Dear Lem," 9 January 1864, Locke Letters, ISHL; Metcalf reminiscences, 126, Harrisburg CWRT Collection, USAMHI.

32. *OR* 31, pt. 1, 94, 145–46, 170–71; Osborn, *Trials and Triumphs*, 123.

33. *OR* 31, pt. 1, 94, 193.

34. Ryder, *Reminiscences of Three Years' Service*, 42; J. L. Locke to "Dear Lem," 9 January 1864, Locke Letters, ISHL.

35. *OR* 31, pt. 1, 227, 229, 234.

36. J. L. Locke to "Dear Lem," 9 January 1864, Locke Letters, ISHL; Ryder, *Reminiscences of Three Years' Service*, 43; Andrew Boies, *Record of the Thirty-third Massachusetts Volunteer Infantry* (Fitchburg, Mass.: Sentinel Printing Company, 1880), 47–48; *OR* 31, pt. 1, 103–4.

37. Hurst, *Seventy-third Ohio*, 87–88.

38. *OR* 31, pt. 1, 109; Hurst, *Seventy-third Ohio*, 88.

39. *OR* 31, pt. 1, 150, 186.

40. Ibid., 147–49, 152, 191.

41. Ibid., 171–73, 206–11.

42. Ibid., 111, 188–89.

43. Howard, "Grant at Chattanooga," 208–9.

44. Ryder, *Reminiscences of Three Years' Service,* 43; J. L. Locke to "Dear Lem," 9 January 1864, Locke Letters, ISHL; *OR* 31, pt. 1, 104.

45. Metcalf reminiscences, 16–27, Harrisburg CWRT Collection, USAM-HI; *OR* 31, pt. 1, 101–2; anonymous letter to "Dear William," 4 November 1863, One Hundred Thirty-sixth New York File, CCNMP.

46. *OR* 31, pt. 1, 234; Underwood, *Thirty-third Massachusetts,* 166.

47. Underwood, *Thirty-third Massachusetts,* 166–68; *OR* 31, pt. 1, 230.

48. *OR* 31, pt. 1, 109, 230; Boies, *Record of the Thirty-third Massachusetts,* 48–49; Ryder, *Reminiscences of Three Years' Service,* 43; Underwood, *Thirty-third Massachusetts,* 167–68.

49. Oates, *War between the Union and the Confederacy,* 283–85.

50. All times given here are purely estimates, deduced from the conflicting reports of participants on both sides and from the acrimonious testimony given during the Schurz court of inquiry. *OR* 31, pt. 1, 228, 234.

51. Metcalf reminiscences, 128, Harrisburg CWRT Collection, USAMHI; *OR* 31, pt. 1, 106; anonymous letter to "Dear William," 4 November 1863, One Hundred Thirty-sixth New York File, CCNMP.

52. J. B. Polley, "A Battle 'above the Clouds,'" *CV* 5, no. 3 (March 1897): 105–6.

53. *OR* 331, pt. 1, 187–94.

54. Howard, "Grant at Chattanooga," 208–9; Hartwell Osborn, "The Eleventh Corps in East Tennessee," in *Military Essays and Recollections: Papers Read before the Commandery of the State of Illinois, Military Order of the Loyal Legion of the United States,* vol. 4 (Chicago: Cozzens and Beaton Company, 1907), 360.

55. Grant, "Chattanooga," 690–91; Wilson, *Under the Old Flag,* 1:278–79; Carpenter, *Sword and Olive Branch,* 60; Hebert, *Fighting Joe Hooker,* 260; *OR* 31, pt. 1, 73.

CHAPTER EIGHT / A GOLDEN THREAD THROUGH
THE TANGLED WEB

1. Longstreet, *Manassas to Appomattox,* 477; *OR* 31, pt. 1, 218–19, 222–23.

2. Oates, *War between the Union and the Confederacy,* 283; Brent, "Notes on the Investment and Operations around Chattanooga," 8, Palmer Collection of Bragg Papers, WRHS.

3. Brent journal, 30 October 1863, Palmer Collection of Bragg Papers, WRHS.

4. *OR* 31, pt. 3, 609; Connelly, *Autumn of Glory,* 262; Brent journal, 31 October 1863, Palmer Collection of Bragg Papers, WRHS; Hughes, *Hardee,* 166–67.

5. Davis, *Jefferson Davis, Constitutionalist,* 6:69–70; Brent journal, 31 October 1863, Palmer Collection of Bragg Papers, WRHS; Connelly, *Autumn of Glory* 262–63; Steven E. Woodworth, *Jefferson Davis and His Generals: The Failure of Confederate Command in the West* (Lawrence: University of Kansas Press, 1990), 248; McDonough, *Chattanooga,* 98.

6. Connelly, *Autumn of Glory,* 263; Herman Hattaway, *General Stephen D. Lee* (Jackson: University of Mississippi Press, 1976), 102–3; Longstreet to Buckner, 5 November 1863, Civil War Papers—Army of Tennessee, Louisiana Historical Association Collection, Tulane.

7. Liddell, *Liddell's Record,* 157.

8. Connelly, *Autumn of Glory,* 264–65; Hay, "Chattanooga," 124; *OR* 31, pt. 3, 632–35; Alexander, *Fighting for the Confederacy,* 311; Longstreet, *From Manassas to Appomattox,* 480–81; Longstreet to Buckner, 5 November 1863, Civil War Papers—Army of Tennessee, Louisiana Historical Association Collection, Tulane; Carroll Henderson Clark Memoirs, 37, Confederate Collection, TSLA; W. J. Worsham, *The Old Nineteenth Tennessee Regiment, C.S.A., June, 1861—April, 1865* (Knoxville, Tenn.: Press of Paragon Printing Company, 1902), 97.

9. Brent journal, 31 October and 1 November 1863, Palmer Collection of Bragg Papers, WRHS; Hughes, *Hardee,* 167; Manigault, *Carolinian Goes to War,* 126–27; Liddell, *Liddell's Record,* 157.

10. Longstreet to Buckner, 5 November 1863, Civil War Papers—Army of Tennessee, Louisiana Historical Association Collection, Tulane.

11. *OR* 31, pt. 3, 635–36, 644, 670–71; Connelly, *Autumn of Glory,* 265; Brent journal, 9–11 November 1863, Palmer Collection of Bragg Papers, WRHS.

12. Brent journal, 11 November 1863, Palmer Collection of Bragg Papers, WRHS.

13. Grant, "Chattanooga," 691; Hattaway and Jones, *How the North Won,* 459.

14. Hattaway and Jones, *How the North Won,* 459; Grant, "Chattanooga," 691.

15. Grant, *Personal Memoirs* 2:49–50; *OR* 31, pt. 3, 10, 15, 60.

16. Smith, "Operations around Chattanooga," 192.

17. *OR* 31, pt. 3, 73; Grant, *Personal Memoirs,* 2:50.

18. Smith, "Operations around Chattanooga," 193.

19. *OR* 31, pt. 1, 156, and pt. 3, 15.

20. *Record of the Ninety-fourth Ohio,* 59; *OR* 31, pt. 2, 554; James Barnes et al., *The Eighty-sixth Regiment, Indiana Volunteer Infantry: A Narrative of Its Services in the Civil War of 1861–1865* (Crawfordsville, Ind.: Journal Company, 1895), 222–23; Black diary, 5 November 1863, Kansas Historical Society; William Burke, *The Military History of Kansas Regiments during the War for the Suppression of the Great Rebellion* (Leavenworth, Kans.: W. S. Burke, 1868), 215; J. H. SeCheverell, *Journal History of the Twenty-ninth Ohio Veteran Volunteers, 1861–1865. Its Victories and Its Reverses* (Cleveland: N.p., 1883), 84.

21. Grant, *Personal Memoirs*, 2:50; Smith, "Operations around Chattanooga," 193–94; Smith, *Autobiography*, 78; McKinney, *Education in Violence*, 281; OR 31, pt. 2, 29, 58–59.

22. Grant, *Personal Memoirs*, 2:50; McDonough, *Chattanooga*, 107; Smith, "Operations around Chattanooga," 189; OR 31, pt. 2, 29.

23. Grant, *Personal Memoirs*, 2:50.

24. Grant, "Chattanooga," 692–93; OR 31, pt. 3, 55.

25. OR 31, pt. 3, 90–91.

26. Green B. Raum, "With the Western Army: Sherman's March to Chattanooga," *National Tribune*, 3 April 1902; Duke, *Fifty-third Ohio*, 117–18; *The Story of the Fifty-fifth Illinois Regiment Illinois Volunteer Infantry in the Civil War, 1861–1865* (Clinton, Mass.: W. J. Coulter, 1887), 278; Jenkin Jones, *An Artilleryman's Diary* (Madison: Wisconsin History Commission, 1914), 126.

27. Jones, *Artilleryman's Diary*, 126.

28. Raum, "Sherman's March to Chattanooga"; Mosman, *Rough Side of War*, 120; M. O. Frost, *Regimental History of the Tenth Missouri Volunteer Infantry* (Topeka, Kans.: M. O. Frost Printing Company, 1892), 186; Jones, *Artilleryman's Diary*, 127.

29. OR 31, pt. 3, 140; Grant, "Chattanooga," 695.

30. William Tecumsah Sherman, *Memoirs of General W. T. Sherman* (New York: Library of America, 1990), 386–87.

## CHAPTER NINE / THE CHAIR OF HONOR?

1. Wilson, *Under the Old Flag*, 1:280; Govan and Livingood, *Chattanooga Country*, 178; Porter, *Campaigning with Grant*, 8; Hoobler, *Cities under the Gun*, 156.

2. Grant, "Chattanooga," 696; Wilson, *Under the Old Flag*, 1:291; Smith, "Operations around Chattanooga," 195, and *Autobiography*, 78.

3. Smith, *Autobiography*, 78, and "Operations around Chattanooga," 195; OR 31, pt. 2, 31.

4. OR 31, pt. 2, 30–31; Grant, "Chattanooga," 695.

5. Howard, "Grant at Chattanooga," 248; Sherman, *Memoirs*, 386.

6. Howard, "Grant at Chattanooga," 248–49.

7. Sherman, *Memoirs*, 373–75; Lewis, *Sherman, Fighting Prophet*, 308–10.

8. Smith, *Autobiography*, 79; Smith, "Holocaust Holiday," 31.

9. Smith, *Autobiography*, 79; Sherman, *Memoirs*, 37–88; Smith, "Holocaust Holiday," 32.

10. Grant, "Chattanooga," 695, and *Personal Memoirs*, 2:70; OR 31, pt. 2, 31; Smith, "Operations around Chattanooga," 195–96, 198.

11. Govan and Livingood, *Chattanooga Country*, 128–34; Grant, "Chattanooga," 695; Smith, *Autobiography*, 79.

12. Smith, "Operations around Chattanooga," 197.

13. Sherman, *Memoirs*, 388; OR 31, pt. 2, 572.

14. Hughes, *Hardee*, 167; Connelly, *Autumn of Glory*, 270–71.

15. *OR* 31, pt. 2, 685; Connelly, *Autumn of Glory*, 270; Govan and Livingood, *Chattanooga Country*, 164–65; Mary Snyder, "Robert Cravens—A Brief History of the Man and His Family," 9–18, Historical Files, CCNMP; Shanks, "Lookout Mountain and How We Won It," 85–87; Walthall, "Walthall on the Battle of Lookout," 562.

16. *OR* 31, pt. 2, 685; Moore, "Battle of Lookout Mountain," 626.

17. Moore, "Battle of Lookout Mountain," 426.

18. *OR* 31, pt. 2, 685–86, 717, and pt. 3, 695.

19. Moore, "Battle of Lookout Mountain," 426; *OR* 31, pt. 2, 717.

20. From Anderson's report of the campaign, in *The Confederate Collapse at the Battle of Missionary Ridge: The Reports of James Patton Anderson and His Brigade Commanders*, ed. John Hoffman (Dayton, Ohio: Morningside, 1985), 34.

21. Manigault, *Carolinian Goes to War*, 128–29.

22. Brent journal, 10 and 18 November 1863, Palmer Collection of Bragg Papers, WRHS; *OR* 31, pt. 3, 694–95.

23. Richard Eddy, *History of the Sixtieth Regiment, New York State Volunteers, from the Commencement of Its Organization in July 1861, to Its Public Reception at Ogdensburgh as a Veteran Command, January 7, 1864* (Philadelphia: Criss and Markley, Printers, 1864), 298–99.

24. Wagner reminiscences, 95–96, CWTI Collection, USAMHI.

25. *OR* 31, pt. 2, 583–84, 630; Sherman, *Memoirs*, 388.

26. Warner, *Generals in Blue*, 146, 441.

27. *OR* 31, pt. 2, 583, 630–31.

28. Aden G. Cavins, *War Letters of Aden G. Cavins Written to His Wife Matilda Livingston Cavins* (Evansville, Ind.: Rosenthal-Kuebler Printing Company, n.d.), 70.

29. *OR* 31, pt. 2, 642–43; Jones, *Artilleryman's Diary*, 129–30; Raum, "Sherman's March to Chattanooga."

30. Edward E. Schweitzer Diary, 17 November 1863, *CWTI* Collection, USAMHI; *Fifty-fifth Illinois*, 269.

31. Jones, *Artilleryman's Diary*, 131; Alonzo Brown, *History of the Fourth Regiment of Minnesota Infantry Volunteers during the Great Rebellion, 1861–1865* (St. Paul: Pioneer Press Company, 1892), 266; *OR* 31, pt. 2, 572, 642–43; Raum, "Sherman's March to Chattanooga."

32. Schweitzer diary, 18 November 1863, *CWTI* Collection, USAMHI.

33. *OR* 31, pt. 2, 64.

34. Wilson, *Under the Old Flag*, 1:288–91; *OR* 31, pt. 3, 145, 154–56, 163, 177, 181; Aquila Wiley, "Sherman's Inaction," *National Tribune*, 16 April 1891.

35. *OR* 31, pt. 2, 587, 631, 643; Theodore Upson, *With Sherman to the Sea: The Civil War Letters, Diaries and Reminiscences of Theodore F. Upson* (Baton Rouge: Louisiana State University Press, 1943), 78–80.

36. *OR* 31, pt. 2, 39; Schweitzer diary, 21 November 1863, *CWTI* Collection, USAMHI; Brown, *Fourth Minnesota*; *OR* 31, pt. 2, 572, 631; Charles

H. Claver Diary, 22 November 1863, IoHS; Grant, *Personal Memoirs*, 2:60; Raum, "Sherman's March to Chattanooga."

37. Hiram Crandell Diary, 19 November 1863, ISHL; *Fifty-fifth Illinois*, 280–81; Underwood, *Thirty-third Massachusetts*, 177; Rice C. Bull, *Soldiering: The Civil War Diary of Rice C. Bull, 123rd New York Volunteer Infantry* (San Rafael, Calif.: Presidio Press, 1977), 99.

38. Lewis, *124th Ohio*, 90.

39. *OR* 31, pt. 2, 39; McDonough, *Chattanooga*, 110.

40. *OR* 31, pt. 2, 94; Grant, *Personal Memoirs*, 2:60.

41. Brent journal, 18 November 1863, Palmer Collection of Bragg Papers, WRHS.

42. *OR* 31, pt. 2, 667.

43. Ibid., 668–72.

44. Ibid., pt. 3, 732–33, 736; Connelly, *Autumn of Glory*, 272.

## Chapter Ten / A Very Gallant Thing

1. Wiley, "Sherman's Inaction"; Thomas J. Wood, "The Battle of Missionary Ridge," in *Sketches of War History, 1861–1865. Papers Prepared for the Ohio Commandery of the Loyal Legion of the United States, 1890–1896, Volume 4* (Cincinnati: Robert Clarke Company, 1896), 26.

2. *OR* 31, pt. 2, 40; Wiley, "Sherman's Inaction."

3. *OR* 31, pt. 2, 64, 136.

4. Ibid., 32–33, 41; Grant, "Chattanooga," 698.

5. Wood, "Battle of Missionary Ridge," 27.

6. *OR* 31, pt. 2, 128–29, 255; Wood, "Battle of Missionary Ridge," 27; Joseph Fullerton, "Army of the Cumberland at Chattanooga," in *Battles and Leaders*, ed. Buell and Johnson, 3:721; Hoffman, ed., *Confederate Collapse*, 35.

7. *Seventy-fourth Illinois*, 123; E. J. Ingersoll to the Editor, Schuyler (Ill.) *Citizen*, 16 December 1863; Edwin C. High, *History of the Sixty-eighth Regiment Indiana Volunteer Infantry, 1862–1865, with a Sketch of E. A. King's Brigade, Reynold's Division, Thomas's Corps in the Battle of Chickamauga* (Metamora, Ind.: Sixty-eighth Indiana Infantry Association, 1902), 134.

8. Wood, "Battle of Missionary Ridge," 28; *OR* 31, pt. 2, 188; Osborn, *Trials and Triumphs*, 128.

9. Fullerton, "Army of the Cumberland at Chattanooga," 721; *OR* 31, pt. 2, 129, 254.

10. Osborn, *Trials and Triumphs*, 128; Fullerton, "Army of the Cumberland at Chattanooga," 721; Gilbert Stormont, *History of the Fifty-eighth Regiment of Indiana Volunteer Infantry, Its Organizations, Campaigns, and Battles, from 1861–1865* (Princeton, Ill.: Press of Clarion, 1895), 213; *OR* 31, pt. 2, 77, 129; John Shellenberger, "With Sheridan's Division at Missionary Ridge," in *Sketches of War History, 1861–1865. Papers Prepared for the Ohio Commandery of the Military Order of the Loyal Legion of the Unit-*

*ed States, 1890–1896, Volume 4* (Cincinnati: Robert Clarke Company, 1896), 52.

11. *OR* 31, pt. 2, 129, 254; Burke, *Military History of Kansas Regiments,* 216; High, *Sixty-eighth Indiana,* 135.

12. John Ely Diary, 23 November 1863, Thirty-sixth Illinois File, CCNMP; Kimberly, *Forty-first Ohio,* 65.

13. *OR* 31, pt. 2, 280–81, 295; Burke, *Military History of Kansas Regiments,* 216.

14. Burke, *Military History of Kansas Regiments,* 216; *History of Battery M, First Illinois,* 111.

15. Hoffman, ed., *Confederate Collapse,* 57–58; Manigault, *Carolinian Goes to War,* 131.

16. Burke, *Military History of Kansas Regiments,* 216–17; *OR* 31, pt. 2, 263; Hoffman, ed., *Confederate Collapse,* 58.

17. Hoffman, ed., *Confederate Collapse,* 58.

18. *OR* 31, pt. 2, 280, 295, 298; Kimberly, *Forty-first Ohio,* 66.

19. Kimberly, *Forty-first Ohio,* 66–67; *OR* 31, pt. 2, 295; Hoffman, ed., *Confederate Collapse,* 58.

20. *OR* 31, pt. 2, 298; Wagner reminiscences, 98, *CWTI* Collection, USAMHI; A. H. Benham, "Climbing Mission Ridge," *National Tribune,* 30 April 1925.

21. Manigault, *Carolinian Goes to War,* 131; *OR* 31, pt. 2, 298.

22. Wood, "Battle of Missionary Ridge," 29; *OR* 31, pt. 2, 24, 95; Howard, "Grant at Chattanooga," 250–51, and "Chattanooga," 212.

23. *OR* 31, pt. 2, 189, 229; Shellenberger, "With Sheridan's Division," 53.

24. Metcalf reminiscences, 136–37, Harrisburg CWRT Collection, USAMHI; *OR* 31, pt. 2, 95, 359, 362–63, 372, 377.

25. Metcalf reminiscences, 137, Harrisburg CWRT Collection, USAMHI.

26. Howard, "Grant at Chattanooga," 212.

27. *OR* 31, pt. 2, 130, 255–56, 301.

28. Kimberly, *Forty-first Ohio,* 67; John S. Roper, "An Interesting Account of the Battle of Missionary Ridge," *Journal of the Illinois State Historical Society* 6 (1914): 499.

29. *OR* 31, pt. 2, 24, 66; Kimberly, *Forty-first Ohio,* 67; Rawlins to Mary E. Hurlbut, 23 November 1863, Rawlins Papers, ChiHS.

30. Manigault, *Carolinian Goes to War,* 131–32.

31. Lyman S. Widney to his sister, 27 November 1863, Widney Letters, Thirty-fourth Illinois File, CCNMP.

32. Manigault, *Carolinian Goes to War,* 131–34; Hoffman, ed., *Confederate Collapse,* 35.

33. Brent journal, 23 November 1863, Palmer Collection of Bragg Papers, WRHS; Smith, "Operations around Chattanooga," 200.

34. *OR* 31, pt. 2, 745–46; Hoffman, ed., *Confederate Collapse,* 36; Irving Buck, "Cleburne and His Division at Missionary Ridge and Ringgold Gap," *SHSP* 8 (1880): 465.

35. *OR* 31, pt. 2, 706, 739.

36. Ibid., 674–75, 718–19.

37. Ibid., 674; Brent journal, 23 November 1863, Palmer Collection of Bragg Papers, WRHS; Roy, "Sketch," 13, Hardee Papers, ADAH.

38. *OR* 31, pt. 2, 675, 687, 718–19, 733–34; Walthall, "Walthall on the Battle of Lookout," 562; Moore, "Battle of Lookout Mountain," 426.

39. Hoffman, ed., *Confederate Collapse*, 36–37, 58–59, 69; Manigault, *Carolinian Goes to War*, 134; *OR* 31, pt. 2, 739; John T. Haley to Mr. and Mrs. Farr, 17 December 1863, Confederate Collection, TSLA.

40. *OR* 31, pt. 2, 676.

41. Shellenberger, "With Sheridan's Division," 53; Ely diary, 24 November 1863, Thirty-sixth Illinois File, CCNMP.

CHAPTER ELEVEN / THE ADVANTAGE WAS GREATLY ON OUR SIDE NOW

1. Grant, "Chattanooga," 699; Rawlins to Mary E. Hurlbut, 23 November 1863, Rawlins Papers, ChiHS.

2. Grant, "Chattanooga," 699; *OR*, 31, pt. 2, 106–7, 142; Peter McLain to "Friend Tom," 4 December 1863, in "Army Correspondence," Keithsburg (Ill.) *Observer*, 7 January 1864; Boynton, "Battles around Chattanooga," *PMHSM*, 8:387.

3. *OR* 31, pt. 2, 95, 329–30; Wilson, *Under the Old Flag*, 1:292.

4. *OR* 31, pt. 2, 490.

5. Ibid., 74, 503; Levis Ross Diary, 21 November 1863, ISHL; J. B. Ridenour, "Ridenour Speaks," *National Tribune*, 21 July 1892.

6. *OR* 31, pt. 2, 77, 589–90; Wilson, *Under the Old Flag*, 1:294; Pirtle, "Three Memorable Days," 36–37.

7. *OR* 31, pt. 2, 503; Schweitzer diary, 24 November 1863, *CWTI* Collection, USAMHI; Allen Fahnestock Diary, 24 November 1863, Eighty-sixth Illinois File, CCNMP; John W. Boyd to E. A. Carman, 9 December 1907, Tenth Missouri File, CCNMP; Brown, *Fourth Minnesota*, 269.

8. N. M. Baker, "Wounding of General Giles A. Smith," *National Tribune*, 24 July 1902; Ross diary, 24 November 1863, ISHL.

9. Baker, "Wounding of General Giles A. Smith"; Ridenour, "Ridenour Speaks"; Fahnestock diary, 24 November 1863, Eighty-sixth Illinois File, CCNMP; Ross diary, 24 November 1863, ISHL; Milton Haney, *Pentecostal Possibilities, or, the Story of My Life* (Chicago: Christian Witness Company, 1906), 191; Schweitzer diary, 24 November 1863, *CWTI* Collection, USAMHI.

10. Schweitzer diary, 24 November 1863, *CWTI* Collection, USAMHI.

11. Samuel Byers, *With Fire and Sword* (New York: Neale, 1911), 104; Maurice J. Seed to E. A. Carman, 23 November 1907, Sixty-third Illinois File, and John W. Boyd to Carman, 9 December 1907, Tenth Missouri File, both in CCNMP; *OR* 31, pt. 2, 643; James Mahan, *Memoirs of James Curtis Mahan* (Lincoln, Neb.: Franklin Press, 1919), 138.

12. Mahan, *Memoirs*, 138; *OR* 31, pt. 2, 77, 572–73, 643; Howard, "Grant at Chattanooga," 214; Wilson, *Under the Old Flag*, 1:294; Mark M. Boatner III, *The Civil War Dictionary* (New York: David McKay, 1959), 820;

Pirtle, "Three Memorable Days," 36–37; Aaron Dunbar, "Civil War Journal, Volume 2," 23, John Huelskamp Collection; Claver diary, 24 November 1863, IoHS; Henry H. Wright, *A History of the Sixth Iowa Infantry* (Iowa City: State Historical Society of Iowa), 234.

13. Brown, *Fourth Minnesota*, 270–71.

14. *OR* 31, pt. 2, 664, 678; J. H. Steinmeyer Diary, 23 November 1863, University of South Carolina; Brent journal, 24 November 1863, Palmer Collection of Bragg Papers, WRHS.

15. D. R. Hundley to Edward Walthall, 6 October 1882, and Walthall to Hundley, 19 October 1882, both in Walthall Papers, MDAH; Connelly, *Autumn of Glory*, 272.

16. *OR* 31, pt. 2, 707, 739, 747; Connelly, *Autumn of Glory*, 272.

17. *OR* 31, pt. 2, 42.

18. Wilson, *Under the Old Flag*, 1:295–96.

19. Howard, "Grant at Chattanooga," 214; *OR* 31, pt. 2, 348; Hurst, *Seventy-third Ohio*, 93.

20. *OR* 31, pt. 2, 74–75, 109, 368, 573; Brown, *Fourth Minnesota*, 269–70; Wright, *Sixth Iowa*, 235; Frank Dennison to Cousin Annie, 9 December 1863, Eighty-third Indiana File, CCNMP. Sherman claims to have advanced at 1:00 P.M.; the accounts of many disinterested participants, however, place the hour at 2:00 P.M.

21. *OR* 31, pt. 2, 678, 746.

22. Ibid., 747; E. J. Sherlock to E. A. Carman, 10 February 1908, One Hundredth Illinois File, CCNMP.

23. *OR* 31, pt. 2, 747; Warner, *Generals in Gray*, 281–82.

24. *OR* 31, pt. 2, 746–47; Wright, *Sixth Iowa*, 235; J. E. Walton, "Mission Ridge: The Thirtieth Ohio's Gallantry in the Battle," *National Tribune*, 1 November 1888.

25. Brown, *Fourth Minnesota*, 269–70; Walton, "Mission Ridge"; Wright, *Sixth Iowa*, 235; *OR* 31, pt. 2, 643–45.

26. *OR* 31, pt. 2, 747; Walton, "Mission Ridge."

27. *OR* 31, pt. 2, 747.

28. Ibid.

29. Ibid., 573; McDonough, *Chattanooga*, 121–23, treats the issue but reaches no real conclusion, neither condemning nor excusing Sherman's actions.

30. Smith, "Operations around Chattanooga," 202.

31. *OR* 31, pt. 2, 707; "Second Hand Pictures for Silly Southerners," *CV* 1, no. 12 (December 1893): 377.

32. "Second Hand Pictures for Silly Southerners," 377–78; *OR* 31, pt. 2, 710–11.

33. Warner, *Generals in Gray*, 346–47.

34. N. M. Baker, "Wounding of General Giles A. Smith," *National Tribune*, 24 July 1902; *OR* 31, pt. 2, 573.

35. Baker, "Wounding of Smith," and Baker to E. A. Carman, 2 January 1908, both in One Hundred Sixteenth Illinois File, CCNMP; Haney, *Pentecostal Possibilities*, 193.

36. Baker, "Wounding of Smith"; Haney, *Pentecostal Possibilities*, 193.

37. Baker, "Wounding of Smith"; *OR* 31, pt. 2, 708.

38. *OR* 31, pt. 2, 573–74, 631–33, 643; Thomas Smout Recollections, 27, Haynes Collection, IoHS; Thomas Hubler to E. A. Carman, 22 December 1907, Twelfth Indiana File, E. J. Sherlock to Carman, 10 February 1908, One Hundredth Indiana File, and Baker to Carman, One Hundred Sixteenth Illinois File, all in CCNMP.

39. Byers, *With Fire and Sword*, 105.


CHAPTER TWELVE / THE MOST CURIOUS BATTLE OF THE WAR

1. *OR* 31, pt. 2, 315.

2. James A. Fowler, "The Most Curious Battle of the War," *National Tribune*, 9 December 1926.

3. *OR* 31, pt. 2, 330, 390; Greene, *Bridgeport to Ringgold*, 28–29.

4. Eugene Powell, "An Incident of the Capture of Lookout Mountain," *Historical and Philosophical Society of Ohio Publications* (1926): 47–48; *OR* 31, pt. 2, 411, 428, 435; Battlefield Marker 261, CCNMP; William Rickards, "Above the Clouds," *National Tribune*, 1 January 1885. Pioneers were soldiers drawn from the ranks of infantry regiments and organized into units equivalent to modern light combat engineer battalions.

5. Powell, "Incident," 48–49; Robert A. Jarman, "History of Company K, Twenty-seventh Mississippi, Its First and Last Muster Rolls," 22, Jarman Papers, MDAH; W. D. Pickett, "Dead Angle—Rules for Burial of Dead," *CV* 16, no. 5 (May 1908): 230–31.

6. Powell, "Incident," 49–50.

7. H. D. Gallagher, "The Storming of Lookout—Honor to Whom Honor Is Due—the Irish Regiment and Its Commander," Madison (Ind.) *Evening Courier*, 30 December 1863, in Thirty-fifth Indiana File, CCNMP; *OR* 31, pt. 2, 154, 162.

8. *OR* 31, pt. 2, 169.

9. Battlefield Markers 252 and 253, CCNMP.

10. *OR* 31, pt. 2, 391, 452; Cozzens, *No Better Place to Die*, 184.

11. *OR* 31, pt. 2, 692, 698, 700–702; Walthall, "Walthall on the Battle of Lookout," 562; Elber Decatur Willet, *History of Company B (Originally Pickens' Planters), Fortieth Alabama Regiment, Confederate States Army, 1862 to 1865* (Anniston, Ala.: Norwood, 1902), 47.

12. Walthall, "Walthall on the Battle of Lookout," 562.

13. *OR* 31, pt 2, 698; Jarman, "History of Company K, Twenty-seventh Mississippi," 21, MDAH.

14. Moore, "Battle of Lookout Mountain," 427; *OR* 31, pt. 2, 704.

15. Moore, "Battle of Lookout Mountain," 427; *OR* 31, pt. 2, 718–19.

16. Hundley to Walthall, 24 October 1882, Walthall Papers, MDAH; *OR* 31, pt. 2, 677, 718.

17. *OR* 31, pt. 2, 719; Boyle, *Soldiers True*, 176; Walthall to Hundley, 20 September 1882, Walthall Papers, MDAH.

18. Powell, "Incident," 49–50; Doan, *Reminiscences of the Chattanoo-*

*ga Campaign,* 13; Rickards, "Above the Clouds"; Greene, *Bridgeport to Ringgold,* 29–30; *OR* 31, pt. 2, 107, 390.

19. *OR* 31, pt. 2, 390–91, 424, 428–29; W. L. Stork, "Lookout Mountain: A Plain Statement from One of Gen. Geary's Staff Officers," *National Tribune,* 19 May 1907; Rickards, "Above the Clouds."

20. *OR* 31, pt. 2, 441, 447; Rickards, "Above the Clouds."

21. *OR* 31, pt. 2, 411–12; Skinner, *Pennsylvania at Chickamauga and Chattanooga,* 287.

22. *OR* 31, pt. 2, 154–55, 159, 160, 166, 391; Charles Partridge, "Lookout Mountain as Seen by a Member of the Ninety-sixth Illinois," *National Tribune,* 15 July 1886.

23. Greene, *Bridgeport to Ringgold,* 30.

24. Stork, "Lookout Mountain, A Plain Statement."

25. *OR* 31, pt. 2, 55; William P. Carlin, "Military Memoirs," *National Tribune,* 23 April 1885.

26. Partridge, *Ninety-sixth Illinois,* 265–66; Battlefield Marker 261, CCNMP; *OR* 31, pt. 2, 391, 441.

27. *OR* 31, pt. 2, 692; Powell, "Incident," 50; W. F. Dowd, "Lookout Mountain and Missionary Ridge," *Southern Bivouac* 1 (1885/1886): 397; Edmund Pettus to Walthall, 3 January 1888, and Walthall to Hundley, 19 October 1882, both in Walthall Papers, MDAH; Edward T. Sykes, "Walthall's Brigade: A Cursory Sketch with Personal Experiences of Walthall's Brigade, Army of Tennessee, C.S.A., 1862–1865," *Publications of the Mississippi Historical Society, Centenary Series* 1 (1916): 539.

28. *OR* 31, pt. 2, 688.

29. Ibid., 677, 692–93, 703; Dowd, "Lookout Mountain and Missionary Ridge," 397.

30. *OR* 31, pt. 2, 143, 169–70, 177; Simmons, *84th Reg't Ill. Vols.,* 133.

31. Simmons, *84th Reg't Ill. Vols.,* 133; William Sumner Dodge, *A Waif of the War; or, the History of the Seventy-fifth Illinois Infantry* . . . (Chicago: Church and Goodman, 1886), 111–12; Peter McLain to an unknown correspondent, "Army Correspondence," Keithsburg (Ill.) *Observer,* 7 January 1864.

32. *OR* 31, pt. 2, 143–44, 169–70, 316, 453, 599; Battlefield Markers 251 and 253, CCNMP.

33. Greene, *Bridgeport to Ringgold,* 31; *OR* 31, pt. 2, 693.

34. *OR* 31, pt. 2, 392; Greene, *Bridgeport to Ringgold,* 31–32; Rickards, "Above the Clouds."

35. J. W. Simmons, "Heroic Mississippians," *CV* 5, no. 2 (February 1897): 73.

36. Collins, *149th Regt. N.Y. Vol.,* 209–10.

37. Ibid., 210.

38. Greene, *Bridgeport to Ringgold,* 32; *OR* 31, pt. 2, 316, 393.

39. Greene, *Bridgeport to Ringgold,* 32; *OR* 31, pt. 2, 393–94, 448; Battlefield Marker 261, CCNMP.

40. *OR* 31, pt. 2, 693–94, 698, 700, 720, 726, 728; Dowd, "Lookout Mountain and Missionary Ridge," 398; Eddy, *Sixtieth New York,* 306.

41. *OR* 31, pt. 2, 224, 436; Rickards, "Battle above the Clouds."

42. Greene, *Bridgeport to Ringgold*, 33; *OR* 31, pt. 2, 424, 436; Boyle, *Soldiers True*, 176–77.

43. *OR* 31, pt. 2, 693–94, 700; Jarman, "History of Company K, Twenty-seventh Mississippi," 22, MDAH.

44. Simmons, "Heroic Mississippians."

45. Dowd, "Lookout Mountain and Missionary Ridge," 398; *OR* 31, pt. 2, 699.

46. Jesse Jones, "Lookout Mountain: Concerning the Two Cannons Captured at the Craven [sic] House," *National Tribune*, 24 December 1891; Rickards, "Above the Clouds"; *OR*, pt. 2, 108, 429, 691, 699; Dowd, "Lookout Mountain and Missionary Ridge," 398; Greene, *Bridgeport to Ringgold*, 33; Boyle, *Soldiers True*, 177–78; Calvin Ainsworth Diary, 24 November 1863, Michigan Historical Collections, Bentley Historical Library, University of Michigan.

47. *OR* 31, pt. 2, 716–17.

48. Thomas Murphy, "Lookout Mountain: The Struggle Again over the Guns Near the Craven [sic] House," *National Tribune*, 30 July 1891; Jesse Jones, "Lookout Mountain: What Took Place after the Battle above the Clouds," *National Tribune*, 7 May 1891; A. M. Mathewson, "Lookout Mountain: Another Account of Who Captured the Guns and Planted the Flag," *National Tribune*, 20 August 1891; *OR*, pt. 2, 436–37, 441, 448; Charles A. Willison, *Reminiscences of a Boy's Service with the 76th Ohio, in the Fifteenth Army Corps, under General Sherman, During the Civil War, by that "Boy" at Three Score* (Menasha, Wis.: Georga Banta Publishing Company, n.d.), 75–76; Mosman, *Rough Side of War*, 125; Greene, *Bridgeport to Ringgold*, 35.

CHAPTER THIRTEEN / GO IN AND GIVE 'EM HELL

1. *OR* 31, pt. 2, 169–70, 599, 607; Willison, *Reminiscences of a Boy's Service*, 75–76; Charles Dana Miller, "Civil War Narrative," 68, CWC, TSLA; Mosman, *Rough Side of War*, 125.

2. J. E. Reynolds, "Heroism of Walthall's Mississippians," *CV* 15, no. 8 (August 1907): 365; *OR* 31, pt. 2, 170, 703; Miller, "Civil War Narrative," 68, CWC, TSLA; Mosman, *Rough Side of War*, 125.

3. *OR* 31, pt. 2, 170, 177–78, 691, 705; Dodge, *Waif of the War*, 111–12; Simmons, *84th Reg't Ill. Vols.*, 133; Walthall, "Walthall on the Battle of Lookout," 562.

4. *OR* 31, pt. 2, 688, 694, 705; Moore, "Battle of Lookout Mountain," 428.

5. *OR* 31, pt. 2, 705.

6. Ibid., 688, 695; Sykes, "Walthall's Brigade," 537.

7. *OR* 31, pt. 2, 720, 725–26, 728; W. W. Carnes, "At Missionary Ridge," *CV* 28, no. 5 (May 1920): 185; Walthall to Hundley, 19 October 1882, Walthall Papers, MDAH; Sykes, "Walthall's Brigade," 537.

8. Moore, "Battle of Lookout Mountain," 428; Willet, *Company B, Fortieth Alabama*, 47.

9. Moore, "Battle of Lookout Mountain," 428; *OR* 31, pt. 2, 448, 688, 705; Willet, *Company B, Fortieth Alabama*, 47.

10. Moore, "Battle of Lookout Mountain," 428; Willet, *Company B, Fortieth Alabama*, 47; *OR* 31, pt. 2, 444.

11. *OR* 31, pt. 2, 155, 164–65; John Beach, "Lookout Mountain: An Energetic Argument in Favor of Proper Credit to Whitaker's Brigade," *National Tribune*, 22 January 1885.

12. *OR* 31, pt. 2, 164–65; J. E. Taylor, "Lookout Mountain," *National Tribune*, 2 January 1890; W. H. Yiro, "Lookout Mountain, One of the Fortieth Ohio Comes to the Front," *National Tribune*, 19 September 1889.

13. Doan, *Reminiscences of the Chattanooga Campaign*, 14; John N. Beach, *History of the Fortieth Ohio Volunteer Infantry* (London, Ohio: Shepherd and Craig, Printers, 1884), 55, and "Lookout Mountain: Sergeant Beach Thinks the White Stars Had Lots of Help Near the Craven [*sic*] House," *National Tribune* 17 December 1891; J. T. Marlin, "Another Claim," *National Tribune*, 5 November 1891; C. S. Bolton to Brother Thomas, 4 December 1863, Lancaster (Pa.) *Church Advocate*, 24 December 1863.

14. C. S. Bolton to Brother Thomas, 4 December 1863, Lancaster (Pa.) *Church Advocate*, 24 December 1863; *OR* 31, pt. 2, 168; Willet, *Company B, Fortieth Alabama*, 47; D. W. Beebout, "Geary Greedy for Guns," *National Tribune*, 19 May 1904; John N. Beach, "The Struggle Over the Guns Near the Craven [*sic*] House," *National Tribune*, 7 February 1891; Mathewson, "Lookout Mountain: Another Account of Who Captured the Guns and Planted the Flag," *National Tribune*, 20 August 1891.

15. H. D. Gallagher, "The Storming of Lookout," Madison (Ind.) *Evening Courier*, 30 December 1863; *OR* 31, pt. 2, 160–61.

16. *OR* 31, pt. 2, 412, 705; Theodore Wilder, *The History of Company C, Seventh Regiment, O.V.I.* (Oberlin, Ohio: J. B. T. Marsh, 1866), 38.

17. "A Remarkable Example of Coolness," 1–2, Manuscript in Thirty-seventh Alabama Infantry Papers, ADAH.

18. *OR* 31, pt. 2, 155, 159, 162; Wright, *Eighth Kentucky*, 211; Partridge, "Lookout Mountain as Seen by a Member of the Ninety-sixth Illinois," *National Tribune*, 15 July 1886.

19. Moore, "Battle of Lookout Mountain," 428; *OR* 31, pt. 2, 159, 705; Partridge, "Lookout Mountain as Seen by a Member of the Ninety-sixth Illinois," *National Tribune*, 15 July 1886; idem, *Ninety-sixth Illinois*, 270.

20. H. D. Gallagher, "The Storming of Lookout," Madison (Ind.) *Evening Courier*, 30 December 1863; "Letter from Henry Gage of the 96th Ills. Regt.," Waukegan (Ill.) *Weekly Gazette*, 19 December 1863; *OR* 31, pt. 2, 159, 162, 164–66, 168; Beach, "Lookout Mountain."

21. *OR* 31, pt. 2, 159, 396, 409, 436; Greene, *Bridgeport to Ringgold*, 37–38; William Zat, "Lookout Mountain: Who Planted the First Flag on the Fort?" *National Tribune*, 12 September 1887.

22. Battlefield Marker 293, CCNMP; *OR* 31, pt. 2, 425, 430–31; Boyle, *Soldiers True*, 178.

23. *OR* 31, pt. 2, 316–17, 331–32.

24. Partridge, *Ninety-sixth Illinois*, 268–69; Rickards, "Above the Clouds."

25. Moore, "Battle of Lookout Mountain," 428; Rickards, "Above the Clouds"; Battlefield Markers 293 and 294, CCNMP; *OR* 31, pt. 2, 155–56, 430–31.

26. Walthall, "Walthall on the Battle of Lookout," 562; *OR* 31, pt. 2, 705, 732; Moore, "Battle of Lookout Mountain," 428; Pettus to Walthall, 3 January 1888, Walthall Papers, MDAH.

27. Mosman, *Rough Side of War*, 126; *OR* 31, pt. 2, 160, 166, 732.

28. *OR* 31, pt. 2, 145, 166, 170–71, 397–98, 422, 695, 728, 732; Skinner, *Pennsylvania at Chickamauga and Chattanooga*, 288–89.

29. Anonymous letter to the editor, in "Army Correspondence," Ottawa (Ill.) *Free Trader*, 19 December 1863; *OR* 31, pt. 2, 95, 109, 333, 462; Carlin, "Military Memoirs"; Anson McCook and R. P. Speer, "In a Tight Place at Lookout," *National Tribune*, 27 December 1923.

30. *OR* 31, pt. 2, 333.

31. Ibid., 332–33.

## Chapter Fourteen / The Shipwreck of Their Hopes

1. J. W. A. Wright, "Bragg's Campaign around Chattanooga," *Southern Bivouac* 2 (1886/87): 467.

2. *OR* 31, pt. 2, 664, 678, 721.

3. Ibid., 690, 720–21, 726, 728–29; Carnes, "At Missionary Ridge," 185; Losson, *Tennessee's Forgotten Warriors*, 125.

4. E. Burk Wylie to David Wylie, 2 December 1863, IoHS; W. H. Moore, "The Thirtieth Iowa at Lookout Mountain," *National Tribune*, 4 August 1889; E. C. Mount, "Osterhaus's Division: It Had a Hand in the Battle of Lookout Mountain," *National Tribune*, 10 February 1887; *OR* 31, pt. 2, 614, 622; G. J. Laing, "Lookout Mountain," *National Tribune*, 20 September 1923; W. D. Bunch, "Saw the Flag Wave," *National Tribune*, 23 August 1923.

5. Carlin, "Military Memoirs"; McCook and Speer, "In a Tight Place at Lookout"; *OR* 31, pt. 2, 334, 398, 462–63, 476; Daniel Griffin, "A Hoosier Regiment at Chattanooga," *Tennessee Historical Quarterly* 22 (September 1963): 281.

6. A. M. Brinkerhoff, "Lookout Mountain: Part Taken by Osterhaus' Division in the Battle," *National Tribune*, 28 November 1889.

7. Greene, *Bridgeport to Ringgold*, 39; Mosman, *Rough Side of War*, 127.

8. Simmons, "Heroic Mississippians," 733; John Washington Inzer, *The Diary of a Confederate Soldier* (Huntsville, Ala.: Strode Publishers, 1977), 41–42.

9. *OR* 31, pt. 2, 721–22, 734; Losson, *Tennessee's Forgotten Warriors*, 125.

10. Connelly, *Autumn of Glory*, 273; Davis, *Breckinridge*, 386.

11. Connelly, *Autumn of Glory*, 273; Davis, *Breckinridge*, 386–87; Brent journal, 24 November 1863, Palmer Collection of Bragg Papers, WRHS; *OR*

31, pt. 2, 664; Buck, "Cleburne and his Division," 466; Hughes, *Hardee,* 171–72; Roy, "Sketch," 14, ADAH.

12. Buck, "Cleburne and His Division," 466–67.

13. *OR* 31, pt. 2, 679, 722, 734.

14. Wright, "Bragg's Campaign around Chattanooga," 468; *OR* 31, pt. 2, 67, 78, 705, 720, 726; C. L. Willoughby, "Eclipse of Moon at Missionary Ridge," *CV* 21, no. 12 (December 1913): 590; Moore, "Battle of Lookout Mountain," 428; Inzer, *Diary,* 42; Arthur Taylor Fielder Diary, 24 November 1863, Confederate Collection, TSLA.

15. William C. Dodson, *The Battle of Missionary Ridge: An Address* (N.p, n.d.), 1–2; Worsham, *Nineteenth Tennessee,* 98.

## Chapter Fifteen / Time Is Everything

1. McKinney, *Education in Violence,* 291; Stormont, *Fifty-eighth Indiana,* 215.

2. Roper, "Interesting Account of Missionary Ridge," 500; Judson Bishop to his mother, 3 December 1863, Bishop Papers, MnHS; Jeremiah C. Donahower, *Lookout Mountain and Missionary Ridge. Paper Read before Minnesota Commandery of the Loyal Legion U. S. December 13th, 1898* (St. Paul: N.p., 1898) 15; J. G. Essington, "The Battle above the Clouds," Noblesville (Ind.) *Republican Ledger,* date unknown, in J. G. Essington Civil War File, InHS.

3. Fullerton, "Army of the Cumberland at Chattanooga," 723; Smith, "Operations around Chattanooga," 202–3; Boynton, "Battles around Chattanooga," 389; Van Horne, *Army of the Cumberland,* 1:423; *OR* 31, pt. 2, 24–25, 78; Grant, *Personal Memoirs,* 2:73.

4. *OR* 31, pt. 2, 44.

5. Smith, "Operations around Chattanooga," 210.

6. Wright, *Eighth Kentucky,* 213–14; Mosman, *Rough Side of War,* 127; Skinner, *Pennsylvania at Chickamauga,* 81; John Wilson, "Lookout Mountain: Captain Wilson's Claim to Planting the First Flag," *National Tribune,* 11 June 1891; *OR* 31, pt. 2, 146, 163; John Hoch Diary, 25 November 1863, John Hoch Papers, Illinois Historical Survey, University of Illinois at Urbana-Champaign; Charles K. Radcliffe, "The Fighting at Lookout," *National Tribune,* 14 June 1923.

7. Stork, "Lookout Mountain: A Plain Statement"; Lewis Blundin, "That First Flag," *National Tribune,* 26 December 1889; Buckner Memoirs, 28, ISHL; Partridge, "Lookout Mountain as Seen by a Member of the Ninety-sixth Illinois"; *OR* 31, pt. 2, 146, 399.

8. *OR* 31, pt. 2, 112–13, 163, 178, 399; Dodge, *Waif of the War,* 114.

9. *OR* 31, pt. 2, 96, 113, 115; McKinney, *Education in Violence,* 292–93, 495; Smith, "Operations around Chattanooga," 220; Wilson, *Under the Old Flag,* 1:296; Carlin, "Military Memoirs"; Charles A. Dana, *Recollections of the Civil War with the Leaders at Washington and in the Field in the Sixties* (New York: D. Appleton, 1902), 148.

10. *OR* 31, pt. 2, 96, 146, 336; Boynton, "Battle around Chattanooga," 392; Hoch diary, 25 November 1863, Hoch Papers, Illinois Historical Survey, University of Illinois at Urbana-Champaign; Carlin, "Military Memoirs"; F. Voss, "On Lookout Mountain," *National Tribune*, 14 June 1923.

11. Boynton, "Battles around Chattanooga," 396–97; Fullerton, "Army of the Cumberland at Chattanooga," 723; Grant, *Personal Memoirs*, 2:75; Wilson, *Under the Old Flag*, 1:296.

12. Jones, *Artilleryman's Diary*, 141; Schweitzer diary, 25 November 1863, *CWTI* Collection, USAMHI.

13. *OR* 31, pt. 2, 574.

14. Ibid., 574, 643; Theodore Jones to E. A. Carman, 2 January 1908, Thirtieth Ohio File, and N. M. Baker to Carman, 1 February 1908, One Hundred Sixteenth Illinois File, both in CCNMP; McDonough, *Chattanooga*, 145; J. Grecian, *History of the Eighty-third Regiment, Indiana Volunteer Infantry. For Three Years with Sherman* (Cincinnati: John F. Uhlhorn, Printer, 1865), 40.

15. McDonough, *Chattanooga*, 145; Schweitzer diary, 25 November 1863, *CWTI* Collection, USAMHI; *OR* 31, pt. 2, 629, 636, 643; Boynton, "Battles around Chattanooga," 389.

16. *OR* 31, pt. 2, 633, 636; Hiram Hall to E. A. Carman, 232 January 1908, Fortieth Illinois File, and R. E. Athearn to Carman, 26 November 1907, One Hundred Third Illinois File, both in CCNMP.

17. A. A. Stuart, *Iowa Colonels and Regiments: History of Iowa Regiments in the War of the Rebellion; and Containing a Description of the Battles in Which They Have Fought* (Des Moines, Iowa: Mills and Company, 1865), 161; Warner, *Generals in Blue*, 94.

18. Many veterans of Corse's brigade claimed that the brigade started forward at daylight, but the weight of evidence does not substantiate that claim. Wright, *Sixth Iowa*, 227, 235; *Reminiscences of the Civil War from Diaries of Members of the 103d Illinois Volunteer Infantry* (Chicago: Press of J. F. Leaming and Company, 1904), 26; *OR* 31, pt. 2, 636; Matthew H. Jamison, *Recollections of Pioneer and Army Life* (Kansas City, Mo.: Hudson Press, 1911), 203; Athearn to Carman, 26 November 1907, One Hundred Third Illinois File, J. W. Baugh to Carman, n.d., and Hall to Carman, 23 January 1908, Fortieth Illinois File, Jesse Brandt to Carman, 18 December 1907, Forty-sixth Ohio File, Jones to Carman, 2 January 1908, Thirtieth Ohio File, all in CCNMP.

19. Jones to Carman, 2 January and 28 February 1908, Louis Lambert to Carman, 29 January 1908, and George Hildt to Carman, 18 January 1908, all in Thirtieth Ohio File, CCNMP; Schweitzer diary, 25 November 1863, *CWTI* Collection, USAMHI.

20. Foster diary, 6, *CWTI* Collection, USAMHI; Jones to Carman, 2 January 1908, Thirtieth Ohio File, CCNMP.

21. Jones to Carman, 2 January and 28 February 1908, Thirtieth Ohio File, CCNMP; Schweitzer diary, 25 November 1863, *CWTI* Collection, CCNMP.

22. Hall to Carman, 17 December 1907, J. B. Smith to Carman, 4 Janu-

ary 1908, and Baugh to Carman, n.d., all in Fortieth Illinois File, CCNMP; *OR* 31, pt. 2, 629.

23. Hall to Carman, 23 January 1908, Fortieth Illinois File, and Lambert to Carman, 8 February 1908, Thirtieth Ohio File, both in CCNMP.

24. Jones to Carman, 2 January 1908, Thirtieth Ohio File, R. E. Athearn to Carman, 26 November 1907, One Hundred Third Illinois File, Jesse Brandt to Carman, 18 December 1907, Forty-sixth Ohio File, all in CCNMP; Wright, *Sixth Iowa*, 235; *Reminiscences of the One Hundred Third Illinois*, 26.

## CHAPTER SIXTEEN / THIS WAS BUSINESS

1. *OR* 31, pt. 2, 726; Thomas J. Key, "Concerning the Battle of Missionary Ridge," *CV* 12, no. 8 (August 1904): 390.

2. *OR* 31, pt. 2, 664, 735, 749; Inzer, *Diary*, 43; John Jackman, *Diary of a Confederate Soldier: John S. Jackman of the Orphan Brigade*, ed. William C. Davis (Columbia: University of South Carolina Press, 1990), 95; Dowd, "Lookout Mountain and Missionary Ridge," 398.

3. The precise alignment of Corse's regiments is speculative, as the deployment indicated in Walcutt's report is at variance with the testimony of several members of the brigade. *OR* 31, pt. 2, 636; Wright, *Sixth Iowa*, 236; *Reminiscences of the 103d Illinois*, 26; R. E. Athearn to E. A. Carman, 26 November 1907, One Hundred Third Illinois File, CCNMP.

4. Foster diary, 56–57, *CWTI* Collection, USAMHI; *OR* 31, pt. 2, 574, 636, 750; Casimer Fortenbacher to Carman, 23 December 1907, Forty-sixth Ohio File, and Carman to R. E. Ahearn, 11 November 1907, One Hundred Third Illinois File, both in CCNMP.

5. *Reminiscences of the 103d Illinois*, 27–28; *OR* 31, pt. 2, 636, 750; Wright, *Sixth Iowa*, 237.

6. Jamison, *Recollections of Pioneer and Army Life*, 203.

7. *OR* 31, pt. 2, 636, 750; Claver diary, 25 November 1863, IoHS; Daniel, *Cannoneers in Gray*, 113; Grammer diary, 25 November 1863, Swett's Battery File, CCNMP; Jesse Brandt to Carman, 18 December 1907, Forty-sixth Ohio File, CCNMP.

8. *OR* 31, pt. 2, 750; Davis, ed., *Diary of a Confederate Soldier*, 95.

9. Foster diary, 58, *CWTI* Collection, USAMHI.

10. Schwietzer diary, 25 November 1863, *CWTI* Collection, USAMHI.

11. Foster diary, 58, *CWTI* Collection, USAMHI.

12. *OR* 31, pt. 2, 636, 750; Smout Recollections, 28, Hayne Collection, IoHS; Hall to Carman, 23 January 1908, Fortieth Illinois File, CCNMP; Wright, *Sixth Iowa*, 237.

13. Sherlock, *One Hundredth Indiana*, 54; Henry Robinson, "Statement Concerning Missionary Ridge," One Hundredth Indiana File, CCNMP; Thomas Hubler to Carman, 22 December 1907, Twelfth Indiana File, CCNMP.

14. *OR* 31, pt. 2, 633, 727, 730; Jacob Vanscoy, "Three Yankee Soldier-

Brothers in the Battle of Chattanooga, Three Letters," *East Tennessee Historical Society Publications* 35 (1963): 103; Robert Scott to Carman, 13 December 1907, Twelfth Indiana File, and Robinson, "Statement Concerning Missionary Ridge," One Hundredth Indiana file, both in CCNMP.

15. *OR* 31, pt. 2, 633; D. G. Duffy to Carman, 14 January 1908, Ninetieth Illinois File, and J. B. Bruner to Carman, 25 November 1907, Twenty-sixth Illinois File, both in CCNMP.

16. *OR* 31, pt. 2, 633.

17. Buck, "Cleburne and His Division," 467–68; *OR* 31, pt. 2, 633; Robinson, "Statement Concerning Missionary Ridge," One Hundredth Indiana File, CCNMP.

18. Robinson, "Statement Concerning Missionary Ridge," One Hundredth Illinois File, CCNMP.

19. *OR* 31, pt. 2, 735, 750; Key, "Concerning Missionary Ridge," 390; Grammer diary, 25 November 1863, Swett's Battery File, CCNMP.

20. Bruner to Carman, 25 November 1907, and Ira Bloomfield to Carman, 21 November 1907, Twenty-sixth Illinois File, Hubler to Carman, 22 December 1907, and Robert Scott to Carman, 13 December 1907, Twelfth Indiana File, Lawrence Morrissey to Carman, 28 February 1908, Ninetieth Illinois File, all in CCNMP; *OR* 31, pt. 2, 727, 731.

21. Vanscoy, "Three Yankeee Soldier-Brothers," 103–4; S. Noble King to Carman, 21 November 1907, Twenty-sixth Illinois File, CCNMP.

22. *OR* 31, pt. 2, 368, 370, 634, 735; Skinner, *Pennsylvania at Chickamauga and Chattanooga*, 160.

23. *OR* 31, pt. 2, 368, 632, 736; Skinner, *Pennsylvania at Chickamauga and Chattanooga*, 160; William Wilson to Carman, 18 April 1908, Thirty-third New Jersey File, CCNMP; Key, "Concerning Battle of Missionary Ridge," 390.

24. Upson, *With Sherman to the Sea*, 86–87; Sherlock, *One Hundredth Indiana*, 55.

25. *OR* 31, pt. 2, 634, 643; Smith, "Operations around Chattanooga," 209.

26. *OR* 31, pt. 2, 736.

27. Ibid., 643–44, 652; Raum, "With the Western Army: Fight on Tunnel Hill," *National Tribune*, 1 May 1902.

28. *OR* 31, pt. 2, 652.

29. Stuart, *Iowa Colonels*, 137.

30. *OR* 31, pt. 2, 653; Aaron Dunbar, "Civil War Journal," 25, John Huelskamp Collection.

31. *OR* 31, pt. 2, 654; Dunbar journal, 25, Huelskamp Collection.

32. W. H. Mengel to Carman, 11 January 1907, Twenty-sixth Missouri File, John T. Crowe to Carman, 26 December 1907, Ninety-third Illinois File, and Carman to Stephen G. Moffat, 6 December 1907, Tenth Iowa File, all in CCNMP; *OR* 31, pt. 2, 652; Byers, *With Fire and Sword*, 106–7.

33. William Carnes to Richard Randolph, 20 November 1931, Carnes's Battery File, CCNMP; Daniel, *Cannoneers in Gray, 113*. Daniel suggests that Stevenson's batteries were not brought to bear against Matthies but

rather reached the ridge only in time to contribute to the cannonade against the subsequent attack of Raum. The weight of evidence, although inconclusive, seems at variance with Daniel's assertion.

34. Dowd, "Lookout Mountain and Missionary Ridge," 399; Key, "Concerning Battle of Missionary Ridge," 390; John H. Bingham, "How Errors Become Historical Facts," *CV* 12, no. 4 (April 1904): 172.

35. *OR* 31, pt. 2, 652, 653, 750; Oliver C. Kinley, "Battle of Tunnel Hill," *National Tribune*, 18 February 1904.

36. *OR* 31, pt. 2, 652, 655; Skinner, *Pennsylvania at Chickamauga and Chattanooga*, 160–61; Civil War Diary of Jabez Banbury, 25 November 1863, John Huelskamp Collection.

37. *OR* 31, pt. 2, 652; A. W. Fritchey to Carman, 11 November 1907, Twenty-sixth Missouri File, CCNMP; *Report of the Adjutant General and Acting Quartermaster General of the State of Iowa. January 1, 1865, to January 1, 1866* (Des Moines: F. W. Palmer, State Printer, 1866), 189; Banbury diary, Huelskamp Collection.

38. John T. Crowe to Carman, 26 December 1907, O. Wilkinson to Carman, 18 December 1907, G. S. Kleckner to Carman, 9 December 1907, and Carman to George W. Booman, 11 November 1907, all in Ninety-third Illinois File, CCNMP; *OR* 31, pt. 2, 653, 750; Bingham, "How Errors Become Historical Facts," 172; Dunbar journal, 26, Huelskamp Collection.

39. James W. Dennis to Carman, 15 December 1907, Twenty-sixth Missouri File, CCNMP; N. C. Buswell to Richard Yates, n.d., Yates Papers, ISHL; Dunbar journal, 26, Huelskamp Collection.

40. *OR* 31, pt. 2, 652; A. W. Fritchey to Carman, 11 November 1907, Twenty-sixth Missouri File, CCNMP; Edward Garland to Carman, 9 December 1907, Stephen Moffat to Carman, 10 December 1907, and James Launier to Carman, 10 December 1907, all in Tenth Iowa File, CCNMP; Stuart, *Iowa Colonels*, 227.

41. *OR* 31, pt. 2, 652; Henry Hicks to Carman, 30 November 1907, Ninety-third Illinois File, CCNMP.

42. Raum, "With the Western Army: Battle of Missionary Ridge," and "With the Western Army: Fight on Tunnel Hill."

43. *OR* 31, pt. 2, 644.

44. Raum, "With the Western Army: Fight on Tunnel Hill"; Stuart, *Iowa Colonels*, 331.

45. Raum, "With the Western Army: Fight on Tunnel Hill."

46. Ibid.; *OR* 31, pt. 2, 648.

47. *OR* 31, pt. 2, 648; Pren Metham to Carman, 10 December 1907, Eightieth Ohio File, and James Ogden III to Ray Erwin, 27 October 1990, Ninety-third Illinois File, both in CCNMP; Christopher Kiser, "Tunnel Hill: Severe Fighting by Raum's Brigade to Turn Rebel Right on Mission Ridge," *National Tribune*, 2 June 1904; Raum, "With the Western Army: Fight on Tunnel Hill."

48. Bingham, "How Errors Become Historical Facts," 172; *OR* 31, pt. 2, 751; Rufus W. Daniel Diary, 37, Civil War Miscellaneous Collection,

USAMHI; W. H. Mengel to Carman, 11 January 1907, Twenty-sixth Missouri File, CCNMP; Buswell to Yates, n.d., Yates Papers, ISHL; A. M. Trimble to Carman, 11 December 1907, Ninety-third Illinois File, CCNMP; Harvey Trimble, *History of the Ninety-third Regiment Illinois Volunteer Infantry from Organization to Muster Out* (Chicago: Blakely Printing Company, 1898), 77–78.

49. *OR* 31, pt. 2, 751; Dowd, "Lookout Mountain and Missionary Ridge," 399; Metham to Carman, 10 December 1907, and George Robinson to Carman, 8 December 1907, both in Eightieth Ohio File, CCNMP; Jacob Darst, "Carried Flag Up Missionary Ridge," *National Tribune*, 4 August 1904; Kiser, "Tunnel Hill."

50. *OR* 31, pt. 2, 735, 751.

51. Ibid., 751; Hughes, *Hardee*, 174–75; "Maney's Brigade at Missionary Ridge," 301.

52. *OR* 31, pt. 2, 751; W. M. Pollard Diary, 6, Civil War Collection, TSLA; William Pollard, "Brief History of the First Tennessee," *CV* 18, no. 11 (November 1909): 544; "Maney's Brigade at Missionary Ridge," 301.

53. *OR* 31, pt. 2, 751.

54. Ibid., 737.

55. Ibid.

56. Ibid., 737, 751.

57. *OR* 31, pt. 2, 737, 751; "Maney's Brigade at Missionary Ridge," 303.

58. Pollard diary, 6, Civil War Collection, TSLA; "Maney's Brigade at Missionary Ridge," 303; Marcus Toney, *Privations of a Private: The Campaign under Gen. R. E. Lee, the Campaign under Gen. Stonewall Jackson, Bragg's Invasion of Kentucky, the Chickamauga Campaign, the Wilderness Campaign, Prison Life in the North . . .* (Nashville: For the author, 1905), 63.

59. Byers, *With Fire and Sword*, 108–9; *OR* 31, pt. 2, 655; Ogden to Erwin, 27 October 1990, Ninety-third Illinois File, CCNMP; John Whitten Journal, 25 November 1863, John Huelskamp Collection.

60. Crandell diary, 25 November 1863, ISHL; *OR* 31, pt. 2, 655.

61. Trimble to Carman, 11 December 1907, Ninety-third Illinois File, CCNMP; Trimble, *Ninety-third Illinois*, 78; *OR* 31, pt. 2, 86–88, 752; Raum, "With the Western Army: Fight on Tunnel Hill"; W. H. Mengel to Carman, 11 January 1907, Twenty-sixth Missouri File, CCNMP.

62. Kiser, "Tunnel Hill"; Stuart, *Iowa Colonels*, 137; Franklin Hobart to Carman, 22 December 1907, Seventeenth Iowa File, CCNMP; *OR* 31, pt. 2, 648.

63. Darst, "Carried Flag up Missionary Ridge"; Metham to Carman, 10 December 1907, and P. W. Wood to Carman, 3 January 1908, both in Eightieth Ohio File, CCNMP; *OR* 31, pt. 2, 737.

64. H. Dudley to Carman, 16 December 1907, Fifty-sixth Illinois File, CCNMP; *OR* 31, pt. 2, 649, 737; A. J. Davis to the Editor, 23 December 1863, Schuyler (Ill.) *Citizen*, 2 January 1864; Frost, *Tenth Missouri*, 189–90; M. O. Frost to Carman, 11 December 1907, Tenth Missouri File, CCNMP; Toney, *Privations of a Private*, 63; "Maney's Brigade at Missionary Ridge," 303.

65. Green B. Raum, "With the Western Army: After the Battle," *National Tribune*, 29 May 1902; *OR* 31, pt. 2, 650.

66. *OR* 31, pt. 2, 360, 371; Skinner, *Pennsylvania at Chickamauga and Chattanooga*, 161.

67. *OR* 31, pt. 2, 737, 751.

68. Kiser, "Tunnel Hill"; *OR* 31, pt. 2, 648, 650, 737, 752; Metham to Carman, 10 December 1907, Eightieth Ohio File, CCNMP.

69. *OR* 31, pt. 2, 634; Ira Bloomfield to Carman, 21 November 1907, Twenty-sixth Illinois File, CCNMP.

70. *OR* 31, pt. 2, 349, 382; Smith, "Operations around Chattanooga," 210.

71. Smith, "Operations around Chattanooga," 210.

72. N. M. Baker to Carman, 2 January and 1 February 1908, One Hundred Sixteenth Illinois File, John Mahle to Carman, 9 December 1907, Sixth Missouri File, John Schmidt to Carman, 9 December 1907, Eighth Missouri File, and George Bailey to Carman, 10 December 1907, Sixth Missouri File, all in CCNMP.

73. Baker to Carman, 1 February 1908, and T. S. Collins to Carman, 14 November 1907, One Hundred Sixteenth Illinois File, Bailey to Carman, 10 December 1907, Sixth Missouri File, and Schmidt to Carman, 9 December 1907, Eighth Missouri File, all in CCNMP; Smith, "Operations around Chattanooga," 210.

74. Preston, "Memoirs of the War," 30, Thirty-third Alabama File, ADAH.

75. Cavins, *War Letters*, 72; Milan Edson to Carman, 18 November 1907, CCNMP; *OR* 31, pt. 2, 382.

## Chapter Seventeen / An Unusual Solemnity Pervades Our Ranks

1. *OR* 31, pt. 2, 318, 600; McKinney, *Education in Violence*, 292.

2. McKinney, *Education in Violence*, 293; Smith, "Operations around Chattanooga," 220; *OR* 31, pt. 2, 78, 96, 116.

3. *OR* 31, pt. 2, 600–601, 607; Willison, *Reminiscences of a Boy's Service*, 77; *Military History and Reminiscences of the Thirteenth Regiment of Illinois Volunteer Infantry in the Civil War in the United States, 1861–1865* (Chicago: Woman's Temperance Publishing Association, 1892), 377.

4. McKinney, *Education in Violence*, 293; Hinman, *Story of the Sherman Brigade*, 459–60; Wilson, *Under the Old Flag*, 1:296; Cope, *Fifteenth Ohio*, 388; Cadwallader, *Three Years with Grant*, 149.

5. Grant, *Personal Memoirs*, 1:75; Wood, "Battle of Missionary Ridge," 33; Cadwallader, *Three Years with Grant*, 149–50.

6. *OR* 31, pt. 2, 34, 507; Grant, *Personal Memoirs*, 2:77; "Correspondence Relating to Chickamauga and Chattanooga," in *PMHSM*, 8:249.

7. High, *Sixty-eighth Indiana*, 149; Wood, "Battle of Missionary Ridge," 34; Thomas J. Wood, "A Thrilling War Chapter. The Battle of Missionary Ridge. Recollections of Gen. Thomas J. Wood," New York *Times*, 16 July 1876; Smith, "Operations around Chattanooga," 216.

8. McKinney, *Education in Violence*, 294; Smith, "Operations around Chattanooga," 221.

9. McKinney, *Education in Violence*, 294; OR 31, pt. 2, 68, 116; "Correspondence Relating to Chickamauga and Chattanooga," 249; Wilson, *Under the Old Flag*, 1:297–98; High, *Sixty-eighth Indiana*, 149; Fullerton, "Army of the Cumberland at Chattanooga," 724; Roper, "Interesting Account of Missionary Ridge," 503.

10. Wilson, *Under the Old Flag*, 1:298; Cadwallader, *Three Years with Grant*, 153–54; Wood, "Battle of Missionary Ridge," 35; "Correspondence Relating to Chickamauga and Chattanooga," 250; W. J. Colburn, "Memorandum," Historical Files, CCNMP; OR 31, pt. 2, 34, 132, 257; Smith, "Operations around Chattanooga," 215–16; High, *Sixty-eighth Indiana*, 149; Fullerton, "Army of the Cumberland at Chattanooga," 724; McKinney, *Education in Violence*, 292.

11. Dodson, "Battle of Missionary Ridge," 3; Davis, *Breckinridge*, 387–88; Hoffman, ed., *Confederate Collapse*, 36, 73; OR 31, pt. 2, 710–11, 740.

12. Davis, *Breckinridge*, 386–87, 394–96; Hazen, *Narrative of Military Service*, 206; OR 31, pt. 2, 664; McDonough, *Chattanooga*, 181–83; Manigault, *Carolinian Goes to War*, 154; John S. Wise, *The End of an Era* (Boston: Houghton Mifflin, 1899), 450–53.

13. Hoffman, ed., *Confederate Collapse*, 36–37, 58–59; Roy, "Sketch," 16, ADAH; Daniel, *Cannoneers in Gray*, 112; OR 31, pt. 2, 739; "Correspondence Relating to Chickamauga and Chattanooga," 252; Davis, *Breckinridge*, 386–87.

14. J. Patton Anderson, "Autobiographical Sketch," 9, J. Patton Anderson Papers, UNC; Hoffman, ed., *Confederate Collapse*, 14–15, 37; Dodson, "Battle of Missionary Ridge," 3; Cornelius Irvine Walker, *Rolls and Historical Sketch of the Tenth Regiment, So. Ca. Volunteers in the Army of the Late Confederate States* (Charleston: Walker, Evans and Cogswell, 1881), 108; Manigault, *Carolinian Goes to War*, 58–59.

15. Hoffman, ed., *Confederate Collapse*, 16.

16. Walker, *Tenth South Carolina*, 108; Hoffman, ed., *Confederate Collapse*, 15–16; Manigault, *Carolinian Goes to War*, 134–35; Dowd, "Lookout Mountain and Missionary Ridge," 398; John Ephraim Gold Questionnaire Data, Confederate Collection, TSLA.

17. Daniel, *Cannoneers in Gray*, 111–12.

18. Ibid., 112–13; "Correspondence Relating to Chickamauga and Chattanooga," 253; OR 31, pt. 2, 740; Colburn, "Memorandum," 9, Historical Files, CCNMP.

19. Hoffman, ed., *Confederate Collapse*, 49, 58–59, 69, 71; Roy, "Sketch," 17, ADAH; Manigault, *Carolinian Goes to War*, 136; OR 31, pt. 2, 739; Davis, *Breckinridge*, 388.

20. Dodson, "Battle of Missionary Ridge," 4; Anderson, "Autobiographical Sketch," 9, Anderson Papers, UNC; William Ralston Talley Autobiography, 34, in Havis's Georgia Battery File, CCNMP; Charles Hemming, "A Confederate Odyssey," *American Heritage* 36 (December 1984): 69.

21. Hoffman, ed., *Confederate Collapse*, 37, 53.

22. Manigault, *Carolinian Goes to War*, 136–37; *OR* 31, pt. 2, 281, 289; Hannaford, *Sixth Ohio*, 506; William Ross Glisan Diary, 25 November 1863, Sixth Ohio File, CCNMP.

23. Manigault, *Carolinian Goes to War*, 136; Hoffman, ed., *Confederate Collapse*, 41, 54, 70–71, 73; *OR* 31, pt. 2, 740.

24. Manigault, *Carolinian Goes to War*, 137; Breckinridge to Bate and Stewart, 1:00 P.M., 25 November 1863, Civil War Miscellaneous Collection, USAMHI; *OR* 31, pt. 2, 740.

25. Wright, "Bragg's Campaign around Chattanooga," 544–45; *OR* 31, pt. 2, 740; "Correspondence Relating to Chickamauga and Chattanooga," 252; Davis, *Breckinridge*, 388–89.

## CHAPTER EIGHTEEN / WE ARE ALL OFFICERS TODAY

1. Hannaford, *Sixth Ohio*, 506–7; *OR* 31, pt. 2, 281, 289; Glisan diary, 25 November 1863, Sixth Ohio File, CCNMP.

2. Kimberly, *Forty-first Ohio*, 68; Shellenberger, "With Sheridan's Division," 56–57; Ely diary, 25 November 1863, Thirty-sixth Illinois File, CCNMP; Cadwallader, *Three Years with Grant*, 150.

3. *OR* 31, pt. 2, 131, 190; Burke, *Military History of Kansas Regiments*, 218–19; McDonough, *Chattanooga*, 168.

4. *OR* 31, pt. 2, 132, 189, 194–95, 281, 228–29; "Correspondence Relating to Chickamauga and Chattanooga," 250; Otho Means to David Horseman, 6 December 1863, James Robinson Papers, IoHS; Ely diary, 25 November 1863, Thirty-sixth Illinois File, CCNMP; Clark, *125th O.V.I.*, 164.

5. *OR* 31, pt. 2, 459.

6. Ely diary, 25 November 1863, Thirty-sixth Illinois File, CCNMP.

7. Lewis, *124th Ohio*, 98–99.

8. Smith, "Operations around Chattanooga," 216; "Correspondence Relating to Chickamauga and Chattanoga," 250; *OR* 31, pt. 2, 508; James A. Connolly, *Three Years in the Army of the Cumberland: The Letters and Diary of Major James A. Connolly* (Bloomington, Ind.: Indiana University Press, 1959), 156.

9. High, *Sixty-eighth Indiana*, 149; Wood, "Battle of Missionary Ridge," 35.

10. Cope, *Fifteenth Ohio*, 381–82; *OR* 31, pt. 2, 264, 286, 304; William Doll Reminiscences, 254, Indiana State Library; Fullerton, "Army of the Cumberland at Chattanooga," 726.

11. *OR* 31, pt. 2, 190; Benjamin T. Smith, *Private Smith's Journal: Recollections of the Late War* (Chicago: R. R. Donnelly, 1963), 121; Philip Henry Sheridan, *Personal Memoirs of P. H. Sheridan*, 2 vols. (New York: Charles L. Webster, 1888), 1:307.

12. *OR* 31, pt. 2, 223, 233, 238; Fullerton, "Army of the Cumberland at Chattanooga," 724; Buckner memoirs, 29, ISHL; High, *Fifty-eighth Indiana*, 218.

13. Carlin, "Military Memoirs."

14. *OR* 31, pt. 2, 132, 199, 207, 213–15, 219, 223, 269–72; E. B. Parsons, "Missionary Ridge," in *War Papers Read before the Commandery of the State of Wisconsin, Military Order of the Loyal Legion of the United States,* 1:196.

15. William Morgan, "Hazen's Brigade at Missionary Ridge," in *War Talks in Kansas, Papers Read before the Commandery of Kansas, Military Order of the Loyal Legion of the United States* (Kansas City, Mo.: Franklin Hudson Publishing Company, 1906), 1:272; Ely diary, 25 November 1863, Thirty-sixth Illinois File, CCNMP; *OR* 31, pt. 2, 195, 230.

16. Shellenberger, "With Sheridan's Division," 58.

17. Walker, *Tenth South Carolina,* 105; Cooper memoirs, 37, Confederate Collection, TSLA; P. D. Stephenson, *Missionary Ridge. A Paper Read before R. E. Camp, No. 1, of Richmond Virginia, February 21, 1913* (N.p., n.d.), 8; Roy, "Sketch," 17, ADAH; Worsham, *Nineteenth Tennessee,* 99, 101.

18. Manigault, *Carolinian Goes to War,* 137.

19. Hemming, "Confederate Odyssey," 69–70.

20. Wagner reminiscences, 100, *CWTI* Collection, USAMHI; Burke, *Military History of Kansas Regiments,* 219; Kimberly, *Forty-first Ohio,* 69; Lewis, *124th Ohio,* 95; Clark, *125th O.V.I.,* 165; Billings D. Sibley to "Dear Anna," 2 December 1863, Billings D. Sibley Papers, MnHS; Shellenberger, "With Sheridan's Division," 59; Hazen, *Narrative of Military Service,* 174.

21. *Seventy-fourth Illinois,* 125–26; *OR* 31, pt. 2, 234; Bircher, *Drummer Boy's Diary,* 85; Kimberly, *Forty-first Ohio,* 696.

22. *OR* 31, pt. 2, 195, 197, 223, 234; Wagner reminiscences, 100, *CWTI* Collection, USAMHI; Shellenberger, "With Sheridan's Division," 58–59; Burke, *Military History of Kansas Regiments,* 219; *Eighty-sixth Indiana,* 246–47.

23. *OR* 31, pt. 2, 309; *Eighty-sixth Indiana,* 247.

24. *Report of the Chickamauga and Chattanooga National Park Commission on the Claim of Gen. John B. Turchin and Others That in the Battle of Chattanooga His Brigade Captured the Position on Missionary Ridge Known as the De Long Place, and the Decision of the Secretary of War Thereupon* (N.p., 1907?), 6; *OR* 31, pt. 1, 508, 512.

25. *OR* 31, pt. 2, 513.

26. Ibid., 741; Hoffman, ed., *Confederate Collapse,* 74.

27. Hoffman, ed., *Confederate Collapse,* 74; John W. Reese to his wife, 6 December 1863, John W. Reese Papers, Duke; *OR* 31, pt. 2, 741; Wagner reminiscences, 100, *CWTI* Collection, USAMHI; Shellenberger, "With Sheridan's Division," 59–60.

28. *OR* 31, pt. 2, 248–49; Robert Watson Diary, 25 November 1863, Seventh Florida File, CCNMP.

29. Shellenberger, "With Sheridan's Division," 59.

30. J. M. Bratty, "They All Got There First," *National Tribune,* 5 January 1885; John D. McKinnie, "Fighting around Chattanooga," *National Tribune,* 14 October 1926; John Lindsley, *The Military Annals of Tennes-*

see. *Confederate. First Series: Embracing a Review of Military Operations, with Regimental Histories and Memorial Rolls* (Nashville: J. M. Lindsley, 1886), 189; Francis M. Carlisle Autobiography, 22, Forty-second Indiana File, CCNMP; *OR* 31, pt. 2, 488–89.

31. Judson Bishop to his mother, 3 December 1863, Bishop Papers, MnHS; *OR* 31, pt. 2, 534; Manigault, *Carolinian Goes to War,* 138.

32. Hoffman, ed., *Confederate Collapse,* 61; Walker, *Tenth South Carolina,* 105; Donahower, "Narrative, Volume 2," 218, Donahower Papers, MnHS; Shellenberger, "With Sheridan's Division," 59–60; Manigault, *Carolinian Goes to War,* 138.

33. Hoffman, ed., *Confederate Collapse,* 49.

34. Ibid.

35. Manigault, *Carolinian Goes to War,* 138–39.

36. Martin Holt Reminiscences, ISHL; James G. Watson, "Middletown Yank's Journey to War and Back," typescript of selected portions of James G. Watson Diary, compiled by Gerald Miller, Champaign County Historical Archives, Urbana, Illinois, 25; High, *Fifty-eighth Indiana,* 212; *Seventy-fourth Illinois,* 122–23.

37. Hazen, *Narrative of Military Service,* 217; *OR* 31, pt. 2, 190, 215, 218, 219, 230, 248, 512–13, 517, 530; Ely diary, Thirty-sixth Illinois File, 25 November 1863, CCNMP; Donahower, "Narrative, Volume 2," 218, Donahower Papers, MnHS; Manigault, *Carolinian Goes to War,* 139; Judson Bishop, *The Story of a Regiment. Being a Narrative of the Services of the Second Regiment, Minnesota Veteran Volunteer Infantry* (St. Paul: N.p., 1890), 126.

38. "Correspondence Relating to Chattanooga," 250; *OR* 31, pt. 2, 278; Bishop, *Second Minnesota,* 126.

39. *OR* 31, pt. 2, 275; Asbury Welsh, "Up the Ridge," *National Tribune,* 28 June 1900; Cope, *Fifteenth Ohio,* 382.

40. *OR* 31, pt. 2, 264.

41. Ibid., 273.

42. Ibid., 264, 267, 270–71, 277–78; Allen Varner's manuscript report, Twenty-fifth Illinois, Stephen W. Calhoun Collection.

43. Daniel Wait Howe and Flavius J. Van Vorhis, *In the Matter of the Location Where Beatty's Brigade of Wood's Division of 4th Army Corps Reached the Crest of Missionary Ridge on November 25, 1863, Before the Commissioners of Chickamauga and Chattanooga National Park* (N.p., n.d.), 16–17, 43; idem, *In the Matter of the Location Where Beatty's Brigade of Wood's Division of 4th Army Corps Reached the Crest of Missionary Ridge on November 25, 1863. Reply Brief. Before the Commissioners of Chickamauga and Chattanooga National Park* (N.p., 1911), 14.

44. *OR* 31, pt. 2, 301, 304–5, 309; *Eighty-sixth Indiana,* 250; Howe and Van Vorhis, *In the Matter of the Location Where Beatty's Brigade Reached the Crest,* 17–19.

45. *OR* 31, pt. 2, 221, 226, 281–82, 290; Hazen, *Narrative of Military Service,* 194, 214–15; Wagner reminiscences, 101–2, *CWTI* Collection, USAMHI; Morgan, "Hazen's Brigade at Missionary Ridge," 273.

46. *OR* 31, pt. 2, 296; Wilson S. Miller to his father, 4 December 1863, Wilson S. Miller Letters, Federal Collection, TSLA; Kimberly, *Forty-first Ohio*, 69–70.

47. Wood, "Battle of Missionary Ridge," 37, 39, 46; High, *Sixty-eighth Indiana*, 149; Shellenberger, "With Sheridan's Division," 67.

48. Shellenberger, "With Sheridan's Division," 45; Wood, "Battle of Missionary Ridge," 67; Hazen, *Narrative of Military Service*, 225.

49. *OR* 31, pt. 2, 213, 217, 221, 223; John L. Richardson, "At Missionary Ridge," *National Tribune*, 14 September 1899; E. T. Hibbard, "Wagner's Brigade: How It Climbed Mission Ridge Along with the Rest of the Boys," *National Tribune*, 6 October 1887; Ephraim Wagley, "Civil War Memoirs," 128, Paul Wagley Collection.

50. Ephraim Wagley, "Civil War Memoirs," 129, Paul Wagley Collection.

51. *OR* 31, pt. 2, 223; Richardson, "At Missionary Ridge."

52. Clark, *125th O.V.I.*, 169; *OR* 31, pt. 2, 230, 234, 238; Shellenberger, "With Sheridan's Division," 62 .

53. *OR* 31, pt. 2, 195, 197; Ely diary, 25 November 1863, Thirty-sixth Illinois File, CCNMP; *Address to the 73rd Regiment Illinois Volunteer Infantry, by Colonel James F. Jaquess, at a Reunion Held in Springfield, Illinois, October 8th–10th, 1890* (N.p., n.d,), 14; William H. Newlin, *History of the Seventy-third Regiment of Illinois Infantry Volunteers, Its Services and Experiences in Camp, on the March, on the Picket and Skirmish Lines, and in Many Battles of the War, 1861–1865* (Springfield, Ill.: Regimental Reunion Association, 1890), 266; Lindsley, *Military Annals of Tennessee. Confederate*, 188–89; Gold questionnaire data, Confederate Collection, TSLA.

54. *OR* 31, pt. 2, 202; Lyman G. Bennett, *History of the Thirty-sixth Regiment Illinois Volunteers during the War of the Great Rebellion* (Aurora, Ill.: Knickerbocker and Hodder, 1876), 527–28.

55. *OR* 31, pt. 2, 133, 190; Smith, *Private Smith's Journal*, 121.

56. *OR* 31, pt. 2, 482; John D. McKinnie, "Fighting around Chattanooga," *National Tribune*, 14 October 1926; Lindsley, *Military Annals of Tennessee. Confederate*, 188; John T. Drion, "Fifth Tennessee Infantry Regiment," 5, manuscript history in Confederate Collection, TSLA.

57. Anonymous letter to the editor in "Army Correspondence," Ottawa (Ill.) *Free Trader*, 19 December 1863; *OR* 31, pt. 2, 463, 468, 474–78; Scribner, *How Soldiers Were Made*, 179–80.

58. *OR* 31, pt. 2, 530, 543–44, 546; *Report on the Claim of Gen. John B. Turchin*, 6; Hazen, *Narrative of Military Service*, 194; Donahower, *Lookout Mountain and Missionary Ridge*, 20–21.

59. *Report on the Claim of Gen. John B. Turchin*, 6, 20; *OR* 31, pt. 2, 512–13, 517; Howe and Van Vorhis, *In the Matter of the Location Where Beatty's Brigade Reached the Crest*, see entire pamphlet, but especially pages 15–17, 26, 55–59.

60. *Report on the Claim of Gen. John B. Turchin*, 6–7; *OR* 31, pt. 2, 532.

61. *OR* 31, pt. 2, 508–9.

62. Ibid., 68. This represents my best estimate of the time. In their battle reports, not one Union troop commander cited precise or even approximate times of events after the attack began, a good indication of the level of confusion.

## CHAPTER NINETEEN / ALMOST UP, SIR

1. Fullerton, "Army of the Cumberland at Chattanooga," 725; *Eighty-sixth Indiana*, 259.

2. High, *Sixty-eighth Indiana*, 149; *Eighty-sixth Indiana*, 259; OR 31, pt. 2, 133; Wood, "Battle of Missionary Ridge," 39; OR 31, pt. 2, 509; Hazen, *Narrative of Military Service*, 235.

3. OR 31, pt. 2, 133; High, *Sixty-eighth Indiana*, 149.

4. OR 31, pt. 2, 133, 190; Smith, *Private Smith's Journal*, 122.

5. Hibbard, "Wagner's Brigade"; OR 31, pt. 2, 223–24; Richardson, "At Missionary Ridge."

6. OR 31, pt. 2, 220.

7. Ibid., 217–18; Asbury L. Kerwood, *Annals of the Fifty-seventh Regiment Indiana Volunteers: Marches, Battles, and Incidents of Army Life* (Dayton, Ohio: W. J. Shuey, 1868), 225.

8. OR 31, pt. 2, 238.

9. Shellenberger, "With Sheridan's Division," 63; Clark, *125th O.V.I.*, 169–70; OR 31, pt. 2, 240.

10. Shellenberger, "With Sheridan's Division," 63; Clark, *125th O.V.I.*, 170; Wood, "Battle of Missionary Ridge," 45.

11. OR 31, pt. 2, 209, 215, 220, 224.

12. Smith, *Private Smith's Journal*, 122; OR 31, pt. 2, 190–91; Parsons, "Missionary Ridge," 199; W. L. Kessler, "Capturing Two Guns: The Seventy-ninth Illinois's Version of the Taking of 'Lady Breckinridge' and 'Lady Buckner,'" *National Tribune*, 15 February 1900; Shellenberger, "With Sheridan's Division," 64; Wood, "Battle of Missionary Ridge," 45.

13. Joshua Horton, *A History of the Eleventh Regiment (Ohio Volunteer Infantry), Containing the Military Record, so Far as It Is Possible to Obtain It, of Each Officer and Enlisted Man of the Command, a List of Deaths, an Account of the Veterans, Incidents of the Field and Camp, Names of the Three Months' Volunteers* (Dayton, Ohio: Horton and Teverbaugh, 1866), 107; Howe and Van Vorhis, *In the Matter of the Location Where Beatty's Brigade Reached the Crest*, 15; Morgan, "Hazen's Brigade at Missionary Ridge," 273; Clark, *125th O.V.I.*, 166–67; Burke, *Military History of Kansas Regiments*, 220; OR 31, pt. 2, 281–82.

14. Scribner, *How Soldiers Were Made*, 180–81.

15. John W. Reese to his wife, 6 December 1863, Reese Papers, Duke; Lindsley, *Military Annals of Tennessee. Confederate*, 452; Dowd, "Lookout Mountain and Missionary Ridge," 399; George E. Brewer, "Why Missionary Ridge Was Lost by the Confederates," *CV* 22, no. 5 (May 1914): 232; OR 31, pt. 2, 741; Worsham, *Nineteenth Tennessee*, 100; Hemming, "Con-

federate Odyssey," 71; Donahower, "Narrative, Volume 2," 223–24, Donahower Papers, MnHS; Francis M. Carlisle Autobiography, 22, Forty-second Indiana File, CCNMP; Scribner, *How Soldiers Were Made*, 181; Hoffman, ed., *Confederate Collapse*, 70–71; Maurice Marcoot, *Five Years in the Sunny South: Reminiscences of Maurice Marcoot* (N.p., n.d.), 42.

16. Hazen, *Narrative of Military Service*, 215; Wagner reminiscences, 102, *CWTI* Collection, USAMHI; William S. Miller to his father, 4 December 1863, Federal Collection, TSLA; Clark, *125th O.V.I.*, 166–67.

17. Cadwallader, *Three Years with Grant*, 152.

18. Howard, "Grant at Chattanooga," 252–53.

## Chapter Twenty / Chickamauga, Damn You!

1. Hoffman, ed., *Confederate Collapse*, 41; Colburn, "Memorandum," 9, Historical Files, CCNMP; J. A. Chalaron, "At Missionary Ridge: Confederate Commander Writes of the Capture of Guns by Union Troops," *National Tribune*, 4 May 1899; William B. Hazen to Chalaron, 22 June 1879, Civil War Papers Collection, Tulane.

2. Hoffman, ed., *Confederate Collapse*, 42.

3. High, *Sixty-eighth Indiana*, 149; Wood, "Battle of Missionary Ridge," 39–40, 47.

4. Frank Erdelmeyer, "Thirty-second Indiana at Missionary Ridge," 2, Thirty-second Indiana File, CCNMP; Hazen, *Narrative of Military Service*, 222.

5. Erdelmeyer, "Thirty-second Indiana at Missionary Ridge," 2, Thirty-second Indiana File, CCNMP; Hoffman, ed., *Confederate Collapse*, 71; Robert Hammond, "The Charge of a Corps," *National Tribune*, 17 August 1899; Cope, *Fifteenth Ohio*, 381; Howe and Van Vorhis, *In the Matter of the Location Where Beatty's Brigade Reached the Crest*, 8–11.

6. Erdelmeyer, "Thirty-second Indiana at Missionary Ridge," 2; *OR* 31, pt. 2, 271; Hazen, *Narrative of Military Service*, 210–11; O. C. Bowen, "Don't Know Who Was There First," *National Tribune*, 18 February 1886; Hannaford, *Sixth Ohio*, 508.

7. Hannaford, *Sixth Ohio*, 508–10; Hoffman, ed., *Confederate Collapse*, 71.

8. Hannaford, *Sixth Ohio*, 508.

9. Erdelmeyer, "Thirty-second Indiana at Missionary Ridge," 2, Thirty-second Indiana File, CCNMP; Hannaford, *Sixth Ohio*, 509; Hazen, *Narrative of Military Service*, 210; Bowen, "Don't Know Who Was There First"; Lewis, *124th Ohio*, 101.

10. Howe and Van Vorhis, *In the Matter of the Location Where Beatty's Brigade Reached the Crest*, 16; S. F. Stewart, *In the Matter of the Location on Missionary Ridge of the Tablets and Markers of the Brigades of Gen. S. Beatty and Gen. J. B. Turchin, Before the Chickamauga and Chattanooga National Park Commission. Brief of Turchin's Brigade. February 10, 1911* (N.p., 1911), 17.

11. *OR* 31, pt. 2, 264, 267–78; Watson, "Middletown Yank," 25–26; Matthew McInerny, "Mission Ridge Again," *National Tribune,* 15 April 1886; Howe and Van Vorhis, *In the Matter of the Location where Beatty's Brigade Reached the Crest . . . Reply Brief,* 39–40.

12. *OR* 31, pt. 2, 264, 268, 278; Watson, "Middletown Yank," 26; High, *Sixty-eighth Indiana,* 148; Burke, *Military History of Kansas Regiments,* 221; Samuel W. Bird, "Mission Ridge: Why They Charged without Orders," *National Tribune,* 18 February 1886; Captain Allen Varner's manuscript report of Missionary Ridge, dated 26 November 1863, Stephen W. Calhoun Collection; William R. Nash, "Missionary Ridge: Another Claim as to Who Was First Up the Big Hill," *National Tribune,* 3 November 1892; Howe and Van Vorhis, *In the Matter of the Location Where Beatty's Brigade Reached the Crest,* 26. For the view from Orchard Knob, see Roper, "Interesting Account of Missionary Ridge," 503–4. Which regimental flag was the first to fly atop Missionary Ridge? It is impossible to say with certainty. My guess—and it is only that—is that the honor should go to the Sixth Kentucky, Sixth Ohio, or Thirty-second Indiana. After the war, scores of articles littered the pages of the *National Tribune* with passionately argued claims to the honor put forward by members of every regiment that participated in the charge. Regimental historians echoed the claims. Only the historian of the One Hundred Twenty-fifth Ohio had the courage to write what all the others, if they were honest with themselves, knew to be true: "According to all precedents in regimental histories, we ought to tell whose flag was first planted on the ridge. A large majority of the survivors of the 125th have lived all these years unshaken in the belief that ours was the first—ahead of all others. Affidavits to that effect could be procured for the asking from men who *saw* our own flag there before they saw that of any other command. A good many other regiments make the same claim, many of them in their official reports. It can never be determined who was first, if any one was. . . . Officers and men would naturally observe their own flag, but would not be apt in that final rush to take note of others." Clark, *125th O.V.I.,* 173–74.

13. Hoffman, ed., *Confederate Collapse,* 71.

14. Hazen, *Narrative of Military Service,* 204, 210; Colburn, "Memorandum," 9, Historical Files, CCNMP.

15. Colburn, "Memorandum," 9, Historical Files, CCNMP; Chalaron, "At Missionary Ridge."

16. Hazen, *Narrative of Military Service,* 215; *OR* 31, pt. 2, 282, 293; Morgan, "Hazen's Brigade at Missionary Ridge," 273.

17. *OR* 31, pt. 2, 290–91; Wagner reminiscences, 102–3, *CWTI* Collection, USAMHI; Morgan, "Hazen's Brigade at Missionary Ridge," 273; A. H. Benham, "Climbing Missionary Ridge," *National Tribune,* 30 April 1925; Kimberly, *Forty-first Ohio,* 71; Colburn, "Memorandum," 9, Historical Files, CCNMP; Thomas J. Wood, "A Thrilling War Chapter. The Battle of Missionary Ridge. Recollections of Gen. Thomas J. Wood," *New York Times,* 16 July 1876.

18. *OR* 31, pt. 2, 290–91; Captain Wilson B. Miller to his father, 4 December 1863, Miller Letters, Federal Collection, TSLA; Kimberly, *Forty-first Ohio*, 71; Hoffman, ed., *Confederate Collapse*, 75. Reynolds claimed that his men put up a stubborn resistance to Hazen and that he actually held out until Bate had fallen back on his left. His report is best dismissed as self-serving fiction.

19. Wagner reminiscences, 103–5, *CWTI* Collection, USAMHI.

20. Massenburg's Battery Marker, CCNMP; Hazen, *Narrative of Military Service*, 231; *OR* 31, pt. 2, 665.

21. *OR* 31, pt. 2, 741–42; Colburn, "Memorandum," 9, Historical Files, CCNMP; Chalaron, "At Missionary Ridge"; Hazen, *Narrative of Military Service*, 189, 195.

22. Colburn, "Memorandum," 3, 9, Historical Files, CCNMP; Chalaron, "At Missionary Ridge"; *OR* 31, pt. 2, 742; Hazen, *Narrative of Military Service*, 205, 231–32.

23. Colburn, "Memorandum," 9–10, Historical Files, CCNMP; Chalaron, "At Missionary Ridge"; Benham, "Climbing Missionary Ridge"; Kimberly, *Forty-first Ohio*, 71; Hazen to Chalaron, 22 June 1879, Civil War Papers Collection, Tulane; Stanley Horn, ed., *Tennessee's War 1861–1865, Described by Participants* (Nashville: Tennessee Civil War Centennial Commission, 1965), 242.

## CHAPTER TWENTY-ONE / WE'VE GOT 'EM IN A PEN

1. Colburn, "Memorandum," 10, Historical Files, CCNMP.

2. *OR* 31, pt. 2, 293; Hazen, *Narrative of Military Service*, 216.

3. Stephen Helmer to his wife, 26 November 1863, Civil War Miscellaneous Collection, USAMHI; Hazen, *Narrative of Military Service*, 191; *OR* 31, pt. 2, 742; Lindsley, *Military History of Tennessee. Confederate*, 452–53; Robert Jamison, *Letters and Recollections of a Confederate Soldier, 1860–1865* (Nashville: N.p., 1964), 165; Horn, ed., *Tennessee's War 1861–1865*, 242.

4. Mebane's Tennessee Battery Marker, CCNMP.

5. *OR* 31, pt. 2, 291, 296, 742; Cooper memoirs, 39, TSLA.

6. *OR* 31, pt. 2, 81–82, 215; Hazen, *Narrative of Military Service*, 226.

7. *OR* 31, pt. 2, 210, 217–18, 224–25; Daniel, *Cannoneers in Gray*, 115; Talley autobiography, 34, Havis's Georgia Battery File, CCNMP; J. D. Lytle, "Capturing Two Cannon," *National Tribune*, 6 April 1899.

8. Hemming, "Confederate Odyssey," 71; Shellenberger, "With Sheridan's Division," 64; Talley autobiography, 34, Havis's Georgia Battery File, CCNMP.

9. Hemming, "Confederate Odyssey," 71–72.

10. Daniel, *Cannoneers in Gray*, 116.

11. *OR* 31, pt. 2, 234; Shellenberger, "With Sheridan's Division," 65; idem, "On Missionary Ridge: The Capture of 'Lady Buckner' and 'Lady Breckinridge' of Cobb's Battery," *National Tribune*, 16 May 1901; Edwin

Porter Thompson, *History of the Orphan Brigade* (Louisville: L. N. Thompson, 1898), 228.

12. Shellenberger, "With Sheridan's Division," 65; Kessler, "Capturing Two Guns"; Solomon Barb, "At Missionary Ridge," *National Tribune*, 6 April 1899.

13. McDonough, *Chattanooga*, 204; Hazen, *Narrative of Military Service*, 206–7; E. William Beitus Recollections, Civil War Papers: Reminiscences, Army of Tennessee, Tulane; W. H. Edsall, "The First on Mission Ridge," *National Tribune*, 25 February 1886; Foster diary, 60–61, *CWTI* Collection, USAMHI.

14. *OR* 31, pt. 2, 191.

15. Ibid., 195, 202, 207; Bennett, *Thirty-sixth Illinois*, 528; Ely diary, 25 November 1863, Thirty-sixth Illinois File, CCNMP; E. J. Ingersoll to the Editor, Schuyler (Ill.) *Citizen*, 6 December 1863; Sheridan, *Personal Memoirs*, 1:308.

16. Lindsley, *Military History of Tennessee. Confederate*, 198; Drion, "Fifth Tennessee Infantry," 5, and Gold questionnaire data, 8, both in Confederate Collection, TSLA.

17. *OR* 31, pt. 2, 195, 203–4, 208; *Seventy-fourth Illinois*, 127; Ingersoll to the Editor, Schuyler (Ill.) *Citizen*, 28 November 1863; A. Lammey, "The Eighty-eighth Illinois: Another Regiment Claims to Have Planted Its Flag First on Missionary Ridge," *National Tribune*, 12 November 1891.

18. Bennett, *Thirty-sixth Illinois*, 529; Gold questionnaire data, 8, Confederate Collection, TSLA.

19. *OR* 31, pt. 2, 202–3; Lammey, "Eighty-eighth Illinois"; McDonough, *Chattanooga*, 199–200; Arthur MacArthur to his father, 26 November 1863, in undated newspaper clipping, "Correspondence of Wisconsin Volunteers, Volume 10," E. A. Quiner Papers, State Historical Society of Wisconsin.

20. Bennett, *Thirty-sixth Illinois*, 529, 531; Belknap, *Michigan at Chickamauga and Chattanooga*, 121; E. J. Ingersoll to the Editor, Schuyler (Ill.) *Citizen*, 6 December 1863; G. W. Sledge, "Battle of Missionary Ridge," *CV* 22, no. 2 (February 1914): 65. The location of Stanford's Mississippi battery is tentative. G. W. Sledge, a member of the battery, places it behind Tyler's brigade, but admits his uncertainty. It does not, however, seem likely that General Stewart—who said his artillery battalion was concentrated at the start of the fighting near the Moore house—would have deployed one of its batteries in support of another division when his own lacked artillery support.

21. Newlin, *Seventy-third Illinois*, 266–67.

22. Thomas J. Ford, *With the Rank and File: Incidents and Anecdotes during the War of the Rebellion, as Remembered by One of the Non-Commissioned Officers* (Milwaukee: Press of the Evening Wisconsin Company, 1898), 28–29.

23. Bennett, *Thirty-sixth Illinois*, 531–32.

24. Ely diary, 25 November 1863, Thirty-sixth Illinois File, CCNMP; James Haynie, *The Nineteenth Illinois: A Memoir of a Regiment of Volun-*

*teer Infantry Famous in the Civil War of Fifty Years Ago for Its Drill, Bravery, and Distinguished Service* (Chicago: M. A. Donahue, 1912), 256

25. Lindsley, *Military Annals of Tennessee. Confederate*, 189, 298; Gold questionnaire data, 8, Confederate Collection, TSLA.

26. *OR* 31, pt. 2, 199; Belknap, *Michigan at Chickamauga and Chattanooga*, 121.

27. Carlin, "Military Memoirs"; Scribner, *How Soldiers Were Made*, 180.

28. Scribner, *How Soldiers Were Made*, 180; William Wirt Calkins, *The History of the One Hundred and Fourth Regiment of Illinois Volunteer Infantry, War of the Great Rebellion, 1862–1865* (Chicago: Donohue and Henneberry), 181.

29. Anonymous letter to the editor in "Army Correspondence," Ottawa (Ill.) *Free Trader*, 19 December 1863; *OR* 31, pt. 2, 463, 476–78.

30. *OR* 31, pt. 2, 474; anonymous letter to editor in "Army Correspondence," Ottawa (Ill.) *Free Trader*, 19 December 1863.

31. *OR* 31, pt. 2, 474.

32. Ibid.; Carlisle autobiography, 22, Forty-second Indiana File, CCNMP; anonymous letter to the editor, in "Army Correspondence," Ottawa (Ill.) *Free Trader*, 19 December 1863.

33. Davis, *Breckinridge*, 389; Wright, "Bragg's Campaign around Chattanooga," 544–45; *OR* 31, pt. 2, 318.

34. Wright, "Bragg's Campaign around Chattanooga," 545; Davis, *Breckinridge*, 545; James Ogden III to Peter Cozzens, 18 March 1993.

35. Inzer, *Diary*, 43–44; Wright, "Bragg's Campaign around Chattanooga," 545–46.

36. *OR* 31, pt. 2, 318, 601, 607, 615.

37. Ibid., 318.

38. In his report, Colonel Williamson credits the Ninth Iowa with netting Cabell Breckinridge. The commander of the Ninth, however, makes no mention of the incident in his report, and other contemporary accounts credit members of the Fourth Iowa with the act. The captors probably came from the latter regiment, as Williamson had shaken it out in a skirmish line to guard his left flank and front. *OR* 31, pt. 2, 615; *Thirteenth Illinois*, 378–79; Fowler, "Most Curious Battle of the War"; Davis, *Breckinridge*, 389.

39. Willison, *Reminiscences of a Boy's Service*, 77; *Thirteenth Illinois*, 379; *OR* 31, pt. 2, 601.

40. *Thirteenth Illinois*, 380.

41. Wright, "Bragg's Campaign around Chattanooga," 546–47.

42. Peter McLain to the editor, in "Army Correspondence," Keithsburg (Ill.) *Observer*, 7 January 1864; Wright, "Bragg's Campaign around Chattanooga," 547; Mosman, *Rough Side of War*, 129; *OR* 31, pt. 2, 171; Alfred Allen, "Helping Hooker at Lookout," *National Tribune*, 8 March 1923.

43. *OR* 31, pt. 2, 147, 171; Wright, "Bragg's Campaign around Chattanooga," 546; Davis, *Breckinridge*, 389.

44. Wright, "Bragg's Campaign around Chattanooga," 546; *OR* 31, pt. 2, 615; Davis, *Breckinridge*, 389–90.

45. Inzer, *Diary,* 44–45.

46. Ibid., 45; Davis, *Breckinridge,* 390.

47. Willison, *Reminiscences of a Boy's Service,* 77; "Correspondence Relating to Chickamauga and Chattanooga," 253; *OR* 31, pt. 2, 745.

48. Carlin, "Military Memoirs"; Inzer, *Diary,* 45; Scribner, *How Soldiers Were Made,* 183; Wright, "Bragg's Campaign around Chattanooga"; Carlisle autobiography, 22, Forty-second Indiana File, CCNMP; *OR* 31, pt. 2, 472, 474.

49. Scribner, *How Soldiers Were Made,* 183.

CHAPTER TWENTY-TWO / SAVE YOURSELF! THE YANKEES
ARE ON YOU!

1. Hoffman, ed., *Confederate Collapse,* 61–62; Manigault, *Carolinian Goes to War,* 139.

2. Manigault, *Carolinian Goes to War,* 139; *OR* 31, pt. 2, 530.

3. Manigault, *Carolinian Goes to War,* 139.

4. Ibid.; Hoffman, ed., *Confederate Collapse,* 63; Walker, *Tenth South Carolina,* 105–6.

5. Manigault, *Carolinian Goes to War,* 139–40; Walker, *Tenth South Carolina,* 108; Hoffman, ed., *Confederate Collapse,* 63.

6. Manigault, *Carolinian Goes to War,* 140; Hoffman, ed., *Confederate Collapse,* 42–43, 63–64; Walker, *Tenth South Carolina,* 108.

7. Manigault, *Carolinian Goes to War,* 140; Hoffman, ed., *Confederate Collapse,* 43, 64–65; Walker, *Tenth South Carolina,* 108; Howe and Van Vorhis, *In the Matter of the Location Where Beatty's Brigade Reached the Crest,* 18.

8. *OR* 31, pt. 2, 267–68, 301–2, 305, 311; Manigault, *Carolinian Goes to War,* 141; R. H. Higgins to S. F. Stewart, Fifty-ninth Ohio File, CCNMP; *History of the Seventy-ninth Regiment Indiana Volunteer Infantry in the Civil War of Eighteen Sixty-one in the United States* (Indianapolis: Hollenbeck Press, 1899), 107.

9. F. G. Jordan, "First on Missionary Ridge," *National Tribune,* 14 June 1888; J. M. Adair, "The First on Mission Ridge," *National Tribune,* 31 December 1885; Leonard A. Heil, "Break on Mission Ridge," *National Tribune,* 29 March 1923; *OR* 31, pt. 2, 268, 311; Higgins to Stewart, 2 January 1905, Fifty-ninth Ohio File, CCNMP; Howe and Van Vorhis, *In the Matter of the Location Where Beatty's Brigade Reached the Crest,* 14, 19; Hoffman, ed., *Confederate Collapse,* 65.

10. Howe and Van Vorhis, *In the Matter of the Location Where Beatty's Brigade Reached the Crest,* 18.

11. Ibid.; Manigault, *Carolinian Goes to War,* 141; *OR* 31, pt. 2, 518.

12. Manigault, *Carolinian Goes to War,* 141; R. W. Reams, "Brief War Incidents," *CV* 22, no. 9 (September 1914): 400; Howe and Van Vorhis, *In the Matter of the Location Where Beatty's Brigade Reached the Crest,* 18–

19; Stewart, *In the Matter of the Location of the Tablets of Beatty and Turchin. . . . Brief of Turchin's Brigade . . . February 10, 1911*, 23–24; OR 31, pt. 2, 311, 530; H. Allspaugh, "Mission Ridge," *National Tribune*, 2 June 1887; Higgins to Stewart, 2 January 1905, Fifty-ninth Ohio File, CCNMP.

13. Hoffman, ed., *Confederate Collapse*, 55; Reams, "Brief War Incidents," 400; J. W. Bishop et al., *In the Matter of the Request for Removal of the Second Minnesota Monument from De Long Point to Strock Knob. Before the Chickamauga and Chattanooga Park Commission. Brief of the Survivors of the Minnesota Monument Commission* (N.p., n.d.), 14; James Walker, "Through a Bullet Storm," *National Tribune*, 17 May 1923.

14. Donahower, "Narrative, Volume 2," 224–25, Donahower Papers, MnHS; OR 31, pt. 2, 535–36; Judson Bishop to his mother, 3 December 1863, Bishop Papers, MnHS; J. W. Bishop et al., *In the Matter of the Request by Survivors of Van Derveer's Brigade for Restoration of Its Historical Tablet to Its Original and Proper Position on De Long Point, Missionary Ridge, Before the Chickamauga and Chattanooga National Park Commission. Brief of the Survivors of the Second Minnesota Regiment* (Saint Paul, Minn.: N.p., 1911), 22.

15. Donahower, "Narrative, Volume 2," 226; Bishop et al., *In the Matter of the Request by Survivors of Van Derveer's Brigade for Restoration of Its Historical Tablet*, 23; Reams, "Brief War Incidents," 400.

16. Quoted in McDonough, *Chattanooga*, 198; Bishop et al., *In the Matter of the Request by Survivors of Van Derveer's Brigade for Restoration of Its Historical Tablet*, 23; Donahower, *Lookout Mountain and Missionary Ridge*, 21–22; Waters's Alabama Battery Marker, CCNMP.

17. Alfred Taylor Fielder Diary, 25 November 1863, Confederate Collection, TSLA; Bishop to his mother, 3 December 1863, Bishop Papers, MnHS; OR 31, pt. 2, 513, 515; Waters's Alabama Battery Marker, CCNMP; Billings D. Sibley to his father, 26 November 1863, Billings D. Sibley Papers, MnHS; Allspaugh, "Mission Ridge"; Frederick Marion to his sister, 1 December 1863, Frederick Marion Letters, ISHL.

18. OR 31, pt. 2, 513, 528; Donahower, "Narrative, Volume 2," 226, Donahower Papers, MnHS; idem, *Lookout Mountain and Missionary Ridge*, 27; Bishop et al., *In the Matter of the Request by Survivors of Van Derveer's Brigade for Restoration of Its Historical Tablet*, 18–19.

19. John Harris to "Dear George," 13 October 1863, John Harris Letters, Confederate Collection, TSLA.

20. Hoffman, ed., *Confederate Collapse*, 43, 51.

21. Ibid., 51; OR 31, pt. 2, 535; Allspaugh, "Mission Ridge."

22. Hoffman, ed., *Confederate Collapse*, 43, 51; Fielder diary, 25 November 1863, CCNMP.

23. OR 31, pt. 2, 528, 535, 541, 544; Scott's Tennessee Battery Marker, CCNMP; Sibley to his father, 26 November 1863, Sibley Papers, MnHS; Peter Kellenberger to "Friend Add," 19 December 1863, Kellenberger Letters, DLC.

CHAPTER TWENTY-THREE / WE ARE FIGHTING THE WORLD

1. Benjamin Franklin Cheatham to Edward C. Walthall, 6 April 1876, Cheatham Papers, TSLA; Losson, *Tennessee's Forgotten Warriors*, 127; Andrew Jackson Neal to his sister, 26 November 1863, McCants's Florida Battery File, CCNMP.

2. *OR* 31, pt. 2, 706; Losson, *Tennessee's Forgotten Warriors*, 125; J. C. Moore, "Some Confederate War Incidents," *CV* 12, no. 3 (March 1904): 117.

3. Donahower, "Narrative, Volume 2," 229, and *Lookout Mountain and Missionary Ridge*, 27; *OR* 31, pt. 2, 528, 532; Losson, *Tennessee's Forgotten Warriors*, 127–28.

4. Tourgee, *Story of a Thousand*, 288; Hartzell, "Autobiography, Part 2," 105–6.

5. *OR* 31, pt. 2, 541, 544, 546, 548; Neal to his sister, 26 November 1863, McCants's Florida Battery File, CCNMP; "Correspondence Related to Chickamauga and Chattanooga," 251.

6. Donahower, "Narrative, Volume 2," 229–31, and *Lookout Mountain and Missionary Ridge*, 28.

7. Donahower, "Narrative, Volume 2," 231, and *Lookout Mountain and Missionary Ridge*, 29; *OR* 31, pt. 2, 528, 530; James G. Essington, "Second Year History of the Seventy-fifth Indiana Volunteer Infantry," Noblesville (Ind.) *Republican Ledger*, 30 October 1885; Floyd, *Seventy-fifth Indiana*, 238.

8. *OR* 31, pt. 2, 528, 541, 544, 548; Hartzell, "Autobiography, Part 2," 106; Peter Kellenberger to "Friend Add," 19 December 1863, Kellenberger Letters, DLC; Henry Davidson to his aunt, 19 December 1864, Davidson Papers, ISHL; Losson, *Tennessee's Forgotten Warriors*, 128.

9. Neal to his sister, 26 November 1863, McCants's Florida Battery File, CCNMP.

10. Ibid.

11. Essington, "Second Year History of the Seventy-fifth Indiana Volunteer Infantry," Noblesville (Ind.) *Republican Ledger*, 30 October 1885; Floyd, *Seventy-fifth Indiana*, 240; *OR* 31, pt. 2, 515, 528.

12. Dowd, "Lookout Mountain and Missionary Ridge," 399; Sykes, "Walthall's Brigade," 541; Jarman, "History of Company K, Twenty-seventh Mississippi," 23; Cheatham to Walthall, 6 March 1876, Cheatham Papers, TSLA; *OR* 31, pt. 2, 697.

13. Roy, "Sketch," 15, MDAH; Sykes, "Walthall's Brigade," 540–42; *OR* 31, pt. 2, 727.

14. *OR* 31, pt. 2, 510, 539, 697, 727; Dowd, "Lookout Mountain and Missionary Ridge," 399; Jarman, "History of Company K, Twenty-seventh Mississippi," 23, MDAH; Donahower, *Lookout Mountain and Missionary Ridge*, 29.

15. *OR* 31, pt. 2, 291, 541; Kellenberger to "Friend Add," 19 December 1863, Kellenberger Letters, DLC.

16. Sheridan, *Personal Memoirs*, 1:312–13.

17. Ibid., 1:313; Ford, *With the Rank and File*, 29; OR 31, pt. 2, 191; E. J. Ingersoll to the editor, Schuyler (Ill.) *Citizen*, 6 December 1863.

18. Sheridan, *Personal Memoirs*, 1:191; Shellenberger, "With Sheridan's Division," 65; OR 31, pt. 2, 231; Clark, *125th O.V.I.*, 170.

19. Hemming, "Confederate Odyssey," 72–73; idem, "Inquiry for an Alabama Soldier," *CV* 15, no. 10 (October 1907): 457; OR 31, pt. 2, 742.

20. Lindsley, *Military History of Tennessee. Confederate*, 452–53; OR 31, pt. 2, 665, 743.

21. Lindsley, *Military History of Tennessee. Confederate*, 453; OR 31, pt. 2, 743.

22. OR 31, pt. 2, 191, 225; Lindsley, *Military History of Tennessee. Confederate*, 453.

23. Davis, *Breckinridge*, 391; Lindsley, *Military History of Tennessee. Confederate*, 453; "Correspondence Relating to Chickamauga and Chattanooga," 252–53.

24. Davis, *Breckinridge*, 391; OR 31, pt. 2, 742–43.

25. Sheridan, *Personal Memoirs*, 1:315.

## CHAPTER TWENTY-FOUR / WHIPPED, MORTIFIED, AND CHAGRINED

1. Manigault, *Carolinian Goes to War*, 142–43; Hoffman, ed., *Confederate Collapse*, 65, 71.

2. Hoffman, ed., *Confederate Collapse*, 43–44, 51.

3. Sykes, "Walthall's Brigade," 542; OR 31, pt. 2, 727; Dowd, "Lookout Mountain and Missionary Ridge," 399.

4. Watkins, *"Co. Aytch,"* 106.

5. OR 31, pt. 2, 753; Doyle, "Recollections of Chattanooga."

6. Watkins, *"Co. Aytch,"* 106–7.

7. OR 31, pt. 2, 679; Davis, *Breckinridge*, 397.

8. OR 31, pt. 2, 666.

9. Buck, "Cleburne and His Division," 469; Connelly, *Autumn of Glory*, 276; Dowd, "Lookout Mountain and Missionary Ridge," 399.

10. Davis, *Breckinridge*, 397.

11. Sykes, "Walthall's Brigade," 542.

12. OR 31, pt. 2, 666, 679.

13. Jarman, "History of Company K, Twenty-seventh Mississippi," 23; Green, *Johnny Green of the Orphan Brigade*, 111.

14. Watkins, *"Co. Aytch,"* 107–8.

15. Smith, *Autobiography*, 80–81; Hartzell, "Autobiography, Part 2," 107–8; Grant, "Chattanooga," 707–8; OR 31, pt. 2, 117; Wilson, *Under the Old Flag*, 1:302. Wilson asserts that Grant rode behind Sheridan's division in its twilight pursuit, but there is no evidence to support this claim, nor would such an act have been logical, given Grant's larger responsibilities.

16. Sheridan, *Personal Memoirs*, 1:315–16; OR 31, pt. 2, 80–83, 134–35.

17. *OR* 31, pt. 2, 116–17, 134.

18. Doyle, "Recollections of Chattanooga"; *OR* 31, pt. 2, 196; Sheridan, *Personal Memoirs*, 1:316–18.

19. *OR* 31, pt. 2, 45, 117; McKinney, *Education in Violence*, 298–99; McFeely, *Grant*, 149–50; Carl Sandburg, *Abraham Lincoln: The War Years*, 4 vols. (New York: Charles Scribners Sons, 1939), 4:477–79.

20. *OR* 31, pt. 2, 45.

21. Korn, *The Fight for Chattanooga*, 108–11; McFeely, *Grant*, 149.

22. Ford, *With the Rank and File*, 29–30; Ely diary, 25 November 1863, Thirty-sixth Illinois File, CCNMP; Hartzell, "Autobiography, Part 2," 108.

23. Hartzell, "Autobiography, Part 2," 108.

24. Ford, *With the Rank and File*, 30–31.

25. High, *Fifty-eighth Indiana*, 224.

26. Claver diary, 26 November 1863, IoHS.

27. High, *Fifty-eighth Indiana*, 223–24; Ely diary, 25 November 1863, Thirty-sixth Illinois File, CCNMP; Thomas W. Connelly, *History of the Seventieth Ohio Regiment, from Its Organization to Its Mustering Out* (Cincinnati: Peak Brothers, 1902), 65; Crandell diary, 25 November 1863, ISHL.

28. Ephraim Wagley, "Civil War Memoirs," 132–36, Paul Wagley Collection.

29. Donahower, "Narrative, Volume 2," 235–39, Donahower Papers, MnHS.

30. Hinman, *Sherman Brigade*, 461–62.

31. Frank Wolfe, "From the Foot of Lookout Mountain," *Civil War Times Illustrated* 22 (June 1983): 38–44.

## CHAPTER TWENTY-FIVE / THEY ARE CROWDING US

1. Sandburg, *Lincoln: The War Years*, 4:446–47, 477–79; *OR* 31, pt. 2, 25, 26.

2. *OR* 31, pt. 2, 350, 491; Sherman, *Memoirs*, 391.

3. *OR* 31, pt. 2, 491; J. M. Branum, "Contemporaneous Accounts of Events in the History of the Ninety-eighth Ohio," *National Tribune*, 17 January 1901; Oscar F. Harmon, *Life and Letters of Oscar Fitzalan Harmon, Colonel of the One Hundred Twenty-fifth Regiment Illinois Volunteers* (Trenton: MacCrelish and Quiqley Company, 1914), 125; Fahnestock diary, 26 November 1863, Eighty-sixth Illinois File, CCNMP.

4. *OR* 31, pt. 2, 350, 491; Harmon, *Life and Letters*, 125; Jackman, *Diary of a Confederate Soldier*, 96; Branum, "Contemporaneous Accounts of the 98th Ohio."

5. *OR* 31, pt. 2, 492.

6. Fahnestock diary, 26 November 1863, Eighty-sixth Illinois File, CCNMP; *OR* 31, pt. 2, 350.

7. Buck, "Cleburne and His Division," 470; *OR* 31, pt. 2, 350; Preston, "Memoirs of the War," 30, ADAH.

8. *OR* 31, pt. 2, 118–19, 319.

9. Ibid., 46.

10. Ibid., 91, 319; for more on the "most thoroughly hated" senior staff officer in the Union army, see Gerard Patterson, "Daniel Butterfield," *Civil War Times Illustrated* 12, no. 7 (November 1973): 12–19.

11. *OR* 31, pt. 2, 319; Peter McLain to the editor, in "Army Correspondence," Keithsburg (Ill.) *Observer*, 7 January 1864.

12. Mosman, *Rough Side of War*, 131–32; *OR* 31, pt. 2, 119, 319.

13. *OR* 31, pt. 2, 119, 319; Mosman, *Rough Side of War*, 132; McLain to the editor, "Army Correspondence," Keithsburg (Ill.) *Observer*, 7 January 1864; Federal Writers' Project, WPA, *Georgia: A Guide to Its Towns and Countryside* (Athens: University of Georgia Press, 1940), 180.

14. Brent journal, 26 November 1863, Palmer Collection of Bragg Papers, WRHS; *OR* 31, pt. 2, 680.

15. Watkins, *"Co. Aytch,"* 108; J. Stokes Vinson, "On Retreat from Missionary Ridge," *CV* 25, no. 1 (January 1917): 28; *OR* 31, pt. 2, 492–93; Jackman, *Diary of a Confederate Soldier*, 96.

16. Scribner, *How Soldiers Were Made*, 185–86.

17. Ibid., 186–88; John McElroy, "Army of the Cumberland and the Great Central Campaign: The Pursuit," *National Tribune*, 27 December 1906.

18. Scribner, *How Soldiers Were Made*, 188; Vinson, "On Retreat from Missionary Ridge," 28; Jackman, *Diary of a Confederate Soldier*, 96.

19. Vinson, "On Retreat from Missionary Ridge," 28; Jackman, *Diary of a Confederate Soldier*, 96.

20. Vinson, "On Retreat from Missionary Ridge," 28; Buck, "Cleburne and His Division," 471; McDonough, *Chattanooga*, 220.

21. *OR* 31, pt. 2, 680; McDonough, *Chattanooga*, 220.

22. Buck, "Cleburne and His Division," 470; Milner, "Lieut. Gen. Hardee," 362; Wiley A. Washburn, "Reminiscences of Confederate Service by Wiley A. Washburn," *Arkansas Historical Quarterly* 35 (Spring 1976): 60.

23. Milner, "Lieut. Gen. Hardee," 362; Buck, "Cleburne and His Division," 471.

## CHAPTER TWENTY-SIX / A SAD AFFAIR

1. Preston, "Memoirs of the War," 30, ADAH; Milner, "Lieut. Gen. Hardee," 362; Washburn, "Reminiscences of Confederate Service," 60.

2. *OR* 31, pt. 2, 320–21, 754; Buck, "Cleburne and His Division," 471.

3. *OR* 31, pt. 2, 754–55; Buck, "Cleburne and His Division," 471–72.

4. J. P. Austin, *The Blue and the Gray. Sketches of a Portion of the Unwritten History of the Great American Civil War. A Truthful Narrative of Adventure with Thrilling Reminiscences of the Great Struggle on Land and Sea* (Atlanta: Franklin Printing and Publishing Company, 1899), 115; Preston, "Memoirs of the War," 31, ADAH; *OR* 31, pt. 2, 321, 603, 755.

5. *OR* 31, pt. 2, 755; Austin, *Blue and the Gray*, 115.

6. Austin, *Blue and the Gray*, 116; *Thirteenth Illinois*, 383; *OR* 31, pt. 2, 320, 603; Preston, "Memoirs of the War," 31, ADAH.

7. *OR* 31, pt. 2, 604, 755; Buck, "Cleburne and His Division," 472; Preston, "Memoirs of the War," 31, ADAH; Washburn, "Reminiscences of Confederate Service," 35.

8. Austin, *Blue and the Gray*, 116; Preston, "Memoirs of the War," 31, ADAH.

9. *OR* 31, pt. 2, 321.

10. Ibid., 755.

11. Charles H. Kibler, *76th Ohio at Ringgold or Taylor's Ridge. A Little History* (N.p., n.d.), 2–3; *OR* 31, pt. 2, 608, 755; *Thirteenth Illinois*, 384; William H. H. Clark, *History in Catoosa County* (N.p., 1972), 232–33.

12. *OR* 31, pt. 2, 608; *Thirteenth Illinois*, 384; Kibler, *76th Ohio at Ringgold*, 2.

13. Elizabeth and Howell Purdue, *Pat Cleburne, Confederate General: A Definitive Biography* (Hillsboro, Tex.: Hill Jr. College Press, 1973), 153–54; *Thirteenth Illinois*, 385.

14. *Thirteenth Illinois*, 385–86; Clark, *Catoosa County*, 231; *OR* 31, pt. 2, 755, Purdue, *Pat Cleburne*, 154.

15. *Thirteenth Illinois*, 386–87.

16. *OR* 31, pt. 2, 757; *Thirteenth Illinois*, 386; Buck, "Cleburne and His Division," 473.

17. Kibler, *76th Ohio at Ringgold*, 3; *OR* 31, pt. 2, 608; Charles Dana Miller, "A Narrative of the Services of Brevet Major Charles Dana Miller in the War of the Great Rebellion, 1861–1865," 68, Civil War Collection, TSLA.

18. *OR* 31, pt. 2, 604, 616, 756.

19. "General Polk's Report of Battle of Taylor's Ridge," *SHSP* 8 (1880): 590; "Report of General M. P. Lowrey of Battle of Taylor's Ridge," *SHSP* 9 (1881 ): 63–64; Clark, *Catoosa County*, 232–33.

20. *OR* 31, pt. 2, 608, 756; Kibler, *76th Ohio at Ringgold*, 4–5; Miller, "Narrative of Services," 68, CWC, TSLA; Willison, *Reminiscences of a Boy's Service*, 78–79.

21. *OR* 31, pt. 2, 403; Skinner, *Pennsylvania at Chickamauga and Chattanooga*, 84.

22. *OR* 31, pt. 2, 616; Skinner, *Pennsylvania at Chickamauga and Chattanooga*, 84.

23. *OR* 31, pt. 2, 616–17.

24. Skinner, *Pennsylvania at Chickamauga and Chattanooga*, 84.

25. *OR* 31, pt. 2, 616–17; "Polk's Report," 590–91.

26. Skinner, *Pennsylvania at Chickamauga and Chattanooga*, 84; Wilder, *History of Company C*, 39; *OR* 31, pt. 2, 604, 756.

27. *OR* 31, pt. 2, 616–17.

28. Ibid., 404, 756.

29. Collins, *149th Regt. N.Y. Vol.*, 215–16; *OR* 31, pt. 2, 405; Eddy, *Sixtieth New York*, 311–12.

30. Collins, *149th Regt. N.Y. Vol.*, 216.

31. *OR* 31, pt. 2, 757.

32. Ibid., 120–21, 149, 322.

33. Ibid., 122, 757; Davis, *Breckinridge*, 392–93; Smith, "Holocaust Holiday," 38–39.

## CHAPTER TWENTY-SEVEN / THE FRUITS ARE BITTER

1. George L. Wood, *The Seventh Regiment: A Record* (New York: James Miller, 1865), 167; OR 31, pt. 2, 70; Harmon, *Life and Letters*, 120.

2. Abraham Lincoln, *The Collected Works of Abraham Lincoln*, ed. Roy Basler, 8 vols. (New Brunswick, N.J.: Rutgers University Press, 1953), 7:30.

3. OR 31, pt. 2, 35, 46–47; Sherman *Memoirs*, 391.

4. OR 31, pt. 2, 48; Sherman, *Memoirs*, 391.

5. OR 31, pt. 2, 49–50, 71–72, 137–38, and pt. 3, 270; Sherman, *Memoirs*, 391–93.

6. Sherman, *Memoirs*, 393; Osborn, "Eleventh Corps in Tennessee," 374.

7. Osborn, "Eleventh Corps in Tennessee," 374; Philip Cornelius Hays, "Campaigning in East Tennessee," in *Military Essays and Recollections. Papers Read before the Commandery of the State of Illinois, Military Order of the Loyal Legion of the United States*, vol. 4 (Chicago: Cozzens and Beaton, 1907), 336; Woodworth, *Davis and His Generals*, 253.

8. Sherman, *Memoirs*, 393–94.

9. Lincoln, *Collected Works*, 7:35, 53; Grant, "Chattanooga," 711.

10. Grant to Elihu B. Washburn, 2 December 1863, Grant Papers, ISHL.

11. "Statement of the Strength of the Army of Tennessee in the Engagements before Chattanooga, the Losses in Those Engagements, the Strength of the Army on Its Arrival at Dalton, Its Strength on the 20th Inst., and the Increase of Effective Strength Since the Retreat and to the 20th of December," Confederate Collection, TSLA; OR 31, pt. 2, 36.

12. OR 31, pt. 2, 81, 88.

13. Shelby Foote, *The Civil War: A Narrative. Fredericksburg to Meridian* (New York: Random House, 1963), 859.

14. OR 31, pt. 2, 34; Grant, "Chattanooga," 705–7; Wood, "Battle of Missionary Ridge," 42; John Shellenberger, "Missionary Ridge, as Seen by an Officer of the Sixty-fourth Ohio," *National Tribune*, 20 May 1886.

15. Wilson, *Under the Old Flag*, 1:304–7; Warner, *Generals in Blue*, 181.

16. Hay, "Battle of Chattanooga," 140–41.

17. OR 31, pt. 2, 682.

18. Ibid., 35, 744; Hallock, *Bragg*, 145–46.

19. John Whitten Journal, 27 November 1863, John Huelskamp Collection.

20. OR 31, pt. 2, 71–72.

21. Ibid., 682; Brent journal, 28–29 November 1863, Palmer Collection of Bragg Papers, WRHS.

22. OR 31, pt. 2, 681.

23. Ibid., 666.

24. Bragg to Davis, 1 December 1863, Palmer Collection of Bragg Papers,

WRHS; Davis, *Breckinridge*, 398; Horn, ed., *Tennessee's War 1861–1865*, 243; McDonough, *Chattanooga*, 225–26.

25. *OR* 31, pt. 2, 775–76; Brent journal, 2 December 1863; Connelly, *Autumn of Glory*, 277; Roy, "Sketch," 17.

26. B. F. Carter to his wife, 5 December 1863, Pope-Carter Family Papers, UNC; Thomas Walker Davis Diary, 79, CWC, TSLA.

27. Davis diary, 79, Civil War Collection, TSLA; Liddell, *Liddell's Record*, 164.

28. Liddell, *Liddell's Record*, 160.

# BIBLIOGRAPHY

## MANUSCRIPTS

Alabama Department of Archives and History, Montgomery
    W. E. Preston Memoirs
    T. B. Roy Manuscript
    Thirty-seventh Alabama Infantry Papers
    Thirty-third Alabama Infantry Papers
Bowling Green State University, Bowling Green, Ohio
    Alexander Family Papers
    Searles Family Papers
Champaign County Historical Archives, Urbana, Illinois
    James G. Watson Diary
Chicago Historical Society
    John Rawlins Papers
Chickamauga and Chattanooga National Military Park Library
    Francis M. Carlisle Autobiography
    William Ross Glisan Diary
    Andrew Jackson Neal Letters
    William Ralston Talley Autobiography
    Robert Watson Diary
    Lyman S. Widney Letters
    Miscellaneous Correspondence, Historical and Regimental Files
Cincinnati Historical Society
    Cist Family Papers
William R. Perkins Library, Duke University, Durham, North Carolina
    John Magee Diary
    Eugene Marshall Papers
    Pope-Carter Family Papers
    John W. Reese Papers
    Samuel Hollingsworth Stout Papers

Emory University, Robert W. Woodruff Library, Atlanta
  John Bratton Papers
  Honnell Family Papers
  A. J. Neal Papers
The Historic New Orleans Collection, Kemp and Leila Williams Foundation, New Orleans
  William C. D. Vaught Collections
Illinois State Historical Library, Springfield
  James Cole Papers
  Hiram Crandell Diary
  Henry G. Davidson Papers
  U. S. Grant Papers
  J. L. Locke Letters
  Richard Yates Papers
Indiana Historical Society, Smith Memorial Library, Indianapolis
  Civil War File of Thomas Small
Indiana State Library, Indianapolis
  George H. Martling Diary
Iowa Historical Society, Des Moines
  Charles H. Claver Diaries
  William T. Coffman Sketch
  Robert W. Henry Papers
  George M. Shearer Papers
  (Mrs.) James Robinson Papers
  Thomas Smout Recollections, Haynes Collection
  E. Burk Wylie Letters
Library of Congress, Washington, D.C.
  Braxton Bragg Papers
  Peter B. Kellenberger Letters
  John Patton Memoirs
Michigan Historical Collections, Bentley Historical Library, University of Michigan, Ann Arbor
  Calvin Ainsworth Diary
Minnesota Historical Society, St. Paul
  Levi B. Aldrich Papers
  John Reed Beatty Papers
  Judson Bishop Papers
  Jeremiah Chester Donahower Papers
  Billings D. Sibley Papers
Mississippi Department of Archives and History, Jackson
  Robert A. Jarman Manuscript
  Edward Cary Walthall Papers
New York Public Library, New York City
  Ezra Carman Papers
Ohio Historical Society, Columbus
  John Sanderson Letter Diary

Private Collections
        Stephen Calhoun Collection
                Battle Report of Allen Varner
        John Huelskamp Collection
                Jabez Banbury Diary
                Aaron Dunbar Journal
                John Whitten Journal
        Paul Wagley Collection
                Ephraim Wagley Civil War Memoirs
State Historical Society of Wisconsin, Madison
        E. A. Quiner Papers
Tennessee State Library and Archives, Nashville
        Benjamin Franklin Cheatham Papers
        Civil War Collection:
                Thomas Walker Davis Diary
                Charles Dana Miller Narrative
                Francis Mohrhardt Field Notes
                W. E. Yeatman Memoirs
                W. M. Pollard Diary
        Confederate Collection:
                Carroll Henderson Clark Memoirs
                James L. Cooper Memoirs
                John T. Drion Manuscript History of Fifth Tennessee Infantry
                Arthur Taylor Fielder Diary
                John H. Freeman Diary
                David George Godwin Letters
                John Ephraim Gold Questionnaire Data
                Joel T. Haley Letters
                John Harris Letters
                William E. Sloan Diary
                C. W. Tyler Manuscript History of Fiftieth Tennessee Infantry
        Federal Collection:
                Francis Mohrhardt Field Notes
                Richard J. McCadden Letters
        Alan Woodworth Diary
Tulane University, New Orleans
        George Brent Papers
        Civil War Papers: Reminiscences, Army of Tennessee
United States Army Military History Institute, Carlisle Barracks, Pennsylvania
        Civil War Miscellaneous Collection:
                John C. Breckinridge Message
                Rufus W. Daniel Diary
                Edward E. Schweitzer Diaries and Correspondence
                Jonathan Wood Memoirs
        Civil War Times Illustrated Collection:

Lyman Daniel Ames Diary
Fergus Elliott Letters
Samuel F. Foster Diary
Henry Henney Diary and Letters
Levi Wagner Reminiscences
Harrisburg Civil War Round Table Collection:
George P. Metcalf Reminiscences
David Nichol Diary
Richard F. Mann Papers:
William Stahl Diary
Wiley Sword Collection:
Andrew McCormick Letter
University of North Carolina, Southern Historical Collection, Chapel Hill
James Patton Anderson Papers
Pope-Carter Family Papers
University of South Carolina, South Caroliniana Library, Columbia
James Nance Papers
J. H. Steinmeyer Diary
Western Reserve Historical Society, Cleveland
William J. Palmer Collection of Braxton Bragg Papers


NEWSPAPERS

Aberdeen (Mississippi) *Examiner*
*The Church Advocate* (Lancaster, Pennsylvania)
Hancock *Courier* (Findlay, Ohio)
Keithsburg (Illinois) *Observer*
Madison (Indiana) *Evening Courier*
New York *Times*
Noblesville (Indiana) *Republican-Ledger*
Ottawa (Illinois) *Free Trader*
Schuyler (Illinois) *Citizen*
Waukegan (Illinois) *Weekly Gazette*


NATIONAL TRIBUNE

The following articles from the *National Tribune*, the precursor of *Stars and Stripes*, were invaluable in my research. The stories and letters from Civil War veterans that appeared regularly in the *National Tribune* form an important body of primary sources for the Union side.

Adair, J. M. "The First on Mission Ridge." 31 December 1885.
Alban, K. J. "Charge of Mule Brigade." 22 February 1923.
Allen, Alfred. "Helping Hooker at Lookout." 8 March 1923.
Allspaugh, H. "Mission Ridge." 2 June 1887.
Ashbaugh, H. V. "Captured by Wheeler in the Sequatchie Valley." 28 May 1903.

Ashmore, H. H. "Around Chattanooga: The Stirring Days of the Latter Part of 1863." 9 November 1899.

B. L. T. "With the Wagon Train: Reminiscences of the Chattanooga Campaign." 27 December 1900.

Baker, N. M. "Wounding of General Giles A. Smith." 24 July 1902.

Banks, Charles. "How Hazen's Brigade Floated Down in Pontoon Boats and Established the Cracker Line." 12 May 1892.

Banks, George. "Storming the Ridge: Shot Down Carrying the Flag—Who Captured Two Rebel Guns." 20 July 1899.

Beach, John. "Lookout Mountain: An Energetic Argument in Favor of Proper Credit to Whitaker's Brigade." 22 January 1885.

Beebout, D. W. "Geary Greedy for Guns." 19 May 1904.

Benham, A. H. "Climbing Mission Ridge." 30 April 1925.

Bird, Samuel W. "Mission Ridge: Why They Charged without Orders." 18 February 1886.

Blundin, Lewis. "Above the Clouds: What a Pennsylvanian Knows about Lookout Mountain." 21 October 1886.

———. "Lookout Mountain: White Star Soldiers at Variance about the Battle." 17 September 1891.

———. "The White Star People: Comrade Blundin Again Brings His Gun into Position." 27 January 1887.

Bowen, O. C. "Don't Know Who Was There First." 18 February 1886.

Brandley, A. "The Cracker Line." 28 May 1885.

Bratty, J. M. "They All Got There First." 5 January 1885.

Brinkerhoff, A. M. "Lookout Mountain: Part Taken by Osterhaus' Division in the Battle." 28 November 1882.

Bunch, W. D. "Saw the Flag Wave." 23 August 1923.

Carlin, William P. "Military Memoirs." 23 April 1885.

Chaffee, James. "Craven-House Guns." 8 October 1891.

Chalaron, J. A. "At Missionary Ridge: Confederate Commander Writes of the Capture of Guns by Union Troops." 4 May 1899.

Conner, D. M. "Who Fought at Lookout." 21 June 1923.

Crammer, C. E. "Carried Flag Up Missionary Ridge." 4 August 1904.

Crowell, Silas. "Missionary Ridge: How 'Dutchy' Captured a Rebel Gun." 5 November 1889.

Curtiss, A. S. "Sherman's Men at Lookout." 26 July 1923.

De Bolt, Rezin S. "Sounded the Advance at Mission Ridge." 11 December 1924.

Dicks, Philip. "The Cracker Line." 30 April 1885

Doyle, William E. "Artillery at Mission Ridge." 19 June 1902.

———. "Recollections of Chattanooga: The Capture and Holding of a Gateway of the Rebellion." 29 June 1899.

Edsall, W. H. "The First on Mission Ridge." 25 February 1886.

Fowler, James A. "The Most Curious Battle of the War." 9 December 1926.

Hammond, Robert. "The Charge of a Corps." 17 August 1899.

Hayworth, George B. "Safety First." 12 July 1923.

478 / Bibliography

Heil, Leonard A. "Break on Mission Ridge." 29 March 1923.

Herriman, A. "The Boat at Brown's Ferry." 3 May 1923.

Hibbard, E. T. "Wagner's Brigade: How It Climbed Mission Ridge Along with the Rest of the Boys." 6 October 1887.

Hicks, Owen. "Above the Clouds: More Backing for Comrade Blundin and the White Star." 31 March 1887.

Hill, Charles W. "At Brown's Ferry." 1 March 1923.

——. "The Boat at Brown's Ferry." 13 September 1923.

——. "Who Fought at Lookout." 24 May 1923.

Hill, H. H. "The Second Minnesota: Reminiscences of Four Years' Service at the Front." 13 and 20 July 1899.

Hobart, Thomas. "Lookout Mountain: Concerning Two Cannon Captured at the Craven House." 24 December 1891.

Jones, Jesse. "Lookout Mountain: An Account of the Battle by a Fighting Parson." 24 October 1889.

——. "Lookout Mountain: Echoes from Comrades about the Fight above the Clouds." 25 June 1891.

——. "Lookout Mountain: What Took Place after the Battle above the Clouds." 7 May 1891.

Jordan, F. G. "First on Missionary Ridge." 14 June 1888.

Kessler, W. L. "At Missionary Ridge." 17 October 1901.

——. "Capturing Two Guns: The Seventy-ninth Illinois Version of the Taking of 'Lady Breckinridge' and 'Lady Buckner.'" 15 February 1900.

Kiser, Christopher. "Tunnel Hill: Severe Fighting by Raum's Brigade to Turn the Rebel Right on Mission Ridge." 2 June 1904.

Laing, G. J. "Lookout Mountain." 20 September 1923.

Lammey, A. "The Eighty-eighth Illinois: Another Regiment Claims to Have Planted Its Flag First on Missionary Ridge." 12 November 1891.

Long, D. E. "Sherman at Lookout." 19 July 1923.

Lucas, E. C. "Lookout Mountain: The Gallant Part Taken by the 8th Ky." 10 June 1886.

Lytle, J. D. "Capturing Two Cannon." 6 April 1899.

McCook, Anson, and R. P. Speer. "In a Tight Place at Lookout." 27 December 1923.

McElroy, John. "Army of the Cumberland and the Great Central Campaign: The Pursuit." 27 December 1906.

McKinnie, John D. "Fighting around Chattanooga." 14 October 1926.

McMahon, James. "Those Captured Cannon." 27 July 1899.

Maine, George. "At Tunnel Hill." 27 July 1911.

Mathewson, A. M. "Lookout Mountain: Another Account of Who Captured the Guns and Planted the Flag." 20 August 1891.

Moore, Joseph. "After the Battle: Removing the Wounded from Ringgold to Chattanooga." 26 November 1891.

Moore, Sheldon. "The 111th Pa.: A Comrade Tells How It, Too, Had a Hand in the Fight on Lookout." 5 May 1887.

Moore, W. H. "The Thirtieth Iowa at Lookout Mountain." 4 August 1887.

Mount, E. C. "Osterhaus's Division: It Had a Hand in the Battle of Lookout Mountain." 10 February 1887.

Murphy, Thomas. "Lookout Mountain: The Struggle Again Over the Guns Near the Craven House." 30 July 1891.

Nash, William R. "Missionary Ridge: Another Claim as to Who Was First up the Big Hill." 3 November 1892.

Paxton, James R. "Osterhaus at Lookout." 23 August 1923.

Powell, Eugene. "The Battle above the Clouds: Ordered to Make a Demonstration, Gen. Geary Bridges Lookout Creek and Assails the Heights." 6 August 1901.

Radcliffe, Charles K. "The Fighting at Lookout." 14 June 1923.

Raum, Green B. "With the Western Army: Relief of Rosecrans." 20 March 1902.

———. "With the Western Army: Opening the Cracker Line." 27 March 1902.

———. "With the Western Army: Sherman's March to Chattanooga." 3 April 1902.

———. "With the Western Army: The First Day's Fight at Chattanooga," 10 April 1902.

———. "With the Western Army: Battle of Lookout Mountain." 17 April 1902.

———. "With the Western Army: Battle of Missionary Ridge." 24 April 1902.

———. "With the Western Army: Fight on Tunnel Hill." 1 May 1902.

———. "With the Western Army: The Army of the Cumberland at Missionary Ridge." 8 May 1902.

———. "With the Western Army: Pursuit of Bragg's Army and Relief of Knoxville." 15 May 1902.

Reynolds, T. P. M. "Lookout Mountain: A Brilliant Account of the Exploits of Osterhaus' Division." 14 July 1883.

Richardson, John L. "At Missionary Ridge." 14 September 1899.

Rickards, William. "Above the Clouds." 1 January 1885.

Ridenour, J. B. "Ridenour Speaks." 21 July 1892.

Scott, Launcelot I. "Brown's Ferry Expedition: Shortening the Ration Line and Helping Save the Starving Army at Chattanooga." 25 January 1912.

Shellenberger, John. "The Capture of 'Lady Buckner' and 'Lady Breckinridge' of Cobb's Battery." 16 May 1901.

Smith, James E. "Confederate Confession: Some Startling and Almost Incredible Statements about Missionary Ridge." 22 October 1903.

Southerland, D. J. "Gen. Rosecrans's Cracker Line." 24 October 1901.

Stork, W. L. "Lookout Mountain: A Plain Statement from One of Gen. Geary's Staff Officers." 19 May 1907.

Taylor, J. E. "Lookout Mountain." 2 January 1890.

Thompson, A. "The 1st Ohio Cav.: What They Accomplished During the Battle at Lookout Mountain." 4 February 1892.

Thompson, F. M. "Lookout Mountain, and the Part the 8th Ky. Took There." 16 September 1886.

Todd, C. M. "Mission Ridge: Its Capture One of the Greatest Feats in History." 9 December 1920.
Todd, H. D. "Up the Ladder at Lookout." 22 February 1923.
Towling, I. B. "Battling above the Clouds." 12 April 1900.
———. "Missionary Ridge: Captain Webster Still Insists That the Night was Very Bright." 7 July 1892.
Voss, F. "On Lookout Mountain." 14 June 1923.
Walker, James. "Through a Bullet Storm." 17 May 1923.
Walton, J. E. "Mission Ridge: The Thirtieth Ohio's Gallantry in the Battle." 1 November 1888.
Welsh, Asbury. "Up the Ridge." 28 June 1900.
Wiley, Aquila. "Sherman's Inaction." 16 April 1891.
Wilson, John. "Lookout Mountain: Captain Wilson's Claim to Planting the First Flag." 11 June 1891.
Yiro, W. H. "Lookout Mountain, One of the Fortieth Ohio Comes to the Front." 19 September 1889.
Zat, William. "Lookout Mountain: Who Planted the First Flag on the Fort?" 12 September 1887.

## OFFICIAL DOCUMENTS

*The War of the Rebellion: A Compilation of the Official Records of the Union and Confederate Armies.* Washington, D.C.: U.S. Government Printing Office, 1880–1901.

## ADDRESSES, ARTICLES, AND ESSAYS

*Address to the 73rd Regiment Illinois Volunteer Infantry, by Colonel James F. Jaquess, at a Reunion Held in Springfield, Illinois, October 8th–10th, 1890.* N.p., n.d.
Atkinson, John. "The Story of Lookout Mountain and Missionary Ridge." In *War Papers Read before the Michigan Commandery of the Military Order of the Loyal Legion of the United States. Volume 2. From December 7, 1893, to May 5, 1898.* Detroit: James H. Stone, 1898.
"The Battle of Lookout Mountain." *Southern Bivouac* 2 (1883/1884): 97–105, 193–201.
Bingham, John H. "How Errors Become Historic Facts." *Confederate Veteran* 12, no. 4 (April 1904): 172–73.
Bishop, J. W., et al. *In the Matter of the Request by Survivors of Van Derveer's Brigade for Restoration of Its Historical Tablet to Its Original and Proper Position on De Long Point, Missionary Ridge, Before the Chickamauga and Chattanooga National Park Commission. Brief of the Survivors of the Second Minnesota Regiment.* Saint Paul, Minn.: N.p., 1911.
———. *In the Matter of the Request for Removal of the Second Minnesota Monument from De Long Point to Strock Knob, Before the Chicka-*

*mauga and Chattanooga Park Commission. Brief of the Survivors of the Minnesota Monument Commission.* N.p., n.d.

Blakely, Archibald. *Address Delivered by Colonel Archibald Blakely, on Sherman Heights, Missionary Ridge, Chattanooga, Tennessee, at the Dedication of the Monument Erected by the Commonwealth of Pennsylvania in Memory of Her Seventy-third Infantry Regiment, November 7, 1903.* N.p., n.d.

"The Bond of Heroism. Blending of the Blue and Gray." *Southern Historical Society Papers* 22 (1894): 67–69.

Brewer, George E. "Why Missionary Ridge Was Lost by the Confederates." *Confederate Veteran* 22, no. 5 (May 1914): 232.

Brinton, Daniel. "Dr. Daniel Garrison Brinton with the Army of the Cumberland." *Pennsylvania Magazine of History and Biography* 90 (October 1966): 466–90.

Buck, Irving A. "Cleburne and His Division at Missionary Ridge and Ringgold Gap." *Southern Historical Society Papers* 8 (1880): 464–75.

Butterfield, Daniel. *Major General Joseph Hooker and the Troops from the Army of the Potomac at Wauhatchie, Lookout Mountain and Chattanooga . . . Address by Major General Daniel Butterfield at the Battlefield Dedication Ceremonies at Chattanooga, September 18, 1895.* New York: Exchange Printing Company, 1896.

Carnes, W. W. "At Missionary Ridge." *Confederate Veteran* 28, no. 5 (May 1920): 185.

Cheavens, Henry Martyn. "A Missouri Confederate in the Civil War." *Missouri Historical Review* 57 (October 1962): 16–52.

Coker, J. L. "Battle of Lookout Valley or Wauhatchie." *Confederate Veteran* 18, no. 10 (October 1910): 473.

Cooper, James Litton. "The Civil War Diary of Captain James Litton Cooper, September 30, 1861 to January, 1865." *Tennessee Historical Quarterly.* 15, no. 2 (June 1956): 141–75.

———. "Service with the Twentieth Tennessee Regiment." *Confederate Veteran* 23, no. 4 (April 1925): 138–39.

"Correspondence Relating to Chickamauga and Chattanooga." In *Papers of the Military Historical Society of Massachusetts. Volume VIII. The Mississippi. Tennessee, Georgia, Alabama, 1861–1864,* 247–72. Boston: Military Historical Society of Massachusetts, 1910.

Cubbison, Douglas R. "Midnight Engagement: Geary's White Star Division at Wauhatchie, Tennessee, October 28–29, 1863." *Civil War Regiments* 3, no. 2 (1993): 70–101.

Doan, Isaac C. *Reminiscences of the Chattanooga Campaign, a Paper Read at the Reunion of Company B, Fortieth Ohio Infantry, at Xenia, O., August 22, 1894, by Sergeant Isaac C. Doan.* Richmond, Ind.: N.p., 1894.

Dodson, William C. *The Battle of Missionary Ridge: An Address.* N.p, n.d.

Donahower, Jeremiah C. *Lookout Mountain and Missionary Ridge. Paper Read before Minnesota Commandery of the Loyal Legion U.S. December 13th, 1898.* St. Paul: N.p., 1898

Dowd, W. F. "Lookout Mountain and Missionary Ridge." *Southern Bivouac* 1 (1885/1886): 397–99.

"General Polk's Report of Battle of Taylor's Ridge." *Southern History Society Papers* 8 (1880): 590.

Gow, June I. "Chiefs of Staff in the Army of Tennessee under Braxton Bragg." *Tennessee Historical Quarterly* 27 (1968): 355–59.

Green, John P. *The Movement of the 11th and 12th Army Corps from the Potomac to the Tennessee. Read by John P. Green before the Commandery of the State of Pennsylvania, Military Order of the Loyal Legion of the United States, March 23d, 1892*. Philadelphia: Allen, Lane and Scott's Printing House, 1892.

Greene, Albert R. *From Bridgeport to Ringgold by Way of Lookout Mountain*. Providence, R.I.: By the Society, 1890.

Griffin, Daniel. "A Hoosier Regiment at Chattanooga." *Tennessee Historical Quarterly* 22 (September 1963): 280–87.

Hay, Thomas Robson. "The Battle of Chattanooga." *Georgia Historical Quarterly* 8 (1924): 121–41.

Hays, Philip Cornelius. "Campaigning in East Tennessee." In *Military Essays and Recollections. Papers Read before the Commandery of the State of Illinois, Military Order of the Loyal Legion of the United States*, 4:318–47. Chicago: Cozzens and Beaton, 1907.

Hemming, Charles. "A Confederate Odyssey." *American Heritage* 36 (December 1984): 69–84.

———. "Inquiry for an Alabama Soldier." *Confederate Veteran* 15, no. 10 (October 1907): 457.

Henry, H. W. "Little War-Time Incidents." *Confederate Veteran* 22, no. 7 (July 1914): 306–7.

Hill, Andrew Malone. "Personal Recollections of Andrew Malone Hill." *Alabama Historical Quarterly* 20 (Spring 1958): 85–91.

Homer, J. W. "They Were Not Cowards." *Confederate Veteran* 24, no. 10 (October 1916): 455.

Howard, Oliver Otis. "Chattanooga." *Atlantic Monthly* 38 (1876): 203–19.

———. "Grant at Chattanooga." In *Personal Recollections of the War of the Rebellion: Addresses Delivered before the New York Commandery of the Loyal Legion of the United States, 1883–1891*, 1:244–57. New York: By the Commandery, 1891.

Howe, Daniel Wait, and Flavius J. Van Vorhis. *In the Matter of the Location Where Beatty's Brigade of Wood's Division of 4th Army Corps Reached the Crest of Missionary Ridge on November 25, 1863, Before the Commissioners of Chickamauga and Chattanooga National Park*. N.p., n.d.

———. *In the Matter of the Location Where Beatty's Brigade of Wood's Division of 4th Army Corps Reached the Crest of Missionary Ridge on November 25, 1863. Reply Brief. Before the Commissioners of Chickamauga and Chattanooga National Park*. N.p., 1911.

———. *In the Matter of the Location Where Beatty's Brigade of Wood's Division of 4th Army Corps Reached the Crest of Missionary Ridge* on *November 25, 1863. Second Reply Brief. Before the Commissioners of Chickamauga and Chattanooga National Park.* N.p., 1911.

————. *In the Matter of the Location Where Beatty's Brigade of Wood's Division of 4th Army Corps Reached the Crest of Missionary Ridge on November 25, 1863. Summary and Recapitulation. Reply. Before the Commissioners of Chickamauga and Chattanooga National Park.* N.p., 1911.

Huelskamp, John W. "Fearless, Yet Forgotten: Colonel Holden Putnam and the 93rd Illinois Volunteer Infantry." Unpublished manuscript, courtesy of author.

Jenney, William Le Baron. "With Sherman and Grant from Memphis to Chattanooga. A Reminiscence." In *Military Essays and Recollections. Papers Read before the Commandery of the State of Illinois, Military Order of the Loyal Legion of the United States,* 4:215–37. Chicago: Cozzens and Beaton, 1907.

Key, Thomas J. "Concerning Battle of Missionary Ridge." *Confederate Veteran* 12, no. 8 (August 1904): 390.

Kniffin, Gilbert C. *Military Order of the Loyal Legion of the United States, Commandery of the District of Columbia. War Papers, 37. The Army of the Cumberland at Missionary Ridge . . . Read at the State Meeting of December 5, 1900.* N.p., n.d.

Leland, J. D. "Capt. B. F. Eddins—A Tribute." *Confederate Veteran* 40, no. 2 (February 1932): 49–52.

Livermore, Thomas. "The Siege and Relief of Chattanooga." In *Papers of the Military Historical Society of Massachusetts. Volume VIII. The Mississippi Valley. Tennessee, Georgia, Alabama, 1861–1864,* 273–340. Boston: Military Historical Society of Massachusetts, 1910.

Livingood, James W. "Chattanooga's Crutchfields and the Famous Crutchfield House." *Civil War Times Illustrated* 20 (November 1981): 20–25.

"Maney's Brigade at Missionary Ridge." *Southern Bivouac* 2 (1883/84): 298–305, 345–48.

Meigs, Montgomery C. *The Three Days' Battle of Chattanooga, 23d, 24th, 25th November, 1863. An Unofficial Dispatch from General Meigs, Quartermaster of the United States, to the Hon. E. M. Stanton, Secretary of War.* New York: U.S. Sanitary Commission, 1864.

Milner, W. J. "Lieutenant General William Joseph Hardee." *Confederate Veteran* 22, no. 8 (August 1914): 360–64.

Moore, J. C. "Battle of Lookout Mountain." *Confederate Veteran* 6, no. 9 (September 1898): 426–29.

————. "Some Confederate War Incidents." *Confederate Veteran* 12, no. 3 (March 1904): 116–17.

Morgan, William A. "Brown's Ferry." In *War Talks in Kansas: Papers Read before the Commandery of Kansas, Military Order of the Loyal Legion of the United States,* 1:343–50. Kansas City, Mo.: Franklin Hudson, 1906.

————. "Hazen's Brigade at Missionary Ridge." In *War Talks in Kansas: Papers Read before the Commandery of Kansas, Military Order of the*

*Loyal Legion of the United States,* 1:271–75. Kansas City, Mo.: Franklin Hudson, 1906.

Munhall, Leander. *The Chattanooga Campaign, An Address Delivered before the Loyal Legion, Commandery of Pennsylvania, May 7, 1902.* N.p., n.d.

Osborn, Hartwell. "The Eleventh Corps in East Tennessee." In *Military Essays and Recollections: Papers Read before the Commandery of the State of Illinois, Military Order of the Loyal Legion of the United States,* 4:348–78. Chicago: Cozzens and Beaton, 1907.

Parsons, E. B. "Missionary Ridge." In *War Papers Read before the Commandery of the State of Wisconsin, Military Order of the Loyal Legion of the United States,* 1:189–200. Milwaukee: Burdick, Armitage, and Allen, 1891.

Patterson, Gerard. "Daniel Butterfield." *Civil War Times Illustrated,* 12, no. 7 (November 1973), 12–19.

Pickett, W. D. "Dead Angle—Rules for Burial of Dead." *Confederate Veteran* 16, no. 5 (May 1908): 230–31.

Pirtle, Alfred. "Three Memorable Days—A Letter from Chattanooga, November, 1863." In *Sketches of War History, 1861 to 1865. Papers Prepared for the Commandery of the State of Ohio, Military Order of the Loyal Legion of the United States, 1903–1908,* 6:35–46. Cincinnati: Monfort, 1908.

Pollard, W. M. "Brief History of the First Tennessee." *Confederate Veteran* 17, no. 11 (November 1909): 543–44.

Polley, J. B. "A Battle 'Above the Clouds.'" *Confederate Veteran* 5, no. 3 (March 1897): 104–6.

Porter, James D. "Hooker Slandered Cheatham's Division." *Confederate Veteran* 12, no. 11 (November 1904): 523.

Powell, Eugene. "An Incident of the Capture of Lookout Mountain." *Historical and Philosophical Society of Ohio Publications* (1926): 44–52.

Reams, R. W. "Brief War Incidents." *Confederate Veteran* 22, no. 9 (September 1914): 400.

"Report of General M. P. Lowrey of Battle of Taylor's Ridge." *Southern Historical Society Papers* 9 (1881): 63–64.

*Report of the Chickamauga and Chattanooga National Park Commission on the Claim of Gen. John B. Turchin and Others That in the Battle of Chattanooga His Brigade Captured the Position on Missionary Ridge known as the De Long Place, and the Decision of the Secretary of War Thereupon.* N.p., 1907?

Reynolds, J. E. "Heroism of Walthall's Mississippians." *Confederate Veteran* 15, no. 8 (August 1907): 365.

Roper, John S. "An Interesting Account of the Battle of Missionary Ridge." *Journal of the Illinois State Historical Society* 6 (1914): 496–505.

Rumpel, John. "Ohiowa Soldier." *Annals of Iowa* 36 (Fall 1961): 110–48.

"Second-Hand Pictures for Silly Southerners." *Confederate Veteran* 1, no. 12 (December 1893): 377–78.

Shanks, William F. G. "Lookout Mountain, and How We Won It." *Harper's New Monthly Magazine* 37 (June 1868): 4–15.

Shellenberger, John. "With Sheridan's Division at Missionary Ridge." In *Sketches of War History, 1861–1865. Papers Prepared for the Ohio Commandery of the Loyal Legion of the United States, 1890–1896, Volume 4,* 51–67. Cincinnati: Robert Clarke, 1896.

Simmons, J. W. "Heroic Mississippians." *Confederate Veteran* 5, no. 2 (February 1897): 73.

Sledge, G. W. "Battle of Missionary Ridge." *Confederate Veteran* 22, no. 2 (February 1914): 65.

Smith, William F. "An Historical Sketch of the Military Operations around Chattanooga, Tennessee, September 22 to November 27, 1863." In *Papers of the Military Historical Society of Massachusetts. Volume VIII. The Mississippi Valley. Tennessee, Georgia, Alabama, 1861–1864,* 149–247. Boston: Military Historical Society of Massachusetts, 1910.

———. *The Re-Opening of the Tennessee River Near Chattanooga, October, 1863, as Related by Major General George H. Thomas and the Official Record.* Wilmington, Del.: Press of Mercantile Printing Company, n.d.

Smith, William Wrenshall. "Holocaust Holiday." *Civil War Times Illustrated* 18, no. 6 (October 1979): 28–40.

Stephenson, P. D. "Missionary Ridge." *Confederate Veteran* 21, no. 11 (November 1913): 540–41.

———. *Missionary Ridge. A Paper Read before R. E. Camp, No. 1, of Richmond Virginia, February 21, 1913.* N.p., n.d.

Stewart, S. F. *General Turchin Vindicated. The Claim of His Brigade to the De Long Point of Missionary Ridge Is Finally Established by the Acting Secretary of War.* N.p., 1907.

———. *In the Matter of the Location on Missionary Ridge of the Tablets and Markers of the Brigades of Gen. S. Beatty and Gen. J. B. Turchin, Before the Chickamauga and Chattanooga National Park Commission. Brief of Turchin's Brigade. February 10, 1911.* N.p., 1911.

———. *In the Matter of the Location on Missionary Ridge of the Tablets and Markers of the Eleven Brigades Engaged in the Assault Nov. 25, 1863, Before the Chickamauga and Chattanooga National Park Commission. Brief of Turchin's Brigade in Reply to Brief of the Beatty Committee Received about March 5, 1911.* N.p., 1911.

———. *In the Matter of the Location on Missionary Ridge of the Tablets and Markers of the Eleven Brigades Engaged in the Assault Nov. 25, 1863, Before the Chickamauga and Chattanooga National Park Commission. Brief of Turchin's Brigade in Reply to the "Second Reply Brief" of the Beatty Committee, Received April 21, 1911, and to the Brief of the Minnesota Monument Commission, dated April 15, 1911.* N.p., 1911.

———. *In the Matter of the Location on Missionary Ridge of the Tablets and Markers of the Eleven Brigades Engaged in the Assault Nov. 25, 1863, Before the Chickamauga and Chattanooga National Park Com-*

mission. *Brief of Turchin's Brigade in Reply to Brief of the Beatty Committee Received about June 1, 1911.* N.p., 1911.

Sykes, Edward T. "Walthall's Brigade: A Cursory Sketch with Personal Experiences of Walthall's Brigade, Army of Tennessee, C.S.A., 1862–1865." *Publications of the Mississippi Historical Society, Centenary Series* 1 (1916): 477–623.

Trice, C. W. "At Missionary Ridge." *Confederate Veteran* 28, no. 2 (February 1920): 78.

Turner, Jim. "Jim Turner Co. G, 6th Texas Infantry, C.S.A. . . . ." *Texana* 12, no. 2 (1974): 149–78.

Vanscoy, Jacob. "Three Yankee Soldier-Brothers in the Battle of Chattanooga: Three Letters." *East Tennessee Historical Society Publications* 35 (1963): 100–105.

Vaughan, Turner. "Diary of Turner Vaughan, Co. C, 4th Alabama." *Alabama Historical Quarterly* 18 (Winter 1956): 573–601.

Vinson, J. Stokes. "On Retreat from Missionary Ridge." *Confederate Veteran* 25, no. 1 (January 1917): 28.

Walthall, Edward C. "Walthall on the Battle of Lookout." *Confederate Veteran* 6, no. 2 (December 1898): 562–64.

Washburn, Wiley A. "Reminiscences of Confederate Service by Wiley A. Washburn." *Arkansas Historical Quarterly* 35 (Spring 1976): 47–90.

Watkins, Samuel. "Battle of Missionary Ridge." *Southern Bivouac* 2 (1883/84): 49–58.

Willoughby, C. L. "Eclipse of Moon at Missionary Ridge." *Confederate Veteran* 21, no. 12 (December 1913): 590.

Wolfe, Frank. "From the Foot of Lookout Mountain." *Civil War Times Illustrated* 22 (June 1983): 38–44.

Wood, Thomas J. "The Battle of Missionary Ridge." In *Sketches of War History, 1861–1865. Papers Prepared for the Ohio Commandery of the Loyal Legion of the United States, 1890–1896, Volume 4,* 22–51. Cincinnati: Robert Clarke, 1896.

Wright, James W. A. "Bragg's Campaign around Chattanooga." *Southern Bivouac* 2 (1886/87): 461–68, 543–49.

## Personal Narratives, Memoirs, and Collected Works

Alexander, E. Porter. *Fighting for the Confederacy: The Personal Recollections of General Edward Porter Alexander.* Edited by Gary Gallagher. Chapel Hill: University of North Carolina Press, 1989.

Austin, J. P. *The Blue and the Gray. Sketches of a Portion of the Unwritten History of the Great American Civil War. A Truthful Narrative of Adventure with Thrilling Reminiscences of the Great Struggle on Land and Sea.* Atlanta: Franklin Printing and Publishing Company, 1899.

Barton, Thomas. *Autobiography of Dr. Thomas H. Barton . . . Including a History of the Fourth Regt. West Va. Vol. Inf'y.* Charleston, W. Va., 1890.

Bircher, William. *A Drummer Boy's Diary*. St. Paul: St. Paul Book and Stationery Company, 1889.

Blackburn, Theodore. *Letters from the Front: A Union "Preacher" Regiment (74th Ohio) in the Civil War*. Dayton, Ohio: Morningside, 1981.

Buell, Clarence, and Robert Johnson. *Battles and Leaders of the Civil War*. 4 vols. New York: Thomas Yoseloff, 1956.

Butler, Marvin. *My Story of the Civil War and the Underground Railroad*. Huntington, Calif.: United Brethren Pub. Est., 1914.

Byers, Samuel. *With Fire and Sword*. New York: Neale, 1911.

Cadwallader, Sylvanus. *Three Years with Grant, as Recalled by War Correspondent Sylvanus Cadwallader*. Edited by Benjamin Thomas. New York: Knopf, 1955.

Cavins, Aden G. *War Letters of Aden G. Cavins Written to His Wife Matilda Livingston Cavins*. Evansville, Ind.: Rosenthal-Kuebler Printing Company, n.d.

Collins, R. M. *Chapters from the Unwritten History of the War between the States; or, Incidents in the Life of a Confederate Soldier, in Camp, on the March, in the Great Battles, and in Prison*. St. Louis: Nixon-Jones Printing Company, 1893.

Connolly, James Austin. *Three Years in the Army of the Cumberland: The Letters and Diary of Major James A. Connolly*. Bloomington: Indiana University Press, 1959.

Coward, Asbury. *The South Carolinians: Colonel Asbury Coward's Memoirs*. New York: Vantage Press, 1968.

Dana, Charles A. *Recollections of the Civil War with the Leaders at Washington and in the Field in the Sixties*. New York: D. Appleton, 1902.

Davis, Jefferson. *Jefferson Davis, Constitutionalist: His Letters, Papers, and Speeches*. Edited by Dunbar Rowland. 10 volumes. Jackson, Miss.: Mississippi Department of Archives and History, 1923.

Dudley, Henry W. *Autobiography of Henry Walbridge Dudley*. Menasha, Wis.: George Banta, 1914.

Foote, Corydon. *With Sherman to the Sea: A Drummer Boy's Story of the Civil War*. New York: John Day, 1960.

Ford, Thomas J. *With the Rank and File. Incidents and Anecdotes During the War of the Rebellion, as Remembered by One of the Non-Commissioned Officers*. Milwaukee: Press of the Evening Wisconsin Company, 1898.

Grant, Ulysses S. *Personal Memoirs of U. S. Grant*. 2 vols. New York: Charles Webster, 1885–86.

Green, Johnny Williams. *Johnny Green of the Orphan Brigade: The Journal of a Confederate Soldier*. Lexington: University of Kentucky Press, 1956.

Haney, Milton. *Pentecostal Possibilities, or, the Story of My Life*. Chicago: Christian Witness Company, 1906.

Harmon, Oscar F. *Life and Letters of Oscar Fitzalan Harmon, Colonel of the One Hundred Twenty-fifth Regiment Illinois Volunteers*. Trenton: MacCrelish and Quiqley, 1914.

Hartzell, John Calvin. "The Autobiography of John Calvin Hartzell, Part II."

Edited by Thomas M. Hartzell. Unpublished manuscript in the possession of Thomas M. Hartzell.

Hazen, William. *A Narrative of Military Service*. Boston: Ticknor, 1885.

Inzer, John Washington. *The Diary of a Confederate Soldier*. Huntsville, Ala.: Strode, 1977.

Jackman, John. *Diary of a Confederate Soldier: John S. Jackman of the Orphan Brigade*. Columbia: University of South Carolina Press, 1990.

Jamison, Matthew H. *Recollections of Pioneer and Army Life*. Kansas City, Mo.: Hudson Press, 1911.

Jamison, Robert. *Letters and Recollections of a Confederate Soldier, 1860–1865*. Nashville: N.p., 1964.

Jones, Jenkin. *An Artilleryman's Diary*. Madison: Wisconsin Historical Commission, 1914.

Joyce, John A. *A Checkered Life*. Chicago: S. P. Rounds, 1883.

Kirkpatrick, George. *The Experiences of a Private Soldier in the Civil War*. Chicago: N.p., 1924.

Liddell, St. John Richardson. *Liddell's Record*. Edited by Nathaniel C. Hughes. Dayton, Ohio: Morningside, 1985.

Lincoln, Abraham. *The Collected Works of Abraham Lincoln*. Edited by Roy Basler. 8 vols. New Brunswick, N.J.: Rutgers University Press, 1953.

Longstreet, James. *From Manassas to Appomattox: Memoirs of the Civil War in America*. Philadelphia: J. B. Lippincott, 1896.

Mahan, James. *Memoirs of James Curtis Mahan*. Lincoln, Neb.: Franklin Press, 1919.

Manigault, Arthur. *A Carolinian Goes to War: The Civil War Narrative of Arthur Middleton Manigault, Brigadier General, C.S.A.* Columbia: University of South Carolina Press, 1983.

Marcoot, Maurice. *Five Years in the Sunny South: Reminiscences of Maurice Marcoot*. N.p., n.d.

Mathis, Ray. *In the Land of the Living: Wartime Letters by Confederates from the Chattahoochee Valley of Alabama and Georgia*. Troy, Ala.: Troy State University Press, 1981.

Maxwell, James Robert. *Autobiography of James Robert Maxwell of Tuscaloosa, Alabama*. New York: Greenburg, 1926.

Mixson, Frank M. *Reminiscences of a Private*. Columbia, S.C.: State Company, 1910.

Mosman, Chesley A. *The Rough Side of War: The Civil War Journal of Chesley A. Mosman*. Edited by Arnold Gates. Garden City, N.Y.: Basin, 1987.

Nisbet, James Cooper. *Four Years on the Firing Line*. Chattanooga: Imperial Press, 1915.

Paver, John M. *What I Saw from 1861 to 1864, Personnel Recollections of John M. Paver*. Indianapolis: Scott-Miller, 1906.

Peddy, George W. *Saddle Bag and Spinning Wheel: Being the Civil War Letters of George W. Peddy, M.D., Surgeon, 56th Georgia Volunteer Regiment, C.S.A. and His Wife, Kate Featherston Peddy*. Macon, Ga: Mercer University Press, 1984.

Porter, Horace. *Campaigning with Grant.* New York: Century Company, 1897.

Potter, John. *Reminiscences of the Civil War in the United States.* Oskaloosa, Iowa: Globe Press, 1897.

Robbins, Edward. *Civil War Experiences, 1862–1865.* Carthage, Mo.: N.p., 1919.

Ryder, John. *Reminiscences of Three Years' Service in the Civil War by a Cape Cod Boy.* New Bedford, Mass.: Reynolds, 1928.

Scribner, Benjamin. *How Soldiers Were Made; or, the War as I Saw It under Buell, Rosecrans, Thomas, Grant, and Sherman.* Chicago: Donohue and Henneberry, Printers, 1887.

Seaton, Benjamin M. *The Bugle Softly Blows: The Confederate Diary of Benjamin M. Seaton.* Waco, Tex.: Texian Press, 1965.

Sheridan, Philip Henry. *Personal Memoirs of P. H. Sheridan.* 2 vols. New York: Charles L. Webster, 1888.

Sherman, William Tecumseh. *Memoirs of General W. T. Sherman.* New York: Library of America, 1990.

Smith, Benjamin T. *Private Smith's Journal: Recollections of the Late War.* Chicago: R. R. Donnelly, 1963.

Smith, William F. *Autobiography of Major General William F. Smith, 1861–1864.* Dayton, Ohio: Morningside, 1990.

Toney, Marcus. *The Privations of a Private, the Campaign under Gen. R. E. Lee, the Campaign Under Gen. Stonewall Jackson, Bragg's Invasion of Kentucky, the Chickamauga Campaign, the Wilderness Campaign, Prison Life in the North . . .* Nashville: For the Author, 1905.

Tuttle, John. *The Union and the Civil War and John W. Tuttle . . .* Frankfort: Kentucky Historical Society, 1980.

Upson, Theodore. *With Sherman to the Sea: The Civil War Letters, Diaries and Reminiscences of Theodore F. Upson.* Baton Rouge: Louisiana State University Press, 1943.

Willison, Charles A. *Reminiscences of a Boy's Service with the 76th Ohio, in the Fifteenth Army Corps, under General Sherman, during the Civil War, by that "Boy" at Three Score.* Menasha, Wis.: George Banta, n.d.

Wilson, James H. *Under the Old Flag: Recollections of Military Operations in the War for the Union, the Spanish War, the Boxer Rebellion, etc.* 2 vols. New York: D. Appleton, 1912.

Wise, John S. *The End of an Era.* Boston: Houghton Mifflin, 1899.

Young, Joseph. *The Personal Letters of Captain Joseph Willis Young.* Bloomington, Ind.: Monroe County Historical Society, 1974.

Young, Lot D. *Reminiscences of a Soldier of the Orphan Brigade.* Paris, Ky., n.d.

## Unit Histories

Alexander, John. *History of the Ninety-seventh Regiment of Indiana Volunteer Infantry.* Terre Haute, Ind.: Moore and Langen, 1891.

Barnes, James, et al. *The Eighty-sixth Regiment, Indiana Volunteer Infantry: A Narrative of Its Services in the Civil War of 1861–1865.* Crawfordsville, Ind.: Journal Company, 1895.

Bennett, Lyman G. *History of the Thirty-sixth Regiment Illinois Volunteers during the War of the Great Rebellion.* Aurora, Ill.: Knickerbocker and Hodder, 1876.

Bishop, Judson. *The Story of a Regiment, Being a Narrative of the Services of the Second Regiment, Minnesota Veteran Volunteer Infantry, in the Civil War of 1861–1865.* St. Paul: N.p., 1890.

Boies, Andrew. *Record of the Thirty-third Massachusetts Volunteer Infantry.* Fitchburg, Mass.: Sentinel Printing Company, 1880.

Boyle, John R. *Soldiers True: The Story of the One Hundred and Eleventh Regiment Pennsylvania Veteran Volunteers, and of Its Campaigns in the War for the Union, 1861–1865.* New York: Eaton and Mains, 1903.

Brown, Alonzo. *History of the Fourth Regiment of Minnesota Infantry Volunteers during the Great Rebellion, 1861–1865.* St. Paul: Pioneer Press Company, 1892.

Brown, Thadeus C. S. *Behind the Guns: The History of Battery I, 2d Regiment Illinois Light Artillery.* Carbondale: Southern Illinois University Press, 1965.

Buck, Irving. *Cleburne and His Command.* Dayton: Morningside, 1982.

Burke, William. *The Military History of Kansas Regiments during the War for the Suppression of the Great Rebellion.* Leavenworth, Kans.: W. S. Burke, 1868.

Calkins, William Wirt. *The History of the One Hundred and Fourth Regiment of Illinois Volunteer Infantry, War of the Great Rebellion, 1862–1865.* Chicago: Donohue and Henneberry, 1895.

Canfield, Silas S. *History of the 21st Regiment Ohio Volunteer Infantry, in the War of the Rebellion.* Toledo: Vrooman, Anderson and Bateman, Printers, 1893.

Chase, John. *History of the Fourteenth History Regiment, O.V.V.I., from the Beginning of the War in 1861 to Its Close in 1865.* Toledo: St. John Printing House, 1881.

Cist, Henry M. *The Army of the Cumberland.* New York: Charles Scribner's Sons, 1882.

Clark, Charles T. *Opdycke Tigers, 125th O.V.I, a History of the Regiment and the Campaigns and Battle of the Army of the Cumberland.* Columbus, Ohio: Spahr and Glenn, 1895.

Coker, James L. *History of Company G, Ninth S.C. Regiment, Infantry, S.C. Army, and of Company E, Sixth S.C. Regiment, Infantry, S.C. Army.* Charleston, S.C.: Press of Walker, Evans, and Cogswell, 1899.

Collins, George K. *Memoirs of the 149th Regt. N.Y. Vol. Inft., 3rd Brig., 2d Div., 12th and 20th A.C.* Syracuse: By the Author, 1891.

Connelly, Thomas W. *History of the Seventieth Ohio Regiment, from Its Organization to Its Mustering Out.* Cincinnati: Peak Brothers, 1902.

Cope, Alexis. *The Fifteenth Ohio Volunteers and Its Campaigns, War of*

*1861–1865.* Columbus, Ohio: Press of the Edward T. Miller Company, 1916.

Cunningham, Sumner Archibald. *Reminiscences of the 41st Tennessee Regiment.* Shelbyville, Tenn.: N.p., 187–.

Davis, William C. *The Orphan Brigade: The Kentucky Confederates Who Couldn't Go Home.* Garden City, N.Y.: Doubleday, 1980.

Dodge, William. *History of the Old Second Division, Army of the Cumberland.* Chicago: Church and Goodman, 1864.

———. *A Waif of the War; or, the History of the Seventy-fifth Illinois Infantry . . .* Chicago: Church and Goodman, 1886.

Duke, John K. *History of the Fifty-third Regiment Ohio Volunteer Infantry, during the War of the Rebellion, 1861–1865.* Portsmouth, Ohio: Blade Printing Company 1900.

Dunkelman, Mark. *The Hardtack Regiment: An Illustrated History of the 154th Regiment, New York State Infantry Volunteers.* Rutherford, N.J.: Fairleigh Dickinson University Press, 1981.

Eddy, Richard. *History of the Sixtieth Regiment, New York State Volunteers.* Philadelphia: By the Author, 1864.

*Eighty-sixth Regiment, Indiana Volunteer Infantry, a Narrative of Its Services in the Civil War of 1861–1865.* Crawfordsville, Ind.: Journal Company, Printers, 1895.

Floyd, David B. *History of the Seventy-fifth Regiment of Indiana Infantry Volunteers, Its Organization, Campaigns, and Battles.* Philadelphia: Lutheran Publishing Society, 1893.

Frost, M. O. *Regimental History of the Tenth Missouri Volunteer Infantry.* Topeka, Kans.: M. O. Frost Printing Company, 1892.

Gibson, Joseph. *History of the Seventy-eighth Pennsylvania Volunteer Infantry.* Pittsburgh: Pittsburgh Printing Company, 1905.

Grecian, J. *History of the Eighty-third Regiment, Indiana Volunteer Infantry. For Three Years with Sherman.* Cincinnati: John F. Uhlhorn, Printer, 1865.

Hannaford, Ebenezer. *The Story of a Regiment, a History of the Campaigns, and Associations in the Field of the Sixth Regiment, Ohio Volunteer Infantry.* Cincinnati: By the Author, 1868.

Haynie, James. *The Nineteenth Illinois, a Memoir of a Regiment of Volunteer Infantry Famous in the Civil War of Fifty Years Ago for Its Drill, Bravery, and Distinguished Service.* Chicago: M. A. Donahue, 1912.

Head, Thomas. *Campaigns and Battles of the Sixteenth Regiment, Tennessee Volunteers.* Nashville: N.p., 1885.

Herr, George. *Episodes of the Civil War, Nine Campaigns in Nine States . . .* San Francisco: Bancroft, 1890.

High, Edwin C. *History of the Sixty-eighth Regiment Indiana Volunteer Infantry, 1862–1865, with a Sketch of E. A. King's Brigade, Reynold's Division, Thomas's Corps in the Battle of Chickamauga.* Metamora: Sixty-eighth Indiana Infantry Association, 1902.

Hinman, Wilbur F. *The Story of the Sherman Brigade: The Camp, the*

*March, the Bivouac, the Battle; and How the Boys Lived and Died during Four Years of Active Field Service.* Alliance, Ohio: Press of Daily Review, 1897.

*History of the Organization, Marches, Campings, General Services and Final Muster Out of Battery M, First Regiment of Illinois Light Artillery.* Princeton: Mercer and Dean, 1892.

*History of the Seventy-ninth Regiment Indiana Volunteer Infantry in the Civil War of Eighteen Sixty-one in the United States.* Indianapolis: Hollenbeck Press, 1899.

Horrall, Spillard. *History of the Forty-second Indiana Volunteer Infantry.* Chicago: Donahue and Company, 1892.

Horton, Joshua. *A History of the Eleventh Regiment (Ohio Volunteer Infantry), Containing the Military Record, so Far as it is Possible to Obtain It, of Each Officer and Enlisted Man of the Command, a List of Deaths, an Account of the Veterans, Incidents of the Field and Camp, Names of the Three Months' Volunteers.* Dayton, Ohio: Horton and Teverbaugh, 1866.

Hurst, Samuel H. *Journal-History of the Seventy-third Ohio Volunteer Infantry.* Chillicothe, Ohio: N.p., 1866.

Keil, Frederick W. *Thirty-fifth Ohio, a Narrative of Service from August 1861 to 1864.* Ft. Wayne, Ind.: Archer, Housh and Company, 1894.

Kerwood, Asbury L. *Annals of the Fifty-seventh Regiment Indiana Volunteers: Marches, Battles, and Incidents of Army Life.* Dayton, Ohio: W. J. Shuey, 1868.

Kibler, Charles H. *76th Ohio at Ringgold or Taylor's Ridge. A Little History.* N.p., n.d.

Kimball, Charles. *History of Battery "A," First Illinois Light Artillery Volunteers.* Chicago: Cushing Printing Company, 1899.

Kimberly, Robert L. *The Forty-first Ohio Volunteer Infantry in the War of the Rebellion, 1861–1865.* Cleveland: W. R. Smellie, 1897.

Kinnear, John. *History of the Eighty-sixth Regiment Illinois Volunteer Infantry, during Its Term of Service.* Chicago: Tribune Book and Job Printing Office, 1866.

Lewis, George W. *The Campaigns of the 124th Ohio Volunteer Infantry.* Akron: Werner, 1894.

Lindsley, John. *The Military Annals of Tennessee. Confederate. First Series: Embracing a Review of Military Operations, with Regimental Histories and Memorial Rolls.* Nashville: J. M. Lindsley, 1886.

Lucas, D. R. *New History of the 99th Indiana Infantry.* Rockford, Ill.: Horner Printing Company, 1900

McMurray, W. J. *History of the Twentieth Tennessee Regiment Volunteer Infantry, C.S.A.* Nashville: Regimental Publication Committee, 1904.

Martin, John. *Military History of the Eighth Kansas Veteran Volunteer Infantry.* Leavenworth, Kans.: Daily Bulletin Printing House, 1869.

*Military History and Reminiscences of the Thirteenth Regiment of Illinois Volunteer Infantry in the Civil War in the United States, 1861–1865.* Chicago: Woman's Temperance Publishing Association, 1892.

Newlin, William H. *History of the Seventy-third Regiment of Illinois Infantry Volunteers, Its Services and Experiences in Camp, on the March, on the Picket and Skirmish Lines, and in Many Battles of the War, 1861–1865.* Springfield, Ill.: Regimental Reunion Association, 1890.

Oates, William C. *War between the Union and the Confederacy and Its Lost Opportunities, with a History of the 15th Alabama Regiment and the Forty-eight Battles in Which It Was Engaged.* New York: Neale, 1905.

Osborn, Hartwell. *Trials and Triumphs: The Record of the Fifty-fifth Ohio Volunteer Infantry.* Chicago: A. C. McClurg, 1904.

Owen, William Miller. *In Camp and Battle with the Washington Artillery of New Orleans. A Narrative of Events During the Late Civil War from Bull Run to Appomattox and Spanish Fort.* Boston: Ticknor, 1885.

Partridge, Charles. *History of the Ninety-sixth Regiment Illinois Volunteer Infantry.* Chicago: Brown, Pettibone, 1887.

Peddycord, Will F. *History of the Seventy-fourth Regiment Indiana Volunteer Infantry.* Warsaw, Ind.: Smith Printery, 1913.

Perry, Henry F. *History of the Thirty-eighth Regiment Indiana Volunteer Infantry. One of the Three Hundred Fighting Regiments of the Union Army.* Palo Alto, Calif.: F. A. Stuart, 1906.

*Record of the Ninety-fourth Regiment, Ohio Volunteer Infantry, in the War of the Rebellion.* Cincinnati: Valley Press, 189–.

*Reminiscences of the Civil War from Diaries of Members of the 103d Illinois Volunteer Infantry.* Chicago: J. F. Leaming, 1904.

Rerick, John H. *The Forty-fourth Indiana Volunteer Infantry, History of Its Services in the War of the Rebellion and a Personal Record of Its Members.* Ann Arbor, Mich.: Courier Printing House, 1880.

Schmitt, William. *History of the Twenty-seventh Illinois Volunteers.* Winchester, Ill.: Standard Printing House, 1892.

SeCheverell, J. H. *Journal History of the Twenty-ninth Ohio Veteran Volunteers, 1861–1865. Its Victories and Its Reverses.* Cleveland: N.p., 1883.

Sherlock, Eli J. *Memorabilia of the Marches and Battles in Which the One Hundredth Regiment of Indiana Infantry Volunteers Took an Active Part, War of the Rebellion, 1861–1865.* Kansas City, Mo.: Gerard-Woody Printing Company, 1896.

Simmons, L. A. *History of the 84th Reg't Ill. Vols.* Macomb, Ill.: Hampton Brothers, 1866.

*Society of the Seventy-fourth Illinois Volunteer Infantry: Reunion Proceedings and History of the Regiment.* Rockford: W. P. Lamb, Printer, 1903.

Stormont, Gilbert. *History of the Fifty-eighth Regiment of Indiana Volunteer Infantry, Its Organizations, Campaigns, and Battles, from 1861–1865.* Princeton, Ill.: Press of Clarion, 1895.

*The Story of the Fifty-fifth Regiment Illinois Volunteer Infantry in the Civil War, 1861–1865.* Clinton, Mass.: W. J. Coulter, 1887.

Stuart, A. A. *Iowa Colonels and Regiments: History of Iowa Regiments in the War of the Rebellion; and Containing a Description of the Battles in which They Have Fought.* Des Moines, Iowa: Mills and Company, 1865.

Todd, George T. *First Texas Regiment.* Waco: Texian Press, 1963.

Tourgee, Albion. *The Story of a Thousand, Being a History of the Service of the 105th Ohio Volunteer Infantry, in the War for the Union.* Buffalo: McGerald and Son, 1896.

Trimble, Harvey M. *History of the Ninety-third Regiment Illinois Volunteer Infantry from Organization to Muster Out.* Chicago: Blakely Printing Company, 1898.

Underwood, Adin. *The Three Years' Service of the Thirty-third Mass. Infantry Regiment, 1862–1865, and the Campaigns and Battles of Chancellorsville, Beverley's Ford, Gettysburg, Wauhatchie, Chattanooga, Atlanta, the March to the Sea and through the Carolinas in Which It Took Part.* Boston: A. Williams and Company, 1881.

Van Horne, Thomas B. *History of the Army of the Cumberland, Its Organization, Campaigns, and Battles.* 2 vols. Cincinnati: Robert Clarke, 1875.

Walker, Cornelius Irvine. *Rolls and Historical Sketch of the Tenth Regiment, So. Ca. Volunteers in the Army of the Late Confederate States.* Charleston: Walker, Evans and Cogswell, 1881.

Watkins, Samuel. *"Co. Aytch," Maury Grays, First Tennessee Regiment; or, a Side Show of the Big Show.* Chattanooga: Times Printing Company, 1900.

Wilder, Theodore. *The History of Company C, Seventh Regiment, O.V.I.* Oberlin, Ohio: J. B. T. Marsh, 1866.

Willet, Elbert Decatur. *History of Company B (Originally Pickens' Planters), Fortieth Alabama Regiment, Confederate States Army, 1862 to 1865.* Anniston, Ala.: Norwood, 1902.

Wilson, Lawrence. *Itinerary of the Seventh Ohio Volunteer Infantry 1861–1864.* New York and Washington: Neale, 1907.

Wood, George L. *The Seventh Regiment: A Record.* New York: James Miller, 1865.

Worsham, W. J. *The Old Nineteenth Tennessee Regiment, C.S.A., June, 1861—April, 1865.* Knoxville, Tenn.: Press of Paragon Printing Company, 1902.

Wright, Henry H. *A History of the Sixth Iowa Infantry.* Iowa City: State Historical Society of Iowa, 1923.

Wright, Thomas J. *History of the Eighth Regiment Kentucky Volunteer Infantry.* St. Joseph, Mo.: St. Joseph Steam Printing Company, 1880.

## SECONDARY SOURCES

Belknap, Charles. *History of the Michigan Organizations at Chickamauga, Chattanooga and Missionary Ridge, 1863.* Lansing, Mich.: Robert Smith Printing Company, 1897.

Boatner, Mark M., III. *The Civil War Dictionary.* New York: David McKay, 1959.

Butterfield, John L., ed. *A Biographical Memorial of General Daniel But-*

*terfield, Including Many Addresses and Military Writings.* New York: Grafton Press, 1904.

Carpenter, John Alcott. *Sword and Olive Branch: Oliver Otis Howard.* Pittsburgh: University of Pittsburgh Press, 1964.

Clark, William H. H. *History in Catoosa County.* N.p., 1972.

Connelly, Thomas Lawrence. *Autumn of Glory: The Army of Tennessee, 1862–1865.* Baton Rouge: Louisiana State University Press, 1971.

Cozzens, Peter. *No Better Place to Die: The Battle of Stones River.* Urbana: University of Illinois Press, 1990.

———. *This Terrible Sound: The Battle of Chickamauga.* Urbana: University of Illinois Press, 1992.

Daniel, Larry J. *Cannoneers in Gray: The Field Artillery of the Army of Tennessee, 1861–1865.* University, Ala.: University of Alabama Press, 1990.

Davis, William C. *Breckinridge: Statesman, Soldier, Symbol.* Baton Rouge: Louisiana State University Press, 1973.

———. *Jefferson Davis: The Man and His Hour.* New York: Harper Collins, 1991.

Fitch, Michael. *The Chattanooga Campaign, with Special Reference to Wisconsin's Participation Therein.* Madison: Wisconsin History Commission, 1911.

Govan, Gilbert E., and James W. Livingood. *The Chattanooga Country, 1540–1976: From Tomahawks to TVA.* Knoxville: University of Tennessee Press, 1977.

Hallock, Judith Lee. *Braxton Bragg and the Confederate Defeat. Volume II.* University, Ala.: University of Alabama Press, 1991.

Hattaway, Herman, and Archer Jones. *How the North Won: A Military History of the Civil War.* Urbana: University of Illinois Press, 1983.

Hebert, Walter H. *Fighting Joe Hooker.* Indianapolis: Bobbs-Merrill, 1944.

Hicken, Victor. *Illinois in the Civil War.* Urbana: University of Illinois Press, 1991.

Hoobler, James A. *Cities under the Gun: Images of Occupied Nashville and Chattanooga.* Nashville: Rutledge Hill Press, 1986.

Horn, Stanley F. *Tennessee's War 1861–1865, Described by Participants.* Nashville: Tennessee Civil War Centennial Commission, 1965.

Hughes, Nathaniel C. *General William J. Hardee: Old Reliable.* Baton Rouge: Louisiana State University Press, 1965.

Korn, Jerry. *The Fight for Chattanooga: Chickamauga to Missionary Ridge.* Alexandria, Va.: Time-Life Books, 1985.

Lamers, William M. *The Edge of Glory: A Biography of General William S. Rosecrans, U.S.A.* New York: Harcourt, Brace, and World, 1961.

Lewis, Lloyd. *Sherman, Fighting Prophet.* New York: Harcourt, Brace, 1932.

Losson, Christopher. *Tennessee's Forgotten Warriors: Frank Cheatham and His Confederate Division.* Knoxville: University of Tennessee Press, 1989.

McDonough, James Lee. *Chattanooga—A Death Grip on the Confederacy.* Knoxville: University of Tennessee Press, 1985.

McFeely, William S. *Grant: A Biography.* New York: W. W. Norton, 1981.

McKinney, Francis F. *Education in Violence: The Life of George H. Thomas and the History of the Army of the Cumberland.* Detroit: Wayne State University Press, 1961.

Purdue, Elizabeth and Howell. *Pat Cleburne, Confederate General: A Definitive Biography.* Hillsboro, Tex.: Hill Junior College Press, 1973.

*Report of the Adjutant General and Acting Quartermaster General of the State of Iowa. January 1, 1865, to January 1, 1866.* Des Moines: F. W. Palmer, State Printer, 1866.

Skinner, George W. *Pennsylvania at Chickamauga and Chattanooga: Ceremonies at the Dedication of the Monuments Erected by the Commonwealth of Pennsylvania to Mark the Positions of the Pennsylvania Commands Engaged in the Battles.* Harrisburg, Pa.: Wm. Stanley Ray, State Printer, 1900.

Stickles, Arndt M. *Simon Bolivar Buckner: Borderland Knight.* Chapel Hill: University of North Carolina Press, 1940.

Walker, Robert Sparks. *Lookout: The Story of a Mountain.* Kingsport, Tenn.: Southern Publishers, 1941.

Warner, Ezra. *Generals in Blue: Lives of the Union Commanders.* Baton Rouge: Louisiana State University Press, 1964.

———. *Generals in Gray: Lives of the Confederate Commanders.* Baton Rouge: Louisiana State University Press, 1959.

Woodworth, Steven E. *Jefferson Davis and His Generals: The Failure of Confederate Command in the West.* Lawrence: University of Kansas Press, 1990.

## MAPS

*Atlas of the Battlefield of Chickamauga, Chattanooga and Vicinity. Published . . . by the Chickamauga and Chattanooga National Park Commissions.* Washington, D.C.: G.P.O., 1901.

*Map of a Portion of Missionary Ridge, Illustrating the Positions of Baird's and Wood's Divisions, Nov. 23, 24, 25, 1863,* in Historical Files, Chickamauga and Chattanooga National Military Park Library.

*Missionary Ridge Crest Road.* Excerpt from *Map of the Preliminary Survey of the Crest Road on Missionary Ridge, dated February 9, 1892, made by E. E. Betts for the Chickamauga and Chattanooga National Military Park Commission from the Tunnel to the Shallow Ford Road,* in Historical Files, Chickamauga and Chattanooga National Military Park Library.

# INDEX

Italicized page numbers at the end of entries in this index refer to the Appendix.

PETER COZZENS is a foreign service officer with the U.S. Department of State. Before joining the Foreign Service, he served as a military intelligence officer in the United States Army. A summa cum laude graduate of Knox College with a degree in international relations, Cozzens also attended the Chinese University of Hong Kong. He has contributed articles to the *Illinois Historical Journal, Civil War Times Illustrated,* and other periodicals. Cozzens is the author of *No Better Place to Die: The Battle of Stones River* and *This Terrible Sound: The Battle of Chickamauga.*